# Lecture Notes in Computer Science    1875

Edited by G. Goos, J. Hartmanis and J. van Leeuwen

**Springer**
*Berlin*
*Heidelberg*
*New York*
*Barcelona*
*Hong Kong*
*London*
*Milan*
*Paris*
*Singapore*
*Tokyo*

Kurt Bauknecht  Sanjay Kumar Madria
Günther Pernul (Eds.)

# Electronic Commerce and Web Technologies

First International Conference, EC-Web 2000
London, UK, September 4-6, 2000
Proceedings

 Springer

Series Editors

Gerhard Goos, Karlsruhe University, Germany
Juris Hartmanis, Cornell University, NY, USA
Jan van Leeuwen, Utrecht University, The Netherlands

Volume Editors

Kurt Bauknecht
IFI, University of Zürich
Winterthurer Str. 190, 8057 Zürich, Switzerland
E-mail: bauknecht@ifi.unizh.ch

Sanjay Kumar Madria
Purdue University, Department of Computer Science
West Lafayette, IN 47907, USA
E-mail: skm@cs.purdue.edu

Günther Pernul
University of Essen, Department of Information Systems
Universitätsstr. 9, 45141 Essen, Germany
E-mail: pernul@wi-inf.uni-essen.de

Cataloging-in-Publication Data applied for


Die Deutsche Bibliothek - CIP-Einheitsaufnahme

Electronic commerce and web technologies : first international
conference ; proceedings / EC Web 2000, London, UK, September 4 - 6,
2000. Kurt Bauknecht ... (ed.). - Berlin ; Heidelberg ; New York ;
Barcelona ; Hong Kong ; London ; Milan ; Paris ; Singapore ; Tokyo :
Springer, 2000
  (Lecture notes in computer science ; Vol. 1875)
  ISBN 3-540-67981-2



CR Subject Classification (1998): C2. J.1, H.3, H.4, J.4, K.6.5


ISSN 0302-9743
ISBN 3-540-67981-2 Springer-Verlag Berlin Heidelberg New York

Springer-Verlag Berlin Heidelberg New York
a member of BertelsmannSpringer Science+Business Media GmbH
© Springer-Verlag Berlin Heidelberg 2000
Printed in Germany

Typesetting: Camera-ready by author
Printed on acid-free paper      SPIN 10722361      06/3142     5 4 3 2 1 0

# Preface

This volume includes the papers accepted for the First International Conference on Electronic Commerce and Web Technologies, which was held in Greenwich, UK, on September 4-6, 2000. The conference is the first of a series of planned conferences on these topics with the goal to bring together researchers from academia, practitioners and commercial developers from industry, and users to assess current methodologies and explore new ideas in e-commerce and web technology.

The conference attracted 120 papers from all over the world and each paper was reviewed by at least three program committee members for its merit. The program committee finally selected 42 papers for presentation and inclusion in these conference proceedings.

The conference program consisted of 14 technical sessions and two invited talks spread over three days. The regular sessions covered topics such as web application design, intellectual property rights, security and fairness, distributed organizations, web usage analysis, modelling of web applications, electronic commerce success factors, electronic markets, XML, web mining, electronic negotiation, integrity and performance, facilitating electronic commerce, and mobile electronic commerce.

There were two invited addresses at the conference. The first was by Anthony Finkelstein, University College London, UK on "A Foolish Consistency: Technical Challenges in Consistency Management". This was a common address to the DEXA, the DaWaK and the EC-Web attendees. The second talk was by Paul Timmers, European Commission, Information Technologies Directorate on "The Role of Technology for the e-Economy".

We would like to express thanks to the people who helped put together the technical program: the program committee members and external reviewers for their timely and rigorous reviews of the papers, the DEXA organizing committee for their help in administrative work and support, and special thanks to Gabriela Wagner for doing most of the organizational work and for always responding promptly.

Finally, we would like to thank all the authors who submitted papers, authors who presented papers, the invited speakers, and the attendees who made this conference intellectually stimulating.

Günther Pernul (University of Essen)
Sanjay Kumar Madria (Purdue University)

# Conference Organization

**General Chair**

K. Bauknecht, Switzerland
University of Zurich

**Program Chair**

**Electronic Commerce**
G. Pernul, Germany
University of Essen

**Web Technologies**
S. Kumar Madria, USA
Purdue University

## Program committee

**Electronic Commerce Track**
K. Aberer, Germany
N.R. Adam, USA
M. Bichler, Austria
W. Cellary, Poland
R. Clarke, Australia
A. Dogac, Turkey
E. Fernandez, USA
J. Gricar, Slovenia
K. Karlapalem, China
S. Klein, Germany
W. König, Germany
R. Kramer, Germany
K. Kurbel, Germany
W. Lamersdorf, Germany
R.M. Lee, The Netherlands
M. Merz, Germany
G. Neumann, Austria
R. Oppliger, Switzerland
A. Röhm, Germany
S. Teufel, Germany
P. Timmers, Belgium
A M. Tjoa, Austria
A. Tsalgatidou, Greece
H. Weigand, The Netherlands
H. Werthner, Austria
J.C. Westland, China
A.B. Whinston, USA
Y. Yesha, USA

**Web Technologies Track**
C. Baru, USA
B. Bhargava, USA
F. Fotouhi, USA
J. Freire, USA
A. Joshi, USA
M. Klusch, Germany
L. Lakshmanan, Canada
G. Lausen, Germany
D. Lee, China
E.P. Lim, Singapore
B. Mobasher, USA
M. Mohania, USA
S. Paraboschi, Italy
E. Pitoura, Greece
G. Psaila, Italy
P.K. Reddy, Japan
G. Samaras, Cyprus
N.L. Sarda, India
P. Scheuermann, USA
C. Shahabi, USA
G. Sindoni, Italy
J. Srivastava, USA
D. Suciu, USA
K.L. Tan, Singapore
K. Vidyasankar, Canada
K. Wee-Ng, Singapore
Y. Zhang, Australia

**Additional Reviewers**

L. Ahmedi, Y. Cao, G. Carchesio, W. Essmayr, R. Grimm, N. Hamali, G. Herrmann, A. Hintoglu, C. Huemer, V. Iravul, S. Lee, J. Lopez, J. Markkula, P.J. Marron, D. Merkl, L. Mutenda, J. Narikka, E. Ojanen, T. Ozen, M. Paolucci, S. Pektas, I. Pramudiono, G. Quirchmayr, K. Rannenberg, T. Schlichting, W. Thoen, A. Tumer, J. Veijalainen, W. Winiwarter, M. Zielinsky

# Table of Contents

## Web Application Design

## Intellectual Property Rights

## Security and Fairness

## Distributed Organisations

## Integrity and Performance

## Facilitating EC

## Mobile E-Commerce

# Construction of Adaptive Web-Applications from Reusable Components

Guntram Graef and Martin Gaedke

Telecooperation Office (TecO), University of Karlsruhe, Vincenz-Priessnitz Str. 1,
76131 Karlsruhe, Germany, Tel.: +49 (721) 6902-79, Fax: -16,
E-Mail: {graef|gaedke}@teco.edu

**Abstract.** The Web has become a ubiquitous environment for application delivery. The originally intended idea, as a distributed system for knowledge-interchange, has given way to organizations offering their products and services using the Web as a global point of sale. The centralized delivery-mechanism enables the construction of E-Commerce applications personalized for each user by using behavior analysis. Current technologies suffer from the Web's legacy and use Log file-analysis or collaborative filtering only to adapt the content to users' needs. Motivated by the results of collaborative filtering algorithms, we describe a construction approach based on the abstract concept of services. To support the fine-grained concept we use the component-based WebComposition Markup Language to support reuse and seamless evolution of E-Commerce applications.

## 1 Introduction

While originally intended as a medium for distributing information in a document-centric form, the World Wide Web [3] has become much more than that. With the introduction of dynamism both on the client-side and the server-side the Web has emerged as a new platform for software applications serving a variety of purposes such as E-Commerce.

An important aspect that distinguishes applications on the Web from PC or work station applications is their central deployment. Software serving a large number of users can be installed and maintained in one single location. This drastically reduces cost and duration needed for deploying new or multiple versions of an application. It also means that the behavior of users can be observed in a single location.

Maes and Shardanand demonstrated in [15] how centrally acquired data about user interests can be utilized to provide users with information adapted to their preferences. With the work presented in this paper we go one step further. Rather than dynamically generating single html pages with information such as product recommendations we adapt complete E-Commerce applications to the needs of individual customers.

A fundamental requirement for the automatic adaptation of applications in a flexible and evolution oriented way is the availability of all necessary functionality and features as independent building blocks or components. The document based implementation model of the Web neither allows for the granularity needed for this kind of components nor does it provide mechanisms for abstraction. Thus it is for example not possible to implement a component as a normal Web resource that represents a feature such as a corporate identity design applicable to all Web applications of an organization. We can overcome this problem with WebComposition, a component-based approach to Web development that we will detail at the beginning of third section of this contribution. After that we will introduce services as higher level functional abstractions and describe how we use a service factory and domain-specific languages to improve productivity and maintainability for service development. We will conclude that section with our mechanism for the automatic adaptation of an application to individual customers' needs. In the fourth section we will detail the algorithm we employ for identifying individual customers' requirements. An evaluation of our work and a conclusion can be found at the end of this contribution. Beforehand, in the following section, we will discuss the current state of art concerning individual and adaptive applications.

## 2 Previous work

The problem of directly addressing a user and his or her personal needs has been subject to research for many years. Much of this work has been centered around user interface development, which is quite natural since this is the part of an application most visible to users. There is also some work related to adaptive Web sites.

Solutions can be divided into adaptive or individual (parts of) applications. An adaptive application presents a general solution that adapts its behavior during run-time to the user. An individual application in contrast has been produced for the specific needs of a user.

### 2.1 Adaptive and Individual User Interfaces

In the user interface design community there has been work on both adaptive user interfaces as well as the development of individual user interfaces. Adaptive user interfaces are widely discussed in contributions like FLEXEL [17] or [14], but their adaptation process is limited to the analysis of a single user's behavior. Individual user interface development has been addressed with TADEUS [13] and ADEPT [11]. These tools include a user model, which is used to automatically produce individual user interfaces or user interface descriptions. A major limitation is that the user model has to be defined manually by the UI developer.

### 2.2 Adaptive Web Sites

In the Web community there has been work on adaptive Web sites following several different approaches. Projects such as WebWatcher [2]or AVANTI [5] use a *path prediction* approach. This technique is closely tied to the structure of hypertext consisting of information resources (documents) and links. Path prediction tries to forecast the next action a user wants to perform after reaching a given state. The notion of state is usually tied to the recently viewed document resource. In a more complex E-Commerce application, state is not limited to currently viewed resources but might also include such things as state of product configurations created by a customer in advance of an ordering process which might make path prediction much more complex. Both examples also rely on manual input from the user about his personal interests.

Another technique is *collaborative filtering*. It is based on user preferences and user behavior in the past rather than navigation between application states. This approach described in [15] uses information about user interests to determine groups of users with similar interests. The calculated results can be used as recommendation of resources for a user based on previously accessed resources by other users in the same group. The idea has been demonstrated in an experimental implementation called Ringo. About 2000 users entered ratings for audio-cd-titles and music artists. This data has been used to dynamically generate html-pages with music recommendations for each user.

While Ringo requires users to actively provide information about their preferences, some commercial applications such as Amazon.com [1] try to infer the likes and dislikes of its customers from observed actions such as ordering a product. This proved to be a feature crucial for user acceptance of any type of adaptive mechanism in E-Commerce applications. In a highly competitive environment such as the Internet it is mandatory to avoid or minimize any customer workload.

## 3 Evolution and Adaptation of E-Commerce Applications

The automatic adaptation of whole applications on the level of code primitives is not feasible with current technology. We need to find proper abstractions and components as application building blocks to reduce the complexity of the application adaptation process. Therefore we divide the construction of software into a supply oriented micro level for providing functional components and a demand oriented macro level where functional components are federated in the application according to user demand.

The only kind of code abstraction ubiquitous on the Web are document resources. Unfortunately these do not satisfy our requirements both in terms of supported granularity and expressive power of inter-document relations. To overcome these limitations we based our approach on the WebComposition programming model.

On top of this general programming model we use the notion of services as higher level building blocks encapsulating functionality required to perform a certain task such as placement of an order or providing customer feedback. In contrast to lower level system components, the function of services can be perceived and described without specific technical knowledge. Service components form the basis for macro level application adaptation and evolution.

To support the development and seamless evolution of a large number of services we introduce a process for service production based on a domain specific language and a service factory. The macro level adaptation of E-Commerce applications is done through a special application service. This service controls how other services are presented to the customer based on the automatic analysis of customer requirements detailed later in this contribution.

## 3.1 WebComposition

The WebComposition programming model is based on the WebComposition Markup Language [8] and the WebComposition approach [10]. It enables us to perform component-based software development for the Web in a platform independent and evolution oriented way.

## 3.2 Reuse oriented programming model

A major productivity factor during all cycles of software development is reuse. The WebComposition programming model aims at facilitating reuse of development artifacts of any kind of granularity on various levels of abstraction. Code fragments of any given target language are modeled as WebComposition components. Components define a first level of code abstraction.

Between WebComposition components it is possible to define reuse relations such as aggregation (has-part) and specialization (inherits-from). Thus the model is object-oriented. More specifically it is based on a *prototype-instance paradigm* [18] instead of a class-based object-oriented model. This means that instantiated objects can inherit the capabilities of components by simply using them as prototypes. It is not necessary to provide class definitions. In the WebComposition model an object is an instance of a component and a component can serve as a prototype for other components. A component may be used like an abstract class, i.e. it could serve as a prototype for a certain type of components.

Prototyping as described in [18] is a mechanism to implement code sharing among objects. Alternatively multiple references of a component could be used to share its code. Sharing is fundamental for efficient reuse and maintenance because it enables us to keep modifications local. This is in contrast to other suggested object-oriented Web models such as WOOM [4].

## 3.3 WebComposition Markup Language

Components are described using the WebComposition Markup Language (WCML). WCML extends the semantics of common Web languages with statements for component definition and inter-component relations. WCML is an application of the eXtended Markup Language (XML). This way we can build on the familiarity of Web developers with markup languages and the availability of various tools such as syntax parsers. Components are organized in *virtual component stores,* which are implemented as documents, database tables or Web server resources. A *component repository* allows for retrieval of components through various access models [7]. WCML components can be mapped automatically to the Web implementation model using a compiler. This mechanism is independent of any specific deployment platform or language as the programming model is generic. Migration to a new implementation language or simultaneous support of several implementation languages can be achieved by using object-oriented concepts like polymorphism and WCML components encapsulating target language specific code.

## 3.4 Services as Functional Abstractions

The typical function of a Web based E-Commerce system is to enable customers to perform tasks such as product ordering or information retrieval. In a more general sense we can abstract from the concrete possibilities a system offers to its customers. Instead we can state that an E-Commerce system provides a set of services to its users. Each product, news channel or item of information can be modeled as a service provided by the system and the organization behind it. As a concrete example we could realize the selling of office chairs through such a service.

This definition of a service provides us with a powerful task oriented abstraction. A service as a whole tends to change very little when technical changes occur as compared to less abstract components.

Services are based on a level of abstraction both familiar to customers as well as domain experts in an organization. Interest in and knowledge about the requirements of a certain service is often found in a single person or small organizational unit. Customer activities most easily can be described as performing a set of tasks. Implementing tasks as service components we can base our application adaptation process on customer access to and federation of a set of components. Changes in an application on a task-level granularity also does not tend to bring the same level of confusion sometimes found when changes occur on a sub-task level. Services usually consist of components describing different aspects such as layout, navigation, language, content and processing. A more detailed description of service components can be found in [9].

## 3.5 Automated Service Production

Due to our practical experience with E-Commerce application environments there tend to be groups of services that only differ from each other in rather limited ways but can account for a large percentage of the total amount of services needed. For the development of this kind of services we try to bridge the gap between less technically sophisticated domain experts and the development system by means of introducing a service factory.

Our service factory uses service descriptions to automatically produce components implementing a service in the WebComposition programming model. A service description contains all information necessary to distinguish a specific service from a general type of services. Thus a service for ordering office chairs might be of the general type of a product order service while possessing numerous specific properties describing its products, configuration options, user interface dialog elements and so on. The service description can be specified using a special visual editor or a simplified human readable markup language. In contrast to many code production tools available, maintenance of the services remains on the service description level.

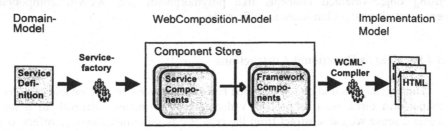

Figure 1: Service production

The service components produced by the service factory inherit from existing WebComposition components that form a component framework for service development. Thus basic changes affecting a larger group of services such as all information services can be done by changing a single set of components in the framework. The service descriptions for single services stay unaffected. This separation of concerns into different components and levels of the system architecture allows for an incremental evolution of individual services and groups of services [6]. The process of service production has been summarized in figure 1.

### 3.6 Adaptation Process

We consider a Web application as a special kind of service that contains all the functionality a system offers to its users. In most cases it will contain other services tailored to more specific tasks. We call this service the application service.

The adaptation process (figure 2) is performed by the application service. It is based on customer requirements data. In the next section we will therefore describe how this data can be obtained and processed automatically. The application service combines other services and makes them available according to their importance to the customer. Thus a service available in the overall system might either be presented to a customer more or less prominently or hidden. In this way the customer's cognitive capacity and the available bandwidth for system to customer interaction can be used in an optimized way.

## 4 Individual Customer Requirements Analysis

Determining the needs of an individual customer is the basis for providing an adaptation mechanism for any kind of Web application. A customer needs certain functionality presented to him or her in a way suiting his or her preferred style of interaction. In this section, we will discuss the selection of functionality in the form of services in more detail.

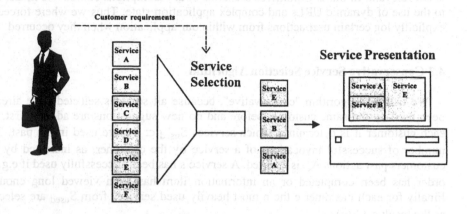

Figure 2: Adaption to customer requirements

## 4.1 The Service Selection Problem

We have a given set of services S, a set of customers C and a set of customer actions A in the past obtained from the observation of customer behavior. Each action $a \in A$ is related to a service $s \in S$ and a customer $c \in C$.

The problem is how to find a set of Services S(c) for a customer c that most accurately reflects those services the customer would use in the future assuming equal exposure of each service to the customer.

A simple approach to this problem is to calculate S(c) directly from the set of services related to past actions of the same customer c. In single user environments this usually is the only possible solution. We will use this method to determine those services that are regularly used by a customer. The algorithm implementing this method will be referred to as the *conservative service selection algorithm*.

Obviously not all services a customer might be willing to use in the future can be derived from the customer's past actions alone. Fortunately in our multi-customer case we have access to multiple customers' activity data. Thus we can employ a second algorithm for determining services of use to a customer, which we call the *social service selection algorithm*.

## 4.2 Observation of Past Customer Behavior

Before we can apply any algorithm for service selection we need to obtain A, the set of past customer actions. A very widespread approach to gathering information about user activity on the Internet is through logging HTTP-requests made to the Web server. This works if each customer action that is of interest is directly related to a set of URLs on the Web server. It also assumes that the result of the action (such as success of subsequent processing on the server) as well as the current application state is not relevant. In our E-Commerce scenarios both assumptions couldn't be made, due to the use of dynamic URLs and complex application state. Thus we where forced to explicitly log certain user actions from within our application when they occurred.

## 4.3 Conservative Service Selection Algorithm

We call this algorithm "conservative", because all services selected have already been used by the same customer before and no new suggestions are added. First, for each customer it is determined which services $S_{used} \subset S$ were used in the past. The number of successful invocations of a service by the customer, as indicated by the customers past actions $A_c$, is counted. A service s has been successfully used if e.g. an order has been completed or an information item has been viewed long enough. Finally for each customer c the n most heavily used services from $S_{used}$ are selected as the result set S(c).

## 4.4 Social Service Selection Algorithm

Our approach for this algorithm is based on the implicit exploitation of recurrent patterns in user behavior. Behavioral patterns state that people that exhibited a certain past behavior $B_p$ are likely to exert a certain behavior in the future $B_f$ with recent and expected future behavior forming a complete behavioral pattern [16]. A simple such pattern might be that a person that once used a service to order a telephone installation will very likely (with probability p) use another service to buy accessories for that telephone.

One way to exploit this for service selection is the explicit definition of association rules [12] capturing these patterns. This requires explicit and up to date knowledge of the existing behavioral patterns, which is usually not available because their number and complexity grow exponentially with the number of Services. Even for the most trivial case where each behavior is only related to one service, the number of possible relations between past user behaviors and predicted user behaviors is O( $|S|^2$ ).

Our approach is based on the implicit exploitation of behavioral patterns. Instead of directly associating observed actions via rules with services, we do so indirectly by deriving associations between customers. The algorithm we suggest consists of the following steps:

1. *Customer Profile Generation*: For each customer c ∈ C generate a profile p based on all actions a ∈ A related to that customer. The set of customer profiles is called P.
2. *Determination of User Profile Similarity Relation*: Calculate a similarity relation between each pair of customer profiles in P.
3. *Target Profile Generation*: For each p ∈ P calculate a target profile t.
4. *Service Selection*: Use the target profile t to determine the service selection S(c).

A customer profile consists of an attribute vector. Each attribute describes the level of usage of a service by the customer. We applied the following mapping of customer activities to profile attributes:

0 = No past actions by the customer related to that service
1 = Service was used by the customer at least once, but never successfully completed
N = Service successfully was used by the customer N-1 times.

To determine the degree of similarity between two customer profiles we applied a distance metric based on the mean squared difference between two profile vectors:

$$\frac{1}{(P_x - P_y)^2}$$

We use the set of profiles and the similarity metric to generate a "target profile" for each user. This profile tries to predict what a customer's profile will develop to if equally exposed to all available services. It is based on the assumption that people who behaved similar in the past will do so in the future. It also assumes that if a customer $C_1$ has only partially completed a pattern of behavior, another customer $C_2$ whose profile shows a high degree of similarity compared to $C_1$'s profile might already have executed the remaining part of that pattern. The optimal way to compute the target profile would be the calculation of a weighted average from all available customer profile vectors, where the weight would be a function of the similarity calculated in the previous step of the algorithm. However, for performance reasons we decided to calculate the target profile as the average vector from the n profiles that are most similar to the considered customer's profile but that are significantly different in at least one attribute. This is to avoid the effect of profile convergence and stabilization if there are many identical profiles (e.g. initial profiles of new customers).

After generating the target profile t we compute a differential profile d = t - p. We then use the relations between profile attributes and customer actions and between customer actions and services to determine the service selection S(c). Our result set contains services that if used by the customer would change his profile to become more similar to the target profile.

## 4.5 Quality of Predictions

We conducted a simple evaluation about the quality of predictions made by the different algorithms. As the basis for the algorithms we took a set of history data about past activities of about 1000 users of the Eurovictor II system described in the next section, and compared our predictions to activities performed by the same users afterwards. The complete set of existing services was equally exposed to each user. Thus every user was subject to the same application experience without any adaptation done during this stage.

We compared the number of selected services that have actually been used during the following two weeks while applying four different selection algorithms: Random, Conservative Service Selection Algorithm (CSSA), Social Service Selection

Algorithm (SSSA) and a combination of both CSSA and SSSA, where each of the two algorithms contributed to the result set.

| Applied algorithm | Predicted services used per customer |
|---|---|
| Random | 0.7 |
| CSSA | 4.5 |
| SSSA | 6.2 |
| CSSA and SSSA combined | 6.8 |

Figure 3: Quality of predictions

Figure 3 shows the results. Please note that the numbers in the table should only be interpreted relative to each other, because the absolute values also depend on the actual type and number of services and the present behavioral patterns. Obviously, both CSSA and SSSA produce useful predictions, while the combination of the two algorithms delivers better results than the application of a single algorithm.

### 4.6 Runtime Complexity

The conservative service selection algorithm's complexity is relatively low. Complexity for one customer scales linear with the number of services in the system, being $O(|S|)$.

Social service selection proves much more complex, since for the selection of services for each customer, data from all other customers has to be considered. Thus the algorithms complexity for one customer basically is $O(|C| * |S|)$.

## 5 Evaluation

The approach presented in this paper has been used to implement a complete service oriented E-Commerce system. Eurovictor II has been developed in the Telecooperation Office at the University of Karlsruhe in a joint project with Hewlett-Packard (HP). The system is currently productive at HP in Europe with more than 10000 regular customers. Eurovictor II has been designed as an evolvable and open system providing services to internal customers at HP.

The system already offers several hundred services mainly in the areas hardware orders, software orders, telecommunication, virtual office and news services. Services have been developed in a decentralized manner by people with moderate technical skills and have automatically been integrated into the system. Eurovictor II is highly flexible and adapts itself to each customer based on past activities of all users. It provides each of its users with an individual application experience.

Figure 4 shows a screenshot from Eurovictor II as it has automatically adapted itself to a specific customer. The application contains Eurovictor II services that have been selected using a combination of the two service selection algorithms described in the previous section. The presentation of the services has also been adapted to the customer's habits. Frequently used services are displayed more prominently or even executed automatically. Right after the start of the Web application the "application changes"-service is automatically invoked, because it has been accessed by the current customer more frequently than other services. This specific service retrieves and displays information about the most recent changes during the evolution of what the customer perceives as personal Eurovictor II application. Another customer might be welcomed by Eurovictor II with a service that displays a stock report or a company news summary.

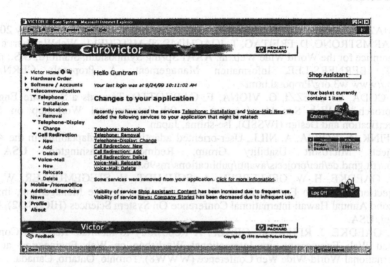

Figure 4: Adaptive Eurovictor II

# 6 Conclusion

In this paper we have described a platform based on the so-called "service" abstraction. The platform uses a component-based development model for the Web. Based on this model we introduced a service factory that enhances productivity during Web service development and allows technically less sophisticated domain experts to enable business processes on the Web. An application service together with a mechanism for the automatic analysis of individual customer requirements enables the automatic adaptation of applications to individual customers' needs. Components implementing solutions to different problems are used and reused as building blocks.

From the individual customer's point of view the application performs an automatic evolution, based on the changing behavior of all customers. The evolution of services due to changes in business logic is separated from this process and centralized. Logic closely related to technology is encapsulated in separate components. Thus, we achieve a clear separation of concerns related to three major sources of change and fields of expertise: customer requirements, technology and business processes.

As a proof of concept we successfully applied our approach in a mission critical E-Commerce environment. The results from Eurovictor II encourage us to look at further issues such as adaptation on a finer granularity optimizing the way individual tasks can be performed by the customer. Another issue would be the detection and consideration of a customer's level of user expertise in addition to the requirements in terms of system functionality.

# References

[1] AMAZON.COM, Amazon Homepage: http://www.amazon.com (accessed: May 2000)

[2] R. ARMSTRONG, D. FREITAG, T. JOACHIMS, T. MITCHELL, WebWatcher: a learning apprentice for the World Wide Web, in: AAAI Spring Symposium, Stanford, U.S., pp. 6-12.

[3] T. BERNERS-LEE, Information Management: A Proposal: CERN. 1998. http://www.w3.org/Proposal.html

[4] F. CODA, C. GHEZZI, G. VIGNA, F. GARZOTTO, Towards a Software Engineering Approach to Web Site Development, in: 9th International Workshop on Software Specification and Design (IWSSD), Ise-shima, Japan.

[5] J. FINK, A. KOBSA, A. NILL, User-oriented adaptivity and adaptability in the AVANTI project: Microsoft Usability Group, Redmond, Washington, USA 1999. http://fit.gmd.de/hci/projects/avanti/publications/ms96.html

[6] M. GAEDKE, H.-W. GELLERSEN, A. SCHMIDT, U. STEGEMÜLLER, W. KURR, Object-oriented Web Engineering for Large-scale Web Service Management, in: Thirty-Second Annual Hawaii International Conference On System Sciences (HICSS-32), Island of Maui, USA.

[7] M. GAEDKE, J. REHSE, G. GRAEF, A Repository to facilitate Reuse in Component-Based Web Engineering, in: International Workshop on Web Engineering at the 8th International World-Wide Web Conference (WWW8), Toronto, Ontario, Canada.

[8] M. GAEDKE, D. SCHEMPF, H.-W. GELLERSEN, WCML: An enabling technology for the reuse in object-oriented Web Engineering, in: Poster-Proceedings of the 8th International World Wide Web Conference (WWW8), Toronto, Ontario, Canada.

[9] M. GAEDKE, K. TUROWSKI, Generic Web-Based Federation of Business Application Systems for E-Commerce Applications, in: Second International Workshop on Engineering Federated Information Systems (EFIS'99), eds. S. Conrad, W. Hasselbring, G. Saake, Kühlungsborn, Germany.

[10] H.-W. GELLERSEN, R. WICKE, M. GAEDKE, WebCompostion: an object-oriented support system for the Web engineering lifecycle, Computer Networks and ISDN Systems Special Issue on the 6th Intl. WWW Conference, Santa Clara, CA, USA 1997 1429-1437.

[11] P. JOHNSON, S. WILSON, P. MARKOPOULOS, J. PYCOCK, ADEPT: Advanced Design Environment for Prototyping with Task Models, in: Human factors in computing systems (CHI'93), Amsterdam, The Netherlands, pp. 56.

[12] R. MILLER, Y. YANG, Association Rules over Interval Data, in: ACM SIGMOD international conference on Management of data, Tucson, Arizona, USA, pp. 452-461.

[13] E. SCHLUNGBAUM, T. ELWERT, TADEUS - a model-based approach to the development of Interactive Software Systems, Rostocker Inform. Berichte 17 1995 93-104.

[14] M. SCHNEIDER-HUFSCHMIDT, T. KÜHME, U. MALINOWSKI, Adaptive user interfaces : principles and practice, Amsterdam; New York, 1993.

[15] U. SHARDANAND, P. MAES, Social information filtering: algorithms for automating "word of mouth", in: Human factors in computing systems (CHI'95), Denver, USA, 210-217

[16] B. F. SKINNER, Science and human behavior, New York, 1953.

[17] C. THOMAS, M. KROGSÆTER, An adaptive environment for the user interface of Excel, in: international workshop on Intelligent User Interfaces (IUI), pp. 123-130.

[18] D. UNGAR, R. B. SMITH, Self: The Power of Simplicity, in: OOPSLA '87, pp. 227-242.

# The WebConsultant - A Flexible Framework for Dynamic Web Applications

Andreas Turk[1], Frank Farnschläder[2],
Horst Silberhorn[2], Herbert Stoyan[2], Stefan Kreutter[2]

[1] SCHEMA GmbH, Andernacher Str. 18, D-90411 Nuremberg, Germany
turk@schema.de

[2] FORWISS (Bavarian Research Center for Knowledge-based Systems)
Am Weichselgarten 7, D-91058 Erlangen, Germany
{ff, silberh}@forwiss.de,
hstoyan@informatik.uni-erlangen.de,
snkreutt@cip.informatik.uni-erlangen.de

**Abstract.** Web-based consultancy and e-commerce are important services in the rapidly growing internet market. The engineering of Web-based consultancy applications is like the engineering of Web applications in general not yet supported by a methodical approach and adequate process models. This article presents a process model for Web software engineering and an appropriate execution model for Web consultancy. The models have been used in the specification and prototypic implementation of the WebConsultant, a tool that collects customer data in a client-server architecture in order to decide on the subsequent course of the interview. The XML-application ISDL is used to define the structure and flow of interviews. The content of an ISDL-document determines the course of an interview dependent on the customer's input. As a result, consultancy Web pages that display relevant extracts of a database are produced.

## 1. Introduction

Web applications differ in several aspects from non-web software. Most Web applications produce changing and incrementally growing hypertext sites - a behaviour, which demands for openness and flexibility. Further typical features are: their client-server architecture, their ability to run in heterogeneous system environments (browsers, databases, operating systems etc.), and their multi-user and anytime capability. They have to consider compatibility requirements raised by current Web communication standards (HTML, HTTP) and integrate smoothly with standard software (HTTP-servers, databases). Web applications offer a different view as well: the *content* of generated Web sites and their structure typically evolve rapidly. In order to keep the sites constantly accessible for the client, the Web site maintainer must be able to change both content and structure easily and quickly at server runtime. There are important factors besides the evolutionary aspect and the fluidity of requirements. According to Lowe [5], cognitive elements deserve particular emphasis. Examples of such cognitive elements are the structure of the information and the sophistication (e.g., user modeling).

The process of *Web engineering* comprises the engineering of Web pages and the engineering of Web software. Web page engineering is commonly regarded as part of the document engineering task [6]. Web software engineering for client- and server-side software shall be investigated in this article more closely in the following. Its major aspects are

- dynamics (generation of pages on request, applets),
- components (integration of different modules, e.g. database, Web server), and
- actuality (the need to ensure relevance of content and structure).

For the purpose of this article, we restrict our attention to interview-based consultancy through the Web. With the *WebConsultant*, a solution for this given class of engineering problems will be presented comprising *reusable modules*. The WebConsultant provides a framework of software modules for dynamic Web applications. It implements a so called *Web execution model*, i.e. a generic model of a specific kind of Web application that determines the way data is computed.

After a short discussion on the major problems of engineering Web software (section 2), we introduce the fundamental process model. This is complemented by the WebConsultant execution model, which includes an abstract machine and a description language for interviews (section 3). We show how to create the WebConsultant from these tools. Next, we compare our approach to others and show benefits and drawbacks of the WebConsultant (section 4). Finally we sum up our results and propose future tasks.

## 2. Problems addressed

This section describes the general problems in automated consulting and presents the WebConsultant as a software solution for the limited problem space of consultancy in the Web. An example illustrates the application of the WebConsultant to the domain of insurance consulting.

### 2.1 Consulting in the WWW

The number of information services and commerce services on the WWW is rapidly increasing. The WWW is well-suited to automating the interaction process between a vendor or consultant on the one side and a customer on the other side.

In order to provide the desired piece of information or product to the client, it is necessary for the interviewing tool to adapt to the client's needs and the client's current state of knowledge. Therefore the aim of the communication process must be to elicit all relevant data from the client. The quality of this elicitation process and its results depend on how well the client is modeled and how well the model is subsequently mapped into the solution space. The modeling in its turn depends firstly on how well the client understands the questions posed by the consultant. If the client faces problems with the wording or lacks background information the input's quality may suffer. The consultant can alleviate this danger by providing additional information on demand (e.g., a glossary). Secondly, it is important how well the consultant's questions cover the problem space. Another factor comes into play if the client's answers need not be of a stereotypical nature but may exhibit a higher degree of expressional freedom, as is the case in freely phrasable text that must be parsed, interpreted and disambiguated. As far as the mapping of the client model into the solution space is concerned, the detail and correctness of the mapping and the data is the decisive factor.

## 2.2 A specialized tool for automated Web consultancy

The WebConsultant covers consulting applications where stereotypical answers to the consultant's questions suffice. It is possible to provide the client with additional information by specifying a glossary. The correctness and the mapping is of course utterly in the hand of the consultant application designer, but the WebConsultant provides means to specify solutions of every detail and scale. Since a tool like the WebConsultant lacks human intelligence and common sense, the client must have a rather clear idea of his problem space and the input parameters the consulting result shall be based on. The WebConsultant guides the client through hypertext interview pages that elicit user data by forms where the user input determines the subsequent course of the interview. If specified in ISDL (see below), the WebConsultant sends intermediate consulting pages that refer to the given answers and display database content. Arbitrary terms (e.g. technical language) may be endowed by the ISDL programmer with hyperlinks to the according explanation in a glossary browser frame. Other links can be inserted that refer to hypermedia-annotations like pictures or audio data. The interview is completed by a final consulting page presenting the final results relevant to the user (client). The structure of the interview is specified using a self-developed XML application named ‚Interview Structure Description Language' (ISDL). ISDL is therefore used to specify questions, the appropriate type of answer forms, pagination and sequence information als well as consulting and glossary data. While the ISDL document and the database provide content, HTML templates with special expandable tags specify the layout of the pages. Thus we accomplish the commonly desired separation of graphical layout and content.

## 2.3 An example application: The Internet Insurance Consultant[1].

Questionable insurance brokers often trick customers into life insurance contracts that unnecessary or of inappropriate size. Since the profit of the insurance seller is deduced from the amount of insurance, sellers try to create as many high contracts as possible. In contrast to an insurance seller the insurance consultant tries to understand the life situation of the client and looks for possibilities to cover the most important risks. He does not work for a specific insurance company and tries to find an optimal contract for his client. He does not press the client to sign a specific contract but presents a set of alternatives from which the client may choose.

The Internet Insurance Consultant is a net application that works along these guidelines. The user is asked about people who depend on their financial power to find out if there is any reason to make a life insurance. If there are children or a partner with a reasonable income, a life insurance is suggested. With input from the user, the sum of the life insurance is proposed. By accessing a database with contract performances and contract characteristics appropriate life insurances are selected and proposed. The user may then call a seller and bargain for optimal conditions.

The question structure of the interview is simple at present. The year of birth of the user is necessary to determine the contract conditions . It serves as a criterion for the probability of a marriage and children. If a marriage is possible, an appropriate question is posed. Independent of this, children can exist. The age of the persons is a trigger to ask about their income. After the consultant has collected the set of persons that are financially dependent, the insurance sum has to be determined. This can be done by asking for the intended life style and the rates the client is willing to pay each month. Now all data are collected to access the data base and present the user a list of life insurance contract versions. In each case a risk insurance is proposed if the user has not already got one.

# 3. The WebConsultant

In order to give a flexible solution for the discussed problem of Web consultancy, we are going to describe a process model of Web software engineering, an appropriate execution model including a dedicated specification language, and a framework of reusable software components that implement the execution model.

## 3.1 The process model

The applied process model is based upon the standard process model of software engineering and thus comprises the well known cycle of analysis, design, implementation and test (see [10] for instance). As opposed to the static aspects of Web engineering, which cover the production of Web pages into persistent files [6], the *Web software engineering* deals with the dynamic generation of Web pages by server side software. Each request from a client may actuate a uniquely created Web

---

[1]  http://faui81.informatik.uni-erlangen.de/IMMD8/WebConsultant

page being sent through the HTTP-stream. As described above, specific maintenance requirements are pressing, hence the process model is centred around a prototype which incrementally evolves during overall lifetime. Prototyping shows even more benefit, when the specific application type of *Web consultancy* is considered. The framework to be presented (section 3.4) releases programmers from re-inventing standards over and over, but focuses their work on maintenance aspects, once the initial system configuration has been established. Regarding the process steps again, the analysis is already finished, since the application domain is fixated. Next, the specification includes setting up the interview structure and the corresponding database schemas. No implementation in form of usual coding is necessary, but the contents of the database and the interview will be determined and tied together by execution rules. Testing has to reveal deficits of contents and relations in the first place, because the combined software components should have been well tested during their creation.

## 3.2 Execution model and system architecture

The given task has been to implement a framework of easily incorporable software components required to automate effective Web consulting. Fig.1 shows the proposed system architecture. Its modules fill in the mentioned framework and thus implement the abstract machine of Web consulting. A particular consulting session is carried out according to the following scheme:

1. System start, initialisation
   - Load the interview structure and rule base (ISDL-Parser).
   - Open the database interface (ODBC).
   - Start the HTTP-Server.

2. Preliminaries
   - The client requests the start page.
   - The server sends initial information about the consulting procedure and technical advice (session interrupt, Undo/Redo by back/forward).
   - The client triggers the interview by clicking on a hyperlink.

3. Interview
   - The server decodes the submitted form content, encoded within the URL (HTML-Generator).
   - The inference engine is fed with the results representing decisions of the client and a follow-up-question is chosen.
   - When the interview is finished, a consultancy page is generated.
   - The server loads the HTML templates (schemata) for interview pages (HTML-Generator).
   - The schemata are instantiated by filling in the content, which consists of the session history (wrapped into hidden forms) and the actual question group (a set of questions to be answered by the client in the next step).

- The generated Web page is transmitted to the client.
- The client receives the page and may request the multimedia annotations by clicking on the responding hyperlinks.
- The client user answers the questions by filling in the forms.
- The client submits the data by clicking on the submit button.

## 4. Consulting
- A server module determines the configuration.
- A corresponding subset of the database is selected.
- The HTML-template for consulting pages is loaded (HTML-Generator).
- The schemata are instantiated (HTML-Generator).
- Eventually an intermediate consulting will be emitted, that refers to the follow-up interview page.
- The server feeds the final consulting page into the HTTP stream to the client.

To build an execution model [11], a specification language has to be supplied. We will define the interview structure description language (ISDL) in the next section.

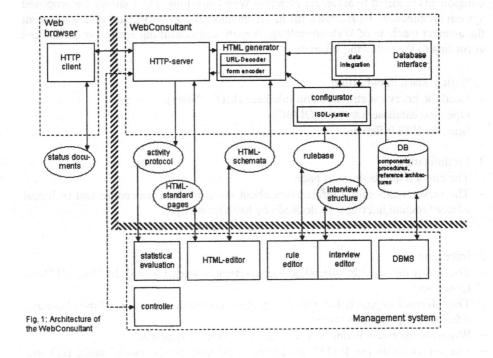

Fig. 1: Architecture of
the WebConsultant

## 3.3 Language definition (ISDL)

We decided to use an XML[2]-application [3] for several reasons. XML provides a human-readable, compact, non-proprietary and platform-independent format with growing tool support. By using XML we adapt to a recent and promising development that may lead to a standardization of specification languages. The structure of an XML-document is easy to define by specifying a Document Type Definition (DTD) and can be validated automatically by standard XML parsers. ISDL provides means to specify interview structures and rules that control the interview flow depending on preceeding questions and answers. ISDL also allows to describe result configurations as well as glossary and multimedia annotations. By virtue of the element-wise definition in XML, questions, rules, glossary and annotations can be conceived and edited independently, thus they become reusable and easily exchangeable.

An ISDL-document can be separated into five types of subdocuments:

*Questions* (tagged <qg>):
This element groups questions in question units (<qunit>) and corresponding answer possibilities (<aunit>). A question group has a status attribute telling whether the questions are to be used at the start of the interview or somewhere within. Notes (<note>) and multimedia annotations (<annotation>) are also expressible. Annotations can appear inlined or referred to by a hypermedia link. Possible answer form types are single choice from a range of given answers, an integer from a range by given upper and lower bounds, a free text (which may be cited at a later point of time but which cannot be used for computing the interview flow), and a generable range of answers with a pre- and a posttext and a quantity attribute specifying the number of the generated possible answers. Answers are attributed with a unique id which is used to reference them from question rules.

*Question rules* (tagged <qrule>):
Question rules determine depending on given client answers which question group will succeed the current one and whether there is an intermediate or final consulting page. Every question rule consists of references to answers and an action. An action can be the selection of a new question unit or the generation of a consulting page.

*Configuration rules* (tagged <crule>):
Result pages are configured by these rules, each of them consisting of references to answers and a configuration action. The action determines an attribute value (<cset>) or the way the results are sorted (<csort>).

*Configuration explanations* (tagged <cexplain>):
They specify how some text and given free text answers can be combined for use in result pages.

*Glossary content* (tagged <glossary>):

---

[2] Specification: http://www.w3.org/TR/1998/REC-xml-19980210

The glossary is a set of glossary entries <gentry> which are referred to by an id specified in answer elements.

At the moment, the XML Schema Working Group (WG) develops the XML Schema definition language and has published several Working Drafts[3] (WD). XML schema is a model for describing the structure of information, similar to DTDs. But XML Schemas are much more expressive than DTDs and will overcome several limitations. The use of XML Schemas will allow to exchange XML data much more robustly. The specification of ISDL by the use of XML Schema may result in additional expressiveness. But XML Schemas are still far from stable and the specification of XML Schema may be significantly changed in future drafts. Therefore the XML Schema Working Group advises developers not to use the XML Schema specification for application development, so far.

### 3.4 Implementation details

The following section explains the architecture of the WebConsultant in more detail and describes some of the components and how they interact (see fig.1 for a graphical illustration of the architecture).

The WebConsultant uses HTTP, the protocol of the WWW, and comprises its own server. The client may be any standard HTTP-client (Web browser). Using only standard HTML achieves the broadest browser and platform compatibility and makes the service available to thin clients. The WebConsultant is implemented in Common Lisp which is suitable for rapid prototyping and allows dynamic compiling of altered code at runtime. As the course of an interview depends on client answers, the contextual state of all ongoing interview sessions must be kept persistent until the consulting process is finished. In a client-server architecture, there are two ways to keep such data, namely by the client and/or by the server. Keeping the session-information on the server would demand a timeout mechanism that disposes of data no longer needed in order to free system resources. Client requests could be identified by fixed-length session-ids transferred to and from the client by employing hidden forms. As a disadvantage, server-sided saving of data can be costly and a timeout could prevent the client from taking up the interview after a pause. We have decided to use the client for persistently holding the session-information. The client transfers the information to the server after a change of state (answering a question) to have it processed and immediately receives the new session state encoded in a Web page. Thus the server is freed from any longtime responsibility for sessions while the client keeps the complete interview history. The client can save the Web page on disk and continue the interview after reloading it at any time. Additionally, the backward-forward-functionality of the browser can be used as a limited undo/redo-mechanism during the session. The costs here lie in the bandwith needed for transferring the data back and forth. In order not to limit the use of the WebConsultant to a specific database, ODBC (Open DataBase Connectivity) [9] was chosen to provide a generic database interface.

---

[3] World Wide Web Consortium (W3C), W3C Working Draft (April 7th 2000): http://www.w3.org/TR/xmlschema-0/.

The Web server integrated server is the Common Lisp server CL-HTTP[4]. It is delivered with the complete source code. An advantage of this package is that computed URLs supersede conventional cgi-scripts and allow to implement the whole server functionality in a homogenous development environment.

The applied validating XML parser was built from the ISDL-DTD by use of an XML parser generator by Schema GmbH. It provides output represented an internal format used as input to the other modules.

The result of a consulting process is assembled from arbitrary elementary data in the database, connected to the other components by the use of ODBC [9]. The underlying database is at present a Microsoft[5] Access® application, but any ODBC-connectable relational database [2] will do. The access is realized by dynamic construction of SQL (Structure Query Language [1]) queries, triggered by specific SQL rules in the ISDL-document. As an example the following crule-element means that the answer to question a1 has been a1.1 and the answer to question a2 has been in range [23..28]:

When triggered, the produced SQL query would look like

```
<crule table="risk (age23-25)">
   <answerref idref="a1.1">
   <rangeref idref="a2">
     <lower>23</lower>
     <upper>25</upper>
   </rangeref>
   <caction>
     <cset>
       <attname>age</attname>
       <attterm>='25-30'</attterm>
       <attname>children</attname>
       <attterm>='2'</attterm>
     </cset>
   </caction>
</crule>
```

```
SELECT * FROM table1
WHERE age='25-30' AND
children='2'
```

and yield the first row of the example table in table 1. Particular rules can combine to single SQL-statements. All attributes of a table are selected by default. A further selection takes place during the generation of consulting pages by use of layout templates. The contents, attributes and table names in the database are not restricted in any way.

Due to a lack of tools, the correspondence of rules specified in ISDL and the database scheme must be assured by hand which makes the process laborious and error-prone. Here a specific integrated development environment (IDE) like the one of the ElementsAdvisor (see section 4) would be a useful extension of the WebConsultant.

| company | age | children | premium rate | amount |
|---------|-----|----------|--------------|--------|
| Neckbreak Inc. | 25-30 | 2 | $400 | $200000 |
| Feelsave Ltd. | 25-30 | 3 | $440 | $230000 |

table 1: table 'risk (age23-25)'

---

[4] http://www.ai.mit.edu/projects/iiip/doc/cl-http/home-page.html
[5] http://www.microsoft.com

### 3.5 The HTML-generator

The generation of Web pages by the HTML-generator is triggered by requests of the client and controlled by templates (HTML-schemata). The files put on the HTTP-stream to the client are partly static files located in the file system and partly generated on-the-fly at runtime. All generated pages are based on one of the five schematas (a frame document and templates for interview-, consulting-, glossary- and annotation-pages). The templates contain special tags that are expanded by the HTML-generator to genuine HTML. A template with expanded special tags is a fully expanded Web page to be sent to the client. Questions and tables derived from database content are marked up with HTML by the generator and then inserted into the Web page at the place of the appropriate special tag. The generator also decodes the BASE64-encoded[6] URL and extracts the information gathered. When a new Web page for the client is produced, the complete history is then packed into *hidden forms* within the page to be transferred back again with the next URL coming from the client to the server.

## 4. Systems and tools with similar objectives

In this section we will look at a couple of outstanding systems and tools that may rival the WebConsultant in one or more aspects. The evolution of Web application development started at producing simple static Web sites edited by hand. They emerged through the generation of static Web sites to dynamically (on-the-fly) generated ones. Now they focus increasingly on integrating interactive elements (Java-Script, Java). Two examples for tools that generate static Web Sites are the The Hyperwave[7] Information Server and SchemaText[8]. Hyperwave is a complete development and runtime environment for Web site generation that comes with an integrated server. Web pages can be generated from a database while layout and content are separated. It supports colloborative authoring and cares for the referential integrity of the generated sites (no broken links). Reusable components and templates help the authors to work efficiently. SchemaText represents a mature authoring tool using an object-oriented approach. Class schemata allow authoring-in-the-large and separation of content, structure and layout. This simplifies the generation of different documentation formats apart from HTML (Framemaker, Word, WinHelp etc.) from one source. Both tools are sophisticated applications for the generation of static sites. The generation of static pages is especially suited for tasks like technical documentation, newspaper archiving and digital libraries. Applications such as e-

---

[6] The allowed characters in an URL are limited to a certain range, therefore Web browsers encode all data transferred with the URL using the BASE64-encoding. See also http://www.w3.org/Addressing/URL/

[7] http://www.hyperwave.de/

[8] http://www.schema.de

commerce, consulting services and customized content delivery demand interactive Web applications. Examples of tools that support engineering such applications are iHTML[9], ColdFusion[10], ElementsAdvisor[11] and ModelCraft[12]. iHTML and ColdFusion provide powerful scripting languages to produce HTML. Both tools allow database access and can interface with other applications. While the development of interactive Web applications with these tools cannot be done without programming, the WebConsultant only needs a specification of the interview structure in ISDL. ElementsAdvisor and ModelCraft are development environments for object-oriented modeling and rule-base development. Both also provide a sophisticated inference engine. By integrating with a Web server and a database, one can build powerful interactive Web applications. The power is tied to complex programming languages which are even harder to conceive and understand than the aforementioned scripting languages. Therefore educated programmers are needed to build and maintain interactive sites. This implies that changing structure and content of a Web application is expensive for the majority of the clients. Adapting general tools for the use in a specific domain like Web consulting inevitably leads to costly and time-consuming programming activities and less maintainability. As a conclusion we see that for our targeted domain the WebConsultant is an reasonably appropriate solution for an avarage client in terms of expressiveness as well as development and maintenance costs.

## 5. Summary and future work and conclusion

We have presented a process model for Web application engineering that expands the model of software engineering and separates the dynamic from the static aspects of Web applications. As an example application of the latter model, the WebConsultant is presented in detail. It represents a generic solution for realizing specific Web consulting applications where the domain knowledge can be specified in a declarative way. A special markup language (ISDL) makes the description of an interview flow as easy as possible. Nevertheless, the correct use of references by ids within an ISDL-document can be a complex and confusing task as the interview size grows. Therefore as a topic for future work, it would be helpful to the engineer to have an integrated development environment that takes over laborious jobs like checking id-consistency. Another desirable feature would be the possibility to use an arbitrary different (e.g. already implemented) HTTP-server instead of CL-HTTP which demands an extended architecture implementing a standard interface.

Our objectives have been to sketch a development method for Web software engineering and to reduce the effort of developing applications to three tasks: a formal system specification, a declarative implementation of logical dependencies and the domain-specific authoring. The feasibility of this method has been shown by the

---

[9] http://www.ihtml.com
[10] http://www.coldfusion.com
[11] http://www.elements.com
[12] http://www.cunav.com

implementation of the WebConsultant, a framework for engineering Web-based consulting services. We have also seen that a declarative way of implementing specific Web applications is – if not impossible - hard to achieve and costly if general Web application engineering tools are to be employed.

## 6. Acknowledgements

We would like to thank Ralf Kokowski for implementing and configuring the ODBC-interface and SCHEMA GmbH for providing the XML-parser generator written by Hans Weber. Thanks also to all external proof-readers, to the *Bundesministerium für Bildung und Forschung* (bmb+f)[13] for the financial support granted and to the coordinators of the DeMeS[14] project.

## 7. References

[1]     Bowman, Judith,S. and Emerson, Sandra,L. and Darnovski, Marcy: The practical SQL handbook, 3rd edition, Addison-Wesley,1996.

[2]     Elmasri, Ramez and Navathe, Shamkant B.: Fundamentals of Database Systems, 2nd edition, Addison-Wesley, 1994.

[3]     Goldfarb,Charles F. and Prescod,Paul: The XML handbook, Prentice Hall, 1998.

[4]     Garzotto, Franca and Paolini, Paolo and Schwabe,Daniel: HDM – A Model-Based Approach to Hypertext Application Design. ACM Transactions on Information Systems, Vol. 11, No. 1, January 1993, p 1-26.

[5]     Lowe, David and Bucknell, Andrew: Tutorial "Hypermedia and Web Development Methods", Hypertext '99

[6]     Kuhnke, Christoph and Schneeberger, Josef and Turk, Andreas: A Schema-Based Approach to Web Engineering. Proceedings of the 33rd Hawaii International Conference on System Sciences, Hawaii 2000.

[7]     Lowe, Hall: Hypermedia and the Web - An Engineering Approach, Wiley, 1999.

[8]     Mallery, John C.: A Common LISP Hypermedia Server, Proceedings of the First International Conference on the World-Wide Web, Geneva: CERN, May 25, 1994.

[9]     Microsoft ODBC 3.0 Software Development Kit and Programmer's Reference, Microsoft Press, 1997.

[10]    Sommerville, Ian: Software Engineering, 4th edition, Addison-Wesley, 1992.

[11]    Stoyan, Herbert: Programmiermethoden der Kuenstlichen Intelligenz, Springer 1988.

---

[13] http://www.bmbf.de

[14] „DeMeS (Development of Media Services), a joint project funded by the German Federal Ministry of Education, Science, Research and Technology (BMBF) (http://demes.darmstadt.gmd.de/project1en.html).

# Security of Electronic Business Applications: Structure and Quantification

Konstantin Knorr[1] and Susanne Röhrig[2]

[1] Department of Computer Science, University of Zurich, Switzerland,
knorr@ifi.unizh.ch
[2] SWISSiT Informationstechnik AG, Zurich, Switzerland,
roehrig@swiss-it.ch

**Abstract.** The rapid growth of the commercial use of the Internet goes along with a rising need for security for both customer and merchant. As many parties and different systems are involved, security becomes a complicated issue. Therefore, the need for definition, structuring, and quantification of security arises. This paper proposes a structured approach to analyze security measures and to quantify the overall security of an electronic business application. The quantifier is calculated through a security matrix which breaks down the assessment of security into smaller parts. These parts correspond to the locations, security objectives, and implemented security mechanisms of the application. The security quantifier can be used to analyze, design the application, and to compare it with other applications.

**Keywords**: security, security quantifier, electronic business application

## 1 Introduction

A central issue in the commercial use of the Internet is security. Surveys state that the economic success of electronic business applications is inhibited because the Internet lacks appropriate security measures [20]. One way to increase the trust of consumers in electronic business applications is to establish a standardized quantification of security. It is important to find a security quantifier – not only to compare systems with one another but also to analyze and design electronic business applications.

Most work related to the quantification of security focuses on special areas of security. Brocklehurst et al. [3] consider the measurement of operational security comparing the security with the reliability of a system. Following this approach it is possible to use existing methods of checking software reliability. Bhargava and Bhargava [2] attempt to quantify the quality of service in electronic commerce software. Security is used as one of several measurements (like convenience, throughput, and reliability) for the quality of service of electronic commerce software. Jøsang [15] deals with a metric of trust needed in public key infrastructures. In this area some research has been done [18, 25]. In contrast, Ting [24] does not define a specific metric but emphasizes the need for a security quantification in information systems regarding the relative and not the absolute value of the data in the system.

Another related topic is the evaluation of systems according to national or international evaluation criteria - like the Common Criteria [6] - where the compliance of systems with predefined protection profiles is assessed and assigned an evaluation assurance level. Even though such an evaluation may be very thorough, the results cannot be compared easily since the protection profiles are quite complex and it is likely that for another system a different protection profile has been used. Schönberg and Thoben [23] develop an evaluation concept that allows to carry out cardinal and ordinal evaluations when doing a risk analysis of workflow-based applications.

Nevertheless, a quantification of the security of an electronic business application is missing. Therefore, this paper introduces a way to quantify the security of Internet based electronic business applications. This is done using a *security matrix* resulting from the security objectives and the major locations of an electronic business application (the merchant's site, the consumer's site, and the transmission way).

The remainder of this paper is structured as follows: Section 2 examines the major security objectives confidentiality, integrity, availability, and accountability. Section 3 defines an electronic business application, and describes security objectives, threats, and measures from the point of view of consumer and merchant, including considerations about the transmission way. Section 4 defines our security quantifier and discusses issues associated with the definition. An example is given, too. Finally, Section 5 gives a conclusion and describes further work.

## 2 General Security Objectives

Traditionally, when talking about data security usually three security objectives are identified: confidentiality, integrity, and availability. To better suit the needs of electronic business with all its legal aspects more security objectives have been identified. The most important one is accountability.

**Confidentiality** describes the state in which data is protected from unauthorized disclosure. A loss of confidentiality occurs when the contents of a communication or a file are disclosed.

**Integrity** means that the data has not been altered or destroyed which can be done accidentally (e.g. transmission errors) or with malicious intent (e.g. sabotage).

**Availability** refers to the fact that data and systems can be accessed by authorized persons within an appropriate period of time. Reasons for loss of availability may be attacks or instabilities of the system.

**Accountability:** If the accountability of a system is guaranteed, the participants of a communication activity can be sure that their communication partner is the one he or she claims to be. So the communication partners can be held accountable for their actions.

# 3 Security of Electronic Business Applications

Electronic commerce is the common use of business information, the maintenance of business relationships, and the execution of business processes and market transactions while using information technology [26]. Gaugler [12] classifies electronic business into business-to-business (if enterprises have established a commercial relationship using electronic communications), business-to-consumer (if the enterprise wants to use electronic means of communication to sell products or services to consumers), business-to-public (if businesses and public administration are communicating), and public-to-consumer (if the public administration offers electronic means of contact to consumers).

In this article we will confine ourselves to business-to-consumer on the Internet. An electronic business application (EBA) is a system consisting of a server system (at the merchant's location), a client system (at the customer's location), and the transmission way in between, which is assumed to be insecure and untrusted.

We will show that the task of carrying out a secure transaction is highly complex. On each side of this communication as well as during the transmission problems may occur. Thus, when talking of security within the context of an EBA all three locations have to be taken into account. Security becomes a complex problem because (1) different systems can be involved, (2) one party cannot influence the other party's system and its security status, and (3) the transmission media – in our case the Internet – is to be regarded as insecure, as it has not been designed for commercial purposes.

## 3.1 Security Requirements

Each partner in an electronic business transaction may have different concepts of security. These interests may even contradict each other. To point this out we will now regard the security from the merchant's and the consumer's point of view. This shows how complex the security of an EBA may become and that the weights assigned to the security matrix (cf. Sect. 4) may shift when being regarded from different points of view.

**The Customer's View** One major reason for a consumer to prefer an Internet merchant over a local shop is the *convenience* of the buying process. She[1] can buy at any given time, can choose and compare between several merchants, and does not have to leave her home when 'browsing' the shops. If security features are difficult to handle, this presents an obstacle in its use. The security functionality must therefore be convenient and easy to use.

A consumer may also be concerned about *privacy* and *confidentiality*. By ordering via the Internet she allows the merchant to find out about her tastes and preferences. In most online transactions today, she even submits her credit card information trusting that the merchant will use it only for

---

[1] In the remainder of this paper the merchant will be male and the customer female.

the specified purpose. The consumer's main security objectives in electronic business therefore are privacy and confidentiality.

**The Merchant's View** The aim of a merchant on the Internet is to create revenue or profit by selling his products. To do so he must establish the *consumer's trust* in his services and products by gaining a *reputation* of good business practice and reliable security measures. This includes the *confidential* use of customer information and the respect of the customer's *privacy*. A breach of security or a published security incident will destroy this trust and influence the merchant's turnover. Since the merchant will send his goods to an unknown customer, he might wish to reliably find out the customer's real identity or at least to get assurance that his goods will be paid for (*accountability*). Another aim is that his service is always *available* in order to reach potential customers at any given time. If his service is not available, the customer will use another merchant's service instead. Furthermore, the information on the web site must be correct and up-to-date, which refers to the *integrity* of the data. In electronic business the merchant is therefore interested in all four security objectives.

## 3.2 Security Threats

For an EBA the following threats can be identified. Table 1 gives a summary.

**Threats to confidentiality** On the consumer's side the confidentiality can be compromised if cookies[2] are collected at a central site, and a profile of the customer's browsing habits is generated without her knowledge. On the merchant's site it may not be guaranteed that only authorized staff may access personal data[3]. A breach of confidentiality might also occur if data about shopping habits of customers or customer groups are published on the merchant's web site[4]. During an unguarded transmission, data are readable to everyone with access to the transmission media.

**Threats to integrity** On the customer's computer the integrity of the data to be transmitted could be put at risk by malicious software such as trojan horses or malicious applets[5]. On the merchant's web site the data presenting

---

[2] Cookies are pieces of data that are stored on the user's computer to introduce the concept of state to the otherwise stateless HTTP. With cookies a server may easily recognize a user visiting his web site for a second time [16].

[3] Recently, even the credit card company VISA had to admit that it was subject to a successful hacking attack where data were stolen from internal servers (http://www.computerworld.com/home/print.nsf/all/000128E45A).

[4] The web site of the Internet bookstore *Amazon* published the preferences of their customers according to their affiliation or residence. The web page in question can be found at http://www.amazon.com/purchase-circles.

[5] In February 1997 the German Chaos Computer Club published an ActiveX control that abused the home banking software *Quicken* to transfer money without the user's knowledge [10].

his merchandise may be compromised by an attacker[6]. A breach of integrity also occurs if an unauthorized user changes another user's data[7]. During the transmission data may also be manipulated. Even though data are protected against transmission errors on the lower layers of the TCP/IP-protocol stack, intentional damage could happen as an attacker could easily recompute the checksums of the protocol [9].

**Threats to availability** The availability of the consumer's computer may be disturbed by malicious software like computer viruses or instable application systems. Attackers aiming to harm a certain merchant might try to attack his web site to set it out of order (e.g. through IP bombing). To guarantee a certain availability of transmission services the Internet was built redundantly. However, current implementations of TCP/IP allow attackers to disturb the operation of computers or parts of the network[8].

**Threats to accountability** Either consumer or merchant could fake a false identity towards each other. Techniques to produce a wrong IP number of the sender's computer are well known (IP spoofing).

**Table 1.** Some security threats and measures in electronic business

| Threats | Confidentiality | Integrity | Availability | Accountability |
|---------|-----------------|-----------|--------------|----------------|
| Customer | cookies | malware (e.g. trojan horses) | malware (e.g. trojan horses) | repudiation |
| Merchant | data protection problems | hacking attacks | hacking attacks | repudiation |
| Transmission | eavesdropping | sequence number guessing | denial-of-service attacks, worms | spoofing attacks |

| Measures | Confidentiality | Integrity | Availability | Accountability |
|----------|-----------------|-----------|--------------|----------------|
| Customer | configuration, awareness | malware scanning | malware scanning | client certificates |
| Merchant | access control | IDS, security tests | IDS, security tests | server certificates |
| Transmission | encryption (SSL, ESP) | SSL | 'redundant network design' | AH |

[6] In February 2000 some Japanese government web sites were changed by hacking attacks (http://www.spiegel.de/netzwelt/politik/0,1518,61238,00.html).

[7] In January 2000 this happened at the Internet bank X.com where any user knowing the account number of another could move and withdraw money from the other's account [17].

[8] In February 2000, the Internet bookstore amazon.com and the Internet auctioneer ebay.com were attacked and could not be accessed for several hours (http://www.spiegel.de/netzwelt/techologie/0,1518,63447,00.htm).

## 3.3 Security Measures

The threats described above must be countered by appropriate security measures. We will describe the measures according to the location where they have to be taken. Table 1 summarizes these security measures. This list cannot be exhaustive.

**Consumer-Side** First of all, the consumer must be aware of possible security problems and act carefully. Her computer has to be configured with care to avoid the threats mentioned above. To maintain confidentiality the consumer's web browser should not send her email address and always ask if a cookie is accepted. To enhance both integrity and availability the consumer's computer should be equipped with an up-to-date version of a virus scanner to detect any malicious software. To prove that she really is the person she claims to be, certificates can be obtained. This may either be client certificates issued by an acknowledged Certification Authority (CA) or PGP[9] keys that are signed by other trusting users. Further security measures to be taken at the consumer's site are listed in [1].

**Merchant-Side** Since on the merchants side the number of computers and applications is probably higher, the security measures to be taken here are much more complex. Moreover the operating system has to be configured carefully. To secure the internal data from being accessed by unauthorized persons an appropriate access control mechanism should be implemented. External access to the merchant's location should be shielded by a firewall system [7]. An intrusion detection system (IDS) should monitor all system activity. Sensitive data should be kept on an internal system that is not accessible via the Internet. To keep the system available, regular checks concerning the state of the security of the applications, the operating system and the network configuration should be carried out using appropriate tools like ISS [14] or SATAN[10] [11]. Server applications such as scripts or servlets should be checked for correctness, to prevent an attacker from using it as an entrance to the system[11]. To prove his identity the merchant should obtain a server certificate from an acknowledged and trusted CA. Integrative approaches to implement secure Internet services are described in [9, 19]. Other measures to enhance the availability are of organizational and infrastructural nature, such as hardware locks to the server rooms and fire protection measures.

**Transmission** During the transmission all sensitive data should be encrypted using a strong cryptographic algorithm. This can be achieved by security protocols on different layers of the TCP/IP protocol stack [22]: On the application layer secure application protocols like S-HTTP[12] or S/MIME[13], on the transport layer the SSL (Secure Sockets Layer) protocol, and on the

---

[9] Pretty Good Privacy, cf. http://www.pgp.com
[10] System Administrator's Tool for Analyzing Networks
[11] A tool which can be used is *Whisker*, cf. http://www.wiretrip.net/rfp/whisker.
[12] Secure Hypertext Transfer Protocol
[13] Secure Multipurpose Internet Mail Extensions

network layer protocols containing security mechanisms – e.g. the AH (Authentication Header) and ESP (Encapsulation Security Protocol) – can be used.

# 4 Quantification

This section presents the quantification of the security of an EBA. Subsection 4.1 gives a formal definition for the security quantifier. Subsection 4.2 focuses on the practical use of this quantifier. The definitions of Subsect. 4.1 are illustrated and interpreted. The security of a sample application is quantified in the last subsection.

## 4.1 Formal Definition

To define the security quantifier we use a *security matrix* with the places and the security objectives of the EBA in its rows and columns. The entries are real numbers representing in how far appropriate measures to implement the security objectives have been made. A high value of the entry/quantifier corresponds to a high security level, a low value to a low level.

To define the security quantifier of an EBA certain formalizations have to be made. The set $S_{obj}$ contains the four security objectives and is defined as follows: $S_{obj} = \{con, in, av, ac\}$. In this definition $con$ represents confidentiality, $in$ integrity, $av$ availability, and $ac$ accountability (cf. Sect. 2). The set $P$ with $P = \{c, m, t\}$ defines the place where the security objective is considered. $c$ symbolizes the consumer's site, $m$ the merchant's site, and $t$ the transmission way (cf. Sect. 3). The *security matrix* $M_{sec}$ can be defined as a function mapping a security objective and a place to a real number in the interval $[0, 1]$:

$$M_{sec} : P \times S_{obj} \longrightarrow [0, 1] \ .$$

The next step in the definition of the security quantifier is the introduction of weights. A weight is a non-negative real number not greater than 1. The sum of all weights in a set of weights has to be equal to 1. Each entry of $M_{sec}$ is assigned such a weight. This can be modeled with a function $w$ mapping each entry in $M_{sec}$ to a real number in the interval $[0, 1]$.

$$w : P \times S_{obj} \longrightarrow [0, 1]$$

The security of an EBA can be quantified as

$$\mu(\text{EBA}) := \sum_{i \in P, \, j \in S_{obj}} w(i, j) * M_{sec}(i, j) \ .$$

$\mu$ will be called the *security quantifier* of EBA. From the definition of $M_{sec}$ and $w$ follows that $0 \leq \mu(\text{EBA}) \leq 1$.

Three special cases can be derived from $\mu$ via the assignment of special sets of weights.

1. If the weights are chosen equally, $\mu_{\text{equi}}(\text{EBA}) := \frac{1}{12} * \sum_{i \in P, j \in S_{\text{obj}}} M_{\text{sec}}(i, j)$. $\mu_{\text{equi}}$ is a very intuitive measure for security. The different values of $M_{\text{sec}}$ are summed up and divided by the total number of entries to normalize the result. This approach is simple but not relevant in practice. In EBAs the different places and security objectives are of different importance which should be borne in mind when choosing the set of weights.

2. The security quantifier $\mu_{\text{weak}}$ follows the paradigm: A chain is as strong as its weakest link. $\mu_{\text{weak}}$ equals to the minimal (or one of the minimal) value(s) of $M_{\text{sec}}$.

$$\mu_{\text{weak}}(\text{EBA}) := \min_{i \in P, j \in S_{\text{obj}}} M_{\text{sec}}(i, j) \ .$$

Even tough the definition of $\mu_{\text{weak}}$ does not contain $w$, weights could be added artificially: all weights are equal to zero except the one corresponding to one of the minimal entries of $M_{\text{sec}}$. The weight corresponding to this entry is set to 1. $\mu_{\text{weak}}$ is propagated by various authors [13, 24].

3. If we apply the paradigm 'The survival of the fittest', a new security quantifier $\mu_{\text{strong}}$ can be introduced, defined as

$$\mu_{\text{strong}}(\text{EBA}) := \max_{i \in P, j \in S_{\text{obj}}} M_{\text{sec}}(i, j) \ .$$

Analogously to $\mu_{\text{weak}}$ weights can artificially be introduced. This approach is unpopular, since usually an attack on a system focuses on its the weaker parts and not on the strong holds.

$\mu$ is defined in a additive manner. Another security quantifier $\pi$ can be defined using multiplication:

$$\boxed{\pi(\text{EBA}) := \prod_{i \in P, j \in S_{\text{obj}}} M_{\text{sec}}(i, j) \ .}$$

On the one hand $\pi$ has the following advantageous characteristics: $0 \leq \pi \leq 1$, $\pi = 0$ if any entry in $M_{\text{sec}}$ is 0, and $\pi = 1$ if all entries are 1. On the other hand $\pi$ will – because of its multiplicative nature – typically be close to 0. The definition can be extended with weights: $\pi(\text{EBA}) := \prod_{i \in P, j \in S_{\text{obj}}} M_{\text{sec}}(i, j)^{w(i,j)}$. Note that (1) the weights do not necessarily have to add up to 1, (2) weights greater than 1 are possible, and (3) a high value of $w$ decreases the importance of the corresponding entry in the matrix and vice versa.

The difficult part in the quantification process is to determine the values in $M_{\text{sec}}$. The numerical calculation of the quantifier is comparatively easy. Therefore, once $M_{\text{sec}}$ has been evaluated, all the proposed quantifiers can be calculated. For the remainder of the paper the discussion is restricted to $\mu$.

## 4.2 Discussion and Use of the Security Quantifier

The last subsection focused on the formal definition of security quantifiers. This subsection will shed some light on the practical use.

**How are the values for the security matrix $M_{sec}$ determined?** After the security threats and measures have been identified (cf. Sect. 3), the measures have to be evaluated. More precisely, a measure for the fulfillment of the security objective at the specific place has to be found. Therefore a real number between 0 and 1 is assigned to the corresponding entry of $M_{sec}$. Examples: $M_{sec}(in, t) = 0$ means that no measures have been taken to guarantee the integrity of the data during transmission. $M_{sec}(m, av) = 1$ means that all relevant precautions to provide the availability of the application have been met at the merchant's site. Values between 0 and 1 represent cases where more than none and less than all security measures have been implemented. The evaluation of the values for $M_{sec}$ requires to know all relevant security measures. The crucial question is: what are all necessary measures?, a question which cannot be answered. Nevertheless there are publications (e.g. [4, 5]) which focus on this topic and give a comprehensive overview.

Another important question is: Who carries out the evaluation? In theory we would need an omniscient evaluator for the three locations. In practice this has to be done by someone familiar with the security measures at the corresponding site. For practical purposes we suggest to switch from continuous to discrete values for the entries of $M_{sec}$, e.g. to work only with the three values 0.1, 0.5, and 0.9 to facilitate the assignment.

**How are the weights determined?** The value of the different weights depends on the importance of the corresponding entries in $M_{sec}$, i.e. the values represent how relevant a security objective at the corresponding place is deemed by the estimator. Table 2 shows an example: most weight is put on the confidentiality and accountability at the merchant's site. In order to compare different applications it is important to use the same weights. A possible solution would be to establish renowned standard weight sets, e.g. a special set of weights for Internet shopping applications.

**How can the security quantifier $\mu$ be interpreted?** The security quantifier $\mu$ maps the security of an EBA to a real number in the interval $[0, 1]$. Therefore, $\mu$ can be interpreted as the percentage of the necessary and implemented security measures. $\mu(\text{EBA}) = 0$ means that none of the necessary security measures have been met, $\mu(\text{EBA}) = 1$ means that all relevant security measures have been implemented. The values in between are interpreted analogously. Note that $\mu(EBA) = 1$ does not mean that EBA is absolutely secure. There is no such thing as absolute security. All security measures rely on their correct implementation and use.

After having described how $\mu$ can be calculated, it is time to think about what to do with $\mu$ after its calculation.

**Analysis** The security quantifier $\mu$ maps the security of an application in an intelligible and intuitive way to a real number. While analyzing an application one can follow the simple rule for $\mu$: the higher the value the better.

**Comparison** After quantifying the security of different applications the quantifiers can be used to compare the applications. The following issues have to be taken into account: (1) The same set of weights has to be used. (2) The evaluation of the values in $M_{sec}$ has to be done on the 'same basis', i.e. there should be no signification difference in the evaluation of security measures. (3) The value of $\mu$ alone without an overview of the evaluation process is of almost no use at all, especially if $\mu$ is used to promote an application. Therefore the tables of threats and security measures, weights, and values of $M_{sec}$ should be available.

**Design** Usually, during the implementation of an EBA not all security measures are implemented at the same point in time. Therefore, a calculation of $\mu$ at various points in time during the implementation can be used to monitor the progress in the system's security.

## 4.3 Example

This section shows the calculation of $\mu$ illustrated through an example of an imaginary bookstore[14]. Let us focus on the following scenario: the book store NOZAMA is selling books over the Internet. The application has a client/server architecture. Clients are the browsers of the consumers, the server side resides at the merchant and consists of one or more HTTP, database, and backup servers. On the server side access control mechanisms are implemented to regulate access to the database(s). Payment is done via credit card. The TCP/IP connections between browser and HTTP server is protected using SSL. The costumers have to possess valid certificates (implemented in their browser) for authentication and have to provide a valid login name and password when accessing the HTTP server. Furthermore the customer's browser is 'fortified' to allow for stronger encryption. $\mu$(NOZAMA) is derived in the following steps:

**Table 2.** Security measures, $M_{sec}$, and the set of weights for the NOZAMA example

| | Confidentiality | Integrity | Availability | Accountability |
|---|---|---|---|---|
| Customer | browser fortification | browser fortification | - | client certificate |
| Merchant | access control mechanisms | plausibility check, checksums | backup servers | server certificate, login/password, log-file |
| Transmission | SSL | SSL | - | log-file, SSL |

| $w$ | $con$ | $in$ | $av$ | $ac$ |
|---|---|---|---|---|
| $c$ | 0.05 | 0.05 | 0.05 | 0.05 |
| $m$ | 0.2 | 0.1 | 0.1 | 0.2 |
| $t$ | 0.05 | 0.05 | 0.05 | 0.05 |

| $M_{sec}$ | $con$ | $in$ | $av$ | $ac$ |
|---|---|---|---|---|
| $c$ | 0.5 | 0.5 | 0.1 | 0.9 |
| $m$ | 0.9 | 0.5 | 0.5 | 0.9 |
| $t$ | 0.9 | 0.9 | 0.1 | 0.9 |

---

[14] The authors tried to find a real example but it turned out that the security mechanisms of an EBA – especially on the merchant's side – are an intimate detail which most companies are not willing to compromise.

1. The first step is to organize the implemented security mechanisms in a table which is shown for the NOZAMA example in Table 2. Note that some security measures reside in several fields of the table. E.g. SSL supports the confidentiality, integrity, and accountability security objective during transmission. Other fields of the table may be empty.
2. Next, the security measures have to be evaluated to get $M_{sec}$ which is shown – due to our evaluation – in Table 2, too. Remarks: We use the 0.1,0.5,0.9-evaluation introduced in Sect. 4.2. $M_{sec}(c, av) = 0.1$ and $M_{sec}(t, av) = 0.1$ since almost no appropriate measures have been taken. For the tuples $(c, con)$, $(c, in)$, $(m, in)$, and $(m, av)$ the value of $M_{sec}$ is 0.5 since the corresponding security measures fulfill the security objectives at the corresponding place to a certain amount, but additional other measures are needed. All remaining entries of $M_{sec}$ are set to 0.9, because the corresponding measures are deemed sufficient.
3. The last step is the numerical calculation of $\mu$. The application of the weights (cf. Table 2) yields $\mu(\text{NOZAMA}) = 0.7$. Remarks: The choice of weights depends on the evaluator. The customer may choose different weights than the merchant and their evaluation may be different, too. In our evaluation we tried to take a 'neutral viewpoint'.

For the NOZAMA example $\mu_{equi} = 0.55$, $\mu_{weak} = 0.1$, and $\mu_{strong} = 0.9$. If no weights are used $\pi(\text{NOZAMA}) = 0.1^2 * 0.5^4 * 0.9^6 \approx 0.332 * 10^{-3}$.

## 5 Conclusion and Further Research

This paper has focused on the security of EBAs. After introducing the notions of security and electronic business, a systematic way to organize security measures in a matrix has been shown. The rows of this matrix give the place and the columns the security objective of the analyzed application. This matrix has been used to define a security quantifier. Its definition and properties have been discussed and illustrated through an example. Summarized, we have given an easy to use and flexible procedure to map the security of an EBA to a real number in the interval $[0, 1]$.

Future work will focus on the extension of our model and its practical use: (1) One way to extend our approach is to examine more security objectives like anonymity, timeliness etc. A problem arising is that there might be significant correlations between the different elements in the extended set of objectives. (2) Another way to extend our approach is to include more places in the security matrix. Example: EBAs may include more than two business partners. Next to the consumer and the merchant there might be a bank, lawyer, or CA involved. Each of these partners may have a different evaluation of the applied security measures. (3) The security quantifier in this paper is of theoretical nature. Therefore, it is of paramount importance to gain an understanding of its practical relevance. Studies can compare different EBAs, but may also analyze and design a system using our quantifier.

# Acknowledgments

The authors would like to thank Prof. K. Bauknecht and the members of the Information and Communication Management Group, University of Zurich for the discussion of this paper. The work was partly funded by the Swiss National Science Foundation under grant SPP-ICS 5003-045359.

# References

[1] Jo Bager, Holger Bleich, Patrick Brauch, and Axel Kossel. Natürliche Abwehrkräfte: Windows- und Internet-Software richtig konfigurieren. *c't*, Feb. 2000, pp. 214–223.

[2] A. Bhargava and B. Bhargava. Measurement and quality of services in electronic commerce software. In *Proc. of the IEEE Symposium on Application-Specific Systems and Software Engineering and Technology*, 1999.

[3] S. Brocklehurst, B. Littlewod, T. Olovsson, and E. Jonsson. On measurement of operational security. In *Proc. of the 9th Annual Conference on Computer Assurance, COMPASS'94*, 1994.

[4] British Standards Institute. *BS7799: Code of Practice for Information Security Management (CoP)*, 1995.

[5] Bundesamt für die Sicherheit in der Informationstechnik (BSI), Bonn. *IT-Grundschutzhandbuch: Maßnahmenempfehlungen für den mittleren Schutzbedarf*, 3 edition, Juli 1997.

[6] Common Criteria for Information Technology and Security Evaluation: Part 1: Introduction and general model. International Standard ISO/IEC 15408, May 1998.

[7] William R. Cheswick and Steven M. Bellovin. *Firewalls and Internet Security — Repelling the Wily Hacker*. Professional Computing Series. Addison Wesley, 1994.

[8] Cheskin Research and Studio Archetype/Sapient. *eCommerce Trust Study*, January 1999.

[9] D. Damm, Ph. Kirsch, Th. Schlienger, S. Teufel, H. Weider, and U. Zurfluh. Rapid Secure Development: Ein Verfahren zur Definition eines Internet-Sicherheitskonzeptes. Tech. Report, Inst. für Informatik, Uni. Zürich, 02/1999.

[10] Lutz Donnerhacke and Steffen Peter. Vorsicht Falle! ActiveX als Füllhorn für Langfinger. *iX*, März 1997.

[11] Dan Farmer and Wietse Venema. Improving the Security of Your Site by Breaking Into it. http://wzv.tue.nl/satan/admin-guide-to-cracking.html, 1993.

[12] Thomas Gaugler. *Interorganisatorische Informationssysteme (IOS): Ein Gestaltungsrahmen für das Informationsmanagment*. PhD thesis, Institut für Informatik, Universität Zürich, 1999.

[13] A.K. Ghosh. Securing E-Commerce: A Systematic Approach. *Journal of Internet Banking and Commerce*, 1997.

[14] Internet Security Systems. *Network and Host-based Vulnerability Assessment*, 1999. http://www.iss.net.

[15] Andrun Jøsang. A subjective metric of authentication. In *Proc. of the 5th European Symposium on Reserach in Computer Security*, LNCS 1485, pages 329–344, Belgium, Sep. 1998.

[16] D. Kristol and L. Montulli. HTTP State Management Mechanism. RFC 2109, February 1997.

[17] John Markoff. Security Flaw Discovered at Online Bank. *The New York Times*, January 2000.

[18] Ueli Maurer. Modelling a public-key infrastructure. In *Proc. of the 5th European Symposium on Reserach in Computer Security*, pages 325–350, Italy, Sep. 1996.

[19] V. McCarthy. Web-Security: How Much Is Enough? *Datamation*, January 1997.

[20] Günter Müller and Detlef Schoder. Potentiale und Hürden des Electronic Commerce — Eine Momentaufnahme. *Informatik Spektrum*, August 1999.

[21] Adam R. Nabil and Yelena Yesha, editors. *Electronic Commerce: Current Research Issues and Applications*. LNCS 1028, Springer, 1996.

[22] Rolf Oppliger. Internet Security: Firewalls and Beyond. *Communications of the ACM*, 40(5), May 1997.

[23] Arndt Schönberg and Wilfried Thoben. Ein unscharfes Bewertungskonzept für die Bedrohungs- und Risikoanalyse Workflow-basierter Anwendungen. In *Sicherheit und Electronic Commerce — Konzepte, Modelle und technische Möglichkeiten (WS SEC'98)*, pp. 47–62, Vieweg-Verlag, 1998.

[24] T. C. Ting. How secure is secure: Some thoughts on security metrics. In *Proc. of the 9th annual IFIP WG 11.3 Working Conference on Database Security*, pp. 3–7, Lake Tahoe, CA, Aug. 1995.

[25] P.R. Zimmermann. *The Official PGP User's Guide*. MIT Press, 1995.

[26] V. Zwass. Electronic Commerce: Structures and Issues. *International Journal of Electronic Commerce*, 1(1):3–23, 1996.

# Towards a Secure and De-centralized Digital Watermarking Infrastructure for the Protection of Intellectual Property

Philipp Tomsich and Stefan Katzenbeisser

Institute of Software Technology, Vienna University of Technology
Favoritenstraße 9–11/188, A–1040 Wien, Austria
phil@ifs.tuwien.ac.at, skatzenbeisser@acm.org

**Abstract.** The advent of the Web, electronic commerce and the creation of electronic distribution channels for content have brought new challenges regarding the protection of intellectual property. As it has become increasingly difficult to protect the distribution medium against copying, techniques for asserting the copyright on information have gained in importance. A particularly promising method is the use of digital watermarking to embed additional copyright information within data. However, central servers or certification authorities are required by most current watermarking protocols, thus limiting the wide-spread application of watermarking in electronic commerce applications.

We propose a secure, distributed watermarking scheme using trusted, tamper-proof hardware. The protocols presented provide support for copyright protection and fingerprinting in a de-centralized fashion. Extensive use of a public-key infrastructure permits the secure exchange of secret keys between trusted devices. The unencrypted, private keys never leave the hardware, rendering them unrecoverable. If adopted, this allows for the establishment of a ubiquitous digital watermarking infrastructure to support and foster e-commerce applications.

## 1 Introduction

With the increasing availability and distribution of media in a digital form, the protection of intellectual property faces new challenges. The possibility to easily and cheaply reproduce content without a loss of quality is undermining the film, music and entertainment industries. As a consequence, the question of how to effectively protect the copyright holder's interests are critical to a wide-spread acceptance of e-commerce in these application domains.

Two fundamentally different approaches exist to counteract the increased risk of copyright infringements:

- **Copy protection** attempts to find ways which limit the access to copyrighted material and/or inhibit the copy process itself. Examples include encrypted digital TV broadcast, access controls to copyrighted software through the use of license servers and technical copy protection mechanisms on the media. However, copy protection is very difficult to achieve in open systems, as recent developments for DVD [2, 11] show.

- **Copyright protection** uses embedded information to encode the copyright owner's identity within the content. Whenever the copyright of a digital document is disputed, this copyright information can be extracted to identify the rightful owner. It is also possible to fingerprint digital content with the identity of its buyer to provide for the tracing of any authorized copies. The most prominent way of embedding information in digital media is the use of digital watermarking [7].

Basically a watermarking scheme consists of two algorithms, one embedding and one extraction algorithm. The embedding algorithm inserts a watermark into digital media using a secret key, thereby generating the watermarked media. Depending on the nature of the extraction algorithm, two types of watermarking schemes can be identified. The extraction process of *private watermarking* systems takes the watermarked media, the original media, the watermark and the secret key and outputs TRUE if the watermark is actually present in. In the case of *blind watermarking* systems, the extractor extracts the watermark given only the watermarked media and the key. Watermark extraction should also be possible in the case small modifications have been applied to the marked media, i.e. the embedding process should be *robust*. Such modifications can be the result of intentional attacks in order to remove the mark or the result of coding schemes (e.g. lossy compression) and errors during the transmission [7]. Whereas secure copy protection mechanisms in open systems seems to be difficult to achieve, copyright protection systems based on watermarks and strong cryptography are feasible. As a result, considerable interest in digital watermaking exists for electronic commerce applications. However, watermarking protocols are yet to experience wide-spread use. Most approaches proposed so far, either make use of a central server to ensure the uniqueness of watermarks [1], require the generation of disjunct keys for every transaction or require the publication of private keys during the dispute resolution [6].

We propose a secure, distributed watermarking scheme using trusted, tamper-proof hardware; however, we this protocol does not attempt to restrict the use of copyrighted material and leaves this to higher level solutions. The protocols presented provide support for copyright protection and fingerprinting in a de-centralized fashion. Extensive use of a public-key infrastructure permits the secure exchange of secret keys between trusted devices. Trust is established using public-key certification and verification. The unencrypted, private keys never leave the hardware, rendering them unrecoverable. Such a distributed solution appears favorable to one based on the availability of a central server, as it is immune to denial-of-service attacks, offers far superior scalability and no-one except for the owner ever has access to the original, unmarked work.

The remainder of this paper is organized as follows: Section 2 discusses the basic requirements and problems of watermarking for copyright protection. The properties of tamper-proof hardware are summarized in section 3 and a protocol using such hardware is given in section 4. An extension to fingerprinting is presented in section 5. Some conclusions are given in section 6.

## 2  Considerations for successful watermarking protocols

Many researchers see watermarks as a cure-all solution to copyright protection problems. However, this protocol is seriously flawed and susceptible to different attacks as depicted in the following scenarios featuring three imaginary person Alice, Bob and Carol, where Alice is the rightful copyright owner, Bob commits an infringement and Carol act as judge or arbitrator:

- **Invertibility.** Bob could try to insert his own watermark in the copy he received and claim the ownership of the newly marked object. One could argue that such an attack has to fail, since Alice's original contained only her watermark whereas Bob's fake original contains both Alice's and Bob's mark, thereby clearly establishing an order of watermark insertion. However, Craver et al. [4] showed that it is—under specific circumstances—possible by an attacker to insert a second watermark in the already marked object in a way that his new mark seems to be present in the copy Alice locked away (although the attacker has no knowledge of the unmarked data). In such "invertibility attacks", Bob "subtracts" (rather than adds) his own watermark from the watermarked data, and claims the result to be the original work. The watermark detector will now detect Bob's watermark in the original object. There is no way to resolve copyright ownership in this case, as it becomes impossible to determine which object is the original.

  In order to prevent such an attack, one has to use *noninvertible marking schemes*, based on hash functions. Another possibility would be the use of a central time-stamping device.

- **Public versus private information.** When Alice is asked to prove the ownership of her works in front of a judge, she has to reveal her private key. Since in most watermarking schemes the key is coupled with the location of the watermark in the digital media, it is then possible to remove the mark once the key is public. Thus, once Alice is asked to prove the ownership of a work, *all other marks generated by the same key are removable*.

  Thus, an asymmetric watermarking system (similar to asymmetric cryptography) would be preferable, where a mark is inserted by a private key but can be checked by a public key. Unfortunately, such schemes do not exist yet. Recently Craver [6] proposed the use of zero-knowledge proofs in watermarking.

- **Buyer/Seller conflict.** Suppose the digital work is not sold by Alice directly, but by a distributor named Carol. Bob can always claim that it was actually Carol who circulates illegal copies containing watermarks identifying Bob as the customer and that he is actually innocent [9]. There is no way for Carol to prove the opposite.

- **Copy attack.** Recently Kutter et al. [8] showed that in some systems a third party is able to copy a watermark from a marked image to another (unmarked) image.

For these reasons a simple watermarking protocol in this section cannot solve the problem of copyright protection. However, a number of general requirements for practical copyright protection protocols can be established.

**Secrecy Criterion:** Watermark verification must be possible *without* revealing the secret key of the owner.

**Rightful Ownership Criterion:** A watermark should uniquely identify the owner of a digital document; thus, it should not be possible to forge watermarks (or copy watermarks between images).

**Noninvertibility Criterion:** It must at least be feasible to reconstruct a strict order of watermark insertion. Thus, if marks $W_1, \ldots, W_n$ are found in the document, it must be possible to determine which mark was the first one (thereby preventing "invertibility attacks").

**Decentralization Criterion:** The copyright protocol should not rely on central infrastructure, but rather on the existing public-key infrastructure.

# 3 Tamper-proof hardware

Software executing within the main memory of a computer is always susceptible to manipulation of observation, weakening the secrecy criterion. An intruder may be able to retrieve secret key information from main memory during the execution of an encryption algorithm. Dedicated hardware may provide a far better protection against attackers by limiting the number of access points. In combination with audited protocols and certified software, attackers can be locked out of the system. During the last few years a number of *tamper-proof* hardware devices have been developed and deployed, the most popular being smart cards used for identification purposes and financial transactions.

The physical security of information stored in tamper-proof hardware usually starts with the combination of computer memory and processor in a single package with a protective enclosure. Given the outer enclosure sufficiently protects such a device against unauthorized access the the chip, it is extremely difficult to examine the contents of the memory cells within the chip. It is also difficult to to intercept the electrical signals passing between the processor and memory. All access to the hardware is carried out using dedicated access points and protocols. The hardware runs a tiny operating system, which implements the communication protocol and provides security. The access to state information of processes running within the tamper-proof hardware thus requires fairly expensive equipment and unhampered access to the hardware under attack.

In order to ensure that the software executing within the tamper-proof hardware is trustworthy, only manual inspection and certification is possible. However, using a read-only memory to store the program code, the hardware remains trustworthy for its entire lifetime. If the distribution of secret information is limited to certified devices, no danger of a public disclosure exists. If a public-key infrastructure is to be built on such devices, the public keys may be signed by a well-known certification authority (e.g. an international standardization organization). Although seemingly centralized, the central authority is only needed prior to the deployment of the hardware—the operation does not require access to any central site or service. Since software updates will likely be necessary, appropriate mechanisms to ensure the integrity and trustworthiness of the new software packages have to be added to updateable hardware. Such a software update infrastructure can be built using public-key cryptography and one-way hash functions.

# 4 Copyright protection protocol based on tamper-proof hardware

We present a copyright protection protocol which is based on tamper-proof hardware and a traditional public-key infrastructure. It is assumed that every user has access to tamper-proof hardware which contains the public key $E_{CA}$ of a certification authority and a certified public/private key pair $E_{H_A}/D_{H_A}$. It is assumed, that every user has a key pair $E_A/D_A$ as part of an infrastructure for legally binding digital signatures. The protocols presented are assumed to be implemented in tamper-proof hardware. Copyright protection is based on four protocols: watermark key generation, watermark insertion, watermark extraction and a dispute resolution protocol.

## 4.1 Watermark key generation

The purpose of this protocol is to generate a "watermark key envelope", which is used in the following protocols. Basically, a watermark key envelope consists of an encrypted random watermark and a string describing the identity of a user, signed by the certification authority.

1. Alice requests the signed public key of the hardware and verifies whether it is signed by an agreed authority which ensures a conforming software within the trusted hardware.
2. Alice sends an encrypted request to her hardware; this request contains the public key $E_A$ of Alice along with a string of her identity $Id$, signed with her private key (we denote this by $D_A(Id)$). Furthermore Alice sends a certificate of her public key $D_{CA}(E_A, Id)$, i.e. her private key and her identify string signed by a certification authority.
3. The hardware generates a random watermark key $K$ and encrypts $K$ with its public key $E_{H_A}$, yielding $E_{H_A}(K)$ and constructs the watermarking key envelope, consisting of the encrypted watermark $E_{H_A}(K)$, the signed user identification $D_A(Id)$ and the certificate $D_{CA}(E_A, Id)$ received:

$$W_K = \langle E_{H_A}(K), D_{CA}(E_A, Id), D_A(Id) \rangle .$$

   The hardware signs the envelope and returns it to the user.
4. Alice checks the signature on $W_K$ to ensure unmodified transmission and stores $W_K$ for future use.

The watermark key envelope provides a secure transfer and storage medium for the secret watermark key and related information identifying the key holder. This ensures the *secrecy criterion*, because the unencrypted key never leaves the hardware. Even the key holder cannot access or manipulate the information contained without using the trusted hardware. This guarantees that only valid operations can be performed. The contained user identification allows the watermark verification process to uniquely identify the key holder (a prerequisite for the *rightful-ownership criterion*) within the limits of current digital signature standards. Signing the key envelope with the secret hardware key ensures that an intruder cannot insert a pre-fabricated watermark envelope, as no direct verification of the envelope's content is possible for the user.

It should be noted that one user can have multiple watermark keys. Furthermore, one user can also have more than one piece of hardware; one hardware device can also be shared between different people.

## 4.2 Watermark insertion

This protocol inserts a watermark in a digital object $O$, thereby using a noninvertible watermarking scheme. We assume a method similar to Craver et al. [5] or Qiao and Nahrstedt [10]. A noninvertible scheme is based on a hash of the original data. Suppose the watermark consists of $n$ watermark bits $w_0, \ldots, w_n$ and the first $n$ bits of a hash of $O$ are $b_0, \ldots, b_n$. Depending on the value of $b_i$, the watermarking algorithm chooses among two possible ways of inserting the watermark bit $w_i$. Assuming a "perfect" hash function $H$ (i.e. a hash function which hashes even perceptually similar images to completely different bit-strings), it is believed that such watermarking schemes are not susceptible to inversion attacks: suppose an attacker wants to "subtract" a fake watermark $W'$ from an already watermarked data $O'$, thereby creating the fake original $O''$. Since in noninvertible marking schemes the location of $W'$ depends of the fake original $O''$ which is not yet known, the attacker has to guess a bit-string $b_1, \ldots, b_n$ and a mark $W'$ in a way that when $W'$ is subtracted from $O'$, the result hashes to $b_1, \ldots, b_n$. This should not be possible when using a one-way hash.

1. Alice requests the hardware public key and verifies it.
2. Alice sends the original data $O$, a string $Desc$ describing $O$ and a previously generated watermarking key $W_K$ back to the hardware. All data must be encrypted using the hardware public key to fend off any attackers intercepting transfers to the trusted hardware.
3. The hardware extracts the encrypted random watermark $E_{H_A}(K)$ out of $W_K$, decrypts it to obtain the watermarking key $K$. It then watermarks $O$ using a noninvertible scheme and watermark key $K$; the watermark itself should consist of a string describing Alice's identity.
4. The hardware sends the watermarked image back to Alice, along with verification token consisting of all information necessary to verify the watermark. This includes the description, the hardware public key, the watermarking key envelope and a one-way hash of the original object used by the non-invertible marking scheme:

$$Ref = \langle Desc, E_{H_A}, W_K, H(O) \rangle .$$

The hardware signs $Ref$, returns it to Alice and clears its memory.
5. Alice retrieves the marked data and stores $Ref$ for use in a watermark verification protocol or a dispute resolution protocol.

Using a non-invertible watermarking scheme ensures the satisfaction of the *noninvertibility criterion*. During the process, a verification token is generated, which encapsulates all the information necessary in the verification and dispute resolution protocols. The verification token returned to the user, contains a watermarking envelope with an encrypted key which can only be decrypted by the original watermarking hardware. In order to use it with a different hardware device, it needs to be decrypted by the original hardware and encrypted for the new hardware device. This is necessary to uphold the *secrecy criterion*.

## 4.3 Watermark verification

The watermark verification protocol is straightforward to implement. The same hardware that was originally used to watermark the data is given a marked media and the verification token. It then verifies the presence of the watermark in the media, using information from the verification token.

1. Alice requests the public key from the hardware and checks whether the hardware is trustworthy.
2. Alice transfers the marked object $O$ and the associated verification token $Ref$ into the hardware. The transferred data is encrypted using the hardware public key in order to prevent attackers from inserting fake data.
3. The hardware checks the signature of the verification token, extracts the hash value $H(O)$ and decrypts the random watermark key $K$ contained in the watermark key envelope $W_K$. After this process, the hardware checks whether Alice's watermark is contained in $O$, thereby using the watermark key $K$ and the hash $H(O)$, and returns the answer TRUE or FALSE. It then clears its memory.
4. If the answer of the hardware was TRUE, it supports Alice's claim that bob infringes her copyright.

Note that there is no need for the hardware to check the identity of its user, which conforms with the *decentralization criterion* as no central directory is necessary. If this identity is in question, authentication will be performed during a dispute resolution protocol. Bob may now confess that he was actually illegally distributing Alice's media. Otherwise, Alice will start a dispute resolution protocol in front of an arbitrator. This arbitrator will again verify the watermark and query the certification authority for the validity of Alice's public keys. The *secrecy criterion* holds for watermark key, as it never leaves the hardware unencrypted.

## 4.4 Dispute resolution protocol

Probably the most difficult protocol is the dispute resolution protocol. This protocol involves three parties: Alice, Bob and an arbitrator/judge Carol. Basically, Carol will verify the watermark in *her* hardware, thereby preventing possible allegations by Bob that Alice is actually cheating in the verification process. For this purpose, the judge asks Alice's hardware to provide a verification token that is suitable for her hardware (i.e. re-encrypt the verification token). Carol's hardware can now verify the validity of the mark and check the identity of Alice.

In fact, the dispute resolution protocol does not attempt to determine the actual holder of the copyright, but rather establishes an strict precedence order on the claims, similar in spirit to the ordering system used for patent rights. The actual copyright holder can only be determined, if he/she participates in the protocol.

1. Alice transmits the public key of her hardware to Carol.
2. Carol verifies that Alice's hardware is trustworthy.
3. Carol then asks Alice's hardware to recode the verification token for her hardware and provides her hardware public key to Alice.
4. Alice verifies Carol's hardware key to determine whether the hardware is trustworthy. If this succeeds, both parties have established that their hardware may communicate using the provided keys.

5. Carol's hardware now receives the verification token, recoded and encrypted to her hardware. The recoding process involves the decryption and re-encryption of the secret watermarking key (contained in the watermarking key envelope). The second layer of encryption ensures that the data can not be manipulated during the transmission. Additionally, the sending hardware signs the token with its private key to uniquely establish the originator.

In more detail, Alice's hardware receives $Ref$, extracts and decrypts the contained information and returns the token

$$\langle Desc, E_{H_A}, H(O), E_{H_C}(K), D_{CA}(E_A, Id), D_A(Id)\rangle$$

where $E_{H_C}$ denotes the public key of Carol's hardware. $Desc$ is a string describing the digital data, $E_{H_A}$ is the public key of Alice's hardware, $E_{H_C}(K)$ is the random watermark encrypted with Carol's public hardware key, $D_{CA}(E_A, Id)$ is a certificate of Alice's public key and $D_A(Id)$ is Alice's signed identity. The entire token is signed by Alice's hardware using the secret hardware key $D_{H_A}$.

6. Carol's device checks the signature on the token received, extracts the necessary information. Then, the device decrypts the random watermark key contained in the watermarking key envelope and verifies the presence of the watermark using the hash. Once the watermark is accepted as genuine, it remains to control the identity of Alice to detect the man-in-the-middle: Carol's hardware checks the signature on the certificate $D_{CA}(E_A, Id)$ using the public key of the certification authority and uses the private key $E_A$ to verify the signature $D_A(Id)$. However, it remains to verify whether the person identified by $Id$ is actually the communication partner expected. Existing infrastructure for legally binding digital signatures can be used in this phase.

7. If all tests passed and Alice's watermark is indeed present, Carol's hardware outputs TRUE.

In a simple case, Bob may now confess that he has actually stolen Alice's data. However, Bob could also claim that he is the rightful owner and that Alice has actually stolen his image and inserted her watermark into it. Carol has to resolve this case by checking the presence of watermarks in the digital data Alice and Bob claim to be the originals. We can distinguish four cases:

- *Bob's original contains Alice's mark but Alice's original does not contain Bob's mark*: in this case, Bob clearly inserted his mark after Alice. The court may conclude that Alice is the rightful owner.
- *Alice's original contains Bob's mark but Bob's original does not contain Alice's mark*: this case is similar to the last one; clearly, Alice inserted her mark after Bob and so the court may conclude that Bob is the rightful owner.
- *Both Alice's and Bob's original contain no detectable watermarks*: in this case, no conclusion can be drawn; either Bob or Alice got an unmarked version of the image owned by the other one or both Alice and Bob independently inserted their own watermarks into an image actually owned by a third person. This third person may have watermarked the image or not.
- *Both Alice's and Bob's original contain both watermarks*: this is the classical *deadlock situation* produced by inversion attacks. Again, no conclusion can be drawn.

In the first two cases, it was possible to resolve the copyright situation; in the last two cases a final conclusion cannot be drawn and the dispute must be settled in a traditional court case.

Even the first two cases are more problematic than they may seem: since the dispute resolution protocol is only a three-party protocol, there might by the possibility that both Alice and Bob have actually stolen the image from another party which does not participate in the protocol. In this case, the claimed originals might contain other watermarks. Since the watermark key of this unknown party would be required to verify that assumption, Carol is not able to exclude this possibility until she has checked all watermark keys from *all possible parties*, which is obviously not feasible.

Obviously the third and fourth cases are most problematic. One could argue that the fourth situation does not happen when using noninvertible watermarking systems. The third case should never happen in reality either, as it always results from neither party having inserted a watermark or from uncontrolled access to the unmarked original, which is then copied by the infringer.

## 5 Fingerprinting protocol

The protocols presented in the last section do not allow the tracing of users selling illegal copies of digital data. In addition to the normal watermarking functionality, it is required that a mark should identify the buyer of the digital object uniquely. No customer should be able to falsely deny that he distributed illegal copies. The fingerprinted media should only be known to the customer to avoid false claims of infringement.

It is straightforward to add such functionalities. However, the marking algorithm has to be modified to avoid *collusion attacks*; assume that several copies of one digital object are sold and that an attacker has access to $n$ such copies. By comparing the copies, he can find least some of the modifications applied during the marking process and try to remove them. To elude this attack, the watermark is encoded prior to the embedding process in such a way that several watermarks have a common intersection which cannot be found by comparison. Boney and Shaw presented an encoding for this purpose in [3]. In order to avoid a buyer/seller conflict, the marked data must not be known to the merchant. This can be provided for in two ways: the sold data can either be marked in the buyer's media or the marked media must leave the merchant's hardware encrypted. The watermark insertion protocol can be modified accordingly.

## 6 Conclusions and future research

We argue that watermarking alone is not sufficient to resolve rightful ownership of digital data; a protocol relying on the existing public-key infrastructure (which is also used for digital signatures) is necessary. It seems that the primary vulnerability of the presented protocol is the watermarking algorithm itself; most known watermarking systems are sensitive to intentional distortions of the digital data and do not merge the digital data and the watermark completely, as copy attacks show. For these reasons, the software used for watermarking will have to be updated regularly. A secure distribution protocol will become necessary to support these updates. Additionally, the presented solution poses open problems, if hardware is rendered inaccessible as the hardware's secret keys are otherwise compromised.

The protocol presented in the previous sections eliminates the problem of revealing the private key in front of a judge when verifying a watermark. A distributed solution overcomes the main disadvantages of a central solution: limited scalability, a single point of failure and the dependence on the trustworthiness of the service provider. Furthermore, extensive use of public key cryptography assures the secure exchange of keys and renders man-in-the-middle attacks very difficult; trusted tamper-proof hardware is used to conceal the actual watermarking operation. It is easy to imagine that a specialized microchip—which could integrate other functionality used to support secure e-commerce, such as secure electronic transactions and public-key cryptography—can be cheaply produced, given the number of potential customers. When a robust and non-invertible watermarking system is used as a building block for the proposed protocol, we believe that this protocol allows the establishment of a sufficiently secure digital watermarking infrastructure to support and foster e-commerce applications.

# References

1. A. Adelsbach, B. Pfitzmann, A.-R. Sadeghi, "Proving Ownership of Digital Content" in *Proc. of the Third Intl. Workshop on Information Hiding*, LNCS 1768, 2000, pp. 117–133.
2. J. A. Bloom, I. J. Cox, et. al., "Copy Protection for DVD Video", in *Proc. of the IEEE*, vol. 87, no. 7, July 1999, pp. 1267–1276.
3. D. Boneh, J. Shaw, "Collusion-Secure Fingerprinting for Digital Data", in *Proc. of the CRYPTO'95*, LNCS 963, 1995, pp. 452–465.
4. S. Craver, N. Memon, B. L. Yeo, M. M. Yeung, "Can invisible watermarks resolve rightful ownership?", in *Proc. of the SPIE 3022, Storage and Retrieval for Image and Video Databases*, 1997, pp. 310–321.
5. S. Craver, N. Memon, B. L. Yeo, M. M. Yeung, "Resolving Rightful Ownerships with Invisible Watermarking Techniques: Limitations, Attacks and Implications", in *IEEE Journal on Selected Areas in Communications*, vol. 16. no. 4, 1998, pp. 573–586.
6. S. Craver, "Zero Knowledge Watermark Detection", in *Proc. of the Third International Workshop on Information Hiding*, LNCS 1768, 2000, pp. 101–116.
7. S. Katzenbeisser, F.A.P. Petitcolas (eds.), *Information Hiding Techniques for Steganography and Digital Watermarking*, Boston, London: Artech House, 2000.
8. M. Kutter, S. Voloshynovskiy, A. Herrigel, "The Watermark Copy Attack" in *Proc. of the SPIE 3971, Security and Watermarking of Multimedia Contents II*, 2000.
9. N. Memon, P. W. Wong, "Buyer-seller watermarking protocol based on amplitude modulation and the El Gamal Public Key Crypto System", in *Proceedings of the SPIE 3657, Security and Watermarking of Multimedia Contents*, 1999, pp. 289–294.
10. L. Qiao, K. Nahrstedt, *Watermarking Schemes and Protocols For Protecting Rightful Ownerships and Customer's Rights*, Research report, Dept. of Computer Science, University of Illinois at Urbana-Champaign, 1997.
11. B. Schneier, *DVD Encryption Broken*, Crypto-Gram Newsletter 11/1999, available at http://www.counterpane.com/crypto-gram-9911.html.

# Selling Bits:
# A Matter of Creating Consumer Value

**Jaap Gordijn[1], Hans Akkermans[12], Hans van Vliet[1], and Edwin Paalvast[3]**

[1] Vrije Universiteit, De Boelelaan 1081a, NL-1081 HV Amsterdam, The Netherlands,
{gordijn,HansAkkermans,hans}@cs.vu.nl
[2] AKMC Knowledge Management, Klareweid 19, NL-1831 BV Koedijk, The Netherlands
[3] Cisco Systems International, Hoogoorddreef 9, NL-1101 BA Amsterdam, The Netherlands,
epaalvas@cisco.com

**Abstract.** Digital goods such as music are vulnerable to illegal use over the internet. Technology-driven IT solutions to protection are useful but limited. Instead, we suggest that incentives to legal forms of consumption can be constructed by redesigning how the e-business model for digital content creates consumer value. We present a general framework that enables a quantified utility analysis and clarifies what parameters, technological as well as market ones, influence consumer value. On this basis, we discuss several business scenarios that show how to make the value gap between legal and illegal offerings as large as possible. This analysis framework is part of our $e^3$-$value^{TM}$ methodology for e-business modelling and decision making in which business and IT considerations are integrated.

## 1 Introduction

An advantage of selling products such as music, video, and information via the internet, is that they can be instantaneously delivered as a bitstream. Unfortunately, the drawback is that digital products can be easily copied against almost zero cost. This allows pirates to resell music or video against a fraction of the original price, or even to give it away for free. Today, illegal copying of digital content occurs at a large scale, decreasing revenues for all creative actors involved.

Clearly, there is a need for approaches that ensure that creative actors benefit from digital sales representing their creative efforts. The technology-driven IT approach is to protect digital content using encryption technology and watermarking [1, 7, 8]. However, all current IT-driven protection methods are vulnerable to attacks. At the other side of the spectrum, business-oriented approaches [9, 2] propose to sell multiple versions of digital content, to update content frequently, or to sell it in bundles with related products. The idea here is that one should focus on the concept of *consumer value*.

This raises the basic question how one might actually *calculate* the multi-faceted notion of consumer value, in such a way that it becomes possible to compare the results across different business-consumer scenarios and so make decisions about the suitability of various possible e-business models. The present paper aims to contribute to this rather ambitious goal.

It presents a practical framework to analyze the various dimensions of value contained within a single product [6], as a basis for understanding how consumers may maximize their expected utility. Next, by evaluating a range of relevant *what-if* scenarios, it supports in uncovering in a *quantifiable* way what the major (IT as well as market) parameters are that influence consumer value. This framework is part of our $e^3$-$value^{TM}$ methodology [4, 5], a business modelling approach that offers an integrated view upon the business as well as IT factors that are relevant to executive decision making concerning e-business strategies.

As an application of our framework for value maximization, we consider a music track download service that enhances value by increasing convenience in terms of search and download time, and we compare this to a service offering illegal content. We use our framework to argue that products represented by bits such as music or video, have value aspects for consumers other than mere content. These aspects can be exploited to create additional consumer value such that consumers are encouraged to buy music or video legally rather than to obtain it from an illegal source. Moreover, this added value is difficult to create for illegal content providers.

This paper is structured as follows. In Sec. 2 we briefly review IT-dominated ways of protecting digital content. We do not argue that protection of content is unnecessary, but rather that creation of additional consumer value *and* protection of digital content should be seamlessly applied to selling bits. In Sec. 3 we discuss business-oriented ways to ensure that digital content is bought rather than illegally copied. One of these is the creation of additional consumer value. In Sec. 4 we analyze illegal copying of music from two perspectives: (il)legality and consumer value. Sec. 5 introduces a practical attempt to quantify the consumer value contained in digital products. It is the foundation for Sec. 6, which evaluates several scenarios for two prototypical consumer segments with respect to consumer value as a way to prevent illegal use of content. We show how these business scenarios help focus executive decision making. Finally, we present our conclusions.

## 2   Protection of Rights on Digital Assets

Protection is a way to discourage the unintended use of digital content (such as copying, unauthorized resale and more), but is, as we will show, not sufficient to prevent a piracy scene, especially if the price of legal content is high enough. Various approaches for *protecting* the intended usage of digital content exist. We distinguish (1) protection by encryption, (2) protection by watermarking, (3) protection by law.

**Protection by Encryption.** Encryption systems offer facilities to *prevent* violations of the intended usage of the music but have a number of weak spots. First, the consumer can *always* make copies by resampling the analog output. There is a small quality loss but all subsequent copies can be made without any further loss. Second, the consumer can intercept the decrypted bitstream and save this stream in a file. Third, the encrypted content itself can be attacked.

**Protection by Watermarking.** A next step is to *watermark* the content. A watermark can be used in court to *prove* violations of intended usage of the content. With watermarking technology it is possible to identify the digital content, to identify the original producer of the content, and to identify the consumer who sold the rights to use the digital content [8]. This information is important to prosecute violations of intended usage of content.

However, in [3], a number of successfull attacks on watermarks are identified, so protection by watermarking is not the only way to go.

**Protection by Law.** The last line of defense is to *prosecute* the person who violates the intended usage of digital content. Protection of digital content by law has a number of weaknesses. First, the law differs between countries. Laws of some countries offer more handles to prosecute illegal use of content than others do. Second, if the violator is in another country than the owner of the content (the prosecutor), it is difficult to prosecute the violator. Furthermore, suing itself does not scale up very well. If a large number of small violators exists (as is actually the case in music copying and downloading), it is not feasible to sue all these violators individually.

In conclusion, if digital content is to be sold, one should bear in mind that a consumer can violate the intended usage of the content, sometimes rather easily. This remains true also when various protection schemes have been applied. Especially if the motivation of the consumer is high enough, s/he is able to obtain digital content from sources other than the legal ones. Hence, protection of digital content alone is not sufficient to address the problem of misuse of digital content.

## 3 Business-oriented Approaches

**Versioning and Bundling.** Various authors, for instance [9] and [2], have proposed business-oriented solutions to ensure that content creators get paid for their creative efforts. However, these solutions are limited in that they are effective only for highly interactive or *time-dependent* digital content, i.e., content of which the value quickly decreases with time. One way to exploit the time dependence of digital content is to create multiple versions, for example a number of remixes of a music track, or different quality levels of images. However, the number of versions a consumer can choose from is usually very limited, and therefore illegal copies of versioned content will become easily accessible as well. A more extreme position is to sell complementary related products which cannot easily be copied such as merchandise of artists, while the content itself is nearly for free. In such a scenario, the digital content plays only the role of attracting consumers to a site: the revenues should come from related sales.

A variation on this theme is *bundling*: a consumer can only buy merchandise if s/he also buys the associated digital content. A general limitation of business-oriented approaches exploiting time-dependent value of digital content is that there are many cases of digital products (e.g., 'classic' songs and movies) that maintain their value over long periods of time. Hence, it is important to analyze the concept of consumer value contained in digital content *itself*, and not solely consider the generation of revenues from complementary products and related sales.

**Dimensions of Consumer Value in Market Research.** We thus want to explore how to exploit the value of digital content itself, in such a way that it creates a value gap between legal and illegal providers of digital content. We suggest that recent 'interpretive' marketing research on consumer value gives some useful initial handles on this topic. In particular, we use Holbrook's value framework [6] that investigates different aspects or dimensions of value resulting from the consumption experience of a product.

In his framework, Holbrook makes a distinction between the *extrinsic* and *intrinsic* value of a product. A product has an extrinsic value component if a consumer uses the product to accomplish some goal that is outside the consumption of the product itself. For example, a consumer values a hammer mainly because it can be used to drive in a nail, rather than that s/he values the hammer in its own right. In contrast, something is valued intrinsically if the consumption experience is valued for its own sake. For example, music has an important intrinsic value component because listening to music, the experience, is of value by itself. In fact, the digital content considered in this paper relates to the *right* to have a, hopefully appreciated, experience. The bits are only the representation of the music that enables the experience.

**Table 1.** Value types in Holbrook's framework.

| Value dimension | Extrinsic | Intrinsic |
|---|---|---|
| Active | EFFICIENCY (I/O function, convenience) | PLAY (fun) |
| Reactive | EXCELLENCE (quality) | ESTHETICS (beauty) |

Another dimension introduced by Holbrook is that value may have an *active* or *reactive* component. A product with an active value component requires that a consumer actively does something with the product (for example, using a music track for karaoke singing) as part of the consumption experience. Consumer value is called reactive if the product itself accomplishes something to or with a consumer as a result of a consumption experience, such as listening to music passively.

Putting together the $2 \times 2$ combinations from these two dimensions of consumer value yields four types of value, as shown in Table 1. Below, we show how such a value typology can be used as an aid in uncovering which different e-business parameters influence consumer value. In addition, we will quantify these value parameters, and analyze their effect on e-business model design through a collection of realistic business-consumer interaction scenarios.

## 4  The e-Business Design Space: Legality vs. Value Creation

We do not suggest that protection of digital content is irrelevant. On the contrary, such a first barrier prevents a number of consumers from committing an illegal act, and makes them aware that unintended use of the digital content is prohibited. However, we do claim that rethinking and redesigning the value to the consumer of a digital content service (e.g. the right to listen to a music track once) can contribute to reducing the illegal ways of consumption. We can exploit the fact that a digital product has valuable aspects in addition to the actual content itself, cf. the Holbrook value typology. For example, convenience in selecting and ordering, receiving the content without delays, enhancing fun by different options to interact with the digital content may all be of great value to the consumer. In Sec. 5, we analyze the multiple aspects of value created by digital content in more depth.

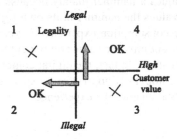

**Fig. 1.** Positioning e-business models: (il)legal content versus created consumer value.

Figure 1 shows how various e-business model options may be positioned in a design space spanned by the degree of legality and the degree to which consumer value is created. The first quadrant, digital content that is legal but offered with a low consumer value, is not interesting from a business point of view. Illegal content with a low consumer value, the second quadrant, is not likely to be very popular with consumers either. If for example the convenience is low, consumers will not be attracted to obtain the illegal content. Thus, offerings in this quadrant can be left alone (note also that from a business point of view, technical or legal protection measures are not really needed here).

The third quadrant, illegal content with a high consumer value, is highly unwanted, however. As indicated in Figure 1, there are ways to make the e-business 'models' positioned in this quadrant less attractive. Illegal content with high consumer value requires high visibility and accessibility in a market. If not, it takes too much effort for consumers to find and select the product. Furthermore, it must be easy and convenient to obtain and consume the content. However, visibility and a high-quality fulfillment infrastructure enable content owners to take corrective action, for example to prosecute suppliers of illegal content or to ask legally operating Internet Service Providers to remove or block illegal content. Such measures do not remove illegal offerings entirely, but result in illegal content with lower consumer value, thus moving illegal offerings from the undesirable quadrant 3 to the uninteresting quadrant 2 (in other words, these measures generate utility destruction). Alternatively, suppliers of such illegal content may decide to set up a legal operation and move up to quadrant 4. This quadrant represents the desired situation: providing legal content with a high consumer value. Finally, Figure 1 shows that legal content providers already in this quadrant may strive to increase the consumer value created by the digital products they offer.

Generally, the approach is *to increase the value gap* between legal and illegal offerings.

# 5 Consumer Value

## 5.1 Receipts and Sacrifices

We will now analyze which factors play a role in the various types of consumer value creation, how they can be quantified, and how they can be used as 'control parameters', so to speak, to design an optimally positioned e-business model.

In marketing literature (e.g., [6]), consumer value is often stated in terms of a *value equation*:

$$Consumer\ Value = \frac{\sum\limits_{i=1}^{n} Receipt_i}{\sum\limits_{j=1}^{m} Sacrifice_j}.$$

The sacrifices comprise all costs a consumer has to make to consume the product; receipts represent the sum total of the benefits s/he experiences from consuming the product. The consumer will only buy the product if the consumer value ratio is greater than one; otherwise, a consumer decides not to buy the product at all, because the sacrifices outweigh the receipts.

Receipts and sacrifices need to be further decomposed. First, we distinguish out-of-pocket costs. These are sacrifices that result in a direct transfer of money from consumer to supplier. Second, there are other value types (in terms of Holbrook's framework) that are not directly payable to someone, but contribute to sacrifices or receipts. An example is the inconvenience for the consumer if the download-time of music is very long.

To focus our analysis, we will concentrate on a specific service in selling bits: the product comprising the right to *listen-once to a track of music*. This product allows a consumer to select a track of music, and after selection the music will be played as soon as possible. We assume a non-streaming service: the track has first to be downloaded completely before the consumer can listen to it.

We illustrate our claim that value creation is a key consideration to enhance legal ways of selling bits, by investigating and quantifying several possible business scenarios in terms of consumer value, for two prototypical consumer segments, viz., yuppies (enough money, but lack of time) and students (scarce money resources, enough time). Each scenario is studied from two perspectives: (1) obtaining the music legally, and (2) obtaining the same music illegally.

## 5.2 Out-of-pocket Costs

If a consumer wants to listen to a track s/he has to pay money directly to others, called out-of-pocket costs. These costs are part of the sacrifices mentioned in the value equation. Here, we distinguish (1) the *data communication costs* to be paid to a telecommunication company and/or Internet Service Provider, and (2) the *price* to be paid for the right to listen to the music track itself.

**Data Communication Costs.** We consider (1) communication costs for selecting content, (2) for downloading content, and (3) for uploading content. The latter costs may appear if a consumer obtains the content illegally. Many illegal sites use a *ratio* scheme. Such a scheme requires that a consumer first *uploads* a music-track, after which s/he can *download* tracks of choice.

**Price.** If the consumer buys the music legally, a fee is paid for the right to listen to the track. We assume this price is known and set by the supplier. In the illegal case, the price is $ 0.00.

## 5.3 Instantiating Value Types

Table 2 shows the value creation parameters, structured according to the discussed Holbrook consumer value framework, for the product *listen-once to a selected track of music*. Such parameters can contribute to either sacrifices or receipts, depending on the valuation by the consumer.

**Table 2.** Value parameters for a *listen-once* service.

| Value dimension | Extrinsic | Intrinsic |
|---|---|---|
| Active | selection time upload time download time | interactive track play |
| Reactive | presentation quality | track beauty |

**Selection Time.** Selection time is the time it takes for a consumer to search for and select a particular track of music s/he wants to listen to. We assume that a consumer already *knows* the title of the music track as well as the performing artist before selection; the selection-time only indicates the time necessary to find a supplier offering the *downloadable* track under consideration. The track should be downloadable because in the piracy scene, it does happen in practice that a site indicates that a particular track is available, but the track itself has disappeared. In such a case, the consumer has to spend additional time to find a new site that offers the track, which increases the total selection time for the track.

The selection time is an important instrument to fight piracy. If the selection time is low for music tracks of illegal content providers, such providers have high visibility and reliability. This enables legal providers, content owners and right organizations to fight such pirates.

**Upload Time.** On an illegal ratio-based site, a music track must be uploaded first before one can obtain one or more tracks. The upload time is the time necessary to complete the upload and to gain the rights for one or more downloads. This includes the time necessary to obtain the track for upload from another medium such as a CD.

**Download Time.** The download time period starts when a consumer decides to listen to a previously selected track, and ends when the track is ready for play at the consumer site. At a ratio-based illegal site, the required upload has to be completed before the consumer can decide to listen to the desired track. The download and upload time depend on factors such as the available bandwidth. A legal provider can influence this factor positively, for instance by co-locating its content server with the Internet access points of its consumers.

**Presentation Quality.** The presentation quality of music is determined by the *bitrate* of the music track. For consumers, perceived quality may be expressed in terms such as CD quality, near-CD quality, radio quality, and telephony quality. A legal provider can influence this parameter by consumer-selectable presentation quality options.

**Interactive Track Play.** The aspect of play, as identified in Holbrook's framework, refers to possibilities for the consumer to actively interact with the product. This interactivity should be of value for its own sake. For the *listen-once to a selected track of music* product we define the play aspect as the presence of functionality to turn on and off music instruments and vocals, allowing consumers to produce the vocals themselves (as in karaoke), or select alternative instruments and vocals so as to create their own version of a song. Such functionality is for example offered by the website of David Bowie (www.davidbowie.com). Legal providers can exploit this creative play and fun element, initially because they can obtain access to alternative instrument and vocal recordings, and subsequently by providing different versions of these. This boils down to a versioning approach as discussed in Sec. 3.

**Track Beauty.** Finally, there is the aspect of beauty, implying that the music itself is valued as a consumption experience for its own sake by the consumer.

We note that we have introduced several independent parameters relevant to value cration. For example, a consumer may like the interactive play element of a David Bowie song, because it gives you the possibility of acting as a creative designer making a new instrumentation of a song, but s/he may not actually like David Bowie's music.

## 5.4 Calculating Consumer Value

To compare scenarios with each other on a consumer value basis, it is necessary to calculate direct out-of-pocket costs (which can be done in a rather objective fashion) as well as the different Holbrook value type aspects (of which the valuation is more subjective with respect to the consumer). As an example, consider the valuation of a short download time by the consumer. One part of this stems from the objective expected download time, which depends on the size of the track in bits and the available bandwidth. Another part may be formulated as an *inconvenience fee* in $/second incurred by the consumer, expressing that the utility of absorbing consumer time also has to be taken into account (as a more subjective, and consumer segment-dependent opportunity cost or nuisance value component). This utility quantification of the various objective and subjective factors is presented in Table 3. To calculate consumer value, we use the following measurable quantities:

- The *bitrate* (bits/second) used to represent the content in a digital way.
- The *duration* of a track in seconds.
- The *bandwidth* (bits/second) available to stream content to the consumer. A provider of music can influence this factor positively, for example by co-locating its servers close to Internet access points of consumers, by having a high-bandwidth connection to the Internet, or even by exploiting an own access infrastructure for consumers. Note that all these measures make the content provider visible for organizations controlling the correct use of digital content. Therefore, enhancing consumer value in this way is not an option for illegal content providers.

– The *data communication costs* or *ticks* ($/second) and a *connection setup fee* ($/connection setup), to be paid by the consumer for a connection to the Internet.
– In the case of an illegal provider, the *ratio* between uploaded and downloaded tracks. The ratio is the number of tracks which need to be uploaded before a consumer can download one track of his choice (typically 0.1).

**Table 3.** Calculation of out-of-pocket costs and Holbrook value type parameters.

| Out-of-pocket costs | Calculation |
|---|---|
| *Data communication costs:* | |
| selection time | *selection-time* $*$ *ticks* $+$ *setup-fee* |
| download time | $\frac{bitrate*duration}{bandwidth} * ticks$ |
| upload time | $\frac{bitrate*duration}{bandwidth} * ticks * ratio$ |
| price | *determined price by supplier* |

| Holbrook value type | Calculation |
|---|---|
| *Inconvenience costs:* | |
| selection time | *selection-time* $*$ *inconvenience-fee*$_{consumer}$ |
| download time | $\frac{bitrate*duration}{bandwidth} * inconvenience\text{-}fee_{consumer}$ |
| upload time | $\frac{bitrate*duration}{bandwidth} * inconvenience\text{-}fee_{consumer} * ratio$ |
| presentation quality | $f_{consumer}(bitrate)$ |
| interactive track play | $f_{consumer}(availability)$ |
| track beauty | $f_{consumer}(content)$ |

## 6  Scenarios

Scenarios constitute an established tool for strategic analysis [10]. We will discuss a number of scenarios representing different kinds of consumers. The first set of scenarios is about a yuppie, a consumer characterized by enough monetary resources but with a lack of time. The second set of scenarios focuses on a student consumer, who has scarce monetary resources but enough time. For both scenario sets, we analyze two situations: (1) the consumer obtains the music from a illegal site, and (2) the consumer buys the music from a legal site.

For the evaluation of the yuppie and student scenarios, we assume values for the consumer utility parameters as summarized in Table 4. Values for some parameters differ between the legal and the illegal case. The rationale for this is that by carefully influencing or controlling such parameters, a legal provider has an opportunity to create additional consumer value. This especially holds for the available bandwidth, selection time, and price. By fighting piracy effectively, the search time for illegal providers can be increased, resulting in a lower consumer value of illegal content. However, some parameters cannot be easily influenced by content providers such as the costs for telecommunication.

**Table 4.** Parameter values for the yuppie and student scenarios.

| Consumer utility parameter | Illegal case | Legal case |
|---|---|---|
| selection time | 60 s | 30 s |
| bit-rate | 128 kb/s | equal |
| mean duration of track | 240 s | equal |
| bandwidth | 30 kb/s | 60 kb/s |
| ticks | $ 0.01/minute | equal |
| connection setup fee | $ 0.05/setup | equal |
| ratio | 0.1 | 0 |

The values of the consumer utility parameters are, where possible, based on realistic empirical estimates. We assume that an illegal site offers only 50% of the bandwidth a legal site offers to its consumers. This bandwidth is measured end-to-end: from music supplier to consumer. The bandwidth is therefore constrained by the bandwidth offered by Internet Service Providers to their end users. We take, for the legal case, a value of 60 kbit/s, which is possible using ISDN. A content provider can fully exploit this bandwidth if its content servers are co-located with the access servers of the ISP. The values for *ticks* and *connection setup fee* are taken from the current standard tariffs of a large Dutch telecoms company. We assume that Internet access itself is for free, as is the case in the Netherlands and the United Kingdom. For the *ratio* we assume a value of 1:10, which is often seen on illegal sites. For *bitrate* we assume a value which is currently typical for MP3 tracks on the Internet.

## 6.1 Scenario A: Yuppie

Table 5 illustrates a valuation of the product *listen-once to a selected track of music* by the yuppie, both for the legal and illegal cases. We call this scenario the null scenario. We have chosen hypothetical but reasonable values, using the following approach. First, a consumer equally values the presentation quality and the beauty aspect for the legal and illegal case, because for both cases a consumer values the same track of music. Second, we assume that the consumer ranks the value of Holbrooks aspects in the following order (from high to low): (1) the beauty aspect (the first priority is to listen to a particular track of a selected artist), (2) the presentation quality aspect, and (3) the interactive play capability. Further, we have assumed that the yuppie inconvenience fee is $ 1.-/hour. Of course, this is an example for which it is difficult to get accurate numbers. However, an important point to note is that these numbers are not intended for exact value calculations *per se*. Instead, we are interested in the much more modest goal of *relative* statements, drawn from a comparative analysis and a sensitivity analysis of relevant business scenarios. As we will see, it is indeed possible to come to strategically relevant conclusions from a quantified analysis based on rough, order-of-magnitude, numbers. This is all we aim for in this paper.

**Table 5.** Yuppie consumer value equation: null scenario.

| Consumer value equation Variables | Illegal Case Receipts | Sacrifices | Legal case Receipts | Sacrifices |
|---|---|---|---|---|
| **Out-of-pocket costs** | | | | |
| (Data communication costs) selection | - | 0.060 | - | 0.055 |
| download | - | 0.17 | - | 0.085 |
| upload | - | 0.017 | - | - |
| price | - | - | - | 0.10 |
| **Holbrook value type parameters** | | | | |
| (Inconvenience costs) selection time | - | 0.017 | - | 0.008 |
| download time | - | 0.28 | - | 0.14 |
| upload time | - | 0.028 | - | - |
| presentation quality | 0.15 (near CD) - | | 0.15 (near CD) - | |
| interactive track play | - (no) | - | 0.05 (yes) | - |
| track beauty | 0.20 | - | 0.20 | - |
| **Consumer value equation results** | **Illegal case** | | **Legal case** | |
| *Total Receipts and Sacrifices:* | 0.35 | 0.572 | 0.40 | 0.388 |
| *Ratio Receipts/Sacrifices:* | **0.61** | | **1.03** | |

**Variations on the Null Scenario.** Several variations on the null scenario are interesting to analyze; they are motivated by expected changes in the null scenario that are likely to occur: (1) nearly equal end-to-end bandwidth for the illegal and illegal case, (2) an increase of the overall bandwidth without changing costs, (3) changes in the play factor of the product, (4) changes in the consumer's inconvenience fee, and (5) a service extension to repeated listenings to the same track.

**Scenario A1: The Bandwidths of the Legal and Illegal Sites Become Nearly the Same.** It is possible that the music industry is not sufficiently capable of fighting the illegal scene, as previously discussed in Sec. 4. Then, a consequence may be that illegal sites are offering music with nearly the same bandwidth as legal sites. If we assume for the illegal site a bandwidth of 50 kbit/s, the consumer value equation ratio for the illegal case becomes 0.93 instead of 0.61, i.e., close to the value for the legal case. If bandwidths are equal (60 kbit/s) the illegal offering is even favored over the legal one in terms of consumer value. Thus, the bandwidth difference is an important parameter to create a value gap between the legal and illegal cases.

**Scenario A2: The Bandwidth Increases.** In the near feature, it is reasonable to expect an increase of available bandwidth nearly without any change in costs. Developments such as xDSL, which offer a high bandwidth connection (order 1 Mbps) over the local loop of a telecoms operator, are now being commercially introduced. A bandwidth increase will heavily cut down both the out-of-pocket and inconvenience sacrifices, especially those related to download times. Compared to the null scenario, a bandwidth increase above about a factor of 5 (both for illegal and legal bandwidth) will start to favor the illegal site over the legal site. Therefore, a differentiation in bandwidth only (scenario A1) is not sufficient in the long run as a means to sell music legally. Because this scenario is very likely to happen in the near future, we analyze the following scenarios in conjunction with this scenario.

**Scenario A3: The Selection Time for the Illegal Case Increases Substantially.** If the music industry is successful in fighting piracy, the selection time for illegal tracks increases. For instance, if it takes 600 seconds to find a downloadable illegal track, the consumer value of the illegal scenario is 0.43 instead of 0.61, whereas the legal case remains the same at a value of 1.03. Moreover, if we additionally suppose that scenario A2 occurs, the consumer value of the illegal case becomes 0.82, while the legal scenario results in a consumer value of 2.46. Consequently, differentiation in selection time is a powerful instrument to have consumers favor the legal offering.

**Scenario A4: The Inconvenience Fee is Nonlinear.** In our model, we assume that the yuppie uses a flat rate for his inconvenience fee. However, it might be more appropriate to assume that the costs associated with waiting for a music track grow more than linearly with time. In this way, we model the likely situation that a consumer wants to have the music fast, and if it takes too long, s/he is not interested anymore. If the inconvenience fee during the first 5 minutes is $1.- per hour, during the second 5 minutes is $ 5.- per hour, and is $ 25.- per hour beyond that, the consumer value for the legal case is 0.64, but for the illegal case 0.086. If we analyze scenarios A2 and A4 in combination, the consumer values of the illegal and legal cases are about equal (1.89 vs. 1.88). If also scenario A3 occurs (selection time differentiation), the consumer will however prefer the legal case (0,46 vs. 1,88).

**Scenario A5: Repeated Listenings of the Same Track.** Our null scenario is based on a *pay-per-listen* product. However, for content such as music and video, *repeated* consumption occurs frequently. A consumer then listens to the same track of music a number of times. If in such a case the consumer stored the music-track locally after the first initial download, communication costs are zero for the subsequent listenings.

In our null scenario, a supplier of legal content differentiates himself from an illegal supplier by offering a fast download service (more bandwidth), so that the legal consumer saves data communication expenses. However, for subsequent listenings, no downloads are necessary if the content is stored locally, and the advantage of a fast download service becomes less significant. Table 6 presents the effect of subsequent listenings on consumer value.

From this table it can be concluded that if a yuppie expects to listen to a track more than twice, it becomes attractive to obtain the track illegally. A way to deal with this issue is to use a nonlinear pricing scheme. In Table 7, the price of $n$ subsequent listenings is calculated as follows:

$$price_{n\text{-}subs.\text{-}list.} = discount\text{-}factor_{n\text{-}subs.\text{-}list.} * price * number\text{-}of\text{-}subs.\text{-}list.$$

**Table 6.** Yuppie valuation of subsequent listenings.

| Consumer Value | Illegal case | Legal case | Total revenue |
|---|---|---|---|
| 1 listening | 0.61 | 1.02 | 0.10 |
| 2 listenings | 1.21 | 1.62 | 0.20 |
| 4 listenings | 2.42 | 2.32 | 0.40 |
| 10 listenings | 6.06 | 3.10 | 1.00 |

Using such a nonlinear pricing scheme, the yuppie will be encouraged to buy the music legally. The drawback of such a scheme is that, after two subsequent listenings, hardly any marginal revenues are generated. If we assume that scenario A2 also applies, the illegal offering becomes attractive. However, if scenario A3 occurs in addition, the legal offering has a higher consumer value. Application of scenario A4 strengthens this conclusion.

**Table 7.** Yuppie valuation of subsequent listenings using a nonlinear pricing scheme.

| Consumer Value | Discount Factor | Illegal case | Legal case | Total revenue |
|---|---|---|---|---|
| 1 listening | 1.00 | 0.61 | 1.02 | 0.10 |
| 2 listenings | 0.90 | 1.21 | 1.69 | 0.16 |
| 4 listenings | 0.50 | 2.42 | 3.26 | 0.16 |
| 10 listenings | 0.21 | 6.06 | 8.07 | 0.17 |

In sum, nonlinear pricing is a useful mechanism to create value for the consumer. Bandwidth differences only help in the short run. Selection time differences turn out to be a key to create a significant value gap between legal and illegal offerings.

## 6.2 Scenario B: Student

The student null scenario assumes that the student's inconvenience fee is $ 0.10/hour (one order of magnitude lower than the yuppie inconvenience fee). We keep all other values the same. The consumer value of the illegal case now becomes 1.25, while the value of the legal case is 1.57. Consequently, for consumer segments that incur a low inconvenience fee (that is, they are willing to spend their own time) illegal offerings become relatively more attractive.

We briefly summarize the results from variations on the null scenario.

– *Scenario B1: The bandwidth of the legal and illegal site is nearly the same.* A lower inconvenience cost results in a lower fee for waiting on a download. Therefore, the difference of bandwidths between the illegal and legal case is of less importance compared to the yuppie scenario. If the bandwidth of the illegal provider is 41 kbit/s and the bandwidth of the legal provider remains 60 kbit/s, the consumer will already opt for the illegal provider, while in the yuppie scenario bandwidths should be nearly equal.

- *Scenario B2: The bandwidth increases.* Because of a lower inconvenience fee, an increase of available bandwidth by a factor of about 2 is already sufficient to favor the illegal case over the legal one. Therefore, bandwidth cannot be exploited very successfully in the student scenario to create additional consumer value.
- *Scenario B3: The selection time for the illegal case increases substantially.* A selection time of 600 seconds for the illegal case makes that the sacrifices outweigh the receipts, favoring the legal offering. This is also the case if we assume both scenario B2 and B3.
- *Scenario B4: The inconvenience fee is nonlinear.* If the inconvenience fee during the first 5 minutes is $0.1/hour, the second 5 minutes is $ 0.5/hour, and beyond that is $ 2.50/hour, the consumer value for the legal case (1.43) is higher than the consumer value for the illegal case (0.56). If bandwidth is no issue (scenario B2, with a 5 times increase of bandwidth), the illegal case will be chosen by the consumer.
- *Scenario B5: Repeated listenings of the same track.* In case of repeated listenings, we find that for two listenings and more, the student chooses to obtain the music illegally. A nonlinear pricing scheme as discussed previously ensures that a student obtains music legally if the discount factor as presented in Table 7 is 1 (1 listening), 0.82 (2 listenings), 0.41 (4 listenings), and 0.17 (10 listenings). A nonlinear pricing scheme plus scenario B2 results in a preference for the illegal case, but scenarios B2, B3 and B4 together favor the legal case.

In sum, our scenario analysis shows that for both consumer segments, selection time differences are a key parameter that must be controlled in order to create a significant value gap between legal and illegal offerings. Nonlinear pricing also is a useful 'control parameter' to make legal offerings attractive to the consumer. The difference between the student and yuppie consumer segments is that for the former, illegal offerings become attractive more quickly due to the lower inconvenience fee. Bandwidth differences only have short-term relevance, because the bandwidth itself is likely to increase strongly in the near future.

## 7  Conclusions

The key point of this paper is that creation of additional consumer value contributes to legal obtainment of digital goods such as music and video, apart from IT-based ways to protect content. To show this in a quantifiable way, we have presented a multi-aspect utility framework, grounded in Holbrook's consumer value approach, that can be used to calculate consumer value for different business-consumer scenarios. Using this framework, we have analyzed two prototypical music consumer groups, yuppies and students, and shown what the major parameters are that affect consumer value.

In this paper we have applied this framework to a comparison of legal and illegal music download services. A major application conclusion is that exploiting end-to-end bandwidth as a way to minimize download time, and thereby inconvenience, only has a short-term effect. This is caused by expectations that end-to-end bandwidth will grow substantially, both for legal and illegal services. If the bandwidth passes a certain threshold, it is not a good way anymore to create additional value for legal providers. Our key long-term conclusion is that legal content providers have to enlarge the gap between the search time for legal and illegal content. If our estimates of the inconvenience fee or 'nuisance value' of long waiting times are order-of-magnitude correct, this promises to be an effective barrier to inhibit consumers from obtaining illegal content. Other interesting results of our analysis are that all successful business scenarios have to be based on a low price for the right to listen to a track of music, and that subsequent listenings to a track should be priced in a nonlinear way to discourage illegal acquisition of music.

More generally, we feel that our framework makes an advance in getting a better, more quantifiable, grip on the many dimensions and parameters in consumer value. There is no claim that it is a tool for calculating consumer value exactly. This is also not needed: as shown, it is adequate if it aids executive decision making, by differentiating and understanding the trade-offs between various conceivable strategic scenarios in e-business. The presented framework is part of ongoing research into our $e^3$-$value^{TM}$ methodology that approaches e-business modelling as designing new value exchange networks enabled by IT methods [4, 5]. Such a value-based approach is in our opinion the most fruitful one to achieve the required integration between business and IT factors in electronic commerce applications.

*Acknowledgement.* This work has been partly sponsored by the Stichting voor Technische Wetenschappen (STW), project nr VWI.4949.

# References

1. Matt Blaze, Joan Feigenbaum, and Jack Lacy. Decentralized trust management. In *Proceedings of the IEEE Conference on Security and Privacy*, Oakland, CA, May 1996.
2. Soon-Yong Choi, Dale O Stahl, and Andrew B. Whinston. *The economics of doing business in the electronic marketplace*. Macmillan Technical Publishing, Indianapolis, 1997.
3. Scott Craver, Boon-Lock, and Minerva Yeung. Technical trials and legal tribulations. *Communications of the ACM*, 41(7):45–54, July 1998.
4. J. Gordijn, J.M. Akkermans, and J.C. van Vliet. Value based requirements creation for electronic commerce applications. In *Proceedings of the 33rd Hawaii International Conference On System Sciences (HICSS-33)*, pages CD–ROM. IEEE, January 4-7 2000.
5. J. Gordijn, H. de Bruin, and J.M. Akkermans. Integral design of E-Commerce systems: Aligning the business with software architecture through scenarios. In H. de Bruin, editor, *ICT-Architecture in the BeNeLux*, 1999.
6. Morris B. Holbrook. *Consumer value: a framework for analysis and research*. Routledge, New York, 1999.
7. Dimitri Konstantas and Jean-Henry Morin. Trading digital intangible goods: the rules of the game. In *Proceedings of the 33rd Hawaii International Conference On System Sciences (HICSS-33)*, pages CD–ROM. IEEE, January 4-7 2000.
8. Nasir Memon and Ping Wah Wong. Protecting digital media content. *Communications of the ACM*, 41(7):35–43, July 1998.
9. Carl Shapiro and Hal R. Varian. *Information Rules*. Harvard Business School Press, Boston, Massachusetts, 1999.
10. Kees van der Heijden. *Scenarios: the arts of strategic conversation*. John Wiley & Sons Inc., New York, 1996.

# A Secure Electronic Software Distribution (ESD) Protocol Based on PKC

Sung-Min Lee[1], Hyung-Woo Lee[2], Tai-Yun Kim[1]

[1] Department of Computer Science & Engineering, Korea University
1, 5-Ga Anam-Dong Seongbuk-Gu Seoul 136-701 Korea
{smlee, tykim}@netlab.korea.ac.kr
[2] Division of Information & Communication Engineering, Chonan University
115, Ansco-Dong Chonan Chungnam 330-180 Korea
hwlee@moon.chonan.ac.kr

**Abstract.** In this paper we propose a secure electronic software distribution and copyright protection protocol for electronic commerce based on public key cryptography (PKC). The proposed protocol considers post-installation security using an authentication agent and electronic license. It prevents software piracy and illegal copying. Even if software is copied illegally, a merchant can trace back to its original owner from the electronic license. The proposed protocol provides consumers, merchants, and producers in the electronic marketplace with confidence, security, and efficiency.

## 1 Introduction

Electronic commerce is a modern business methodology that addresses the necessity of organizations, merchants, and consumers to cut costs while improving the quality of their goods and services and increasing the speed of service delivery. E-commerce provides consumers the ability to bank, invest, purchase, distribute, communicate, and research from home, work, bookstores, or virtually anywhere an Internet connection can be made[1,2]. The international data corporation predicts that by 2000, at least 46 million Americans will have purchased products or services online, spending an average of $350 per person per year[9].

Owing to an improvement in E-commerce technology, users can get software easily through an on-line software distribution using the Internet. As the purchase and downloading of software are processed via an on-line batch process, the time and cost necessary for software purchase and installation can be reduced considerably. However, there are several problems for online software distribution. As Internet access becomes available in the workplace, online piracy rapidly grows. The protection of computer software and other creative property transmitted over the Internet remains problematic for international trade as well. Millions of dollars in pirated software can be downloaded and distributed illegally in a matter of minutes. Online, pirates are reaping profits on a grand scale – stealing the creative output of hardworking software designers, programmers and engineers, authors, and producers – and thereby removing their economic incentive for creation and innovation.

Worldwide software business losses due to piracy are estimated at nearly $11 billion in 1998. More than 38% of all software in use is illegally copied[9], so strong copyright protection for creative works is crucial to the success of E-commerce.

In this paper we propose a secure electronic software distribution (ESD)[12] protocol for electronic commerce. The protocol provides a secure software installation and illegal copy protection scheme based on public key cryptography (PKC), which was first proposed by the Diffie and Hellman in 1974[5]. The goals of our protocol are piracy prevention and intellectual property protection of software producers, as we keep users from copying and redistributing the software by using an electronic license and authentication agent (AA). As the proposed protocol uses an authentication agent, it automatically checks whether a user is authorized or not when a software is installed or executed. When a user executes software, authentication is transparently processed using a multi-thread mechanism. Even if the software and electronic license are copied and redistributed to unauthorized users, a merchant can trace back to original owner of the software using the found electronic license. The proposed protocol provides consumers, merchants, and producers in the electronic marketplace with confidence, security, and efficiency.

The remainder of this paper is organized as follows. Section 2 discusses previous technologies and their problems. Section 3 describes the proposed ESD protocol. In section 4, the proposed protocol is analyzed and compared with existing models. Finally section 5 provides the conclusion of this paper.

## 2 Previous Technologies

In this section we describe existing technologies such as hardware-based models and software-based models for electronic software distribution and software protection. We also discuss their problems.

### 2.1 Hardware-based Technologies

One of the copyright protection approaches is based on tamper-resistant modules in the buyers' machines that at least prevent the copying of the internal representation of the data. Physically protected special computers for each task can eliminate the problem of software piracy. However, this approach is limited and special hardware for protection is too expensive[3]. Several theoretical models based on special hardware have been proposed, such as PIM and RAM models[4].

### 2.2 Software-based Technologies

We describe two types of software-based model. One is Symantec software[10] and the other is S.O.Shop[11]. If a customer buys software from the Symantec corporation on-line, she should purchase and then unlock the wrapped software. A customer can download the software before or after she completes the purchase process (by filling in and submitting the online order form), whichever she prefers. For security reasons, the downloaded software has been packaged in a locked "wrapper". Once a customer purchase has been approved, she will receive an email message containing an electronic license certificate (ELC)[10] that allows her to unlock and install the software for use. A customer should not make any changes to the ELC since it is digital signature that may not work if altered. The procedure of unlocking wrapped software is as follows: to install downloaded software, a customer first gets the electronic license certificate (ELC) from an email message and copies the ELC onto the Windows clipboard. Then the downloaded software file (*.EXE) is run. A window requesting the electronic license (ELC) appears. In this window, the ELC is pasted. A message confirming the intended product and the person licensed to use the ELC appears. If the digital signature is valid, the product's setup program starts automatically. The problem of this model is that an ELC can be copied and redistributed to unauthorized users easily.

S.O.Shop is a program for electronic software distribution. It separates license from software as it is based on dynamic software license control system (DSLC)[11], so users can download software free but they cannot install the software without a license. In order to check an authorized user, it uses an authentication server. The authentication server checks the signed license when software is executed. The license file is signed by using the private key of S.O.Shop, then encrypted by using a customer's public key. However, the manner may not be secure since a buyer can decrypt the signed license using her private key, then redistribute the signed license to others who are unauthorized without exposing her private key.

# 3 Proposed ESD Protocol

In this section the overall architecture of the proposed protocol is described. In addition, a PKC-based secure installation scheme and illegal copy protection scheme are proposed. We assume that a buyer of software never publishes her private key and that an operating system guarantees that the port reserved by the authentication agent of the proposed protocol is never used by any other programs. We also assume that the merchant server of our protocol is a trusted party.

## 3.1 Overall Architecture

There are several variations for software licenses such as a CPU license, user license, site license, and server license. A CPU license is granted to specific computers. A user license is granted to specific users. Use of the software only by licensed users is permitted. A site license is granted to a specific site (location or office). A server license is granted to all clients connected to a server.

The proposed protocol has been designed based on a user license and electronic software distribution concept, so users may download software free via the Internet but only authorized users can install and execute it. The protocol authenticates an authorized user based on public key cryptography (PKC). Figure 1 shows the overall architecture of the proposed protocol. Four types of principals are involved in our protocol: producer, customer, merchant server, certificate authority (CA). Producers register their own software and its information such as product-ID, corporation, and so on, in a merchant server via web. Customers select a software that they want to buy and register information such as name, id, password, email address, and so forth after purchasing the software. A merchant server issues an electronic license for each customer using the merchant server's private key used for a digital signature and a customer's public key used for encryption then sends it to the customer. The electronic license is in following form : $S_{merchant}$ $(P_{customer}(Product\_Code,$ $License\_No.))$, where $P_x(y)$ denotes the result of applying $x$'s public key function, such as RSA[6], to $y$. $S_x(y)$ denotes the result of applying $x$'s private key function (that is, the signature generation function) to $y$. The merchant server gets the customer's public key from a certificate which is obtained from a CA who is a trusted third party. The certificate contains $x$'s identity and signature public key, plus trusted server CA's signature $S_{CA}$ over these. $Cert_x$ denotes a public key certificate[7,8]: $cert_x = (I_x, P_x,$ $S_{CA}(I_x, P_x))$ , where $I_x$ denotes the identity of $x$ and $P_x$ denotes the public key of x. The proposed protocol uses Java servlet as a web interface since it is more efficient than CGI-bin script[13,14].

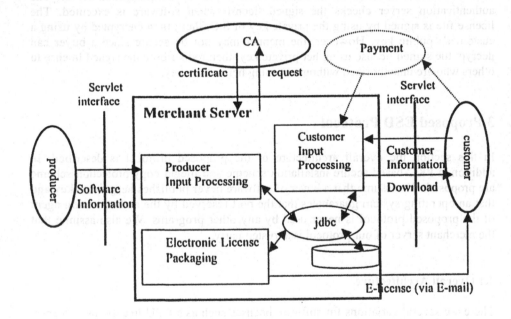

**Figure 1.** Overall Architecture of Proposed Protocol

## 3.2 Secure Installation Scheme

After purchasing software on the web, a customer should install an authentication agent to install and execute the software. An authentication agent (AA) is a program which checks a customer's electronic license. An AA is working always in a customer's computer as an authentication server using a loopback address (127.0.0.1) and predefined port. An AA has two functions for authentication: one is an authentication function when a customer installs downloaded software; the other is an authentication function when a user executes installed software. When a customer completes a software purchase, a merchant server sends an electronic license to the customer via email. The customer then puts the electronic license in a specific directory for the AA's reference to check whether the user is authorized or not. The electronic license comprises 3 components : $H(secret, Customer\_ID, passwd)$, $S_{merchant}(P_{customer}(Product\_Code, License No.))$, $S_{merchant}(Product\_Code, License\_No.)$. In the first component, the secret is a random string that is stored in the source code of the AA statically, so only the merchant server and AA know the secret. A message digest of secret, registered *Customer_ID*, and password is generated using a hash function $H$ such as MD5 and SHA algorithms[7,8]. In the second component, *Product_Code* and *License_No.* of software are encrypted by using the customer's public key, then signed by using the merchant server's private key. The third component of the electronic license is signed *Product_Code* and *License_No.* using the merchant server's private key.

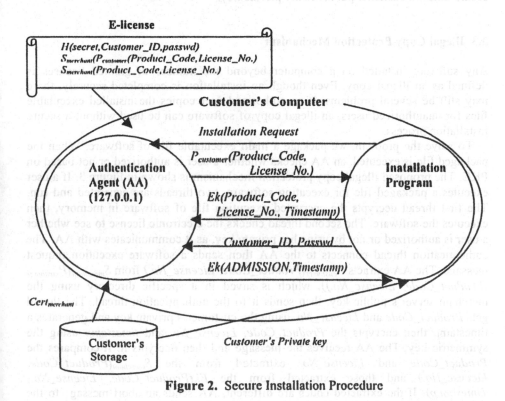

**Figure 2.** Secure Installation Procedure

Software installation procedures are shown in Figure 2. When a customer executes an installation program, the program (install shield) first connects to an AA using a loopback address and predefined port and then sends an installation request message to AA. The AA decrypts $S_{merchant}(P_{customer}(Product\_Code, License\_No.))$ using a merchant server's public key obtained from $Cert_{merchant}$, then sends the obtained message to the installation program. The installation program then extracts *Product_Code* and *License_No.* from the received message using the buyer's private key. It also extracts the message from $S_{merchant}(Product\_Code, License\_No.)$. If the two extracted messages are the same, it continues authentication, and it generates a timestamp as a nonce to prevent replay attack. Then it encrypts the *Product_Code*, *License_No.*, and timestamp using a symmetric key shared with the AA and sends it to the AA. The symmetric key is hard coded into the source code of the AA and installation program initially. In addition, a customer inputs her ID and password registered on the merchant server's web page. The AA receives *Customer_ID* and her password then computes the message digest for them and the secret using hash function and compares it with $H(secret, Customer\_ID, passwd)$ in the E-license. If the two messages are the same, the AA sends the installation admission message. Otherwise the installation program is aborted. Finally, the installation program can check the timestamp matches that was sent in the previous message. This method is secure unless a customer publishes her private key.

## 3.3 Illegal Copy Protection Mechanism

Any software installed on a computer beyond the number of granted licenses is defined as an illegal copy. Even though an installation is completed securely, there may still be several problems. If an authorized user copies the installed executable files for unauthorized users, an illegal copy of software can be used without a secure installation process.

To solve the problem, we package a main executable file of software. When the packaged file is executed, an AA checks whether a user is authorized or not based on PKC. The proposed illegal copy protection mechanism is shown in Figure 3. If a user executes a packaged file for executing software, two threads are generated and run. The first thread decrypts the encrypted execution file of software in memory, then executes the software. The second thread checks the electronic license to see whether a user is authorized or not by using her private key, as it communicates with AA. The authentication thread connects to the AA then sends a software execution request message. The AA extracts $P_{customer}(Product\_Code, License\_No.)$ from $S_{merchant}(P_{customer}$ $(Product\_Code, License\_No.))$, which is saved in a specific directory using the merchant server's public key, then sends it to the authentication thread. The thread gets *Product_Code* and *License_No.* using the customer's private key and generates a timestamp then encrypts the *Product_Code*, *License_No.* and *timestamp* using the symmetric key. The AA receives the message and then decrypts it. It compares the *Product_Code* and *License_No.* extracted from the $S_{merchant}(Product\_Code, License\_No.)$ and those extracted from the $Ek(Product\_Code, License\_No., Timestamp)$. If the extracted codes are different, AA sends an abort message to the thread. Then the other thread is aborted. In this manner does the proposed protocol prevent software illegal use. The use of timestamp prevents the reuse of messages transferred and guarantees the freshness of message received. If we first authenticate the license and then execute the software sequentially, it is very time consuming for a user since the speed of encryption and decryption of public key algorithm is slow. To solve this problem, the proposed protocol uses a multi-thread. The authentication procedure is processed transparently for users since two threads of the protocol are run simultaneously.

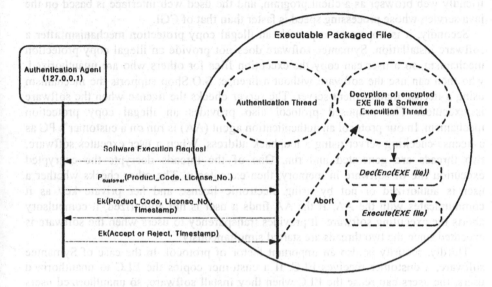

**Figure 3.** Illegal Copy Protection Protocol using Multi-thread

## 4 Comparison with Existing Models

In this section, we analyze and compare the proposed protocol with existing models such as Symantec software and S.O.Shop. Table 1 shows the compared results. The items compared are including client type, support of post installation security, security level, and support of illegal copier tracing mechanism.

**Table 1.** Comparison with Software-based Models

| Items / Models | Client Type | Post Installation Security | Security Level | Illegal Copier Tracing |
|---|---|---|---|---|
| Symantec | Web Browser | X | X | X |
| S.O.Shop | Specific Client | O | Δ | X |
| Proposed Protocol | Web Browser | O | O | O |
| O : Possible (High), X : Impossible (Low), Δ : Moderate | | | | |

Firstly, we compare used client types for shopping and software download. In the case of Symantec software, a customer uses a web browser for shopping and selecting software download. In the case of S.O.Shop, a customer should use the client program that is made and provided by the producer of S.O.Shop. A customer should therefore install the client program for shopping in advance. The proposed protocol uses a user-friendly web browser as a client program, and the used web interface is based on the java servlet, whose processing speed is faster than that of CGI.

Secondly, it is important to provide an illegal copy protection mechanism after a software installation. Symantec software does not provide an illegal copy protection mechanism, so a user can copy the execution files for others who are unauthorized, who then can use the software without a license. S.O.Shop supports the mechanism using a license management server. The server checks the license when the software is executed. The proposed protocol also provides an illegal copy protection mechanism. In our protocol an authentication agent (AA) is run on a customer's PC as a license-checking server using a loopback address. When a user executes software, two threads are generated and run. One of the threads decrypts the encrypted execution file of software in memory, then executes it. The other checks whether a user is authorized or not by using electronic license and her private key as it communicates with the AA. If the AA finds a user is not authorized, it compulsory aborts the executing software. It provides transparency to users when the software is executed since the two threads are started simultaneously.

Thirdly, security is also an important factor of protocol. In the case of Symantec software, a customer receives ELC. If a customer copies the ELC to unauthorized users, the users can reuse the ELC when they install software, so unauthorized users can successfully install software without payment. In the case of S.O.Shop, the electronic license is first encrypted using the merchant server's private key, then encrypted again using a customer's public key; so a customer can thereafter decrypt the message using her private key, and then distribute the message to unauthorized users. Therefore, unauthorized users can encrypt the message using her public key then use it as an authorized electronic license. The proposed protocol is based on PKC. The electronic license is encrypted with a buyer's authentic public key, then signed with the merchant server's private key. The proposed protocol is thus secure, unless a buyer publishes her electronic license and private key.

Finally, we discuss an illegal copier tracing scheme. When a copied and redistributed electronic license is found, existing models do not provide a copier tracing scheme. In the case of the proposed protocol, even if a software buyer copies and redistributes her electronic license and private key to unauthorized users, it can be traced back to its original owner through identification by the ID, password, and public key when the copied electronic license is found. This threat of detection will deter users from releasing unauthorized copies. Therefore, the proposed protocol provides strong security and safety.

The drawback of the proposed protocol is that a user must install an AA on her PC, and the process of the AA always resides in memory for authentication. An operating system should prevent other programs from replacing the AA as it protects the port used by the AA. It therefore needs the AA to be embedded in the operating system for enhanced security. The proposed protocol is more secure and efficient than existing software-based models, but to guarantee perfect security and maximum efficiency, it needs to work in tandem with feasible hardware-based technologies.

# 5 Conclusion

Although there are diverse efforts for enhancing electronic software distribution and software copyright protection technologies, the existing models have several problems in security and efficiency. Most existing methods leave the software product vulnerable to the unauthorized use and redistribution by customers once the product has been unlocked.

In this paper we have proposed a secure electronic software distribution and copyright protection protocol based on PKC. The proposed protocol considers post-installation security using an authentication agent and electronic license. When a user executes software, authentication is transparently processed since a multi-thread mechanism is used. The proposed protocol is secure unless a buyer distributes her electronic license and private key to unauthorized users. Even if software is copied illegally, a merchant can trace back to its original owner once the electronic license is found. The proposed protocol provides consumers, merchants, and producers in the electronic marketplace with confidence, security, and efficiency.

# References

1. Kalakota and Whinston, *Frontiers of Electronic Commerce*, Addison Wesley, 1996.
2. Anup K. Ghosh, *E-commerce Security*, Wiley, 1998.
3. Rafail Ostrovsky, "An Efficient Software Protection Scheme," Advances in Cryptology-CRYPTO '89 Proceedings, Springer-Verlag, pp. 610-611, 1990.
4. Oded Goldreich, "Towards a Theory of Software Protection," Advances in Cryptology-CRYPTO '86 Proceedings, Springer-Verlag, pp. 426-437, 1987.
5. W. Diffe and M. Hellman, "New Directions in Cryptography," IEEE Transactions on Information Theory, November 1976.
6. R.L. Rivest, A. Shamir and L. Adleman, "A Method for Obtaining Digital Signatures and Public-Key Cryptosystems," Comm. ACM, Vol. 21, No. 2, pp. 120-126, Feb. 1978.
7. Bruce Schneier, *Applied Cryptography*, Second Edition, Wiley, 1996.
8. Alfred J. Menezes, Paul C. van Oorschot, Scott A. Vanstone, *Handbook of Applied Cryptography*, CRC Press, 1997.
9. Software Piracy, URL: http://www.nopiracy.com.
10. Symantec Software, URL : http:www.symantec.com
11. S.O.Shop, URL : http://www.soshop.co.kr
12. ESD, URL : http://www.spa.org/sigs/internetesdpoli.htm
13. Sun Microsystems, "Servlet Tutorial," URL: http://java.sun.com/products/jkd/1.2/docs/ext/servlet
14. Phil Inje Chang, "Inside the java web server," URL: http://java.sun.com/features/1997/aug/jws1.html

# An Equitably Fair On-Line Auction Scheme*

Emmanouil Magkos[1], Mike Burmester[1,2], Vassilios Chrissikopoulos[1]

[1] Department of Informatics, University of Pireaus, Greece
{emagos, chris}@unipi.gr
[2] Information Security Group, Royal Holloway, University of London, UK
mikeb@dcs.rhbnc.ac.uk

**Abstract.** We present a sealed-bid electronic auction scheme that is *equitably fair* for the bidders and the seller. In this scheme, the interests of both the bidders and the seller are safeguarded: the identity of the non-winning bidders and their bidding behavior are protected (anonymity), and the bidders cannot withdraw their bids without being detected (non-repudiation). The scheme fulfills the requirements of a secure auction scheme and is verifiable. It extends the Stubblebine & Syverson auction scheme that is *not* equitably fair (it does not prevent bid withdrawals). Our scheme employs a Registrar and an Auctioneer for which no special trust assumptions are made.

## 1 Introduction

Electronic auctions are increasingly popular among the members of the Internet community. Many auction houses adopt security mechanisms that are fortified by, and result in, the non-anonymity of bidders and/or the non-privacy of their bids. To hold bidders accountable, bids are authenticated and transactions are logged. As a result, buying profiles may be constructed and the personal information of users (e.g., their bidding behavior) may be used in several ways.

In this paper we propose a cryptographically secure scheme for sealed (first or second-price) electronic auctions that is *equitably fair* [4] for the bidders and "society". That is, while the identity of the bidders and their bidding behavior are protected, bidders are accountable for their actions (i.e., they cannot withdraw their bids). This protects "society" (the seller or/and the auctioneer) from being abused by irresponsible bidders. Therefore, our system treats the bidder and the seller/auctioneer equitably: bidders cannot withdraw their bids, and the Auctioneer cannot find out the identity of a bidder.

We built a sealed-bid auction protocol, which satisfies all the requirements of a secure auction system and differs from [33] in that, while preserving anonymity and privacy prior to the auctioneer's commitment, it prevents bidders from withdrawing their bids. We believe that *bid-withdrawal*, even if the bid has not yet been revealed, may be *fair* for the bidder but is not *equitable* [4] towards "society" (e.g., the seller/auctioneer). As argued in [4], if altered circumstances make a bid unprofitable

---

* Research supported by the Secretariat of Research and Technology of Greece.

or loss making, and a bidder is allowed to withdraw a bid, then "society" is threatened by the individual. Allowing bid withdrawal is as fair as allowing a seller to withdraw the item being auctioned, because altered circumstances make the sale unprofitable.

In our approach, bid-withdrawal can be traced after the auction has ended. For this purpose we make use of Time-Lock Puzzles[1] [29] for non-repudiation. We also make use of Blind Signatures[2] [9] for anonymity, a Cut-and-Choose[3] technique [9] for correctness, and a Certified-Delivery mechanism [5] to prevent denial-of-service attacks. Checks are also made to ensure that only eligible bidders submit valid bids.

**Our Scenario.** We consider sealed auctions where non-winning bidders retain their anonymity, but no bidder can withdraw a bid. There are several applications in which the anonymity of bidders is an important design feature of auctioning. For example, the bidding behavior of non-winning bidders might be of commercial value. Furthermore, by preventing bid withdrawals, bidders cannot dynamically control an auction by withdrawing their bids when altered circumstances make these unprofitable. Our scenario is appropriate for high security level auctions, where correctness and anonymity are important.

## 1.1 Related Work

Franklin and Reiter [17] designed and implemented a distributed service for performing sealed-bid auctions. This makes use of *Threshold Secret Sharing* [31] and *Verifiable Signature Sharing* [18] for protection against faulty auction servers, and off-line *Digital Cash* [7] for non-repudiation. Franklin and Reiter also proposed a modification of their protocol to establish anonymity for loosing bidders, but in this case, a coalition between either two faulty servers from different auctions or a faulty server and the bank, may reveal the identity of loosing bidders. Furthermore, threshold mechanisms are not applicable for auctions run by small organizations where all parties involved may be corrupted [25]. Finally, the use of Digital Cash creates an opportunity cost, especially in the case of large bids.

Harkavy, Tygar and Kikuchi [21] used *Verifiable Secret Sharing* [11] and *Secure Distributed Computations* [2] to perform sealed-bid electronic auctions. Their protocol establishes privacy for all but the winning bidder, even after the end of the bidding period. They also suggested the use of *Identity Escrow* [23] mechanisms to establish non-repudiation while preserving anonymity. Their protocol cannot handle tie-breaking (i.e., when several bidders tie for the highest bid) without sacrificing privacy. In [22], they deal with the tie-breaking problem by adding an extra auction

---

[1] With Time-Lock Puzzles, a message is encrypted so that it cannot be decrypted without running a computer continuously for at least a certain amount of time.

[2] Blind Signatures are the equivalent of signing carbon-paper-lined envelopes. A user seals a slip of a paper inside such an envelope, which is later signed on the outside. When the envelope is opened, the slip will bear the carbon image of the signature.

[3] Cut-and-Choose techniques are used to establish correctness in a blind signature protocol. The signer opens all but one envelope and then signs the remaining envelope.

round. In both protocols, as well as in [17], security relies on the fact that no more than a threshold of auction servers behave maliciously.

Stajano and Anderson [32] propose an anonymous ascending auction between mistrustful principles with no trusted arbitrator. Their protocol assumes that the seller and the bidders anonymously broadcast messages over a Local Area Network, using the Chaum's *Dining-Cryptographers* scheme [8]. The bid submission and the seller's commitment are made by using the *Diffie-Hellman* key exchange [16]. While there is no privacy for the bids, due to the nature of the auction, all loosing bidders remain anonymous and the identity of the winner is revealed to the seller (provided that the seller commits to the highest bid). For non-repudiation, the public keys are *escrowed* [3,12], while accuracy is achieved with a Cut-and-Choose mechanism. The protocol can be implemented in local networks, and is not practical for open networks (such as the Internet).

Stubblebine and Syverson [33] propose a high-level ascending scheme for on-line auctions. The auction is fair in that the auctioneer commits to the submitted bids prior to their disclosure and cannot selectively close the auction after a particular bid is received. To achieve fairness, the protocol makes use of public notaries [34] and certified-delivery services [6]. A bidder constructs a message that consists of the bid and information binding the bid back to the bidder, then commits to this message by using a *Secret Bit Commitment* scheme [30] and finally submits the commitment to the auctioneer using a certified-delivery service. The auctioneer commits to the bid by using a trusted time source (i.e., a public notary) and the bidder opens his commitment. If the communication channel is anonymous the bidder has a choice not to open his commitment. This provides for limited bid-withdrawal.

**Summary of Results.** This paper presents an *equitably fair* auction scheme, which protects the bidders and their bidding behavior by concealing their identity, while at the same time preventing bidders from abusing the scheme. In particular, (a) non-winning bidders remain anonymous, (b) no bidder is able to withdraw a bid without being detected.

The paper is organized as follows. In Section 2, we overview various auction types presented in the literature. We present a list of desirable properties for secure electronic auctions. In Section 3 we list the basic security assumptions for our scheme and in Section 4 we describe our auction protocol. In Section 5 we show that this protocol satisfies the requirements of Section 2. We conclude in Section 6.

## 2 Background: Auction-Types and Requirements

In this paper we are mainly concerned with *sealed* auctions, first or second-price [36]. In such auctions bidders submit their bid before the end of a previously agreed bidding period. Each bidder is allowed one bid. After the bidding period ends, bids are opened and the winner is determined. The highest bidder wins and pays the amount bid (first price) or an amount equal to the second highest bid (second-price). We focus on *one-sided* auctions for which there is one seller and many buyers.

There are several other types of auctions such as *ascending* (English) auctions [15], *descending* (Dutch) auctions and their variants (for a survey of auction types see [24, 35]). In ascending auctions, bidders submit bids to overcome the current highest bid, and the auction ends when, within a time interval, no bidder submits a higher bid. In descending auctions, the auctioneer starts the bidding at a high price that lowers gradually, and the first bidder that bids the current price wins the item at that price. Ascending auctions are strategically equivalent to second-price sealed auctions under some preconditions [24].

Sealed bid electronic auctions emphasize security issues inherent in every e-commerce activity, while ascending electronic auctions pose novel problems because of their time-dependence [21]. Agent technology promises to ameliorate these temporal issues [37]. Our system, when used in a second-price auction, achieves both the price-discovery virtue of an ascending auction and the simplicity of a sealed-bid mechanism.

Depending on the type of auction, there is a need to adopt the following requirements.

**Anonymity.** During the auction, the identity of bidders is not revealed to anyone. After the auction ends, the identity of the winner (this could be a pseudonym) is revealed to the auctioneer, while the identity of loosing bidders remains secret.

**Privacy.** Bids are not revealed to anyone unless a precondition is satisfied. In a sealed-bid auction, this may be the end of the bidding period.

**Correctness.** The following properties must be satisfied to achieve correctness:
- Only eligible bidders can submit bids.
- No one can impersonate a bidder.
- Valid bids cannot be altered/eliminated by the auctioneer.
- Bids are valid only for the specified auction.
- The winner of the auction is always the highest bidder.

**Non-Repudiation.** Bidders cannot repudiate (withdraw) submitted bids.

**Verifiability.** All participants are able to verify the fairness of the results.

# 3 Basic Security Assumptions

Our protocol uses cryptographic tools and techniques that are publicly known and have been proposed during the past years, such as *Time-Lock Puzzles* [29] for non-repudiation, *Blind Signatures* [9] for anonymity and *Cut-and-Choose* techniques [7] for correctness. We make the following assumptions:

**Certificate Infrastructure.** There is a *Certificate Infrastructure* and the users are legally bound by their signature. Mechanisms to establish non-repudiation for digitally signed messages are discussed in [38]. We also assume that bidders, prior to their registration, possess a private/public key pair and a corresponding certificate, issued by a trusted Certification Authority (CA). This means that they have already proved to a trusted authority their ability to pay for a transaction.

**Channel Anonymity.** There is an *anonymous* channel where bidders can send/accept messages that cannot be traced (e.g., by using traffic analysis). For example, e-mail anonymity can be established using *Mixmaster* re-mailers[4] [10, 14]. HTTP anonymity can be established by using services such as the *Anonymizer* [13], *Crowds* [28], the *Lucent Personalized Web Assistant* (LPWA) [26], and *Onion-Routing* [20]. LPWA and Onion-Routing can handle e-mail as well as HTTP. Onion-Routing also supports "reply onions" that allow anonymous replies to be sent in response to a previously received anonymous e-mail.

**Asynchronous Communication.** Communication during the auction is *asynchronous* i.e. messages by the sender are received within a bounded (but unknown) time interval [1]. Thus, all bids are supposed to be received before the closing of the bidding period.

**Certified Delivery.** All entities participating in the protocol agree on a *Certified-Delivery* Service. We assume that this Service provides for anonymity and *atomicity* [1, 5]. This means that a bidder can prove, while preserving his anonymity, that a bid has been submitted to the auctioneer and that the auctioneer accepted the bid at a specific time, with no intermediate situations (in which, for example, the auctioneer would have a proof of origin while the bidder would not have a proof of receipt). Optionally, the seller may be allowed to submit test-bids periodically, in order to ensure that the auctioneer is operational [33].

**Tie Breaking.** We assume that bids submitted during the protocol are in a "dollars//cents" form (e.g. "one thousand nine hundred and ninety-nine dollars and ninety-nine cents") so that the possibility of a tie between two bidders is practically impossible. This assumption can be circumvented by using *Coin Flipping* [30] in order to determine a winner, or the techniques used in [22].

## 4 The Auction Protocol

Our system employs two authorities, a Registrar and an Auctioneer. The Registrar blindly authenticates eligible bidders while the Auctioneer processes valid bids. The auction requires six steps that we describe below –see Fig. 1.

---

[4] A Mixmaster re-mailer re-mails the messages it gets after a random time-interval (latency). It also re-mails messages in a different order.

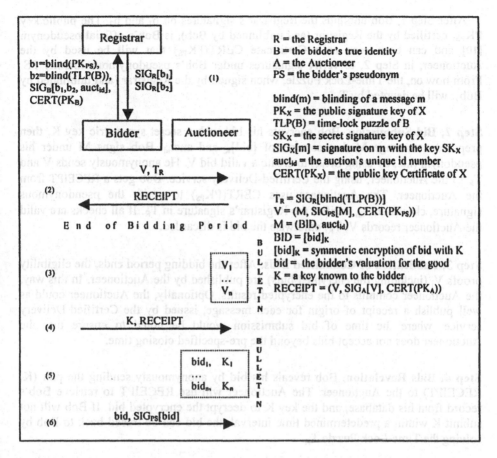

**Fig. 1.** A First/Second price auction protocol

**Step 1, Registration.** A bidder, say Bob, gets a pseudonym that will identify him to the Auctioneer. To do that, Bob creates a private/public key pair (SK$_{PS}$ , PK$_{PS}$) and a Time-Lock Puzzle[5] of his real identity, TLP(B). Bob blinds (e.g., see [30]) both PK$_{PS}$ and TLP(B) to create the blindings $b_1$ and $b_2$ respectively, and then signs a message consisting of the blindings $b_1$, $b_2$, and the unique auction identification number auct$_{id}$. Bob sends these to the Registrar and gets the blindings authenticated by the Registrar. For the correctness of the blindings, a Cut-and-Choose[6] protocol is used. This guarantees that TLP(B) can be solved back to Bob's identity in case of repudiation, while at the same time the Registrar cannot link the puzzle with Bob directly.

---

[5] There are several ways to implement Time-Lock Puzzles. In [20], the message (Bob's identity) is encrypted with an appropriately large symmetric key, which in turn is encrypted in such a way that it cannot be decrypted in a parallelizable way.

[6] Bob sends *n* blinded messages to the Registrar, then unblinds any n-1 indicated by the registrar. The Registrar signs the remaining message. There is a tradeoff between choosing a large n (strong correctness), and a small n (efficiency).

After Step 1, Bob unblinds the Registrar's signatures on $b_1$ and $b_2$. The public key $PK_{PS}$, certified by the Registrar (and unblinded by Bob), is Bob's official pseudonym [10] and can been seen as a Certificate $CERT(PK_{PS})$ that will be used by the Auctioneer, in Step 2, to verify signatures under Bob's pseudonymous identity PS. From now on, the Time-Lock Puzzle, when signed by the Registrar (and unblinded by Bob), will be denoted by $T_R$.

**Step 2, Bid Submission.** Bob encrypts his bid with a secret symmetric key K, then prepares a message M that consists of $[bid]_K$ and $auct_{id}$. Bob signs M under his pseudonym (i.e., by using $SK_{PS}$) to create a valid bid V. He anonymously sends V and $T_R$ to the Auctioneer, using the Certified-Delivery service. Bob gets a RECEIPT from the Auctioneer. The Auctioneer uses $CERT(PK_{PS})$ to verify the pseudonymous signature, checks $auct_{id}$, verifies the Registrar's signature in $T_R$. If all checks are valid the Auctioneer records V, $T_R$, otherwise the bid is discarded.

**Step 3, Publication of Committed Bids.** After the bidding period ends, the eligibility proofs $V_i$ (including the encrypted bids) are published by the Auctioneer. In this way, the Auctioneer commits to the encrypted results. Optionally, the Auctioneer could as well publish a receipt of origin for each message, issued by the Certified-Delivery service, where the time of bid submission would be noted to ensure that the Auctioneer does not accept bids beyond the pre-specified closing time.

**Step 4, Bids Revelation.** Bob reveals his bid by anonymously sending the pair (K, RECEIPT) to the Auctioneer. The Auctioneer will use RECEIPT to retrieve Bob's record from his database, and the key K to decrypt the encrypted bid. If Bob will not submit K within a predetermined time interval, the bid can be traced back to Bob by solving the Time-Lock Puzzle $T_R$.

**Step 5, Final Results.** The Auctioneer publishes all decrypted bids and the keys used to decrypt them. The winner is then determined and all parties are able to verify the auction results.

**Step 6, The Winner's Proof.** If Bob is the winner, he sends in Step 6 his signature on the winning bid. If Bob repudiates the winning bid, his identity can be retrieved by solving the Time-Lock Puzzle $T_R$.

## 5 Security Analysis

Our auction scheme provides protection for the bidders, the Auctioneer and the Registrar against malicious behavior by any number of participants. We do not make any special trust assumptions for the Registrar and the Auctioneer: both authorities may misbehave. We evaluate the security of our protocol by examining the requirements listed in Section 2.

## 5.1 Anonymity

The Registrar checks the identity of a bidder who submits a pseudonym (the pseudonym is authenticated by the bidder). However, the pseudonym is blindly signed in Step 1. Consequently, the Registrar cannot trace any encrypted bid, published in Step 3, back to the bidder's real identity.

The Auctioneer receives messages that cannot be traced back to the sender (the communication channel is anonymous) and that are signed under a certified pseudonym. The Auctioneer cannot link the pseudonym with the bidder's real identity, so the only way to find out the bidder's identity is by solving the puzzle $T_R$, submitted with the encrypted bid in Step 2.

If the Auctioneer conspires with the Registrar, they cannot learn more than they each know separately. However, if a bidder submits a bid to the Auctioneer in Step 2 immediately after Step 1, the two conspiring authorities might guess correctly which bidder bids what. This problem can be solved in part by using a Mixmaster re-mailer that incorporates *latency* and *reordering* mechanisms [14]. Additionally, bidders may be instructed not to submit their bids to the Auctioneer immediately after registration in Step 1. The time-independence of the auction type being proposed (i.e., a sealed-bid) favors this solution.

## 5.2 Privacy

After Step 1 and until the end of the bidding period, bids are protected by symmetric encryption. One has to break the symmetric encryption in order to break the bidder's privacy. After Step 4, when all bidders reveal the encryption keys, there is no bid privacy. This poses no security threats because at this stage the auction is essentially completed and the hidden bids already committed by the Auctioneer. Furthermore, bids are revealed to enable verification. Finally, anonymity throughout the auction procedure compensates for the loss of privacy.

## 5.3 Correctness

**Only eligible bidders can submit bids.** There are two things that determine the user's eligibility through the auction procedure: the certificate CERT(PK$_{PS}$) and the Time-Lock Puzzle $T_R$ (signed by the Registrar).

The Auctioneer uses CERT(PK$_{PS}$) to verify that the bidder is a valid user and rejects all bids that are not authenticated. This filtering makes the auction procedure flexible, saves the Auctioneer from useless bid storage and processing time, and discourages denial-of-service attacks. Independent users also use CERT(PK$_{PS}$) to verify that the auction results are correct (e.g., they verify that bids published in Step 3 have been submitted by eligible bidders and not by the Auctioneer).

The Time-Lock Puzzle $T_R$ is used by the Auctioneer in case of bid repudiation. A bidder gets $T_R$ from the Registrar in Step 1 by proving, during the Cut-and-Choose protocol, that it is linked to his identity. Only the bidder can unblind $T_R$, so the

Auctioneer knows that the owner of $T_R$ is an eligible bidder whose identity will be uncovered in case of repudiation.

**No one can impersonate a bidder.** There are several reasons why someone would want to link their bid to another bidder, say Bob. For example, a bidder may wish to incriminate Bob in case of bid withdrawal, or for high bogus bids.

The Registrar knows Bob's identity so can make a fake $T_R^*$ and impersonate Bob to the Auctioneer (or give $T_R^*$ to a friend). However, $T_R^*$ does not establish non-repudiation for Bob if the fake bid is the winning bid (or if it is withdrawn). Bob can later prove his innocence by revealing his own Time-Lock Puzzle $T_R$. If $T_R$ is different than $T_R^*$ (and it will be, with a very high probability since the bidder got $T_R$ in Step 1 using a Cut-and-Choose protocol) then everybody knows that the Registrar has cheated.

The Auctioneer sees Bob's Time-Lock Puzzle $T_R$ after Step 2, so he might want to use it to create a fake bid (e.g., by giving it away to a friend) in order to establish non-repudiation for Bob. Normally, the Auctioneer should check his database and reject all bids containing a $T_R$ already submitted. Even if the Auctioneer is not supposed to check his database and just accepts bids, Bob can prove that the Auctioneer has cheated: when Bob submits his bid along with the authentic $T_R$, he gets a proof of receipt, signed at a time determined by an external trusted source such as the Certified-Delivery Service. This enables Bob to prove that his bid was submitted earlier.

**Valid bids cannot be altered/eliminated by the Auctioneer.** The use of the Certified-Delivery Service in Step 2 prevents the Auctioneer from altering or eliminating valid bids. The service enables bidders to prove to an arbitrator that, for example, the Auctioneer received a message M at time t. Consequently, the Auctioneer cannot eliminate a correct bid pretending that it is incorrect (or that it has not been submitted). In addition, the Auctioneer cannot reject a bid pretending that it has been submitted at a time later than the end of the bidding period. After the publication in Step 3, the Auctioneer commits to the encrypted results of the auction and cannot alter them without being detected.

**Bids are valid only for the specified auction and cannot be reused.** During the protocol, $auct_{id}$ is used as a freshness indicator. The Auctioneer rejects all messages that are signed by the bidder and do not contain a valid $auct_{id}$ number. In Step 3, $auct_{id}$ is published next to the encrypted bid, as part of message V.

**No one but the highest bidder is the winner of the auction.** This requirement is always satisfied because of the *verifiability* feature discussed next.

## 5.4 Verifiability

All participants can independently verify the results of the auction. The encrypted results are published in Step 3, prior to the decryption of bids in Step 4. In Step 5 all decrypted bids are published along with the keys used to decrypt them. The results in Step 5 are the Auctioneer's commitment to the outcome of the auction so they must be consistent with the results in Step 3. The Auctioneer will be responsible for any inconsistency. A bidder can verify the results concerning other bidders by decrypting the encrypted bids with the published keys and by verifying the signed bids.

## 5.5 Non-Repudiation

The "point of no return" for a bidder can be either the anonymous bid submission in Step 2, before the closing of the bidding period (*strong non-repudiation*) or optionally the anonymous sending of the decryption key K in Step 4, after the closing of the bidding period (*weak non-repudiation*).

In any case the winner cannot repudiate his bid. If the winner does not initiate Step 6 within a pre-specified time interval, then the Auctioneer can discover the identity of the winner by solving the Time-Lock Puzzle. The winner will then be subject to a penalty price, *a priori* known and agreed upon by all participants [33]. For example, this penalty price could be equal to the cost of solving the puzzle, plus the unpaid (repudiated) bid.

**Strong Non-Repudiation (no Bid-Withdrawal).** Bidders commit to the bids published in Step 3. All bidders whose bids are published in Step 3 must provide the keys necessary to decrypt them. For each bidder who does not submit K the Auctioneer solves the Time-Lock Puzzle to retrieve the bidder's identity. By not allowing bidders to repudiate submitted bids, the auction is *equitably fair* for both bidders and the auctioneer/seller, as argued in Section 1.

**Weak Non-Repudiation (Bid-Withdrawal).** Each bidder may be allowed not to reveal the key K necessary to decrypt the encrypted bid published in Step 3 (i.e., to withdraw his bid). In this case, at least one bidder has to initiate Step 4 for the Auctioneer to declare a winner. All bids for which a key K has been submitted within a predefined time interval are published in Step 5. Bidders commit only to the bids published in Step 5.

# 6 Conclusion

We have presented an equitably fair sealed on-line auction scheme with no special trust assumptions. The system is equitable in that, while preserving anonymity for the non-winning bidders, it does not allow the withdrawal of any submitted bid. The bidders use one-time pseudonyms and commit to their identity in such a way that one has to solve a Time-Lock Puzzle in order to reveal it, for non-repudiation. Because the pseudonyms and the identity commitments are one-time, it is not possible to trace the identity of loosing bidders, except by solving a time-consuming computational problem. Our scheme extends the Stubblebine & Syverson auction scheme [33] that does *not* prevent bid withdrawals.

Our protocol, while quite efficient, uses a Cut-and-Choose mechanism to establish correctness, which requires a certain number of interactions. This can be costly. Obviously there is a trade-off between security and efficiency. Our protocol is designed for auctions that require a high security level, and is not suitable for low value auctions for which correctness and anonymity are of little consequence.

It is easy to see how to extend this scheme to equitable ascending auctions. It is also possible to extend this scheme to support equitable *Double Auctions* [19] and equitable *Continuous Double Auctions* (with multiple sellers and buyers) [27].

# References

1. Asokan, N., Shoup, V., Waidner, M.: Asynchronous Protocols for Optimistic Fair Exchange. In: Proceedings of 1998 IEEE Symposium on Security and Privacy. IEEE CS Press (1998) 86-99
2. Ben-Or, M., Goldwasser, S., Wigderson, A.: Completeness Theorems for Non-Cryptographic Fault-Tolerant Distributed Computing. In: 20th Annual ACM Symposium on Theory of Computing. ACM (1988) 1-10
3. Boneh, D., Franklin, M.: Efficient Generation of RSA keys. In: Advances in Cryptology – CRYPTO 97, Lecture Notes in Computer Science, Vol. 1233. Springer-Verlag (1997) 425-439
4. Burmester, M., Desmedt, Y., Seberry, J.: Equitable Key Escrow with Limited Time Span (or How to Enforce Time Expiration Cryptographically). In: Advances in Cryptology - ASIACRYPT '98, Lecture Notes in Computer Science, Vol. 1514. Springer-Verlag (1998) 380-391
5. Camp, J., Harkavy, M., Tygar, K., Yee, B.: Anonymous Atomic Transactions. In: 2nd USENIX Workshop on Electronic Commerce. USENIX Press (1996) 123-133
6. Certmail: The Certified Electronic Mail System, http://www.certmail.com/
7. Chaum, D., Fiat, A., Naor, M.: Untraceable Electronic Cash. In: Advances in Cryptology – CRYPTO 88, Lecture Notes in Computer Science, Vol. 1440. Springer-Verlag (1988) 319-327
8. Chaum, D.: The Dining Cryptographers Problem: Unconditional Sender and Recipient Untraceability. Journal of Cryptology, Vol. 1(1), (1988) 65-75
9. Chaum, D.: Security Without Identification: Transaction Systems to Make Big Brother Obsolete. Communications of the ACM, Vol. 28(10), (1985) 1030-1044
10. Chaum, D.: Untraceable Electronic Mail, Return Addresses, and Digital Pseudonyms. Communications of the ACM, Vol. 24(2), (1981) 84-88
11. Chor, B., Goldwasser, S., Micali, S., Awerbuch, B.: Verifiable Secret Sharing and Achieving Simultaneity in the Presence of Faults. In: 26th IEEE Symposium on the Foundations of Computer Science. IEEE Press (1985) 383-395
12. Cocks, K.: Split Knowledge Generation of RSA Parameters. In: 6th IMA Conference on Cryptography and Coding. Springer-Verlag (1997) 89-95
13. Community ConneXion, Inc., http://www.anonymizer.com
14. Cottrell, L.: Mixmaster and Remailer Attacks. Available from http://obscura.obscura.com/~loki/remailer/remailer-essay.html
15. Crampton, P.: Ascending Auctions. European Economic Review, Vol. 42, (1998) 745-756
16. Diffie, W., Hellman, M.: New Directions in Cryptography. IEEE Transactions on Information Theory, Vol. 22(6), (1976) 644-654
17. Franklin, M., Reiter, M.: The Design and Implementation of a Secure Auction Service. IEEE Transactions on Software Engineering, Vol. 22(5), (1996) 302-311

18. Franklin, M., Reiter, M.: Verifiable Signature Sharing. In: Advances in Cryptology – EUROCRYPT 95, Lecture Notes in Computer Science, Vol. 921. Springer-Verlag (1995) 50-63

19. Friedman, D., Rust, J.: The Double Auction Market: Institutions, Theories and Evidence. Addison-Wesley, MA (1993)

20. Goldschlag, D., Reed, M., Syverson, P.: Onion Routing for Anonymous and Private Communications. Communications of the ACM, Vol. 42(2), (1999) 39-41

21. Harkavy, M., Kikuchi, H., Tygar, J.: Electronic Auctions with Private Bids. In: 3rd USENIX Workshop on Electronic Commerce. USENIX Press (1998) 61-74

22. Harkavy, M., Kikuchi, II., Tygar, J.: Multi-Round Anonymous Auction Protocols. In: 1st IEEE Workshop on Dependable and Real-Time E-Commerce Systems (DARE 99). IEEE Press (1999) 62-69

23. Kilian, J., Petrank, E.: Identity Escrow. In: Advances in Cryptology – CRYPTO 98, Lecture Notes in Computer Science, Vol. 1462. Springer-Verlag (1998) 169-185

24. Klemperer, P.: Auction Theory: A Guide to the Literature. Journal of Economic Surveys, Vol. 13, (1999) at http://econwpa.wustl.edu:8089/eps/mic/papers/9903/9903002.pdf

25. Kumar, M., Feldman, S.: Internet Auctions. In: 3rd USENIX Workshop on Electronic Commerce. USENIX Press (1998) 49-60

26. The Lucent Personalized Web Assistant. Available from http://lpwa.com

27. McCabe, K., Rassenti, S., Smith, V.: Auction Institutional Design: Theory and Behavior of Simultaneous Multiple-Unit Generalizations of the Dutch and English Auctions. American Economic Review, Vol. 80(5), (1990) 1276-1283

28. Reiter, M., Rubin, A.: Crowds, Anonymity for Web Transactions. DIMACS Technical Report 97-15, (1997) available from http://www.research.att.com/projects/crowds/

29. Rivest, R., Shamir, A., Wagner, D.: Time-Lock Puzzles and Timed-Release Crypto. LCS Tech. Memo MIT/LCS/TR-684, (1996) available from http://theory.lcs.mit.edu/~rivest/RivestShamirWagner-timelock.ps

30. Schneier, B.: Applied Cryptography, Second Edition: Protocols, Algorithm and Source Code in C. John Wiley and Sons (1996)

31. Shamir, A.: How to Share a Secret. Communications of the ACM, Vol. 22(11), (1979) 612-613

32. Stajano, F., Anderson, R.: The Cocaine Auction Protocol: On the Power of Anonymous Broadcast. In: 3rd International Workshop on Information Hiding. Lecture Notes in Computer Science, Vol. 1768. Springer-Verlag (1999) 434-448

33. Stubblebine, S., Syverson, P.: Fair On-line Auctions Without Special Trusted Parties. In: Financial Cryptography 99, Lecture Notes in Computer Science, Vol. 1468. Springer - Verlag (1999) 231-241

34. Surety Technologies, Inc., http://www.e-timestamp.com/

35. Ungar, L., Parkes, D., Foster, D.: Cost and Trust Issues in On-line Auctions. In: Agents-98 Workshop on Agent-Mediated Electronic Trading, Minneapolis. MN (1998) 161-172

36. Vickrey, W.: Counterspeculation, Auctions, and Competitive Sealed Tenders. Journal of Finance, Vol. 16(8), (1961) 8-37

37. Wellman, M., Wurman, P.: Real time Issues for Internet Auctions. In: 1st IEEE Workshop DARE 98, (1998) available from http://ftp.eecs.umich.edu/people/wellman/dare98.ps

38. You, C., Zhou, J., Lam, K.: On the Efficient Implementation of Fair Non-Repudiation. In: Proceedings of the 1997 IEEE Computer Security Foundations Workshop. IEEE CS Press (1997) 126-132

# An Optimistic Fair Exchange E-commerce Protocol with Automated Dispute Resolution*

Indrakshi Ray and Indrajit Ray

Department of Computer and Information Science
University of Michigan-Dearborn
Email: {iray, indrajit}@umich.edu

**Abstract.** In this paper we propose an e-commerce protocol with the following features: (1) ensures true fair exchange, (2) does not require manual dispute resolution in case of unfair behavior by any party, (3) does not require the active involvement of a trusted third party, (4) allows the customer to verify that the product he is about to receive is the one he is paying for, and (5) can be used for the fair exchange of any two digital items.

## 1 Introduction

Researchers have identified a number of desirable properties of e-commerce protocols: (i) should ensure fair exchange, (ii) should not require manual dispute resolution in case of unfair behavior by one party, (iii) each party should have the assurance that the item he is about to receive is the correct one, and (iv) should not require the active involvement of a trusted third party. In this paper we propose an e-commerce protocol that satisfies all these properties.

Fair exchange protocols have been proposed in the context of electronic mails [9, 19] and electronic transactions [8, 14]. Most of these works [8, 9, 19] focus on storing evidence that is to be used in case one party misbehaves. If a dispute occurs, a judge looks at the evidence and delivers his judgment. The dispute resolution is done after the protocol execution, that is, after the customer has obtained his product or the merchant his money. However, such "after-the-fact" protection [14, 15] may be inadequate in an e-commerce environment where the customer and the merchant may simply disappear.

The need for such "after-the-fact" dispute resolution does not arise if protocols provide *true fair exchange* – under all circumstances, either the two parties get each other's items or none do. Protocols providing true fair exchange [14] typically use an online trusted third party. The third party receives the items from each party, verifies the items, and then forwards them to the other party. As a result if any party misbehaves or prematurely quits, no harm is caused to the other party. Moreover, each party has the assurance that the item he is about to receive is indeed the correct one. However, the third party is a source of bottleneck for these protocols. Not only is the performance of the third party an issue, but also its vulnerability to denial of service attacks.

---

* This work has been partially supported by the NSF grant EIA 9977548, and by the University of Michigan-Dearborn Faculty Research Grant and Summer Research Grant.

Several protocols have been proposed [1–3, 5] that do not use the third party unless a problem, such as, a party misbehaving or prematurely aborting, occurs. Such protocols are termed optimistic [1–3]. Some of these protocols provide "after-the-fact" protection [1] and others [5] are restricted to the exchange of digital signatures.

This motivates us to propose an e-commerce protocol satisfying all the above mentioned desirable properties. The protocol is based on the theory of cross validation using which each party can verify that the item he is about to receive is indeed the correct one. The protocol does use a trusted third party to ensure fair exchange. The merchant escrows the encrypted product and a pair of keys with the trusted third party. If the merchant disappears after receiving the payment, the trusted third party can always give the customer the keys for decrypting the product. But the third party is not involved unless a problem, such as, a party misbehaving or prematurely aborting occurs. Thus, the use of the third party is kept to a minimum level.

The rest of the paper is organized as follows. Section 2 describes some related work. Section 3 briefly presents the theory of cross validation and describes how the product validation takes place. Section 4 describes the optimistic protocol. Section 5 discusses how the protocol is extended to handle misbehaving parties. Finally, section 6 concludes the paper.

## 2 Related Work

Previous work on fair exchange schemes can be classified under two categories: (i) gradual exchange protocols and (ii) third party protocols. Gradual exchange protocols [4, 6, 10] gradually increase the probability of fair exchange over several rounds of message exchanges; these protocols have extensive communication requirements and assume that both the parties have equal computational power.

The third party protocols [8, 9, 11, 19] make use of a trusted on-line third party. The idea of using a trusted on-line third party to obtain non-repudiation of origin and delivery of a mail message was proposed by Deng et al. [9] and Zhou and Gollmann [19]. Dispute resolution is outside the scope of these protocols; however, the protocols do specify what evidence must be stored for the dispute to be resolved in a fair manner.

Using a trusted third party to ensure fair exchange in the context of sale of low-priced network goods has been proposed in the NetBill system [8]. The trusted third party is the NetBill server that maintains financial accounts for the customers and the merchants. The customer, if interested, requests the merchant for a good. The merchant, in response, sends the encrypted good. On receiving the encrypted good, the customer sends the merchant payment information. The merchant forwards this information and the decrypting key to the NetBill server. The NetBill server then debits customer's account, credits merchant's account and sends a receipt to the merchant. Finally, the merchant forwards this receipt containing the decrypting key to the customer. Note that, the NetBill protocol is not optimistic and a merchant who has provided a worthless good is detected only after the exchange occurs; this is in contrast to our work.

A fair exchange protocol ensuring the consistency of the document but requiring the active participation of a trusted third party has been proposed by Ketchpel [14]. The merchant and the customer after agreeing upon the product and the price sign a contract which is forwarded to the third party. Each party then sends his item to the third party. The third party verifies that the items satisfy the contract, and then forwards them to the respective parties.

Franklin and Reiter [11] also propose a set of fair exchange protocols that verify the consistency of a document before the exchange takes place. The protocols use a one-way function $f$ which has the property that there exists another efficiently computable function $F$ such that $F(x,(f(y))) = f(xy)$. The function, $f$, is known by both the parties, and $F$ is known by the third party. X and Y wish to exchange some secret information $K_X$ and $K_Y$. Before the protocol is initiated, it is assumed that X and Y know $f(K_Y)$ and $f(K_X)$ respectively. The first step involves X sending a random number $x_1$ to Y, and Y sending $y_1$ to X. In the second step X sends the following to the third party: $f(K_X)$, $f(K_Y)$, $K_X x_1^{-1}$, and $f(y_1)$; Y also sends the corresponding components to the third party. The third party makes some comparisons to ascertain that each is sending the correct components, and then forwards $K_X x_1^{-1}$ to Y and $K_Y y_1^{-1}$ to X. Y and X can multiply these by $x_1$ and $y_1$ respectively to get the items. One contribution of this paper is that the third party is semi-trusted (one that can misbehave on its own but will not collude with the participating parties) and will not be revealed the information that X and Y are trying to exchange. However, this protocol requires the active participation of the third party. We invoke the third party when a problem occurs; however, when invoked it is provided with all information pertaining to the items exchanged.

Three fair exchange protocols that do not require the involvement of the third party unless there is a problem, have been proposed by Bao et al. [5]. The important contribution of this paper is that the authors provide a theory based on which each party is able to verify that the signature he is about to receive is indeed the correct signature, before actually receiving the signature. However, the protocol is not general, and does not apply when both the parties want to exchange digital items other than signatures. Asokan et al. [3] also provide an optimistic protocol for the fair exchange of digital signatures.

A more general optimistic protocol that allows exchange of any two digital items has been proposed by Asokan et al. [1]. The protocol begins by the two parties promising each other an exchange of items. If they agree on the terms of the exchange, the exchange takes place. In case of any failure or any party misbehaving, the recovery phase which involves the third party is initiated. One difference with our work is that our protocol provides true fair exchange whereas that by Asokan et al. does not. For this reason, the dispute resolution is outside the scope of Asokan's protocol. Another difference is that in Asokan's protocol a party can verify whether he has received the correct item after receiving the item; in our work, we can do this before receiving the item.

## 3 Theory for Cross Validation

Before presenting our protocol, we provide some background about the theory of cross-validation on which the protocol is based. For details the reader is referred to [18].

**Definition 1.** *The set of messages $\mathcal{M}$ is the set of non negative integers $m$ that are less than an upper bound $N$, i.e. $\mathcal{M} = \{m | 0 \leq m < N\}$.*

**Definition 2.** *For positive integers a, b and N, we say a is* equivalent *to b, modulo N, denoted by $a \equiv b$ mod n, if a mod $n = b$ mod n.*

**Definition 3.** *For positive integers a, x, n and $n > 1$, if $\gcd(a,n) = 1$ and $a.x \equiv 1$ mod n, then x is referred to as the* multiplicative inverse *of a modulo n. Two integers a, b are said to be* relatively prime *if their only common divisor is 1, that is, $\gcd(a,b) = 1$. The integers $n_1, n_2, \ldots, n_k$ are said to be* pairwise relatively prime, *if $\gcd(n_i, n_j) = 1$ for $i \neq j$.*

**Definition 4.** *The Euler's totient function $\phi(N)$ is defined as the number of integers that are less than N and relatively prime to N.*

**Definition 5.** *A key K is defined to be the ordered pair $< e, N >$, where N is a product of distinct primes and e is relatively prime to $\phi(N)$; e is the* exponent *and N is the* base *of the key K.*

**Definition 6.** *The* encryption *of a message m with the key $K = < e, N >$, denoted as $[m, K]$, is defined as $[m, < e, N >] = m^e$ mod N.*

**Definition 7.** *The* inverse *of a key $K = < e, N >$, denoted by $K^{-1}$, is an ordered pair $< d, N >$, satisfying $ed \equiv 1$ mod $\phi(N)$.*

**Theorem 1.** *For any message m, where $K = < e, N >$ and $K^{-1} = < d, N >$,*

$$[[m,K],K^{-1}] = [[m,K^{-1}],K] = m \qquad (1)$$

**Corollary 1.** *An encryption, $[m, K]$, is* one-to-one *if it satisfies the relation*

$$[[m,K],K^{-1}] = [[m,K^{-1}],K] = m$$

**Definition 8.** *Two keys $K_1 = < e_1, N_1 >$ and $K_2 = < e_2, N_2 >$ are said to be* compatible *if $e_1 = e_2$ and $N_1$ and $N_2$ are relatively prime. If two keys $K_1 = < e, N_1 >$ and $K_2 = < e, N_2 >$ are compatible, then the* product key, $K_1 \times K_2$, *is defined as $< e, N_1 N_2 >$.*

**Lemma 1.** *For positive integers a, $N_1$ and $N_2$, $(a$ mod $N_1 N_2) \equiv a$ mod $N_1$.*

**Theorem 2.** *For any two messages m and $\hat{m}$, such that $m, \hat{m} < N_1, N_2$, $K_1$ is the key $< e, N_1 >$, $K_2$ is the key $< e, N_2 >$, $K_1$ and $K_2$ are compatible, and $K_1 \times K_2$ is the product key $< e, N_1 N_2 >$, the following holds:*

$$[m, K_1 \times K_2] \equiv [\hat{m}, K_1] \text{ mod } N_1 \text{ if and only if } m = \hat{m} \qquad (2)$$

$$[m, K_1 \times K_2] \equiv [\hat{m}, K_2] \text{ mod } N_2 \text{ if and only if } m = \hat{m} \qquad (3)$$

## 3.1 Product Validation

Our protocol performs product and payment token validation using the results of theorem 2. The product validation takes place as follows. Let $m$ be the product to be delivered. The third party generates keys $K_{M_1}$ and $K_{M_1}^{-1}$ and provides $K_{M_1}$ to the merchant. The merchant provides the product $m$ to the third party to be encrypted with $K_{M_1}$ (where

$K_{M_1} = < e, N_1 >$) and placed at a public place, which we call the catalog, as an advertisement for $m$. When the customer decides to purchase $m$ from the merchant, the customer acquires $T = [m, K_{M_1}]$ from the catalog and keeps it for future validation of the product received.

To sell $m$ to the customer, the merchant selects a second set of keys ($K_{M_2}$, $K_{M_2}^{-1}$) such that $K_{M_2}$ is compatible with $K_{M_1}$ according to definition 8. The merchant provides the customer with $T' = [m, K_{M_1} \times K_{M_2}]$. The customer verifies that $[m, K_{M_1}]$ and $[m, K_{M_1} \times K_{M_2}]$ are encryption of the same message $m$ by verifying: $T \equiv T' \mod N_1$ as per equation (2). When satisfied, the customer sends the payment token. The merchant, in return, sends the decrypting key $K_{M_2}^{-1}$. The customer obtains $m$ using $m = \left[ T', K_{M_2}^{-1} \right]$. The proof of correctness follows from theorem 2. Using the same principle the bank can validate the payment token before signing it.

## 3.2 Security

In the theory presented in Section 3 if $e$ is chosen small and a customer can guess $e$ correctly, we have a security problem.[1] Assume that the exponent $e$ is small, say e=3. A customer starts as if he is buying the same product $m$ three times, but always stops after having received $[m, K_{M_1} \times K_{M_2}]$, $[m, K_{M_1} \times K_{M_3}]$, $[m, K_{M_1} \times K_{M_4}]$, where $K_{M_2} =< e, N_2 >$, $K_{M_3} =< e, N_3 >$ and $K_{M_4} =< e, N_4 >$.

Let $N = N_1 \times N_2 \times N_3 \times N_4$. Knowing $m^e \mod N_i$, for i $= 1 \ldots 4$, the attacker can, using the Chinese remainder Theorem [16], compute $m$. Thus a customer can get the product, without paying for it. Note that this attack is similar to the low exponent attack on the RSA cryptosystem [13]. However, since the customer does not know the value of $e$, this problem will not arise. Below we provide an additional mechanism using which the security will not be compromised even if the customer can guess $e$ correctly.

For every transaction that the merchant performs, the merchant chooses a random number $r$ such that $r$ is relatively prime to $N_2$. The customer downloads $[m, K_{M_1}]$ from the third party. Rather than sending $[m, K_{M_1} \times K_{M_2}]$ to the customer, the merchant sends the following: $[m.r, K_{M_1} \times K_{M_2}]$, $[r, K_{M_1}]$, where $m.r$ is the product of $m$ with $r$. To validate the product, the customer multiplies $[m, K_{M_1}]$ with $[r, K_{M_1}]$ and the resulting product is compared with $[m.r, K_{M_1} \times K_{M_2}]$. If both match, the customer is confident that the product he is about to receive is the one he is going to pay for. Finally, instead of sending just $K_{M_2}^{-1}$, the merchant now sends $K_{M_2}^{-1}$ and $r^{-1}$ where $r^{-1}$ is the multiplicative inverse of $r$ modulo $N_2$. Using the decrypting key $K_{M_2}^{-1}$, the customer obtains $m.r \mod N_2$. Multiplying this by $r^{-1}$ the customer can retrieve $m$.

## 4 The Basic Protocol

We make the following assumptions in the protocol:

1. Encrypted messages cannot be decrypted without proper keys. Digital signatures cannot be forged. Cryptographic checksums ensure the integrity of messages.

---

[1] Although we use an asymmetric cryptographic system in this protocol, unlike public key cryptosystems we do not disclose the exponent $e$.

2. All parties use the same algorithm for encryption and for generating cryptographic checksums.
3. Payment for product is in the form of a token, $PT$, that is accepted by the merchant.
4. A constant time out period known to all parties is used when a party waits for a message from another party.

The following table lists the notations used in the description of the protocol.

Table 1: Symbols used in protocol description

| SYMBOL | INTERPRETATION |
|---|---|
| $C, M, B$ and $TP$ | Customer, Merchant, Bank and Trusted Third Party |
| $A_{prv}, A_{pub}$ | A's private and public keys |
| $X \Longrightarrow Y : P$ | $X$ sends $P$ to $Y$ |
| $[X, K]$ | Encryption of $X$ with key $K$ |
| $CC(X)$ | Cryptographic Checksum of $X$ |
| $K_{C_1}$ | Key given by the customer's bank $B$ |
| $K_{C_1}^{-1}$ | Decrypting key corresponding to $K_{C_1}$ kept with $B$ |
| $K_{C_2}$ | Key generated by $C$ that is compatible with $K_{C_1}$ |
| $K_{C_2}^{-1}$ | Decrypting key corresponding to $K_{C_2}$ |
| $K_{M_1}$ | Key given by $TP$ to $M$ |
| $K_{M_1}^{-1}$ | Decrypting key corresponding to $K_{M_1}$ held with $TP$ |
| $K_{M_2}$ | Key generated by $M$ that is compatible with $K_{M_1}$ |
| $K_{M_2}^{-1}$ | Decrypting key corresponding to $K_{M_2}$ |
| $r$ | Random number chosen by $M$ for current transaction |
| $r^{-1}$ | Multiplicative inverse of $r$ modulo $N_2$, where $N_2$ is the base for key $K_{M_2}$ |
| $m$ | Product the customer purchases |
| $PO$ | Purchase order used by $C$ to order product $m$ |
| $PT$ | Payment token used to pay for the product |

Before the protocol begins, we assume that the following steps have already executed that sets up the environment in which the protocol operates.

1. **$C$ opens an account with $B$.** $B$ generates a key pair $K_{C_1}$, $K_{C_1}^{-1}$, provides $C$ with $K_{C_1}$ and escrows $K_{C_1}^{-1}$ with itself. For any transaction that involves payment via $B$, $C$ is obligated to use *product keys* $K_{C_1} \times K_{C_2}$, $K_{C_1} \times K_{C_3}$ ..., and so on, where $K_{C_j}$, $j \neq 1$, is compatible with $K_{C_1}$. In this paper, we assume $C$ uses the *product key* $K_{C_1} \times K_{C_2}$.
2. **$M$ registers with $TP$.** $TP$ generates the key pair $K_{M_1}$, $K_{M_1}^{-1}$, provides $M$ with $K_{M_1}$ and escrows $K_{M_1}^{-1}$ with itself. For every product, $m$, that $M$ wants to advertise in the catalog at this $TP$, $M$ sends $m$ and its description. $TP$ performs the encryption before uploading $[m, K_{M_1}]$ on the catalog. In this manner $TP$ is able to certify that the product meets its claim.

3. **C selects a product to purchase.** $C$ downloads $[m, K_{M_1}]$ from the $TP$. Note that $C$ does not have the product $m$, because he does not have the decrypting key $K_{M_1}^{-1}$. This $[m, K_{M_1}]$ will be used later by $C$ to validate the product received from $M$.

4. **C and M agree upon a price for the product.** This step may require several messages exchanged between $C$ and $M$ at the end of which they agree upon a price.

**Protocol Description**

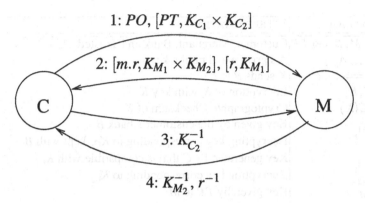

1: $PO, [PT, K_{C_1} \times K_{C_2}]$

2: $[m.r, K_{M_1} \times K_{M_2}], [r, K_{M_1}]$

C

M

3: $K_{C_2}^{-1}$

4: $K_{M_2}^{-1}, r^{-1}$

**Fig. 1.** The Basic Protocol

The protocol executes in the following four steps when no party misbehaves or prematurely quits. The messages exchanged in the protocol are shown in figure 1. Note that only the major contents of each message is shown in the figure.

**Message 1** $C \Longrightarrow M : PO, [CC(PO), C_{prv}], [[PT, K_{C_1} \times K_{C_2}], B_{prv}]$.

$C$ initiates the e-commerce transaction by sending $M$ the following items:

(a) The purchase order, $PO$, containing information about the product identifier, price of the product, identities of $C$ and $M$, and a nonce to prevent replay attacks.

(b) A digitally signed cryptographic checksum of $PO$. (In this and the following messages, the purpose of a signed cryptographic checksum is twofold: (i) it can be used as evidence of what the sender has actually sent and (ii) it also ensures the integrity of the message while in transit.)

(c) The payment token, $PT$, containing information about the identities of $B$, $C$, customer's account information, price of the product and a nonce. The payment token is first encrypted with the *product key* $K_{C_1} \times K_{C_2}$ and then digitally signed by $B$. $B$'s signature ensures that $C$ has sufficient funds to pay for the product. Note that, since $B$ has the key $K_{C_1}^{-1}$, it is able to verify the contents of $PT$ before signing.

**Message 2** $M \Longrightarrow C : [Abort, M_{prv}]$

**OR**

$M \Longrightarrow C : [CC(PO), M_{prv}], [m.r, K_{M_1} \times K_{M_2}], [CC([m.r, K_{M_1} \times K_{M_2}]), M_{prv}],$
$[r, K_{M_1}], [CC([r, K_{M_1}]), M_{prv}]$

$M$ checks to see if $PO$ is to its satisfaction – that is, $M$ agrees to all its contents and is able to verify $B$'s signature on $[PT, K_{C_1} \times K_{C_2}]$. If not, $M$ aborts the transaction and sends $C$ a signed abort message. A signed abort message provides a proof that the sender of the abort message is indeed terminating the transaction.

Otherwise, $M$ sends the following to $C$: (a) a signed cryptographic checksum of the purchase order, (b) encrypted product, (c) signed cryptographic checksum of the encrypted product, (d) encrypted random number, and (e) signed cryptographic checksum of the encrypted random number.

**Message 3** $C \Longrightarrow M : [Abort, C_{prv}]$

**OR**

$C \Longrightarrow M : [K_{C_2}^{-1}, M_{pub}], [CC([K_{C_2}^{-1}, M_{pub}]), C_{prv}]$

After receiving **Message 2** from $M$, $C$ checks to see if it is an abort message or the encrypted product. If it is an abort, $C$ aborts the transaction.

Otherwise $C$ validates the product as outlined in Section 3.2. If the product is not validated, $C$ aborts the transaction and sends $M$ a signed abort message.

If the two compare, $C$ sends the payment token decryption key encrypted by $M$'s public key and a signed cryptographic checksum of the encrypted product decryption key.

Finally, $C$ starts a timer and waits for **Message 4**. If the timer expires $C$ executes the extended protocol given in Section 5.

**Message 4** $M \Longrightarrow C : [K_{M_2}^{-1}, C_{pub}], [CC([K_{M_2}^{-1}, C_{pub}]), M_{prv}], [r^{-1}, C_{pub}],$
$[CC([r^{-1}, C_{pub}]), M_{prv}]$

If $M$ receives an abort message from $C$ in **Message 3**, it terminates the transaction. Otherwise, if $M$ receives the decrypting key $K_{C_2}^{-1}$ from $C$, he decrypts the payment token $PT$ and sends the following to $C$: (a) the product decryption key encrypted with the $C$'s public key, (b) signed cryptographic checksum of the encrypted product decryption key, (c) the multiplicative inverse of the random number $r$ also encrypted with $C$'s public key, and (d) signed cryptographic checksum of the encrypted multiplicative inverse of the random number. Encrypting with $C$'s public key in (a) and (c) ensures that no one else can get these items and decrypt the product.

Using the product decryption key and the multiplicative inverse of the random number, $C$ can get the product as outlined in Section 3.2. The transaction terminates after $C$ gets the product.

# 5 Extension for handling misbehaving parties and disputes

Note that if any party misbehaves or quits before $C$ has send out the key, $K_{C_2}^{-1}$, for decrypting the payment token, fair exchange is not compromised. If any party misbehaves or quits after $C$ has send out $K_{C_2}^{-1}$, then the extended protocol must be executed to ensure fair exchange. Note that since $M$ sends the decryption key only after it has received payment in a satisfactory matter, it will always be the case that $C$ initiates the extended protocol after the timer used in **Message 3** has expired. In the extended protocol $C$ sends $TP$ all the messages it received from $M$ and the key $K_{C_2}^{-1}$ required to decrypt the payment token.

*M* **behaves improperly** This includes the following scenarios: (i) *M* receives **Message 3** but does not send the correct product decryption key $K_{M_2}^{-1}$ in **Message 4**, (ii) *M* receives **Message 3** but disappears without sending the product decryption key, and (iii) *M* claims that it did not send the correct decryption key because it has not received payment. In each case, $TP$ asks *M* to send the product decryption key and starts a timer. If *M* does not respond within the timeout period, $TP$ sends the key $K_{M_1}^{-1}$ to *C* and takes appropriate action against *M*. If *M* responds within the timeout by sending $K_{M_2}^{-1}$, $TP$ forwards it to *C*. *M* can also respond by saying that the reason it did not send the product decryption key in the first instance, is because it did not receive proper payment, that is $K_{C_2}^{-1}$. In this case, *M* still has to provide the $TP$ with $K_{M_2}^{-1}$. $TP$ sends $K_{C_2}^{-1}$ to *M* and $K_{M_2}^{-1}$ to *C*.

*C* **behaves improperly** This scenario occurs only when $TP$ has sent $K_{C_2}^{-1}$ but that key still does not decrypt the payment token $[PT, K_{C_1} \times K_{C_2}]$. In this case, $TP$ gets in touch with *B* to obtain $K_{C_1}^{-1}$. It then forwards this key to *M*.

Note that the following two disputes are not entertained: (i) *M* claims that it has received inadequate payment. The reason why it is not entertained is that *M* always sends the product decryption key after it has an opportunity to ensure that proper payment has been received. (ii) *C* claims after decrypting the product that the correct product was not provided by *M*. The reason why this is not entertained is that the validated receipt property allows the product to be validated. In other words if the product does not validate, *C* always has the option of aborting the transaction without paying.

# 6 Conclusion

In this work we have proposed an e-commerce protocol for performing business over the Internet. Our protocol has the following features. First, it provides true fair exchange under all circumstances. The customer does not get the product unless he pays for it and the merchant does not get paid unless he delivers the product. Note that fairness is always ensured and is not compromised if any party misbehaves or prematurely aborts. Second, the protocol does not require any manual dispute resolution in case any party behaves unfairly. Third, the protocol uses a third party; however, the third party does not become involved unless a problem occurs. Fourth, the protocol allows the customer to be confident that he is paying for the correct product before actually paying for it. Fifth, the protocol can be generalized and used for the fair exchange of any two digital items, not necessarily electronic goods and electronic payment.

In future we plan to address how the many different forms of electronic payment schemes [17], can be incorporated in our protocol. Another important future work is evaluating the correctness of the protocol using formal methods of software verification like model checking [12] and theorem proving [7].

# References

1. N. Asokan, M. Schunter, and M. Waidner. Optimistic Protocols for Fair Exchange. In T. Matsumoto, editor, *Proceedings of the 4th ACM Conference on Computer and Communications Security*, pages 7–17, Zurich, Switzerland, April 1997.

2. N. Asokan, V. Shoup, and M. Waidner. Asynchronous Protocols for Optimistic Fair Exchange. In *Proceedings of the IEEE Symposium on Security and Privacy*, pages 86–99, Oakland, California, May 1998.

3. N. Asokan, V. Shoup, and M. Waidner. Optimistic Fair Exchange of Digital Signatures. In *Proceedings of the Workshop on the Theory and Application of Cryptographic Techniques, Eurocrypt '98*, pages 591–606, Helsinki, Finland, June 1998.

4. A. Bahreman and J. D. Tygar. Certified Electronic Mail. In *Proceedings of the Internet Society Symposium on Network and Distributed Systems Security*, pages 3–19, February 1994.

5. F. Bao, R. H. Deng, and W. Mao. Efficient and Practical Fair Exchange Protocols with Off-line TTP. In *Proceedings of the IEEE Symposium on Security and Privacy*, Oakland, California, May 1998.

6. M. Blum. How to Exchange (Secret) Keys. *ACM Transactions on Computer Systems*, 1:175–193, 1983.

7. D. Bolignano. Towards the Formal Verification of Electronic Commerce Protocols. In *Proceedings of the 10th IEEE Computer Security Foundations Workshop*, June 1997.

8. B. Cox, J. D. Tygar, and M. Sirbu. NetBill Security and Transaction Protocol. In *Proceedings of the 1st USENIX Workshop in Electronic Commerce*, pages 77–88, July 1995.

9. R. H. Deng, L. Gong, A. A. Lazar, and W. Wang. Practical Protocols for Certified Electronic Mail. *Journal of Network and System Management*, 4(3), 1996.

10. S. Even, O. Goldreich, and A. Lempel. A Randomized Protocol for Signing Contracts. *Communications of the ACM*, 28(6):637–647, June 1985.

11. M. K. Franklin and M. K. Reiter. Fair Exchange with a semi-trusted Third Party. In T. Matsumoto, editor, *Proceedings of the 4th ACM Conference on Computer and Communications Security*, pages 1–6, Zurich, Switzerland, April 1997.

12. N. Heintze, J. Tygar, J. Wing, and H. Wong. Model Checking Electronic Commerce Protocols. In *Proceedings of the 2nd USENIX Workshop in Electronic Commerce*, pages 146–164, November 1996.

13. B. Kaliski and M. Robshaw. The Secure Use of RSA. *CryptoBytes*, 1(3):7–13, 1995.

14. S. Ketchpel. Transaction Protection for Information Buyers and Sellers. In *Proceedings of the Dartmouth Institute for Advanced Graduate Studies '95: Electronic Publishing and the Information Superhighway*, 1995.

15. S. Ketchpel and H. Garcia-Molina. Making Trust Explicit in Distributed Commerce Transactions. In *Proceedings of the 16th International Conference on Distributed Computing Systems*, pages 270–281, 1996.

16. I. Niven and H. S. Zuckerman. *An Introduction to the Theory of Numbers*. John Wiley and Sons, 4th edition, 1980.

17. D. O'Mahoney, M. Peirce, and H. Tewari. *Electronic Payment Systems*. Artech House, 1997.

18. I. Ray, I. Ray, and N. Narasimhamurthi. A Fair-Exchange Protocol with Automated Dispute Resolution. In *Proceedings of the 14th Annual IFIP WG 11.3 Working Conference on Database Security*, Schoorl, The Netherlands, August 2000.

19. J. Zhou and D. Gollmann. A Fair Non-repudiation Protocol. In *Proceedings of the IEEE Symposium on Security and Privacy*, pages 55–61, Oakland, California, May 1996.

# Secure PC-Franking for Everyone

Gerrit Bleumer

Francotyp-Postalia, D-16547 Birkenwerder, Germany

**Abstract.** PC franking systems allow customers to download postage value into their PCs and to print postage value onto envelopes or mailing labels by using regular desktop printers connected to their PCs. In emerging standards, such as the IBIP program of the US postal services, the resulting imprints are called *indicia*, and they are printed as 2-D bar codes that are easy and reliable to scan while passing through the mail delivery system. In contrast to the IBIP program, which requires a tamper responsive postal security device for each customer, we propose a pure software solution for PC franking systems that is more secure for the postal services, gives more privacy to the customers and has the potential of being much cheaper than any IBIP compliant franking system. In contrast to existing PC-franking products that require no hardware postal security device, our solution works off-line. Customers are not required to be online while printing indicia. Our solution operates an existing offline e-cash scheme over certain elliptic curves rather than over finite fields.

**Keywords:** Open franking systems, offline electronic cash, blind signature, elliptic curves.

## 1 Introduction

Many companies are moving towards electronic commerce and so do the postal services in many countries around the world. Traditionally, larger companies and organizations use postage meter machines for franking mail. These meter machines are licensed to identified individuals and require some dedicated connection to the postal service in order to be charged with postage (*closed franking systems*). For instance, mechanical meter machines are charged via physical tokens. More recent electronic meter machines are charged by using leased lines or telephone lines to download postage off of a postage server. Furthermore, postage meter machines are sold or leased to registered customers only, and the machines are inspected by the postal services on a regular basis. There are about 1.7 million meter machines installed in the US and they comprise about 30% of the US mail volume. In 1998, postage meters accounted for more than 21 of 60 billion dollar in revenue of the USPS. At the same time, the USPS suffers about a 100 million dollar loss per year from meter fraud. The quest is—not only in the US—for more secure and more cost efficient franking systems.

While more and more small offices and home offices (soho) have enough computing and printing power sitting right on their desktops (more than 40% of US households) and Internet access is cheap, the time has come for franking systems that allow to download postage via open networks such as the Internet (*open franking systems*) and do not require dedicated hardware and regular inspections. A PC can be used to download postage and a standard printer can be used to print out postage onto regular paper envelopes, labels, etc. The resulting printouts are called *indicia*. These are scanned and verified when the respective mail pieces pass the postal sorting centers. The US postal service is one of the first who has specified open franking systems in their Information Based Indicia Program [IBIP99o]. Commercial products complying to the IBIP standard are appearing on the US market, e.g., e-stamp (www.e-stamp.com), stamps.com, etc. Open franking systems should be more robust against fraud than closed systems because users of open franking systems are not registered and their equipment is not undergoing regular postal inspections. However, open franking systems must be substantially cheaper than closed franking systems because otherwise they will not enter the mass market. We call this the *low-cost-high-security dilemma* of open franking systems.

Our proposal features (i) a pure software solution, (ii) offline franking in the sense that the sender can produce and print indicia without having an online connection to any other participant such as a trusted third party, (iii) security as strong as state-of-the-art cryptographic payment systems and (iv) strong customer privacy protection. Such a software solution has the potential of being cheaper than today's closed franking systems and also cheaper and more privacy protecting than any PC franking system complying to the IBIP program. That is because the IBIP program requires each customer to use a tamper responsive hardware security module to hold the signature keys necessary to produce customer specific indicia. Our solution can save the additional cost of producing such hardware security modules and yields more customer privacy because it avoids customer specific indicia. Obviously this escapes the low-cost-high-security dilemma.

We first give a brief overview of open franking systems before we identify the relevant security requirements (Section 2). The new ideas of this work are described in Section 3. All notation used throughout is introduced in Section 4. The details of the new proposal are presented in Section 5. A comparison with the open franking system specification according to the IBIP program is given in Section 7. Design and Performance Options are discussed in Section 6. Finally, the results are summarized in Section 8.

## 2 Security Requirements on Franking Systems

Before discussing the security requirements, we run through a typical franking cycle. The postal service in each country acts in two simultaneous capacities. The postal accounting system ($P$) maintains a special currency, stamps namely, and the mail delivery system ($M$) collects, sorts and distributes mail and invalidates the respective stamps in return. For electronic franking, $P$ provides a postage server (usually through some third party) from which a sender ($S$) can download postage electronically whenever she likes. The postage can be stored on a PC harddrive, a chipcard or any other persistent storage medium. Typically, senders are charged for the postage at download time. Frequent senders may use postal accounts, occasional senders may pay by credit card, debit card, wire, check or electronic cash. Regular letter envelopes or postcards can be printed directly, and labels can be used for larger mail pieces. Printed indicia must at least contain their face value and an electronic signature to authorize this value. In addition, they may support certain functions of the mail delivery system including fraud prevention. For example, they may contain the delivery address, an expiration date, etc. From a privacy perspective, the sender's identity should not be included, unless the sender wishes so. The indicium contains a human readable portion and a machine-only readable portion, which is typically displayed using a two-dimensional bar code such as Data Matrix or PDF417 (see section 6.3). Once it is printed and the piece of mail is sent, it passes through the mail delivery system $M$ where the indicia are scanned and invalidated.[1] If an indicium shows sufficient face value, the mail piece is delivered to the recipient (Fig. 1). The

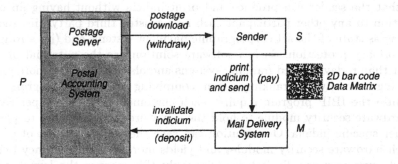

**Fig. 1.** Franking System

postal services require a franking system to counter fraud as much as possible. Customers require that their postal accounts are secure against false access, and they usually like the option of sending mail anonymously, i.e., without disclosing personal data. These security requirements are listed in more detail below:

UNFORGEABILITY: At any point in time the mail delivery system shall not deliver more mail than what has been paid for (since system startup). Important sub-requirements of unforgeability are the following.

DOUBLE SPENDING PREVENTION: After a sender has downloaded $x$ \$ of postage, she shall not be able to print out indicia whose overall value

---

[1] For performance reasons, the mail sorting centers might verify only a small percentage of indicia.

exceeds $x$. In open franking systems the recipient's address (e.g. in the form of a 9-digit ZIP code) and a time stamp are usually included in the indicium. This way, re-using a previous indicium allows little fraud, even without further cryptographic protection. In closed franking systems, the franking process is more separate from the mail addressing process, so including the recipient in the indicia is not an option. In this case, Xerox copies of indicia can be detected (and thereby discouraged) if the mail delivery system maintains a database of indicia which have been processed and delivered. Whenever an indicium turns up a second time it can be rejected. Another way of countering Xerox copies is by using red fluorescent ink, which is hard to reproduce with regular Xerox equipment.

DOUBLE SPENDER DETECTION: After a sender has used the same piece of postage more than once, he can be identified, for example by means of the postal account from which the piece of postage was downloaded.

UNFRAMEABILITY: This requirement makes sense for schemes with double spender detection only. It means that the postal services cannot wrongfully accuse anyone of double spending.

INDICIA UNLINKABILITY/SENDER ANONYMITY: Any two indicia shall not reveal whether they originate from the same sender, unless the sender wishes so. This requirement implies the weaker requirement of sender anonymity, which means that indicia do not reveal their sender's identity.

For general purpose payment systems it has been argued that unconditional unlinkability of payments and therefore unconditional payer anonymity is too strong in practice, because it encourages money laundering, etc. [SN92]. For electronic postage, however, a strong privacy requirement like indicia unlinkability is an interesting option. There is minimal risk of misuse because postage values are relatively small, and indicia will hardly attract big money. In addition there are some convenience requirements:

DIVISIBILITY: After downloading an amount $x$ of postage, a sender should be able to produce any set of indicia which together represent no more postage value than $x$. This escapes the annoying situation with conventional stamps where, for example, a sender cannot produce the value 60c if he has only a number of 33c stamps.

ONLINE PRINTING: There is no separate download transaction, but each time senders wants to print indicia, they connect to a postal server in order to compute and print a proper indicium. This approach is taken for example by Pastor's CRYPTOPOST system [P91] or the more recent PC franking solutions of stamps.com.

OFFLINE PRINTING: The sender downloads postage in advance and is then able to produce and print indicia without having an online connection to any postal server or other trusted third party. Offline printing is probably more convenient for senders.

# 3   What's New

In order to obtain an efficient cryptographic solution for open franking systems, we consider prepay e-cash schemes and map the principals of a franking system as follows: The sender takes the role of a *payer* and the mail delivery system $M$ takes the role of a *merchant*. The postal accounting system $P$ takes the role of the *payer's bank* and of the *merchant's bank* at the same time. Downloading postage off the postage server corresponds to withdrawing money from the sender's account. Printing an indicium and putting the corresponding piece of mail into a mailbox corresponds to buying a service and paying for it. Finally, the mail delivery system invalidates the indicium. This roughly corresponds to a merchant depositing coins into his bank, i.e., the postal accounting system. Since the mail delivery system is a centrally run organization, it can be viewed as one huge merchant.

One of the critical issues in e-cash schemes is double spending, i.e., payers who try to pay more than once with the same coin. In e-cash schemes this can be prevented (*double spending prevention*) by requiring a trusted third party to be online during the payment transaction (*online e-cash*), or by requiring some trusted tamper resistant hardware in the payer's hand that overlooks the payment transaction (*offline e-cash*). Should double spending occur nevertheless, then the double spender can be efficiently identified with both types of systems (*double spender detection*) [B93,BC97].

In open franking systems double spending prevention seems not by all means necessary, because the incentive for double spending can be brought close to zero by non-cryptographic means. In fact, the mail delivery system may require a customized indicia currency where a different type of indicia is required for each recipient each day or each week.[2] This way, a fraudster who has sent a letter to recipient $R$ could re-use that indicia only for a second letter sent to the same recipient $R$ on the same day or week. Only in this rare case is re-using not detectable. However, re-using can be detected if the second indicium is compared to all previous indicia scanned by the postal services, which is possible in $\log n$ time, where $n$ is the number of all indicia previously scanned. The double spending detection mechanism can reveal the fraudster's identity, e.g., his postal account, and appropriate measures can be taken. For example, the fraudster could be charged a penalty fee and if he pays in time, his mail piece could be delivered to the specified recipient. This specialized indicia currency can be used in franking systems, because the postal accounting service knows all the specifics, i.e., recipient, time of mailing, etc., anyway and can use them for verifying the indicia. Thus we can meet the DOUBLE SPENDING PREVENTION requirement by properly customized indicia and the DOUBLE SPENDER DETECTION and the OFFLINE PRINTING requirements by employing an offline e-cash scheme.

---

[2] If this appears too weak against organized groups who are geographically distributed, the sender's mailing area could be used in addition to recipient address and time of mailing.

In order to achieve INDICIA UNLINKABILITY we use ideas from an untraceable e-cash scheme by Brands [B93,B94,B96], where payment transactions cannot be linked to corresponding withdrawal transactions. Thus, the postal service cannot figure out which indicium corresponds to which postage download nor whether two indicia originate from the same sender.

## 4 Notation and Definition

Since all the following protocols are based on the intractability of computing discrete logarithms, the following definitions are useful. Let $q$ be prime. Let $G_q$ be a family of finite, multiplicative, Abelian groups of order $q$. Furthermore, let integral powers ($g^x$ with $g \in G_q$ and $x \in \mathbb{Z}$) be defined by iterated group multiplication. Given a generator $g \in G_q$ and a randomly chosen element $z \in G_q$, the smallest non-negative integer $x$ that satisfies $z = g^x$ is called the *discrete logarithm* of $z$ with respect to $g$, if such $x$ exists. More generally, if $g_1, \ldots, g_l$ are generators of $G_q$, then the tuple $(x_1, \ldots, x_l)$ is called a *discrete representation* of $z$ with respect to $g_1, \ldots, g_l$ if $z = \prod_{i=1}^{l} g_i^{x_i}$ holds.

In the following we consider families of groups $G_q$ that have efficient algorithms for multiplying, choosing group elements uniformly at random and testing equality, and in which computing discrete logarithms and discrete representations is hard, i.e., computing discrete logarithms and discrete representations is not polynomial-time in the bitlength of $q$. Yet no candidates have been proven to exist with respect to the latter requirement, but there are candidates for which many believe that that the *discrete logarithm assumption* DLA and the (*discrete representation assumption* DRA hold. Both assumptions are equivalent [CHP91,B93].

One candidate for the family $G_q$ are the large cyclic subgroups of the multiplicative groups $\mathbb{Z}_p^*$ of residues modulo a large prime $p$ [S91]. Other candidates are suitable elliptic curves over finite fields [MOV97,IEEE]; more precisely large subgroups of prime order $q$ of suitable elliptic curves. [3] It is generally believed that computing discrete logarithms over a cyclic subgroup of residues modulo a prime $p$ of length 1024 bit is approximately as hard as computing "discrete logarithms" over a suitable elliptic curve on an order the size of 160 bit [O99]. (We use quotation marks, because by convention, elliptic curves are written additively.) In the following, elliptic curve notation is obtained by replacing products and powers in $G_q$ by curve addition and scalar multiplication.

We denote protocols and algorithms by a declaration and a definition. A *protocol declaration* consists of (i) the formal output parameters, followed by (ii) an assignment arrow, followed by (iii) the protocol name and (iv) the formal input parameters in parenthesis. To enhance readability, all input and output parameters of a participant are enclosed in square brackets labeled by the participants initial. Values of formal input parameters are called *private input* or

---

[3] Which elliptic curves are suitable is subject to ongoing research. By time of writing, no super-singular or anomalous elliptic curves, or curves of high genus are suitable because they have efficient algorithms to compute discrete logarithms [O99].

*common input* if these parameters are given to only one or to all participants of the protocol. A *protocol definition* is denoted in matrix form. Actions of each participant are listed in columns, and each column is labeled by its participants name. Consecutive actions are displayed in consecutively numbered rows, which are called the *steps* of the protocol.

Protocol actions are denoted by usual mathematical notation and a few special symbols. Choosing an element uniformly at random from a set $A$ and assigning it to a variable $a$ is denoted $a \in_R A$. Evaluating an expression $E$ and assigning the result to $a$ is denoted by a left arrow $a \leftarrow E$. By $\mathcal{H}$ we denote a pseudo-random hash function [FS87] that, on input any binary string, returns a value in $\mathbb{Z}_q$. We relax the notation by allowing any number of arguments to $\mathcal{H}$ meaning that their binary representations are concatenated and then fed to $\mathcal{H}$. Arithmetic operations are either in $G_q$, i.e., multiplication mod $p$ or in $\mathbb{Z}_q$, i.e., addition and multiplication mod $q$. We omit the "(mod $p$)" and "(mod $q$)" whenever the modulus is clear from the context. Transmitting the value of a variable $a$ from participant Alice to participant Bob is simply denoted by a labeled arrow $\xrightarrow{\;a\;}$[4] that stretches from Alice's to Bob's column. Calls of protocols or algorithms are denoted as usual, i.e., by instantiating their formal parameters with respective actual parameters. The phrase "proceed iff $P$" with $P$ a Boolean predicate indicates that the protocol execution proceeds if and only if $P$ holds. Otherwise, the protocol is aborted and the participants return a corresponding exception.

# 5   A Software Solution

Let $g_1, g_2, G, G_0$ be four generators of $G_q$, which are chosen independently and uniformly at random at system startup time. The postage server chooses a private key $x \in \mathbb{Z}_q^*$ uniformly at random and computes the corresponding public key $y = G^x \bmod p$. The values $G_q, g_1, g_2, G, G_0, y$ are publicly available.

The following proposal employs two types of currency. *Pieces of postage*, which are downloaded off the postage server, and *indicia*, which are printed onto the mail. Indicia occur in digital and printed form. The printed form is an easy to scan graphical encoding of the digital form, e.g., a two-dimensional bar code. Each piece of postage and each indicium has a monetary value, but indicia constitute a more specialized currency in that they contain additional information about the mailing recipient, the date and time of sending and possibly also about the origin from where the indicium is sent.

Pieces of postage $PoP$ are tuples $(A, B, \sigma)$, where $A, B$ are elements of $G_q$, and $\sigma = (z, a, b, r)$ is a digital signature from the domain $G_q \times G_q^2 \times G_q^2 \times \mathbb{Z}_q$. A piece of postage is called *valid* if it satisfies the following predicate:

$$verifyPoP(y, A, B, (z, a, b, r)) \equiv \left(G^r \overset{?}{=} (ya_1)^c b_1 \;\wedge\; m^r \overset{?}{=} (za_2)^c b_2\right)$$

$$\text{where } c = \mathcal{H}(A, B, z, a, b) \ . \tag{1}$$

---

[4] We abstract here from essential fault-tolerant mechanisms like typing and (logically) time-stamping messages.

Indicia, in their digital form, are tuples $(A, B, (z, a, b, r), s, rcpt, d/t)$, where $(A, B, (z, a, b, r))$ is a piece of postage, $s \in \mathbb{Z}_q^3$, and the components $rcpt, d/t$ denote the recipient and the date and time of the indicium. Additional data about the sender may be included. An indicium is *valid* if it satisfies the following predicate:

$$verifyInd(y, A, B, (z, a, b, r), s, rcpt, d/t) \equiv \left( AB \neq 1 \ \wedge \ g_1^{s_1} g_2^{s_2} G_0^{s_3} \stackrel{?}{=} AB^c \right)$$

$$\text{where } c = \mathcal{H}(A, B, z, a, b, r, rcpt, d/t) \qquad (2)$$

## 5.1 Opening a Postal Account

Before a sender can open a postal account, she chooses a private digital identity $(u_1, u_2) \in \mathbb{Z}_q^{*2}$ and computes her corresponding public digital identity $I \leftarrow g_1^{u_1} g_2^{u_2} \bmod p$. She identifies herself to the postal services, e.g., by means of a passport, and asks to open an electronic postal account $I$ in her name. She furthermore proves to know a representation of $I$ with respect to the generators $g_1, g_2$ by means of the following interactive proof of knowledge (Fig. 2). If the postal service accepts her application and finds the protocol *prove* to succeed ($acc = $ TRUE), it binds $I$ to the applicant's name and makes this pair a new entry in its account database.

---

$$([acc]^P) \leftarrow prove([u_1, u_2, I]^S, [I]^P)$$

---

| | **Sender** | | **Postal Server** |
|---|---|---|---|
| (1) | Choose $w_1, w_2 \in_R \mathbb{Z}_q$; | | |
| | $a \leftarrow g_1^{w_1} g_2^{w_2} \bmod p$ | $\xrightarrow{\ a\ }$ | |
| (2) | | $\xleftarrow{\ c\ }$ | $c \in_R \mathbb{Z}_q^*$ |
| (3) | $r_1 \leftarrow cu_1 + w_1 \bmod q$ | | |
| | $r_2 \leftarrow cu_2 + w_2 \bmod q$ | $\xrightarrow{\ r_1, r_2\ }$ | |
| (4) | | | $acc \equiv (g_1^{r_1} g_2^{r_2} \stackrel{?}{=} h^c a \ (\bmod\ p))$ |

---

**Fig. 2.** Proving knowledge of a representation of $I$

## 5.2 Downloading a Piece of Postage

The postage server uses its private key $x \in \mathbb{Z}_q^*$ to provide pieces of postage. If a sender $I$ wants to download a piece of postage from her account, she performs the following interactive protocol with the postage server. The identity $I$ and the postage server's public key $y$ are common inputs, and the postage server uses $x$ as private input. Finally in step (12), the sender can verify the resulting piece of postage by using the verifying predicate (1).

$$([A', B', \alpha, \beta, \sigma']^S) \leftarrow download([u_1, u_2, y, I]^S, [x, I]^P)$$

| | **Postal Server** | **Sender** |
|---|---|---|
| (1) | | $([acc]^P) \leftarrow prove([u_1, u_2, I]^S, [I]^P)$ |
| | | proceed iff $acc$ |
| (2) | Choose $t \in_R \mathbb{Z}_q$ | $u \in_R \mathbb{Z}_q^*, v \in_R \mathbb{Z}_q$ |
| (3) | $z \leftarrow (IG_0)^x$ | |
| (4) | $(a, b) \leftarrow (G^t, (IG_0)^t) \xrightarrow{z, a, b}$ | |
| (5) | | Choose $\omega \in_R \mathbb{Z}_q, \alpha \in_R \mathbb{Z}_q^3$ |
| | | $(I', z') \leftarrow ((IG_0)^\omega, z^\omega)$ |
| (6) | | $A' \leftarrow g_1^{\alpha_1} g_2^{\alpha_2} G_0^{\alpha_3}$ |
| | | $\beta \leftarrow (u_1\omega - \alpha_1, u_2\omega - \alpha_2, \omega - \alpha_3)$ |
| | | $B' \leftarrow g_1^{\beta_1} g_2^{\beta_2} G_0^{\beta_3}$ |
| | | {note that now: $A'B' = I' \bmod p$} |
| (7) | | $(a', b') \leftarrow (a^u g^v, b^{\omega u} I'^v)$ |
| (8) | | $c' \leftarrow \mathcal{H}(A', B', z', a', b')$ |
| (9) | $\xleftarrow{c}$ | $c \leftarrow \frac{c'}{u} \bmod q$ |
| (10) | $r \leftarrow cx + t \xrightarrow{r}$ | |
| (11) | | $r' \leftarrow ru + v$ |
| (12) | | proceed iff $verifyPoP(y, A', B', (z', a', b', r'))$ |
| (13) | | $\sigma' \leftarrow (z', a', b', r')$ |

**Fig. 3.** Downloading a Piece of Postage

In step (6), the sender splits the new identity $I'$ into two factors $A', B' \in G_q$ for which she knows respective representations $\alpha_1, \alpha_2, \alpha_3$ and $(\beta_1, \beta_2, \beta_3) = (u_1\omega - \alpha_1, u_2\omega - \alpha_2, \omega - \alpha_3)$ with respect to $g_1, g_2, G_0$.

### 5.3 Making Indicia

When the sender wants to send some mail, she chooses a suitable piece of postage $(A, B, \alpha, \beta, \sigma)$ and computes the corresponding indicium[5]. The computation depends on the recipient $rcpt$, the actual date and time $d/t$ and possibly other postal relevant data items (see Subsection 6.5). In addition to the piece of postage, the sender also needs to input the representations $\alpha, \beta$ of $A$ and $B$, respectively (Figure 4).

### 5.4 Detecting Double Spenders

When a piece of mail passes the mail delivery system, the respective indicium can be verified according to predicate (2).

---

[5] Note that in the previous subsection, pieces of postage have been denoted as $(A', B', \alpha, \beta, \sigma')$, where the primes are used for technical reasons. From here on we drop the primes

$$(s) \leftarrow indicium(A, B, \alpha, \beta, (z, a, b, r), rcpt, d/t)$$

**Sender**
(1)     $c \leftarrow \mathcal{H}(A, B, z, a, b, r, rcpt, d/t)$
(2)     $s = (s_1, s_2, s_3)$, where $s_i \leftarrow \alpha_i + c\beta_i$ for $i = 1, 2, 3$

**Fig. 4.** Computing an Indicium

When a customer uses any downloaded piece of postage $(A, B, (z, a, b, r))$ to print out more than one indicium, then the mail delivery system can detect the fact of "double spending" by simply checking whether the components $(A, B)$ have occured in previous indicia. If so, we denote the challenges of the two indicia as $c_1, c_2$ (cf. step (1)) in Fig. 4 and the corresponding $s$-components as $s_1 = (s_{11}, s_{12}, s_{13})$ and $s_2 = (s_{21}, s_{22}, s_{23})$. (Note that each $s_i$ is a triple of numbers.) Then the mail delivery system can figure the double spender's private digital identity $(u_1, u_2)$ as follows (Figure 5):

$$(u_1, u_2) \leftarrow identifyDS(c_1, s_1, c_2, s_2)$$

**Mail Delivery System**
(1)   $(u_1, u_2) \leftarrow \left( \frac{s_{11}(c_2-1)+s_{21}(1-c_1)}{s_{13}(c_2-1)+s_{23}(1-c_1)} \bmod q, \ \frac{s_{12}(c_2-1)+s_{22}(1-c_1)}{s_{13}(c_2-1)+s_{23}(1-c_1)} \bmod q \right)$

**Fig. 5.** Identifying a Double Spender

## 5.5 Remarks on Elliptic Curve Implementation

Koblitz has shown a very efficient method that picks a suitable curve of prime order $q$ and a point $P$ at the same time [K87]. In this case, the elliptic curve is cyclic and any point (except infinity) is a generator. Once, a generator $P$ on the curve is known, it is easy to compute more generators uniformly at random by multiplying $P$ by a randomly chosen integer $a \in \mathbb{Z}_q$.

## 5.6 Security

The proposed implementation of an offline e-cash scheme follows ideas of Brands' [B93,B94]. Applying his results ensures that the above scheme is effective and meets UNFORGEABILITY, DOUBLE SPENDING DETECTION, UNFRAMEABILITY and INDICIA UNLINKABILITY. It also achieves OFFLINE PRINTING because indicia can be produced and printed by the sender alone (see algorithm *indicia*). Unlike Brands' proposal using tamper resistant hardware to prevent double spending, we only require that each indicium contains the recipient's name, address or ZIP and the date and time of producing the indicium. This works because these specific data items are known to the mail delivery system anyway and can therefore be used to verify indicia.

# 6 Design and Performance Options

## 6.1 Multiple Denominations

The above scheme handles only one type of piece of postage, i.e., one denomination of postage, and at the same time, it handles only one denomination of indicia. In practice, a small number of different denominations are desirable, e.g., 24c, 33c, 60c, 1\$, etc., and this set of denominations changes every time postage rates are changed. One way to implement several denominations is to use a number of different key pairs for the postage server. Each key then corresponds to one denomination. An alternative was proposed by Brands. He suggests to represent denominations in binary and to use a separate generator analogous to $G_0$ for each binary digit of the denomination. For example, if all denominations between 1 and 255 cents may occur and we like to express a denomination of $v = 60_{10}$ cents, then the Postal Server can use eight generators $G_0, \ldots, G_7$ instead of only $G_0$. In steps (3) and (4) of Figure 3 the Postal Server uses the product $I \prod_{i=0}^{7} G_i^{v_i}$ instead of $IG_0$ to build components $z$ and $b$. Note that $(v_7, \ldots, v_0) = (0, 0, 1, 1, 1, 1, 0, 0)$ is the binary representation of $v$. Analogously, the Sender chooses $A', B'$ in step (6) so that she can represent them according to $G_7, \ldots, G_0$.

The first alternative is preferable if the set of necessary denominations at each time is relatively small. If the set is larger, then an equally large set of public keys of the Postal Server must be managed. In this case, some additional computing effort of the Postal Server (steps (3) and (4)) and of the Sender (step (6)) during download is justified. The number of additional exponentiations is $\log m$ for the postal server and $2 \log m$ for the sender, where $m$ is the maximum denomination.

## 6.2 Divisibility

With the above proposal, senders can download any number of pieces of postage of any denominations available at the postage server. A straightforward implementation allows to use one at a time to print an indicium. It is more convenient though if senders can produce indicia of denominations not necessarily the same as those of the pieces of postage they have downloaded in the first place. One option is to combine more than one denomination in one indiciumsimilar to conventional stamps, which can be combined on an envelope. This is straightforward and combinations are limited only by the bit capacity of printable indicia. The above back of the envelope calculation indicates that there is probably room for more than one elliptic curve signature of the proposed system even in a 1 square inch indicium. If that is not enough, 2 by 1 inch indicia might also be acceptable.

Another option is to obtain divisible pieces of postage that a sender can download as a whole and later decide how to split them up. A solution has been proposed by Brands[B93] for the e-cash scheme underlying our proposal in Section5.

## 6.3 Graphical Requirements of Indicia

Indicia in digital form are tuples $(A, B, (z, a, b, r), s, rcpt, d/t)$ of 5 elements from $G_q$, namely $A, B, z, a, b$, 4 elements of $\mathbb{Z}_q$, namely $r, s_1, s_2, s_3$, and further data items such as $rcpt, d/t)$ each 32 bit long. If $p$ is a 1024 bit prime, $q$ at least 160 [O99] bit prime divisor of $p - 1$ and $G_q$ is a subgroup of $\mathbb{Z}_p^*$, then the digital representation of an indicium is 5904 bits = 738 bytes long. Add 50 bytes of plaintext for recipient address or ZIP, date and time, etc. [IBIP99o], then an indicium must encode about 788 bytes. If a Data Matrix code of RVSI Acuity CiMatrix (figure 1) is used (including suitable Reed-Salomon error correction ECC200) [DM96], an indicium can be printed in one square inch at a resolution of about 104 rows × 104 columns per inch, which corresponds to $4 \times 104 = 416$ dpi. (Note that rows and columns need to be at least 3-4 dots wide, in order for black unit elements to appear as squares rather than circles.) Alternatively, if $G_q$ is a suitable elliptic curve of an order the size 160 bit, i.e., where computing discrete logarithms is assumed to be as hard as in the former example, then the digital representation of an indicium is 1504 bits = 188 bytes long. Add again 50 bytes of plaintext, and an indicium must encode 238 bytes. Using the Data Matrix code above, such an indicium can be printed in one square inch at a minimum resolution of about $4 \times 128 = 256$ dpi. This appears perfectly realistic to reproduce with a standard inkjet printer at 300 dpi, let alone with a laser printer. For comparison, to implement IBIP compliant indicia using ECDSA or RSA signatures requires a minimum resolution of about $4 \times 40 = 160$ dpi or $4 \times 52 = 208$ dpi respectively (see Table 1).

**Table 1.** Minimal Print and Scan Resolutions

|  |  | size of indicium | min. resolution |
| --- | --- | --- | --- |
| New | over finite field | 738 byte | 416 dpi |
| proposal | over elliptic curve | 238 byte | 256 dpi |
| IBIP | RSA | 178 byte | 208 dpi |
| compliant | ECDSA | 90 byte | 160 dpi |

## 6.4 Storing and Refunding Pieces of Postage

Senders will usually feel more comfortable if they need not rely on their PC hard-drives alone to store their pieces of postage. Regular backups by tape, diskette or Palmtop are the most conventional solution. Where smartcard readers are available, smartcards can be used as a handy storage medium. Palmtops that provide sufficient computing power and a printer interface on their own, could also serve as a postage wallet themselves.

Pieces of postage that are not needed any longer can be returned to the postage server by transmitting the indicia data electronically instead of printing them out. Indicia printed in error can be sent in by conventional mail.

## 6.5 Copy Protection

The above proposal requires a huge distributed database in which the postal services store and maintain all past indicia that are still not expired. Each time an indicium is scanned off of a mailpiece it needs to be looked up in the database. If it is found, then it is either identical to one that has been scanned before, or it originates from the same piece of postage as another indicium that has been scanned before. In the former case, an exact copy is found. In the latter case, the attacking customer can be identified using Figure 5.

From the point of view of an attacker, Xerox copies of indicia are a no-risk game. If they go undetected, the attacker has sent mail without paying, otherwise at worst the mail is not delivered. This problem can be reduced by reading a fingerprint of a mailpiece and including it in the indicium. In our solution, the fingerprint can be used in addition to the recipient address and the time/date stamp to produce the indicium (see operation indicium in Figure 4). Recent work of Joshua Smith (http://www.escherlabs.com) uses the ridges at the surface of a paper envelope to produce a unique fingerprint. This concept requires that each customer must have additional equipment to scan the fingerprint of his envelopes, and so must the mail delivery system be equipped. It is important to note that it may be acceptable to apply a unique fingerprint to an envelope or box by means of a label. In this case, an attacker can use a Xerox copy of an indicium only if he removes the fingerprinting label from the original envelope to re-apply it to the copy envelope. This might be acceptable because the indicium works only for a given address ZIP code within a given time limit. The relabeling attack works only if a sender $S_1$ mails an envelope with fingerprint label $L$ to a recipient $R$, $R$ physically returns the fingerprint label $L$ together with the indicium back to a sender $S_2$, which may be different from $S_1$, and finally $S_2$ applies label $L$ to a new envelope, copies the indicium onto this new envelope and mails it to $R$ within the time limit of the indicium. If the lifetime of an indicium is strict enough, this burden for an attacker is probably not worth the gain. In this case various hard to copy label technologies could be used such as holograms, watermarks, imprints, etc.

## 7 IBIP in a Nutshell

The IBIP Program specifies an architecture for open and closed franking systems [IBIP99o,IBIP99c]. Both approaches are very similar and totally different from the proposal above. In a nutshell, the IBIP architecture is as follows.

Each customer basically holds a physical tamper responsive wallet, which stores all postage for its customer. This wallet is called postal security device (*PSD*) and it is intended to remain seated in the customer's PC (open system) or meter machine (closed system). Basically, each PSD houses a postage counter and a private signature key, which is used to produce indicia. During download, a PSD's postage counter is incremented. Upon command of its customer and if sufficient postage value is indicated by the internal counter, the PSD produces an indicium by signing the postage value, the PSD ID, the sender's ZIP code, the postage counter content and a number of other data items with the PSD's individual indicium signing key. This data and signature are then encoded into a 2-D bar code, which is easy and reliable to scan by the mail delivery system when printed. Finally, the internal postage counter is decremented by the amount of postage printed. The main difference between the open and closed system architecture is that for open systems, indicia must contain the recipient address or ZIP, whereas for closed systems they need not. This reveals the main advantages of the proposed software solution:

1. NO CRYPTO DEVICE: Customers can simply use their normal PCs, Laptops or PalmTops. No additional PSD, is needed. For cost reasons, mass market availability and tamper responsiveness of PSDs are contradictory requirements. Striving for both means to constantly maintain the fragile balance between cost and security, which probably results in frequent design changes and little customer satisfaction and acceptance.

2. NO FIPS CERTIFICATION OF CUSTOMER SOFTWARE: Customers are not required to use any private key for a public or secret key cryptosystem, and therefore the customer software needs no FIPS certification.

3. MINIMAL PKI: The senders and the mail delivery system only need to know the postage servers' public key(s). Both can lookup these keys at the postal services' webpage, and the respective Postal Services' certificates can be preloaded into the standard web browsers. In contrast, the IBIP Specification requires senders to use their individual indicium signing keys, which implies a significant amount of public key management.

4. NO HARDWARE ASSUMPTION: The key assumption underlying the IBIP specification is that PSD's cannot be tampered with. IBIP requires PSDs be FIPS 140-1 (level 3-4) certified. If an attacker should break a PSD anyway, he can forge any amount of postage, and it will be very hard to even detect the fraud, let alone to identify the attacker. In contrast, the key assumption underlying the above software solution is a cryptographic assumption, which has been established in 1991 by Chaum, Pedersen [CP92] and Brands [B94] and has not been defeated since. The fundamental difference between a cryptographic and a hardware assumption is that a cryptographic assumption can be formally stated if not formally proven. A hardware assumption however is principally unprovable and tends to invoke an arms' race between those looking for new hardware implementations they believe meet the assumption and those who penetrate existing hardware implementations.

As a result of these advantages, the cost of development, production and running of the proposed software solution should be significantly below any IBIP compliant implementation. The costly constraints imposed by IBIP [IBIP99o] on a franking system architecture serve primarily the security interests of the postal services, but must be paid for by the customers. Our software based solution is probably more competitive because it serves the security requirements of both postal services and customers better and reduces the price tag for the customer. It is conceivable that this software solution escapes the low-cost-high-security dilemma mentioned in the introduction.

## 8 Conclusion

We have proposed a software solution for open franking systems that is an extension of a well-known offline e-cash scheme proposed by Brands [B94] and later used by the ESPRIT project Cafe [BBCM94]. The new solution also applies to low-end postage meter machines that include the recipient address or ZIP within the indicia. The new software solution is a) unforgeable, b) effectively discourages double spending of downloaded postage, c) detects double use after the fact, and gives c) unframeability and d) indicia unlinkability to the customer. Unforgeability and double spending detection rely on a cryptographic assumption, which stands since about a decade. The main advantages of this software solution over the emerging IBIP Specification of the USPS are as follows: No tamper responsive hardware is needed at the customer's site, no full-blown public key infrastructure is needed because customers do not use individual public keys, and different levels of customer privacy up to strong indicia unlinkability can be provided.

The proposed software solution also reveals that the IBIP Specifications [IBIP99o,IBIP99c] by the US postal services are essentially an overspecification. They prescribe a system architecture down to a level of detail such that any implementation meeting the IBIP Specification is inherently vulnerable to hardware tampering. Our software solution shows that the high level requirements of IBIP can be met by a non-compliant implementation that does not observe the above vulnerability and in addition allows to give more privacy to the customers. In terms of cost, IBIP compliant solutions are very likely to be more expensive than the software solution proposed.

## 9 Acknowledgment

It is a pleasure for me to thank Andreas Wagner and Dieter Pauschinger for introducing me to franking systems and for supporting this work in particular. Dahlia Malkhi made interesting comments on an early version of this work.

## References

[B93]      Stefan Brands: An Efficient Off-line Electronic Cash System Based On The
           Representation Problem; Centrum voor Wiskunde en Informatica, Com-

|          | puter Science/Departement of Algorithmics and Architecture, Report CS-R9323, March 1993. |
|----------|---|
| [B94]    | Stefan Brands: Untraceable Off-line Cash in Wallet with Observers; Crypto '93, LNCS 773, Springer-Verlag, Berlin 1994, 302-318. |
| [B96]    | Stefan Brands: Privacy-Protected Transfer of Electronic Information; United States Patent 5,521,980, issued 05/28/1996. |
| [BBCM94] | Jean-Paul Boly, et al: The ESPRIT Project CAFE High Security Digital Payment Systems; ESORICS 94 (Third European Symposium on Research in Computer Security), Brighton, LNCS 875, Springer-Verlag, Berlin 1994, 217-230. |
| [BC97]   | Stefan Brands, David Chaum: 'Minting' electronic cash; IEEE Spectrum 34/2 (1997) 30-34. |
| [CHP91]  | David Chaum, Eugne van Heijst, Birgit Pfitzmann: Cryptographically Strong Undeniable Signatures, Unconditionally Secure for the Signer; Crypto '91, LNCS 576, Springer-Verlag, Berlin 1992, 470-484. |
| [CP92]   | David Chaum, Torben Pryds Pedersen: Wallet Databases with Observers. Crypto '92, LNCS 740, Springer Verlag, Berlin 1993, 89-105. |
| [CP94]   | Ronald J. F. Cramer, Torben P. Pedersen: Improved Privacy in Wallets with Observers (Extended Abstract); Eurocrypt '93, LNCS 765, Springer-Verlag, Berlin 1994, 329-343. |
| [DM96]   | ANSI/AIM BC11: International Symbology Specification - Data Matrix; 11/96, http://www.rvsi.com/cimatrix/DataMatrix.html |
| [FS87]   | Amos Fiat, Adi Shamir: How to Prove Yourself: Practical Solutions to Identification and Signature Problems; Crypto '86, LNCS 263, Springer-Verlag, Berlin 1987, 186-194. |
| [IBIP99c]| The United States Postal Services: Information-Based Indicia Program (IBIP)—Performance Criteria For Information-Based Indicia and Security Architecture For Closed IBI Postage Metering Systems (PCIBI-C); Draft January 12, 1999, http://ibip.tteam.com/html/programdoc.html |
| [IBIP99o]| The United States Postal Services: Information-Based Indicia Program (IBIP)—Performance Criteria For Information-Based Indicia and Security Architecture For Open IBI Postage Evidencing Systems (PCIBI-O); Draft June 25, 1999, http://ibip.tteam.com/html/programdoc.html |
| [IEEE]   | IEEE P1363: Standard Specifications for Public-Key Cryptography; http://grouper.ieee.org/groups/1363/ |
| [K87]    | Neal Koblitz: A Course in Number Theory and Cryptography; Graduate Texts in Mathematics GTM 114, Springer-Verlag, Berlin 1987. |
| [SN92]   | Sebastiaan von Solms, David Naccache: On Blind Signatures and Perfect Crimes; Computers & Security 11/6 (1992) 581-583. |
| [MOV97]  | Alfred J. Menezes, Paul C. van Oorschot, Scott A. Vanstone: Handbook of Applied Cryptography; CRC Press, Boca Raton 1997. |
| [O99]    | Andrew Odlyzko: Discrete Logarithms: The Past and the Future; Designs, Codes, and Cryptography (1999). http://www.research.att.com/ amo/doc/discrete.logs.future.ps |
| [P91]    | José Pastor: CRYPTOPOST, A Cryptographic Application to Mail Processing; Journal of Cryptology 3/2 (1991) 137-146. |
| [S91]    | Claus P. Schnorr: Efficient Signature Generation by Smart Cards; Journal of Cryptology 4/3 (1991) 161-174. |

# Contracts for Cross-Organizational Workflow Management[*]

Marjanca Koetsier, Paul Grefen, Jochem Vonk
{marjanca,grefen,vonk}@cs.utwente.nl
Center for Telematics and Information Technology
University of Twente

**Abstract.** Nowadays, many organizations form dynamic partnerships to deal effectively with market requirements. As companies use automated workflow management systems (WFMSs) to control their processes, a way of linking workflow processes in different organizations is required for turning the co-operating companies into a seamless operating virtual enterprise. The CrossFlow Esprit project aims at developing information technology for advanced workflow support in dynamic virtual organizations with contract based service trading. Contracts are necessary for flexible service outsourcing. This paper presents contracts as the basis for finding suitable partners, connecting WFMSs of different kinds, controlling outsourced workflow, and sharing an abstraction of the workflow specification between partners. CrossFlow contracts define the data, process, and conditions relevant to the co-operation and the outsourced workflow process on an abstract level. This information can be fed through an interface to the WFMSs of partners in a virtual enterprise to automate the co-operation between the partners completely.

## 1  Introduction

In today's businesses, the application of workflow management systems (WFMSs) is widespread. The use of WFMSs ensures a well-structured and standardized handling of processes within an organization. Traditionally, the emphasis of workflow management has been on processes within the boundary of a single organization. In the context of close co-operation between companies, where companies combine their efforts and become virtual enterprises, processes crossing organizational boundaries have to be supported. This implies extending the functionality of workflow support so that workflow management systems in different organizations can be linked to manage integrated cross-organizational processes. This extended workflow support should be able to deal effectively with heterogeneous workflow environments, well-specified levels of autonomy of partners in a virtual enterprise, and dynamic formation of new and dismantling of existing collaborations.

A typical pattern of collaboration in virtual enterprises is that of service outsourcing. In this pattern, an organization, called the service consumer, outsources part of its process to another organization, called the service provider, to obtain a result collaboratively. The resulting co-operation is called a virtual enterprise. In specific business sectors (vertical markets), standard types of services exist. This opens the

---

[*] The work presented in this paper is supported by the European Commission as ESPRIT project No. 28635.

possibility of dynamic outsourcing of parts of processes. Based on a common understanding of standard services, services to be outsourced can be exchanged on electronic markets through service trading facilities. Parameterization of standard services is necessary to cater for required flexibility in service enactment.

To enable flexible service trading, detailed contracts are required for both service trading and service execution. These contracts provide the structure for specification and parameterization of complex workflow-supported services. To link workflow management systems properly in the enactment of outsourced services, these contracts should not only specify static parameters of the service being traded, but also service process structures and enactment clauses. Process structures allow a mapping of service execution to workflow management systems on both service consumer and service provider sides. High-level enactment clauses allow the specification of additional execution characteristics, like monitoring quality of service parameters or explicitly controlling outsourced services by the consumer.

To allow high-level, flexible enactment of dynamically specified services, an infrastructure is required on top of traditional workflow management functionality that can handle both contract making and contract enactment. To effectively match the dynamic nature of contracts, this infrastructure should be dynamic as well. Its configuration should be determined by the contents of the contracts. For this purpose, a well-structured contract specification language is required. XML was chosen as the basis for this language, as it allows the specification of complex structures.

In the CrossFlow ESPRIT project [10], contract-based support for cross-organizational workflow is developed for dynamic virtual enterprise settings. Along the lines presented in this paper, a conceptual contract model and contract specification language have been developed to model and specify flexible outsourcing. On top of a commercial workflow management system, a contract making and contract enactment infrastructure has been designed to advertise contracts via a trader, search for contracts matching outsourcing requirements, make contracts, and enact services specified in contracts.

This paper focuses on the contract model and language developed in the CrossFlow project. The contribution of this paper to the state of the art is threefold: it shows that contracts are required for flexible workflow based outsourcing, it explains what form contracts should have by describing a contract model and specification language, and it shows the application of the approach in a real world context.

Below, we start with a discussion of related work, in which we position our work with respect to other work in the fields of cross-organizational workflow management and structured information exchange. In Section 3, we describe the context in which we propose the use of contracts as the basis for cross-organizational workflow management. The conceptual structure of contracts is discussed in Section 4. Here we see how requirements from the context are mapped into a conceptual contract structure. In Section 5, we show how this conceptual structure can be operationalized into an XML-based contract specification language. Next, the application of contracts in the CrossFlow project context is presented as a concrete application of our ideas. We end the paper with conclusions and a description of future work.

## 2    Related Work

In the past decade, workflow management technology has emerged as a basis for structured process management [7]. The emphasis has mainly been on workflow management in homogeneous environments within the boundaries of an organization. With the advent of virtual enterprises and electronic commerce, however, cross-organizational workflow management is attracting much attention these days [17]. Basic interoperability between WFMSs has been addressed by the Workflow Management Coalition [21], but realistic virtual enterprise settings require more. The FlowJet project at Hewlett-Packard aims at coupling various types of WFMSs in E-business contexts [19]. Dynamic resource brokering is within the scope of the project, but explicit contracts for detailed service specification are not considered. The WISE project is comparable to FlowJet as it uses cross-organizational WFM technology for business-to-business E-commerce scenarios [1]. Electronic trading of workflows is also considered in other research efforts [4]. Our work distinguishes itself by the use of contracts as fine-grain specifications of the workflows to be traded.

In the past, a substantial amount of effort has been dedicated to electronic description and communication of structured information. Most notable are developments in the context of EDI [3] and EDIFACT [5]. This work generally concentrates on electronic exchange of product specifications, whereas our work focuses on trading, exchange and enactment of service specifications, including execution characteristics. The work in the XML community aims at structured information specification [8, 23]. We see this as input to our work, as our contract specification language is based on XML.

## 3    Context

In this section, we discuss the context in which contracts for cross-organizational workflow are used. First, we describe the concept of contracts. We will then describe a case situation that we use as an illustration in the rest of the paper. Next, we give an overview of the cross-organizational environment in which contracts are applied. From concept and environment, the requirements for contracts follow. These requirements are the basis for the conceptual contract structure presented in Section 4.

### 3.1    The Concept of Contracts

Contracts are needed in many types of business transactions. In the first place, the contract should specify exactly the product or service to be exchanged in such a way that buyer and seller know what they can expect and what is expected of them. In the second place, a contract establishes the rules of the engagement. In case of disagreements, the contract must contain information to judge who is right. Contract making has been done and studied for centuries, so in itself this is nothing-new [2].

In a vertical market, where the same products or services are traded on a regular basis, standard form contracts can be used [18]. These are contracts with standard wording, leaving fields empty for specifying individual characteristics of each transaction. By using standard form contracts, making a contract is less complicated than when the text of the entire contract has to be formulated with each agreement.

In this paper, we discuss contracts for dynamic outsourcing of workflow. We present contracts that are an electronic variation of standard form contracts for trading standardized workflow processes. This electronic form offers more flexibility in specifying contracts than traditional standard form contracts, as they can be dynamically composed from contract elements.

## 3.2 Example

In order to clarify the following sections we present an example of a virtual enterprise. This is a simplified version of one of the CrossFlow Scenarios and illustrates the concepts in this paper well.

A mail order company uses a transport company to transport the ordered goods for them. The basic process is depicted in Fig. 1a.

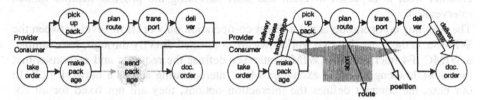

**Fig. 1a.** The mail order process        **Fig. 1b.** Interaction in the mail order process

The mail order company takes the order of the customer and prepares a package containing the goods that the customer has ordered. Then, the sending of the package is outsourced to a provider. After the transport, the mail order company documents all the information on the order in case complaints or questions arrive.

The mail order company wants to provide extra services for its clients. The company wants to be able to inform their clients of the progress of the package delivery, should they phone during the transportation of the package. Also, if a client decides to cancel their order they want to be able to cancel the transport and have the package returned to them as soon as possible. The mail order company expects the transporting company to provide the possibilities for these extra services. The mail order company wants to accomplish all this by connecting their workflow process to the process of the transporting company, with interaction taking place during the execution of the transporting process. This way, the companies form a virtual enterprise.

Fig. 1b shows the interaction between the consumer and the provider. The transporting company requests the delivery address and the type of transport as input for their process. It will send the route of the package to the mail order company, as soon as it is planned. The mail order company can request the position of the package during the transporting, which, together with the route, is an indication of the progress of the package transport. The transporting company allows aborting the transport, while the activity 'Deliver' is not yet started. When the deliveryman is already on his way to the destination address, they cannot contact him and ask to hold back a certain package. During the entire process the consumer can request the state of the process.

### 3.3 An Environment for Contracts

We focus on an environment where transactions take place between automated systems. Contracts are used to define these transactions. The goal is to have a fully automated co-operation that is set up and managed without human intervention. The contracts are established automatically and interpreted by automated systems.

The product that is traded is a service implemented by a workflow process. The automated systems on both sides are Workflow Management Systems (WFMSs), extended with contract handling facilities such that they can deal with the outsourcing interaction. On one side there is a consumer WFMS that wants to outsource a process, on the other side a provider WFMS that can execute this process.

The outsourcing starts when the consumer WFMS notices that it must outsource part of its process. In the mail order case, this happens when the process encounters the activity 'send package'. The consumer WFMS then, through its outsourcing infrastructure sends out a contract search to an automatic matchmaker [12] that results in a contract with a provider. Both the provider and consumer WFMS read from the contract what is expected of them and start executing the process without human intervention.

The resulting co-operation is not a direct co-operation on workflow level between the WFMSs, in the sense that two workflows are connected directly through, for example, a WfMC IF4 interface. The WfMC interface defines the requests and responses that two workflow engines must exchange when interoperating across a network [22]. In our case, the contract defines the interaction options, they are not fixed for all co-operations in advance. Both WFMSs have a contract enactment infrastructure, which can translate the relevant contract information into concepts that can be interpreted by the WFMS. The level of co-operation is elevated to the level of the contract (Fig. 2).

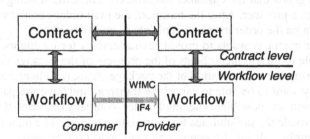

**Fig. 2.** Contract and workflow levels

This is a flexible situation, which is required for dynamic outsourcing. If workflow systems are connected directly, a static situation is created. By elevating the co-operation to the contract level, new links can be made at any moment, without reorganizing the basic workflow infrastructure. Such flexibility means, for example, that different providers can be used each time a specific service is needed, depending on the requirements and offers at that moment. It means that our mail order company can use different providers, depending on which one of them has the best offer for that particular destination and on that particular time. The implications of such an environment for contracts are discussed in the next section.

## 3.4 Requirements to Contracts

In order to have contracts that can be used as a basis for automatic co-operation, these have to comply with several requirements:

*Structured and complete contents.* The contract must be searchable and interpretable by electronic systems. This means the contract must have a clear structure and use unambiguous naming conventions. Also, every interaction issue that can possibly occur must be described in the contract.

*Flexibility.* The contract must be flexible in respect to usage and reusability. For example it may be practical to reuse the same contract for multiple uses of a service. The contract must also be flexible with respect to the enactment characteristics, allowing adaptation of contracts to organizations and circumstances.

*Heterogeneity.* The WFMSs on both sides read, through the outsourcing infrastructure, the specifics of the transaction from the contract. The contract should therefore be stated in such a way that each WFMS on the market can map the contract view to its own process specification language.

*Encapsulation.* The process specification in the contract should be an encapsulated view on the process, leaving out implementation details and summarizing small detailed activities as one larger activity. An abstracted high level description of the process still allows the consumer to track the progress of the process and synchronize its own activities with it, but hides details only of interest to the provider.

*Fine-grained control.* The contract must offer a way of describing the interactions that are possible during the workflow process. Since these interactions may vary depending on the phase of the process, the contract must be able to relate these interaction options to the process stage.

*Legality.* The contract should be a legally binding document that defines the co-operation between the companies. In case of conflict the contract should contain the information for settlement.

With five basic contract elements these requirements can be met. These elements and the way they are structured in the contract are described in the next section.

## 4 Contract Structure

From the requirements, five basic contract elements can be identified, which together describe all aspects of automatic workflow outsourcing. Fig. 3 shows the structure of the contract. The contract elements are not independent, since they refer to each other. How will become clear in the elaboration of the contract structure in Section 4.1-4.3.

The most interesting parts, the concept model, the process model, and the enactment model are explained further in the next subsections. In addition to this there are the:

*Usage model.* The usage model defines manners in which the contract can be used. The simplest case is where one contract is made to start one instance of the service immediately. Other possibilities are contracts made to purchase multiple executions of the service, or contracts made to reserve the resources of the provider for a service execution at a later moment. The usage model describes the different usage possibilities of the contract and their conditions.

*Natural Language Description.* This is a piece of text that is not meant for electronic interpretation, but for human reading. This text can be used to describe the service in an understandable way and to refer to the legal context of the transaction.

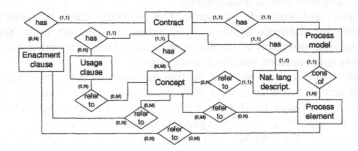

**Fig. 3.** contract structure in EER notation [6]

### 4.1  The Concept Model

The concept model establishes the terminology for the contract. This is the case in traditional non-electronic contracts also, for example a statement: 'Mr. X. who will be referred to as CUSTOMER from now on'. In the rest of the contract the reader can mentally substitute the name of Mr. X. every time the phrase CUSTOMER is used.

For our purpose, the concepts of the contract are defined as a list of parameters. The parameters are defined with their name, type and a description. Such a list makes it possible for the cross-organizational infrastructure to automatically read out this information from the contract. The concept model consists of three parts:

• *General parameters*, that are applicable to each contract.

This part standardizes contracts. It insures that parameters that are used in any service always have the same name and structure, like CONSUMER, PROVIDER, and SERVICENAME. Having this part makes it easier to search for a contract on generally accepted terms.

• *Service specific parameters*, applying only to a particular service.

Parameters like DELIVERY ADDRESS, PACKAGEWEIGHT, etc, will only be applicable to a transport scenario. These parameters are necessary for the input of the provider process, like in our process the delivery address and the transport type (see Fig.2). The consumer should specify the values of these parameters in the contract, so the provider process can read them from the contract and start the workflow instance.

• *Process variables,* used for exchanging information during the service execution.

These parameters define workflow data that can be exchanged between the provider and consumer during the workflow execution. An example of this is 'ROUTE', the route is the result of the workflow activity 'plan route'. The contract states that the consumer will be notified of the value of this data item after it is established in the 'plan route' activity. The structure of this parameter is defined in the contract, even though the value is not yet known. This information facilitates the automatic intercepting and processing of the parameter by the consumer.

Elements of the concept model are used in other parts of the contract, like in the process model, described in the next section.

## 4.2 The Process Model

The contract contains a workflow specification of the traded process. This specification ensures that both parties have the same view on the outsourced process. The contract specification is an abstraction of the exact implementation of the process on the provider's side. In our example, the activity 'transport' undoubtedly has a much more complicated internal structure. The transport company has well worked out procedures for shipping a package, with activities like scanning packages, sorting them, etc. These details, however, are not interesting to the consumer.

To comply with the heterogeneity requirement, the workflow specification must be set in a language that allows mapping to any workflow specification model of a particular WFMS. The Workflow Management Coalition (WfMC) process description language is used for this [21].

The full WfMC workflow specification model contains activities, transitions, workflow relevant data, roles, and application definitions. In the contract, we only use activities and transitions to specify the process. This is sufficient information for the consumer WFMS to track the process. The other aspects of the WfMC specification language are of interest when a workflow must actually be implemented, but would add unnecessary detail to the workflow specification in the contract.

## 4.3 The Enactment Model

The enactment clauses in the contract define additional functionality, required for tight collaboration in a virtual enterprise, that is provided during the execution of the process. These options go beyond a plain connection of two WFMSs and need support from the connection infrastructure. These can include:

- Control operations, allowing the consumer to exercise control on the running provider's workflow process. The consumer may ask to abort the process, pause it, or rollback (part of) the process. In the transport scenario, the consumer can abort the service before the activity 'Deliver' has started.
- Monitoring, allowing the consumer to observe data of the provider's workflow process during the execution. This includes both active notifications of values by the provider (push) and requests for information by the consumer (pull). In the transport example, the value of ROUTE is pushed to the consumer, while the consumer can pull the value of the POSITION of the package during the 'transport package' activity. This also shows how the enactment model refers both to the concept model (the data items ROUTE and POSITION) and to the process model (the 'transport' activity).
- Control of service flexibility, giving the consumer possibilities to adapt the provider's workflow. The consumer may ask to add an extra check in the process, or leave out non-vital activities in order to comply with time constraints.
- Other options, like workflow transaction mechanisms [20], offering the possibility of cross-organizational workflow transactions, remuneration, offering mechanisms for handling of service payments, or authentication, offering security mechanisms.

Enactment clauses are grouped into modules that can be added to and removed from to the contract when they are applicable for a given context.

# 5   Contract Specification Language

Basically, the contract is a highly structured electronic document that is transferred between different kinds of information systems. The obvious language solution for such a situation is XML, since XML is particularly designed to deliver structured content over a network. In the next two sections we will explain how XML was used as the basis for the contract language.

## 5.1   XML as the Basis for Contract Specification

XML is a markup language for documents containing structured information [23, 8]. XML is not unlike HTML, however in XML one can define one's own tags. A Document Type Definition (DTD) is used to define for a set of documents the tags, the order of these tags, and the attributes belonging to those tags. An XML document can be mapped to a tree structure, with elements consisting of other elements.

The contract model has been mapped to a contract DTD, establishing the content and structure for all contracts. The root of the contract DTD is:

```
<!ELEMENT  Contract  (DataSection,   NaturalLanguageDescr?,   WorkFlow,
Enactment, UsageClauses? )>
```

This DTD fragment establishes that the contract consists of a data section, a natural language description (optional), a workflow specification, an enactment specification, and usage clauses (optional). Each element in the contract is specified into detail in turn, defining a complete structure that all contracts must conform to.

However, a DTD alone cannot offer adequate constraints for specifying a complete contract language. Additional constraints have been identified, for example constraints that relate the attribute values of an element to its content. XML in itself cannot impose constraints on text content within elements. These additional constraints form, together with the DTD, the complete contract language.

## 5.2   Mapping the Conceptual Contract Structure to XML

In mapping the contract model to the contract language, explicit design decisions were made to make the contract operationally more suitable. Some features defined as attributes in the model were implemented as individual elements in the XML structure, since it is for the co-operation infrastructure more straightforward to look up explicit tags in the XML contract than to search for a specific value.

Below, the DTD specification of the workflow process, as discussed in Section 4.2, is given. This structure is obtained by mapping its conceptual model into XML.

```
<!ELEMENT WorkFlow (Activity | Transition )+ >
<!ELEMENT Activity (Name, Description?) >
<!ATTLIST Activity ActID ID  #REQUIRED>
<!ELEMENT Name (#PCDATA) >
<!ELEMENT Description (#PCDATA) >
<!ELEMENT Transition (Name, Description?, To, From,    Condition?)>
<!ATTLIST Transition  TransID  ID  #REQUIRED>
<!ELEMENT To (ActRef) >
<!ELEMENT From (ActRef) >
<!ELEMENT Condition (#PCDATA | ParamRef | ActRef)*>
```

```
<!ATTLIST Condition type CDATA #REQUIRED>
<!ELEMENT ActRef EMPTY >
<!ATTLIST ActRef ActID IDREF #REQUIRED>
```

Because of the encapsulation principle (see Sect. 3.3), this is a relatively simple DTD fragment. The activities have an identifier attribute, to enable referring to them in the rest of the document. The parameters, which are defined in the concept part of the DTD, have this too. Conditions are attributed with a type in order to configure the proper evaluators in the infrastructure. The conditions can refer to both activities and parameters, enabling statements that refer to a particular state of an activity, or to a parameter value. A condition language is an additional constraint to the contract language, prescribing the statements that can be used in this mixed content element.

# 6 Contracts in CrossFlow

In this section, we explain how the contract model and language described in the previous sections are developed and used in the CrossFlow ESPRIT project.

Seven European institutes form the consortium of the CrossFlow ESPRIT project [24]. The project researches dynamic outsourcing of workflow processes. An infrastructure is developed to connect workflow systems dynamically, based on contracts. High level support is obtained by abstracting services and offering advanced co-operation support.

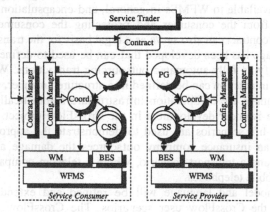

**Fig. 4.** The CrossFlow architecture

The CrossFlow architecture supports both contract making and contract enactment. The architecture uses commercial WFMS technology as a basis, shielded by an interface layer from the CrossFlow technology. In the project, IBM's MQSeries Workflow is used [13]. The CrossFlow architecture is shown in Fig. 4.

The architecture is related to the contracts in the following way. On both sides of the infrastructure, there is a contract manager that can contact the trader and make contracts. A finished contract is interpreted on both the consumer and provider side by the configuration manager. The configuration manager creates Co-operative Service Support units (CSS's), a coordinator and a Proxy Gateway (PG). The coordinator manages the communication between the CSS's themselves, the underlying workflow system and, through the PG, the opposite party. The underlying WFMS is shielded from the CrossFlow architecture through an interface layer, the Workflow Module (WM). The CSS's can define a service by themselves, but can also be supported by Back End Systems (BES).

Each participant has an Internal Enactment Specification (IES), that contains the mapping from the contract language to infrastructure elements. With the IES the configuration manager creates and configures the appropriate CSS modules, that will support the enactment services. The IES on the provider's side also contains the mapping from the encapsulated contract process specification to the actual implemented process on the provider's side. This insures a consistent relation between the contract process and the implemented process.

# 7 Conclusions

By the use of contracts, highly flexible dynamic outsourcing in virtual enterprises is possible. Contracts enable flexibility in the outsourcing by moving the level of co-operation to a higher level. By providing an abstracted view on the interaction on a level above the basic workflow level, process details are shared between the co-operation partners, offering more transparency than with a black box approach. This abstraction approach results in the means to deal with heterogeneity, making this type of co-operation available to WFMSs in general, and encapsulation, shielding private provider details from the consumer and protecting the consumer from irrelevant information. The contract can also serve as a legal basis for the transaction.

A contract language has been developed that can be used to define contracts that are suitable for specifying fully automated outsourcing transactions. With this language, all aspects of the interaction can be defined in a structured manner, making it possible to set up and manage the co-operation infrastructure automatically. A prototype of this infrastructure is under development in the CrossFlow project. In the CrossFlow project, two real-life scenarios are used to demonstrate the approach: an insurance scenario, where an insurance company outsources the damage assessment for car accident claims, and a transport scenario, where a telecom company outsources the distribution of mobile telephones.

In future, the model and language will be refined and extended, based on the experience with the CrossFlow user scenarios. The CrossFlow prototype will be implemented as proof of concept. Contract enactment mechanisms will be developed further. Tools will be developed to edit and create contracts, validate them, and present contracts in an easily readable form.

**Acknowledgments**

All members of the CrossFlow consortium are acknowledged for their contribution to the contract framework. Special thanks go to Yigal Hoffner and Heiko Ludwig of IBM Research for their feedback on contract model and contract language. Furthermore, we thank Roel Wieringa for his feedback on this paper.

# References

1. G. Alonso, U. Fiedler, C. Hagen, A. Lazcano, H. Schuldt, N. Weiler, 'WISE: Business to Business E-Commerce', *Proc. Int. Workshop on Research Issues in Data Engineering*, Sydney, Australia, 1999, pp. 132-139.
2. H.G. Beale, W.D. Bishop, M.P. Furmston, *Contracts, Cases and Materials*, Butterworths, London, 1990.
3. E. Cannon, *EDI guide : a step by step approach*, Van Nostrand Reinhold, New York, 1993.
4. K. Dittrich, D. Tombros; 'Workflow Management for the Virtual Enterprise', *Proc. Int. Process Technology Workshop*, Villard de Lans, France, 1999.
5. *The UN/EDIFACT directories*, http://www.unece.org/trade/untdid/welcom1.htm
6. R. Elmasri, S.B. Navathe, *Fundamentals of database systems*, The Benjamin/Cummings Publishing Company, Inc., 1994.
7. D. Georgakopoulos, M. Hornick, A. Sheth, 'An Overview of Workflow Management: From process Modeling to Workflow Automation Infrastructure', *Journal of Distributed and Parallel Databases*, Vol. 3, No. 2, 1995.
8. I. Graham, L. Quin, *XML Specification Guide*, Wiley Computer Publ, New York, 1999.
9. P. Grefen, R. Remmerts de Vries, 'A Reference Architecture for Workflow Management Systems', *Journal of Data & Knowledge Engineering*, Vol. 27, No. 1; North-Holland - Elsevier, 1998; pp. 31-57.
10. P. Grefen, Y. Hoffner, 'CrossFlow: Cross-Organizational Workflow Support for Virtual Organizations', *Proc. 9th IEEE Int. Workshop on Research Issues in Data Engineering*, Sydney, Australia, 1999, pp. 90-91.
11. P. Grefen, B. Pernici, G. Sanchez, *Database support for workflow management, The WIDE project*, Kluwer Academic Publishers, 1999.
12. Y. Hoffner, 'Supporting Contract Match-Making', *Proc. 9th IEEE Int. Workshop on Research Issues in Data Engineering*, Sydney, Australia, 1999, pp. 64-71.
13. *IBM MQseries Workflow*, http://www-4.ibm.com/software/ts/mqseries/workflow/
14. J. Klingemann, J. Wäsch, K. Aberer, 'Adaptive Outsourcing in Cross-Organizational Workflows', *Proc. 11th Int. Conf. CAiSE'99*, Heidelberg, Germany, June 1999, pp. 417-421.
15. M. Koetsier, P. Grefen, J. Vonk, *Contract Model*, CrossFlow Deliverable D4b, University of Twente, 1999 (on request available via www.crossflow.org).
16. M. Koetsier, P. Grefen, J. Vonk, *Contract Language*, CrossFlow Deliverable D4c, University of Twente, 1999 (on request available via www.crossflow.org).
17. H. Ludwig, C. Bussler, M. Shan, P. Grefen, 'Cross-Organisational Workflow Management and Co-ordination – WACC '99 Workshop Report', *ACM SIGGROUP Bulletin*, Vol. 20, No. 1, 1999, pp. 59-62.
18. New Jersey Law Revision Commission, *Final Report Relating to Standard Form Contracts*, 1998 (available via www.lewrev.state.nj.us).
19. M. Shan, 'FlowJet: Internet-Based E-Service Process Management', *Proc. Int. Process Technology Workshop*, Villard de Lans, France, 1999.
20. J. Vonk, W. Derks, P. Grefen, M. Koetsier, Cross-Organizational Transaction Support for Virtual Enterprises', *Proc. 5th Int. Conf., CoopIS'2000*, Eilat, Israel, September 6-8, 2000.
21. WorkGroup1, *Workflow Management Coalition, Workflow Standard-Interface 1: Process Definition Interchange Process Model*, Doc. nr WfMC TC-1016-P, Nov 12, 1998.
22. *The Workflow Management Coalition*, http://www.aiim.org/wfmc/mainframe.htm
23. *.XML.com website*, http://www.xml.com
24. The CrossFlow Website, http://www.CrossFlow.org

# AllianceNet: Information Sharing, Negotiation and Decision-Making for Distributed Organizations

Jean Marc Andreoli[1], Stefania Castellani[1], and Manuel Munier[*2]

[1] Xerox Research Centre Europe, Grenoble Laboratory, F-38240 Meylan, France,
{andreoli,castella}@xrce.xerox.com
[2] IUT des Pays de l'Adour, Dept. GTR, 40004 Mont de Marsan, France,
munier@marsan.univ-pau.fr

**Abstract.** We explore issues in providing support for information sharing, negotiations and decision-making to distributed autonomous organizations, grouped in alliances to improve their own ability to accomplish customers' requests. In particular, we consider the case of an alliance of printshops offering similar and/or complementary print competencies and capabilities, competing but also collaborating with each other to perform print jobs.

We present a typical scenario of the activities within such an alliance, where the main task of the printshop managers is to schedule their portfolio of jobs. We then introduce a multi-agent architecture, called *AllianceNet*, allowing a manager to flexibly negotiate with the allied printshops some jobs that s/he cannot or does not wish to perform locally. The purpose of the agents in AllianceNet is not to replace the printshop managers, but rather to assist them in the decision process by making available the information needed in the negotiations and by automating the tasks implementing the committed decisions. In particular, we discuss the kind of information used and shared among printshops, the support offered to printshop managers to make informed decisions and to consistently enact and monitor their execution.

**Keywords**: Negotiation, Protocols, Decentralized systems, Agent models and architecture, "Business-to-business" electronic commerce.

## 1 Introduction

We explore issues in providing support for information sharing, negotiations and decision-making to distributed autonomous organizations grouped in alliances. We consider here alliances of organizations offering similar and/or complementary competencies and capabilities, competing but also collaborating with each other to improve their own ability to accomplish customers' requests. In particular, we are interested in an alliance of printshops executing print jobs (simply

---

* Work performed while visiting the Xerox Research Centre Europe in Grenoble

called jobs in the sequel). Each printshop may act sometimes as an "outsourcing" entity, submitting job requests to other printshops in the alliance, and sometimes as an "insourcing" entity, accepting such requests. In fact, the interactions we consider between the printshops are very general "business-to-business" interactions, so that our approach applies to any alliance of organizations, whatever their domain (the case of printshops has been chosen mainly because of its close links to Xerox core business).

The collaborations within an alliance can be partially formalized and automated as workflows, but they cannot be satisfactorily modeled by simple activity diagrams with rigid dependencies defining only synchronizations and ordering between "blackbox"-like activities. More realistically, the printshop managers should be flexibly supported in scheduling and negotiating their portfolio of jobs. For example, a printshop manager may wish to outsource a job and then select, among the printshops making insourcing offers, those providing the best cost/color-quality performance ratio. Also, the manager of an insourcing printshop may need to re-negotiate with the outsourcing printshop the commitment for a job, e.g. for changing a deadline. To be successful, an information technology tool supporting such an alliance should satisfy two constraints: it should be non-disruptive, i.e. respect the actual work practice, and at the same time it should create new opportunities.

Printshops in an alliance are fully autonomous organizations and, as such, each of them is responsible for managing its own jobs and resources. This precludes a straightforward approach to the management of the alliance, in which each partner is requested to declare to the alliance all its available resources (both human and machines), and the alliance handles all the customer requests, splitting and dispatching them in an optimal way among the different partners, using, for example, planning and job-shop scheduling techniques. Indeed, this highly centralized approach, based on a "super-scheduler", is not adapted to the situation we consider for several reasons: (*i*) given the competitive context, the printshop managers are unlikely to give up control over their job portfolio and their resources; (*ii*) many decisions on how to best manage the jobs in a printshop must take into account information that can only be provided by the people working in that printshop itself: this information comes from their experience and the printshop local interests and is difficult to formalize and integrate in a super-scheduler; (*iii*) a "super-scheduler" solution in a distributed context is usually difficult to scale-up and to evolve dynamically.

Sec. 2 describes in more details the activities of a single printshop and its interactions with the alliance. Sec. 3 introduces a multi-agent architecture, called *AllianceNet*, supporting the negotiations occurring in the scenario previously described. In particular, we discuss the kind of information used and shared among printshops, the support offered to printshop managers to make informed decisions and to consistently enact and monitor their execution. Sec. 4 describes our current directions of investigations.

# 2 A Printshop Alliance Scenario

The following scenario is a simplified, though non-trivial description of the activities in a printshop including its interactions with the customers and possibly with other printshops. Building upon the description of a variety of print work processes (in [6] and [4]), we have defined a model for printshop activities which could be modified to encompass/exclude some activities and refine role assignments, but which attempts to model significant kinds of behaviors.

A printshop may receive print requests from both customers and other printshops (outsourcing requests in the latter case). Conversely, the printshop manager may wish to outsource some of her/his jobs, totally or in part, to the alliance. When a print request reaches the printshop with given parameters (e.g. deadline), a first estimation is established. The manager analyses the job description to understand how it can be accomplished, taking into account the current job schedule, the availability of the resources, and trying to optimize the global cost. Existing ad-hoc scheduling tools can be used here. Based on the results of this evaluation, the manager decides either to reject or to accept the print request. In the former case, the negative decision is communicated to the requester. In the latter case, the job has to be allocated. If the current schedule of the printshop allows inclusion of the new job, the manager may decide to perform it locally. However, it may be possible that the job cannot be locally performed (at least not as a block), given the requirements, the printshop resource availability and technical capabilities. For example, if the request includes a color print and the printshop has only black and white printers, then at least the part requiring a color printer should be outsourced. Moreover, even if the execution of the job is consistent with the printshop schedule and equipment, the manager might still decide to outsource (part of) the job, for example, in order to save some of the available resources for a job currently under negotiation with a major customer.

If the manager decides that (part of) the job has to be performed remotely, (s)he will start a negotiation with the partner printshops. The outcome of a negotiation can be "success" (the job was fully outsourced), "failure" (no outsourcing agreement could be reached) or "partial" (only part of the job could be outsourced). An elementary negotiation scheme relies on an "invitation to tender". The manager decides if and how to split the job into slots and notifies the other printshops in the alliance about the outsourcing requests for the different slots. The manager collects quotations from partner printshops, evaluates them and chooses a solution. The outsourced job (or slots) is (are) then sent to the selected insourcer(s). If no "good" solution is found, the manager may accept a sub-optimal offer anyway (and possibly face delays), or re-allocate local resources in order to perform the job locally, or revise the splitting of the job. In any case, the process of choosing a solution is far from trivial and we do not try here to automate it (using so called "intelligent" agents). Once a solution is adopted, it must be implemented and monitored.

The main requirement for the architecture is that it must offer a lot of flexibility in the negotiations occurring in the scenario described above. The manager of a printshop is responsible for issuing the quotations and for allocating the jobs of that printshop. So, (s)he needs to make informed decisions based upon the estimations, the job schedule of the printshop and the knowledge (s)he has about the other printshops technical capabilities and actual resources availabilities.

The manager should be able to negotiate jobs in several ways, and choose a negotiation model on a case by case basis. For example, if a job cannot be performed as a unique block, the manager must split the job and make outsourcing requests of (some of) the pieces. The splitting may be decided a priori, on the basis of the structure of the job, and thus entirely precede the submission of the outsourcing requests, but, more realistically, the two processes have to occur in parallel, the splitting being revised as potential insourcers produce offers.

The manager may also need to re-negotiate the commitment for a job, e.g. when a customer changes requirements and the manager has already committed with an insourcing printshop, or when an insourcing printshop is unable to respect a deadline.

## 3   An Architecture for AllianceNet

The architecture described here mainly focus on the distributed negotiation aspects of the previous scenario.

### 3.1   The Agent Infrastructure

We consider a distributed architecture (Figure 1) where each printshop is a site at a node of the network, allowing collaboration among them. The alliance itself may have resources of its own, to store the state of the negotiations, which may be dispatched on some of the partners' sites, or at some distinct alliance specific sites. Other partners in the alliance, which are not printshops but offer complementary services, are also represented as different sites.

Several kinds of existing tools can support a printshop manager when issuing job quotation and managing the job schedules. For example, in a UK commercial printshop, the manager and her/his collaborators make use of a forward loading board, as reported in the case study in [4]. Another possibility could be to adopt a simulation tool like Zippin [2], that allows to simulate job schedules with alternative configurations for jobs and resources and to evaluate benefits and drawbacks. In all cases, the architecture must be able to integrate existing tools which may not have been developed according to its own model. A coordination infrastructure, with wrapping capabilities, is thus needed.

In the case study cited above, negotiations among printshops are performed by non computer supported means, e.g. through telephone calls between printshop managers. On the contrary, our architecture seeks to provide the managers with a computer support for flexible negotiations. The idea is to benefit from the distributed setting to create a computer supported "market" inside the alliance. In *AllianceNet*, this market is modeled by business objects and business rules implemented on an agent based virtual enterprise development platform called

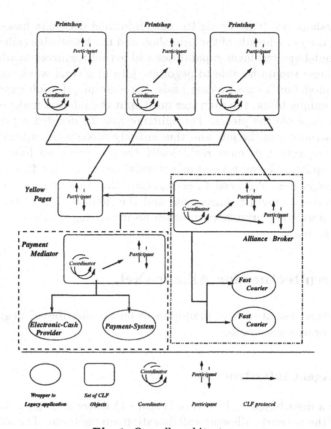

**Fig. 1.** Overall architecture

CLF [1]. CLF offers two major features that are adapted to our needs: a library of business objects and a portable scripting language.

CLF (and in particular its subsystem called Mekano [1]) offers a library of ready-made customizable business objects, as well as facilities to devise new objects without starting from scratch. These new objects can then be integrated into Mekano for later re-use. Compared to other platforms with similar goals, such as Jini, Enterprise Java Beans or Corba, the main characteristic of CLF is that it is built around a rich object model ("objects as resource managers") in which basic features enabling negotiation are accounted for at the lowest interaction protocol level, through eight interaction "verbs" (*a la* KQML) similar to speech acts as found in many agent models. There are two main classes of verbs, allowing respectively to search for distributed resources and to consistently enact distributed resource manipulations. The sequencing of the verb occurrences must conform to a correctness criterion, and a state diagram captures the possible states of the participants in an interaction and their transitions (a classical technique to specify negotiation protocols, e.g. see [7, 9]). The complexity of the diagram is hidden to the programmer by a set of tools provided by the Mekano library.

We make use of the following CLF objects. For each printshop, a CLF *Print-shop* object (new to Mekano) manages job descriptions and time slots, held as resources. A general description of each partner printshop in the alliance is made available through a CLF *Yellow pages* object (customized from an existing Mekano component), which is an alliance-level object. It is thus possible to search for and establish connections with any printshop in the alliance on the basis of its capabilities (e.g. its equipments). Dynamic registration or deregistration of printshops in/from the alliance is directly accounted for by the CLF object model and does not require special treatment. CLF "Fast Delivery" objects offer distributed delivery services and a CLF "Payment Mediator" object provides payment facilities [1]. These two kinds of objects are provided by Mekano (but not yet integrated in our prototype).

## 3.2  Negotiation using CLF Scripts

One of the most salient feature of CLF is its powerful coordination facilities, provided by a highly portable scripting language, adapted to describe business rules. Interpreters of this language are CLF objects called coordinators which manipulate rule-based scripts as resources, allowing reflexivity and a lot of flexibility in the organization of the interactions between the partners of the alliance (for outsourcing, insourcing, job splitting and services combinations, e.g. printing and delivering). We outline here the scripts used in our prototype to support some forms of negotiation. For lack of space, we cannot describe in detail the general behavior of CLF scripts. The interested reader is referred to [1]. Basically, CLF scripts are made of rules which have a purely declarative interpretation in terms of resource manipulations (see the examples below), together with a corresponding operational interpretation that makes use of the resource oriented primitives offered by the CLF protocol (the eight verbs). Not surprisingly, rules have often been used for the flexible coordination of tasks in workflow management or transactions in federated databases.

For example, a simple outsourcing mechanism is implemented in CLF by the following rule:

```
JobRequest(job) @ Partner(job,dest) @
Offer(dest, job, offer) @ Accept(job, dest, offer)
  <>- OutJob(job, dest, offer)
```

This rule asynchronously builds a search-tree of all the possibilities to outsource a job request, and enacts one of them. The left-hand side of the rule (left of <>-) specifies the resources needed (in combination) to achieve outsourcing: (*i*) a job to outsource: **JobRequest** provided by a *PrintShop* agent, (*ii*) a partner printshop that could potentially insource the job: **Partner** provided by the *Yellow pages* agent, (*iii*) an offer: **Offer** made by that partner for that job, and (*iv*) an acceptance of that offer: **Accept** generated by the partner who initiated the outsourcing. All these resources are searched in their respective agents using the search capabilities of the CLF protocol. During this search phase, the agents may asynchronously provide an unbounded number of resources to match the tokens in the rule: for example, the *Yellow page* agent may return a stream of potential partners that are a-priori suitable for the job, and may asynchronously fill the stream as new partners join the alliance or change their description. Hence, the execution of the rule builds a search tree, with new branches being created each time a new matching resource is found. When one branch is complete, the enactment capabilities of the CLF protocol are used to ensure the atomic consumption of the resources. Each agent is asked to reserve (if possible) the resource it returned in this branch of the search phase, and if all the reservations succeed, they are all confirmed, otherwise the transaction (for that branch) is aborted, but the other branches are still concurrently active. This allows to account for missing resources, which are available at search time but not anymore at enactment time, e.g. a job request which was finally allocated locally instead of outsourced, or an offer which relied on a machine which then became out-of-order, or a printshop that retracted from the alliance, etc. Other verbs of the CLF protocol are used to propagate failure information in the construction of the search tree (and thus avoid developing branches that are doomed to fail), and to notify the successful enactment of a branch (insertion of the OutJob resource on the right-hand side of the rule).

A printshop manager may also wish to split jobs into slots and outsource them separately. This could be done by a new rule for the splitting and the rule above for the outsourcing. However, that would force the decision to split or not to be taken a-priori. Instead, a manager may wish to try at the same time to outsource the job as one block and by pieces, making sure of course that in the end, only one of the two solutions is actually adopted. This is realized by the following CLF script, which fully exploits the transactional facilities of the CLF protocol.

```
JobRequest(job) @ SplitJob(job, part1, part2) @
Partner(part1, dest1) @ Offer(dest1, part1, offer1) @
Partner(part2, dest2) @ Offer(dest2, part2, offer2) @
Accept(part1, dest1, offer1) @ Accept(part2, dest2, offer2)
   <>- OutJob(part1, dest1, offer1) @ OutJob(part2, dest2, offer2)
```

This rule can (and will) safely run in parallel with the previous rule for the non-splitting case. Indeed, the splitting rule will be effectively enacted for a given job only if insourcers for both pieces of the split job are found and accepted by the outsourcer. If the splitting rule is finally enacted, the JobRequest resource is removed, thus disabling the non-splitting rule for that job (and vice-versa). Also, several resources may match the SplitJob token in the rule, corresponding to different ways to split the job, e.g. by the bulk, or according to the structure of the job (coversheet vs content or color pictures vs black and white text). All these possibilities will be explored in parallel in the construction of the search tree, but again, in the end, at most one possibility will be effectively enacted.

Other mechanisms for outsourcing jobs can as easily be implemented using CLF scripts. For example, the "Dutch auction" mechanism can be captured by a slight modification of the above scripts. Consider the case without splitting.

In a Dutch auction session, the outsourcer publishes the information concerning the job to be outsourced, as in the previous case, but instead of waiting for insourcing offers, it also publishes a proposed bargain for the job. Potential insourcers may then accept the bargain as such, and the first one to do so gets it. If the bargain is not taken by anyone, the outsourcer may then revise it and propose a new bargain (eventually with more appealing conditions). The following script implements such a behavior.

```
JobRequestDA(job,bargain) @ Partner(job,dest) @
@ AcceptDA(job, dest, bargain)
   <>- OutJob(job, dest, offer)
```

Here, the resources involved are: (*i*) a job to outsource under the Dutch auction mechanism, together with a bargain: `JobRequestDA` provided by a *PrintShop* agent, (*ii*) a partner printshop that could potentially insource the job: `Partner` provided by the *Yellow pages* agent, (*iii*) an acceptance of the bargain attached to the initial request: `AcceptDA` generated by the partner who potentially wishes to insource the job.

The CLF scripts given above can be refined, customized at each partner site. That can even be done dynamically while the system is running, using the reflective features of CLF that allow to manipulate scripts as resources. It is thus very easy to de-activate a rule and activate a new, replacement rule. For instance, the splitting rule could thus be dynamically replaced by a variant in which a control token is inserted in the left-hand side, making some basic automatic cross-checks on the offers made by the partners. Again, the resource-oriented transactional semantics of the CLF ensures that the de-activation of a rule does not generate inconsistencies: de-activation of a rule is treated as a missing resource.

Rules can also be combined in various ways, to achieve more complex behaviors, e.g. heterogeneous splitting where a job is split and one part is outsourced under the Dutch auction mechanism while the other part is outsourced by the usual mechanism; or arbitrary joining of jobs, where two, *a priori* independent jobs are joined together to be considered as one outsourcing job request.

## 3.3 The Printshop Manager Interface

Figure 2 shows the interface for a printshop manager in the alliance. It shows the local jobs ("List of my jobs") and the job requests issued by remote printshops ("Job requests from partners"). Jobs that are intended to be done locally or jobs for which job requests have not yet been defined, are shown as type "J" in the "List of my jobs". Jobs for which the manager has issued a job request are shown as type "JR". Upon selection of a job from the list, the interface displays details about that job.

In the case of a "Job request" (type JR), the detailed view includes the list of the offers for that request (if any) made by the alliance partners. For example, in Figure 2 the job `job01` has been selected and the corresponding detailed view has been displayed. This view allows the manager to: (1) accept an offer; or (2) retrieve the job; or (3) split it.

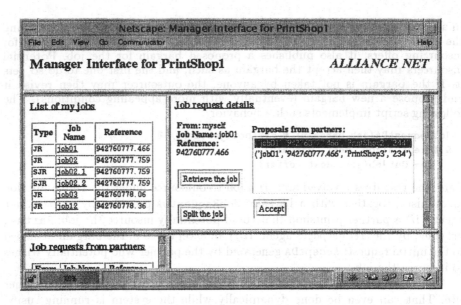

**Fig. 2.** The User Interface: Viewing partners' proposals for an outsourced job

If the manager *accepts* an offer, the job is assigned to the partner who made that offer (the job entry in the "List of my jobs" view is removed and the job appears in the partner's "List of my jobs" view). If the manager *retrieves* the job then the corresponding job request is removed and the job becomes a local job (the job status in the "List of my jobs" changes to "J"). Finally, if the manager *splits* the job in two slots, two new corresponding requests are created (see job02 in Figure 2). The non-split job request is not removed, so that the manager can still choose between splitting or non-splitting offers. Of course, if one of the two alternatives is accepted and succeeds, the other one disappears from the view. In that case, if the manager mistakenly accepts the other alternative before it disappears (which may happen given the asynchronous infrastructure), (s)he will anyway be notified of the error since the transaction will abort (the job request is already consumed).

In the case of a local job (type J), the detailed view shows a description of the selected job and allows the manager to turn it into a job request for outsourcing.

Finally, the "Job request from partners" view shows information about the job requests sent by the other printshops in the alliance (e.g. the printshop that made the request). Upon selection of a remote request from this list, a detailed view of the job is displayed that allows the manager to: (1) see the offers (s)he already made (if any) for that request (but not proposals from other partners, thus preserving confidentiality); (2) make an offer or a new offer; and (3) delete a previous offer.

# 4 Perspectives

The basic negotiation mechanism illustrated in the previous section is essentially an extension of the Contract Net protocol [12] (or similar mechanisms such as the Dutch Auction) with transactional facilities, which enable the coordinated execution of a collection of concurrent, interdependent Contract Nets (e.g., in the case of splitting, there are Contract Nets for the job request as a whole and for the pieces).

However, each Contract Net, in the system presented here, is rather rudimentary, in that the end decision in the protocol is made on the basis of the offers that have been received, with a priori no possibility to request revisions of the offers (e.g. to make counter-offers, as in [8]), except of course by outside means, such as direct (e.g. phone) conversations between the printshop managers. The first step to overcome this limitation is to refine the structure of the offers and replace them by *negotiation objects*. The most simple negotiation object is a price: an outsourcing request specifies the description of a job and the insourcing offers specify a price. But negotiation objects may be more sophisticated. They may include refinements of the specification wherever it was left free (e.g. color quality or price range), thus allowing unbounded chains of successive refinements. The refinement process is multi-phase and based, again, on speech acts [5]. At each stage, the negotiation may progress in two ways: either by refining the negotiation object, or by simply giving it up and replacing it by several alternative negotiation objects (e.g. black-and-white in two days or color in three) which may then be negotiated concurrently. Thus, we still have a search tree, developed asynchronously, whose branches represent the different ways to proceed. The transactional semantics ensures that only one solution will be selected at the end. Inactive branches of negotiation may be saved, so as to be re-activated in case of re-negotiation. Thus, we move from a uni-directional "announce/collect/decide" paradigm to a multi-directional "announce/refine/decide" paradigm.

Note that the refinement process for negotiation objects is similar to propagation in distributed constraint satisfaction [13, 11]. No deep assumption is made here about the nature of the propagated information. In usual DCSP, it may be choices of value or no-goods, propagated according to a static or dynamic prioritization on the agents [3]. Here, the propagated information, held by the negotiation objects, is defined in a negotiation *language*, known to all the partners in the alliance, e.g. capable of constraining prices, print quality, deadlines, delivering conditions, etc. The negotiation object could also include a history of its evolution, and not only static attribute-value informations. This would allow to constrain not only the values of the attributes concerning the job at hand, but also the ordering in which decisions about that job have been taken. Finally, the ordering of the propagations itself could be constrained by some negotiation *protocols* known to all the partners in the alliance (e.g. turn-taking or master-slave propagation; see [10] for a detailed investigation of these schemas), and which could themselves be negotiated.

# 5 Conclusion

In this paper, we have presented an infrastructure providing support for information sharing, negotiations and decision-making to distributed autonomous organizations, grouped in alliances. Flexibility, an absolute requirement in this context, is achieved by combining techniques coming mainly from three different domains: (*i*) multi-agent systems, (*ii*) (relaxed) transaction models and workflows, (*iii*) (distributed) constraint satisfaction.

*Acknowledgement* We are grateful to François Pacull, Jean-Luc Meunier and Christer Fernstrom for helpful comments on this paper.

# References

1. J-M. Andreoli, D. Arregui, F. Pacull, M. Riviere, J-Y. Vion-Dury, and J. Willamowski. CLF/Mekano: a framework for building virtual-enterprise applications. In *Proc. of EDOC'99*, Manheim, Germany, 1999.
2. J-M. Andreoli, S. Castellani, U. Borghoff, R. Pareschi, and G. Teege. Agent-based decision support for managing print tasks. In *Proc. of PAAM'98*, London, U.K., 1998.
3. A. Armstrong and E. Durfee. Dynamic prioritization of complex agents in distributed constraint satisfaction problems. In *Proc. of IJCAI'97*, 1997.
4. G. Button and W. Sharrock. The production of order and the order of production. In *Proc. of ECSCW'97*, Lancaster, U.K., 1997.
5. M. Chang and C. Woo. A speech act based negotiation protocol: Design, implementation and test use. *ACM Transactions on Information Systems*, 12(4):360–382, 1994.
6. C. Eliezer and D. Zwang. Print production workflow: Defining the issues. *Patricia Seybold Report on Publishing Systems*, 27(3), 1997.
7. J-L. Koning, G. Francois, and Y. Demazeau. An approach for designing negotiation protocols in a multi-agent system. In *Proc. of IFIP'98*, pages 333–346, Wien, Austria, 1998.
8. C. Koo. A commitment-based communication model for distributed office environments. In *Proc. of the Conference on Office Information System*, New-York, NY, U.S.A., 1988.
9. S. McConnell. Negotiation facility, 1999. OMG final revised submission for a Corba service.
10. M. Munier. *Une Architecture pour Intégrer des Composants de Controle de la Coopération dans un Atelier Distribué*. PhD thesis, Université Henri Poincaré, Nancy, France, 1999.
11. C. Petrie, H. Jeon, and M. Cutkosky. Combining constraint propagation and backtracking for distributed engineering. In *Proc. of the AAAI'97 workshop on Constraints and Agents*, Providence, RI, U.S.A., 1997.
12. R.G. Smith. The contract net protocol: High level communication and control in a distributed problem solver. *IEEE Transactions on Computing*, 29(12):1104–1113, 1980.
13. M. Yokoo, E. Durfee, T. Ishida, and K. Kuwabara. Distributed constraint satisfaction for formalizing distributed problem solving. In *Proc. of the 12th Int'l Conference on Distributed Computing Systems*, pages 614–621, 1992.

# MIERA: Method for Inter-Enterprise Role-Based Authorization

Heiko Ludwig[1], Luke O'Connor[1], and Simon Kramer[2]*

[1] IBM Research, Zurich Research Laboratory, 8803 Rüschlikon, Switzerland
hlu@zurich.ibm.com
[2] École Politechnique Fédérale de Lausanne, 1015 Lausanne, Switzerland

**Abstract.** This paper addresses the problem of inter-enterprise transaction authorization, as required when an employee of one organization
commissions work to another organization. On receiving an order from
another organization, a company wants to be sure that the sender is
actually entitled to do so within his or her organization. The MIERA
scheme can be used for both intra- and inter-enterprise authorization
and bases the decisions on roles. We define an authorization tree for a
transaction type that determines which combination of roles can authorize such transactions. This tree allows the order-receiving organization
to verify whether the order-sending employee was properly authorized.

## 1 Introduction

Traditionally, authorization was considered a security service that controls who
may access resources and in what manner. This service is implemented via an
access control matrix [1] or a related concept such as access control lists [2]
or capabilities [3]. These mechanisms typically assume that fine-grained control
over resources is required, such as explicitly specifying which users can read a
given file $F$, which group can write to $F$ and so on. This approach is referred
to as the subject-object paradigm [1, 4], which specifies access control in terms
of $(s, o, a)$ triples (subject, object, access rights) and is commonly integrated
quite closely with the underlying operating system. Whereas this model is appropriate for single or closed systems, the subject-object paradigm is less suited
to distributed and general e-commerce applications which require authorization
decisions based on non-local information and credentials [5, 6]. Considering an
inter-enterprise workflow application, authorization is more likely to be based
on a combination of general policies, company affiliation, roles, group privileges,
delegated rights, location information and possibly third-party credentials rather
than on read/write file permissions, for example [5, 7].

### 1.1 Transaction Authorization between Organizations

A major issue is to determine how credentials (or authorization attributes) issued
in one security domain (say company $A$) are to be interpreted in another distinct

---

* Simon Kramer stayed with the IBM Zurich Research Laboratory as a summer student for the MIERA project from August to October of 1999.

security domain (say company $B$). Security frameworks such as Kerberos [8, 9], OSF DCE and Sesame [10, 11] permit trust relationships to be specified between domains. Whereas such a solution is potentially feasible in controlled environments such as between departments of one company, the business-to-business e-commerce promotes access to services where no standard authorization attributes exist. For these environments the trend is towards service requestors providing their credentials to service providers who decide whether the request is authorized based on the credentials supplied and a given access policy [12–15]. Much of the emphasis on credentials coincides with the introduction of public key cryptography [16], which permits authorities to issue statements that can be digitally signed and verified at the time of presentation. Attribute certificates [17] are a means of collecting authorization attributes into a format similar to the standard X.509 certificate for representing public keys [18].

The approach to distributed authorization that we take in this paper is to consider the middle ground between all service requestors and providers agreeing on common authorization attributes on the one hand, and service requestors processing arbitrary requestor credentials on the other. For example, consider the scenario in which two companies—$A$ and $B$—have a formal agreement for making business transactions. In the context of this paper we use the term transaction for any legally binding action between organizations, such as an offer or an order. We denote the possible set of transaction types between $A$ and $B$ by $T(A, B) = \{T_1, T_2, \ldots, T_n\}$, where for example $T \in T(A, B)$ may denote $T \longrightarrow$ "purchase $X$ units of product $Y$ at price $P$ per unit".

We assume that the transaction types denoted by the set $T(A, B)$ are general, and that when the particular transaction takes places, additional details beyond those given in the transaction descriptions of $T(A, B)$ must be provided. A typical situation would be for a person $U_A$ from company $A$ to receive a transaction of type $T \in T(A, B)$ from a person $U_B$, who purports to be from company $B$. As the request originates from a public network, there are several security issues that $U_A$ may consider:

- Should the details of transaction $T(A, B)$ be confidential and encoded for integrity?
- How can one verify that the person $U_B$ requesting the transaction is in fact an employee of company $B$?
- Even if it is known that the person requesting the transaction is $U_B$ from company $B$, how can it be verified that $U_B$ is authorized to request such a transaction for the given values of $X$, $Y$ and $P$?

The first two points are addressed by standard security protocols and cryptographic algorithms [16]. In particular, with public key cryptography each user $U$ can be issued with one or several certificates [18] that can be used to demonstrate their identity (and employer) through the use of digital signatures [16]. In this paper we address the point of *authorization* of the transaction.

From a legal point of view, many countries maintain company registers that (among other things) list the employees who are entitled to act legally on behalf of an organization. If a transaction is signed by a registered employee it is legally enforceable by transaction partners. However, this is usually only a very small group of people, e.g. the CEO and senior management. Daily business would be bottlenecked if every little purchase transaction must be signed by a member of this group. Therefore, senior management sets up internal authorization rules that must be observed to reduce their own authorization work, and authorize employees to send orders if they adhere to these rules. However, the order-accepting person must trust the order-sending person in good faith. In an e-business environment our problem is: How can a transaction requestor $(U_B)$ convince a transaction verifier $(U_A)$ that the requestor is authorized to request a specific transaction $T$? We call this the *transaction authorization problem* (TAP).

## 1.2 The Problem of Interpreting of Authorization Information

Let us assume that $U_A$ is Alice and $U_B$ is Bob. We expect that the authorization information obtained by Bob to request $T$ is specific to his company and, more than likely, not meaningful to Alice. For example, Bob may have discussed the transaction details with his manager and department head, and lastly someone from the purchasing department, who all agreed that he could request the transaction from company $A$. Alice will then receive the transaction details from Bob along with some indication that the transaction was approved by people in company $B$ assuming the roles of "manager", "department head" and "representative of purchasing department". Alice has to believe that the consent of these three people in the stated roles constitutes authorization for the transaction.

Thus we see that the TAP consists of two distinct but related problems. The first is that before Bob can send the transaction to company $A$, he must follow local procedures in his company to obtain authorization for making the transaction. The second is that once Bob has obtained the required authorization from his company, he must then convey this approval to Alice in some meaningful way as Alice is not aware of how transactions are authorized internally in company $B$. In fact, company $B$ will probably be interested in concealing its internal authorization process from other companies.

Whereas it is difficult to imagine how authorization information from company $B$ can be exported discretely and meaningfully to company $A$, it is likely that (users from) company $A$ can verify digital signatures produced by (users from) company $B$. The supporting data structure for signing operations is a *certificate*, which binds a name (key owner) to a signing verification key. Authorization attributes for the key owner could be included in a certificate, but this appears to overload the notion of a certificate beyond its original intention, and therefore dedicated attribute certificates [17] have been introduced as a companion authorization data structure. Nonetheless, whereas certificates provide a convenient solution to the authentication problem, the problem of interpreting authorization attributes remains even if the attributes are signed—we are simply more certain as to who created the attributes, not what they mean.

## 1.3 Overview of the Approach

In this paper we propose the *MIERA* (pronounced meer-rah, *Method for Inter-Enterprise Role-based Authorization*) scheme. We address the TAP for transactions of type $T$ by introducing the concept of an *authorization tree* $A(T)$, which is a data structure produced by the requestor's company and signed by a person that is legally entitled to do so. The authorization tree is sent by the requestor along with the transaction details to the verifier such that in the act of verifying the signature on $A(T)$, the verifier also determines that the requestor is authorized to make the request for the transaction. Thus the only authorization semantics the verifier needs consider is that the requestor is authorized to make the request if and only if the signature on $A(T)$ can be verified. This verification is performed without regard for the identity and position of the requestor in the company as well as for the details of the transaction itself. Although this information is important, particularly to the company of the requestor, it is implicitly encoded into the signature verification process performed by the verifier. Thus the TAP is addressed not by exporting authorization attributes from one domain (company) to another, but by encoding the attributes into a signature verification process that produces a universally recognizable authorization decision: the request is authorized if and only if the signature on $A(T)$ verifies. Returning to our example, Bob will send the transaction details to Alice along with $A(T)$. The $A(T)$ will encode the information that people of company $B$ acting in the roles "manager", "department head" and "representative of purchasing department" can jointly authorize transactions of this type. The $A(T)$ may also encode that the "CEO" alone or "two vice presidents" could authorize such a transaction, but this additional authorization information need not be apparent to Alice.

In MIERA, users authorize transactions by signing some representation of the transaction, and conversely, verifiers determine that a transaction is authorized by verifying signatures. Central to MIERA is the notion that users can assume roles and sign transactions to confer the authority of these roles (such as "department head" and "CEO"). Which collection of roles and in what combinations can authorize a given transaction $T$ will be specified by the structure of $A(T)$. The verifier determines that a transaction of type $T$ is authorized by checking role signatures against the information specified in $A(T)$, and, in essence, this checking operation means checking a signature on $A(T)$ produced by the requestor's company.

## 2   Anonymous Role Certificates

We assume that company $B$ has defined a set of roles $\mathcal{R}_B = \{R_1, R_2, \ldots, R_m\}$, such as "user", "accountant", "manager" and "department head", and that each user $U$ in company $B$ is assigned one or several roles $U_R \subseteq \mathcal{R}_B$. The tasks or activities that a user $U$ can perform will be directly related to the authority of the roles that $U$ can assume. For our purposes we assume that each user $U$ has a X.509 public key certificate $Cert_{CA}(U)$, which contains his or her name, public key and other fields, signed by some local certificate authority $CA$ [18].

As X.509v3 certificates contain extension fields for general information such as an e-mail address, alternatives to X.500 names, and policy information, a role could be included as an extension field. Let $Cert_{CA}(U, R)$ be a certificate for $U$

containing an extension for role $R$. User $U$ is then able to authorize a request or action $T$ based on the authority of role $R$ by signing some representation $T$ of the activity with the private key associated with $Cert_{CA}(U, R)$. A verifier can determine the correctness of the signature using $Cert_{CA}(U, R)$; furthermore, an authorization decision can be based on the role extracted from $Cert_{CA}(U, R)$. With certificates of the form $Cert_{CA}(U, R)$ it is clear that the verifier can link the signer's name and role because this information is unambiguously bound to the same certificate. If the verifier belongs to company $A$ (different from $B$), we expect that any authorization decision will be based on $R$ rather than on the name of $U$. Furthermore, company $B$ may consider the fact that $U$ can authorize activities in the capacity of role $R$ as private information. Thus to break the link between the name of $U$ and the authority of $U$ based on role $R$ we use the notion of an *anonymous role certificate* $Cert_{CA}(R_U)$ for user $U$, which is an X.509v3 certificate with the following changes: 1 the name field represents a fictitious user; 2 there is an extension field containing the role $R_U$ of $U$, and 3 there is an extension field that contains a forward reference from $Cert_{CA}(U)$ to $Cert(U_R)$.

The forward reference can take the form of $E(B, U, passwd)$, which denotes the public key encryption of the concatenation of $U$ and a password by company's $B$ public key or the local $CA$'s public key. The forward reference is a mechanism for company $B$ to identify the owner of a role certificate. Users can have several roles. Each role certificate has a public and a corresponding private key so that users may authorize activities in the capacity of role $R$ without revealing their identity. Thus each user will have at least two certificates, a standard X.509v3 certificate $Cert_{CA}(U)$ that binds his or her name to a public key, and an anonymous role certificate $Cert_{CA}(R_U)$ that binds his or her role to a public key. The link between $Cert_{CA}(U)$ and $Cert_{CA}(R_U)$ can be resolved by the company of $U$ using the forward reference, but given $Cert_{CA}(U, R)$ there is no obvious way to determine $Cert_{CA}(U_R)$ or the identity of $U$. We refer to a signature produced by a private key associated with a role certificate $Cert_{CA}(R_U)$ as *role signature*.

For a user $U$ to obtain authorization to request a particular transaction $T$, let company $B$ have an authorization policy that states that $U$ must obtain approval from his or her manager and department head. In practice the policy can be implemented as $U$ creating an digital representation $D(T)$ of $T$ and obtaining signatures on $D(T)$ from the manager and then the department head.

# 3 Authorization Trees

Using the anonymous role certificates defined in Sect. 2, we now proceed to define a role-based structure $A(T)$ that defines which role signatures are required to deem a request for a transaction of type $T$ authorized. Furthermore, a modified version of $A(T)$ will be made available to the verifier for the purpose of deciding whether a requested transaction of type $T$ is authorized. Thus $A(T)$ will be used by the requestor for preparing a transaction and by the verifier for authorizing a transaction.

Recall that for each transaction $T$ we assume that there is some (electronic) document $D(T)$ representation of $T$, which will basically be some template specifying the (mandatory and optional) information to be provided by the requestor. Also, let $D(T, U)$ denote $D(T)$ after the requestor (some user $U$) has supplied the requested information [$D(T)$ may be an HTML form, and $D(T, U)$ after $U$ has completed the fields of the form]. For any transaction type $T$ we assume that it is possible to distinguish between the details of transaction in $D(T, U)$ and the authorization information for $T$, which will be stored separately in another structure $A(T)$.

*Example 1.* Consider the task $T =$ "travel request" and let $D(T)$ be an HTML form that indicates that user $U$ making the travel request must provide his/her name, department, reason for travel, travel details, and costs. When user $U$ has decided on this information, this information plus $D(T)$ is denoted as $D(T, U)$. Assuming that travel requests require signatures on $D(T, U)$ from user $U$, a manager $(M)$ and a department head $(DH)$, then $A(T)$ will encode information about the roles "user", "manager" and "department head".                    □

In Example 1, we will call the set $P_{T,1} = \{U, M, DH\}$ a *permission set* for transaction $T =$ "travel request". In this case transaction $T$ has only one permission set, but in general a transaction may have several permission sets, which we will denote $P_{T,1}, P_{T,2}, \ldots, P_{T,k}$. Each permission set consists of a set of roles (that is, $P_{T,i} \subseteq \mathcal{R}$, potentially a multiset), with the meaning that any user $U$ is *authorized for a transaction of type $T$ represented by $D(T, U)$* if, for some permission set $P_{T,i} = \{R_1, R_2, \ldots, R_m\}$ of $T$, $m$ users sign $D(T, U)$, where the union of the roles in the corresponding anonymous role certificates for these signatures are exactly the set $P_{T,i}$. The purpose of $A(T)$ is to encode the permission sets $P_{T,i}$ of $T$. Permission sets $P_{T,i}$ then represent sets of roles whose *joint* authority is deemed sufficient to authorize transactions of type $T$. We will represent the permission sets $P_T = \{P_{T,1}, P_{T,2}, \ldots, P_{T,k}\}$ with a two-level tree as follows: For each transaction type $T$, an authorization tree $A(T)$ is created such that there are $k$ nodes at level 1 from the root, corresponding to the $k$ permission sets $P_T = \{P_{T,1}, P_{T,2}, \ldots, P_{T,k}\}$ for transaction type $T$. The nodes at level 2 are leaves, and represent the roles of each permission set.

*Example 2.* If the permission sets $P_T$ for $T$ are $P_{T,1} = \{R_1, R_2\}$, $P_{T,2} = \{R_3, R_4, R_5\}$ and $P_{T,3} = \{R_6\}$, then $A(T)$ has two levels, where level 1 represents $P_{T,1}$, $P_{T,2}$ and $P_{T,3}$ with three nodes and each $P_{T,i}$ has the same number of leaves as there are roles in its permission set. Thus, $P_{T,1}$ would have two children (both leaves) representing $R_1$ and $R_2$, as shown in Fig. 1.                    □

As $T$ is considered authorized if for at least one permission set $P_{T,i}$ signatures are acquired for each role in $P_{T,i}$, we may consider the nodes representing $P_{T,i}$ as AND nodes and the root of $A(T)$ as an OR node. By an AND node we mean that all children of the node must agree to the request $D(T, U)$ (all roles of a permission set must sign), whereas an OR node means at least one child must agree to the request $D(T, U)$ (at least one permission set must jointly sign).

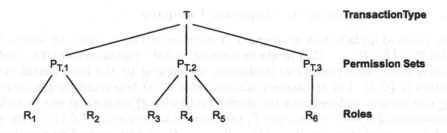

**Fig. 1.** An authorization tree for Example 2.

Alternatively, we may interpret $A(T)$ as a disjunctive representation of the roles that can authorize task $T$, such that $A(T)$ of Example 2 could be written as $A(T) = R_1 R_2 + R_3 R_4 R_5 + R_6$.

The authorization tree $A(T)$ can be thought of as being an example of a Merkle hash tree [19]. We can then define a hashing process $H(T)$ that produces a hash value for $A(T)$, and we can define a signature on $A(T)$ as being the signature on the hash value produced by $H(T)$. The hash $H(T)$ of $A(T)$ is computed in the following standard way. Let $h(\cdot)$ be a hash function such as SHA-1 [16]. If a leaf represents role $R_i$, then label the leaf as $h(R_i)$, and repeat this for all leaves. Then at level 1, label each node with the hash of the concatenation of the labels for its children; lastly, label the root of the tree by the hash of the concatenation of the labels for its children, and let this hash be $H(T)$ (Fig. 2).

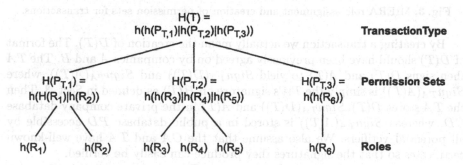

**Fig. 2.** Structure of a hashed authorization tree for Example 2.

## 4 MIERA Scheme

As mentioned in the introduction, we assume that there are two companies $A$ and $B$ that have agreed upon a set of transaction types $T(A, B) = \{T_1, T_2, ..., T_n\}$ they will cooperate on, such that $T \in T(A, B)$ will be represented by the template $D(T)$. For a transaction type $T$, assume that $U_B$ from $B$ will request $U_A$ from $A$ to perform $T$, and that $U_A$ should be assured that $U_B$ is authorized to make such a request. In fact we will denote $U_A$ by $V$ to emphasize that $U_B$ is the verifier, and denote $U_B$ simply by $U$.

## 4.1 MIERA Setup at the Requestor Company

The required initialization at company $B$ is shown in Fig. 3. Users are assigned roles $\mathcal{R} = \{R_1, R_2, \ldots, R_m\}$ by the user acting as Role Administrator ($RA$), and corresponding anonymous role certificates are created by the local Certificate Authority ($CA$). The transaction administrator ($TA$) is responsible for creating transactions and assigning the correct (authorizing) permission sets to each transaction. For each transaction $T$, the transaction authority $TA$ of company $A$ defines permission sets $P_T = \{P_{T,1}, P_{T,2}, \ldots, P_{T,k}\}$ with respect to company roles as in Fig. 3. "$P_{T,i} \longleftarrow \subseteq \mathcal{R}$" denotes the assignment of a subset of roles to the multiset $P_{T,i}$ (a permission set is a multiset because it may require signatures from two different users assuming the same role). Then the $TA$ creates the authorization tree $A(T)$ from $P_T$.

> $RA$:  **for each** user $U$, **assign** $U$ role $R_U \in R$ ;
> $CA$:  **for each** user $U$, **create and store** $Cert_{CA}(R_U)$ ;
> $TA$:  **for each** transaction type $T$ **do**
>   create the transaction template $D(T)$;
>   sign $D(T)$ to yield $Sign_{TA}(D(T))$
>   $P_{T,i} \longleftarrow \subseteq \mathcal{R}$,  $1 \le i \le t_k$ ;
>   hash the authorization tree to yield $H(T)$ ;
>   sign $H(T)$ to yield $Sign_{TA}(A(T))$ ;
>   store $Sign_{TA}(A(T))$ in a public company database $PD$;
>   store $D(T), Sign_{TA}(D(T)), A(T)$ in a private company database $CD$;

**Fig. 3.** MIERA role assignment and creation of permission sets for transactions.

By creating a transaction we actually mean the creation of $D(T)$. The format of $D(T)$ should have been previously agreed on by companies $A$ and $B$. The $TA$ then signs $D(T)$ and $A(T)$ to yield $Sign_{TA}(D(T))$ and $Sign_{TA}(A(T))$, where $Sign_{TA}(A(T))$ is simply the $TA$'s signature on $H(T)$ as defined in Sect. 3. Then the $TA$ stores $D(T), Sign_{TA}(D(T))$ and $A(T)$ in the private company database $CD$, whereas $Sign_{TA}(A(T))$ is stored in a public database $PD$ accessible by all potential verifiers. We also assume that the $CA$ and $TA$ have well-known certificates so that the signatures they produce can easily be verified.

In summary, at the requesting company $B$, users are assigned roles with corresponding certificates for signing in these roles, and the transaction authority creates and signs transactions with corresponding authorization trees. The anonymous role certificate of each user $Cert_{CA}(R_U)$ is made available by the certificate authority $CA$, and the signed authorization tree $Sign_{TA}(A(T))$ is also made available for each transaction $T$.

## 4.2 Preparing a Transaction at the Requestor Company

Imagine now that a requestor (user $U$) of company $B$ wishes to prepare an authorized transaction for processing by some verifier $V$ at company $A$. The steps followed by $U$ are shown in Fig. 4. First $U$ retrieves the template $D(T)$

of $T$ from the (company's) private database $CD$, and verifies its correctness by checking the $TA$'s signature on $D(T)$. If the signature is correct, $U$ supplies the required transaction information for $D(T)$ to obtain $D(T, U)$, and then signs $D(T, U)$ with its role $U_R$ to yield $Sign_{U_R}(D(T, U))$. Here we assume that any transaction request by $U$ initially requires the role signature of $U$, which should be reflected in the permission sets for $T$. $U$ then retrieves the authorization tree $A(T)$ for $T$ from the private database, and again checks the signature produced by the $TA$. If it is correct, $U$ proceeds to obtain role signatures for $D(T, U)$.

> $U$:      requires authorization for transaction $T$ ;
>          retrieve $D(T), Sign_{TA}(D(T))$ from $CD$;
>          check signature $Sign_{TA}(D(T))$ and exit if fails;
>          complete transaction details to give $D(T, U)$ ;
>          sign $D(T, U)$ to give $Sign_{U_R}(D(T, U))$;
> $U$:      retrieve $A(T), Sign_{TA}(A(T))$ from $CB$;
>          check signature $Sign_{TA}(A(T))$ and exit if fails;
>          $PS = \{U_R\}$ ;
> $U$:      **repeat**
>          $U$ requests $U'$ to sign $D(T, U)$ given current role signatures from $PS$;
>          **if** $U'$ signs $D(T, U), PS$ **then** $PS \longleftarrow PS \cup \{U'_R, Sign_{U'_R}(D(T, U))\}$ ;
>          **until** $\exists i, 1 \leq i \leq t_k, P_{T,i} \subseteq PS$ ;
> $U$:      store $D(T, U), PS$ and $path(i, H(T))$;

**Fig. 4.** User $U$ obtaining authorization for a transaction of type $T$.

In Fig. 4 $PS$, the permission set, is the set of users who have currently used one of their role certificates to sign $D(T, U)$. $U$ needs to request further signatures until $PS$ is equal to one of the permission sets for transactions of type $T$. We also note that when $U$ attempts to acquire an additional signature from user $U'$, user $U'$ may want to see the roles and signatures of the users who have previously signed $D(T, U)$. This reflects the requirement that $U'$ may not only be signing the contents of $D(T, U)$ but also the existing role signatures denoted by the set $PS$. In Fig. 4, we have chosen to use a **repeat** loop to represent the problem of collecting role signatures. This is a simplification of the process as in practice several users may, for example, be contacted in parallel, e.g. by using a workflow system. Once the role signatures have been collected, $U$ stores the request $D(T, U)$ along with the collected role signatures $PS$.

At this point the user has provided the transaction details in $D(T, U)$ and has collected signatures constituting a permission set in $PS$. It now remains to store some additional information, which can be used to convince the verifier that $PS$ is indeed a permission set for transactions of type $T$. The hashed tree $H(T)$ will be used for this purpose. As defined, $A(T)$ has three levels: leaves representing roles, internal nodes representing permission sets, and the root representing the union of the permission sets. For a given transaction $T$ with $k$ permission sets $P_T = \{P_{T,1}, P_{T,2}, \ldots, P_{T,k}\}$ let $P_{T,i}$ be the permission set for which user $U$ has obtained the role signatures with which $D(T, U)$ is to be authorized (that is, $P_{T,i}$

is represented in $PS$). Then $H(T)$ can be reconstructed from the $k-1$ hashes

$$path(i, H(T)) = \{H(P_{T,1}), \ldots, H(P_{T,i-1}), H(P_{T,i+1}), \ldots, H(P_{T,k})\},$$

knowledge of the roles in $P_{T,i}$ and of the hashing process. $U$ then stores $path(i, H(T))$ for later use by the verifier, as shown in the final step of Fig. 4.

*Example 3.* If for example the permission sets for $T$ are $P_{T,1} = \{R_1, R_2\}, P_{T,2} = \{R_3, R_4, R_5\}$ and $P_{T,3} = \{R_6\}$, and two users representing roles $R_1$ and $R_2$ have signed $D(T, U)$ at the request of user $U$, $H(T)$ can be reconstructed from the roles certificates of $R_1$ and $R_2$ (which contains the roles as fields) and $path(1, H(T)) = \{h(P_{T,2}), h(P_{T,3})\}$. □

### 4.3 Transaction Authorization at the Verifier

When the requestor $U$ is ready to initiate the processing of the transaction, $U$ sends $D(T, U)$, $PS$ and $path(i, H(T))$ to the verifier $V$. The process of $V$ checking the authorization of the transaction request is shown in Fig. 5. As the companies of the $U$ and $V$ have agreed on transactions of type $T$, and in particular on $D(T)$, $V$ first obtains a signed local copy of $D(T)$ to determine whether $D(T, U)$ is formatted correctly.

| | |
|---|---|
| $U$: | send $V$ the message $D(T, U), PS, path(i, H(T))$ ; |
| $V$: | verify format of $D(T, U)$ with local copy of $D(T)$ and exit if fails; |
| | fetch and verify certificates $Cert_{CA}(U_{R_j})$ for signatures in $PS$ |
| | exit if any certificate fails; |
| | verify each signature on $D(T, U)$ and exit if any signature fails ; |
| | extract roles $R_j$ from certificates $Cert_{CA}(U_{R_j})$ ; |
| | hash the roles with $path(i, H(T))$ to form $H(T')$ ; |
| | fetch $Sign_{TA}(A(T))$ from requestor company's public database ; |
| | fetch and verify $Cert_{CA}(TA)$ and exit if fails ; |
| | verify the signature $Sign_{TA}(A(T))$ using $Cert_{CA}(TA)$ to yield $H(T)$ ; |
| $V$: | sends to $U$ message that authorization is verified if $H(T) = H(T')$; |

**Fig. 5.** Transaction verification with MIERA.

Next $V$ checks the signatures in $PS$ on $D(T, U)$. Let us assume that the permission set selected by $U$ was $P_{T,i}$ which consisted of the $m$ roles $P_{T,i} = \{R_1, R_2, \ldots, R_m\}$, i.e. $PS$ should consist of $m$ signatures on $D(T, U)$. We assume that the signatures in $PS$ are appropriately formatted so that for each signature $Sign_{R_j}(D(T, U))$, the certificate $Cert_{CA}(U, R_j)$ holding the corresponding verification key can be retrieved (from the certificate authority $CA$). If each such certificate $Cert_{CA}(U, R_j)$ is valid (neither expired nor revoked, for example), and each signature of $PS$ of $D(T, U)$ can be verified, then $V$ proceeds to authorization step. Based on checking the signatures from $PS$ on $D(T, U)$, $V$ can extract a list of the roles $R_1', R_2', \ldots, R_t'$ from which users acting in these roles approved the transaction. Next $V$ can hash these roles to form $P_{T,i}' = h(R_1', R_2', \ldots, R_t')$, and then using $path(i, H(T))$ concatenates the hashes to form $H(T')$, the hash of some tree. $V$ fetches $Sign_{TA}(A(T))$ from the public database of the requestor company along with the $TA$'s certificate. Assuming that roles $R'_1, R'_2, \ldots, R'_t$ actually constituted the permission set $P_{T,i}$, and $path(i, H(T))$ were the hashes of the other $k-1$ permission sets of $T$, then $H(T') = H(T)$. Verification of the signature $Sign_{TA}(A(T))$ will then produce $H(T)$, and $V$ determines the transaction to be authorized if and only if $H(T') = H(T)$. Thus we see that verification is a two-step process: check the signatures on $D(T,U)$ as provided in $PS$, and then extract the roles from these signatures and verify them for authorization against the signed copy of $A(T)$. The explicit link between the two steps is that the roles specified in the certificates used to sign $D(T,U)$ are the same roles that will be used to form a candidate hash tree corresponding to $H(T)$, and hence the signature on $A(T)$. Checking the signatures on $D(T,U)$ demonstrates the approval of a permission set $PS$ on the transaction, while checking $H(T')$ against $A(T)$ demonstrates the approval the $TA$ on the given permission set.

## 5 Conclusion

In this paper we have presented the MIERA solution to the inter-enterprise transaction authorization problem. MIERA makes use of anonymous role certificates, hash trees, and a new construct called an authorization structure. The goal is for company $B$ to encode sufficient information in the authorization structure so that $U_A$ from company $A$ can trust that $U_B$ from company $B$ is authorized to perform a given transaction. The issue of interpreting credentials is avoided by the encoding semantics of the authorization structure: if the signature on the authorization structure can be verified based on the signatures provided by $U_B$ and the signature on the authorization structure itself, then $U_A$ assumes that the transaction is authorized, irrespective of which credentials $U_B$ has. This enables organizations to exchange verifiably authorized electronic transactions, and still avoids the bottleneck of a central transaction authorizer in the requestor organization. The MIERA schema has been implemented as a Java package that can be used by developers to apply the scheme to an e-business system. A detailed description of the implementation is contained in [20].

Further work is required to determine how to minimize the information on the decision procedures of a company that leaks through the authorization structure. The current solution will eventually reveal the entire structure of the authorization tree through frequent use. Further investigation is needed to determine whether a stronger anonymity can be built into an authorization structure.

## References

1. Lampson, B. W.: Protection. In: Proc. 5th Princeton Symposium of Information Sciences and Systems, Princeton University (1971) 437–443; reprinted in ACM Operating Systems Rev. 8(1) (1974) 18–24
2. Denning, D. E.: Cryptography and Data Security. Addison–Wesley, Reading, MA (1982)

3. Dennis, J. B., VanHorn, E. C.: Programming Semantics for Multiprogrammed Computations. Commun. ACM **9**(3) (March 1966) 143–155
4. Graham, G. S., Denning, P. J.: Protection – Principles and Practice. In: AFIPS Spring Joint Computer Conference, Vol. 40 (1972) 417–429
5. Thomas, R., Sandhu, S.: Task-based Authorization: A Paradigm for Flexible and Adaptable Access Control in Distributed Applications. In: Proc. 16th NIST-NCSC National Computer Security Conference, Baltimore, MD (1993) 409–415
6. Woo, T. Y. C., Lam, S. S.: Authorization in Distributed Systems: A New Approach. J. Computer Security **2**(2,3) (1993) 107–136
7. Thomas, R. K., Sandhu, R. S.: Task-based Authorization Controls (TBAC): A Family of Models for Active and Enterprise Oriented Authorization Management. In: T.Y. Lin, S. Qian (Eds.) Database Security XI: Status and Prospects, IFIP TC11 WG11.3 11th Int'l Conf. on Database Security (Chapman & Hall, 1998) 166–181
8. Neuman, B. C., Ts'o, T.: Kerberos: An Authentication Service for Computer Networks. IEEE Commun. **32**(9) (1994) 33–38
9. Trostle, J. T., Neuman, B. C.: A Flexible Distributed Authorization Protocol. In: Proc. Symposium on Network and Distributed Systems Security (1996): http://bilbo.isu.edu/sndss/sndss96.html
10. Kaiser, P., Parker, T., Pinkas, D.: SESAME: The Solution to Security for Open Distributed Systems. Computer Commun. **17**(7) (1994) 501–518
11. McMahon, P. V.: SESAME V2 Public Key and Authorization Extensions to Kerberos. In: Proc. Symposium on Network and Distributed System Security (NDSS). IEEE Computer Society Press, Los Alamitos, CA (1995) 114–131
12. Blaze, M., Feigenbaum, J., Keromytis, A. D., Ioannidis, J.: The KeyNote Trust-Management System. Internet draft, draft-ietf-trustmgt-keynote-00.txt, Trust Management Working Group, August 1998
13. Blaze, M., Feigenbaum, J., Lacy, J.: Decentralized Trust Management. In: Proc. IEEE Symposium on Privacy and Security. IEEE Computer Society Press, Los Alamitos, CA (1996) 164–173
14. Ching, N., Jones, V., Winslett, M.: Authorization in the Digital Library: Secure Access to Services across Enterprise Boundaries. In: Proc. Advances in Digitial Libraries '96. IEEE Computer Society Press, Los Alamitos, CA (1996) 110–119
15. Woo, T. Y. C., Lam, S. S.: Designing a Distributed Authorization Service. In: Proc. IEEE INFOCOM '98, San Francisco (April 1998)
16. Menezes, A., van Oorschot, P., Vanstone, S.: Handbook of Applied Cryptography. CRC Press, Boca Raton, FL (1996)
17. Farrell, S.: An Internet AttributeCertificate Profile for Authorization, August 20, 1998: http://www.ietf.org/internet-drafts/draft-ietf-tls-ac509prof-00.txt
18. ISO/IEC 9594, Information Technology - Open Systems Interconnection – The Directory: Authentication Framework, 1993. Also published as ITU-T X.509 (1997 E) Recommendation, June 1997
19. Merkle, R. C.: A Certified Digital Signature. In: Brassard, G. (Ed). Advances in Cryptology, CRYPTO 89, Lecture Notes in Computer Science, Vol. 218. Springer, Berlin Heidelberg (1989) 218–238
20. Ludwig, H., O'Connor, L., Kramer, S.: MIERA: A Method for Inter-Enterprise Role-Based Authorization. IBM Research Report, RZ 3208, Zurich, February 2000

# Visualization and Analysis of Clickstream Data of Online Stores with a Parallel Coordinate System

Juhnyoung Lee and Mark Podlaseck

IBM T. J. Watson Research Center
P. O. Box 218
Yorktown Heights, NY 10598
{jyl, podlasec}@us.ibm.com

**Abstract.** Clickstreams are visitors' path through a Web site. Analysis of click-streams shows how a Web site is navigated and used by its visitors. Clickstream data of online stores contains information useful for understanding the effectiveness of marketing and merchandising efforts. In this paper, we present a visualization system that provides users with greater abilities to interpret and explore clickstream data of online stores. The system visualizes a large number of clickstreams by assigning parallel coordinates to sequential steps in click-streams. To demonstrate how the presented visualization system provides capabilities for examining online store clickstreams, we present a series of parallel coordinate visualizations, which display clickstream data from an operating online retail store.

## 1 Introduction

Clickstream is a generic term to describe visitors' path through one or more Web sites. A series of Web pages requested by a visitor in a single visit is referred to as a *session*. Clickstream data in a Web site is a collection of sessions in the site. Clickstream data can be derived from raw page requests (referred to as *hits*) recorded in Web server log files. Analysis of clickstreams shows how a Web site is navigated and used by its visitors. In an e-commerce environment, clickstreams in online stores provide information essential to understanding the effectiveness of marketing and merchandising efforts, such as how customers find the store, what products they see, and what products they buy.

Analyzing such information embedded in clickstream data is critical to improve the effectiveness of Web marketing and merchandising in online stores. Interest in interpreting Web usage data in Web server log files has spawned an active research and market for Web log analysis tools that analyze, summarize, and visualize Web usage patterns [2, 3, 4, 5, 6, 8, 9, 10, 11, 12]. While useful to some extent, most of existing tools have the following shortcomings: (1) the summaries they provide obscure useful detail information, (2) the static displays such as histograms and pie charts restrict users to passive interpretation, and (3) the weak (or lack of) connection between purchase data and navigation data limits the ability to understand the site's effectiveness in terms of return on investment.

In this paper, we present an interactive *parallel coordinate* system that can be used to provide users with greater abilities to interpret and explore clickstream data of online stores in the Web. Parallel coordinates are a visualization method developed for displaying multivariate data sets to identify the relationship among the variables [7]. A parallel coordinate system comprises a series of parallel lines that are placed equidistantly and perpendicular to the x-axis of a Cartesian coordinate system. Each parallel axis is assigned a specific dependent variable and dependent variable values are plotted along the respective axis. The independent variable is represented by polygonal lines which connect the corresponding dependent variable values relating to the independent variable.

The parallel coordinate system presented in this paper uses the multiple axes of the system to represent sequential steps which sessions take during their navigation in a Web site, and displays a large number of individual sessions as polygonal lines. That is, the clickstream of a session is represented by a polygonal line which intersects its value in each axis. With one or more variables such as referrers and host names that categorize sessions assigned to axes, the system can visualize the relationship between session categories and navigation paths. By looking at which axis a polygonal line ends at, it is straightforward to see at what point sessions leave the site. In order to help users actively explore and interpret data of interest, this system augments parallel coordinates with summary information. Also, by maintaining connection between visualizations and source database, it can dynamically update the summary information.

To demonstrate how the presented system provides capabilities for examining online store clickstreams that exceed those of traditional Web log analysis tools, we present a series of parallel coordinate visualizations which displays clickstream data from an operating online retailer. The visualizations reflect the framework developed for understanding online merchandising efforts in [8]. Especially, a set of metrics referred to as *micro-conversion rates*, which are defined for online merchandising analysis, is used for the visualizations. The results show that the interactive parallel coordinate system is useful in validating various hypotheses about Web merchandising as well as finding interesting patterns in clickstreams that are not identified previously.

The rest of this paper is structured as follows: Section 2 explains a framework and metrics for understanding Web merchandising. Section 3 discusses the types of data required for visual analysis of Web merchandising, and briefly describes how the data can be collected and integrated in an online store. Section 4 discusses how parallel coordinates can be used to visualize online store clickstream data, and help understanding the effectiveness of merchandising tactics. Section 5 summarizes an empirical study of analyzing clickstreams from an operating online store by using the parallel coordinate visualization. Finally, in Section 6, conclusions are drawn and further work is outlined.

# 2 Analysis of Web Merchandising

Web merchants generally analyze their sites' effectiveness from two perspectives: marketing and merchandising. Marketing on the Web is broadly defined as the activities used to acquire customers to online stores and retain them. Metrics that are used for answering these questions include banner ad *clickthrough rate* (the percentage of viewers who click on a banner ad), *conversion rate* (the percentage of visitors who purchase from the store), and banner ad *return on investment* (the amount of revenue and profit generated by visitors referred by a banner ad). The area of analyzing Web marketing is relatively well-understood, while useful metrics and analysis tools for Web merchandising lag behind. In this paper, we focus on the analysis of Web merchandising.

Merchandising consists of the activities involved in acquiring particular products and making them available at the places, times, and prices and in the quantity to enable a retailer to reach its goals [1]. In general, there are four areas for Web merchandising analysis: product assortment, merchandising cues, shopping metaphor, and Web design features [8]. The first analysis area, *product assortment*, deals with whether the products in an online store appeal to the visitors. If the product assortment is not optimal, the merchants may adjust, for example, brands, quality, selection, inventory or price of the products they carry. *Merchandising cues* are techniques for presenting and/or grouping products to motivate purchase in online stores. Examples of merchandising cues are cross-sells, up-sells, promotions and recommendations. Merchandising cues are associated with hyperlinks on Web pages. *Shopping metaphors* in an online store are the means that shoppers use to find products of interest. Examples include browsing through the product catalog hierarchy, various forms of searching, and configuration for "build-to-order" products. Like merchandising cues in online stores, shopping metaphors are associated with hyperlinks on Web pages. This allows one to categorize and group together hyperlinks in an online store by their types of merchandising cue and shopping metaphor. The effectiveness of *Web design features* presents another area of analysis for Web merchandising. The design features of hyperlinks include media type (e.g., image or text), font (if text), size, color, and location.

Just as Web marketing uses banner ads and/or referral sites to attract customers from external sites to an online store, online merchandising uses hyperlinks and image links within the store to lead customers to click to Web pages selling products. Web merchants employ a variety of tactics for merchandising by using hyperlinks. From this perspective, the problem of tracking and measuring the effectiveness of different merchandising tactics in an online store can be partitioned into three sub-problems:

i.   classifying hyperlinks by their merchandising purposes,
ii.  tracking traffic on hyperlinks and analyzing their effectiveness, and
iii. attributing the profit of hyperlinks to their merchandising cue types, shopping metaphor types, and design features.

Having identified the areas of Web merchandising analysis, we now introduce a set of metrics, referred to as *micro-conversion rates*, which can be used for measuring the effectiveness of efforts in these merchandising areas. The metrics are based on the conversion rate which is used for measuring online marketing performance. The conversion rate of an online store indicates the percentage of visitors who purchase from the store. While this measure is useful for evaluating the overall effectiveness of the store, it does not help understand the possible factors within the store that may affect the sales performance. The notion of a micro-conversion rate extends this traditional measure by considering the four general shopping steps in online stores, which are:

i. *product impression*: the view of hyperlink to a Web page presenting a product.
ii. *clickthrough*: the click on the hyperlink and view the Web page of the product.
iii. *basket placement*: the placement of the item in the shopping basket.
iv. *purchase*: the purchase of the item - completion of a transaction.

Basic micro-conversion rates are computed for each adjacent pair of these measures, resulting in the first three rates in the following list. In addition, the aggregation of the first three is also interesting:

i. *look-to-click rate*: how many product impressions are converted to click-throughs.
ii. *click-to-basket rate*: how many click-throughs are converted to basket placement.
iii. *basket-to-buy rate*: how many basket placements are converted to purchases.
iv. *look-to-buy rate*: what percentage of product impressions are eventually converted to purchases.

Note that the first of these, look-to-click rate, is similar to the clickthrough rate used for measuring the amount of traffic on banner ads. Also note that the micro-conversion rates relate the traffic-related measure to sales which happen later in the shopping process. By precisely tracking the shopping steps with these metrics, it is possible to spot exactly where the store loses how many customers. The micro-conversion rates extend the traditional measure by considering the merchandising purposes associated with hyperlinks viewed in the first shopping step, i.e., product impression. In this way, the micro-conversion rate is related to tactics of merchandising, and can be used for evaluating the effectiveness of different merchandising aspects of the store.

# 3 A Data Mart for E-Commerce Analysis

In this section, we briefly describe several data requirements for the analysis of Web merchandising explained in the previous section. First, the visualization of merchandising effectiveness based on micro-conversions requires the combination of the site traffic data and sales data. In most online stores, the two types of data are typically stored in separate storage systems in different structures: the traffic data in Web server logs in a file format, and the sales data in the database of the associated commerce server. It is important to combine data from the two different sources with a common key and to construct an integrated database system or a data mart system for business visualizations.

Second, showing a complete set of micro-conversions requires product impression data. Capturing product impressions involves tracking the content of served Web pages, which is challenging because more and more Web pages are dynamically generated. Currently, the standard Web server logging mechanism does not capture the content of Web pages. One possible method is to enhance the Web server logging as a way to dynamically parse the content of served Web pages and extract useful data such as product impressions and information on hyperlink types.

Finally, it is important to classify and identify hyperlinks by their merchandising purposes, so that later to attribute the profit generated from the hyperlinks to their merchandising cue types, shopping metaphor types, and/or design features. For this purpose, Web pages and hyperlinks in an online store need to be tagged with semantic labels describing their merchandising features. Semantic labels for hyperlinks in a site may be either explicitly provided in a form of meta-data during the site creation or inferred from various sources such as URLs of Web pages.

Figure 1 illustrates a data mart system which provides a single analysis environment that places various e-commerce activities into their business context by integrating data from disparate. The figure shows the types of source and target data of the data mart system, and the steps in transforming source to target data. During the data transformation process, data from various sources is cleansed, normalized, integrated, and then loaded into a multidimensional data model for use by business analysts who seek answers to their business questions by using techniques such as data mining, OLAP (On-Line Analytical Processing), and the visualization of micro-conversions which is presented in this paper.

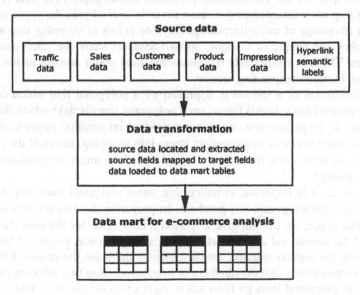

**Fig. 1.** Data mart architecture for e-commerce analysis

# 4  A Parallel Coordinate System for Clickstream Data

Clickstream data of an online store can be visualized by displaying the progression of sessions in terms of micro-conversions among shopping steps described earlier. This approach provides visualizations that help users identify where the store loses how many customers, understand and compare the shopping behavior of different groups of customers, and understand the effectiveness of different merchandising tactics. In this section, we introduce a set of parallel coordinates visualizing the micro-conversions of sessions in an online store.

The system of parallel coordinates was developed for displaying multivariate data sets to identify the relationship among the variables in the set [7]. A parallel coordinate system comprises a series of parallel lines that are placed equidistantly and perpendicular to the x-axis. Each parallel axis is assigned a specific dependent variable and dependent variable values are plotted along the respective axis. The independent variable is represented by polygonal lines which connect the corresponding dependent variable values relating to the independent variable and illustrate a relationship between an independent variable and the dependent variables appearing on each axis

Figure 2 illustrates how we use parallel coordinates to display clickstream data of an online store. In this figure, each polygonal line represents a single session and its progression in the online store. The first parallel axis represents a session categorizer, in this figure, the referrer of each session. In Figure 2, the data points in the categorizer axis are the names of referrers, and there are two different referrers shown. The next three parallel axes represent shopping steps in the online store, i.e., clickthrough, basket placement, and purchase. (The product impression data was not available for the data set used for the visualizations presented in this paper.) For data points in the shopping step axes, timestamps (i.e., start times in second granularity) of sessions are used. An advantage of using timestamps for data points in shopping step axes is that because they are unique to sessions, no two sessions share the same data points in these axes. The last parallel axis represents the total dollar amount of the completed transaction in the corresponding session.

The clickstream of a session is displayed by a polygonal line which connects its values in parallel lines. In this figure, each polygonal line displays where the customer came from, if the person saw one or more product information pages in the store, if the person inserted one or more product items into shopping basket, if the person purchased one or more items from the store, and if so, how much the purchase value was in dollar amount?

In Figure 2, it is important to notice that some polygonal lines stop before they reach the last shopping step, i.e., purchase. In preparing the data set for the visualizations in this paper, we did not give a session a data value for the next shopping step and on, if the session did not convert to the next step. Hence, polygonal lines stops at the last step the session reached, which indicates the point the session left the store. Figure 2 clearly shows that the numbers of lines connecting two adjacent parallel axes decrease, as polygonal lines go from left to right up to the purchase line. Dropouts of polygonal lines visualize where the store loses its customers. Also, the micro-conversion rates can be computed directly from the visualization by using the numbers between two adjacent axes. That is, the click-to-basket rate is the ratio of the number of lines connecting the clickthrough and basket axes to the number of lines connecting the referrer and clickthrough axes. The basket-to-buy rate is the ratio of the number of lines connecting the basket and buy axes to the number of lines connecting the clickthrough and basket axes.

The parallel coordinate system presented in paper is augmented with a summary of the micro-conversions and average order values of the selected session groups presented in a table at the bottom. The idea is that presenting parallel coordinate visualizations together with summary information help users understand the data better, because the two different types of information complement with each other: visualizations give users insight into the relationship among multiple variables and their patterns, while summary information delivers specifics.

## 5 An Empirical Study

In order to understand the applicability and usefulness of the proposed interactive parallel coordinate system, we have performed an empirical study with clickstream data from an online retailer, creating a series of parallel coordinate visualizations. For a five day period during May 1999, the data set consists of over 35,000 sessions and 7,500 basket placements and 3,500 completed transactions. In an attempt to generate meaningful clickstream data, basic Web usage data, i.e., raw hits recorded in Web server log files was processed and cleansed in a way similar to one described in [5].

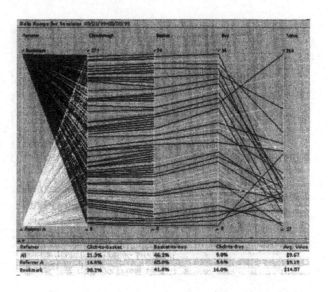

Fig. 2. Micro-conversions of sessions categorized by referrer

Then the generated session data was integrated with data of basket placements and transactions extracted from the commerce server. Because the online store actively uses cookies for identifying customers and their visits, and records them in both Web server logs and commerce server database, the processes of sessionization and data integration were done in an accurate and reliable fashion.

Various attributes of sessions that can be used to categorize them were identified. The session categorizers include referrers, host names, timestamps, the length of time spent in the store, the types and numbers of shopping metaphors used, the types and numbers of merchandising cues used, and the categories and numbers of products viewed and purchased. Visualizations presented in this section are for a demonstration purpose, only a small subset of the visualizations that could be generated from the available data. The visualizations in this section were created for the following two session categorizers: referrers and ISPs.

Figure 2 provides a series of visualizations of sessions categorized by their referrers. Figure 2 visualizes two groups of sessions: sessions that came from a well-known portal site which was labeled as A in the figure, and sessions that came to the store through bookmarks. Note that the number of sessions that had clickthroughs in the visualization are arranged to be roughly the same for a balanced visual comparison. It is commonly believed that the sessions that came to the store through bookmarks are visits from repeate customers who shop at the store frequently, and probably, know what they want to buy from the store. Figure 2 confirms this speculation by showing a relatively high number of click-to-basket conversions. The summary table in the figure also confirms the high micro-conversion rates: the click-to-basket rate of the bookmark group is almost two times higher than that of the baseline, while the click-to-basket rate of the Referrer A group is a few points lower than that of the baseline.

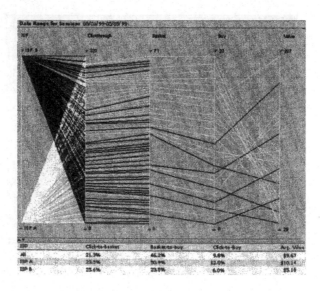

Fig. 3. Micro-conversions of sessions categorized by ISP

The baseline data was computed for the entire data set which include over 35,000 sessions, 7,500 basket placements, and 3,500 transactions. While the basket-to-buy rate of the bookmark group is slightly lower than that of the baseline, the basket-to-buy rate of Referrer A is about 40% higher than that of the baseline. Overall, the click-to-buy rate of the bookmark group is about 60% higher than that of the baseline, while the click-to-buy rate of the Referrer A group shows the roughly the same number as the baseline. In addition, the average order value of all sessions in the bookmark group is about 60% higher than that of the baseline.

Figure 3 shows the micro-conversions and average order values of sessions which are from two different ISPs. One group, labeled as A and colored white, consists of sessions from an ISP that provides connection through regular telephone modems, and the other, labeled as B and colored black, consists of sessions from an ISP that provides service through television-based clients. Again, the number of sessions in each group is balanced for visual comparison. This figure shows that, for this specific period of time, the micro-conversions of Group B is about 50% lower than the other group. The difference in micro-conversions in the two session groups is clearly illustrated by the numbers of the lines connecting adjacent shopping steps colored blue and yellow, respectively. Note that, as in the previous example, a linear relationship is observed between two metrics, the click-to-buy rates and the average order value of all sessions.

Sample visualizations presented in Figures 2 and 3 show results consistent with summary information about a few interesting, but unproven speculations in e-commerce. Also, the visualizations of a large number of individual clickstreams against multiple dimensions show a potential for identifying previously unknown patterns. Visualizations presented in this section are only a small subset of the visualizations that could be created from the available data and further work is required for a better understanding of Web merchandising. However, the visualizations presented in this section clearly demonstrated the applicability and usefulness of the interactive parallel coordinate system for understanding the effectiveness of merchandising efforts in online stores.

# 6 Concluding Remarks

In this paper, we have presented a parallel coordinate system that provides users with abilities to actively interpret and explore clickstream data of online stores in the Web. By using an information structure specifically devised for presenting online store clickstream data, we showed the potential use of parallel coordinates for analyzing the effectiveness of various merchandising efforts in Web stores.

More specifically, clickstream data of an online store is arranged to represent four sequential shopping steps: product impressions, clickthrough, basket placement and purchase. The parallel coordinate system displays a number of individual sessions (as polygonal lines) and their shopping activities (as parallel axes). The system visualizes the progression of sessions in the store, i.e., the conversions from one shopping step to another, and so provide insight into the effectiveness of each step's design. By associating the sessions with attributes that categorize sessions such as the referrers, host names, length, and the shopping metaphors and merchandising cues they used, the sessions and their conversions can be subdivided. Categorization of sessions helps understand how sessions with different category values react to the site differently. An empirical study we performed with clickstream data from an online retailer validated the usefulness of the proposed parallel coordinate system for understanding online store performance.

# References

1. B. Berman and J. R. Evans, *Retail Management: A Strategic Approach, 7th Edition*, Prentice-Hall, Inc., 1998.
2. A. G. Büchner and M. Mulvenna, "Discovering Internet Marketing Intelligence through Online Analytical Web Usage Mining," *SIGMOD Record*, 27(4):54-61, December 1998.
3. M. S. Chen, J. S. Park, P. S. Yu, "Data Mining for Traversal Patterns in a Web Environment," *Proc. of the 16th International Conference on Distributed Computing Systems*, 1996.
4. E. Chi, J. Pitkow, J. Mackinlay, P. Pirolli, R. Gossweiler, and S. Card, "Visualizing the Evolution of Web Ecologies," *ACM CHI Conference on Human Factors in Computing Systems*, 1998, pp. 400-407.
5. R. Cooley, B. Mobasher and J. Srivastava, "Data Preparation for Mining World Wide Web Browsing Patterns," *Journal of Knowledge and Information Systems*, 1(1), 1999.
6. H. Hochheiser, and B. Schneiderman, "Understanding Patterns of User Visits to Web Sites: Interactive Starfield Visualizations of WWW Log Data," *Technical Report*, CS-TR-3989, Department of Computer Science, University of Maryland, 1999.
7. A. Inselberg and B. Dimsdale, "Parallel Coordinates A Tool for Visualizing Multivariate Relations," *Human-Machine Interactive Systems*, Plenum Publishing Corporation, 1991, pp. 199-233.
8. J. Lee, M. Podlaseck, E. Schonberg and R. Hoch, "Visualization and Analysis of Clickstream Data of Online Stores for Understanding Web Merchandising," To appear in the special issue of the *International Journal of Data Mining and Knowledge Discovery* on E-Commerce and Data Mining, Kluwer Academic Publishers, 2000.
9. N. Papadakakis, E. P. Markatos, and A. E. Papathanasiou, "Palantir: a Visualization tool for the World Wide Web," *INET 98 Proceedings*, 1998.
10. J. Pitkow, "In Search of Reliable Usage Data on the WWW," *Technical Report*, College of Computing, Graphics, Visualization, and Usability Center, Georgia Tech, 1996.
11. L. Tauscher and S. Greenberg, "Revisitation Patterns in World Wide Web Navigation," *ACM CHI Conference on Human Factors in Computing Systems*, 1997, pp. 399-406.
12. T. Wilson, "Web Site Mining Gets Granular," *InternetWeek*, March 29, 1999.

# A Heuristic to Capture Longer User Web Navigation Patterns

José Borges and Mark Levene

Department of Computer Science, University College London,
Gower Street, London WC1E 6BT, U.K.
{j.borges, mlevene}@cs.ucl.ac.uk

**Abstract.** In previous work we have proposed a data mining model to capture user web navigation patterns, which models the navigation sessions as a hypertext probabilistic grammar. The grammar's higher probability strings correspond to the user preferred trails and an algorithm was given to find all strings with probability above a threshold. Herein, we propose a heuristic aimed at finding longer trails composed of links whose average probability is above the threshold. A dynamic threshold is provided whose value is at all times proportional to the length of the trail being evaluated. We report on experiments with both real and synthetic data which were conducted to assess the heuristic's utility.

## 1 Introduction

Web usage mining [4] is a recent research field which studies techniques that use log data to find patterns in user web navigation sessions. These *sessions* take the form of sequences of links followed by the user, which we call *trails*. Understanding user navigation behaviour is an essential step in the process of customising web sites to the user's needs either by improving its static structure or by providing adaptive web pages [9]. Moreover, since log data is collected in a raw format it is an ideal target for being analysed by automated tools. Currently several commercial log analysis tools are available; however, these tools have limited analysis capabilities producing results such as summary statistics and frequency counts of page visits. In the meantime the research community has been studying data mining techniques to take full advantage of the information available in log files. There have so far been two main approaches for mining user navigation patterns from log data. One approach is to map log data onto relational tables and an adapted version of standard data mining techniques, such as mining association rules, is invoked, see for example [3, 14]. In the other approach techniques are developed which are invoked directly on the log data, see for example [2, 11, 12].

The work reported herein is part of a ongoing research with the long term goal of specifying a set of techniques to identify relevant web trails [1, 2, 8, 15].

In [2] we presented a new model for handling the problem of mining log data which models the web as a regular grammar; the grammar states correspond to web pages and the production rules to hyperlinks. The navigation sessions are then incorporated into the model in order to build a *hypertext probabilistic grammar* (or simply a HPG). Data mining techniques are used to find the higher probability strings which correspond to the user's preferred navigation trails. The HPG model provides a simple and sound tool to summarise the user interaction with the web and which is potentially useful both to the web site designer and to the individual user.

On the one hand, a HPG can be used as an off-line tool to analyse server logs. The web site designer can benefit from having a better understanding of the users' browsing behaviour, characterised by the set of most popular trails. By understanding the users preferences the designer can provide adaptive web pages or improve the site structure according to the business objectives. Such objectives can be, for example: to personalise web pages, to increase the average time a user spends in the site, or to introduce new pages in places which make them highly visible. To increase the average time a user spends on the site links can be created between pages of popular trails. A new product can be given good exposure by placing links to its pages from a popular trail which includes related products. Knowing the popular trails also allows to identify the pages where users frequently terminate their sessions so that the contents of such pages can be improved. On the other hand, a HPG can be implemented as a browser plug-in to incrementally store and analyse the user's individual navigation history. Such a HPG would be a representation of the user's knowledge of the web and could act as a memory aid, be analysed in order to infer the user preferred trails, or work as a prediction tool to prefetch in advance pages the user may be interested in. In addition the user would be able to compare and/or exchange his HPG model with those of his peers and, for example, identify the preferred trails which are unknown to him but are among the preferences of his peers.

Herein we present a new heuristic for HPGs which aims at finding longer strings composed of links with average probability above a given threshold. In fact, although the algorithm proposed in [2] to find all the strings with probability above a cut-point is efficient it yields an unmanageable number of rules if the confidence is set too low and a small set of very short rules if the confidence is set too high (for the definition of confidence see Section 2). A large rule-set limits the ability of running the algorithm in main memory, with the consequent degradation of its performance, and also demands the existence of large storage space and database access time. This is particularly important when the analyst is interactively experimenting with various different model configurations. These drawbacks led us to investigate a heuristic to compute a relatively small set of long rules. The method is called *inverse fisheye* and makes use of a dynamic threshold which imposes a very strict criterion for small rules and becomes more permissible as the trails get longer.

Section 2 presents an overview of HPGs, while Section 3 presents the proposed heuristic. Section 4 details the results of experiments we performed with both heuristics. Finally, in Section 5 we give our concluding remarks.

## 2 The Hypertext Probabilistic Grammar Model

A log file consists in a per-user ordered set of web page requests from which are inferred the user navigation sessions. A *navigation session* is a sequence of page requests made by a user; techniques to infer the sessions from log data are given in [5]. We model a collection of user sessions as a *hypertext probabilistic language* [8] generated by a *hypertext probabilistic grammar* (or simply HPG) [2] which is a proper subclass of probabilistic regular grammars [13]. In a HPG, a non-terminal symbol corresponds to a web page and a production rule corresponds to a hypertext link. Two additional artificial states, $S$ and $F$, represent the start and finish states of the navigation sessions. The probability of a string is given by the product of the probabilities of the productions used in its derivation. We call the productions with $S$ on its left-hand side *start productions* and we call the productions corresponding to links between pages *transitive productions*.

From the collection of navigation sessions we obtain the number of times a page was requested, the number of times it was the start of a session, and the number of times it terminated a session. The number of times a sequence of two pages appears in the sessions gives the number of times the corresponding link was traversed. The probabilities of the start productions are weighted by a parameter $\alpha$. If $\alpha = 0$ only states that were the first in a session have a start production with probability greater than zero, if $\alpha = 1$ the probability of a start production is proportional to the number of times the corresponding state was visited; $\alpha$ can take any value between 0 and 1. In the example of Figure 1 state $A_1$ was visited 4 times, 2 of which as the first state in a session and for $\alpha = 0.5$ we have that the probability of its start production is $p(A_1) = (0.5 \cdot 4)/24 + (0.5 \cdot 2)/6 = 0.25$. Page $A_4$ was visited 4 times, 1 of which as the last page in a session, once on the way to page $A_6$ and twice on the way to page $A_1$, therefore, $p(A_4A_1) = 2/4$, $p(A_4A_6) = 1/4$ and $p(A_4F) = 1/4$.

The grammar strings correspond to the user navigation trails. (We use the terms trail and string interchangeably.) A trail is in the language if its derivation probability is above a *cut-point*, $\lambda$. The set of trails with probability above the cut-point is the *rule-set*. The cut-point is composed of two thresholds $\lambda = \theta \cdot \delta$; $\theta \in (0, 1)$ is the *support* threshold and $\delta \in (0, 1)$ the *confidence* threshold. The support is the factor of the cut-point responsible for pruning out the strings whose first derivation step has low probability; the confidence is responsible for pruning out strings whose derivation contains transitive productions with small probabilities. The values of the support and confidence thresholds give the user control over the number and quality of trails to be included in the rule-set.

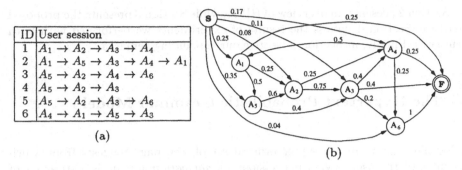

| ID | User session |
|----|--------------|
| 1 | $A_1 \to A_2 \to A_3 \to A_4$ |
| 2 | $A_1 \to A_5 \to A_3 \to A_4 \to A_1$ |
| 3 | $A_5 \to A_2 \to A_4 \to A_6$ |
| 4 | $A_5 \to A_2 \to A_3$ |
| 5 | $A_5 \to A_2 \to A_3 \to A_6$ |
| 6 | $A_4 \to A_1 \to A_5 \to A_3$ |

(a)

(b)

**Fig. 1.** A set of trails and the corresponding HPG for $\alpha = 0.5$.

The use of a Markovian model is sometimes criticised by arguing that it does not represent exactly the actual user navigation sessions. However, we view that as an advantage of the model since the probability of a long trail being often followed in exactly the same manner is low. Moreover, the contents of a page viewed recently should have more influence in choosing the next link to follow than a page viewed in the early steps of the session. On the other hand, the probability of choosing a link is not completely independent of the browsing history. Thus, we make use of the $N$gram concept where $N, N \geq 1$, determines the user memory when navigating the web, implying that when visiting a page only the $N$ previously visited pages influence the next link choice, see [2]. In an $N$gram each state corresponds to a sequence of $N$ pages visited leading to a trade-off between the model accuracy and its complexity, since when the order of the model increases so does its size, measured in the number of states.

In [2] we reported the results of experiments with a modified Breadth-First Search (BFS) algorithm that induces all HPG's strings with probability above a cut-point. Although the BFS is very efficient it has the drawback of potentially returning a very large rule-set for small values of the cut-point and the rules are too short when the cut-point is close to one. Figure 2 (a) shows the variation of the number of rules with the confidence threshold and (b) the variation of the average (ARL) and maximum (MRL) rule length with the same threshold. It can be seen that in order to obtain long rules the threshold has to be set with a low value and that leads to a very large number of rules. Although it is possible to rank the rules in a large rule-set by their length and probability, or by some other criteria, in order to identify the best rules, the manipulation of a large rule-set limits the algorithm's ability to run in main memory. These problems led us to the study of the inverse fisheye heuristic.

## 3 The Inverse Fisheye Heuristic

Herein, we propose a method to find a relatively small set of long rules composed of links with high probability on average. To that effect, we make use of

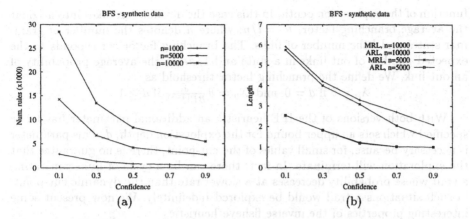

**Fig. 2.** Characteristics of the rule-set induced with the BFS algorithm.

a dynamic cut-point which imposes a very strict criterion for short trails and becomes more permissible as the trails get longer. This idea was motivated by the fisheye-view concept of Furnas [6], which is a method to visualise large information data structures on small computer displays. In a fisheye view the detail with which a document is shown is proportional to the global importance of the document and inversely proportional to its distance from the current document. We call our heuristic the *inverse fisheye* (IFE), since, as opposed to the Furnas concept, our method benefits those pages that are further away from the start of the trail being evaluated. With the IFE heuristic the cut-point becomes more permissible as the trails get longer. We propose two different ways of setting the dynamic cut-point. In the first the cut-point keeps its value proportional to the depth of exploration, and in the second the cut-point is devalued by a factor proportional to the expected decrease in the trail probability. We call the first method the *geometric cut-point* version. The initial value for cut-point is set by means of its two components, the support $\theta$ and the confidence $\delta$ thresholds, and an exploration tree is incrementally built from the start state while the value of the cut-point is updated as a function of the depth of the exploration. The geometric cut-point is defined to be

$$\lambda_G = \theta \delta^d ,$$

where $d$ is the depth of the exploration tree measured by the number of links. The geometric cut-point is devalued geometrically in a way that keeps its value proportional to the trail's length. When the depth of the tree is 0, and the start productions are evaluated, the cut-point corresponds to the support threshold value. In the subsequent stages of the exploration the cut-point incorporates the confidence threshold a number of times corresponding to the number of transitive productions which derive the trails being evaluated.

We call the second method for setting the dynamic cut-point the *branching factor* version. An exploration tree is built and the cut-point is devalued as a function of the exploration depth. In this case the devaluation takes into account the average branching factor, $BF = l/n$, where $n$ denotes the number of grammar states and $l$ the number of links. The branching factor corresponds to the expected number of out-links in a state and $1/BF$ to the average probability of an out-link. We define the branching factor threshold as

$$\lambda_B = \theta \text{ if } d = 0 \quad \text{and} \quad \lambda_B = \theta \frac{\delta}{BF^{(d-1)}} \text{ if } d \geq 1 .$$

With both versions of the IFE heuristic an additional parameter has to be specified which sets an upper bound for the exploration depth, $\bar{d}$. This parameter is necessary because, for small values of the cut-point, there is no guarantee that the exploration will terminate. In fact, there can be a cycle of links generating a trail whose probability decreases at a slower rate than the dynamic cut-point, in such situations a trail would be explored indefinitely. We now present some interesting properties of the inverse fisheye heuristic.

**Proposition 1.** If $\delta = \frac{1}{BF}$ then $\lambda_G = \lambda_B$.

**Proof.** If $d = 0$ we have $\lambda_G = \theta \delta^0 = \theta = \lambda_B$, $\forall \delta$. If $d = 1$, $\lambda_G = \theta \delta^1 = \theta \delta \frac{1}{BF^0} = \lambda_B$. If $d > 1$ we have $\lambda_G = \lambda_B \equiv \theta \delta^d = \theta \delta \frac{1}{BF^{d-1}} \equiv \delta = \sqrt[d-1]{\frac{1}{BF^{d-1}}} = \frac{1}{BF}$. $\square$

**Proposition 2.** If $\delta > \frac{1}{BF}$ then $\lambda_B < \lambda_G$.

**Proof.** $\lambda_B < \lambda_G \equiv \theta \delta \frac{1}{BF^{d-1}} < \theta \delta^d \equiv \delta > \frac{1}{BF}$. $\square$

**Proposition 3.** For $\lambda_G$ and a trail $t = b a_1 \ldots a_l$, where $b$ and $a_i$, $1 \leq i \leq l$ are the links composing the trail, we have: $\frac{p(a_1) + p(a_2) + \ldots + p(a_l)}{l} \geq \delta \left( \frac{\theta}{p(b)} \right)^{\frac{1}{l}}$.

**Proof.** $p(b)p(a_1)p(a_2) \ldots p(a_l) \geq \theta \delta^l \equiv \left( \frac{p(b)p(a_1)p(a_2) \ldots p(a_l)}{\theta} \right)^{\frac{1}{l}} \geq \delta \equiv$

$\equiv \left( \frac{p(b)}{\theta} \right)^{\frac{1}{l}} (p(a_1)p(a_2) \ldots p(a_l))^{\frac{1}{l}} \geq \delta \equiv (p(a_1)p(a_2) \ldots p(a_l))^{\frac{1}{l}} \geq \delta \left( \frac{\theta}{p(b)} \right)^{\frac{1}{l}}$

and by the theorem of the geometric means, [7] it follows that:

$$\frac{p(a_1) + p(a_2) + \ldots + p(a_d)}{l} \geq \delta \left( \frac{\theta}{p(b)} \right)^{\frac{1}{l}}. \quad \square$$

The first property shows that the two methods for setting the dynamic cut-point are equivalent when $\delta = 1/BF$. The second property shows that when $\delta > 1/BF$ the branching factor version is more permissible than the geometric version since its value decreases faster. The third property implies that when $p(b) = \theta$ the average link probability of a rule induced by the geometric version is greater than or equal to the confidence threshold $\delta$, that is, the rule-set is composed of rules whose average link probability is greater than the confidence threshold. Note, that the property is not complete since not all trails with average link probability greater than $\delta$ are induced by the inverse fisheye property.

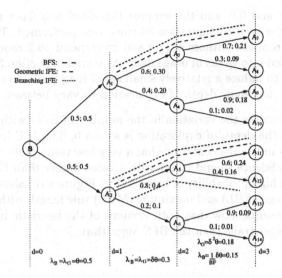

**Fig. 3.** A exploration tree for the inverse fisheye heuristic with $\theta = 0.5$ and $\delta = 0.6$.

Figure 3 shows an example of an exploration tree where $BF = 2$, $\theta = 0.5$, and $\delta = 0.6$. The cut-point values for the two versions are given in the figure, as well as the rules induced by the heuristic and by the BFS algorithm. A pair of numbers next to a link represents the probability of the link and the probability of the trail beginning in state $S$. When $d = 0$ the cut-point corresponds to the support value, when $d = 1$ it corresponds to the product of the confidence and the support $\delta\theta$; the inverse fisheye property only starts having effect for $d \geq 2$. With the geometric version only trails whose average link probability is above $\delta = 0.6$ are induced; trail $A_2 A_5 A_{12}$ is not a rule since its average link probability is just 0.6. Moreover, trail $A_1 A_4 A_9$ meets the acceptance criterion for $d = 2$ since its probability of 0.18 is above the cut-points, however, the trail is not a rule since it is rejected at an early stage when $p(A_1 A_4) = 0.2 < 0.3$. Finally, the example also shows that in this case the BFS is ineffective since it induces a single short rule, i.e., $A_2 A_5$. On the other hand, if the BFS algorithm is set up to run with the cut-point $\lambda = 0.18$ (the final value for the geometric version) the gain relative to the geometric version would only be the short rule $A_1 A_4$.

## 4 Experimental Results

To assess the effectiveness of the IFE heuristic, experiments were conducted with both synthetic data and real log files. The synthetic data generation method consisted in randomly creating HPGs given a number of pages, an average number of out-links per page, and a probability distribution for the links' weights. The number of states, $n$, varied between 1000 and 20000 states, the confidence threshold between 0.1 and 0.9, and the support threshold was fixed to $1/n$ for each grammar size. For each configuration 30 runs were performed. The real log files were obtained from the authors of [10] and correspond to 2 months of log data which was divided into weeks of usage data. As stated in Section 3 the goal of the IFE heuristic is to induce a relatively small set of long trails. In the experiments we have set the maximum depth of exploration to vary between 3 and 6.

Figure 4 (a) shows the variation in the number of rules with the confidence threshold when the depth of exploration is set to 6. The IFE heuristic induces smaller rule-sets unless the confidence has a very low value. Note that for the IFE heuristic the confidence should be set with a value higher than $1/BF$, otherwise every trail has a high probability of being a rule. Figure 4 (b) shows the variation of both the average (ARL) and maximum (MRL) rule length with the confidence threshold. The results show that both versions of the heuristic induce a smaller rule-set with longer trails than the BFS algorithm.

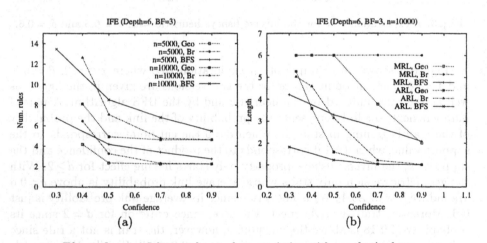

**Fig. 4.** Inverse fisheye rule-set characteristics with synthetic data.

Figure 5 (a) shows the variation in the number of iterations with the number of states where it can be seen that both versions present linear behaviour. Figure 5 (b) shows the variation of the number of rules obtained with the depth of exploration for the geometric version of the IFE heuristic. This results show that it is possible to have some control over the number of rules obtained by setting the both the dynamic cut-point and the exploration depth.

Figure 6 shows the distribution of the rules' length for the real data; each result corresponds to the average for the weekly data sets. The results show that with this real data set the branching version gives rule-sets that are too large, even for very high values of the initial cut-point. The geometric version of the heuristics achieves better results, especially for higher values of the support

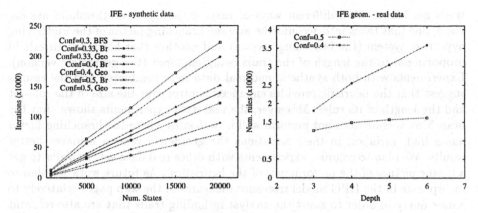

**Fig. 5.** Performance of the heuristics with synthetic data.

threshold where smaller rule-sets are obtained which contain longer rules. The analysis of the structure of the real data revealed that in spite of the real data sets having an average branching factor similar to the specified for the synthetic data, its standard deviation is very high (9 on average). This explains why in this case the BFS algorithm induces long rules for high values of the cut-point, since there is a considerable number of states with just one out-link.

| | | | | Rule length | | | | | |
|---|---|---|---|---|---|---|---|---|---|
| $\delta$ | Algorithm | Tot. | Avg. | 1 | 2 | 3 | 4 | 5 | 6 |
| 0.5 | BFS | 1289 | 1.9 | 414 | 567 | 277 | 31 | | |
| 0.5 | Geometric | 1623 | 3.4 | 131 | 343 | 460 | 323 | 175 | 191 |
| 0.7 | BFS | 933 | 1.8 | 335 | 423 | 162 | 13 | | |
| 0.7 | Geometric | 871 | 2.3 | 188 | 349 | 251 | 62 | 18 | 3 |
| 0.9 | BFS | 714 | 1.78 | 276 | 325 | 107 | 6 | | |
| 0.9 | Geometric | 681 | 1.87 | 234 | 312 | 124 | 11 | | |
| 0.9 | Branching | 14749 | 5.8 | 234 | 77 | 175 | 371 | 836 | 13056 |

*Real data, aggregated weeks with $\theta = 1/n$*

**Fig. 6.** Distribution of the rules' length with real data having $\theta = 1/n$.

## 5 Conclusions

We propose a new heuristic which aims at providing the analyst with more control over the number, length, and probability of the rules induced by a hypertext probabilistic grammar. The heuristic makes use of a dynamic threshold which is very strict when evaluating short trails and becomes more permissible as the trails get longer. Two different ways of varying the dynamic threshold are devised, one that takes into account the average branching factor of the underlying hypertext system (the branching version) and another that keeps the threshold proportional to the length of the trails being explored (the geometric version). Experiments with both synthetic and real data were conducted and the results suggest that the heuristic provides enhanced control over the size of the rule-set and the length of its rules. Moreover, the real data experiments shown that the branching version does not perform well in web sites where the branching factor has a high variance; in these situations the geometric version achieves better results. We plan to conduct experiments with other real data sets in order to get a better picture of the performance of the heuristics . As future work we plan to incorporate in the HPG model relevance measures of the web pages relatively to a user query in order to assist the analyst in finding trails that are also relevant to a given set of keywords.

# References

1. J. Borges and M. Levene. Mining association rules in hypertext databases. In *Proc. of the 4th Int. Conf. on Knowledge Discovery and Data Mining*, pages 149–153, New York, 1998.
2. J. Borges and M. Levene. Data mining of user navigation patterns. In *Proc. of the Web Usage Analysis and User Profiling Workshop*, pages 31–36, San Diego, 1999.
3. M. Chen, J. Park, and P. Yu. Efficient data mining for traversal patterns. *IEEE Transactions on Knowledge and Data Engineering*, 10(2):209–221, 1998.
4. R. Cooley, B. Mobasher, and J. Srivastava. Web mining: Information and patterns discovery on the world wide web. In *Proc. of the 9th IEEE Int. Conf. on Tools with Artificial Intelligence*, pages 558–567, 1997.
5. R. Cooley, B. Mobasher, and J. Srivastava. Data preparation for mining world wide web browsing patterns. *Knowledge and Information Systems*, 1(1):5–32, 1999.
6. G. Furnas. Generalized fisheye views. In *Conf. proc. on Human factors in computing systems*, pages 16–23, 1986.
7. N. Kazarinoff. *Geometric Inequalities*. Random House, 1961.
8. M. Levene and G. Loizou. A probabilistic approach to navigation in hypertext. *Information Sciences*, 114:165–186, 1999.
9. M. Perkowitz and O. Etzioni. Adaptive web sites: an AI challenge. In *Proc. of 15th Int. Joint Conf. on Artificial Intelligence*, pages 16–21, Nagoya, 1997.
10. M. Perkowitz and O. Etzioni. Adaptive sites: Automatically synthesizing web pages. In *Proc. 15th Nat. Conf. on Artificial Intelligence*, pages 727–732, 1998.
11. S. Schechter, M. Krishnan, and M. D. Smith. Using path profiles to predict http requests. *Computer Networks and ISDN Systems*, 30:457–467, 1998.
12. M. Spiliopoulou and L. Faulstich. WUM: a tool for web utilization analysis. In *Proc. Int. Workshop on the Web and Databases*, pages 184–203, Valencia, 1998.
13. C. Wetherell. Probabilistic languages: A review and some open questions. *Computing Surveys*, 12(4):361–379, 1980.
14. T. Yan, M. Jacobsen, H. Garcia-Molina, and U. Dayal. From user access patterns to dynamic hypertext linking. In *Proc. of the fifth Int. World Wide Web Conference*, pages 1007–1014, Paris, 1996.
15. N. Zin and M. Levene. Constructing web-views from automated navigation sessions. In *Proc. of the ACM Digital Libraries Workshop on Organizing Web Space*, pages 54–58, Berkeley, 1999.

# Integrating Web Usage and Content Mining for More Effective Personalization

Bamshad Mobasher, Honghua Dai, Tao Luo, Yuqing Sun, and Jiang Zhu

School of Computer Science, Telecommunications, and Information Systems,
DePaul University, Chicago, Illinois, USA
mobasher@cs.depaul.edu

**Abstract.** Recent proposals have suggested Web usage mining as an enabling mechanism to overcome the problems associated with more traditional Web personalization techniques such as collaborative or content-
based filtering. These problems include lack of scalability, reliance on
subjective user ratings or static profiles, and the inability to capture
a richer set of semantic relationships among objects (in content-based
systems). Yet, usage-based personalization can be problematic when little usage data is available pertaining to some objects or when the site
content changes regularly. For more effective personalization, both usage
and content attributes of a site must be integrated into a Web mining
framework and used by the recommendation engine in a uniform manner. In this paper we present such a framework, distinguishing between
the offline tasks of data preparation and mining, and the online process
of customizing Web pages based on a user's active session. We describe
effective techniques based on clustering to obtain a uniform representation for both site usage and site content profiles, and we show how these
profiles can be used to perform real-time personalization.

## 1 Introduction

The intense competition among Internet-based businesses to acquire new customers and retain the existing ones has made Web personalization an indis-
pensable part of e-commerce. Web personalization can be defined as any action
that tailors the Web experience according to the users' preferences. Automatic
personalization requires the ability to capture behavioral patterns and interests
of users from, potentially anonymous, Web transaction data. We believe that
the solution lies in the creation of a flexible framework and the development of
new techniques for unsupervised and undirected knowledge discovery from Web
usage data, and the integration of content information and meta-data with the
discovered usage patterns.

Personalization based on Web usage mining has several advantages over more
traditional techniques. The type of input is not a subjective description of the
users by the users themselves, and thus is not prone to biases. The profiles are
dynamically obtained from user patterns, and thus the system performance does
not degrade over time as the profiles age. Furthermore, using content similarity

alone as a way to obtain aggregate profiles may result in missing important relationships among Web objects based on their usage. Thus, Web usage mining will reduce the need for obtaining subjective user ratings or registration-based personal preferences. Web usage mining can also be used to enhance the effectiveness of collaborative filtering approaches [6, 16]. Collaborative filtering is often based on matching, in real-time, the current user's profile against similar records (nearest neighbors) obtained by the system over time from other users. However, as noted in recent studies [10], it becomes hard to scale collaborative filtering techniques to a large number of items, while maintaining reasonable prediction performance and accuracy. One potential solution to this problem is to first cluster user records with similar characteristics, and focus the search for nearest neighbors only in the matching clusters. In the context of Web personalization this task involves clustering user transactions identified in the preprocessing stage.

Recent work in Web usage mining has focused on the extraction of usage patterns from Web logs for the purpose of deriving marketing intelligence [1–4, 12, 19, 20], as well as the discovery of aggregate profiles for the customization or optimization of Web sites [9, 11, 14, 17, 18]. For an up-to-date survey of Web usage mining systems see [13]. Despite the advantages, usage-based personalization can be problematic when little usage data is available pertaining to some objects or when the site content may change regularly. For more effective personalization, both usage and content attributes of a site must be integrated into a Web mining framework and used by the recommendation engine in a uniform manner.

In [7, 8], we presented a general framework for usage-based Web personalization, and proposed specific techniques based on clustering and association rule discovery to obtain dynamic recommendations from aggregate usage data. In this paper, we extend this framework to incorporate content profiles into the recommendation process as a way to enhance the effectiveness of personalization actions. We discuss specific preprocessing tasks necessary for performing both content and usage mining, and present techniques based on clustering to derive aggregate profiles. Our goal is to create a uniform representation for both content and usage profiles that can be effectively used for personalization tasks by a recommendation engine in a consistent and integrated fashion. We show how the discovered knowledge can be combined with the current status of an ongoing Web activity to perform real-time personalization. Finally, present the results of our experiments with the proposed techniques using real Web data.

## 2 A Web Mining Framework for Personalization

### 2.1 System Architecture

Figure 1 depicts a general architecture for Web personalization based on usage and content mining. The overall process is divided into two components: the offline component which is comprised of the data preparation and specific Web mining tasks, and the online component which is a real-time recommendation

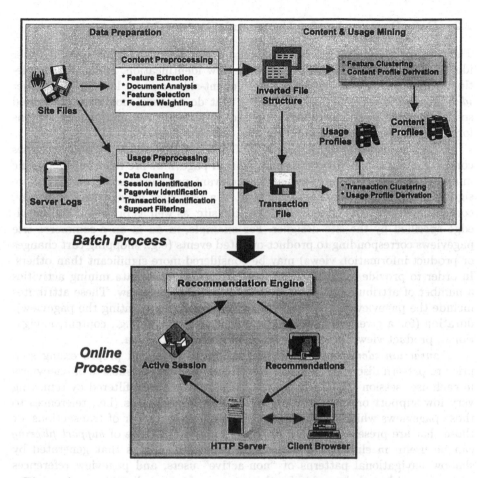

**Fig. 1.** A general framework for automatic personalization based on Web Mining

engine. The data preparation tasks result in aggregate structures containing the preprocessed usage and content data to be used in the mining stage. Usage mining tasks can involve the discovery of association rules, sequential patterns, pageview clusters, or transaction clusters, while content mining tasks may involve feature clustering (based on occurrence patterns of features in pageviews), pageview clustering based on content or meta-data attributes, or the discovery of (content-based) association rules among features or pageviews. In this paper, we focus on the derivation of usage profiles from transaction clusters, and the derivation of content profiles from feature clusters. In the online component of the system, the recommendation engine considers the active server session in conjunction with the discovered profiles to provide personalized content. The personalized content can take the form of recommended links or products, targeted advertisements, or text and graphics tailored to the user's perceived preferences as determined by the matching usage and content profiles.

## 2.2 Data Preparation for Usage and Content Mining

The required high-level tasks in usage data preprocessing are data cleaning, user identification, session identification, pageview identification, and path completion. The latter may be necessary due to client-side or proxy level caching. *User identification* is necessary for Web sites that do not use cookies or embedded session ids. We use the heuristics proposed in [3] to identify unique user sessions form anonymous usage data and to infer cached references.

*Pageview identification* is the task of determining which page file accesses contribute to a single browser display. Not all pageviews are relevant for specific mining tasks. Furthermore, among the relevant pageviews some may be more significant than others. The significance of a pageview may depend on usage, content and structural characteristics of the site, as well as prior domain knowledge specified by the site designer. For example, in an in an e-commerce site pageviews corresponding to product-oriented events (e.g., shopping cart changes or product information views) may be considered more significant than others. In order to provide a flexible framework for a variety of data mining activities a number of attributes must be recorded with each pageview. These attributes include the pageview id (normally a URL uniquely representing the pageview), duration (for a given user session), static pageview type (e.g., content, navigational, product view, index page, etc.), and other meta-data.

*Transaction identification* can be performed as a final preprocessing step prior to pattern discovery in order to focus on the relevant subsets of pageviews in each user session [3]. The transaction file can be further filtered by removing very low support or very high support pageview references (i.e., references to those pageviews which do not appear in a sufficient number of transactions, or those that are present in nearly all transactions). This type of *support filtering* can be useful in eliminating noise from the data, such as that generated by shallow navigational patterns of "non-active" users, and pageview references with minimal knowledge value for the purpose of personalization.

Usage preprocessing ultimately results in a set of $n$ pageview records appearing in the transaction file, $P = \{p_1, p_2, \cdots, p_n\}$, with each pageview record uniquely represented by its associated URL, and a set of $m$ user transactions, $T = \{t_1, t_2, \cdots, t_m\}$, where each $t_i \in T$ is a subset of $P$. To facilitate various data mining operations such as clustering, we view each transaction $t$ as an $n$-dimensional vector over the space of pageview references, i.e., $t = \langle w(p_1, t), w(p_2, t), \cdots, w(p_n, t) \rangle$, where $w(p_i, t)$ is a weight, in the transaction $t$, associated with the pageview represented by $p_i \in P$. The weights can be determined in a number of ways, for example, binary weights can be used to represent existence or non-existence of a product-purchase or a document access in the transaction. On the other hand, the weights can be a function of the duration of the associated pageview in order to capture the user's interest in a content page. The weights may also, in part, be based on domain-specific significance weights assigned by the analyst.

Content preprocessing involves the extraction of relevant features from text and meta-data. Meta-data extraction becomes particularly important when dealing with product-oriented pageviews or those involving non-textual content. In the current implementation of our framework features are extracted from meta-data embedded into files in the form of XML or HTML meta-tags, as well as from the textual content of pages. In order to use features in similarity computations, appropriate weights must be associated with them. For features extracted from meta-data, we assume that feature weights are provided as part of the domain knowledge specified by the site designer. For features extracted from text we use a standard function of the term frequency and inverse document frequency (tf.idf) for feature weights as commonly used in information retrieval [5, 15].

Specifically, each pageview $p$ is represented as a $k$-dimensional feature vector, where $k$ is the total number of extracted features from the site in a global dictionary. Each dimension in a feature vector represents the corresponding feature weight within the pageview. Thus, the feature vector for a pageview $p$ is given by: $p = \langle fw(p, f_1), fw(p, f_2), \cdots, fw(p, f_k) \rangle$ where $fw(p, f_j)$, is the weight of the $j$th feature in pageview $p \in P$, for $1 \leq j \leq k$. For features extracted from textual content of pages, the feature weight is obtained as the normalized tf.idf value for the term. Finally, in order to combine feature weights from meta-data (specified externally) and feature weights from text, proper normalization of those weights must be performed as part of preprocessing. The feature vectors obtained in this way are organized into an inverted file structure containing a dictionary of all extracted features and posting files for each feature specifying the pageviews in which the feature occurs along with its weight. Conceptually, this structure can be viewed as a feature-pageview matrix in which each column is a feature vector corresponding to a pageview.

## 2.3 Discovery of Aggregate Usage Profiles

The transaction file obtained in the data preparation stage can be used as the input to a variety of data mining algorithms. However, the discovery of patterns from usage data by itself is not sufficient for performing the personalization tasks. The critical step is the effective derivation of good quality and useful (i.e., actionable) "aggregate profiles" from these patterns. Ideally, a profile captures an aggregate view of the behavior of subsets of users based their common interests. In particular, aggregate profiles must be able to capture possibly overlapping interests of users, since many users have common interests up to a point (in their navigational history) beyond which their interests diverge. Furthermore, they should provide the capability to distinguish among pageviews in terms of their significance within the profile.

Based on these requirements, we have found that representing usage profiles as weighted collections of pageview records provides a great deal of flexibility. Each item in a usage profile is a URL representing a relevant pageview, and can have an associated weight representing its significance within the profile. The profiles can be viewed as ordered collections (if the goal is to capture the navigational path profiles followed by users [12]), or as unordered (if the focus is on capturing associations among specified content or product pages). This uniform representation allows for the recommendation engine to easily integrate different kinds of profiles (i.e., content and usage profiles, as well as multiple profiles based on different pageview types). Another advantage of this representation is that the profiles, themselves, can be viewed as pageview vectors, thus facilitating the task of matching a current user session with similar profiles using standard vector operations.

Given the mapping of user transactions into a multi-dimensional space as vectors of pageview, standard clustering algorithms, such as k-means, generally partition this space into groups of transactions that are close to each other based on a measure of distance or similarity. Such a clustering will result in a set $TC = \{c_1, c_2, \cdots, c_k\}$ of clusters, where each $c_i$ is a subset of the set of transactions $T$. Ideally, each cluster represents a group of users with similar navigational patterns. However, transaction clusters by themselves are not an effective means of capturing an aggregated view of common user profiles. Each transaction cluster may potentially contain thousands of user transactions involving hundreds of pageview references. Our ultimate goal in clustering user transactions is to reduce these clusters into weighted collections of pageviews which represent aggregate profiles.

An effective method for the derivation of profiles from transaction clusters was first proposed in [8]. For each transaction cluster $c \in TC$, we compute the mean vector $m_c$. The mean value for each pageview in the mean vector is computed by finding the ratio of the sum of the pageview weights across transactions in $c$ to the total number of transactions in the cluster. The weight of each pageview within a profile is a function of this quantity thus obtained. In generating the usage profiles, the weights are normalized so that the maximum weight in each usage profile is 1, and low-support pageviews (i.e. those with mean value below a certain threshold $\mu$) are filtered out. Thus, given a transaction cluster $c$, we construct a usage profile $pr_c$ as a set of pageview-weight pairs:

$$pr_c = \{\langle p, weight(p, pr_c)\rangle \mid p \in P, weight(p, pr_c) \geq \mu\}$$

where the significance weight, $weight(p, pr_c)$, of the pageview $p$ within the usage profile $pr_c$ is given by:

$$weight(p, pr_c) = \frac{1}{|c|} \cdot \sum_{t \in c} w(p, t)$$

and $w(p, t)$ is the weight of pageview $p$ in transaction $t \in c$. Each profile, in turn, can be represented as a vector in the original $n$-dimensional space.

## 2.4 Discovery of Content Profiles

We use precisely the same representation for content profiles (i.e., weighted collections of pageviews). In contrast to usage profiles, content profiles represent different ways pages with partly similar content may be grouped together. Our goal here is to capture common interests of users in a group of pages because specific portions of their contents are similar. Different groups of users may be interested in different segments of each page, thus content profiles must capture overlapping interests of users.

Clusters of pageviews obtained using standard clustering algorithms which partition the data are not appropriate as candidates for content profiles. To obtain content profiles, instead of clustering pageviews (as $k$-dimensional feature vectors, where $k$ is the number of extracted features in the global site dictionary), we cluster the features. Using the inverted feature-pageview matrix obtained in the content preprocessing stage, each feature can be viewed as an $n$-dimensional vector over the original space of pageviews. Thus, each dimension in the pageview vector for a feature is the weight associated with that feature in the corresponding pageview. We use multivariate k-means clustering technique to cluster these pageview vectors. Now, given a feature cluster $G$, we construct a content profile $C_G$ as a set of pageview-weight pairs:

$$C_G = \{\langle p, weight(p, C_G)\rangle \mid p \in P, \; weight(p, C_G) \geq \tau\}$$

where the significance weight, $weight(p, C_G)$, of the pageview $p$ within the content profile is obtained as follows:

$$weight(p, C_G) = \frac{\sum\limits_{f \in G} fw(p, f)}{\sum\limits_{i=1}^{n} \sum\limits_{f \in G} fw(p_i, f)}$$

and $fw(p, f)$ is the weight of a feature $f$ in pageview $p$. As in the case of usage profiles, we normalize pageview weights so that the maximum weight in each profile is 1, and we filter out pageviews whose weight is below a specified significance threshold, $\tau$. Note that the representation of content profiles as a set of pageview-weight pairs is identical to that for usage profiles discussed earlier. This uniform representation allows us to easily integrate both types of profiles with the recommendation engine.

## 3 Integrating Content and Usage Profiles for Personalization

The recommendation engine is the online component of a Web personalization system. The task of the recommendation engine is to compute a *recommendation set* for the current (active) user session, consisting the objects (links, ads, text, products, etc.) that most closely match the current user profile. The essential aspect of computing a recommendation set for a user is the matching of current user's activity against aggregate profiles. The recommended objects are added to the last page in the active session accessed by the user before that page is sent to the browser. Maintaining a history depth is important because most users navigate several paths leading to independent pieces of information within a session. In many cases these sub-sessions have a length of no more than 2 or

3 references. We capture the user history depth within a sliding window over the current session. The sliding window of size $n$ over the active session allows only the last $n$ visited pages to influence the recommendation value of items in the recommendation set. Finally, the structural characteristics of the site or prior domain knowledge can also be used to associate an additional measure of significance with each pageview in the user's active session.

In our proposed architecture, both content and usage profiles are represented as sets of pageview-weight pairs. This will allow for both the active session and the profiles to be treated as $n$-dimensional vectors over the space of pageviews in the site. Thus, given a content or a usage profile $C$, we can represent $C$ as a vector $C = \langle w_1^C, w_2^C, \cdots, w_n^C \rangle$, where

$$w_i^C = \begin{cases} weight(p_i, C), & \text{if } p_i \in C \\ 0, & \text{otherwise} \end{cases}$$

Similarly, the current active session $S$ is also represented as a vector $S = \langle s_1, s_2, ..., s_n \rangle$, where $s_i$ is a significance weight associated with the corresponding pageview reference, if the user has accessed $p_i$ in this session, and $s_i = 0$, otherwise. We can compute the profile matching score using a similarity function such as the normalized cosine measure for vectors:

$$match(S, C) = \frac{\sum\limits_k w_k^C \cdot S_k}{\sqrt{\sum\limits_k (S_k)^2 \times \sum\limits_k (w_k^C)^2}}.$$

Note that the matching score is normalized for the size of the clusters and the active session. This corresponds to the intuitive notion that we should see more of the user's active session before obtaining a better match with a larger profile. Given a profile $C$ and an active session $S$, a recommendation score, $Rec(S, p)$, is computed for each pageview $p$ in $C$ as follows:

$$Rec(S, p) = \sqrt{weight(p, C) \cdot match(S, C)}.$$

If the pageview $p$ is in the current active session, then its recommendation value is set to zero. We obtain the usage recommendation set, $UREC(S)$, for current active session $S$ by collecting from each usage profile all pageviews whose recommendation score satisfies a minimum recommendation threshold $\rho$, i.e.,

$$UREC(S) = \{w_i^C \mid C \in UP, \text{and } Rec(s, w_i^C) \geq \rho\},$$

where $UP$ is the collection of all usage profiles. Furthermore, for each pageview that is contributed by several usage profiles, we use its maximal recommendation score from all of the contributing profiles. In a similar manner, we can obtain the content recommendation set $CREC(S)$ from content profiles. Different methods can be used for combining the two recommendation sets depending on the goals of personalization and the requirements of the site. In our case, for each pageview we take the maximum recommendation value across the two recommendation sets. This allows, for example, content profiles to contribute to the recommendation set even if no matching usage profile is available and vice versa.

## 4 Experimental Results

We conducted a series of experiments with real usage data from the site for the newsletter of the *Association for Consumer Research* (from July 1998 to June 1999). The site contains a variety of news items, including President's columns, conference announcements, and call-for-papers for a number of conferences and journals. The usage preprocessing steps described earlier resulted in a user transaction file containing 18430 user transactions with a total of 62 pageviews represented uniquely by their associated URLs. The transaction clustering process yielded 16 transaction clusters representing different types of user access patterns. A threshold of 0.5 was used to derive usage profiles from transaction clusters (i.e., profiles contained only those pageviews appearing in at least 50% of transactions). In the content preprocessing stage, a total of 566 significant features were extracted with each document contributing at most 20 significant features to the global dictionary (normalized term frequency was used for measuring feature significance). Feature clustering using multivariate k-means resulted in 28 feature clusters from which the corresponding (overlapping) content profiles were derived.

Figure 2 depicts an example of two overlapping content profiles. The top significant features where listed for each document for illustrative purposes. These features indicated why each of the pageviews were included in each content profile. The first profile captures those documents in which a portion of the content relates to global and international business management and marketing. On the other hand, the second profile includes documents about consumer behavior and psychology in marketing. Note that documents which contain content related to both topics have been included in both profiles. Usage profiles are represented in the same manner, but they capture overlapping aggregate usage patterns of the site users.

| Weight | Pageview ID | Significant Features (stems) |
|--------|-------------|----------------------------|
| 1.00 | CFP: One World One Market | world challeng busi co manag global |
| 0.63 | CFP: Int'l Conf. on Marketing & Development | challeng co contact develop intern |
| 0.35 | CFP: Journal of Global Marketing | busi global |
| 0.32 | CFP: Journal of Consumer Psychology | busi manag global |
| Weight | Pageview ID | Significant Features (stems) |
| 1.00 | CFP: Journal of Psych. & Marketing | psychologi consum special market |
| 1.00 | CFP: Journal of Consumer Psychology I | psychologi journal consum special market |
| 0.72 | CFP: Journal of Global Marketing | journal special market |
| 0.61 | CFP: Journal of Consumer Psychology II | psychologi journal consum special |
| 0.50 | CFP: Society for Consumer Psychology | psychologi consum special |
| 0.50 | CFP: Conf. on Gender, Market., Consumer Behavior | journal consum market |

**Fig. 2.** Two Overlapping Content Profiles

The recommendation engine was used for a sample user session using a window size of 2. Figure 3 shows the system recommendations based only on usage profiles, while Figure 2 shows the results from only the content profiles. In these tables, the first column shows the pageviews contained in the current active session. The last pageview in each session window represents the current location of the user in the site. The right-hand column gives the recommendation score obtained using the techniques discussed in the previous section. It is clear from these examples that the combination of recommendations from both content and usage profiles can provide added value to the user. For example, in the usage-based recommendations, the user's visit to "ACR Board of Directors Meeting" did not yield any recommendations with a score above the specified threshold (0.5), while content-based recommendations produced some pages with related content. On the other hand, navigating to the page "Conference Update" resulted in content-based recommendations for pages with only general information and news about conferences, while usage profiles yielded a number of specific recommendations that the site users interested in conferences and calls for papers tend visit.

| Pages in Active Session Window | Recommendations | Score |
|---|---|---|
| * ACR Board of Directors Meeting | NO RECOMMENDATIONS | |
| * ACR Board of Directors Meeting | ACR 1999 Annual Conference | 0.57 |
| * Conference Update | CFP: ACR'99 Asia-Pacific Conf. | 0.53 |
| | CFP: Int'l Conf. on Marketing & Development | 0.52 |
| | CFP: ACR'99 European Conf. | 0.51 |
| | President's Column - December, 1998 | 0.50 |
| * Conference Update | ACR News Special Topics | 0.64 |
| * CFP: Journal of Psych. & Marketing | ACR 1999 Annual Conference | 0.57 |
| | CFP: Int'l Conf. on Marketing & Development | 0.53 |
| | CFP: ACR'99 European Conf. | 0.53 |
| | CFP: Winter 2000 SCP Conference | 0.52 |
| | CFP: Int'l Research Seminar in Marketing | 0.50 |
| * CFP: Journal of Psych. & Marketing | ACR News Special Topics | 0.59 |
| * CFP: Journal of Global Marketing | | |

**Fig. 3.** Recommendations Based on Usage Profiles

# 5 Conclusions and Future Work

We have presented a general framework for personalization based on usage and content mining, in which the user preference is automatically learned from Web usage data and integrated with domain knowledge and the site content. This has the potential of eliminating subjectivity from profile data as well as keeping it up-to-date. Furthermore, the integration of usage and content mining increases the usefulness and accuracy of the resulting recommendations. Our experimental results indicate that the techniques discussed here are promising, each with its own unique characteristics, and bear further investigation and development. Our future work in this area will include automatic classification of pageview

| Pages in Active Session Window | Recommendations | Score |
|---|---|---|
| * ACR Board of Directors Meeting | Special Topics - ACR Letters and Special Topics | 0.70 |
| | Special Topics - ACR Board of Directors Agenda | 0.55 |
| | Special Topics - ACR Appointments | 0.52 |
| * ACR Board of Directors Meeting | Call for Papers | 0.67 |
| * Conference Update | ACR News Updates | 0.54 |
| | ACR News Special Topics | 0.51 |
| * Conference Update | Call for Papers | 0.67 |
| * CFP: Journal of Psych. & Marketing | CFP: Journal of Consumer Psych. I | 0.59 |
| | CFP: Journal of Psych. & Marketing | 0.56 |
| | CFP: Journal of Consumer Psych. II | 0.51 |
| | CFP: Journal of Global Marketing | 0.50 |
| * CFP: Journal of Psych. & Marketing | CFP: Journal of Consumer Psych. I | 0.77 |
| * CFP: Journal of Global Marketing | CFP: Journal of Psych. & Marketing | 0.73 |
| | CFP: Journal of Consumer Psych. II | 0.59 |
| | CFP: Marketing & Public Policy Conf. | 0.56 |
| | CFP: Conf. on Gender, Marketing , Consumer Behavior | 0.54 |

**Fig. 4.** Recommendations Based on Content Profiles

types and better integration of a variety of pageview types (such as those representing different e-commerce or product-oriented events) into the mining and recommendation process.

# References

1. A. Buchner and M. D. Mulvenna. Discovering internet marketing intelligence through online analytical Web usage mining. *SIGMOD Record*, (4) 27, 1999.
2. R. Cooley, B. Mobasher, and J. Srivastava. Web mining: Information and pattern discovery on the world wide web. In *International Conference on Tools with Artificial Intelligence*, pages 558–567, Newport Beach, 1997. IEEE.
3. R. Cooley, B. Mobasher, and J. Srivastava. Data preparation for mining World Wide Web browsing patterns. *Journal of Knowledge and Information Systems*, (1) 1, 1999.
4. M. S. Chen, J. S. Park, and P. S. Yu. Data mining for path traversal patterns in a Web environment. In *Proceedings of 16th International Conference on Distributed Computing Systems*, 1996.
5. W. B. Frakes, R. Baeza-Yates. *Information Retrieval Data Structures and Algorithms*. Prentice Hall, Englewood Cliffs, NJ, 1992.
6. J. Herlocker, J. Konstan, A. Borchers, and J. Riedl. An algorithmic framework for performing collaborative filtering. In *Proceedings of the 1999 Conference on Research and Development in Information Retrieval*, August 1999.
7. B. Mobasher, R. Cooley, and J. Srivastava. Creating adaptive web sites through usage-based clustering of urls. In *IEEE Knowledge and Data Engineering Workshop (KDEX'99)*, November 1999.
8. B. Mobasher. A Web personalization engine based on user transaction clustering. In *Proceedings of the 9th Workshop on Information Technologies and Systems (WITS'99)*, December 1999.
9. O. Nasraoui, H. Frigui, A. Joshi, R. Krishnapuram. Mining Web access logs using relational competitive fuzzy clustering. In *Proceedings of the Eight International Fuzzy Systems Association World Congress*, August 1999.

10. M. O'Conner, J. Herlocker. Clustering items for collaborative filtering. In *Proceedings of the ACM SIGIR Workshop on Recommender Systems*, Berkeley, CA, 1999.
11. M. Perkowitz and O. Etzioni. Adaptive Web sites: automatically synthesizing Web pages. In *Proceedings of Fifteenth National Conference on Artificial Intelligence*, Madison, WI, 1998.
12. M. Spiliopoulou and L. C. Faulstich. WUM: A Web Utilization Miner. In *Proceedings of EDBT Workshop WebDB98*, Valencia, Spain, LNCS 1590, Springer Verlag, 1999.
13. J. Srivastava, R. Cooley, M. Deshpande, P-T. Tan. Web Usage Mining: Discovery and Applications of Usage Patterns from Web Data. *SIGKDD Explorations*, (1) 2, 2000.
14. S. Schechter, M. Krishnan, and M. D. Smith. Using path profiles to predict HTTP requests. In *Proceedings of 7th International World Wide Web Conference*, Brisbane, Australia, 1998.
15. G. Salton, M.J. McGill. *Introduction to Modern Information Retrieval*. McGraw-Hill, 1983.
16. U. Shardanand, P. Maes. Social information filtering: algorithms for automating "word of mouth." In *Proceedings of the ACM CHI Conference*, 1995.
17. C. Shahabi, A. Zarkesh, J. Adibi, and V. Shah. Knowledge discovery from users Web-page navigation. In *Proceedings of Workshop on Research Issues in Data Engineering*, Birmingham, England, 1997.
18. T. Yan, M. Jacobsen, H. Garcia-Molina, and U. Dayal. From user access patterns to dynamic hypertext linking. In *Proceedings of the 5th International World Wide Web Conference*, Paris, France, 1996.
19. K. Wu, P. S. Yu, and A. Ballman. Speedtracer: A web usage mining and analysis tool. *IBM Systems Journal*, 37(1), 1998.
20. O. R. Zaiane, M. Xin, and J. Han. Discovering web access patterns and trends by applying olap and data mining technology on web logs. In *Advances in Digital Libraries*, pages 19-29, Santa Barbara, CA, 1998.

# Extending Content-Based Recommendation by Order-Matching and Cross-Matching Methods

Yasuo Hirooka[1], Takao Terano[2], Yukichi Otsuka[3]

[1] NTT DATA Corp., Shinjyuku ParkTower 24F 3-7-1 Nishi-Shinjyuku
Shinjyuku-ku Tokyo 163-1024 Japan
hirookay@nttdata.co.jp
[2] University of Tsukuba, 3-29-1 Otsuka, Bunkyo-ku
Tokyo 112-0012, Japan
terano@gssm.otsuka.tsukuba.ac.jp
[3] Skysoft Inc., 2-7-24 Nihonbashi Chuo-ku Tokyo 103-0027 Japan
yotsuka@skysoft.co.jp

**Abstract.** We propose TwinFinder: a recommender system for an on-line bookstore. TwinFinder provides two recommendation methods, the Order-Matching Method (OMM) and the Cross-Matching Method (CMM). TwinFinder profiles a customer's interest based on his/her purchase history. Thus, it generates a vector of keywords from titles, authors, synopses, and categories of books purchased. OMM keeps this vector to each category the books belong to. Thus, OMM avoids recommending books that share only one or two keywords but belong to the categories in which the customer has no interest. When a customer has purchased several books that range over two or more categories, TwinFinder generates recommendations based on CMM. CMM looks for books in a category based on the keywords generated from the purchased books in other categories. Thus, TwinFinder can generate rather useful and surprising recommendations by OMM and CMM. We have implemented and validated TwinFinder in the e-business system of a bookstore in Japan.

## 1   Introduction

The rapid spreading of the Internet has made it easy for a firm to develop a new style of e-business via One-To-One Marketing. One of the issues required to establish good relations between a firm and its customers is how to provide appropriate information which matches the implicit and/or explicit needs of customers. This requires automated recommender systems.

As for the on-line book market, on-line bookstores deal with a tremendous number of books, however each customer buys only a few of them. Customers usually use some search methods to find which books to purchase from a huge database of books. However, conventional search methods are convenient only when they know the exact title or ISBN of the books to be purchased. They have very little chance to come across un-thought of and/or unexpected books while searching in a database at an on-line bookstore, though it often happens that we are able to find surprisingly good books in a real bookstore. It is ironic that to come across un-thought of books is difficult in an on-line bookstore because so many books are provided. Therefore, it is important to provide customers with information about books that they desire to purchase by using their purchase histories and a database of books.

In Japan, the foreign (Non-Japanese-language) book market is so small that there are only a few real bookstores, which deal with foreign-books. Therefore, it is more important for on-line bookstores to provide information about their books, because Japanese customers hardly ever take a book in hand when deciding to purchase it or not. Furthermore, the number of Japanese customers in the foreign-book market is relatively small when compared to the number of foreign-books thereby limiting the effectiveness of recommendations based on conventional collaborative filtering techniques.

TwinFinder is a recommender system for an on-line bookstore in Japan. It generates recommendations based on customers' purchase histories and the book information in the databases. We consider that TwinFinder has to have two important characteristics. First, it can generate unexpected and/or un-thought of recommendations to customers. Second, it can work well even when the number of customers is small. We use a content-based recommendation technique and propose an Order-Matching Method (OMM) and a Cross-Matching Method (CMM) to improve it. TwinFinder can generate rather useful and surprising recommendations by OMM and CMM. We have implemented TwinFinder at Skysoft[1]: an on-line foreign-book store in Japan. To validate TwinFinder in the practical environment, we have conducted controlled experiments on the system to apply it to real customers. The results have suggested that our approach is very effective.

This paper is organized as follows: In section 2, we discuss the current issues of recommendation systems. In section 3, we explain the architecture of TwinFinder. In section 4, we describe the experimental setup, the results, and discussions. In section 5, we give some concluding remarks and future work.

## 2 Issues on Recommender Systems

We can find comprehensive surveys on recommender systems in CACM [1,2,5,6,10,12,15], most of which are concerned with social processes of recommendation activities among customers. They have reported (1) roles of volunteers to make recommendation information and receivers of them, (2) cost structures and tradeoffs between good and bad recommendations provided, (3) personal privacy problems when generating recommendations, (4) the qualities of recommendations when so many attendees exist in the target domain (e.g., "vote early and often phenomena"), and (5) business models to develop and maintain recommender systems. Although these issues must be discussed further in detail, in this paper, we will focus on the technical side. In the technical side, there are mainly three kinds of methods in a recommender system: Contents-Based Recommendation, Collaborative-Filtering Recommendation and Hybrid Recommendation.

---

[1] http://www.skysoft.co.jp

## 2.1 Content-Based Recommendation

Conventional Content-Based Recommendation generates recommendations based on a comparison between the representations of content's features and user profiles. A user profile is built up by analyzing accumulated user rating content based on past purchasing behavior. In this method, the techniques of Information Retrieval (IR) are used for content analysis. For example, TFIDF (term frequency times inverse document frequency) [13], a vector space model [13] are often used. Examples of Content-Based Recommendation are found in the systems: InfoFinder[7], NewsWeeder[8] and Syskill & Webert[3].

Two shortcomings of this method are pointed out [2].

- The kind of content depends on the content analysis techniques. At present, it is restricted to the text document to which Information Retrieval techniques are applicable.
- A Content-Based Recommendation system tends to generate over-specialized recommendation. The information provided with users is restricted to the contents which is similar to those already rated.

## 2.2 Collaborative-Filtering Recommendation

Collaborative-Filtering Recommendation is another approach different from Content-Based Recommendation. This method recommends items which other similar users liked, rather than recommend items, which are similar to items a user has rated in past behavior. Thus, in this method, we analyze ratings of items by users to classify the users into groups, so that users in a group share similar interests. Then, a user is recommended items, which his/her similar users have rated highly and he/she has not seen before.

Examples of Collaborative-filtering recommendation are found in the systems: GroupLens[11] and Firefly[14].

This method deals with all kinds of content, because the system need not analyze content to generate recommendation. On the other side, the shortcomings are summarized in the following [2];

- We need to have a large enough number of users and rating information compared with the number of items. When the number of users is small, recommended items will be limited.
- If we have a new item, which we want to recommend, there is no way to recommend it until a user rates it.

## 2.3 Hybrid Recommendation

Hybrid Recommendation[2] combines the techniques of Content-Based Recommendation and Collaborative-Filtering Recommendation to incorporate the advantages of both. In this method, a user is recommended items, which his/her similar users have rated highly, based on the techniques of Collaborative-Filtering.

The similarities between users are based on comparisons between user profiles, which are generated by analyzing content.

# 3 TwinFinder System

## 3.1 Advantages of TwinFinder

Both Content-Based Recommendation and Collaborative-Filtering Recommendation could be applied for recommendation services on a bookstore. However, the shortcomings of both methods pointed in 2.1 and 2.2 suggest that the following problems must be coped with.

- In Content-Based Recommendation, customers are restricted to seeing recommended books similar to the ones they have purchased.
- In Collaborative-Filtering Recommendation, a large number of books will require a large number of customers to make recommendations; otherwise, high quality recommendations cannot be expected.

As we will discuss later in the following sections, TwinFinder basically uses Content-Based Recommendation. However, in order to avoid over-specialized recommendations, initial information gathering of customers, and free riding problems, we will improve conventional Content-Based Recommendation. In the foreign book store domain, we are required to provide high quality recommendation services even when the number of customers is small compared with the number of books.

## 3.2 Process of TwinFinder to generate recommendation

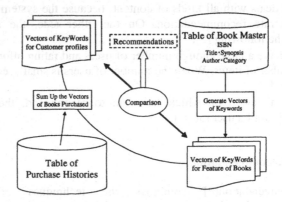

**Fig. 3.1** Basic process to generate recommendations on the TwinFinder system

Generally, as for Content-Based Recommendation focusing on text documents, we use a vector of keywords to represent a customer's profile, which alternates customers' interests and feature of books. TwinFinder also follows the process. First, TwinFinder generates a vector of keywords for customer profiles based on a customer's purchase history and information of books. Then, it computes similarities between the customer profile and feature of books, and it also recommends books, which have a high level of similarity.

## 3.3 Generating customer profiles

### 3.3.1 Utilizing book categories information

In Skysoft, they classify books into 49 categories such as Art, Business and Economics, Cooking, Computers, and so on, according to BISAC [2] Subject Categories. Each category has sub-categories. The total number of sub-categories is 3700. Fig. 3.2 shows that the more books the customers purchase, the more the number of categories increases. Thus, the range of customer's interest with many books becomes very broad. This is different from the case of conventional information retrieval problems in a library context.

In the case of a customer who has an interest in several categories, it is easy to imagine that he or she uses different keywords to search in different book categories. Thus, when we generate a customer profile, which represents the customer's interests, we must generate several sets of keywords for each category that the customer has interests.

In TwinFinder, we assume that one book category represents one of the customer's interests. Therefore, we decide to generate the customer profile from several vectors whose elements contain keywords used in each book category.

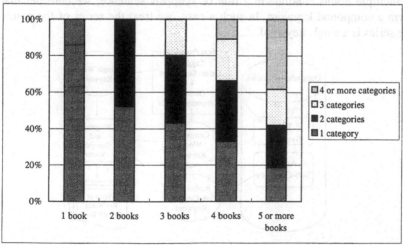

**Fig. 3.2** The number of categories to which purchased books belong by the total number of purchased books

---

[2] The acronym of Book Industry Systems Advisory Committee

### 3.3.2 Utilizing keywords vector

In TwinFinder, we generate a vector of keywords from titles, authors, synopses, and sub-categories of books purchased. Fig. 3.3 shows the process to generate vectors of keywords for a customer profile. First, the system generates a vector of keywords for each book purchased by a customer. Then, it generates vectors of keywords for the customer profile by summing up vectors of keywords in each category to which books purchased belong.

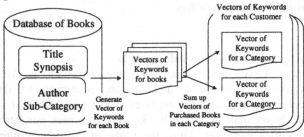

**Fig. 3.3** Process to generate customer profile from vectors of keyword for books

Fig. 3.4 shows the process to generate a vector of keywords for each book. We decompose titles and synopses into separated keywords as follows:

- Tag each word in the title and synopsis word category. For this purpose, we use Brill's English tagger[4].
- To delete stop words, use the information of the word category and a stop word list.
- We adopt remaining words as single word keywords.
- If multiple nouns continue in a title or synopsis sentence, we consider that they form a compound keyword. In such a case, we treat the series of the nouns as if the series is a single keyword.

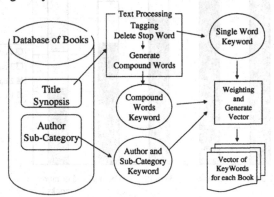

**Fig. 3.4** The process to generate a vector of keywords for each book

Then, we give weights to keywords, which consist of single words, compound words, authors, and sub-categories. We use TFIDF(term frequency times inverse document frequency)[13] as a keyword weighting method.

Let $f_{ij}$ be the frequency of a keyword $t_j$ in a book $d_i$, $n_j$ denote the number of books which contain keyword $t_j$, and $N$ denotes the number of all books in a corpus. $k$ is a weight parameter for each kind of keyword. We set the parameter $k=2$ for sub-category keywords and $k=1$ for the others. We define $TF_{ij}$ as

$$TF_{ij} = \log_2(f_{ij} \cdot k + 1) . \tag{1}$$

We define $IDF_j$ as

$$IDF_j = \log_2(N/n_j) . \tag{2}$$

Thus, the weight $w_{ij}$ of keyword $t_j$ in a book $d_i$ is represented by equation (1) and (2) as

$$w_{ij} = TF_{ij} \times IDF_j = \log_2(f_{ij} \cdot k + 1) \cdot \log_2(N/n_j) . \tag{3}$$

A vector of keywords for each customer is the sum of vectors of keywords for books purchased. We define weight $w'_{jkl}$ of keyword $t_j$ for a category $C_l$ and customer $U_k$ as

$$w'_{jkl} = \sum_i (w_{ij} \cdot b_{ik} \cdot s_{il}) , \tag{4}$$

where $b_{ik}=1$, if a customer $U_k$ has purchased a book $d_i$, otherwise $b_{ik}=0$, and $s_{il}=1$, if a book $d_i$ belongs to a category $C_l$., otherwise we set $s_{il}=0$.

### 3.3.3 Measuring similarities among books and customers

To generate recommendation, TwinFinder compares the customer profile with the feature of books. Recommend rating $r_{ikl}$ of a book $d_i$ for a customer $U_k$ in a category $C_l$ is computed by using the cosine vector formula and equations (3) and (4) as follows:

$$r_{ikl} = \frac{\sum w_{ij} w'_{jkl}}{\sqrt{\sum w_{ij}^2} \sqrt{\sum w'_{jkl}^2}} \qquad (0 \le r_{ikl} \le 1) . \tag{5}$$

## 3.4 Order-Matching Method

In 3.3.2, we have described how TwinFinder generates vectors of keywords for a customer profile in each category to which books purchased belong. Fig. 3.5 shows how to use these vectors to generate recommendations on the Order-Matching Method (OMM). OMM compares a customer's vector for one category with vectors of books in the same category. Thus, OMM avoids recommending books that share only one or two keywords, but belong to the categories in which a customer has no interest.

For example, suppose a customer who has purchased some books about 'cake' and 'cookie' in the category of *cooking*. OMM uses the key word: 'cake' and 'cookie' to search books in the category of *cooking* to recommend books, which mainly refer to 'cake' and 'cookie'. OMM avoids recommending books such as "Mrs. Jeffries Takes the Cake" in the category of fiction, "Cookies"[3] that refers to web programming in the category of computers, and so on.

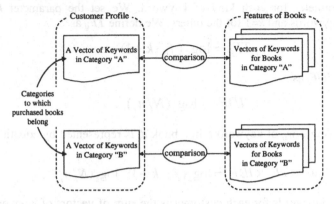

**Fig. 3.5** How to use vectors to generate recommendations on Order-Matching Method

## 3.5 Cross-Matching Method

The Cross-Matching Method (CMM) aims to avoid generating over-specialized recommendations. Fig. 3.6 shows how to use vectors of keywords to generate recommendations with the CMM. CMM compares a customer's vector for one category with vectors of books that are in the other categories but belong to the categories in which the customer has purchased books in past.

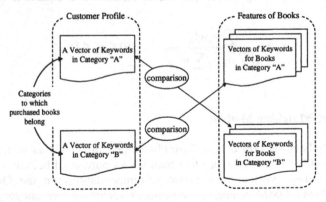

**Fig. 3.6** How to use vectors to generate recommendations on the Cross-Matching Method

We give a simple example to clarify this idea. Suppose a customer who has purchased some books on Star Trek in the category of *fiction* and some books in the

---

[3] "Cookie" is one of web programming techniques to make functional web pages.

category of *cooking*. CMM uses the key word: "Star Trek" to search books in the category of *cooking* to recommend "Star Trek Cookbook" that is indeed in print. Thus, CMM can link two interests of a customer with each other. Then, we expect CMM will give customers rather surprising and unexpected impressions.

## 4 Experiments of TwinFinder System

### 4.1 Experimental setup

We have implemented an experimental recommendation system for Skysoft bookstore: an on-line foreign-book store in Japan, and have conducted experiments from the December of 1999 to January of 2000 (see Fig. 4.1). Our purpose of this series of the experiments is to validate the performance of TwinFinder being able to generate rather useful, surprising and un-thought of recommendations.

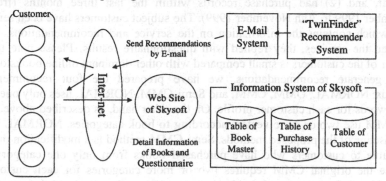

Fig. 4.1 Outline of experimental recommendation service in the e-business system of Skysoft

The experimental recommend services are summarized as follows.
1. TwinFinder displays recommended books for each customer by analyzing book information, customers' information, and customers' purchase histories in the database of Skysoft.
2. We provide each customer with information about recommended books by e-mail two times. The e-mail service is a good way of the experiments, because we are required to develop push-type services in operation. At the first time, the best three books generated by the Normal matching method are recommended. At the second time, the best eight books are recommended. The four books are generated by OMM and the other four books are generated by CMM. For the customers to whom we cannot apply CMM because the purchased books are only in one category, the recommendations are generated by Semi-CMM. These e-mails contain the title, author, synopsis, price, publishing date, binding, and links to not only each book's web page but also a corresponding questionnaire about this service.

3. Customers can click and jump to the web pages, and easily to get more information about the book, and, of course, he or she can purchase it.

**Table 4.1** Statistics of Expriments

| | |
|---|---|
| the number of subject customers | 396 |
| the number of recommendations sent | 2 recommendation mails per customer |
| the number of responses | 1st: 185    2nd:150 |
| Recommendation methods | NORMAL, OMM, CMM, Semi-CMM |
| the number of evaluations for each recommendation method | NORMAL:503, OMM:633, CMM:319, Semi-CMM:228 |

Table 4.1 shows the summary of our experiment statistics. We have selected 396 real customers to offer this service, who have (1) accepted to receive e-mails from SkySoft, and (2) had purchase records within the last three months (from 1st September 1999 to 30th November 1999). The subject customers have been sent an e-mail, which contains the information on the service and recommendations. If they accepted the services, they replied with questionnaire results. Please note that the number of the customers is small compared with other dominant online bookstore.

To generate recommendations, we have prepared the four recommendation methods: NORMAL, OMM, CMM, and Semi-CMM. NORMAL uses only one vector of keywords for each customer profile. On the other hand, as described above, OMM and CMM use two or more vectors according to book categories. NORMAL is used as a baseline of the proposed methods. Semi-CMM method is a modification of CMM applicable to customers who have purchased books from only one category. It is because the original CMM requires two or more categories for each customer to which his or her purchased books belong. We used customers' information of interested categories in the database, which had been registered when they subscribed to Skysoft.

We have conducted survey studies twice using questionnaire forms on the web. For each experiment, 185 and 150 among 396 subject customers replied to the first and second questionnaires respectively.

## 4.2  Experimental Results and Discussion

Fig. 4.2 shows the frequency distribution of the rating points of usefulness to our recommendation service. Customers evaluated the usefulness on a five point rating; poor, not-useful, fair, useful, and excellent. The first experiments have shown that 87% of the subject customers chose 'excellent' or 'useful'. The result clearly states that customers have strong needs for information about foreign-books and our recommendation service is desirable.

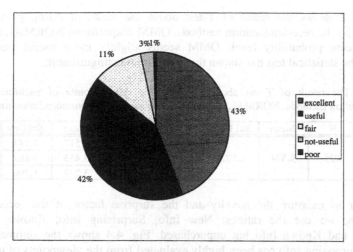

**Fig. 4.2** The frequency distribution of the rating points of usefulness to our recommendation service

Fig. 4.3 shows the frequency distribution of rating points of the usefulness to each recommended information by the recommendation methods. Subject customers have evaluated the usefulness on a five point rating; poor, not-useful, fair, useful, and excellent. NORMAL is used as a baseline of them. OMM, CMM, and Semi-CMM have clearly outperformed NORMAL at the rate 'excellent'. Fig. 4.3 has suggested that OMM and CMM have recommended less irrelevant recommendations compared with NORMAL ones at the rate of 'poor'. Semi-CMM has shown that is the worst one at the rate of 'poor', however, free verbal comments given by the subjects have revealed that the initial profiles by the customers are often irrelevant, because they have not believed that the information will be used for the recommendation.

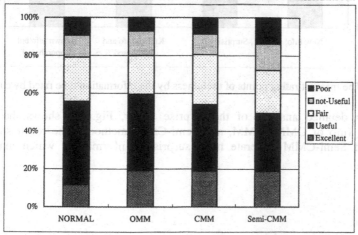

**Fig. 4.3** The frequency distribution of rating points of the usefulness to each recommended information by the recommendation methods

Table 4.2 shows the result of T-test about the mean of rating points of the usefulness by the recommendation methods. OMM outperforms NORMAL at 95% of the significant probability level. OMM seems slightly more useful than CMM, however, the statistical test has shown that they are indistinguishable.

**Table 4.2** The result of T-test about the mean of rating points of usefulness by the recommendation methods. NORMAL is used as a baseline of the recommendation methods.

| Method | N | Mean | Std Dev | Method | N | Mean | Std Dev | Prob>|T| |
|---|---|---|---|---|---|---|---|---|
| | | | | OMM | 619 | 3.517 | 1.147 | 0.037 |
| NORMAL | 495 | 3.374 | 1.122 | CMM | 319 | 3.455 | 1.167 | 0.324 |
| | | | | Semi-CMM | 228 | 3.272 | 1.296 | 0.307 |

In order to measure the novelty and the surprise factor of the recommended information, we use the ratings: New Info, Surprising Info, Known Info and purchased, and Known Info but unpurchased. Fig. 4.4 shows the summary of the answers. Surprising Info has been highly evaluated from the viewpoints of usefulness of the recommendations.

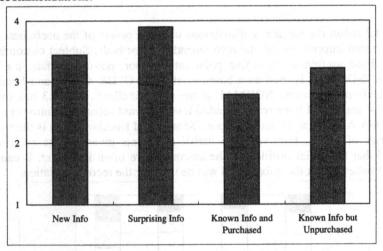

**Fig. 4.4** The mean of rating points of usefulness by the information type rated by customers

For the detailed analysis of the surprise factor, Fig. 4.5 shows the ratio of Surprising Info of OMM, CMM, and Semi-CMM methods. The result shows that CMM and Semi-CMM generate more surprising information, which may attract customers.

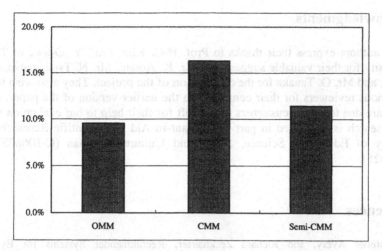

**Fig. 4.5** The ratio of Surprising Info of OMM, CMM, and Semi-CMM methods

# 5. Concluding Remarks

This paper has proposed TwinFinder: a novel content-based recommendation system and has described the experimental results as tested on Skysoft an on-line bookstore. The assumption we made in order to implement the recommendation system is that the quality improvement of recommendation services requires the facility to give both surprising and interesting information to enhance the categories of book selection of the intended users. TwinFinder has been developed based on that assumption and will be a new method to achieve the objective.

The experiments in a real environment have suggested that

1. The system is useful even if there are very small number of users compared with the large number of service items;
2. The OMM (Order-Matching Method) designed to enhance the accuracy of the recommendation has outperformed conventional content-based recommendation methods from the viewpoint of the usefulness of the recommended information;
3. The CMM (Cross-Matching Method) designed to link multiple kinds of interests of users has provided surprising and unexpected information with the customers.

During the experiments, Skysoft reported that 41 books were been sold. When considering the volume of sales at Skysoft, the number is relatively significant. Currently, we have a plan to put TwinFinder into operational use. We are also developing a hybrid type recommendation system for a purpose, which will couple with both of the Content-Based and Collaborative-Filtering type recommendation methods into the architecture of TwinFinder. The results will be reported elsewhere. However, there remain some problems to include Collaborative-Filtering recommendation methods into our system. We must further develop new such methods that are applicable when the number of customers is small. The future work includes the development of fine-tuning methods of the proposed matching algorithms to meet the marketing requirements in general e-commerce environments.

## Acknowledgments

The authors express their thanks to Prof. H.C. Kim, Prof. Y. Osawa of Tsukuba University for their valuable suggestions, Mr. K. Aotani, Mr. N. Tsunematsu, Mr. M. Santou, and Mr. O. Tanaka for the cooperation of the project. They also wish to thank anonymous reviewers for their comments to the earlier version of the paper. Special thanks are due to all the customers of Skysoft for their help to our evaluation studies. This research is supported in part by a Grant-in-Aid for Scientific Research of the Ministry of Education, Science, Sports and Culture of Japan (C-10680370 and 11792025).

## References

1. Christpher Avery, and Richard Zeckhauser, Recommender Systems for Evaluating Computer Messages. *Commnications of the ACM*, 1997, Vol. 40, No.3, pp. 88-89
2. Marko Balabanovic, and Yoav Shoham, Content-Based, Collaborative Recommendation., *Commnications of the ACM*, 1997, Vol. 40, No.3, pp. 66-72
3. D. Billsus, and M. Pazzani, Revising user profiles: The search for interesting Web sites., *Proceedings of the Third International Workshop on Multistrategy Learning* (MSL '96), 1996
4. Eric Brill, Rule Based Tagger, *http://www.cs.jhu.edu/~brill/home.html*, 2000
5. Henry Kauts, Bart Selman, and Mehul Shah, Conbining Social Networks and Collaborative Filtering. *Commnications of the ACM*, 1997, Vol. 40, No.3, pp. 63-65
6. Joseph A. Konstan, Applying Collaborative Filtering to Usenet News. *Commnications of the ACM*, 1997, Vol. 40, No.3, pp. 77-87
7. Krulwich, B., and Burkey, C., Learning user information interests through extraction of semantically significant phrases. *Proceedings of the AAAI Spring Symposium on Machine Learning in Information Access*, 1996
8. Lang, K., Newsweeder: Learning to filter netnews. *Proceedings of the 12th International Conference on Machine Learning,*1995,
9. Luhn, H.P., A Statistical Approach to Mechanized Encoding and Searching of Literary Information. *IBM Journal of Research & Development*, 1957, Vol.1, No. 4, pp. 309-317
10.Paul Resnick and Hal R. Varian, Recommender Systems. *Commnications of the ACM*, 1997, Vol. 40, No.3, pp. 56-58
11.Paul Resnick, Neophytos Iacovou, Mitesh Suchak, et al., GroupLens: An Open Architecture for Collaborative Filtering of Netnews. *Proceedings of the Conference on Computer Supported Cooperative Work*, 1994, pp. 175-186
12.James Rucker and Marcos J.Polanco,Personalized Navigation for the Web. *Commnications of the ACM*, 1997, Vol. 40, No.3, pp. 73-76
13.G. Salton and C. Buckley, Term-weighting approaches in automatic text retrieval., *Information Processing and Management*, 1988, Vol.14, No.5, pp. 513-523
14.Shardanand, U. and P. Maes, Social Information Filtering: Algorithms for Automating 'Word of Mouth'. *Proceedings of the CHI-95* (ACM Press), 1995
15.Loren Terveen, Will Hill, Brian Amento, David McDonald, and Josh Creter, *A System for Sharing Recommendations. Commnications of the ACM*, 1997, Vol. 40, No.3, pp. 59-62

# Global and Local in Electronic Commerce

# (invited talk)

Paul Timmers

paul.timmers@ccc.eu.int
European Commission, Directorate-General Information Society

**Abstract.** The question whether electronic commerce is most successfully applied globally or instead is best suited for local application is gradually becoming more articulated. The analysis is more firmly founded in commercial reality with the growing take-up of electronic commerce. The question gets broken down into many more issues of interest. This paper addresses some of these current issues related to "global and local in electronic commerce' such as the types of global e-markets, barriers to globalization in electronic commerce, and successful global e-commerce business models.

## 1    Issue Definition: Global and Local in e-Commerce

The 'global versus local' question is being debated since a few years in the electronic commerce research community [1]. The central issue has been for a while whether e-commerce is intrinsically global, following the logic of the global nature of the Internet, or whether the largest impact and benefits of electronic commerce would manifest itself through local use of the Internet for business. As it is still early days for electronic commerce in many parts of the world, this question has not yet been answered decisively since evidence is anecdotal rather than systematic. The examples given in the literature tended to illustrate that after a first wave of global approaches many successful local uses of e-commerce were emerging. The question was also addressed from the point of view of regional development, amongst others at the 1999 European Commission / Tekes Information Society Technologies Conference [2].

Recently the debate has moved on stimulated by the rapid growth of e-commerce worldwide and especially by of the emergence of large business-to-business e-marketplaces. These marketplaces and exchanges are typically being created by international alliances of purchasers within industry sectors such as automotive, retail, aerospace, chemicals, agriculture, etc.[1] They also emerge across industry sectors such as in MRO and generic services purchasing in which case they are more likely

---

[1] B2B marketplaces such as AutoXChange, GlobalNetXchange, and others; if they realize their turnover, these widely publicized marketplaces alone will transact in the order of €500-1000 billion in a few years time.

operated by a third party[2]. It is predicted that many more of such marketplaces will arise, in virtually every industry sector[3]. These marketplaces seem naturally best placed to become global electronic trading environments. Questions then arise about the opportunities for growing such e-markets globally and about barriers and marketing strategies. This has been the subject of debate amongst others at the recent CommerceNet B2B Big Bang Conference series [3].

An additional factor in the debate has been the huge market capitalization of Internet companies. This gives these 'dotcoms' the financial basis to execute a business strategy of global presence through acquisitions and mergers or through investing in global branding and global delivery infrastructure.

Finally, the debate is also moving to a macro-economic level, in terms of e-commerce as a factor in global competitiveness. The European Union's March 2000 Lisbon Summit was focused on accelerating the European Union's participation in the digital economy and improving the EU's potential to shape that new economy vis-à-vis the United States.

Therefore the global – local issue has stayed center stage while becoming more articulated and less academic and more based on actual business reality.

To summarize, some of the questions at this stage of the debate are about:

Barriers to global e-commerce
Marketing strategies to go global
Types of global e-markets
Global e-commerce business models

As well as:

Impact of e-commerce on global competitiveness
First-mover advantage of countries and regions
E-commerce and global trade flows
Role of governments in global e-commerce.
Changes in structure of global industries
Global presence based on regional development.

In this paper the first set of questions will be addressed, by providing an overview of barriers to go global in e-commerce and relevant marketing strategies, followed by a typology of global e-markets, and concluded by an assessment of how such barriers are addressed in the wider context of business models. Answering the other, equally interesting, questions will be deferred to a further paper.

---

[2] Examples are TradeZone and Barclays B2B.
[3] Gartner Group estimated that there will be 3000 B2B marketplaces and exchanges within a few years.

# 2 Barriers to Global e-Markets

There are several barriers to creating global e-markets and global business models such as:

- Inadequate global delivery and fulfillment systems
- Differences in culture, language, commercial practice
- Fragmentation in the industry
- Incomplete global legal and self-regulatory framework
- Barriers specific to small companies.

These barriers are addressed in some more detail below.

**Inadequate global delivery and fulfillment systems**
A (limited) survey by Forrester Research in the USA in 1999 revealed that 85% of respondents did not fulfill orders internationally because of complications with customs, tax, shipping, etc [4]. The main barrier expected for 2001 by respondents was in global distribution. The difficulty of handling smaller package delivery and returns were other factors identified as a barrier. Likewise surveys in the European Union point to the complications of international shipping and fragmentation of cross-country logistics as an important remaining barrier to global e-commerce. Large transport, logistics, and postal operators see a natural business opportunity in providing seamless delivery across borders, enriched by value-added services such as identification, clearance etc. Smaller operators in the transport and logistics sector consider to team up by interconnecting their systems. An example of the latter, with a focus on the impact of business process organization, is the EU TRANS2000 project [5].

**Differences in culture, language, commercial practice**
Differences in culture and language remain significant barriers to the globalization of e-markets. This also includes differences in business culture and commercial practice. Sometimes such differences are founded in different legal systems. Global e-markets in legal services for example will not easily be created, except for niche areas like international legal practice for large corporates. To bridge culture, language, and commercial practice differences a role remains for trading intermediaries such as banks, trading companies, international supply chain managers, chambers of commerce, etc. Support is provided by harmonization of trade terms and international trade contracts, for example as undertaken by the UN and the International Chambers of Commerce. However, technology can lend a helping hand too, for example to support negotiation in a situation of diversity of business practice, cf. the EU MEMO, COBRA and COSMOS projects.

**Fragmentation in the industry**
Fragmentation in the industry is another barrier to creating global e-markets. Where the industry is split up in many small companies it may be particularly hard to achieve

economy of scale to create a global e-market, even if the underlying product-market is potentially global. The Internet and e-markets may create additional pressure to consolidate fragmented industries such as in retail financial services or insurance or travel and tourism.

## Incomplete global legal and self-regulatory framework

Differences in law and self-regulatory schemes across the world form another barrier to going global. Over the past years significant progress has been achieved in adapting legal frameworks to the reality of electronic commerce and in developing self-regulation such as codes of conduct and trust marks. The development of these has been conditioned by discussions and guidelines from international bodies such as the WTO, UN, OECD and GBDe. However, often laws and codes of conduct have a single-country focus rather than being multi-country, let alone that they have global applicability. The exception to this is the European Union, which could build upon the common Internal Market framework and therefore has managed to rapidly put a 15-country framework for electronic commerce in place [6]. Another multi-country approach is the common management of domain names by ICANN. Efforts are underway in the aforementioned international bodies to lift national and regional frameworks to the global level and to bridge gaps amongst others by alternative (that is, out-of-court) means of arbitration and mediation of disputes, a priority in the recent eEurope initiative of the European Union[4].

## Barriers specific to small companies

Finally, small companies experience specific barriers to either participate in or set up global e-markets. Clearly resources matter, in terms of capital and personnel. For small companies also lack of brand visibility is another obstacle. And in particular when the business model is that of a marketplace operator it is the number and quality of business relationships that is key. Small companies therefore choose specific strategies to *set up* global e-markets, such as leveraging strategic partnerships, offering sharing arrangements like franchising and affiliate schemes (cf TradeZone), focusing on niche markets (cf Schelfhout), and cooperation with other small companies (e.g. setting up common export-promotion Website as in the furniture sector in Spain). As individual *participants* to global e-markets small companies may face a hard task since at the initial phase of such e-markets especially price transparency will increase rather than transparency of product characteristics in general, such as quality, delivery time, service level, knowledge of the business, etc. Current e-markets are not good at making visible non-price attributes. This may at least initially narrow the base for small companies to compete on. However, this is at this stage a hypothesis, which would be interesting to see validated by empirical research.

A practical example that illustrates most of these barriers to globalization of e-markets is online health services, as recently analyzed by the Economist [7]. Several challenges were listed to deliver such services internationally e.g. from a US base into

---

[4] eEurope initiative is a major political initiative to promote the Information Society for all in the European Union, http://europa.eu.int/comm/information_society/eeurope/index_en.htm.

the European market, or between EU countries, including culture (ethics), different medical practices, different regulations for selling drugs online and advertising, as well as fragmentation in the health and insurance industry.

# 3   Marketing strategies

Companies that wish to pursue global e-commerce will exploit their assets globally in view of the business opportunity and at the same time need to overcome the barriers in the business environment mentioned above, where these occur in their business, as well as address its own internal weaknesses. Marketing strategies to go global in e-commerce have been listed in the 1999 World Markets Research Centre Business Report on electronic commerce and in 'Electronic Commerce' by Timmers [8]:

1. Addressing a global product-market;
2. Being part of a global supply-chain;
3. Offering multiple language support;
4. Setting up global networked franchising;
5. Complementing global physical presence with Internet presence;

To which can be added:

6. Building global presence through mergers and acquisitions.

Each of these strategies may be relevant to the barriers in the business environment, as summarized in Table 1 and brief explained below.

Table 1 Barriers and Marketing Strategies

| Barrier→<br><br>Strategy↓ | Global fulfillment | Culture / language | Industry fragmentation | Legal / self-regulatory | Small companies |
|---|---|---|---|---|---|
| Global product-market | + | n.a. | + | + | + |
| Global supply-chain | + | n.a. | + | - | + |
| Multi-lingual support | - | + | - | - | - |
| Global franchising | + | + | + | + | + |
| Physical + virtual presence | + | + | n.a. | + | - |

Legend: + : the strategy is relevant to overcome the barrier; - : the strategy does not help to overcome the barrier; n.a. : the barrier is not present.

If the strategy is to focus on a global product-market, barriers to be surmounted are more likely to be of an operational nature such as in organizing global delivery. An approach to this may be subcontracting. If products and services can be delivered online, e.g. software or news for professionals, global fulfillment is a non-issue. Barriers may also be in differences in legal/self-regulatory frameworks between countries. For instance, selling technical books online means dealing with a global product-market where issues to be resolved are global small package shipping and taxation/customs differences. Addressing a global product-market may also be an adequate marketing strategy for small companies in case they focus on a niche where their high level of expertise forms a barrier to entry.

For the second marketing strategy, being a partner in a global supply chain, fulfillment is less of an issue as the rest of the supply chain or the supply chain manager takes care of that, but industry fragmentation may be a barrier. This too is a strategy in which small companies can overcome their disadvantages, as is the case for second-tier or third-tier suppliers in the automotive industry sector.

The third strategy, multiple language support, is currently still too costly for small companies. In practice only large companies provide multiple language support, although it is not inconceivable that affiliate schemes may be a route to multiple language support as well. Also, multi-linguality addresses only one of the barriers, and usually there are other barriers that come along with differences in language as well.

The global franchising strategy or more generally global partnering in one form or the other including affiliate schemes, may have the greatest potential to address the full range of barriers. However, it is a complicated strategy to execute, as it requires dealing with global and local issues at the same time. The concept to be implemented is global presence, which requires certain globally shared elements such as brand, catalogue definition, service approach, or others. At the same time the franchisees are local and need to conform to the global elements while they also need to be responsible for local added value.

Extending physical global presence with virtual presence is a route to market for large companies. It is a way to piggyback in the virtual world on solutions to fulfillment problems that have already been arranged for by physical presence (subsidiaries, distributors etc). Knowledge of the local situation is applied to the virtual presence to overcome cultural barriers and address specific local legal/self-regulatory requirements.

# 4    Typology of global e-markets

Global e-marketplaces as currently being realized can be classified in a four types:

A.  **Intrinsically global e-markets**, that deal with global products, customers, and suppliers, e.g. MRO or automotive;
B.  **Globally replicated local markets**, e.g. auctions of perishable products;
C.  **Local markets with a global infrastructure**, e.g. location-dependent m-commerce;
D.  **e-Ports**, where products are exported globally by a collaboration of producers.

Let's look at these four types in more detail.

## 4.1 Intrinsically global e-markets

Intrinsically global e-markets are those that deal with products that are of a global nature and customers and suppliers who themselves are present globally. Many of the recently announced large B2B exchanges are of that nature. For example, the automotive sector is already to a large extent a global industry, where supply chains span the globe and component suppliers and automotive plants cooperate with partners worldwide. AutoXchange, the large automotive marketplace already brings together manufacturers from Europe, Japan and the USA (Renault, Toyota, DaimlerChrysler, Ford, GM). Another example is the trading of routine business products or so-called non-productive goods (MRO – Maintenance, Repair, Operations). These are needed by business worldwide, while there are often many suppliers all over the world for such products. Marketplaces that provide a uniform view on the products on offer (cf. TradeZone, Barclays B2B) are intrinsically global.

To some extent this is of course a simplified picture: the operation of marketplaces does not end with ordering. Fulfillment will increasingly become part of e-markets, and with fulfillment local and location factors will come play a role, ranging from delivery time and cost depending on transportation distance, to import/export regulation, to differences in business practice. The challenge for intrinsically global marketplaces is to move beyond the straightforward role of matching demand and supply, to also provide fulfillment, while avoiding fragmentation of the marketplace into a set of local markets.

## 4.2 Replicated local markets

Some e-markets are necessarily geographically bounded. However, the same approach as followed in one region can be replicated in other regions, thereby achieving global leverage. An example is in fisheries, where e-auctions have been set up, amongst others by as a result of the European Infomar project[5]. Internet-based auction software has made it possible to interconnect auctions all across Europe. Fish that has been caught is traded at the e-auction while the vessel is still at sea. Depending upon the deal that is made the ship can choose the port to unload the catch. Effectively a single auction is being created across a region (a number of neighboring European countries). While it makes no sense to extend the auction by involving ever more countries without limits, the same approach is pursued by the providers involved in other parts of the world, likewise on a regional basis.

---

[5] The provider of auction software is Schelfhout from Belgium specialising on perishable goods trading, www.schelfhout.com.

## 4.3   Local markets built on a global infrastructure

When we talk about global e-markets not all of a market needs to be truly global. The actual representation and trading function could be fully local, while access, payment, security and delivery functions could be global. A convincing example is mobile electronic commerce or m-commerce. Location-specific services are likely to become a key feature of m-commerce, e.g. obtaining through the mobile phone a taxi upon arrival in a city. While this is a function that is highly location-dependent it requires access to a widely – preferably globally –available mobile network infrastructure. The infrastructure should support global roaming for access. Moreover, it is likely that 'services roaming' will be introduced more generally[6]. An example is the roaming of taxi-services, potentially creating a 'global' taxi-service on the basis of local offers and roaming agreements[7]. The infrastructure is also likely to support payments globally. It is an interesting question to consider which infrastructure services minimally have to be available on a global basis, and which services could be made available globally in order to increase efficiency and convenience for local markets that build upon these global infrastructure services.

## 4.4   e-Ports

As another example of markets with a global dimension that nevertheless retain a strong local element, 'e-ports' can be mentioned. The concept is that of a number of suppliers within a common geographic region who seek global presence but are not able to go global individually. They set up a joint export facility that deals on their behalf with the complexity of international trade such a multi-language catalogues, import/export regulations, multi-currency financing, international shipping, etc. Effectively they create a common marketplace, with global presence, which could be as simple as an e-mall or have the much richer functionality of a third-party marketplace[8]. An example is a group of furniture producers in Spain that have set up FurnitureNet. Because of the export orientation of this marketplace it is called an 'e-port'.

# 5   global e-business models and marketing strategies

E-markets usually implement one or more business models. Business models analysis combined with the insight in the marketing strategies mentioned before provides further guidance in the global – local issue.

---

[6]  I am grateful to Bror Salmelin at the European Commission for pointing this out to me.

[7]  Strictly speaking this need not be an e-market, in the sense that an intermediary brings several suppliers and buyers together: it could also be realized as a collection of e-shops (see business models below).

[8]  For these and other business models see section 5.

A business model should give product/service, information and money flows. It should also list the business actors involved, what their role is and which benefits they get. A business model together with the companies' marketing strategies enables to assess the commercial viability of the business model and to answer questions like: how is competitive advantage being built, what is the positioning, what is the marketing mix, which product-market strategy is being followed. Therefore it is useful to define beyond a business model also the 'marketing model' of a company, which consists of a business model in combination with the marketing strategy of the company. A short description is provided below, for a more profound analysis see the 'Electronic Commerce' book by Timmers [8] or the paper on 'Business Models for Electronic Markets' also by Timmers [9].

In principle very many new business models can be conceived by breaking down the value chain or the set of business processes that make up a business, followed by re-constructing the value chain again using electronic commerce technologies to build up the business operation. In practice a limited number only is being realized in Internet electronic commerce as qualitatively presented in Figure 1. The dimensions in this mapping are the degree of innovation relative to the non-electronic way of doing business, and the degree of integration of business functions. Also indicated in that diagram are the business models that individually or in combination are the basis of e-markets today. A number of business models are described below. For each of them comments are added as to their suitability to be applied for global e-commerce.

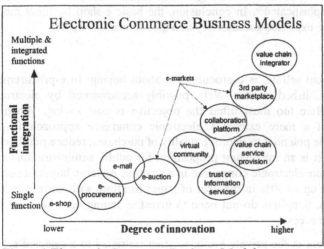

Figure 1 Electronic Commerce Business Models

**e-shop**

Most companies make their first steps in electronic commerce by displaying their company brochure and product offer on a Web site, creating an e-shop. Often this amounts to not much more than an electronic version of the traditional marketing/sales brochure. The hope is that this will lead to reduced cost in sales because shopping becomes more of a self-service operation. Usually only the sales department is affected by the e-shop, which tends to see it as an additional medium to bring the company message (next to paper or personal contact) rather than as a new channel in its own right, let alone as a new way of doing business[9]. If only limited effort is spent on this form of electronic commerce, cost-reduction should be the prime objective. Potentially, however, an e-shop can be the visible part of a more extensive electronic commerce system, which is integrated throughout the company with the objective to improve quality, reduce time-to-market, and gain access to new markets.

Regarding that last aspect of market access, setting up e-shop has been seen for a while as the easy and immediate route for companies to achieve the venerable global reach. Reality is more complicated than that, though. Even if the e-shop is visible globally, actual communication with customers worldwide and especially delivery and payment internationally is for most e-shops still far too difficult. This is not only a matter of technical complexity. It is also more than once the internal company organization that is not at all adjusted to international business. This observation is in line with Venkatraman's analysis of the extent of value innovation versus the extent of integration of IT in the company and its business network. Venkatraman states that access to new markets requires transformation of business processes inside the company as well as transformation of the way its network of partners operates [10]. As an illustration, for Weekend a Firenze, an e-shop selling artifacts from Florence, Italy, it was necessary to work closely with Japanese publishers in order to provide proper advertising to its important Japanese clientele. Delivery and returns complexity had to be resolved as well as credit card invoicing, which made that this e-shop had to become increasingly sophisticated[10]. In conclusion, the basic e-shop business model faces many hurdles to be exploited successfully as a global business model.

**e-procurement**
Where an e-shop is about selling, is e-procurement about buying. In e-procurement calls for tender are published on the Web, possibly accompanied by electronic submission of bids. Here too most often the objective is cost saving. When e-procurement is part of a more extensive electronic commerce approach in the company there is also the potential to improve quality of purchases, reduce purchasing time, etc. E-procurement is an interesting proposition for public administrations and more generally to promote electronic commerce in a country. As large buyers a public administration can save up to 50% in the cost of paper handling with corresponding savings for its suppliers. Suppliers do not need to invest in setting up a Website, all that is needed is Internet access.

In practice, e-procurement in the private sector is often restricted to a selected set of supplier (contrary to the generally more open e-marketplaces), and is therefore not the most obvious way to get involved as a supplier in global e-commerce. A company

---

[9] In fact, it is often not even sales & marketing that is in the lead in setting up an e-shop. In 1998 a UK survey showed that still 70% of all electronic commerce initiatives were being driven by the IT people in companies rather than by marketing or by the CEO.

[10] Private communication Alessandro Naldi founder of Weekend a Firenze, http://www.weekendafirenze.com/.

would first have to get onto the list of preferred suppliers. Public e-procurement would seem more attractive in that sense. However, public procurement is still rather limited, and there are still restrictions in international public procurement. The EU has committed itself to improving access to and usage of online public procurement as part of the eEurope action plan. Without fully transparent and simplified rules and procedures for e-procurement, this business model is bound to stay dominated by a local approach, and moreover, in which small companies are underrepresented.

## e-malls

Electronic malls are in their basic form no more than a collection of e-shops, accessible from a common entry point on the Internet. E-mall providers can add value by common branding and e-shop presentation, possibly adding quality guarantees, an attractive presentation of the shops in the mall, and payment support (cf BarclaysSquare). With further functionality e-malls can become third party marketplaces. The 'archetypal' industry e-mall is Industry.Net. Basic e-malls do not seem to be very attractive as a global business model, probably because the complications of international commerce such as international fulfillment require added-value services that go beyond this simple business model. A local or regional orientation is prevalent. Although basic e-malls can bring many small companies together and thus have a potential to overcome industry fragmentation, they do not exploit this asset as a critical mass for additional services (contrary to third party marketplaces for fragmented markets, see below).

## e-auctions

Electronic auctions receive much attention, especially B-to-C auctions such as eBay in the USA and UK's QXL. However, B-to-B auctions have at least as much potential, especially where spare capacity and surplus stocks are concerned. Here too the prime objective is increased efficiency, reduced wastage and overall cost-reduction. Auctions can be applied in any situation where there is fluctuation of demand or supply. Examples that can be considered are in areas as diverse as electricity production to surplus electronic components to advertising space. A European B-to-B example in perishable goods (fruit, fish) is the Multitrade system of SCS, a result of the EU Infomar project[11]. In this particular case the e-auction is also successful globally, in the sense of global replication of the local / regional market approach. This illustrates that certain B-to-B e-auctions can overcome some of the barriers to globalization.

Consumer-to-consumer auction tend to stay local or national. Global identification of consumers as parties in the transaction is virtually non-existent today. Global payment and delivery from consumer to consumer is perceived is unreliable. Third party services such as escrow can alleviate this to some extent. Effectively, C-to-C e-auctions cover a limited geography. Consequently many geographic e-auctions lack liquidity as they have insufficient customers. Consumer auctions are therefore, until now, of limited success globally. As for B-to-B auctions local replication with

---

[11] See www.schelfhout.com. As a case study this is analysed in-depth in Timmers (1999).

adaptation is an approach that is followed, cf. QXL's presence in several countries in Europe and elsewhere.

### virtual communities

Virtual communities are both a business model and a facility that can be added to almost any other business model. The concept is to gather participants around an area of common interest and to let *themselves* contribute to the information base, inciting them to make public their experience. The business model is often based on advertising revenues and membership fees. Although they are now abundant on the Web, many of them are not profitable[12]. Groups with a common area of interest can be found almost anywhere. For example, these could be ethnic groups, industry sectors, professionals, hobbies, etc. Some of them attract a lot of interest from investors. A virtual community depends upon several factors: the number of people that share the same interest, the possibility to reach them, their willingness and interest to share information so that a rich collection of content can develop, and ultimately the interest of advertisers or the willingness of community members to pay a membership fee or the opportunity to add further paid-for services. Depending upon those factors a virtual community can be a successful global business model and equally well there are successful local virtual communities.

### collaboration platforms

Collaboration platforms are a business model of a different kind: they fit the wider definition of electronic commerce, namely that it is 'about doing business electronically including collaborative work'. Examples are collaborative design or construction, collaborative virtual consultancy, collaborative export marketing, etc. All these examples involve technology to support the collaboration (such as common databases, project management, search tools, etc). The platform must support integration of several functions such as market research, contact management, negotiation, contracting, IPR management, possibly payments, etc. The business model for the provider of the platform often is based on membership fees.

Collaboration platforms are particularly interesting for small companies to pool their limited resources. In Spain furniture companies have thus set up a joint export site as mentioned before. In Germany small automotive suppliers are looking at collaborative design and engineering. The European SUPPLYPOINT project dynamically pools the resources of small companies in construction so that they too can bid for larger construction projects. Commercial examples in construction include Buildcom.com and Bidcom.com.

According to some industry analysts the future of B-to-B marketplaces is in collaborative e-commerce [11]. This seems a logical step in order to add value to straightforward transaction handling (but see third party marketplaces, below). However, collaboration often extends deep into business processes that may have a

---

[12] Advertising as a revenue stream is common to many business models. This, however, is to some extent self-defeating: there is now more advertising space on the Web than advertisers.

strong local orientation. Collaboration in the construction industry for example has to take into account the many differences in local practices, rules and regulations, as well as simply physical parameters like distance between suppliers and buyers.

Collaboration platforms, in conclusion, are often a promising approach to 'going global', overcoming industry fragmentation and promoting the involvement of small companies, provided that the platform provider addresses legal and self-regulatory issues and differences in business conventions.

**third party marketplaces**
A very important business model is the third party marketplace (TPM). The provider of a TPM puts the catalogues of suppliers online, and offers catalogue search, ordering and payment facilities in a secure environment to purchasers. The TPM provider might add branding, one-to-one marketing support, and even logistics to this, as well as more advanced functions such as pre- and post-financing, risk management and insurance, tax/customs handling, and product bundling. In short, the TPM provider relieves suppliers and buyers of much of the burden to go online.

The business model is based on a combination of subscription fees, transaction fees and service fees. This approach is so important as it is particularly suited for volume trading of routine supplies between businesses. These supplies are often called MRO goods – maintenance, repair and operations. The MRO market is estimated to be 60% of all B-to-B electronic commerce, which itself is 80% of all electronic commerce. In other words, MRO trading is 50% of all electronic commerce. Estimates for the value of MRO trading vary widely but are predicted to be huge (hundreds of billions of euros/dollars in a few years time).

The approach is also very interesting for small companies that do not want to be bothered with the online world, but nevertheless wants to sell online. In that case the small company can rely completely upon a TPM (at a price of course). Third party marketplace operators also address fragmented markets like hospital products or construction. With their added value of uniform access to products and suppliers as well as to buyers they create economy of scale.

A TPM that bases its revenue model on transaction fees only may soon find that these do not provide enough differentiation. Therefore TPMs can be expected to move into value added services. One of those is global transaction support, e.g. for payments and logistics. Therefore routine business trading supported by a (third party) marketplace operator is likely to be an important kind of global e-market development.

In summary, third party marketplaces are one of the most promising routes to global e-markets.

**value chain integration**
Value chain integrators focus on integrating multiple steps of the value chain, with the potential to exploit the information flow between those steps for further added value. In particular this may include customized advice to buyers of components about new applications, as well as customized advice to the manufacturers about demand patterns

and customer requirements for new products. Revenues are coming from consultant fees or transaction fees. Tight value chain integration is close to 'traditional' supply chain management, where a limited number of qualified suppliers are involved in deep information sharing and information systems integration. Value chain integration as a global business model therefore is likely to be limited.

**value chain service provision**

Value chain service providers specialize on a specific function for the value chain, such as electronic payments or logistics, with the intention to make that into their distinct competitive advantage. Banks for example have been positioning themselves as such since long, and now may find new opportunities using the open Internet network. New approaches are also emerging in production/stock management where the specialized expertise needed to analyze and fine-tune production is offered by new intermediaries. A fee- or percentage based scheme is the basis for revenues. Addressing global fulfillment problems is claimed to be the expertise of global value chain service providers such as FedEx, UPS, or postal operators that are offering global shipping with internet access to order and track package delivery.

**trust and specialized information services**

Finally amongst the innovative specialized functions and services that business and consumers need, there are trust services and specialized information brokerage. Typically any party with a trusted image can consider becoming a trust service provider. Banks, telecom companies, chambers of commerce, insurance companies and notaries are all considering setting up a trust business or have already moved into this. With the new European legislation on electronic signatures now adopted the time is ripe for mutual recognition of such services across borders and Europe-wide trust services are already emerging. There is still scope for national added value in trust services, as trust is likely to remain a quality with a strong local and cultural dimension. However, global trust provision is a natural business model for pure play trust providers. Their added value is limited in comparison to click-and-mortar trust providers such as banks unless they can support their customers internationally or globally[13].

# 6 Summary

The global – local analysis of electronic commerce points to a rich set of questions, of which only a few could be addressed in this paper. Following an analysis of barriers to global electronic commerce, a typology was provided of global e-markets as well as an assessment of how well current electronic commerce business models are suited to support global e-commerce.

---

[13] Example trust providers seeking global presence are Verisign and Globalsign.

# References

1. Proc. of the Bled 1998 and 1999 conferences, P. Timmers in the World Market Research Centre Business Briefing on Electronic Commerce, Sept 1999, and the International Journal of Electronic Markets, Vol. 9, No. 1&2, June 1999

2. Global versus Local, session report in the IST99 Final Report, http://europa.eu.int/comm/information_society/ist/conference_en.htm#finalreport and www.ist99.fi for the IST99 conference

3. http://www.b2bbigbang.com/

4. http://www.forrester.com/

5. www.cordis.lu/ist, as well as the compilation of about 350 projects in 'Accelerating Electronic Commerce in Europe', http://www.ispo.cec.be/ecommerce/books/aecebook.html

6. www.ispo.cec.be/ecommerce

7. The Economist, 'Health Online in Europe', 25 March 2000

8. Timmers, P. (1999); 'Electronic Commerce: Strategies and Models for Business-to-Business Trading', Wiley & Sons Ltd, ISBN 0 471 720291

9. Timmers, P. (1998); 'Business Models for Electronic Markets', International Journal of Electronic Markets, Vol. 98/2, http://www.electronicmarkets.org/

10. Venkatraman, N. (1994); 'IT-Enabled Business Transformation: From Automation to Business Scope Redefinition', Sloan Management Review, (35:2), Winter 1994

11. E.g. Morgan, Stanley, Dean, Witter (April 2000) in "The B2B Internet Report: Collaborative Commerce", http://www.msdw.com/techresearch/index.html

# Object-Oriented Conceptual Modeling of Web Application Interfaces: The OO-$\mathcal{H}$Method Abstract Presentation Model

Cristina Cachero[1]*, Jaime Gómez[1], and Oscar Pastor[2]

[1] Departamento de Lenguajes y Sistemas Informáticos
Universidad de Alicante. SPAIN
{ccachero,jgomez}@dlsi.ua.es
[2] Departamento de Sistemas Informáticos y Computación
Universidad Politécnica de Valencia. SPAIN
opastor@dsic.upv.es

**Abstract** Object-oriented conceptual modeling approaches must be reconsidered in order to address the particulars associated with the design of web application interfaces. In this context, the paper introduces the presentation layer of OO-$\mathcal{H}$Method, an extension of the OO-Method conceptual modeling approach that is devoted to the specification of this kind of interfaces. The OO-$\mathcal{H}$Method presentation approach is based on the concept of templates. Each page template may fall into one among a set of categories, which together cover the different presentation perspectives captured in the model. In order to better define the page template structure, a new diagram is introduced: the Abstract Presentation Diagram (APD). The APD does not need to be drawn from scratch: the navigation structure previously defined in the OO-$\mathcal{H}$Method Navigation Access Diagram (NAD) provides the information needed to automatically generate a default APD. This skeleton template structure may be further refined and enriched with the aid of the OO-$\mathcal{H}$Method Interface Pattern Catalog. As a result, a web application interface is generated in an automated way.

## 1 Introduction

The research effort inverted by the scientific community in hypermedia modeling approaches specifically devoted to the development of web sites has led to different projects and products. Some of the most relevant examples studied so far are HDM [7], HDM-lite [6], OOHDM [17], RMM [9], ADM [1, 11] or Strudel [5]. However there is still, as far as we know, a gap to be filled: that of web applications' interaction issues. In this context our research efforts have been focused on the proposal of 'Not Yet Another Method' for web modeling, but on a set of semantics and notation that allows the development of web-based interfaces for existing OO-Method [14, 15] applications. This proposal, known as

---

\* This article has been written with the sponsorship of the Conselleria de Cultura, Educació i Ciència de la Comunitat Valenciana

OO-$\mathcal{H}$Method [8], extends OO-Method with two new diagrams: (1) the Navigation Access Diagram (NAD) and (2) the Abstract Presentation Diagram (APD).

Both the NAD and the APD can be further enriched and refined by means of a set of interface patterns, which are defined in the OO-$\mathcal{H}$Method Pattern Catalog[2]. The OO-$\mathcal{H}$Method Pattern Catalog provides a user-centered Hypermedia Interface Pattern Language [16] that offers alternative solutions to well-known hypermedia problems, considered from the user point of view. Furthermore, its use allows the designer to choose the most suitable among a set of possible implementations. The patters can fall into one of the following three categories: (1) Information patterns, that provide the user with useful context information, (2) Interaction Patterns, which cover user-interface communication issues such as protocol-related features for invoking services and (3) Navigation Patterns, that determine the way the user is going to move through the system. The information and patterns captured at the NAD level suffice to automatically generate a default APD, which provides the designer with the skeleton page template structure on which to perform further refinements. This article introduces the APD main semantic and structural features.

The remainder of the article is structured as follows: section 2 gives an overview of the NAD and the concepts captured there, which are the basis for the generation of the default APD. Section 3 introduces the APD and describes in detail, by means of an example, both the concepts and the template constructs associated with this diagram. It also defines its construction process (automatic default generation and refinement). The web interface that is generated from the information captured both in the NAD and in the APD is shown in section 4. Section 5 makes a comparison with related work, and section 6 presents the conclusions and further work.

## 2  OO-$\mathcal{H}$Method Navigation Access Diagram

For a more general perspective of the approach, a small example is going to be employed all along the paper: a Chat Management System. As a basic explanation (for reasons of brevity) it is assumed that there are several possible chat topics. Each message corresponds to a single topic. Besides, messages are hierarchically structured so that a message can be the start point of a new discussion line inside its topic or, otherwise, be a response to another previous message. The chat user, whose behaviour we will model, is able to read messages and reply to an existing message. OO-$\mathcal{H}$Method associates a different NAD diagram with each agent (user-type). This diagram is based on the following constructs:

1. Navigation Classes (NC): they are domain classes whose attributes and methods have been filtered and enriched in order to better accommodate the specific features of hypertext. This enrichment causes different types of attributes to appear: V-Attributes (attributes that are always visible), R-Attributes (available to the user on demand, by means of any kind of

reference) and H-Attributes (attributes hidden to the user except on very specific occasions, such as when displaying detailed views of the system).

2. Navigation Targets (NT): they group the elements of the model that collaborate in the coverage of a certain user navigation requirement. In our example (see Fig. 1) there is one NT, corresponding to the user requirement 'Participate in Chat'. Inside it, we can observe two navigation domain classes: the 'Chat' class, which determines the available discussion topics, and the 'Messages' class, which contains the messages stored in the system. We can observe that the 'Chat' class has a single attribute ('nameChat'), which is labelled as 'Visible' (V) and specifies the identifying name for each discussion topic.

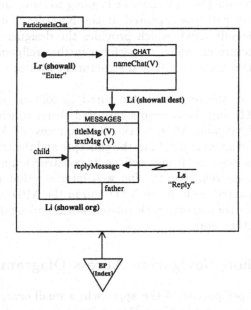

**Figure1.** *NAD Diagram of a Chat Manager System*

3. Navigation Links (NL): they define the navigation paths through the information. They have a set of associated Dynamic Flow Navigation Patterns, which are defined in the Pattern Catalog and qualify the user navigation behaviour. Also, they are accompanied by a set of Navigation Filters, which restrict and qualify the target information. We can distinguish among four different link types: I-Links (Internal Links), which provide navigation paths among objects inside a given NT, T-Links (Traversal Links), which are defined between navigation classes belonging to different NT, R-Links (Requirement Links), which define the entry point to each NT and S-Links (Service Links), which determine the available services for the user-type as-

sociated to that NAD. In Fig. 1 we can observe three out of the four possible link types. The structural relationship (composition) that exists between 'Chat' and 'Messages' allows the designer to define a Li that makes possible the access to all the messages corresponding to a given chat topic. The Lr 'Enter' shows the navigation entry point to the NT. Also, an example of the Ls link type is provided, associated with the 'Reply' service.

4. Collections: they group objects following certain criteria under hierarchical, either static or dynamic, structures. They have a set of Dynamic Flow Navigation Patterns and Navigation Filters associated, which define both the traversal behaviour of the link structure and the set of objects on which this collection will apply. In OO-HMethod there are three main collection types: C-Collections (Classifying Collections), which provide an access structure, hierarchical or not, to groups of related objects, T-Collections (Transaction Collections), which group navigation services that are offered to the user as a whole and S-Collections (Selector Collections), which group objects that conform to a set of values gathered from the user. In our example we can observe a special kind of C-Collection, the EP (Entry Point), which, as every collection, is drawn as an inverted triangle. An EP determines the entry point to the application.

The NAD captures the navigation paths and the services the user can activate when working with the interface, and so a different NAD should be defined for each user type. From there a web interface might be generated without further work, because OO-HMethod provides a set of default values for the main presentation features. That allows the designer to shorten the time needed to develop application prototypes. However, once an agreement between designer and client has been reached, the designer will most probably need to modify this default structure in order to improve both its appearance and usability features. In order to do so, OO-HMethod defines another diagram: the APD, which will be detailed in next section. In order to get more information about the NAD diagram, interested readers are referred to [8].

## 3 The Abstract Presentation Diagram

We agree with [1, 5, 6, 11] in the adoption of a template approach for the specification of not only the visual appearance but also the page structure of the web. OO-HMethod defines five template types, expressed as XML (eXtensible Markup Language) documents[4, 10]. In order to define the tags and the structure of the documents we have associated a Document Type Definition (DTD)[1] with each type of template. For reasons of space, the five DTD specifications are left out of the article. Interested readers are referred to [3].

---

[1] A new proposal, called XML-SCHEMA, is being discussed at [4] as an alternative to the DTD definition language

## 3.1 Template Types

The five template types defined in our approach are, namely: (1) tStruct, which defines the information that will appear in the materialized page, (2) tStyle, which reflects the visual features of the page, (3) tForm, which defines the data required from the user in order to interact with the system, (4) tFunction, which captures language-independent client functionality and is based on the DOM (Document Object Model) specification[4] and (5) tWindow, which reflects two or more simultaneous views of the information. With this approach, the addition of new document types to our model simply consists on the addition of (1) a new DTD defining the structure of such document, and (2) a set of mapping rules to each one of the different target environments. Furthermore, defining a common set of XML templates could serve as a framework for comparison among different proposals.

The default template structure can be derived from the information captured in the NAD by using a set of default APD generation rules. Following these rules, V-Attributes, I-Links, T-Links and R-Links are automatically transformed into link-elements inside the tStruct page. Also C-Collections and S-Collections generate a new tStruct abstract page that contains a tree-like structure made up of link elements pointing to other tStruct elements, and so on. In our example, the abstract template pages Home Page, Chat List, Message View and Reply Message (which can be seen in Fig. 2) have been automatically derived from the NAD diagram, together with its corresponding links. Also a general Style page has been automatically added to the template structure. In the following section we will present the possible ways of refinement that cause the template structure to evolve towards its final appearance.

## 3.2 APD Refinement

The default APD provides the user with a functional interface, that can serve as a prototype on which to validate the user-requirements. But, in order to get a more sophisticated appearance, the designer will probably need to perform further refinements. OO-$\mathcal{H}$Method provides the user with two refinement mechanisms, the simpler one consisting on manually adding structures and/or individual pages to the default APD diagram. As an example, in Fig. 2 we have added a TWindow structure that adds a multi view capability to the default one-view-at-a-time interface. The other mechanism consists on the application of a series of APD-related patterns captured in the Pattern Catalog. These patterns provide the designer with additional hypermedia features and techniques, which are known to be useful to improve the interface quality. Also, the use of patterns makes possible the automation of the refinement process. APD-related patterns have a set of application rules that drive the APD evolution when they are applied. As an example of this second approach, in Fig. 2 the application of the 'head and food' implementation corresponding to the 'Location Pattern' has caused two new abstract pages (head and foot) of type tStruct, to appear on the diagram.

These two pages are connected to every page where the designer wants them to be included. In fact patterns might cause the appearance and/or modification of any kind of abstract page. For instance, the generated 'ChatList' tStruct abstract page, after applying the refinements, is as follows:

```
<?XML version="1.0"?>

<!DOCTYPE tStruct SYSTEM "tStruct.dtd" encoding="UTF-8">
<tStruct>
    <label style="" text="List of available chats" />
    <link name="error" type="automatic" show="new"
        pointsTo="tStruct" dest="errorPage"/>
    <link name="head" type="automatic" show="here"
        pointsTo="tStruct" dest="head"/>
    <collection format="ulist" style="schatlist">
        <object type="chat">
            <attrib name="nameChat" type="STRING">
            </attrib>
            <call event="onClick" function="validate">
        </object>
    </collection>
    <link name="foot" type="automatic" show="here"
        pointsTo="tStruct" dest="foot"/>
</tStruct>
```

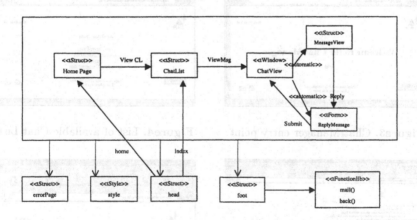

**Figure2.** *Simplified APD of the Chat User Agent*

Once the selected patterns have been applied to the diagram, a set of interaction tasks and techniques[2] will define the implementation constructs for a given environment. Last, but not least, we can enrich the model with redundant implementations for the same pattern: e.g. the Navigation Observer Pattern, which

---

[2] both concepts will be introduced in the following section

allows the interface to keep track of the navigation path followed by a given user, might be present in the interface by both a 'back' and a 'reload' mechanism.

## 4 Implementation of the APD

We might define an Interaction Task as a mechanism that groups, according to the action to be performed, the set of Abstract Interaction Objects (AIO's) that collaborate in the coverage of such action. These elements might have been explicitly chosen by the designer or might be part of any pattern applied to these models. On the other hand, we define an 'Interaction Technique' as each one of the materialization possibilities an Interaction Task has. Interaction Techniques are always associated with a concrete strategy and/or programming environment, and are made up of Concrete Interaction Objects (CIO's). The complexity of the mapping among the abstract pages in the APD and the final constructs (first to AIO's and then to CIO's [12]) goes beyond the purpose of this article. In Fig. 3 to 5 the interface generated from the APD of Fig. 2, which corresponds to the Chat Manager example, is shown.

**Figure3.** Chat Manager entry point  **Figure4.** List of available Chat Lists

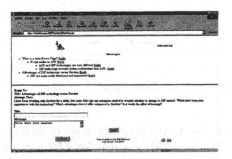
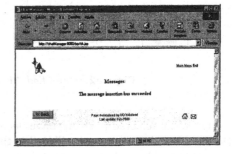

**Figure5.** Adding an opinion to the chat

The process is as follows: first, the generator tool looks for the page template derived from the Application Entry Point (see Fig. 3). Note that every page of the diagram has the same head/foot associated, which provides the interface with a common visual context (Location Pattern). When the user clicks on the 'Enter' link, the ChatList tStruct page is populated with the active application objects and the materialized HTML page is shown (see Fig. 4). Again, when the user clicks on the name of one of the Chat topics, the materialization of the tWindow abstract page is performed. This template defines the generation of the, from now on, two different and simultaneously available views of the system by means of two 'automatic' links, that is, links that don't require the user interaction in order to be activated. Those views are (1) the messages kept on the system (again a tStruct abstract page) and (2) a tForm abstract page that encapsulates the fields required to add a new message to the application. The replyMessage function returns a Boolean value, which provokes the final Ok message to appear once the operation has been successfully fulfilled (see Fig. 5).

The sample application has been developed using JavaServer Pages and Bean components [18] as the chosen server technology, and HTML as the chosen client technology.

## 5  Comparison with Related Work

Many commercial applications make use of some kind of templates in their hypermedia development approach. IDC's or ASP's from Microsoft, or Cold Fusion from Allaire are some examples. The main drawback of these approaches is that they remain too close to the implementation space, and thus the designer has to deal with error-prone activities such as specifying exact names of database fields, or explicitly managing the linkage of pages. Our template structure on the contrary follows, like others [6, 13, 17] a declarative approach that covers every aspect of the interface, from content to style. As an example, the tStyle template type adds a further level of abstraction to the CSS approach, followed in many traditional applications: while CSS pages work on documents with a definite hypermedia structure, tStyle templates act on abstract pages on which the hypermedia structure is not still defined. CSS are, again, just a possible final materialization (among many others) of tStyle templates.

Although the template approach is not the only possible approach (see for example [17]), it however provides us with the required flexibility and extensibility we consider vital for our method in such a changing environment as the web. Our template concept shares with other models studied so far [1, 5, 6, 11, 17] many similarities: it implicitly assumes a page visualization schema and somehow specifies the data it is going to show. But there are just as many features in which our work is different: generally speaking, we consider mixing in a single template features regarding structure, content, presentation and behaviour, overdimensions such templates, and difficults the designer task. On the contrary, the OO-$\mathcal{H}$Method taxonomy of templates facilitates to focus on complementary aspects of the final implementation. We also claim that the separation of content and layout [6] doesn't suffice to deal with the different aspects involved in presentation, such as client functionality, interaction with logic or several simultaneous views of the system. We haven't found, up to now, any other abstraction proposal for such characteristics apart from that included in OO-$\mathcal{H}$Method. Also, the definition of the different aspects of the interface by means of a set of patterns greatly simplifies both the construction and modification of the APD, and also improves its usability.

# 6 Conclusions and further work

OO-$\mathcal{H}$Method is an extension of the OO-Method conceptual modeling approach to address the particulars associated with the design of web interfaces. In this article we have presented a new diagram, the APD, based on the concept of constructive templates, which provides the designer with an intuitive way of refining the default interface structure, previously captured in the NAD diagram. We have also proposed an interface enrichment process driven by patterns. Furthermore, the article illustrates how OO-$\mathcal{H}$Method captures application interaction issues that, in spite of its relevance in web application interfaces, we have found missing in other proposals.

Summarizing, the most relevant contributions of this paper are the following:

1. A taxonomy of templates, defined in XML, that separates the different complementary views involved in the complete definition of the interface.
2. A process for the APD refinement.
3. A set of ways in which the use of the OO-$\mathcal{H}$Method Interface Pattern Catalog improves and facilitates the diagrams construction and refinement and influences the user interface quality.

At the moment we are applying this method to an e-commerce application. The experience gained in the development of this interface will surely enrich our pattern catalog and refine our template structure. Also, a taxonomy of interaction tasks and techniques (already in the solution space) is being defined.

*Acknowledgments* We would like to thank the anonymous referees for their valuable comments to this work

# References

[1] P. Atzeni, G. Mecca, and P. Merialdo. Design and Maintenance of Data-Intensive Web Sites. In *Advances in Database Technology - EDTB'98*, pages 436–449, 03 1998.

[2] C. Cachero. The OO-$\mathcal{H}$Method Pattern Catalog. Technical report, Universidad de Alicante, 12 1999.

[3] C. Cachero. The OO-$\mathcal{H}$Method Template Taxonomy. Technical report, Universidad de Alicante, 02 2000.

[4] eXtensible Markup Language (XML). http://www.w3.org/XML/.

[5] F. M. Fernández, D. Florescu, J. Kang, A. Levy, and D. Suciu. Catching the Boat with Strudel: Experiences with a Web-Site Management System. In *Proceedings of ACM SIGMOD International conference on Management of data*, pages 414–425, 10 1998.

[6] P. Fraternali and P. Paolini. A Conceptual Model and a Tool Environment for Developing more Scalable, Dynamic, and Customizable Web Applications. In *Advances in Database Technology - EDBT'98*, pages 421–435, 1998.

[7] F. Garzotto and P. Paolini. HDM A Model-Based Approach to Hypertext Application Design. *ACM Transactions on Information Systems (TOIS)*, 11(1):1–26, 01 1993.

[8] J. Gómez, C. Cachero, and O. Pastor. Extending a Conceptual Modelling Approach to Web Application Design. In *CAiSE '00 (to appear)*. 12$^{th}$ *International Conference on Advanced Information Systems*. Springer-Verlag. Lecture Notes in Computer Science, 06 2000.

[9] T. Isakowitz, E. A. Stohr, and V. Balasubramanian. RMM: A Methodology for Structured Hypermedia Design. *CACM: Communications of the ACM.*, pages 34–44, 08 1995.

[10] S. McGrath. *XML by Example. Building e-commerce Applications*. Prentice Hall, 1998.

[11] G. Mecca, P. Merialdo, P. Atzeni, and V. Crescenzi. The ARANEUS Guide to Web-Site Development. Technical report, Universidad de Roma, 03 1999.

[12] P. Molina. Especificación de la Interfaz de Usuario en OO-Method. Technical report, Universidad Politécnica de Valencia, 1998.

[13] M. Nanard, J. Nanard, and P. Kahn. Pushing Reuse in Hypermedia Design: Golden Rules, Design Patterns and Constructive Templates. In *HYPERTEXT '98. Proceedings of the ninth ACM conference on Hypertext and hypermedia: links, objects, time and space—structure in hypermedia systems*, pages 11–20, 1998.

[14] O. Pastor, E. Insfrán, V. Pelechano, J. Romero, and J. Merseguer. OO-METHOD: An OO Software Production Environment Combining Conventional and Formal Methods. In *CAiSE '97. International Conference on Advanced Information Systems*, pages 145–158, 1997.

[15] O. Pastor, V. Pelechano, E. Insfrán, and J. Gómez. From Object Oriented Conceptual Modeling to Automated Programming in Java. In *ER '98. International Conference on the Entity Relationship Approach*, pages 183–196, 1998.

[16] G. Rossi, D. Schwabe, and A. Garrido. Design Reuse in Hypermedia Applications Development. In *Proceedings of the eight ACM conference on HYPERTEXT '97*, pages 57–66, 1997.

[17] D. Schwabe, G. Rossi, and D. J. Barbosa. Systematic Hypermedia Application Design with OOHDM. In *Proceedings of the the seventh ACM conference on HYPERTEXT '96*, page 166, 1996.

[18] The source for java technology. http://java.sun.com.

# Representing Web Data as Complex Objects*

Alberto H.F. Laender, Berthier Ribeiro-Neto,
Altigran S. da Silva†, and Elaine S. Silva

Department of Computer Science
Federal University of Minas Gerais
31270-901 Belo Hrizonte MG Brazil
{laender,berthier,alti,elaine}@dcc.ufmg.br

**Abstract.** The popularization of the Web has made a huge volume of data available for a large audience. In a large number of Web sites, such as bookstores, electronic catalogs, travel agencies, etc., the pages constitute documents which are composed of pieces of data whose overall structure can be easily recognized. Such pages are called data-rich and can be seen as collections of complex objects. In this paper, we show how such objects can be represented by nested tables, which are simple, intuitive, and quite convenient for expressing their implicit structure. The assumption is that, for most sites of interest, only few examples are required to reveal the structure of the objects. To corroborate our assumption, we describe a data extraction tool that adopts this approach and present results of some experiments carried out with this tool.

## 1 Introduction

Despite the huge volume of data made available through the Word Wide Web, manipulating such data effectively is not a simple problem. In fact, traditional database operations, such as querying, view generation, and data integration, are usually very difficult to carry out with the data available on the Web.

One of the main reasons for such a difficulty is the lack of knowledge on the structure of textual data in general. In fact, the structure associated with this type of data is usually left undeclared. However, such structure is usually present in some inherent form. For example, Web sites such as bookstores, electronic catalogs, and travel agencies include pages which are composed of pieces of data whose overall structure can be easily recognized. Such structure has not been declared anywhere but is clearly identifiable. Such pages are said to be *data rich* and *narrow in ontological breadth* [6]. Usually, the data found in them do not have a rigid structure and therefore is said to be *semistructured* [2]. Such pages are the main target of our study and, for convenience, are referred to simply as data rich pages.

---

*This work is supported by Project SIAM (grant MCT/FINEP/PRONEX 76.97.1016.00) and by individual research grants from CNPq and CAPES.
†On leave from the University of Amazonas, Brazil.

In this paper, we propose a new approach for revealing the structure of data present in data rich Web pages. The general idea is to let the user assemble example objects taken from a Web page into a nested table according to her/his perspective and then to automatically analyze the structure of the resulting table to determine the structure of the assembled object. Nested tables [7, 10, 17] are interesting because they are simple, intuitive, and are expressive enough to represent the semistructured data normally present in common Web pages. Using this idea, we developed a tool for semistructured data extraction called *DEByE (Data Extraction By Example)* [8, 15, 16], whose graphical user interface (GUI) allows assembling an example object using simple "cut-and-paste" operations. The structure of the example object can then be used to identify new objects in the page or in other similar pages. In case of the structure of the objects vary, more than one example must be provided. The complexity and the "size" of the structural information required depend on the number of objects having distinct structures and on how distinct these structures are. We expect habitual Web users to be able to identify noticeable structural differences between objects and provide more example objects whenever necessary. We notice, however, that our aim in this paper is to present our approach for revealing the structure of Web data. Therefore, we do not address details of the extraction strategy of our tool.

Several data models have been proposed to represent semistructured data [3, 4, 14]. These models are, in general, based on labeled directed graphs and aim at capturing the irregular structure inherent to such data. OEM (Object Exchange Model) is an object-based model adopted by the TSIMMIS project [14]. An OEM object can be of type either atomic or complex. The value of an OEM object of type complex is a set of object references to its components and these references can be cyclic. The data model proposed in [3] for the UnQL query language is quite similar to OEM. The difference is that the UnQL data model lacks the notion of an object, describing data by means of a set of trees whose leaf nodes have the actual instances associated with them. The model presented in [4] also represents data as a directed labeled graph in which each node corresponds to an object. But unlike the other two, this model is deterministic in the sense that the edges emanating from any node (that describes data) must be distinctly labeled. However to properly use these data models, we need to previously know the structure of the objects.

Many different approaches have been proposed in the literature to discover structural information from implicit objects found in data rich Web pages [6, 11, 12, 18]. The work in [11] presents a method to derive hierarchies of types and to assign objects to the derived types in a given OEM database. In [12] the authors discuss the trade-offs between having a large, but very precise, structural description of the data and having a more compact one, but that is possibly imperfect. The approach proposed in [18] aims at determining structural patterns matching the majority of objects in a OEM database, and using this information to determine a typical structure for the objects composing it. The work in [6] presents a method for the discovery of one-level structures (records) in Web pages based on HTML formating tags. More recently, some proposals have been put forward to address the problem of finding structural constraints in semistructured data [13].

Our approach is remarkably distinct from previous works because it relies on the user's perception of the object's structure. That is, instead of trying to derive structural (semantic) matches from the formating (syntax), we induce the user to inform the structure as she/he perceives it. We believe that in those situations in which the user is available to provide the information (for example, when browsing a Web site), this approach works better than alternative methods based on "blind" heuristics [11, 12, 18]. Furthermore, our approach is not tied to any specific formating system (e.g. HTML, XML, LaTex, etc.). Instead, it takes advantage of any type of markups surrounding the data of interest.

The remainder of the paper is organized as follows. Section 2 presents the modeling concepts adopted to describe the structure of data present in data rich Web pages. In Section 3 we discuss the notion of nested tables and its correspondence to complex objects types. The *DEByE* tool is covered in Section 4. Section 5 presents the results of an experiment carried out with the tool. Our conclusions are presented in Section 6.

## 2 Complex Objects in Web Pages

In this section, we discuss the data modeling concepts that we adopt to describe the structure of data present in data rich Web pages. These modeling concepts rely on the assumption that such pages can be seen as collections of *complex objects* which have an inherent implicit structure. In many cases, these objects are composed of sub-objects, that also have themselves an implicit structure yielding a hierarchy of objects.

Consider, for instance, the excerpt of a page from the **Murder by the Book** bookstore Web site (http://www.murderbythebook.com) shown in Fig. 1. There

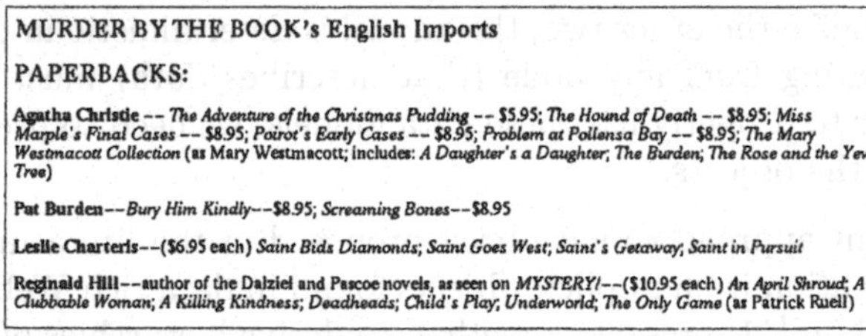

MURDER BY THE BOOK's English Imports

PAPERBACKS:

Agatha Christie -- *The Adventure of the Christmas Pudding* -- $5.95; *The Hound of Death* -- $8.95; *Miss Marple's Final Cases* -- $8.95; *Poirot's Early Cases* -- $8.95; *Problem at Pollensa Bay* -- $8.95; *The Mary Westmacott Collection* (as Mary Westmacott; includes: *A Daughter's a Daughter; The Burden; The Rose and the Yew Tree*)

Pat Burden--*Bury Him Kindly*--$8.95; *Screaming Bones*--$8.95

Leslie Charteris--($6.95 each) *Saint Bids Diamonds; Saint Goes West; Saint's Getaway; Saint in Pursuit*

Reginald Hill--author of the Dalziel and Pascoe novels, as seen on *MYSTERY!*--($10.95 each) *An April Shroud; A Clubbable Woman; A Killing Kindness; Deadheads; Child's Play; Underworld; The Only Game* (as Patrick Ruell)

**Fig. 1.** Excerpt of a page from the Murder by the Book bookstore Web site.

is an inherent structure to the text on this page. For instance, we are able to identify distinct portions of data on books by four authors. Each one of these portions can be regarded as a distinct implicit *object*. For each of these objects, we can distinguish an author name and a corresponding list of books. For the books in this list, we can identify information on book titles and prices. Thus, there is an inherent structure associated with the objects implicitly present in the Web page of Fig. 1. Such structure has not been declared anywhere but is clearly identifiable. The implicit objects have a multi-level structure and, because of that, are said to be *complex objects*.

In what follows, we present the data modeling concepts that we use for the definition of complex object types with arbitrarily deep nesting levels. They follow the ideas described in [1] and [9], and can be seen as extensions to the relational data model.

A set of similar complex objects is described by the notion of an *object type*. An object of a specific type is called an *instance* of the type. We consider the following object types:

- *atomic type*: an object of an atomic type can only assume atomic values;
- *tuple type*: an object of a tuple type is an aggregation of other objects called its *components*;
- *list type*: an object of a list type is an ordered set of objects of the same type, called its *elements*.

To each type $\tau$ is associated a *domain*, denoted by $dom(\tau)$.

We now describe more precisely the syntax and the semantics of these object types.

**Definition 1** *If $\tau$ is an **atomic type** or **a-type**, $dom(\tau)$ is given by the enumeration of its elements, i.e., $dom(\tau) = \{e_1, e_2, e_3, \ldots, e_m\}$ ($m \geq 1$). We assume that for every a-type $\tau$, $\lambda \in dom(\tau)$, where $\lambda$ denotes a null value. We also refer to a-types as **attributes**.*

Alternatively, and for the sake of simplicity, we allow for atomic types domains to be defined as the domains of usual programming languages basic types such as *int*, *float* or *string*.

**Definition 2** *Let $\tau_1, \tau_2, \ldots, \tau_n$ ($n \geq 2$) be types. The notation $\tau : (\tau_1, \tau_2, \ldots, \tau_n)$ will be used to define a **tuple type** or **t-type**. The domain of a t-type $\tau$ is defined as $dom(\tau) = dom(\tau_1) \times dom(\tau_2) \times \ldots \times dom(\tau_n)$.*

**Definition 3** *Let $\tau$ be a type. The notation $\{\tau\}$ will be used to define a **list type** or **l-type**. The domain of an l-type $\{\tau\}$ is defined as $dom(\{\tau\}) \subseteq \{i \rightarrow dom(\tau) \mid i \in \{1, \ldots, |dom(\tau)|\}$.*

When dealing with data rich Web pages, semantically similar objects can present variations in their structures. To capture this semistructured [2] nature of such objects, we adopt the notion of a *variant type* [9]. Objects of a variant type are objects of any type from a list of types called the *alternatives* of the variant type. The syntax and the semantics of a variant type are defined in what follows.

**Definition 4** *Let $\tau_1, \tau_2, \ldots, \tau_n$ ($n \geq 2$) be types. The notation $\tau : [\tau_1, \tau_2, \ldots, \tau_n]$ will be used to define a **variant type** or **v-type**. The domain of a v-type $\tau$ is defined as $dom(\tau) = dom(\tau_1) \cup dom(\tau_2) \cup \ldots \cup dom(\tau_n)$.*

An example of a complex object type composed of several sub-types is:

$$\text{Author:}[(\text{Name},\{\text{Book:}(\text{Title,Price})\}), \\ (\text{Name,Collection:}(\text{UnitPrice},\{\text{BookTitle}\}))] \tag{1}$$

This v-type, Author, has as alternatives two distinct t-types (we omit their names). The first alternative is composed by an a-type Name and by an l-type defined over a t-type Book. The second alternative is similar to the first one, but its second component is a t-type Collection, whose internal components differ from the t-type Book composing the first alternative. This v-type can be used to describe the structure of the data found in the sample page of Fig. 1. Two instances of Author present in this page are described in Fig. 2.

[Author:(⟨Name,*Agatha Christie* ⟩,
        {Book:(⟨Title,*The Adventure of the Christmas Pudding*⟩,⟨Price,*5.95*⟩));
        Book:(⟨Title,*The Hound of Death*⟩,⟨Price,*8.95*⟩));
        Book:(⟨Title,*Miss Marple's Final Cases*⟩,⟨Price,*8.95*⟩));
        Book:(⟨Title,*Poirot's Early Cases*⟩,⟨Price,*8.95*⟩));
        Book:(⟨Title,*Problem at Pollensa Bay*⟩,⟨Price,*8.95*⟩))})]

[Author:(⟨Name,*Leslie Charteris*⟩,
      Collection: (⟨UnitPrice,*6.95* ⟩,
           {⟨BookTitle,*Saint Bids Diamonds*⟩;
           ⟨BookTitle,*Saint Goes West*⟩;
           ⟨BookTitle,*Saint in Pursuit*⟩}))]

**Fig. 2.** Two possible instances of Author found in the sample page.

## 3 Representing Complex Objects Through Nested Tables

The types defined in Section 2 are powerful enough to describe arbitrarily complex object types. At the down side, describing such types may not be a trivial task. As a result, users might find it difficult to describe the structure of objects of their interest in such a way.

Motivated by this difficulty, we propose in this section the adoption of nested tables [7, 10, 17] as a paradigm for facilitating the description of complex objects by the user. This paradigm is the base of the tool presented in Section 4.

Regarding the correspondence between nested tables and complex objects, as we shall see, every table scheme can indeed be defined in terms of complex objects, although the contrary is not necessarily true. Thus, nested tables are not as powerful as complex object types. However, they provide a simple, intuitive, and expressive enough paradigm to describe the structure of complex objects normally found in the Web. For this matter, we extend the usual notion of nested tables to allow for variations in their structure.

Intuitively, a table can be defined as an l-type (list type) object defined over a t-type (tuple type) object. For "flat" tables (i.e., pure relational tables) each t-type object component is an a-type (attribute type) object. Multi-valued attributes are handled by defining t-type object components as l-type objects defined over a-type objects. To represent nested tables, one can recursively define t-type object components as l-types over t-type objects.

Consider the type defined in (1). We can define an l-type

$$\{\text{Author}:(\text{Name},\{\text{Book}:(\text{Title},\text{Price})\})\} \tag{2}$$

over it to "store" data on many author entries having a structure similar to this. This type corresponds to a table named Author, where the values of one of its columns, Book, are themselves tables. Fig. 3a illustrates such a table containing two instances of this type.

**(a)**

| Author | |
|---|---|
| **Name** | **Book** |
| Agatha Christie | Title / Price: The Adventure of the ... 5.95; The Hound of Death 8.95; Miss Marple's Final Cases 8.95; Poirot's Early Cases 8.95; Problem at Pollensa Bay 8.95 |
| Pat Burden | Title / Price: Bury Him Kindly 8.95; Screaming Bones 8.95 |

**(b)**

| Author | |
|---|---|
| **Name** | **Book** |
| Agatha Christie | Title / Price: The Adventure of the ... 5.95; The Hound of Death 8.95; Miss Marple's Final Cases 8.95; Poirot's Early Cases 8.95; Problem at Pollensa Bay 8.95 |
| Leslie Charteris | UnitPrice 6.95 / Title: Saint Bids Diamonds; Saint Goes West; Saint in Pursuit |

**Fig. 3.** Nested tables representing instances of Author according to (2) and (3).

A table where rows may have many alternative structures can be defined by using an l-type defined over a v-type, provided that each alternative t-type of this v-type has the same components. The components of the alternative t-type, however, may have different structures. For example, the table illustrated in Fig. 3b represents an instance of the following l-type:

$$\{\text{Author}:[(\text{Name},\{\text{Book}:(\text{Title},\text{Price})\}), \\ (\text{Name},\{\text{Book}:(\text{UnitPrice},\{\text{BookTitle}\})\})]\} \tag{3}$$

This l-type was built over a modified version of the v-type defined in (1), in which the second component of the second alternative of Author is now a list over a different t-type Book.

From our discussion so far, it should be clear that not all complex object types defined in Section 2 can be represented by nested tables. This is the case of the v-type defined in (1). To precisely characterize this we define the notion of a *table scheme*, as follows.

**Definition 5** *An l-type defined over a v-type $\{\tau : [\tau_1, \tau_2, \ldots, \tau_n]\}$ $(n > 0)$ is a* **table scheme** *only if all of its alternative types $\tau_i$ $(0 < i \leq n)$ are of the form*

$\tau_i = (\gamma_1, \gamma_2, \ldots, \gamma_m)$ $(m > 0)$, where each $\gamma_j$ $(j \geq 0)$ is an a-type, an l-type defined over an a-type or a table scheme.

Given the definition of a table scheme, we can now define a table as follows.

**Definition 6** *A* **table** *is defined by using the notation* $\mathsf{T}\{\tau : [\tau_1, \tau_2, \ldots, \tau_n]\}$, *where* $\mathsf{T}$ *is the table name and* $\{\tau : [\tau_1, \tau_2, \ldots, \tau_n]\}$ *is its scheme. Further, we define an* **instance** *of a table* $\mathsf{T}$ *as a subset of* $dom(\tau)$.

One way of defining complex object types that can always be derived from the structure of a nested table is to use pre-defined operations for manipulating table schemes. These operations are such that, applying any sequence of them, we will always have as a result a complex object type that satisfies Definition 5.

There are six operations that can be used for table scheme manipulation: *add-to-v-type*, *add-to-t-type*, *group-components*, *remove-from-v-type*, *remove-from-t-type* and *ungroup-components*. These operations always modify a given table scheme by adding or removing types that compose it. The *add-to-v-type* operation adds a new t-type to the list of t-types that compose a given v-type, i.e., it adds a new alternative t-type to the v-type, observing the conditions of Definition 5. The *add-to-t-type* operation adds a new component to each t-type that composes a given v-type, i.e., it adds a new column in the table. The *group-components* operation adds a nested table scheme as a new component of every t-type $\tau$ that composes a given table scheme. Fig. 4(b) shows the result of applying the *group-components* operation to the table in Fig. 4(a). The *remove-from-v-*

| Author | | |
|---|---|---|
| **Name** | **Title** | **Price** |
| *Agatha Christie* | *The Hound of Death* | *8.95* |
| *Leslie Charteris* | *Saint Bids Diamonds* | *6.95* |

(a)

| Author | | |
|---|---|---|
| **Name** | **Book** | |
| *Agatha Christie* | **Title** · *The Hound of Death* | **Price** · *8.95* |
| *Leslie Charteris* | **Title** · *Saint Bids Diamonds* | **Price** · *6.95* |

(b)

**Fig. 4.** Table Author before (a) and after (b) the *group-components* operation.

*type*, *remove-from-t-type*, and *ungroup-components* operations are, respectively, symmetric to the *add-to-v-type*, *add-to-t-type* and *group-components* operations. A more precise discussion of these operations are out of the scope of this paper and can be found in [5].

## 4    The DEByE Tool

The graphical user interface (GUI) of our semistructured data extraction tool, *DEByE (Data Extraction By Example)** [8, 16], adopts the nested table paradigm,

---

\* The name of our tool is an homage to Moshé Zloof, creator of the QBE (Query By Example) language, who suggested us the example-based approach we use to specify the data to be extracted.

as discussed in Section 3 to describe the structure of complex objects found in data rich Web pages. By using this GUI, users can easily assemble example of complex objects using, so that their implicit structure, as perceived by them, can be determined. For such data rich pages, it it is expected that just a couple of different examples are required to determine the structure of most objects in the page or even in other similar pages (e.g., pages of a same site).

Once this structural information is available, the tool adds to it information on the textual context of the example objects to build data structures called *Object Extraction (OE) patterns*. The OE patterns can then be fed to an *Extractor* module that uses them to identify and to extract new objects whose structure and textual context are similar to the example objects provided. Fig. 5 presents an overview of the major modules which compose the *DEByE* tool and their role in the data extraction process. The details of the *Extractor* module are out of

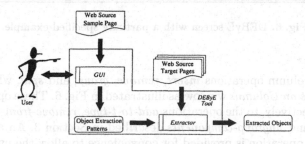

**Fig. 5.** Modules of the DEByE tool and their role in a data extraction process.

the scope of this paper and can be found in [5, 8, 15]. In this section we focus our discussion on the use of the *DEByE* GUI to assemble proper example objects.

Fig. 6 presents a snapshot of the main screen provided by the GUI to the user. The screen includes three main windows: the *Source Window*, the *Table Window*, and the *Pattern Builder Window*. The *Source Window* displays a Web page selected by the user. In this case, the page is from the Murder by the Book bookstore Web site which we have been using throughout our discussion. The *Table Window* is used to assemble the nested table that describes the structure of the example objects. The *Pattern Builder Window* is used by the user to trigger the generation of the OE patterns for the example object given.

Formally, in the *Table Window* each row corresponds to an alternative t-type that composes a v-type which is defined inside an l-type that corresponds to the outermost table, in a way similar to the l-type defined in (3). The names of the types composing these t-types appear as the heading of the table columns. This forces every row to have the same attributes, according to our definition of table scheme (Definition 5). The same is true for each nested table.

To assemble an example object, the user must mark pieces of data in the text in the *Source Window* and copy them into the columns of the *Table Window*. This is done separately for each piece of data. To allow the user to specify the (nested) table which embeds the structure of her/his example object, the tool

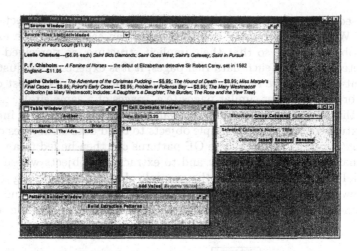

**Fig. 6.** DEByE screen with a partially specified example.

provides the column operations *insert*, *remove*, *group*, and *split*, which compose the *Operations on Columns* window as illustrated in Fig. 6. These operations correspond, respectively, to the operations *add-to-t-type*, *remove-from-t-type*, *group-components*, and *ungroup-components* described in Section 3. An additional *rename* column operation is provided for convenience to allow the user to rename a column. For instance, in Fig. 6, the user has executed the *insert* column operation to add a new column (Price) and the *rename* column operation to assign the labels Name, Title, and Price to the three columns. The other two operations are discussed in the immediately following.

In Fig. 7, the user has advanced in her/his example specification task. Having observed that *Agatha Christie* has written many books, she/he decided to compose the attributes Title and Price into a nested table, called Book, which can be used to hold various books written by *Agatha Christie*. To create this nested table, the user applies the *group* operation on the attributes Title and Price, and the *rename* operation to assign the label Book to it.

For pages with non-homogeneous objects (as the pages of the Murder by the Book site), the user might have to specify more than one example object to cover a larger fraction of the (implicit) objects in the page. For instance, in Fig. 7 the user specified a second example object to indicate that, in the case of the author *Leslie Charteris*, the price of all her books is the same. This is indicated by assembling the book titles written by *Leslie Charteris* in a list. This is done by an *insert* row operation, which corresponds to the operation *add-to-v-type* and results in the inclusion of a new row into the (nested) table. Likewise, there is also a *remove* row operation, which corresponds to the *remove-from-v-type* operation. We stress that each row in a (nested) table corresponds in fact to an alternative t-type of a v-type.

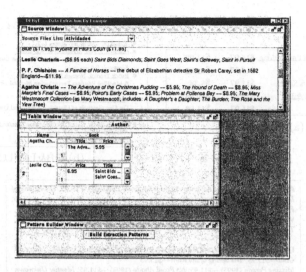

**Fig. 7.** Specification of two distinct example objects for a sample page.

## 5  Experimental Results

In this section, we present the results of some experiments we carried out using the DEByE tool. The goal was to investigate how useful is the DEByE *GUI* in assisting the user with the specification of example objects. In the experiment sixteen undergraduate Computer Science students used the DEByE *GUI* to specify example objects for three Web sites: CDNow (http://www.cdnow.com), ACM TODS from DB&LP (http://www.informatik.uni-trier.de/~ley/db), and Murder by the Book (http://www.murderbythebook.com). Fig. 8 illustrates excerpts of pages from these three sites.

According to an increasing order of complexity, the users were first presented with a page from CDNow, followed by a page from DB&LP and, at the end, with a page from Murder by the Book. In each case, each user was asked to specify a set of example objects (in a number of her/his choosing). Each set of example objects yielded a separate set of OE patterns. We notice that the (implicit) objects in the CDNow pages are flat (i.e., their structure is given by a one-level hierarchy), while the (implicit) objects in the DB&LP TODS and Murder by the Book pages can be interpreted as a two-level hierarchical structure. Further, the objects in the DB&LP TODS pages are homogeneous, while the objects in the Murder by the Book pages present structural variations.

To evaluate the user example objects specified by our 16 users, we compared each example object with all others and separated them in 3 groups. The first group is called *complete* and is composed of objects that have all a same structure and whose structure is the most complex (among all the example objects specified), according to the perception of the users. The second group is called *partial* and is composed of objects that have a structure which is only a part of the structure of the objects in the first group. The third group is called *incorrect*

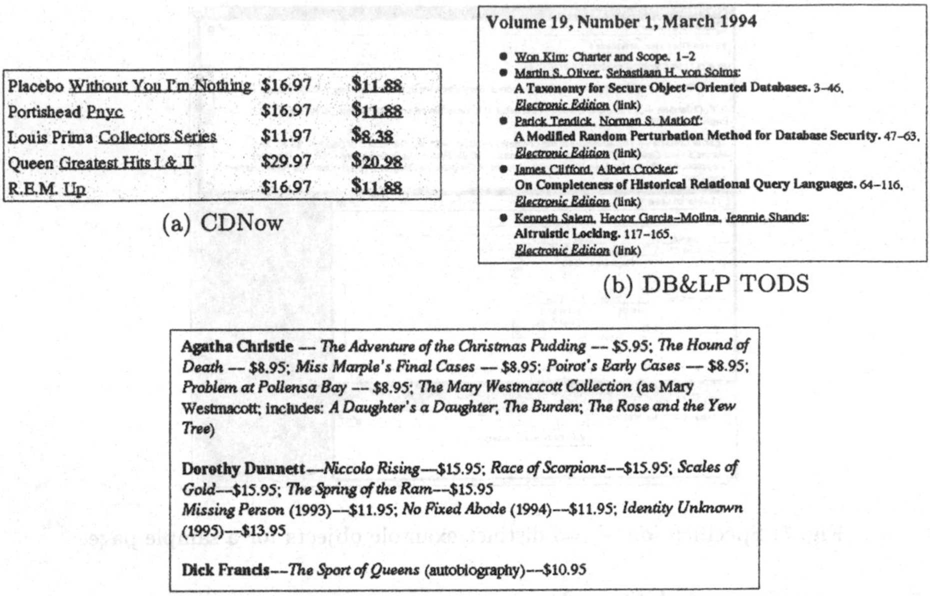

| Placebo Without You I'm Nothing | $16.97 | $11.88 |
| Portishead Pnyc | $16.97 | $11.88 |
| Louis Prima Collectors Series | $11.97 | $8.38 |
| Queen Greatest Hits I & II | $29.97 | $20.98 |
| R.E.M. Up | $16.97 | $11.88 |

(a) CDNow

Volume 19, Number 1, March 1994

- Won Kim: Charter and Scope. 1–2
- Martin S. Oliver, Sebastiaan H. von Solms:
  A Taxonomy for Secure Object–Oriented Databases. 3–46.
  *Electronic Edition* (link)
- Patick Tendick, Norman S. Matloff:
  A Modified Random Perturbation Method for Database Security. 47–63.
  *Electronic Edition* (link)
- James Clifford, Albert Crocker:
  On Completeness of Historical Relational Query Languages. 64–116.
  *Electronic Edition* (link)
- Kenneth Salem, Hector Garcia–Molina, Jeannie Shands:
  Altruistic Locking. 117–165.
  *Electronic Edition* (link)

(b) DB&LP TODS

**Agatha Christie** — *The Adventure of the Christmas Pudding* — $5.95; *The Hound of Death* — $8.95; *Miss Marple's Final Cases* — $8.95; *Poirot's Early Cases* — $8.95; *Problem at Pollensa Bay* — $8.95; *The Mary Westmacott Collection* (as Mary Westmacott; includes: *A Daughter's a Daughter; The Burden; The Rose and the Yew Tree*)

**Dorothy Dunnett**—*Niccolo Rising*—$15.95; *Race of Scorpions*—$15.95; *Scales of Gold*—$15.95; *The Spring of the Ram*—$15.95
*Missing Person* (1993)—$11.95; *No Fixed Abode* (1994)—$11.95; *Identity Unknown* (1995)—$13.95

**Dick Francis**—*The Sport of Queens* (autobiography)—$10.95

(c) Murder by the Book

**Fig. 8.** Excerpts of pages from three Web sites used in our experiments.

and is composed of all the objects that have a structure which does not seem to make sense. The results of our 16 user sessions are summarized in Table 1.

| Web Site | User Specified Example Objects | | | Percentage of Objects Extracted |
| --- | --- | --- | --- | --- |
| | Complete | Partial | Incorrect | |
| CDNow | 15 | - | 1 | 100% |
| DB&LP ACM TODS | 16 | - | - | 92% |
| Murder by the Book | 9 | 3 | 4 | 89% |

**Table 1.** Summary of the results of our experiments.

As can be observed, the users were very effective in providing examples for the CDNow and DB&LP Web sites. Surprisingly, one user miss-interpreted the CDNow page which is the least complex one. Not surprisingly, the users found it more difficult to deal with the Murder by the Book Web site. Even though, the majority of the users was able to successfully specify the example objects properly. Table 1 also presents the percentage of objects extracted from a set of pages of each Web site when we submitted complete examples to the DEByE *Extractor* module. As we can see, the tool was very effective and extracted a high percentage of the existing objects in these pages. The results of a larger set of extraction experiments on pages of several popular Web sites are reported in [8, 15].

# 6 Conclusions

In this paper, we proposed a new approach for revealing the structure of data present in data rich Web pages. This approach relies on the assumption that such pages can be seen as collections of similar complex objects and that the user can give her/his interpretation of the data structure by providing examples of such objects.

To be able to create abstractions for collections of similar objects, we defined a set of object types, including a special type, called *v-type*, which allows us to capture the semistructured nature of the data involved. The types defined are powerful enough to describe very complex data structures. Here, however, we discussed the use of nested tables as a form of representation for such structures. Nested tables are not as powerful as the defined object types, but they have the avdantage of being simple, intuitive, and quite convenient for expressing multi-level hierarchical structures [10]. We also showed that every table scheme corresponds to a complex object type, although the contrary is not necessarily true.

Based on the above ideas, we implemented a semistructured data extraction tool, called *DEByE*, whose GUI allows the assembling of example objects into a nested table by using simple "cut-and-paste" operations. The structure of the example object can then be used to identify new objects in the page or in other similar pages. As we discuss in [8, 15], this approach is very effective and usually only a couple of examples is sufficient to extract a high percentage of the objects existing in the pages.

The approach we presented is remarkably distinct from previous works because it relies on the user's perception of the object's structure. That is, instead of trying to derive structural (semantic) matches from the formating (syntax), we induce the user to inform the structure as she/he perceives it. We believe that in those situations in which the user is available to provide the information (for example, when browsing a Web site), this approach works better than alternative methods based on "blind" heuristics. Furthermore, our approach is not tied to any specific formating system (e.g. HTML, XML, LaTex, etc.). Instead, it takes advantage of any type of markups surrounding the data of interest.

# References

[1] ABITEBOUL, S., HULL, R., AND VIANU, V. *Foundations of Databases*. Addison-Wesley, Reading, Massachusetts, 1995.

[2] BUNEMAN, P. Semistructured Data. In *Proceedings of the Sixteenth ACM SIGMOD Symposium on Principles of Database Systems* (Tucson, Arizona, 1997), pp. 117–121.

[3] BUNEMAN, P., DAVIDSON, S., HILLEBRAND, G., AND SUCIU, D. A Query Language and Optimization Techniques for Unstructured Data. In *Proceedings of the ACM SIGMOD International Conference on Management of Data* (Quebec, Canada, 1996), pp. 505–516.

[4] BUNEMAN, P., DEUTSCH, A., AND TAN, W. A Deterministic Model for Semistructured Data. In *Proceedings of the Workshop on Query Processing for Semistructured Data and Non-Standard Data Formats* (Jerusalem, Israel, 1999).

[5] DA SILVA, A. S. *Example-based Extraction and Integration of Semi-Structured Data.* Ph.D. Thesis Proposal, Departament of Computer Science, Federal University of Minas Gerais, Belo Horizonte, Brazil, 2000. In preparation.

[6] EMBLEY, D. W., CAMPBELL, D. M., JIANG, Y. S., LIDDLE, S. W., NG, Y.-K., QUASS, D., AND SMITH, R. D. Conceptual-model-based data extraction. *Data & Knowledge Engineering 31*, 3 (1999), 227–251.

[7] JAESCHKE, G., AND SCHEK, H.-J. Remarks on the algebra of non first normal form relations. In *Proceedings of the ACM Symposium on Principles of Database Systems* (Los Angeles, California, 1982), ACM, pp. 124–138.

[8] LAENDER, A. H. F., RIBEIRO-NETO, B., AND DA SILVA, A. S. DEByE – Data Extraction By Example. Technical Report, Department of Computer Science, Federal University of Minas Gerais, Belo Horizonte, Brazil, 2000.

[9] LIBKIN, L. A Relational Algebra for Complex Objects Based on Partial Information. In *Proceedings of the Third Symposium on Mathematical Fundamentals of Database and Knowledge Systems* (Rostock, Germany, 1991), pp. 29–43.

[10] LORENTZOS, N. A., AND DONDIS, K. A. Query by Example for Nested Tables. In *Proceedings of the 9th International Conference in Database and Experts Systems Applications* (Vienna, Austria, 1998), pp. 716–725.

[11] NESTOROV, S., ABITEBOUL, S., AND MOTWANI, R. Inferring Structure in Semistructured Data. *SIGMOD Record 26*, 4 (1997), 39–43.

[12] NESTOROV, S., ABITEBOUL, S., AND MOTWANI, R. Extracting Schema from Semistructured Data. In *Proceedings of the ACM SIGMOD Conference on Management of Data* (Seatle, Washington, 1998), pp. 256–306.

[13] P. BUNEMAN AND W. FAN AND S. WEINSTEIN. Interaction between Path and Type Constraints. In *Proceedings of ACM Symposium on Principles of Database Systems (PODS)* (Philadephia, Pennsylvania, 1999), pp. 56–67.

[14] PAPAKONSTANTINOU, Y., GARCIA-MOLINA, H., AND WIDOM, J. Object Exchange Across Heterogeneous Information Sources. In *Proceedings of the Eleventh International Conference on Data Engineering* (Taipei, Taiwan, 1995).

[15] RIBEIRO-NETO, B., LAENDER, A. H. F., AND DA SILVA, A. S. Extracting Semi-Structured Data Through Examples. In *Proceedings of the Eighth ACM International Conference on Information and Knowledge Management - CIKM'99* (Kansas City, Missouri, 1999), pp. 94–101.

[16] SILVA, E. S. Example-Based Semi-Structured Data Extraction. Master's Thesis, Departament of Computer Science, Federal University of Minas Gerais, Belo Horizonte, Brazil, 1999. In Portuguese.

[17] VAN GUCHT, D., AND FISCHER, P. C. Multilevel nested relational structures. *Journal of Computer and System Sciences 36*, 1 (1988), 77–105.

[18] WANG, K., AND LIU, H. Schema Discovery for Semistructured Data. In *Proceedings of the Third International Conference on Knowledge Discovery and Data Mining (KDD-97)* (Newport Beach, California, 1997), pp. 271–274.

# Applying the Resource Description Framework to Web Engineering

Reinhold Klapsing and Gustaf Neumann

Information Systems and Software Techniques
University of Essen, Universitätsstraße 9, D–45141 Essen, Germany
Tel.: +49 (0201) 183 4078, Fax: +49 (0201) 183 4073
{Reinhold.Klapsing,Gustaf.Neumann}@uni-essen.de
http://nestroy.wi-inf.uni-essen.de/

**Abstract.** Generally, a multitude of tools is used for the management of
a Web application life cycle. It is highly desirable to provide an exchange
format for such tools to enable interoperability. This paper presents an
eXtensible Web Modeling Framework (XWMF), which applies the Resource Description Framework (RDF) to Web engineering to provide an
interoperable exchange format. Our proposed framework makes use of
one and the same (meta- ) data model to specify the structure and content of a Web application, to make statements *about* the elements of a
Web application, and to reason about the data and metadata. XWMF is
extensible, because schemata defining additional vocabulary to integrate
new design artifacts can be added. The XWMF tools are able to convert
the Web application (metadata) description into the corresponding Web
implementation.

## 1 Introduction

Approaches for the structured and formal development of Web applications can
be summarized by the term Web engineering (see for example [10, 15]). Web
engineering should provide artifacts to manage a Web application life cycle. A
formal model for defining a Web application should be expressed in an interoperable format that can be exchanged easily, so that a developer can use the suitable
tool for each phase of a Web application life cycle. The exchange of (parts of)
a Web application model is also necessary for the distributed development of a
Web application.

This paper presents such a formal Web application description model called
the eXtensible Web Modeling Framework (XWMF). XWMF is an application of
the Resource Description Framework (RDF) [4, 9] or, more precisely, XWMF consists of an extensible set of RDF schemata and descriptions. RDF [4] is an open
standard available from the World Wide Web Consortium (W3C), providing
a model for processing metadata, which is expressed in an interoperable and
machine-understandable format, that can be exchanged on the Web. In XWMF,
metadata is used to describe the properties and the relationships of Web resources. The distinction between "data" and "metadata" depends on the application domain. XWMF applies a (meta-) data model to define the Web resources

and to make statements *about* the resources of a Web application. This formal model results in machine-understandable *content* and *metadata* descriptions of a Web application. Design concepts and the final product are described by one and the same graph-based data model. The basic model of XWMF is extensible, thus a Web developer can introduce new design artifacts corresponding to unforeseen requirements. XWMF bridges the gap between high-level Web design concepts and the low-level file-based Web implementation model. A Web application is modeled in terms of classes and objects in contrast to files. XWMF supports the separation of layout and content information and the reuse of artifacts.

We have developed exemplary tools (the XWMF tools) which are able to automatically convert a Web application description into the corresponding Web implementation. Additionally, the tools implement a query system that supports querying the Web application metadata but also the data of the application.

The remainder of this paper is structured as follows. Section 2 discusses related Web engineering approaches and tools. Section 3 describes the components of XWMF. Section 4 discusses the Web object composition model of XWMF. The implementations of the supporting XWMF tools are presented in Sect. 5. A discussion in Sect. 6 concludes the paper.

## 2 Related Work

XWMF avoids the constraints of a file-based approach for the modeling of Web applications. There are several (Web) design approaches that provide more sophisticated abstractions than the file-based Web implementation model. Examples include OOHDM [14] and RMM [8]. These approaches are mainly used for the design phase of the life cycle of a Web application. In contrast to the approaches above XWMF provides a standardized exchange format for a Web application design as a foundation to support the whole life cycle of a Web application.

The Web Object Oriented Model (WOOM) [5] provides a generative model for describing Web applications in terms of objects arranged in a directed acyclic graph (DAG). For each object a transformer method is used to convert the object into its Web implementation. In the Web object composition model of XWMF, objects are also arranged in a DAG. In contrast to WOOM, XWMF assigns a property to classes which provides information used to convert objects into its Web implementations, in order to avoid that modeling information is hidden in a transformer method and, thus, not part of the Web application model.

Like the objects in WOOM the objects in WebComposition [7] encapsulate the conversion into a Web implementation in a dedicated method. A WebComposition application model is expressed in XML [2] and thus in a standardized programming language independent exchange format. In XWMF the standardized RDF is applied, thus it is possible to reason about the data and metadata of a Web application, which is not directly supported if XML is used.

Many commercial tools do exist for Web authoring, Web development, and Web site management. However, many of these tools are rather self-contained

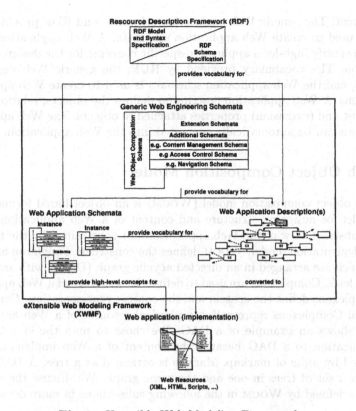

**Fig. 1.** eXtensible Web Modeling Framework

and thus difficult to integrate with other tools in the development process. The following section presents a model applying a standardized exchange format, which can be used to integrate Web engineering tools.

# 3 eXtensible Web Modeling Framework

XWMF (see Fig. 1) is an extensible set of RDF schemata and RDF descriptions defining the properties of a Web application. On the top of Fig. 1 RDF is shown. RDF provides the vocabulary necessary to create new RDF schemata and descriptions. The generic Web engineering schemata shown in the middle of Fig. 1 are expressed by using the RDF vocabulary. The generic schemata define application independent vocabularies to support Web engineering tasks. The generic Web object composition schema (WOCS) provides the vocabulary to define structure and content of a Web application in terms of objects. The WOCS vocabulary and the corresponding model are described in Sect. 4. XWMF is extensible because additional generic Web engineering schemata can be included. Such extension schemata can provide vocabulary for various application areas such as advanced navigation modeling, access control modeling, or content management. The generic Web engineering schemata and RDF provide the vocabulary used to create Web application schemata. A Web application schema is used to specify high-level application-specific concepts for the design of a Web application. The vocabulary provided by RDF, the generic Web engineering schemata, and the Web application schemata is used to create Web application descriptions. A Web application description defines the objects, relationships of the objects, and (extension) properties attached to objects. The Web application descriptions can be automatically converted into the Web application.

## 4  Web Object Composition Model

The Web object composition model (WOCM) is an object-based formal (meta) data model for designing structure and content of a Web application. WOCM gives an abstract view of the Web application not constrained by the file-based Web implementation model. WOCM defines the constructs *Simplexon* and *Complexon* which are arranged in an directed acyclic graph (DAG), with simplexons being the leafs. Complexons are used to define the structure of a Web application while simplexons define the content and the content representation. *Components* are special Complexons representing a physical resource of a Web application. Figure 2 shows an example of a DAG. We chose to map the structure of a Web application to a DAG because the content of a Web implementation is represented by units of markup. Markup is arranged as a tree. A DAG is able to express a set of trees in one and the same graph. We discuss the modeling constructs defined by WOCM in the following subsections in more detail.

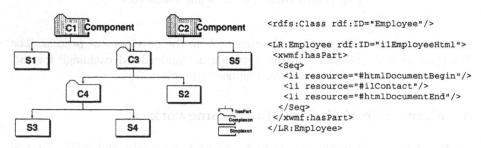

```
<rdfs:Class rdf:ID="Employee"/>

<LR:Employee rdf:ID="i1EmployeeHtml">
 <xwmf:hasPart>
  <Seq>
   <li resource="#htmlDocumentBegin"/>
   <li resource="#i1Contact"/>
   <li resource="#htmlDocumentEnd"/>
  </Seq>
 </xwmf:hasPart>
</LR:Employee>
```

**Fig. 2.** DAG of a Component          **Fig. 3.** Complexon (Employee)

### 4.1  Complexons

Complexons are containers for simplexons and complexons. Circular containment is not allowed. Complexons support separation of concerns in the way that they allow to define the structure of a Web application independently from the organization of the files of a Web application. The containment relationship is modeled with the property *hasPart* which is defined by WOCS. Figure 3 shows the definition of the complexon class Employee (in abbreviated RDF/XML syntax). The complexon instance i1EmployeeHtml of type Employee has the predicate hasPart referring to a sequence of instances of simplexons. The type concept allows to query the model to show all instances of a certain type (of type Employee for example).

## 4.2 Simplexons

A simplexon class is used to define an abstract data type. In addition a simplexon class defines the Web implementation for objects of that class. Thus the separation of concerns (separate content from its Web implementation) is supported because an object's content can be defined independently from its Web implementation. A Web application developer defines which predicates a simplexon should have. Figure 4 shows the definition of the simplexon class Contact and the property name which is assigned to the simplexon class Contact. A property is defined independently from a simplexon class and the same property can be assigned to many simplexon classes. This property-centric approach enables multiple use of already defined properties in different contexts. For simplexons,

```
<rdfs:Class rdf:ID="Contact"/>

<rdf:Property rdf:ID="name">
  <rdfs:domain rdf:resource="#Contact"/>
  <rdfs:range  rdf:resource=
  "http://.../PR-rdf-schema-19990303#Literal"/>
</rdf:Property>
```

**Fig. 4.** Class Contact with an assigned Property

subclassing is supported. The subclassing relationship allows the developer to model property inheritance. Figure 5 shows an example where the simplexons HtmlContact and WmlContact inherit the property name. Figure 6 shows the corresponding RDF/XML serialization defining the subclass relationship of class Contact and HtmlContact by the predicate subClassOf. A simplexon class which should be instantiated must have a predicate *implementation*. The value of the predicate *implementation* is used to convert a simplexon into the Web implementation model. The predicate *implementation* can be respecified by a subclass to refine the Web implementation model in regard of the properties a subclass adds. WOCS defines any markup or string as a value for the property *implementation*. Thus, for example, HTML [13], XML [2], WML [16] are allowed. In addition to model (parts of) Web pages, simplexons can be used to model (parts of) program code for the client side (e.g. ECMAScript [6]) or server side (e.g. XOTcl [12]). Markup or program code at any granularity are allowed as value of the property *implementation*. Thus ad-hoc design is supported by defining a whole (parameterized) Web page with a single simplexon. A more sophisticated design

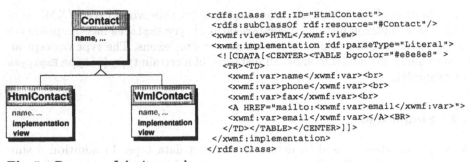

```
<rdfs:Class rdf:ID="HtmlContact">
  <rdfs:subClassOf rdf:resource="#Contact"/>
  <xwmf:view>HTML</xwmf:view>
  <xwmf:implementation rdf:parseType="Literal">
  <![CDATA[<CENTER><TABLE bgcolor="#e8e8e8" >
    <TR><TD>
      <xwmf:var>name</xwmf:var><br>
      <xwmf:var>phone</xwmf:var><br>
      <xwmf:var>fax</xwmf:var><br>
      <A HREF="mailto:<xwmf:var>email</xwmf:var>">
      <xwmf:var>email</xwmf:var></A><BR>
    </TD></TABLE></CENTER>]]>
  </xwmf:implementation>
</rdfs:Class>
```

**Fig. 5.** Property Inheritance by means of Subclassing

**Fig. 6.** Simplexon Class HtmlContact

is achieved by defining a simplexon per concept embodied in a Web page and by composing these simplexons by a complexon.

The XML element *var* can be used as a placeholder inside a value of the property *implementation*. For example **<xwmf:var>name</xwmf:var>** is used as a placeholder for a value of the predicate **name** of an instance of class **HtmlContact**. Figure 6 shows an example with several placeholders. Defining a part of a Web

```
<lr:HtmlContact rdf:ID="i1Contact">
  <lr:name>Reinhold Klapsing</lr:name>
  <lr:phone>+49 (201) 183 4078</lr:phone>
  <lr:fax>+49 (201) 183 4073</lr:fax>
  <lr:email>
  Reinhold.Klapsing@uni-essen.de
  </lr:email>
</lr:HtmlContact>
```

```
<CENTER><TABLE bgcolor="#e8e8e8" ><TR>
  <TD>Reinhold Klapsing<br>
  +49 (201) 183 4078<br>
  +49 (201) 183 4073<br>
  <A HREF=
  "mailto:Reinhold.Klapsing@uni-essen.de">
  Reinhold.Klapsing@uni-essen.de</A><BR>
</TD></TABLE></CENTER>
```

**Fig. 7.** Simplexon Instance i1Contact

**Fig. 8.** Web Implementation of i1Contact

resource is done by instantiating a simplexon class. The Web implementation is generated by merging the values of an object via the *var-construct* with the value of the property *implementation* defined by the class an object is related too. Reuse is supported because (many) objects related to a simplexon class are using the same Web implementation (value of the property *implementation*). Figure 7 shows the object **i1Contact** which is an instance of the class **HtmlContact**. Figure 8 shows the Web implementation (in this case HTML) of the object **i1Contact**, composed of values of the object and the value of the predicate **implementation** of class **HtmlContact** (see Fig. 6). Figure 3 shows the usage of the simplexon instance **i1Contact** as part of the complexon **Employee**. An object may be an instance of more than one simplexon class. This indicates that the object has all the characteristics that are to be expected of an object of each super class. This, in conjunction with the *view* property, which is defined in WOCS, allows to define different views for an object according to the context (see Sect. 4.3) in which an object is used. Additionally, object reuse is supported because

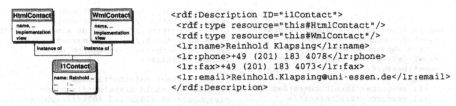

```
<rdf:Description ID="i1Contact">
  <rdf:type resource="this#HtmlContact"/>
  <rdf:type resource="this#WmlContact"/>
  <lr:name>Reinhold Klapsing</lr:name>
  <lr:phone>+49 (201) 183 4078</lr:phone>
  <lr:fax>+49 (201) 183 4073</lr:fax>
  <lr:email>Reinhold.Klapsing@uni-essen.de</lr:email>
</rdf:Description>
```

**Fig. 9.** Multiple Types of an Object   **Fig. 10.** Simplexon Instance with Multiple Types

only one object has to be defined for possibly many views. Figure 9 shows the object i1Contact which is an instance of the simplexon classes HtmlContact and WmlContact and Fig. 10 shows the corresponding RDF/XML serialization syntax (note: in contrast to the examples above no abbreviated RDF syntax is used because multiple type predicates are not expressible in abbreviated RDF syntax). The simplexon class HtmlContact defines, for the predicate view, the value HTML (see Fig. 6), thus the instance i1Contact may be used in an HTML context. In the same way the class WmlContact defines the view WML thus the instance i1Contact may also be used in a WML context.

### 4.3 Components

A component is a special complexon representing a physical entity (e.g. a Web page stored in a file) of a Web application. A component is a complexon with an *isComponent* predicate. A Web application consists of a set of components. For each component the corresponding complexons and simplexons are arranged in a tree, where the complexon which has an assigned *isComponent* predicate is the root container (see Fig. 2). More precisely, the complexon having an *isComponent* predicate is a representative for the whole component (tree composed of complexons and simplexons). WOCS defines an URI as an allowed value of an *isComponent* predicate which gives a reference to where a component should be stored. Additionally, for a component the value of the (optional) predicate *isView* defines in which context the simplexons of a component have to be instantiated. A component must have a predicate *isView* if it contains simplexons which are instances of more than one class.

Figure 11 shows the complexon instance i1EmployeeHtml which is also a component. After the generation process this component will be stored in the file /htdocs/Klapsing.html. The value HTML of the predicate isView defines the context in which the simplexons of the component have to be interpreted. The context HTML defines that the implementation of the simplexon class HtmlContact (and not of the simplexon class WmlContact) has to be used during the generation process.

### 4.4 Integrating Extension Models

Integrating extension models into XWMF is supported by utilizing XML namespaces [3]. An XML namespace refers to the corresponding RDF schema

```
<WP:Employee rdf:ID="ilEmployeeHtml">
  <xwmf:inComponent rdf:resource=
  "file:/htdocs/Klapsing.html"/>
  <xwmf:isView>HTML</xwmf:isView>
  <xwmf:hasPart>
    <Seq>
      <li resource="#htmlDocumentBegin"/>
      <li resource="#ilContact"/>
      <li resource="#htmlDocumentEnd"/>
    </Seq>
  </xwmf:hasPart>
</WP:Employee>
```

**Fig. 11.** Complexon which is also a Component

```
<RDF xmlns="http://.../22-rdf-syntax-ns#"
  xmlns:rdf="http://.../22-rdf-syntax-ns#"
  xmlns:rdfs="http://.../PR-rdf-schema-19990303#"
  xmlns:xwmf="http://.../schema/xwmf.rdf#"
  xmlns:cm="http://.../schema/cm.rdf#"
  xmlns:lr="this#">
  ...
  <lr:HtmlContact rdf:ID="ilContact">
    <lr:name>Reinhold Klapsing</lr:name>
    <lr:phone>+49 (201) 183 4078</lr:phone>
    <lr:fax>+49 (201) 183 4073</lr:fax>
    <lr:email>
    Reinhold.Klapsing@uni-essen.de
    </lr:email>
    <cm:expires>31 Dec 2000</cm:expires>
  </lr:HtmlContact>
</RDF>
```

**Fig. 12.** Integrating Extension Schemata

which defines the vocabulary used to apply the extension model. To extend WOCM, properties are assigned to complexons, simplexons, and components. Figure 12 shows the RDF/XML serialization syntax of the extension of the simplexon object ilContact. The predicate expires defines the expiration date of the information represented by that object. A content management software can query the model by means of the property expires to determine which information became obsolete. The property expires is defined in the RDF schema http://.../schema/cm.rdf. The content management schema is bound to the XML namespace prefix cm.

Note the possibility to store an extension description separated from the WOCM description. Thus, a content management tool only needs to operate on the content management description, possibly stored on a remote system.

# 5 Implementation

We developed a set of tools to create (GRAMTOR), process (Web application generation tools) and analyze (WebObjectBrowser, RDF-Handle) the RDF description of a Web application. The Web application generation tools are written in the object-oriented scripting language XOTcl [12]. For reading RDF models we developed an RDF parser which uses the TclXML parser [1]. The RDF parser produces the triples of an RDF model. The RDF-Handle operates on the triples and provides an interface to modify an RDF model and to store the model in triple notation and RDF/XML serialization syntax. Additionally, the RDF-Handle provides an interface to query an RDF model. The query interface is used by the WebObjectComposer to analyze the Web application description. The WebObjectComposer generates XOTcl classes and objects representing the simplexons, complexons and components of a Web application and is able to generate the corresponding Web implementation.

GRAMTOR is an RDF editor for the graphical development of RDF models. GRAMTOR is able to save RDF models in different formats including the triple notation and the XML/RDF serialization syntax.

The WebObjectBrowser provides a graphical interface which shows the class hierarchy and the objects of a Web application as a graph. A developer can browse the simplexons, complexons, and components to analyze the current state of the classes and objects. The main parts of the GRAMTOR and the Web-ObjectBrowser are written in XOTcl. The graphical user interfaces have been developed with the Motif version of $W_a f^e$[11] which provides a Tcl interface for the XToolkit.

## 6  Conclusion, Future Work and Acknowledgements

Web engineering is a complex task that makes it necessary to use a multitude of artifacts for the development of a Web application. In this paper we presented XWMF which provides a vocabulary defined by a set of RDF schemata that can be used to describe Web applications. XWMF enables inter-operation of various Web engineering artifacts by applying a standardized machine-understandable exchange format. Both data and metadata of a Web application are represented in one and the same graph-based model. Machine-supported reasoning about data and metadata is enabled. In order to meet the requirements of additional Web engineering tasks XWMF can be extended by new generic Web engineering schemata. XWMF provides concepts of a higher-level for the definition of a Web application than the file-based Web implementation model by supporting the definition of concepts in Web application schemata. To support not only ad-hoc development but also more sophisticated designs the grade of granularity of concepts is left to the developer. The content of a Web resource is separated from the presentation layout. For the same content different views can be specified. XWMF supports any text-based implementation language, including HTML and XML in its various applications. Adaption of the Web application to new Web implementation technologies is supported as the access to the implementation definitions in the design model is granted. Reuse is supported as a Web implementation template is shared by (possibly many) objects. This also supports maintenance, as a modification of a Web implementation template results in a modification of the Web representation of all objects related to the template. XWMF supports modularity as extension descriptions can be separated from a WOCM. Distributed development and control of a Web application are supported as extension descriptions can be stored on a remote system.

We plan to support more sophisticated navigational user guidance by defining vocabulary for guided tours. This together with the XWMF query system will allow such tasks as generating a guided tour of all resources of a certain type. To support a wider range of reuse of concepts and Web implementation templates we plan to develop a repository mechanism and to extend the XWMF tools accordingly. Future versions of the tools and a longer version of this paper can be obtained from the XWMF home page [17]

We thank Wolfram Conen and Eckhart Köppen for many useful discussions regarding XWMF. Alexander Block developed significant parts of the GRAMTOR and the RDF-Handle as part of his diploma thesis. Fredj Dridi is author of a tool called Inspector. The WebObjectBrowser is a re-adjustment of this tool.

# References

1. St. Ball: The "native" TclXML parser. http://www.zveno.com/zm.cgi/in-tclxml/.
2. T. Bray, J. Paoli, C. M. Sperberg-McQueen: Extensible Markup Language (XML) 1.0. W3C, 1998. http://www.w3.org/TR/1998/REC-xml-19980210.
3. T. Bray, D. Hollander, and A. Layman: Namespaces in XML. W3C, 1999. http://www.w3.org/TR/1999/REC-xml-names-19990114/.
4. D. Brickley, R.V. Guha: Resource Description Framework (RDF) Schema Specification. W3C, 1999. http://www.w3.org/TR/1999/PR-rdf-schema-19990303.
5. F. Coda, C. Ghezzi, G. Vigna, F. Garzotto: Towards a Software Engineering Approach to Web Site Development. In *9th International Workshop on Software Specification and Design (IWSSD)*. IEEE, 1998.
6. ECMA General Assembly: ECMAScript Language Specification. Standard ECMA-262, ECMA, 1998. http://www.ecma.ch/stand/ECMA-262.htm.
7. H.-W. Gellersen, R. Wicke, M. Gaedke: WebComposition: an object-oriented support system for the Web Engineering Lifecycle. In *6th International World-Wide Web Conference*, volume 29 of *Computer Networks and ISDN Systems*, pages 1429–1437. IW3C2, 1997.
8. T. Isakovitz, E. A. Stohr, P. Balasubramanian: RMM: A Methodology for Structured Hypermedia Design. *Communications of the ACM*, 38(8):34–44, 1995.
9. O. Lassila, R. R. Swick: Resource Description Framework (RDF) Model and Syntax Specification. W3C, 1999. http://www.w3.org/TR/1999/REC-rdf-syntax-19990222.
10. S. Murugesan, Y. Deshpande: Web Engineering. In *International Conference on Software Engineering (ICSE99)*, pages 693–694. ACM, 1999.
11. G. Neumann, St. Nusser: $W_a f^e$- An X Toolkit Based Frontend for Application Programs in Various Programming Languages. In *USENIX Winter 1993 Technical Conference*, 1993.
12. G. Neumann, U. Zdun: XOTcl, an Object-Oriented Scripting Language. In *Proceedings of 7th Usenix Tcl/Tk Conference (Tcl2k)*, 2000.
13. D. Raggett, A. Le Hors, I. Jacobs: HTML 4.01 Specification. W3C, 1999. http://www.w3.org/TR/1999/REC-html401-19991224.
14. D. Schwabe, G. Rossi, S. D.J. Barbosa: Systematic Hypermedia Application Design with OOHDM. In *Hypertext 1996*. ACM, 1996.
15. L. A. Shklar, J. G. Davis, S. Murugesan, C. F. Enguix: International Workshop Web Engineerung '99: Eighth International World Wide Web Conference. http://budhi.uow.edu.au/web-engineering99/web_engineering.html, 1999.
16. Wireless Application Protocol Forum: WAP WML - Version 1.2. Approved specification, WAP-Forum, 1999. http://www1.wapforum.org/tech/terms.asp?doc=SPEC-WML-19991104.pdf.
17. XWMF-Home-Page http://nestroy.wi-inf.uni-essen.de/xwmf/.

# E-commerce Site Evaluation: A Case Study

Luis Olsina[12], Guillermo Lafuente[1], Gustavo Rossi[23]

[1] GIDIS, Department of Computer Science, Faculty of Engineering, at UNLPam,
Calle 9 y 110, (6360) General Pico, LP, Argentina
E-mail [olsinal, lafuente]@ing.unlpam.edu.ar
[2] LIFIA, Informatics School at UNLP, Calle 50 y 115, (1900) La Plata, Argentina
[3] CONICET - Argentina
E-mail grossi@info.unlp.edu.ar

**Abstract.** Recent surveys on e-commerce sites confirm the increased use of the Web for shopping. The reasons of these trends have been attributed to different factors such as convenience, saving time, absence of sales pressure, among others. However, an essential site characteristic that should also be taken into account is the quality in use. In this paper, we present a case study on five e-bookstores in order to assess characteristics and attributes that influence quality in use utilizing for such an end the Web-site Quality Evaluation Methodology (QEM). The main goal of this work is to show the level of accomplishment of required quality characteristic like usability, functionality, reliability, efficiency and derived sub-characteristics and attributes, regarding the user standpoint. In addition, we focus on sub-characteristics and attributes concerning e-commerce site functionality.

## 1 Introduction

E-commerce (EC) is nowadays a growing reality in the Web. Interestingly, recent field studies on EC sites confirm the increased use of the Web for shopping. For instance, the tenth edition of GVU's WWW User Survey [4] reports that both personal and professional shopping are up by significant percentages (10.3% and 23.7%, respectively) since the ninth survey. The major reasons for using the Web for personal shopping was convenience factor (21% of reason given), followed by saving time (18.8%), the presence of vendor information (18.7%), and the absence of sales pressure (16%).

Besides, surveys and evaluations on EC sites' attributes and factors have also drawn initial and interesting outcomes. For example, to cite only some, Lohse and Spiller [6] measured 32 attributes on 28 Web stores that influence store traffic and sales. The authors identified six principal categories for a Web store, namely: Merchandise, Service, Convenience, Store Navigation, Promotion, and Checkout, regarding a previous classification [1]. In addition, Tilson et al [11] surveyed factors and principles affecting the decision to purchase by analyzing four sites; the 16 participants rated the importance of fifty factors on a scale from 1 to 7.

However, considering the evaluation viewpoint, an essential site (product) issue that should be emphasized is the characteristics and attributes that influence the quality in use. Process quality contributes to improving product quality, and product quality contributes to improving quality in use. Thus, one of the main goals to website evaluation and comparison is to understand the extent which a given set of product characteristics and attributes fulfills a set of explicit and implicit needs in consideration of specific audiences. In this direction, the proposed Web-site QEM methodology [10] can be an useful approach in providing this understanding, in a rather objective and quantitative way. In addition, by analyzing the intermediate and final product quality indicators recommendations can be suggested. That is, the evaluation process generates elemental, partial, and global quality indicators (or preferences) that can be easily backward and forward traced, justified, and efficiently employed in recommendations tasks.

Therefore, the aim of this paper is to show the level of accomplishment of selected quality characteristic like *Usability, Functionality, Reliability, Efficiency* and derived sub-characteristics and attributes in five e-bookstores, from a general user standpoint. With regard to quality characteristics and attributes for assessment purposes, over a hundred and forty ones were taken into account, considering attributes directly or indirectly quantifiable. Furthermore, we build the quality requirement tree starting from the same high-level quality characteristics as those prescribed in ISO/IEC 9126 standard [5], -a new version of this standard is in draft state.

In this work, sub-characteristics and attributes concerning EC functionality and a recursive decomposition mechanism are also discussed. For instance, the *Functionality* characteristic is split up in *Searching and Retrieving, Navigation and Browsing,* and *EC Functionality and Content* sub-characteristics. Regarding the latter, attributes for *Product Information, Purchase, Customer* and *Store Features,* and *Promotion Policies* sub-characteristics were in turn specified.

The structure of this paper is as follows: in the next section, we put the e-bookstores case study in context, and in Section 3, we present the evaluation process regarding Web-site QEM's main steps. In sub-section 3.1, the decomposition mechanism and the EC functionality sub-characteristic are analyzed. In the two following sub-sections the elementary and global criteria and methods are outlined. In sub-section 3.4, we discuss and compare partial and global outcomes. Finally, in Section 4, concluding remarks are considered. An Appendix depicts the whole requirement tree employed in this case study.

## 2 The E-Commerce Case Study on Bookstores

In order to prepare the study on e-bookstores domain five established sites were selected (the reader can also refers to the case studies carried out on museums and academic sites domains [8, 9]). Likewise, the chosen sites should be typical and well known regionally and/or internationally as well as they should specifically allow domestic and international shopping. One of the primary goals of this study is the understanding and comparison of the current level of fulfillment of essential quality characteristics and attributes given a set of requirements with regard to a general audience. Particularly, we assessed the level of accomplishment of standardized characteristics as previously mentioned (and derived sub-characteristics and attributes), and compare partial and global preferences in order to analyze and draw conclusions about the state-of-the-art of e-bookstores quality. Important conclusions (mainly, domain specific as well as general ones) can emerge as it will be seen, later.

We selected the following e-bookstore sites, namely: Amazon (US, http://www.amazon.com), Cúspide (Argentina, http://www.cuspide.com.ar), Barnes and Noble (US, http://www.bn.com), Díaz de Santos (Spain, http://www.diazdesantos.es), and Borders (US, http://www.borders.com). The data collection activity was performed from the 15th Sep. to the 20th Oct., 1999. In this period, Díaz de Santos site changed its look & feel, so we evaluate the new interface.

Speaking in a wider sense, software artifacts are generally produced to satisfy specific user's needs, and Web artifacts are not the exception. In designing e-bookstore sites, there are many challenges that should not be neglected. For instance, when users enter the first time at a given home page they may want to find a piece of information quickly. There are two ways to help them in doing that: browsing or searching. Moreover, to get a time-effective mental model of the overall site, i.e., its structure and content, there are attributes like a table of contents or an index (a catalog) that help in getting a quick global site understandability, facilitating browsing. On the other hand, a searching function (quick and advanced ones), provided in the main page and remaining permanent in all pages can effectively help retrieving the desired piece of information and avoid browsing. So, the two functions can be complemented. In addition, first time visitor help (or a guided tour) and general information attributes can allow quick understanding about content information, common procedures, and policies. Fig. 1, shows a screenshot of a home page and highlights some attributes. There are a lot of such attributes both general and domain specific that contribute to quality, so designers should take into account when building for intended audiences (for a wider specification, see the list in Appendix A).

**Fig. 1.** Partial view of Cúspide's home page, where some attributes are highlighted. These are generally available in e-bookstore sites.

# 3 The Evaluation Process

The proposed stepwise, expert-driven methodology, Web-site QEM, is essentially quantitative, flexible and robust, and it covers most of the activities in the evaluation, comparison, and ranking process of websites. These steps are grouped in the following major technical phases:

1. *Quality Requirement Definition and Specification,*
2. *Elementary Evaluation: Definition and Implementation,*
3. *Global Evaluation: Definition and Implementation,*
4. *Analysis, Conclusions and Documentation*

As said above, these phases are composed by activities. Even if we do not describe and discuss thoroughly the steps here (for a broader description, see [9]), the next fourth sub-sections deal with some activities, strategies, models, methods, and tools employed in the EC study regarding the previous listed stages.

## 3.1 The E-bookstore Requirement Tree

In the first phase, the evaluators should clarify the evaluation goals and user standpoint. They should select the sites to assess and compare, and, finally, agree and specify the quality requirement tree. In the latter step, the ISO-prescribed characteristics give evaluators a conceptual model for quality requirements and provide a baseline for ulterior decomposition. Thus, a quality characteristic can be decomposed in a list of sub-characteristics recursively, and so, a sub-characteristic can be refined in a set of direct or indirect measurable attributes. Therefore, regarding the domain, the specific goals, and the user standpoint (i.e., the user implicit and explicit needs), quality characteristics and attributes should be specified in a requirement tree. The whole-intervened characteristics and measurable attributes for this study are outlined in Appendix A. Next, we discuss some characteristics and attributes and the decomposition mechanism.

The *Usability* high-level characteristic is decomposed in sub-characteristics such as *Global Site Understandability, Feedback and Help Features,* and *Interface and Aesthetic Features.* The *Functionality* characteristic is split up in *Searching and Retrieving Issues, Navigation and Browsing Issues,* and *EC Functionality and Content* sub-characteristics. The same decomposition mechanism is applied to *Reliability and Efficiency* factors.

Focusing on *EC Functionality and Content* characteristic, we have grouped five main components: *Product Information* (2.3.1 coded), *Purchase Features* (2.3.2), *Customer Features* (2.3.3), *Store Features* (2.3.4), and *Promotion Policies* (2.3.5). Regarding *Product Information* sub-characteristic, we see at the same level *Product Description, Price Evaluation,* and 2.3.1.3, 2.3.1.4, 2.3.1.5 attributes. For example, the *Product Description* (2.3.1.1 coded), is compounded by a *Basic Description* attribute, *Book Content & Structure,* and *Product Image* sub-characteristics. The *Basic Description* attribute takes into account the availability of information such as book title, author, edition, format, pages, size/weight, ISBN, price and availability (e.g., we can use a discrete multi-variable criterion in order to evaluate this attribute). On the other hand, the *Price Comparison Availability* (2.3.1.2.1) mechanism allows users to compare prices in different stores. According to the recent GVU's WWW User Survey [4] it informs that for professional shopping *Detailed Information* was cited as important when selecting a product or service on the Web for 30.6% of responses out of a choice of 6 possible ones; *Information about Availability* was cited as the next most important (26.7%), followed by ability to make *Price Comparisons* (26.5%) by the user. Unfortunately, no evaluated site had this desirable attribute.

Focusing on *Purchase Features* (2.3.2 coded), we can observe two main sub-characteristics: *Purchase Mode* (2.3.2.1), and *Purchase Policies* (2.3.2.2). Regarding the *Purchase Mode* sub-factor, online and offline modalities are feasible, however, the former is becoming more preferred as long as confidence in security is increasing. For purchase online, the *Shopping Basket*, *Quick Purchase*, and *Checkout* features are modeled. The shopping basket mechanism (also known as a design pattern in [12]) is generally used to decouple the selection process from the checkout process of products or services. For example, we evaluate the availability, the continue buying feedback, and the edit/recalculate feature of the *Shopping Basket* sub-characteristic. On the other hand, the *Purchase Policy* (2.3.2.2) sub-factor, should contain a sound and concise information for potential and current customers, as cancellation and return policies information, shipping and handling costs (separating domestic from international information), payment policy information, and, optionally, a resent purchase or gift service facility.

As previously said, there are a lot of such attributes that contribute to site quality in use that designers should consider when building for some domain and intended audiences. Finally, focusing on *Feedback and Help Features* characteristic (where Usability is the super-characteristic), we have grouped five main components: two of them are *Link-based Feedback* (1.2.3) and *Form-based Feedback* (1.2.4). *FAQ* and *What's New Feature* are attributes of 1.2.3 sub-characteristic; *Questionnaire Feature*, *Comments/Suggestions* and *Subject-Oriented Feedback* (like in Barnes & Noble and Borders sites) are attributes of 1.2.4 sub-characteristic. They partially contribute to the communicativeness and learning process.

## 3.2 The Elementary Evaluation

In the second phase, the evaluators should define the basis for elementary evaluation criterion (for each attribute), and perform the measurement and mapping process. For each direct or indirect attribute $A_i$, we can associate a variable $X_i$, which can take a real measured or calculated value. Besides, for each variable it is necessary to establish a scale and unit [3], and set a criterion function, called the elementary criterion function. This function models a mapping among the measured or calculated value to the value of the new numerical representation, resulting afterwards in an elementary quality preference. The elementary preference $EQ_i$ is frequently interpreted as the percentage of satisfied requirements for a given attribute, and it is defined in the range between 0, and 100% [2]. In this way, the scale and unit become normalized.

There are two kinds of general criteria: absolute and relative. Regarding absolute criteria, a basic taxonomy decomposes preference variables in continuous and discrete. Continuous variable criteria are classified in direct preference assessment, single, normalized and multi-variable criteria. Discrete variable criteria are classified in binary, multi-level, subset-structured, and multi-variable criteria. In the following specification two types of criteria are shown. On the other hand, to ease the preferences interpretation, we group them in three categories or acceptability levels, namely: unsatisfactory (from 0 to 40%), marginal (from 40 to 60%), and satisfactory (from 60 to 100%) -or red, gray, and green ranges respectively. Next, for the e-bookstore study two attributes are documented following a hierarchical and descriptive specification framework as in previous case studies.

Title: Customized Recommendations; Code: 2.3.3.2; Type: Attribute
Higher-level characteristic: Functionality ; Super-characteristic: Customer Features
Definition / Comments: It is a mechanism that provides customers with personalized recommendations of products according previous buying preferences. These recommendations are automatically generated each time he/she enters to the e-store.
Elementary Criteria: It is an absolute and discrete binary criterion. We only ask if it is available (1), or not (0).
Preference Scale: see Fig. 2; Data Collection Type: Manual, Observational
Example/s: Only Amazon site provided this facility.

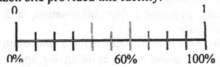

**Fig. 2.** Customized Recommendations attribute represented by a preference scale.

Title: Broken Links; Code: 3.1.1.1; Type: Attribute
Higher-level characteristic: Reliability; Super-characteristic: Link Errors
Definition/Comments: It represents found links that lead to missing destination nodes (also called dangling links). *"Users get irritated when they attempt to go somewhere, only to get their reward snatched away at the last moment by a 404 or other incomprehensible error message"* [7].
Elementary Criteria: It is an absolute and continuous normalized-variable criterion, where if BL = number of broken links found, and TL = number of total site links, then, the formula to compute the variable is: $X = 100 - (BL * 100/TL) * 10$; where, if $X < 0$ then $X = 0$; Preference Scale: see Fig. 3; Data Collection Type: Automated.
Example/s: Cúspide yielded an elementary preference of 99.83 %, Amazon, 98.40 %, and Barnes and Noble site 97.45 %.

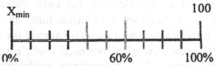

**Fig. 3.** Broken Links attribute represented by a preference scale.

Ultimately, once all elementary criteria were defined and data collected, the elementary preferences can be yielded and documented. The final hyperdocument links the requirement tree with the specification cards and elementary outcomes. Table 1, shows the preferences of some attributes for each e-bookstore site.

**Table 1.** Partial outcomes of elementary preferences for the five e-bookstores.

| | Amazon | Barnes & Noble | Cúspide | Díaz de Santos | Borders |
|---|---|---|---|---|---|
| **1. Usability** | | | | | |
| 1.2.3.1 | 100 | 100 | 100 | 0 | 100 |
| 1.2.3.2 | 100 | 100 | 80 | 80 | 100 |
| 1.2.4.1 | 0 | 0 | 0 | 100 | 0 |
| 1.2.4.2 | 0 | 100 | 0 | 70 | 70 |
| 1.2.4.3 | 0 | 100 | 0 | 0 | 70 |
| **2. Functionality** | | | | | |
| 2.1.1.1 | 100 | 100 | 100 | 0 | 100 |
| 2.1.1.2 | 100 | 100 | 100 | 100 | 70 |
| 2.3.1.1.1 | 100 | 100 | 40 | 24 | 70 |
| 2.3.1.1.2.1 | 100 | 100 | 50 | 50 | 0 |
| 2.3.1.1.2.2 | 42 | 42 | 12 | 12 | 21 |
| 2.3.1.2.1 | 0 | 0 | 0 | 0 | 0 |
| 2.3.2.1.1.1.1 | 100 | 100 | 100 | 100 | 100 |
| 2.3.2.1.1.1.2 | 100 | 70 | 0 | 0 | 40 |
| 2.3.2.1.1.1.3 | 100 | 100 | 100 | 100 | 100 |
| 2.3.2.1.1.2 | 100 | 0 | 0 | 0 | 100 |
| 2.3.2.1.1.3.1 | 100 | 100 | 100 | 0 | 100 |
| 2.3.2.1.1.3.2 | 100 | 100 | 100 | 0 | 0 |
| **3. Reliability** | | | | | |
| 3.1.1.1 | 98.4 | 97.45 | 99.83 | 60.07 | 76.34 |
| **4. Efficiency** | | | | | |
| 4.1.1 | 100 | 77.75 | 100 | 99.75 | 99.70 |

Even if they are only elementary values where no aggregation mechanism and computation were yet applied, some observations can be done all the same. For instance, we see the five sites having *What's New* (1.2.3.2) attribute resolved (the greater preference arises if, to the newest additions -generally in the home page, is also included a summary and links to the information objects). Nevertheless, in the book *Basic Description* (2.3.1.1.1) attribute, two sites fall in the red range. The elementary result is worse in the book *Content Description* (2.3.1.1.2.2), as the reader can observe. We evaluate the availability and richness of content description. The greater richness is for Amazon, B&N, and Borders, but the availability is varying. Notice that a review of a product is considered in the *Customer Revision of a Book* (2.3.3.4) attribute.

Lastly, focusing on the *Shopping Basket* sub-characteristic, we observe the *Shopping Basket Availability* (2.3.2.1.1.1.1) in all selected sites. However, the *Continue Buying Feedback* attribute is absent in Cúspide and Díaz de Santos, and unsatisfactory (40%) in Borders site. The *Quick Purchase* (2.3.2.1.1.2) attribute is implemented efficiently only in Amazon and Borders (it is absent in the other sites). Unfortunately, Díaz de Santos site has no *Checkout Security* attribute, and the *Checkout Canceling Feedback* (2.3.2.1.1.3.2) one is only explicitly considered in Amazon, B&N, and Cúspide sites, in all pages at checking out time.

### 3.3 The Global Evaluation

In order to obtain a global quality indicator for each website, the evaluators should define, in the third phase, the aggregation process and implement it. In the process, the type of relationships among attributes, sub-characteristics, and characteristics and the relative weights might be considered. For this purpose, it was agreed as in previous case studies the use of a robust and sensible model such as the Logic Scoring of Preference (LSP) model (regarding the amount of intervening characteristics and attributes, i.e., over a hundred and forty ones). LSP is based in a weighted power means mathematical model [2]. However, in simpler cases a merely additive scoring model can be used where indicators can be computed using the following structure: *Global/Partial Indicator* = $\sum$ *(Component Weight * Elementary Indicator)*. The strength of LSP model over merely additives ones resides in the power to deal with different logical relationships and operators to reflect the evaluation needs. The basic relationships modeled are: 1) Replaceability, when it is perceived that two or more input preferences can be alternated; 2) Simultaneity, when it is perceived that two or more input must be present simultaneously; 3) Neutrality, when it is perceived that two or more input preferences can be grouped independently (neither conjunctive nor disjunctive relationships).

On the other hand, the major LSP operators are the arithmetic means (A) that models neutrality relationship, and week (C-), medium (CA), and strong (C+) quasi-conjunction functions, that model simultaneity relationships. In addition, we can tune these operators to intermediate values, e.g., C-- is positioned between A and C-operators, and C-+ is between CA and C- operators, and so on. The above operators (except A) mean that, given a low quality of an input preference can never be well compensated by a high quality of some other inputs to output a high quality preference. Similarly to conjunctive operators, we can also use the quasi-disjunction operators that model replaceability relationships. That is, a low quality of an input preference can always be compensated by a high quality of some other input.

Regarding the aggregation process, it follows the hierarchical structure of the requirement tree, from bottom to top. Applying a stepwise aggregation mechanism, the elementary preferences can be partially structured; in turn, repeating the aggregation process at the end can be obtained a global schema. This aggregation model allows computing partial and global preferences. For example, Fig. 4a) depicts a partial aggregation structure for the *EC Functionality and Content* (2.3) sub-characteristic. The 2.3 output (0.5 weighted), produced by means of C-- operator, together with 2.1 and 2.2 outputs, are inputs to the C- operator in order to compute the *Functionality* (2) preference (do not shown in the figure). The rectangles on the left side of the figure contain the coded elementary preferences. For instance, the values of 2.3.1.1.2.1 and 2.3.1.1.2.2 preferences yield the 2.3.1.1.2 output. The C-- operator does not model mandatory requirements, i.e., a zero in one input does not produces a zero at the output even though it punishes the outcome. The interpretation is we need a *Book's Content Description* and *Table of Contents* simultaneously (however, in this case, an "and" weak relationship is used). Finally, Fig. 4b) shows the final aggregation of the characteristics coded as 1, 2, 3, and 4 respectively, to produce the global preference. The global quality preference represents the total degree of satisfaction of quality requirements.

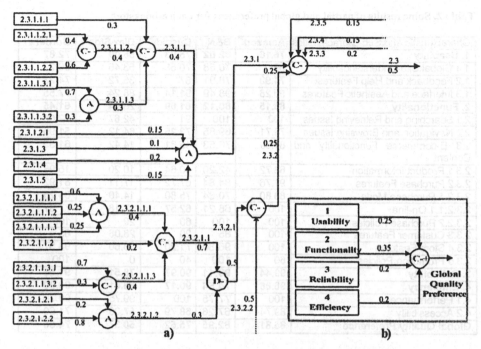

**Fig. 4.** Aggregation of preferences by using the LSP Model. a) Depicts a partial aggregation structure for the 2.3 sub-characteristic; b) Shows the final aggregation structure.

## 3.4 The Analysis of E-bookstore Sites

In the fourth phase, the evaluators analyze and compare the elementary, partial and global outcomes regarding the goals and user standpoint. Partial and final values dumped, for instance, in tables 1, and 2, and schemas as in Fig. 4, are useful sources of information to analyze, justify, and draw conclusions about the quality of e-bookstore sites. Besides, Fig. 5 b) represents the final ranking.

The colored quality bars at the left side of the Fig. 5b), indicate the levels of acceptability, as previously commented. For instance, a scoring within a gray bar can be interpreted as though improvement actions should be considered (this is the case for the global preference of Díaz de Santos site), as long as an unsatisfactory rating level can be interpreted as though necessary and urgent change actions must be taken. A scoring within a green bar can be interpreted as a satisfactory quality of the artifact as a whole. However, partial results for each high-level characteristic or sub-characteristic could indicate some kind of improvement.

The global quality preference was satisfactory for Amazon (86.81%), B&N (82.95%), Cúspide (75.52%), and Borders (74.86%) sites (see Fig. 5b). Díaz de Santos site should plan improvement actions due to the marginal score (50.37%). In the following paragraphs, we focus the discussion mainly on the *Functionality* factor.

**Table 2.** Some results of partial and global preferences for each e-bookstore

| Characteristic and Sub-characteristics | Amazon | B&N | Cúspide | Díaz Stos | Borders |
|---|---|---|---|---|---|
| **1. Usability** | **76.16** | **82.62** | **75.93** | **56.09** | **72.87** |
| 1.1 Global Site Understandability | 59 | 70.58 | 70.58 | 53.46 | 66.22 |
| 1.2 Feedback and Help Features | 74.99 | 78.91 | 67 | 35.72 | 74.23 |
| 1.3 Interface and Aesthetic Features | 95.28 | 98.49 | 91.14 | 88.24 | 77.55 |
| **2. Functionality** | **83.15** | **80.12** | **61.69** | **28.64** | **61.45** |
| 2.1 Searching and Retrieving Issues | 100 | 100 | 91 | 42.67 | 72.06 |
| 2.2 Navigation and Browsing Issues | 70.71 | 69.85 | 73.25 | 64.12 | 51.95 |
| 2.3 E-commerce Functionality and Content | 81.99 | 76.53 | 45.81 | 14.42 | 61.55 |
| 2.3.1 Product Information | 63.72 | 42.20 | 40.64 | 10.20 | 15.98 |
| 2.3.2 Purchase Features | 91.76 | 84.84 | 67.72 | 17.11 | 81.92 |
| 2.3.2.1 Purchase Mode | 83.80 | 70.64 | 75.80 | 14.40 | 65.25 |
| 2.3.2.1.1 On-line | 100 | 66.21 | 62.57 | 17.18 | 77.87 |
| 2.3.2.2 Purchase Policies | 100 | 100 | 60 | 20 | 100 |
| 2.3.3 Customer Features | 100 | 85 | 20 | 28.08 | 65 |
| 2.3.4 Store Features | 100 | 96.80 | 71.20 | 33.60 | 93.57 |
| 2.3.5 Promotion Policies | 60 | 100 | 40 | 0 | 100 |
| **3. Reliability** | **99.44** | **99.11** | **90.97** | **78.51** | **91.66** |
| **4. Efficiency** | **96.88** | **74.54** | **90.17** | **86.01** | **90.90** |
| 4.1 Performance | 100 | 77.75 | 100 | 99.75 | 99.70 |
| 4.2 Accessibility | 89.74 | 67.26 | 68.79 | 57.08 | 71.60 |
| **Global Quality Preference** | **86.81** | **82.95** | **75.52** | **50.37** | **74.86** |

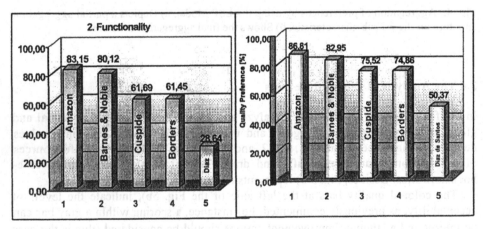

**Fig. 5.** Scores and rankings for the five e-bookstores: a) to the Functionality characteristic; b) to the final Quality

Regarding the *Functionality* characteristic, the highest score was to Amazon site (83.15%), and the lowest to Díaz de Santos (28.64%); i.e., the quality is unsatisfactory for this factor (see Fig 5a). For instance, Amazon and B&N sites have reached the outstanding score of 100% in *Searching and Retrieving* sub-characteristic (e.g., in-site quick and advanced searching, and level of retrieving customization and feedback attributes). Nonetheless, Díaz de Santos site has no quick search, and the retrieving customization and feedback mechanisms are weak (drawing a partial preference of 42.67% -see Table 2). On the other hand, the bigger differences among sites are observed in the *EC Functionality and Content* (2.3) sub-characteristic. Only Amazon, B&N, and Borders sites show a satisfactory score of 81.99, 76.53, and 61.55% respectively. The quality for Cúspide is below the satisfactory level (45.81%), and Díaz de Santos site is very poor (14.42%).

The strength of Web-site QEM methodology is that by generating elemental, partial, and global quality indicators the evaluation process can be easily analyzed, traced, and justified, as well recommendations can be made. For example, comparing the strongest and the weakest sites, we observe 63.72% of the preference to Amazon, and 10.20% to Díaz de Santos, considering *Product Information* sub-characteristic. Looking for the causes in Table 1, the book *Basic Description* (2.3.1.1.1) score was 100% to the former and 24% to the latter. Besides, Díaz de Santos has lower scores in 2.3.1.1.2.1, 2.3.1.1.2.2, and 2.3.1.1.3.1 attributes. In addition, it has neither *Related Product/Author Recommendations*, nor *Product Rating Availability*. On the other hand, looking at the schema in Fig. 4a), the 2.3.1.1 output (Product Description) is produced by means of a C-- operator, which punishes low input preferences, as previously commented.

Likewise, in the *Online Purchase Mode* (2.3.2.1.1), we observe tremendous differences among both sites. Unfortunately, Díaz de Santos site has available neither *Quick Purchase*, nor *Checkout Security*, nor *Checkout Canceling Feedback* among other needed or desirable attributes. Conversely, Amazon site has an excellent *Online Purchase* preference (100%). Besides, in Table 2, the reader can observe and compare the partial preferences for *Customer Features* (2.3.3), *Store Features* (2.3.4), and *Promotion Policies* (2.3.5) sub-characteristics, among intervening e-bookstores. Analyzing each attribute that composes these sub-characteristics, recommendations to improvement can be made, when necessary.

Finally, considering the *Efficiency* characteristic, the highest score was to Amazon (96.88%), and the lowest was to B&N (74.54%), however, all scores have fallen in the satisfactory range. The reader can observe that four out of five sites have surpassed the 99% in the *Performance* sub-characteristic. Here, we measure the *Quick Access Pages* attribute [9]. With regard to the *Accessibility* sub-characteristic, the highest preference was again to Amazon (89.74%). Unfortunately, one out of five sites have implemented the *Text-only Version* (4.2.1.1) attribute. This capability would be necessary because users would have total information accessibility on pages, mainly for people with disabilities, or when speed is a drawback [13].

## 4 Final Remarks

As commented in the Introduction Section, there are some factors that influence quality in use, particularly, internal and external product attributes. Nowadays, it is widely recognized that process quality contributes to improving product quality, and product quality contributes to improving quality in use. However, the evaluation of the Web as a product has often been neglected in the web engineering community. Hence, to understand, control, and improve the quality of Web-based products we should increasingly use software engineering methods, models, techniques, and tools. In this direction, the proposed expert-driven Web-site QEM methodology, can be a useful approach to assess the quality in the different phases of a Web product lifecycle. As frequently said, if we don't know where we are standing, a map won't help.

Specifically, in this work, we have illustrated the Web-site QEM steps, by analyzing the state-of-the-art of the quality of five e-bookstores sites. The case study has resulted that the state-of-the-art of the quality of typical e-bookstores sites, from a general user standpoint, is rather high (particularly, for four out of five evaluated sites, which surpass the lower satisfactory limit of 60%). The sites satisfied globally a range from 50% and 87% of the specified quality requirements. However, the partial and final results show that the wish list because of poor-designed or absent attributes, is not empty. Each assessed site has at least a sub-characteristic in the red and/or gray quality bar, where improvement actions should be considered. Hence, engineers and designers have a powerful and flexible tool to redirect their efforts on the weaker characteristics and attributes of the site. Moreover, the strengths and weaknesses can be well understood, so, in this case, a map would help.

Finally, the proposed quantitative methodology can be used to assess diverse application domains regarding different user viewpoints and evaluation project goals. It should be noticed though, that the definition and the specification of quality requirements are key activities in the evaluation process. For instance, from an EC site developer viewpoint, some other internal and external attributes should be considered; besides, the ISO-prescribed characteristics like *Portability* and *Maintainability* should be taken into account. Lastly, according to our recent studies, many attributes and sub-characteristics can be reused among different website domains, if we consider a particular kind of user. Some others are unavoidably domains specific. On the other hand, the precision of the assessment process can be adjusted selecting the appropriate metrics and, ultimately, the appropriate evaluation criteria and procedures. Moreover, the subjectivity can substantially be minimized in the evaluation process but can not be eliminated at all.

# References

1. Arnold, S.; Ma, S; Tigert, D.: A comparative analysis of determinant attributes in retail store selection, Advances in Computer Research. Assoc. for Consumer Research (5), (1977) 663-667.
2. Dujmovic, J.J.; Bayucan, A.: A Quantitative Method for Software Evaluation and its Application in Evaluating Windowed Environments, IASTED Software Engineering Conference, San Francisco, US (1997).
3. Fenton, N.E.; Pfleeger, S.L.: Software Metrics: a Rigorous and Practical Approach, 2nd Ed., PWS Publishing Company (1997).
4. GVU's WWW User Survey, The tenth edition, http://www.gvu.gatech.edu/user_surveys/survey-1998-10/tenthreport.html
5. ISO/IEC 9126-1991 International Standard, "Information technology - Software product evaluation - Quality characteristics and guidelines for their use" (1991).
6. Lohse, G.; Spiller, P.: Electronic Shopping, Communications of the ACM 41,7 (1998) 81-86.
7. Nielsen, Jakob; The Alertbox, http://www.useit.com/alertbox/
8. Olsina, L.: Web-site Quantitative Evaluation and Comparison: a Case Study on Museums, Workshop on Software Engineering over the Internet, at Int'l Conference on Software

Engineering, http://sern.cpsc.ucalgary.ca/~maurer/ICSE99WS/ICSE99WS.html, Los Angeles, US (1999).
9. Olsina, L., Godoy, D; Lafuente, G.J; Rossi, G.: Assessing the Quality of Academic Websites: a Case Study, In: New Review of Hypermedia and Multimedia (NRHM) Journal, Taylor Graham Publishers, UK/USA Vol 5, ISSN 1361-4568 (1999).
10. Olsina, L.; Rossi, G.: Towards Web-site Quantitative Evaluation: defining Quality Characteristics and Attributes, Proceedings of IV Int'l WebNet Conference, World Conference on the WWW and Internet, Hawaii, USA, Vol.1, (1999) 834-839.
11. Tilson, R., Dong, J., Martin, S., Kieke, E.: Factors and Principles Affecting the Usability of Four E-commerce Sites", 4th Conference on Human Factors & the Web, Baking Ridge, NJ, US (1998).
12. Rossi, G., Schwabe, D.; Lyardet, F.: Improving Web Information Systems with navigational Patterns, Proceedings of WWW8 Congress, Toronto, Canada, Elsevier Ed. (1999) 589-600.
13. W3C, W3C Working Draft, WAI Accessibility Guidelines: Page Authoring, http://www.w3c.org/TR/WD-WAI-PAGEAUTH/ (1999).

# Appendix A: Quality Requirement Tree for E-Bookstores

**1. Usability**
1.1 Global Site Understandability
1.1.1 Book-domain Organization Scheme
1.1.1.1 *Table of Content*
1.1.1.2 *Alphabetical Subject Index*
1.1.2 *Quality of Labeling System*
1.1.3 *Guided Tour for First Time Visitors*
1.2 Feedback and Help Features
1.2.1 Quality of Help Features
1.2.1.1 *Global Help for First Time Visitors*
1.2.1.2 *Specific Help*
1.2.1.2.1 *Search Help*
1.2.1.2.2 *Purchase Help*
1.2.1.2.3 *Check-out Help*
1.2.2 Addresses Directory
1.2.2.1 *E-mail Directory*
1.2.2.2 *TE/Fax Directory*
1.2.3 Link-based Feedback
1.2.3.1 *FAQ Feature*
1.2.3.2 *What's New Feature*
1.2.4 Form-based Feedback
1.2.4.1 *Questionnaire Feature*
1.2.4.2 *Comments/Suggestions*
1.2.4.3 *Subject-Oriented Feedback*
1.2.5 Miscellaneous Features
1.2.5.1 *Foreign Language Support*
1.3 Interface and Aesthetic Features
1.3.1 *Cohesiveness by Grouping Main Control Objects*
1.3.2 Presentation Permanence and Stability of Main Controls

1.3.2.1 *Direct Controls Permanence*
1.3.2.1.1 *Main Controls Permanence*
1.3.2.1.2 *Search Control Permanence*
1.3.2.1.3 *Browse Permanence*
1.3.2.1.4 *Account Control Permanence*
1.3.2.1.5 *Shopping Basket Control Permanence*
1.3.2.2 *Indirect Controls Permanence*
1.3.2.3 *Stability*
1.3.3 *Style Issues*
1.3.3.1 *Link Color Style Uniformity*
1.3.3.2 *Global Style Uniformity*
1.3.4 *Aesthetic Preference*
**2. Functionality**
2.1 Searching and Retrieving Issues
2.1.1 Web-site Search Mechanisms
2.1.1.1 *Quick Search*
2.1.1.2 *Advanced Search*
2.1.2 Retrieve Mechanisms
2.1.2.1 *Level of Retrieving Customization*
2.1.2.2 *Level of Retrieving Feedback*
2.2 Navigation and Browsing Issues
2.2.1 Navigability
2.2.1.1 Orientation
2.2.1.1.1 *Indicator of Path*
2.2.1.1.2 *Label of Current Position*
2.2.1.2 *Average of Links per Page*
2.2.2 Navigational Control Objects
2.2.2.1 Presentation Permanence and Stability of Contextual (sub-site) Controls
2.2.2.1.1 *Contextual Controls Permanence*

# Loyalty Program Scheme
# for Anonymous Payment Systems

Arrianto Mukti Wibowo[1], Kwok Yan Lam[2] and Gary S.H. Tan[2]

Computer Science Department, School of Computing
National University of Singapore
[1]arrianto@comp.nus.edu.sg, amwibowo@yahoo.com
[2]{lamky, gtan}@comp.nus.edu.sg

**Abstract.** Loyalty program is a marketing effort by the merchant to keep customers loyal to their stores. It tries to keep track of the purchasing-behavior of a customer by recording customer's purchase information, including his credit card number, as a key identifier to the customer. While it may benefit the customer, the drawback is that the privacy of the customer is intruded. If the customer is using an anonymous payment system such as electronic cash / digital coins, his privacy is protected, but he will not get any benefit from the loyalty program which tries to record his payment information. This paper suggests several solutions to solve merchant's need to gather statistical data from customer's purchasing behavior versus customer's need for privacy. Among the solutions, we present the idea of *blindly signed pseudo digital certificates*, which satisfies our requirement for a loyalty program scheme with an anonymous payment system.

## 1 Introduction

A recent article by Barefoot [1] explicitly mentioned a real world problem, where banks and merchants are gathering information on customer's purchases. Although the reason for mining the sales data is to provide better customer service such in loyalty programs, the drawback is that the privacy of the customer is intruded.

Of course, if the customer is using an anonymous payment system, which the identity of the customer is concealed, his privacy is guaranteed. However, the customer will loose the benefit of the extra customer service offered by the merchant, since the merchant will not be able to track down the purchasing-behavior of each customer.

In this paper, we propose several methods to allow a merchant to keep track of its customer purchasing-behavior, even if the customer uses an anonymous payment system such as electronic cash. Thus, *the seemingly two conflicting interests, which are customer's privacy versus merchant's need to gather statistical data from customer's behavior, can be resolved.*

We begin by describing loyalty program, or some call it 'customer retention program', in section 2, along with its importance. We also examine how merchant can gather the needed information for loyalty program. In section 3, we take a detour to illustrate various anonymous payment systems along with its motivations. At this point, we will see incompatibility to use anonymous payment system with a loyalty program. Section 4 digs deeper in our apparent problem and then formally defines the basic problem. Section 5 shares our preliminary thoughts and describes detailed requirements. In section 6, we discuss several plausible solutions to the requirement and therefore answer the basic problem. Finally, we end our discussion with the conclusion.

## 2 Loyalty Program

### 2.1 Definitions and Importance

Sharp and Sharp define *loyalty programs* as structured marketing efforts that reward, and therefore encourage, loyal behavior (of the customer), for the benefit of the merchant [26]. Another term for loyalty program is *customer retention program*, which Harris defines as a continuous attempt to satisfy and keep current customers actively involved in conducting business [13].

The objective of a customer loyalty program is to keep existing customer and to increase their repeat-purchase loyalty, in contrast to other marketing activities on winning new customers. The loyalty program tries to minimize the chance the customers would switch to another competing products or services. Bolton, Kannan, and Bramlett study on credit card loyalty program [2], showed that the existing customer in a loyalty program are less sensitive to some issues which others might consider important, such as a low quality rating of customer's current credit card company, or if the billing scheme is not the best among the credit card companies. One possible reason was probably they perceive that they are getting better quality and service for the price or, in other words, good value.

Intimate and interpersonal relationship between salesperson and the customer is a very important aspect in customer loyalty. The salesperson must have an understanding of each customer's needs. As shown by Macintosh and Lockshin in their study on retail relationship and store loyalty [18], customer's trust and commitment to the salesperson are directly linked with purchase intention. Without interpersonal salesperson relationship, store loyalty is influenced only by customer's trust in the store. Therefore, knowing exactly what *each* customer wants - as apparently done by a good salesperson - is an important factor in customer loyalty to the merchant. The argument complement Harris' argument that a well-developed loyalty program plan should create an environment which current customers' needs are met and new needs are explored [13].

The financial importance of loyalty program was underlined by Pearson in [23], since loyalty program gives something of guarantee of future earnings. Even if current earnings are high, a low level of customer loyalty means that future earnings may be at risk.

## 2.2 Mining Data for Loyalty Program

Among several methods to obtain information of existing customers' needs, one of them is by 'mining' the historical point of sales data. It must be noted here that there are several ways to look at the data. The merchant may want to observe the buying pattern for a typical *single* purchase. For example, the merchant may want to know when customers buy a box of cereal, what are the other products bought along with it. It may find out that for nearly every cereal purchased, many customers also bought fresh milk.

Alternatively, the merchant can gather the shopping pattern of *each* particular customer from time to time, and can intelligently give specific suggestions to a particular customer, depending on his previous purchasing-behavior. For example, if a particular customer buys cereals regularly, the merchant may offer a discount prices for cereals, or suggest a brand new cereal for the customer to try. The merchant can also suggest which cereal is the best buy and suggest other microwave breakfast foods for complement. The merchant may choose not to offer these suggestions to a customer who rarely buys cereals or any breakfast foods, since the person may usually have a brunch at 10.30 AM.

Bolton, Kannan, and Bramlett research on loyalty programs by credit card companies [2] is another good example for us. They observe that the loyalty programs, allow the credit card companies to observe the purchasing pattern of each cardholder. In the loyalty program, members can accumulate points with each dollar transacted with their credit card. Those points are later redeemable for a wide variety of goods and services such as air certificates, car rental, vacation options, and retail gifts. It is worth to note, that even some of these credit card companies charge about US$40 to a customer who wants to join the loyalty program.

From the merchant's point of view, using credit card number as the key identification for each customer in a loyalty program seems natural. Firstly, the merchant does not need to ask every customer to participate in the loyalty program. It merely records every credit card transaction. It is a very convenient way to automatically enable loyalty program. As a matter of fact, many credit card companies have partnerships with merchants. Secondly, credit card is a very popular payment method, but every payment transaction is *traceable*. Which means, we can identify who made certain purchases. If the merchant has partnership with an issuing credit card company, it can even gather more valuable information about the customers. Debit cards, now gaining wide acceptance, also has the same properties as credit cards, in which every transaction is traceable.

In contrast, *untraceable* payment like cash payments would not allow the merchant to keep track which customer made certain purchases. We can also say that cash payments are one form of anonymous payment system.

# 3 Anonymous Payment System Revisited

## 3.1 Motivations for Anonymity

In [5], Chaum argues that untraceable payment is very important, since it will protect the privacy of the payer (customer). Third parties, such as merchants or service companies, can keep track of the behavior of their customers, if the customers use some sort of a traceable payment system such as credit card, check, or debit card. Furthermore, all of these payment records can be linked so that they constitute in effect a single dossier on a customer's life [6]. The customer may wish that his personal lifestyle, whereabouts and associations remain private.

Apparently, Chaum's advocacy in anonymous payment system was supported by a more recent survey by GVU WWW Surveying Team, Georgia Institute of Technology [12]. The survey revealed that just over half of respondents agree that they prefer anonymous payment systems (51%), a quarter are neutral (25%). In general, people prefer an anonymous payment system or they have no preference, few actually prefer a user-identified system. Either people who already know, or who have just been told what an anonymous payment is, both have similar opinions, in that most prefer anonymous payment.

## 3.2 Two Aspects of Anonymity

In our paper, we are interested in two aspects of anonymity. The first aspect, as we mentioned before, is *untraceability*, in which the privacy of the user is protected, such that no one can trace the relation between a customer and his purchases. The identity of the payer (customer) in a particular payment cannot even be traced although the merchant colludes with the issuing financial institution (such as bank).

We are also concerned about the aspect of *unlinkability* of an anonymous payment system. According to Tsiounis' definition in his paper about anonymous digital coins [27], unlinkability is the property in which given a set of coins (or in our case, a set of payments), one cannot identify whether those coins (payments) came from the same customer account or not. Tsiounis continued to argue that if several payments are linkable (although anonymous), identification can be performed by conventional means, such as correlating payment's locality, time, size, type, frequency, or by finding a single payment in which the user identified himself.

The first breed of proposed anonymous payment systems were electronic cash. Untraceability is a universal feature of electronic cash. Some called it digital coins, since in the real world, payment with coins are really untraceable.

However, when it comes to the unlinkability issue, several proposed digital coins are unlinkable [4, 3, 10, 17, 27], but others are actually linkable digital coins [9, 21, 22, 24, 29]. Some of the linkable digital coin authors proposed to 'rotate' several digital coin 'licenses' to obtain pseudo-unlinkability. Note that some unlinkable digital coins protocols can be modified to be spendable $n$-times, but it will make all the payments done using a single digital coin and its 'children' be linkable [3, 11].

The idea of anonymous electronic cash also lead to the development of other anonymous payment systems, such as anonymous check (which is actually an extension of e-cash protocols), anonymous credit card protocols [16] and anonymous bank account [8].

From the discussion above, it is clear that any anonymous payment system must have untraceability as its properties, but not all anonymous payment systems have unlinkability as one of their properties.

# 4   Problem Statement

At this point, we can notice the apparent conflicting interest. Banks or merchants want to gather statistical data of customers' behavior from customer's payment information, but customers may want to use an anonymous payment system.

Before we formalize our problem, let us try to comprehend a closely related real world problem. Barefoot in [1] stated that the current issue is how the banks (or in our context, credit card companies) will be able to safeguard customer privacy completely, without undermining the most exciting innovations in banking. She argued that there are at least four focal points of privacy intrusion risk:

1. information transmitted over the Internet;
2. third-party relationships (such as partnership with merchants);
3. computerized credit scoring; and
4. data mining and customer relationship management (e.g. loyalty program).

She gave an example of Amazon.com, the largest Internet book store in the world:

*"After months of glowing publicity regarding its trailblazing role and progress in bringing happy consumers into e-commerce, Amazon found itself attacked for compiling and disclosing data on customer reading habits. To the embarrassment of some parties, it publicly listed the books most frequently purchased by certain affinity groups, including the employees of specific companies. One well-known company's best seller was a book critical of its CEO, while another large firm's employees seemed quite interested in reading about sex. Amazon's assurance that the lists were disclosed in the spirit of "fun" did not dispel the unease of critics, some of whom had never realized that their own purchase information might be tracked and used."* [1]

While her example may not perfectly exemplify our discussion (we are interested in the behavior of a particular customer, not a group of customers), it may well illustrate what we should be aware of. Please be reminded that Amazon may actually try to give better customer service, but it does so by intruding the privacy of its customers.

To worsen things, even some of the merchants know exactly the amount of pre-approved credit the customers have [14], especially those who have partnership with credit card companies.

We also noticed that many e-commerce websites now require the customers to register their credit card information and their proper address, or else they will not deliver the goods. From a practical point of view, this security measure to prevent credit card fraud and misuse seems acceptable. But there is no guarantee that the merchant is not going to make use of customers' credit card information to track customers purchasing-behavior.

Barefoot's approach to solve the problem was apparently more legalistic, rather than technical. She suggested the banks and the merchants should be ready to comply with the newly proposed act, which let the customers exclude their records from internal usage and external sharing arrangements, including third parties. She also suggested that voluntary privacy protection steps should be taken and privacy consciousness must become ingrained in the banking culture.

If the merchant used to gather credit card numbers (or any other traceable payment method) as the key identifier of each customer, then the merchant can use this key to gather more statistical information on its customers. But because of the inherent problem of traceability of those payment systems, eventually some of the customers may prefer to use anonymous payment system to protect their privacy. However, the merchant will loose valuable marketing information.

Now we formally define our problem.

**Problem.** *Given a set of customers who are using anonymous payment system, devise solution(s), to let the merchant still be able to keep track of the purchasing-behavior of each customer.*

## 5    Basic Idea and Detailed Requirements

Since we were doing research in anonymous digital coins, we originally thought of making the digital coins inherently support loyalty programs. Apparently, since a typical payment consist of multiple coins, we thought that it would be a lot easier if we can mint another 'coin' with an encrypted identity on it. Then we shall prove that the coin with the encrypted identity is in the same group as the other coins.

It came out that the coin with an encrypted identity, is crucial in our study. The coin with the encrypted identity was minted nearly the same way as the other coins using a certain blind signature protocol, but without any nominal value. We reduce the digital coin with an encrypted identity 'problem', simply into a signed pseudo identity, which may be created using a blind signature protocol. *Signed* pseudo identity implies that the pseudo identity should be trusted. Therefore, our main solution relies on the use of *blindly signed pseudo digital certificates* or *digital unforgeable pseudonyms*, among other solutions to consider. Take note that three out of four suggested solutions actually rely on the use of another 'authenticated token', external to the payment itself.

A pseudonym is defined as:

*"person's name that is not his real name, especially one used by an author, a pen-name"*
[15]

Of course in our context, the individual is not a book author or pen-pal, but a customer.

Now let us formally define the requirement of the proposed protocol to answer the stated problem above.

**Requirements.** The proposed solution, should have these following properties:

1. The protocol should allow merchant (payee) to link several payments made in different places and time to a particular customer (payer).

2. The protocol should conceal the true identity of the customer even if the merchant colludes with financial institution responsible for the payment system (i.e., the bank).

3. A pseudonym for a particular customer cannot be used by another customer. A pseudonym is unique for each customer. In another word, the pseudonym is unforgeable.

4. A pseudonym is produced by the customer to the merchant, only under customer's will. It also means that the merchant would not be able to extract the pseudonym without customer's consent.

5. The protocol should be able to be mounted on any anonymous payment system, including anonymous check, anonymous credit card and anonymous account.

6. A pseudonym may only be used after the customer's true identity has been verified/authenticated by the merchant. The customer then creates his own pseudonym, such that any other party cannot link the pseudonym to the true identity. For example, a credit card company with its merchant partners may only let a customer be a member in their loyalty program, only if the customer show his credentials or has already been registered before.

7. To give some sort of flexibility, ideally, the protocol should be able to be implemented with several different kinds of cryptographic primitives.

Please note that in our discussion, we limit our focus and concern to the customer authentication protocol. Therefore, we leave other security issues such as transmission privacy as another problem.

# 6    Solutions

There are different solutions to the basic problem previously stated, but not all of these solutions address all of the formal requirements mentioned.

## 6.1    Cookies

Cookies are a standard mechanism that allows a website (or server) to deliver simple data to a client (end user); request that the client store the information; and, in certain circumstances, return the information to the website [20]. Cookies are a way of storing persistent client data so that a website can maintain information on a user across HTTP stateless connections.

Using cookies is a simple and practical way to resolve our problem. At the simplest model, the merchant web server merely checks whether the customer (client) already has a cookie or not. If not, then the merchant server creates a cookie for the customer in the client's computer hard disk. The merchant then stores the customer profile in the cookies, including his 'purchasing-behavior'. Whenever the merchant needs to get the customer profiles, it merely gets the information from the cookie.

To a certain degree, cookies are quite secure. Its specification defines that only the website that creates the cookie can retrieve it back again, so other websites cannot peek at another cookie which was not theirs [28]. To enable server authentication and communication privacy, it may even optionally use SSL.

It has several drawbacks, though. If the client computer is shared for several users, and the operating system inherently has a low level security, such as Microsoft Windows 95/98, other users can see other user's cookies. In addition, cookies are not stored encrypted. They are just ordinary, editable, text files. If the customer authentication scheme is not well design, a customer can pretend to be another customer.

For some web applications, using cookies is probably sufficient. It definitely meets the first and fifth requirement. Its basic design does not rely on cryptographic protocols (other than SSL), so the seventh requirement is not applicable. Basically the client does not control the cookies (there exist applications to let users manually control cookies), so the fourth and the sixth requirement are generally not met. Depending on the application, the second requirement may or may not be met. Moreover, without proper security support from the operating system or the browser, the third requirement may not be achievable.

We must underline that cookie's basic security pretty much relies on a non-cryptographic HTTP specification. For some other applications, using cookies is not possible or just not sufficient, especially non-Web applications and those that demands much stronger cryptographic client authentication scheme.

## 6.2    Pseudo Digital (Public-Key) Certificates

Digital certificate, or to be more precise *public-key certificate,* is a vehicle by which public key may be stored, distributed or forwarded over unsecure media without the danger of manipulation [19]. Digital certificates are commonly used as a digital identification or authentication means over an unsecure public network such as the Internet. In general, it helps to tell us that the person named 'Alice' over the network is really Alice as we know her. As its name implies, public-key digital certificates employ a certain asymmetric cryptographic algorithm such as RSA, El-Gamal, DSA, etc.

To create a digital certificate, initially an entity generates his public-key pairs. He keeps his private key secret, then sends his public key along with his personal information to a *certificate authority* (CA). The CA then creates the digital certificate by signing the public key and necessary information with CA's private key. In its very basic form, a certificate is only a public key signed by a CA. However, usually it also contains other necessary information such as entity's personal information/address, expiry date, serial number, algorithm used, policies, etc. Any other entity who wants to verify the validity of the certificate needs to have CA's public key. A challenge-and-response protocol is usually employed to authenticate entities holding the digital certificates. Readers are encouraged to read more on public-key cryptography and digital certificates in [19, 25].

Digital certificates may have different 'authenticity' levels. Class 1 certificates are the least authentic digital certificates. Higher class-number generally denotes higher certificate authenticity. Class 1 digital certificates, are created by the CA without verifying the identity of the entity that requested the certificate. The only security measure is forcing the entity to enter his e-mail address at registration, since usually the client will receive his requested certificate from an e-mail from the CA. However, with this type of digital certificates, Alice can pretend to be Bob, by submitting Bob's name, his personal information and *her* (newly created) e-mail address *honestlyiambob@e-mail.com* to the CA at registration.

The process of obtaining higher authenticity digital certificates, such as the ones that are used for commercial web servers, is a lot more complicated. Obtaining the highest quality certificates requires the entity to register at the CA office *in person* to produce their original documents to support their authenticity. With this kind of digital certificates, the CA guarantees that a certificate with the name XYZ Co. Ltd., New York, USA, is really the XYZ Co. Ltd. which operated in New York, in the United States. The CA usually offers some insurance just in case the high authenticity digital certificate is misused.

In our discussion, we are particularly interested with the least authentic kind of digital certificates, such as (but not necessarily) class 1 digital certificates. It actually lets someone (e.g., a customer) declare his own pseudonym by letting him decide by what name shall he be known, which is fortunately unforgeable (by the definition of a digital certificate).

Our point is, therefore, if the CA does not examine the validity of the entity's (customer's) personal identity, the issued digital certificate is actually an unforgeable pseudo digital identity. This pseudo digital certificates actually complies to all of our requirements, except the sixth requirement, since the merchant never had a chance to verify the true identity of the customer. Nevertheless, for most applications that do not require the true identity of the customer to be known prior to gathering data, definitely this scheme solves our problem.

## 6.3    Linkable Anonymous Payment Systems

As we have previously mentioned, there are several anonymous but linkable payment systems. In general, these linkable digital coin protocols try to speed up the minting process and minimize storage requirements. Many of them do so by letting the user (customer) have an electronic anonymous 'license' to mint a series of coins. The license acts like a 'head' or 'root' of a graph of coins, extendible 'on the fly' to the children.

If we were to use linkable anonymous payment system for the sake of the loyalty program, ideally the customer should use one license for all payments in each particular merchant. Therefore, the merchant can still keep track of purchasing-behavior of each particular customer, although each of them is only known by its anonymous license.

Since in several payment protocols the license is limited to a certain amount of money, each license automatically expires when it has used all of its license to use that certain amount of money. In this case, the relation between an anonymous customer with his identity may not be persistent. In another words, the first requirement cannot be achieved permanently. However, there is a way to tackle this difficulty. If the customer is using his subsequent license (as the old license expires), customer merely proves in front of the merchant, that he can 'open' digital coins derived from both licenses. Of course if the old license has expired, the merchant should not accept the coins derived from the old license. The merchant will be required to keep track of the licenses that each customer used.

The second requirement is met, because basically the license is a blinded identification signed by the issuer (bank). The third requirement is also achieved. The forth requirement is not met, because the customer implicitly shows his pseudo identity (the license) to the merchant at payment phase. In addition, since this method uses the inherent properties in the payment system, it cannot be used in another payment method (fifth requirement). The sixth requirement cannot be achieved because the merchant may not be able to authenticate the true identity of the customer using the linkable digital coins. Finally, it generally cannot use other cryptographic algorithms other than the one used in the payment protocol (seventh requirement).

## 6.4   Blindly Signed Pseudo Digital Certificates

The basic idea of this solution is to use a blindly signed pseudo digital certificate as the pseudonym for each customer. Note that this solution is very much the same as our previously described (least authentic) pseudo digital certificate. Except now, the merchant (or any other trusted party, such as the bank or the credit card company) can verify the true identity of the customer, before the customer request a certificate to the trusted party. Signing blindly, implies that the signer (trusted party) do not have any knowledge whatsoever of the signed message, at anytime (prior, after or at the moment of signing).

Here we sketch how it works:

*Setup phase:*

1. A trusted party $T$ (it can be the bank or the merchant itself) authenticates the customer in some certain way, such as using digital certificates, or other physical proof. This step is very important to correctly identify the customer, since not everyone is allowed to the loyalty program. Please be reminded, if the protocol is conducted over unsecure public network, then the exchanged messages in following steps must be signed to protect integrity and authenticity.
2. The customer generates a pair of public and private keys. The customer keeps the private key secret.
3. The customer blinds his public key and executes a blind signature protocol to let $T$ blindly sign his public key. Both customer and $T$ perform necessary steps in the agreed blind signature protocol.
4. At the end of the protocol, the customer will obtain a signature of $T$ on his public key key (i.e., the blindly signed pseudo digital certificate), without $T$ ever knowing his public key.

After executing the setup phase protocol, the customer receives a signed public key (a digital certificate). But since the key was blinded when the trusted party $T$ signed it, $T$ cannot correctly correlate the signed public key to a particular setup phase transcript. Because no one is able to link a particular setup phase transcript to a particular blindly signed digital certificate, it also mean that no one can link a blindly signed digital certificate to a true identity. It is actually this property which satisfies the sixth requirement.

The authentication process is just a digital certificate verification and authentication.

*Authentication on payment phase:*

1. Before a customer pays, the merchant asks the customer to present his blindly signed pseudo digital certificate.
2. The customer complies by sending the blindly signed pseudo digital certificate to the merchant.
3. The merchant verifies the validity of the public key in the certificate by using the appropriate verification process, depending on the algorithm used. The merchant will accept if the signature in the certificate is valid. The merchant sends back a challenge to the customer to prove his pseudo authenticity.
4. The customer complies by sending an appropriate response to the merchant. Refer to [19, 25] for more information on authentication process using digital certificates.
5. After verifying the response, the merchant tells the customer that the merchant is ready to accept the payment.
6. The customer pays.
7. Merchant records the blindly signed pseudo digital certificate (or just the public key) along with the purchase information, as data source for the loyalty program.

Optionally, the authentication process can be done before the customer browses the shop, so the merchant can offer suggestions while the customer shops.

The solution satisfies all of our seven requirements. If the customer keeps using just one blindly signed pseudo digital certificate, the merchant can link his payments to his 'blinded identity', so the first requirement is met. The 'blinded identity' implies that the true identity of the customer is shrouded, so the second requirement is met. Since only the rightful holder of the corresponding private key can comply to a challenge-and-response authentication process, the third requirement is met. The solution also meets the fourth requirement, since the customer may not choose to use his blindly signed digital certificate if he does not want his behavior be tracked. The fifth requirement is also addressed, because it is basically an authentication token outside the payment protocol. The sixth requirement is met by the blind signature process in the setup phase. And since the signing process can use several kind of blind signature protocols, it may be implemented with different primitive cryptographic algorithms.

To prevent several merchants cooperating together to monitor the behavior of a customer, the customer should create multiple blindly signed pseudo digital certificate, one for each merchant, by executing the setup phase several times. Alternatively, the customer may also use the same blindly signed digital certificate for several merchants, which have integrated loyalty program for added benefit.

Several variants of blind signature protocols based on RSA [5] and discrete log in [7] can be used to create blindly signed digital certificates. Note that the customer, may also include a pseudonym of his own choice along with the public key, before those information is blinded at setup phase.

# 7 Conclusions

We have shown in this paper that it is possible for the merchant to conduct a customer loyalty program although the customers are using an anonymous payment system. Several solutions exist, such as using cookies, least authentic type of digital certificates (pseudo digital certificates), linkable anonymous payment system, and blindly signed pseudo digital certificates. Amongst those solutions, the blindly signed pseudo digital certificates satisfies all of our requirements and is the most versatile one.

Three of the solutions basically rely on an additional 'authentication token', which might be considered 'external' or not inherent in the payment protocol. Despite several requirements which are not addressed, the solution to use linkable anonymous payments still makes use of the inherent design of the payment protocol itself.

We also acknowledge several limitations. One of the most obvious limitations is that the merchants still do not have the ability to gather maximum information it can get, such as customer's mailing address. Of course, the customers can fill those information, only if they are willing to do so and know the consequences. The second limitation is, especially with the blindly signed pseudo digital certificate, that these solution may require the customer to willingly join the loyalty program. From a practical point of view, probably the setup can be awkward for the customers, if not well designed. On the other hand, this limitation may also be an advantage, since law in several states may prohibit merchants to observe the customers' behavior without customers' consent.

It should also be noted that mining historical point of sale data is not the only way to gather information for loyalty program. Other possibilities exist as well, such as conducting survey, or asking the customers to fill in complain forms or registration forms.

# References

1. Jo Ann S. Barefoot. Privacy under scrutiny. In *Banking Strategies*, Nov/Dec 1999.
2. Ruth N. Bolton, P. K. Kannan and Matthew D. Bramlett. Implications of loyalty program membership and service experiences for customer retention and value. In *Journal of Academy of Marketing Science*. Greenvale, Winter 2000.
3. Stefan Brands. An efficient off-line electronic cash system based on the representation problem. Report CS-R9323, Centrum voor Wiskunde en Informatica, March 1993.
4. David Chaum, Amos Fiat and Moni Naor. Untraceable electronic cash. In *Advances in Cryptology – proceedings of CRYPTO 88*, Lecture Notes in Computer Science 403, Springer-Verlag, 1990.
5. David Chaum. Blind signatures for untraceable payments. In *Advances in Cryptology – proceedings of CRYPTO 82*, Plenum Press, New York, 1983.
6. David Chaum. Achieving Electronic Privacy. In *Scientific American*, August 1992.
7. David Chaum and Torben Pryds Pedersen. Wallet databases with observers. In *Advances in Cryptology – CRYPTO 92*. Lecture Notes in Computer Science 740, Springer-Verlag, 1993.
8. Jan L. Camenish, Jean-Marc Piveteau and Markus A. Stadler. An Efficient Electronic Payment System Protecting Privacy. In *Proceedings of ESORICS '94*. Lecture Notes in Computer Science 875, Springer-Verlag, 1995.

9. Tony Eng and Tatsuaki Okamoto. Single term divisible electronic coins. In *Advances in Cryptology – EUROCRYPT 94*. Lecture Notes in Computer Science 960, Springer-Verlag, 1995.

10. Niels Ferguson. Single term off-line coins. In *Advances in Cryptology – EUROCRYPT 93*, Lecture Notes in Computer Science 765, Springer-Verlag, 1994.

11. Niels Ferguson. Extensions of single term coins. In *Advances in Cryptology – CRYPTO 93*, Lecture Notes in Computer Science 773, Springer-Verlag, 1994.

12. GVU WWW Surveying Team, Georgia Institute of Technology, *GVU's 8th WWW User Survey*. Available at *http://www.gvu.gatech.edu/user_surveys/*, 1997.

13. Elaine K. Harris. *Customer Service: A Practical Approach*, Prentice Hall, Upper Saddle River, 1996.

14. Denison Hatch. Privacy: how much data do direct marketers really need?. In Rob Kling (ed.), *Computerization and Controversy: Value Conflicts and Social Choices, 2nd edition*. Academic Press, San Diego, 1996.

15. A.S. Hornby and A.P. Cowie (editor), *Oxford Advanced Learner's Dictionary of Current English*, Oxford University Press, Oxford, 1992

16. Stephen H. Low, Nicholas F. Maxemchuk and Sanjoy Paul. Anonymous Credit Cards. In *Proceedings of the 2nd ACM Conference on Computer and Communication Security*. 1994.

17. Anna Lysyanskaya and Zulfikar Ramzan. Group blind digital signatures: A scalable solution to electronic cash. In *Financial Cryptography, 2nd International Conference, FC 98*, Lecture Notes in Computer Science 1465, Springer, 1998.

18. Gerrard Macintosh and Lawrence S. Lockshin. Retail relationship and store loyalty: A multi-level perspective. In *International Journal of Research in Marketing*, vol. 14, 1997.

19. Alfred J. Menezes, Paul C. van Oorschot, and Scott A. Vanstone. *Handbook of Applied Cryptography*, CRC Press, Boca Raton, 1997.

20. Netscape Communications Security, Cookies and Privacy FAQ, available at *http://www.cookiecentral.com/n_cookie_faq.htm*, 1997

21. Tatsuaki Okamoto. An efficient divisible electronic cash scheme. In *Advances in Cryptology – CRYPTO 95*. Lecture Notes in Computer Science 963, Springer-Verlag, 1995.

22. Tatsuaki Okamoto and Kazuo Ohta. Universal electronic cash. In *Advances in Cryptology – CRYPTO 91*. Lecture Notes in Computer Science 576, Springer-Verlag, 1992.

23. S. Pearson. How to achieve return on investment from customer loyalty – part 1. In *Journal of Targeting, Measurement and Analysis for Marketing*, vol. 3 no.1, 1994.

24. Cristian Radu, René Govaerts and Joss Vandewalle. Efficient electronic cash with restricted privacy. In *Financial Cryptography, 1st International Conference, FC 97*, Lecture Notes in Computer Science 1318, Springer, 1997.

25. Bruce Schneier. *Applied Cryptography: Protocols, Algorithms, and Source Code in C, 2nd edition*, John Wiley & Sons. Inc., New York, 1996.

26. Byron Sharp and Anne Sharp. Loyalty programs and their impact on repeat-purchase loyalty patterns. In *International Journal of Research in Marketing*, vol. 14, 1997.

27. Yiannis S. Tsiounis. Efficient electronic cash: new notions and techniques. Ph.D. thesis. Department of Computer Science, Northeastern University, 1997.

28. David Whaler, The Unofficial Cookie FAQ, available at *http//www.cookiecentral.com/faq/*, 1999.

29. Yacov Yacobi. Efficient electronic money. In *Advances in Cryptology – ASIACRYPT 94*. Lecture Notes in Computer Science 917, Springer-Verlag, 1995.

# OpenSource in Electronic Commerce —
# A Comparative Analysis

Markus Konstroffer[1], Torben Weis[2], and Sascha Braun[1]

[1] Institut für Wirtschaftsinformatik, Johann Wolfgang Goethe–Universität, Frankfurt
am Main, Germany
{konstrof, sbraun}@wiwi.uni-frankfurt.de,
http://www.wiwi.uni-frankfurt.de/iwi
[2] K Desktop Environment
weis@kde.org
http://www.kde.org

**Abstract.** We discuss the advantages and disadvantages of OpenSource
e-commerce software from the perspective of a company wanting to be
present on the World Wide Web. The OpenSource movement, its license
model and its development model are explained. The functionality of
commercial e-commerce solutions and OpenSource e-commerce solutions
are compared. Security issues are discussed. An approach to customizing
an e-commerce solution taken by consultants is described. After that
the total cost of ownership of e-commerce software is analyzed and a
conclusion is drawn.

## 1 OpenSource

The OpenSource movement has become increasingly popular within the computer industry lately. Projects like Linux, a free UNIX like operating system
and Apache, the most often used WWW server on the net, have proven that
OpenSource projects can be real competitors to conventional commercial products.

The word "OpenSource," which is today a registered trademark, is com-
parably new. The roots of the movement go back to the FSF (Free Software
Foundation) and their very popular GNU [Stallmann 98] (GNU is not Unix)
project. The goal of the FSF was to develop free software. The meaning of free
does not mean "at no cost." It means that everybody has the freedom to take
the software, improve it and share the results with others.

The FSF published two very popular licenses, the GPL [FSF 89] and the
LGPL [FSF 89a]. The task of these licenses is to ensure that the code stays free
and that no developer can be sued for damage done by the software. This shows
the first big difference to commercial software. There is no company which can
offer a support contract and is liable.

However, to be able to discuss the use of OpenSource software for the e-
commerce business, one needs to clarify what OpenSource really is. We will
focus on three different aspects:

1. OpenSource licenses
2. The OpenSource development model
3. OpenSource as a business model

## 1.1 Open Source licenses

Whether a license may call itself an OpenSource license or not depends on certain criteria which can be found at [Perens 97]. The license says nothing about the development model, which means the way software is developed nor does it directly imply any kind of a business model. The most important issues of the licenses are:

- Everybody is able to read, modify and redistribute the software.
- The license may not discriminate against anybody.
- Changes made to free software must be made available to the community.

For companies which intend to base their development on existing free software, the last topic is very important. It means that every extension or addition made to free software is in turn free. That makes it for example impossible sometimes to combine free software with commercial software modules or modules which are licensed from a third party under a different license.

The details depend on the license chosen by the developers. The most common license, the GPL (GNU general public license) is very strict when it comes to the question of to what extent free software can be mixed with non–free modules. The LGPL (GNU library general public license) is less strict and can be used in combination with non–free software, while modifications to LGPL code still have to be freely available.

That means if a company wants to develop new E-commerce software and has to decide whether it uses existing OpenSource technology or not, then an intensive study of the licenses is needed. The project management has to evaluate whether technology from third parties is required and whether licenses allow to combine them with the free software. And the managers have to decide whether they want to publish their code or whether or not they can unleash the technology which is put in the project.

## 1.2 OpenSource development model

Software development models are still an interesting research topic in computer sciences. A bad development model can make software expensive to develop and maintain, having great impact on the quality of the code and release schedules.

The OpenSource development model [Raymond 99] has shown that it can produce high quality software. Apache [Apache] and Linux (see http://www.kernel.org) have proven to be more reliable and secure than competing products from well–known companies. This success made professionals look at the way OpenSource software is developed in the hope of finding a revolutionary new way of writing software.

However, it is often ignored that there is a lot of free software which has very low quality, especially with regard to usability and documentation or that is never completed.

Even well known and very successful projects like Linux and KDE are known to be released long after the original time schedule which can be disastrous for a commercial project, since a delay of the release date can cost enormous amounts of money.

We claim that the OpenSource development model is not deterministic enough to be used in a commercial project. It works too much like the kind of evolution we know from nature. Many people work on heaps of projects trying all kinds of more or less genuine ideas, and finally they often come up with an excellent piece of software. However, it is not predictable when this is going to happen and how the result will look. No investor will put money in a project that claims to produce some excellent software but is unable to say when it will be finished and how it should finally look.

Another idea people often have about OpenSource is that one only needs to publish some source code and hundreds of free developers may help to improve it. An example is the Mozilla (see http://www.mozilla.org) project. The goal of this project is to write a free WWW browser based on the sources of the well known Netscape Navigator. While the project is still alive it makes progress at very low speed and has not managed to get many developers working on it.

## 1.3 OpenSource Business Model

As we have shown above, the licenses and the development model used by the community of free developers is only seldom interesting for commercial developers. So the question arises whether one can make money with OpenSource at all.

One answer is that companies usually do not make money by *developing* free software. If a company releases some of its source code under an OpenSource license then it is because they do not intend to make money with the software itself. For example, SGI puts some of its technology in Linux to finally get a good operating system for their server hardware. They make money with the hardware, not with the software. Another example is IBM. Big Blue actively supports the Apache project. They in turn do not make money by selling the Apache, since everybody can download the software for free. Instead, they earn money with consulting and service contracts, which is financially even more interesting then just selling software licenses.

Another reason for releasing software under an OpenSource license may be to increase the level of awareness. A small software company may quickly become well known all over the Web, in case they release an OpenSource software in a field where there is a large demand for the software.

An example of companies that make money by selling OpenSource software are Linux distributors like SuSE, Red Hat, Caldera and Corel. In fact they do not get money for software licenses, but they get their money for putting the software on CD-ROM, writing documentation and making it easy to install and configure. Other possible business models are presented at [OpenSource.org].

We conclude that a company which intends to develop its own e-commerce software would rather decide not to give the source code to the public. But often it is not necessary to develop new software. Using existing open source software to build an e-commerce business seems to be very attractive for multiple reasons:

- The software does not cost anything.
- OpenSource software has proven that it can be of excellent quality.
- If the project is still maintained or has a big user base, then there is a good chance that reported bugs or problems can be solved very quickly.
- Since the source code is available, it is possible to fix bugs or tailor the software for special needs.
- The availability of the source code allows one to port the software to other hardware platforms.

Whether the initial costs of a software is important or not depends on the size of the e-commerce shop. Big shops with thousands of customers a day spend much money on maintaining existing software and on increasing availability and robustness of the system. Compared to that license costs are often negligible. For small, new companies, instead, it makes a big difference whether they can get the software for free or not.

Two of the most important topics are security and reliability. Commercial WWW servers like the Microsoft IIS server are known for their security problems (see http://www.eeye.com/html/advisories/AD19990608-3.html). Hackers always find some way to lock or crash the server, and in some cases they manage to get confidential data like credit card numbers or a list of customers. The free Apache server, in contrast, is known to be one of the most reliable servers on the market. The same applies to the Linux operating system. Their advantage is not only that they have a lower number of bugs. If an error shows up, developers are extremely fast in releasing a patch that solves the problem. Commercial companies are often either slow in fixing bugs or they want to sell expensive support contracts.

We believe that standard OpenSource software is often the better choice since it is more secure and reliable. However, by default that only applies to software that is used by many users already. If only a few people are using the software, then it is much less likely that an error becomes quickly detected and fixed. That means: The more popular a free project is, the better the support becomes, and the shorter the time between error detection and the release of a patch.

Sometimes a software package needs to be tailored for special needs. With closed source software that is very limited, since one can only configure the things which the developers made configurable. For more sophisticated changes one needs to modify the source code. Companies often do not ship their source code to their customers. One reason is that they fear that the code may be stolen. And usually the companies do not want to support hacked versions of their software since they do not want to fix bugs introduced into the code by the customer.

Another problem when setting up a computer system is finding the correct combination of software and hardware. If a commercial company does not support a certain hardware architecture, then it is unlikely that they will do so because a single customers demands it. OpenSource software can be adapted and recompiled on new hardware much more easily. Usually free developers have already made the software compile on a wide range of hardware ranging from Intel machines to big IBM, HP or Sun servers.

When the e-commerce shop grows, then it might be necessary to buy new hardware in order to handle more transactions. That often means exchanging the hardware platform for example from an Intel based system to a big UNIX server. In this case the system administrators just need to recompile the software. If the provider of a commercial software package does not support the new hardware platform, then there is little hope. This is especially a problem when the software used to run on Windows NT or Windows 2000 since these operating systems only work on Intel. Not every software vendor can offer a version that runs on big UNIX servers.

Large amounts of free software are written for UNIX operating systems. Using a UNIX based system makes sure that scalability is easier to achieve since the same software can usually be compiled on cheap Intel servers and very powerful servers with only a few modifications. That means an e–commerce shop can start with some cheap Intel servers running Linux, and later they can easily switch to more expensive but more powerful hardware while still using the same software.

To sum up: There is no general answer to the question whether one should choose OpenSource software over closed source software when building an e-commerce business. It depends on the special needs and on the concrete software packages available on the market. In the following paragraphs we will compare software packages from both worlds – closed source and OpenSource.

## 2 Attributes of E-Commerce Software

The success of a real (non–virtual) shop is, for instance, affected by its physical conditions, rental payments or its attractiveness to potential customers. Companies that want to start a virtual business on the Internet must pay attention to almost the same attributes. The quality of an e-commerce software can be the decisive factor whether a webshop is efficient and successful or not. E-commerce software provides the user with many different functionalities. The importance of these features for the user depends on how intensively one wants to use the Internet as a distribution channel.

Every shop consists of a storefront and the back office[Ludewig 99]. The storefront consists of all that customers see. To that belong different features that make shopping easier and more pleasurable for the customer, like a categorized array of products, a shopping cart or various payment types. Different ways to customize the shop allow the shopkeeper to adapt the shop's layout and look to his or her desires or the corporate design to stand out among the competitors. Better shops provide one with advanced features like marketing functionalities (e.g. cross selling facilities), multilinguality, the use of different regional settings (languages, dimensions, currencies, date and time), to create statistics, inventory tracking and shipping tools, which calculate shipping by using a per item price or by weight and destination.

The back office consists primarily of customer data files and the inventory control system [Ludewig 99]. Some shops have an integrated database for this purpos or offer interfaces to connect with existing systems. Furthermore the shop system should be compatible with the operating system used[Ludewig 99].

## 2.1 Interfaces to Inventory Control Systems

The complex structures and operations of commercial enterprises are supported by electronic inventory control systems. Computer–supported inventory tracking control in commercial enterprises means the exact collection of quantities and values of sale of goods, storage and disposition/booking. Furthermore the system provides one with information for financial accounting, inventory support and management information [Scheer 90, p.226 ].

Due to the needs of different enterprises, these inventory control systems often are developed or individually customized. This is the reason why these systems often differ much from standard solutions and why they become inflexible.

The success of an e-commerce installation depends on how integrated it is with other in–house applications and how strong the business process becomes supported by the whole IT environment [Albers et al. 99, p.157].

If interconnecting both systems is not possible, the enterprise must change to another inventory control system if it wishes to optimize its business process and not to enter orders manually in the old system. This change leads to high expenditures and wastes personnel resources.

By connecting a webshop to an inventory control system customers may verify availibility of items. Orders are processed immediately by the system and the sold item subtracted from the inventory. In this way customers always receive current information. Some systems provide tools for customers to check the status of orders and for the business to process and check the status of payment.

Intershop Software can be integrated into existing inventory control systems, Intershop Software also includes an inventory control system. Intershop 4 comes delivered with the databases Oracle 8.0 or Sybase Adaptive Server XI. Both databases follow the Open Database Connectivity (ODBC) Standard, which allows access for external systems via appropriate ODBC drivers [Liedke 99]. ODBC allows the interactive import and export of data between applications [Kauffels 98].

## 2.2 Scalability

Webopedia (www.webopedia.com) gives the following definition for the word "scalable": "A popular buzzword that refers to how well a hardware or software system can adapt to increased demands. For example, a scalable network system would be one that can start with just a few nodes but can easily expand to thousands of nodes. Scalability can be a very important feature because it means that you can invest in a system with confidence you won't outgrow it."

Scalability of a software means its ability to be run on computers of different magnitudes. One requirement is, that the software can be used without changes when switching whole computers or merely various components. A former expression for scalability was upward compatibility [Stahlknecht 97].

Scalability of a software is a pre-condition so that the architecture of the selected e-commerce solution can grow with the enterprise. Clearly stated is that the upgradability of existing solutions with a rising number of transactions or data traffic exists without the need to change to new software. This attribute is present with multiple-processor systems, whose power can be raised by adding additional processor cards. Software with high scalability is also compatible on lower systems.

Software with low scalability can cause a company to change to other programs, which may lead to high expenditures and the wasting of personnel resources.

Intershop itself advertises the high scalability of its products, which has been always confirmed by various analysts[Kauffels 98]. Partnerships with e.g. Compaq or Fujitsu Siemens Computers shall contribute to enhance the scalability of Intershop products on their hardware.

## 2.3 Security

We do not intend to discuss pure TCP/IP security mechanisms. Instead we focus on application layer security. There are questions on different levels about security in the context of software. Besides an external attack (Hacking) a safety problem can be present with the program. The two most popular cases were that of Microsoft and RealNetworks. Both Microsoft's Media-Player and RealNetworks's RealPlayer and RealJukebox secretly submitted a Global Unique Identifier (GUID) to a server when one played a multimedia file from the Internet which allowed one to identify a PC. Something similar would be possible with e-commerce Software. A program could, due to the fact that it is always online, submit company data or client data anywhere on the Web. Even if such methods are not the standard, a user of"closed source" software must believe in what the producer says. OpenSource software enables the user to modify a program so that no data will be submitted to unwanted places. This is very important to one who runs a webshop, because a company's client data (and hopefully a loyal clientele) can be a decisive competitive factor and therefore is the most guarded value of the company. This problem is alleviated to some extent by different laws in different countries, if a law for this exists at all. In Europe, governments prefer laws for data protection, while the USA believes in a self–regulating economy.

## 2.4 Comparision of available solutions

In the following section we will give examples of differences between closed source and OpenSource e-commerce software.

Intershop from Jena in Germany is one producer of commercial e–commerce systems. With its products Intershop provides companies of all sizes with solutions for setting up electronic commerce and running a webshop. To their product line "Intershop 4" belong "ePages", "Hosting" and "Merchant." ePages and Hosting Intershop are attractive to Internet Service Providers (ISP's) which want to provide their customers with Shops to rent in the Internet [Maddox et al. 98]. The provider can run some thousands of shops on one server parallel. Customers pay e.g. a monthly rent to the provider (from about 20 Euros per month, dependant on the provider and the desired features and services) but do not need to invest in their own hardware and software. Customers can organize, manage and customize their shops online via a standard web browser. Compared to ePages, Hosting offers more functionalities. The higher version, "Merchant," is similar to Hosting but is a dedicated–server solution for companies which want to run their shop in–house. Intershop supports the platforms Microsoft Windows NT, Sun Solaris, Linux, SGI Irix and Compaq Tru64.

For individual extension of the functionalities Intershop provides customers with two "Developer Tools." The Cartridge Developer Kit (CDK) enables one to develop junctions between Intershop software and applications or payment systems of third parties. To use the CDK one must have knowledge of e.g. Perl5 and SQL, participated successfully at the "CDK-Training" and become a member "Intershop Integrated Technology Partner (ITP) Program." The "Intershop Developer Kit (IDK)" is a set of development tools that allows one to integrate Intershop technology into existing business systems.

"Intershop Enfinity" is the largest and with a price of 300,000 USD per license is the most expensive program provided by Intershop. The program targets large enterprises and supports e.g. financial transactions, machine–to–machine commerce, transactions on other websites and protocols like WAP.

Besides this commercial e-commerce software, there is a wide range of open–source software. Some of them are licensed under the Generel Public License GPL by the Free Software Foundation. Several of them are Yams (Yet Another Merchant System), OpenMerchant, MySQLShopper, MiniVend or CiberTienda.

CiberTienda was developed two years ago by the Spanish bank Banesto and is now OpenSource licensed under the GPL. The program can be downloaded from the homepage (http://www.cybertienda.org) free of charge. To be compliant with the idea of the GPL, Bansto has signed an agreement with Onirica. This company's task is to set up a community where "the software can be improved with the collaboration of the community" and names various "main goals of the development." The CGI based program was developed under Linux and runs as well under Unix. PostgreSQL (www.posgresql.org) is the only supported database. The support of additional databases is planned as well as the possiblity of running the program on Windows NT. Banesto provides the program "Virtual POS" for the use of different payment methods. To use this, one must register and certify. Banesto is the certifying authority; one condition is that one has an account at Banesto.

Yams (Yet Another Merchant System) is written in Perl (www.perl.org) and uses a MySQL (www.mysql.com) database. It features a persistent shopping cart, the ability to handle different types of products including various kinds of physical and electronic products as well as the ability to showcase "affiliate" products. Additionally, Yams provides support for authorization of credit cards through Signio, a commercial company earning money with its e–commerce payment platforms. Yams is licensed under the GPL. A mailing list is distributed on its homepage (http://yams.sourceforge.net/) to get support or to take part in the community.

What both Yams and Cibertienda have in common with Intershop Merchant is that they run on dedicated servers. Therefore they can be run in–house without the need of a e–commerce service provider. Both Yams and Cibertienda are licensed under the GPL, the source code can be downloaded for free from the Internet. The license for Intershop Merchant costs about $5,000. All programs provide one with different features that a modern shop system should include. They allow, for instance, the use of different payment systems, they generate statistics and allow the use of various marketing functionalities like cross selling. Both Yams and Cibertienda have payment systems which prefer specific authorities with the allocation of certificates, in this case Banesto or Signio.

On the criterion of the compatibility with different databases and operating systems, Merchant is the more developed solution. Yams and Cibertienda are each limited to one database. While support of the GPL licensed programs is conducted via mailing lists, Intershop products are supported by CSP's.

As Yams and Cibertienda source codes are free, one can customize or enhance the programs as desired. With the use of Intershop one must use the mentioned developer tools. The target group of these tools seems not to be a single shop operator but suppliers of applications that want to integrate their programs into Intershop technology and thus reach more potential customers.

Most OpenSource solutions require more know–how about the software and software development than commercial software, which is something that should be considered when selecting a webshop. But even if installing and running a shop for the first time is often easier with commercial products, the use of more complex functionalities or the integration of third party applications also requires more expertise.

## 3  E-Commerce Consulting

To continue our evaluation of OpenSource e–commerce software it is important to get an idea of how e-commerce projects are currently handled. One of the leading IT-consultants, referred to as "the consultant" from now on, has agreed to outline the major steps taken in an average e-commerce project.

**Functionality compared**

|  | Intershop Merchant | Cibertienda | Yams |
|---|---|---|---|
| Credit Card Processing | x | x | x |
| Database | x | x | x |
| Inventory Control | x | | |
| Support | x | | |
| Price | USD 5000,- | Free | Free |
| License | commercial | GPL | GPL |

*While Intershop is offering professional support, users of the OpensSource shops have to rely on the Usenet or mailing lists until some company will offer professional support. An interface, e.g. XML–based, from the OpenSource-shops to inventory control systems, can be easily developed by a programmer.*

### 3.1 Services of consultants

The basic approach to all e-commerce projects by the consultant is the following:

1. Vision
2. Plan
3. Fulfillment

where fulfillment is the major part. The consultant follows the principle of efficiency and uses state of the art technology. The consultant does not use complete solutions, but only components of different manufacturers that are being combined. Intershop products are not used at all, because the consultant is unwilling to use proprietary solutions written in the Practical Extraction and Report Language (PERL).

In addition to the standardized software–components, self–developed Java-software is used. The consultant stresses that these pieces of software are applied to distinct parts of the overall solution. For example, certain interfaces are programmed in Java and small tasks are handled by Java programs. It is also possible, that certain transaction systems are developed using Java.

To sum up, the main approach is the use of software components of large software manufacturers, e.g. database–servers of IBM, Oracle or Informix, application servers of BEA, IBM or SUN and the Netscape Enterprise Server as web-server. The Netscape Enterprise Server includes an application interface (API) which the consultant uses to apply a self–made tool. This tool is used to increase the security of the webserver. Asked whether any OpenSource products are being used, the consultant replied that the IBM webserver is also being used and that the IBM webserver is basically an imitation of the Apache webserver, but OpenSource products are not used at all.

### 3.2 Cost of consulting

The consultant is developing, installing and configuring software, after the vision and the plan have been established. Whether standardized software components are used or OpenSource software, the cost of the consultants work is hardly affected, as long as the software used fulfills its purpose and enables the consultant to use his philosophy of efficiency. The cost of licensing the software is generally negligible compared to the cost of the consultant.

By introducing self–developed software we believe the consultant is enhancing the link of the customer to the consultant, because usually another consultant will not have the same insight into this software as the consultant himself.

## 4  Management Analysis

### 4.1  Risks of Purchasing Software

**Flaws in Software** Unfortunately it can happen that software does not have the features that the box says it has. In that case, usually the price is the amount refunded. The price of purchasing can be large or small compared to the work hours invested. The work hours for installation and configuration still have to be paid. The resources used up in this process are part of the risk of the buyer, in case he realizes at an early time that the product does not fulfill the requirements. If the flaws are very serious, the manufacturer of commercial software can be sued; the developers of OpenSource software cannot be sued.

This is the reason some organizations do not use OpenSource software. The case of Microsoft does however show that suing a software company can absorb very much time and money. The safety of having the option of suing does not necessarily imply to win in an appropriate time. Therefore, from our point of view, this apparent safety should not lead to an exclusion of OpenSource software prior to evaluation of software products for a certain purpose.

**Discontinuation** In commercial as well as OpenSource software there is a risk that the software of your choice will no longer be produced or supported after a very limited time. In that case there are no new versions of the software available that e.g. incorporate the use of new technologies. In case the software is critical to daily work, a new investment will become necessary.

While the user of OpenSource software can become the head of the headless software project, the user of commercial software does not have this option, because neither the source code of the software nor the legal prerequisites are available to him or her.

### 4.2  Total Cost of Ownership

There are many different ways of defining the total cost of ownership of IT. We will discuss the immediate costs induced by an investment in a certain kind of software. A more in–depth discussion about the Total Cost of Ownership is provided by [Cappucio et al. 96].

**Installation, Configuration, Maintenance and Support** The cost of software beyond the initial price of software may be divided into cost of installation, configuration, maintenance and support. These costs exist no matter if the software had a price or was given away for free.

Of the four costs mentioned, the costs occuring after installation and configuration are of special interest. While widely used OpenSource software usually serves the user with the advantage of very quick bug fixes, the user of commercial software has to wait for the new release of a bug fix by the manufacturer. The support of OpenSource software is not institutionalized in the form of call center hotlines, but usually there will be a lot of support offered by other users and developers via usenet. Today, the first companies have been founded that are specializing in giving services and support for OpenSource software. From our own experience we would like to state that this type of support works. In case you have ever tried to reach someone with enough know–how in a call center of a software vendor to give an answer to your question, you might have experienced that it takes a lot of time and patience, if you get the correct answer at all.

**Training** The cost of training employees occurs no matter if the software is OpenSource or not. Training might be necessary to aquaint users with new software or with new releases and new functionality added to software already in use.

**Human Resources** To support the IT-infrastructure one needs personnel. It is of some importance which software products have to be supported. If, for example, a company does not use the latest version of Lotus Notes, it is often harder to find support staff for this company than it is to find support staff for the current release of Lotus Notes. The reason for this is that the support staff is in fear of loss of their market value, if they are not up to date and know the latest hints with the current release.

OpenSource software offers the staff the possibility to always be up to date with the product they offer support for. Because the source code is available, after every new release it can be judged whether the installation and configuration of the new release is worthwhile. The support staff never has to stick to the old version of a software because of budget constraints for software licenses and also never has to fear a loss of their own market value for such a reason.

## 5 Conclusion

OpenSource software is software. Therefore, all services that are provided for software are also possible for OpenSource software.

Let us assume for a moment that suing a manufacturer of commercial software only has a very limited chance of success. In that case, functionality, security and the total cost of ownership are the key factors for the decision maker. When it comes to security, OpenSource software has an advantage. Only if you know the source code you can check if any back doors are included in the software. In e-commerce, there are many OpenSource products that are enabling a rapid developement of complex websites. There are also software packages available, that implement basic shop–functionality and can be modified, because the sourcecode is freely available. Such a website coud be, just like it is the case today, planned and fulfilled by a consultant. After purchasing the service of a consultant, the owner of the webiste is not bound to that consultant by licenses or other agreements - he can freely chose who will be the next one working on the site. This may lead to more competition and better services, although the one first creating a website will always have the advantage of a deeper insight into the product.

We conclude that customers are not free from the task of testing the available products. Open Source software adds some additional choices to the market which are worth being considered. Open Source products are especially interesting for small businesses because of the low price, and it may be a good starting point for one's own developments, as long as the license is no problem. When it comes to integration with other proprietary systems like ERP software, then closed source software may offer the better choices currently.

# References

[Albers et al. 99]   Albers, Sönke; Clement, Michel; Peters, Kay; Skiera, Bernd:*eCommerce - Einstieg, Strategie und Umsetzung im Unternehmen*, F.A.Z.-Institut für Management-, Markt- und Medieninformationen GmbH, Frankfurt am Main, 1999

[Apache]   Apache HTTP Server Project: *About the Apache HTTP Server Project*, http://www.apache.org/ABOUT_APACHE.html, 1999

[Brooks 95]   Brooks, Frederick P.:*The Mythical Man-Month : Essays on Software Engineering*, Anniversary Edition, Addison–Wesley, 1995

[Cappucio et al. 96]   Cappucio, D.; Keyworth, B.; Kirwin, W.: *Total Cost of Ownership: The Impact of System Management Tools*, Gartner Group Strategic Analysis Report, http://gartner5.gartnerweb.com/public/static/software/rn/00031136.html, 1996

[FSF 89]   Free Software Foundation: *GNU General Public License*, http://www.fsf.org/copyleft/gpl.html, 1989

[FSF 89a]   Free Software Foundation: *GNU Library General Public License*, http://www.fsf.org/copyleft/lgpl.html, 1991

[Kauffels 98]   Kauffels, Franz-Joachim: *E-Business: Methodisch und erfolgreich in das E-Commerce-Zeitalter*, MITP-Verlag, Bonn 1998

[Liedke 99]   Liedke, Bernd: *Praxishandbuch Internet Business: Online Marketing, Electronic Commerce and Intranet*, Interest Verag, Augsburg, 1999

[Ludewig 99]   Ludewig, Bernd: *Existenzgründung im Interet: Auf- und Ausbau eines erfolgreichen Online Shops*, Vieweg, Wiesbaden, 1999

[Maddox et al. 98]   Maddox, Kate; Blankenhorn, Dana:*Web commerce: building a digital business*, John Wiley & Sons Inc., Canada, 1998

[OpenSource.org]   OpenSource.org: *The Business Case for Open Source*, http://www.opensource.org/for-suits.html

[Perens 97]       Perens,       Bruce:       *The       OpenSource       Definition*,
                  http://www.opensource.org/osd.html, 1997

[Raymond 99]      Raymond, Eric S.: *The Cathedral and the Bazaar*,
                  http://www.tuxedo.org, 1999

[Raymond 98]      Raymond,       Eric       S.:       *Homesteading       the       Noosphere*,
                  http://www.tuxedo.org, 1998

[Raymond 99a]     Raymond, Eric S.: *The Magic Cauldron*, http://www.tuxedo.org,
                  1999

[Stahlknecht 97]  Stahlknecht, Peter: *Einführung in die Wirtschaftsinformatik*,7.
                  Edition, Springer-Verlag, Berlin Heidelberg New York, 1997

[Stallmann 98]    Stallman,       Richard:       *The       GNU       Project*,
                  http://www.fsf.org/gnu/thegnuproject.html, 1998

[Scheer 90]       Scheer, August-Wilhelm: *EDV-orientierte Betriebswirtschaft-*
                  *slehre: Grundlagen für ein effizientes Informationsmanagement*,7.
                  Edition, Springer-Verlag, Berlin Heidelberg New York London
                  Paris Tokyo Hong Kong, 1990

# Electronic OTC Trading in the German Wholesale Electricity Market

Stefan Strecker, Christof Weinhardt*

University of Giessen, Information Systems
Licher Str. 70, D-35394 Giessen, Germany
{stefan.strecker, christof.weinhardt}@wirtschaft.uni-giessen.de

**Abstract.** Recent changes in the German energy policy initiated a deregulation process from a monopolistic to a competitive market, fundamentally changing the market structure, transaction relationships and trading processes. While the mutual exchange of electric energy has been a
business activity between vertically integrated utilities for a long time,
wholesale electricity trading in an open market only recently started
to gain momentum. Electricity becomes a commodity traded at power
exchanges and off-exchange on over the counter (OTC) markets. In Germany, the wholesale electricity market is dominated by OTC trading.
Trading in OTC markets is usually performed via telephone and facsimile which leads to a limited price transparency, a limited liquidity,
an ex ante restricted number of potential market partners and, last but
not least, substantial transaction costs. Market participants are therefore searching for new trading mechanisms to circumvent the problems
of the current trading processes. The electronization of trading activities
promises to reduce the disadvantages of current OTC trading processes
through the automation of tasks within the transaction chain. In this
context, electronic markets for electricity trading are coordination mechanisms for the market exchange of electricity and electricity derivatives,
i. e., a virtual market place where supply and demand meet and trade.
An important feature of electronic markets is an automated dynamic
pricing which is currently not supported by electronic markets available
for electricity trading in the German wholesale market. A concept for an
Electronic Electricity Trading System is therefore proposed with a main
focus on automated price discovery.

## 1 Introduction to the German Electricity Markets

The German Energy Act of 29 April 1998 fundamentally changed the policy
for the German energy sector. Following the EU directive 96/92/EC, the new
energy legislation breaks up the regulated monopoly and transforms the electric
utility industry into a competitive electric power industry [1, p. 14].

* The research presented in this paper is funded by the Deutsche Forschungsgemeinschaft (DFG) under project no. WE 1436/4-1. We would like to thank the four
anonymous referees for their valuable suggestions and helpful comments. The authors are responsible for all remaining deficiencies.

For more than 100 years, electric energy supply was deemed to be a sector where competition does not achieve the objectives of energy policy makers, i. e., a reasonably priced and secure supply. The German energy policy therefore accepted a regulated monopoly and explicitly excepted exclusive, vertical concession agreements between municipalities and utilities as well as horizontal, interutility demarcation agreements from anti-trust law. This policy led to closed supply areas in Germany prohibiting competition among local, regional and nation-wide utilities. The Energy Act of April 1998 changed this policy radically. Concession and demarcation contracts are now prohibited by antitrust provisions which results in the right to freely choose a supplier. Unbundling of generation, transmission, distribution and trading is enforced whereas only the "wires" business, i. e., the transmission and distribution lines, remains a regulated monopoly due to its natural monopoly characteristics [2, p. 19]. Access to the transmission and distribution lines, i. e., to the grid, must be granted to third parties by the respective grid operator according to an association agreement. As a consequence to the new energy policy, competition was introduced in the generation and trading business [3]. Germany has the largest net electricity demand (483 TWh in 1998) and, hence, the largest market volume in Europe, created by nearly 43 million small-size (mainly private households), and 295,000 medium-size to large-scale (industrial) consumers [4, p. 39]. The size of the market is numbered on 60 billion Euro [5] and the expected overall trading volume (physical and financial) exceeds every other market in Europe by an estimated total of 5 to 10 times the demand, i. e., between 2,415 and 4,830 TWh. Given these figures, electricity trading clearly marks the most prominent effect of the deregulation process.

To discuss the chances for the automation of trading activities in the German electricity market, we describe the commoditization process as a consequence to the deregulation of the German energy policy (section 2). Then, we visualize the changes in the market structure to demonstrate the impact on the trading process (section 3). By describing the current status of electricity trading in Germany (section 4), we motivate a need for electronic markets as coordination mechanisms for the market exchange of electricity and electricity derivatives (section 5). The deficits of existing electronic markets for OTC trading in Germany (section 6) serve as a starting point for our concept for an electronic market for electricity trading (section 7). The concluding section briefly summarizes the research layed out in this paper.

## 2 Commoditization of Electricity in Germany

Even though the mutual exchange of electric energy has been a business activity between vertically integrated utilities in Europe for a long time, wholesale electricity trading in an open market only recently started to gain momentum.[1]

---

[1] Electricity trading is the process of purchase, sale and mediation of electricity and financial derivatives based on electricity, independent of generation assets, transmission and distribution lines [6].

The deregulation in Germany initiated a commoditization process, i. e., electric energy becomes a tradable, negotiable entity, valued by price signals emerging through negotiations between supply and demand. Yet, electric energy differs significantly from other commodities like grain or metals: Electricity is a non-storable, conduction-bound commodity with unique physical charateristics. Trading electricity therefore requires market participants to obey the economic and physical constraints but also compels specific trading mechanisms. Specifically, contracts for the delivery of electric energy contain additional negotiable terms such as load, delivery period, delivery time, maturity, etc. By combining various contract terms, distinguishable products emerge and become tradable. Historically, the commoditization process perceptible started in 1999 when price indices were freely published on the World Wide Web (WWW). Power traders and power brokers started to use the Internet as a media to indicate prices. Grid operators communicated prices for access to their grid using the Internet. WWW-sites addressing retail customers appeared in the second half of 1999. Electronic market places are common means to facilitate wholesale trading in liberalized markets. Last but not least, power exchanges use Internet services for order entry, order routing and deal settlement.

## 3  The Impact of Market Structure on Electricity Trading

Before the deregulation in 1998, the market structure was characterized by a high degree of concentration which led to unique, directed supply chains and a hierarchical market structure with simple transaction relationships: the eight nation-wide utilities generated 80 per cent of the total production in Germany and supplied 33 per cent of the demand to end consumers (mostly large-scale industrial consumers). 80 regional utilities generated 9 per cent of the total production and supplied 36 per cent of the end consumer demand while the majority of 900 local and municipal utilities generated 11 per cent of electric energy in Germany and supplied 31 per cent of the end consumer demand. A similiarly high degree of concentration exists in the "wires" business [7, pp. 242, 270]. As depicted in Fig. 1, today, the German electricity market has a completely different structure. Although a noticeable degree of concentration in the generation and transportation business still remains, a major structural change runs through the deregulated power industry. Primarily, new participants enter the market, i. e., new institutions such as power exchanges and new intermediaries such as wholesale broker affect the way, the electricity business is carried out. The number of potential transaction relationships increased in comparison to the monopolistic structure and, hence, the complexity and risk of conducting business in the electricity industry have grown significantly.

Trading processes have to be differentiated with respect to two market segments: the retail and the wholesale market. Because a common definition for either market has not been established yet, we briefly define retail as well as wholesale electricity trading.

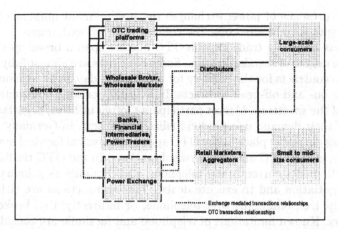

**Fig. 1.** Market structure and transaction relationships in the competitive German electricity market

Retail electricity trading is conducted at the level of distribution lines (in Germany 110 kV and lower) with reseller-to-end consumer transaction relationships. Market participants in the retail market are small- to mid-size end consumers, typically private households, as well as small and medium enterprises with an electricity consumption, that does not allow them to manage their own energy contract portfolio. A typical contract for electricity delivery in the retail market covers electric energy plus affiliated services like maintenance, metering, energy and load management. Wholesale electricity trading, on the other hand, denotes electricity trading at the level of transmission lines (in Germany 380 kV, sometimes 220 kV) with transaction relationships between generators, intermediaries and large-scale industrial consumers as depicted in Fig. 1. A typical wholesale transaction covers pure energy without affiliated services. Furthermore, wholesale trading requires each market participant to manage and control his own energy contract portfolio, i. e., each wholesale market participant ensures that the portfolio meets his consumption and delivery needs. In the further discussion, we will concentrate on the wholesale market.

## 4 The Status Quo of Electricity Trading in Germany

The German wholesale electricity market is dominated by OTC trading. Only a few market participants trade at foreign power exchanges. In Germany, the first institutionalized power exchanges are scheduled to start in Leipzig at the Leipzig Power Exchange (LPX) in June 2000 and in Frankfurt at the European Energy Exchange (EEX) in August 2000 with a spot market. Futures markets are planned at the EEX for the fourth quarter of 2000 and at the LPX for the end of 2000. Also, the Amsterdam Power Exchange (APX) started a market in Germany on 1 January 2000. Yet, experiences in deregulated markets show that even in the presence of power exchanges the predominant amount of deals (70 to 80 per cent) is contracted over the counter, i. e., off-exchange.

Contracts currently traded in the OTC market span a broad spectrum considering the degree of standardization. Some contracts are almost fully standardized such as contracts for the delivery for a complete day, week or month around the clock or on- and off-peak contracts. Individual portfolio contracts mark the other end of the spectrum. Market participants, often utilities, negotiate on a full coverage of their demand using individualized contracts. In Germany, electricity trading takes currently place in the OTC spot and physical forward markets and, increasingly, in the OTC financial forward markets. In the OTC trading process, market participants currently use telephone and facsimile as primary media to conduct negotiation and to execute deals. OTC transactions are either negotiated directly, i. e., bilaterally over telephone, or indirectly, i. e., brokered by an intermediary. Known limitations of telephone and facsimile are considered to be responsible for various disadvantages in the OTC trading process: limited price transparency and liquidity, an ex ante restricted number of potential contract partners and, hence, substantial transaction costs, among others [8, p. 255]. A demand for new market coordination mechanisms, i. e., new ways to bring supply and demand together, arises to cope with the increasing complexity and to comply with the commodity's and participant's requirements. Electronic markets automate the trading process by an electronic support for tasks in the transaction chain and therefore represent potential solutions towards an electronic electricity trading in the German wholesale power market.

## 5  Electronic Trading Systems for Electricity Wholesale Trading

The term "trading system" with respect to electricity trading has no unique meaning and a definition often depends on the perspective of the author. At least, two different meanings of the trading systems have to be differentiated: risk management and trade processing (RMTP) software and electronic markets for electricity trading. RMTP software supports the trading activities of a single market participant, i. e., the front, middle and back office tasks on a trading floor, either for the management of physical (generation, dispatch and scheduling software) or financial trading (risk management software) [9]. In contrast, electronic markets for electricity trading are coordination mechanisms for the market exchange of electricity and electricity derivatives, i. e., a virtual market place where supply and demand meet and trade [10]. Following Picot et. al. [11], electronic electricity markets are computer systems for electronic electricity trading which enable the trade between several, possibly an arbitrary number of, market partipants with electricity and electricity derivatives using information and communication technology (ICT) to automate (parts of) the transaction chain.

A trading or market process consists of a transaction chain of sequential transaction phases. Different phase models have been proposed to capture the semantics of trading processes. Schmid suggests different phase models for electronic markets [12, 13]. Similiar models exist for market processes in securities trading [14, 15]. Typically, phase models subdivide the market process into four successive transaction phases: the knowledge, bidding, negotiation and settlement phase. In the *knowledge* or *information* phase, a market participant searches for quotes, product qualities and contract terms suiting his transaction desire. Assuming a potential deal attracted the participants interest, the specification and transmission of an order to the point of execution takes place in the *bidding phase* (or orderrouting phase). Once placed in the market, the negotiation over contract terms starts and will possibly end in an agreement (*negotiation* phase). Subsequently, the contract partners exchange money for the contracted commodity in the settlement phase. The negotiation phase itself consists of three interdependent processes: product matching (or matching of contract terms), counterparty matching and price discovery [16] whereas alternative pricing procedures exist for the price discovery process:[2] The discovery of prices could either be a manual, requiring human intervention, or an automated, i. e., computerized process. In this respect, dynamic pricing as an umbrella term refers to price discovery mechanisms where a price emerge over time.

Electronic markets differ by the level of automation within the transaction chain and their support for processes in a specific transaction phase [18]. The critical process when automating the transaction chain is the price discovery. A core component of electronic markets are electronic trading systems (ETS) as they automate the price discovery and trade execution process by an electronic support for the bidding and negotiation phase through an automated order routing, price matching and trade execution [19, p. 27]. Electronic trading systems are operated by computer exchanges and electronic OTC markets. In the financial markets, electronic off-exchange trading systems are called proprietary trading systems (PTS) or alternative trading systems (ATS) [20]. We link this terminology to electronic markets for electricity trading and separate two groups of electronic trading systems:

- Electronic Electricity Trading Systems (EETS) are alternative trading systems in the OTC electricity markets
- Power Computer Exchanges (PCE) are fully automated and integrated commodity exchanges for electricity trading

# 6 Electronic OTC Trading in the German Wholesale Market

Eight electronic markets are available for wholesale electricity trading in Germany as of 10 March 2000 (see Tab. 1). The markets differ regarding technology, current status and operator type. Existing electronic markets are based on three technologies: Electronic Data Interchange (EDI), W3C standards (HTTP, HTML, etc.), and pure TCP/IP with proprietary client/server technology.

---

[2] According to Domowitz, "enabling this process of price discovery is a basic function of any trading market mechanism" [17].

**Table 1.** Technology, current status and operator type of existing electronic markets

| | Electronic Markets for Electricity Trading | Technology | Current Status | Operator Type |
|---|---|---|---|---|
| Electronic OTC Markets | NetStrom | W3C | Testing | Consulter |
| | pbi powerbroker | W3C | Price Indication | Broker |
| | Enron Strommarkt | W3C | Price Indication | Marketer |
| | SKM Marketplace | TCP/IP | Price Indication | Broker |
| | Enron Online | W3C | Transaction | Marketer |
| Power Exchange | Nord Pool | EDI | Transaction | Exchange |
| | APX | W3C | Transaction | Exchange |
| | OMEL | W3C | Transaction | Exchange |

The current status shows the primary focus of the systems whereas the operator type demonstrates the diversity of market participants interested in electronic (OTC) trading. If we sort the available electronic markets by their support for the transaction phases, a lack of support for the negotiation and settlement phase for OTC transactions becomes apparent (see Tab. 2): ICT is primarily used to support the knowledge and bidding phase. Electronic OTC markets are commonly used within the knowledge phase for price indication and within the bidding phase for posting offers in closed user group extranet systems. Yet, as of today, negotiation and bargaining takes place over telephone. Only two systems offer first approaches to an electronic support for the negotiation phase: Enron Online and SKM Marketplace. Enron Online, a system originating from the liberalized U.S. power markets, offers standardized contracts on a WWW-based electronic market where subscribers are able to post bid and ask offers to conclude a contract with the operating company, Enron. Negotiable contract terms are restricted to price and quantity. SKM Marketplace uses a proprietary client interface to display bid and ask offers entered by SKM brokers. The negotiation phase is supported by an electronic chat system which aims to replace telephone conversations.

**Table 2.** Support for transaction phases by electronic markets available to German participants

| | Electronic Markets for Electricity Trading | Knowledge | Bidding | Negotiation | Settlement |
|---|---|---|---|---|---|
| Electronic OTC Markets | NetStrom | √ | √ | | |
| | pbi powerbroker | √ | √ | | |
| | Enron Strommarkt | √ | √ | | |
| | SKM Marketplace | √ | √ | (√) | |
| | Enron Online | √ | √ | (√) | |
| Power Exchanges | Nord Pool | √ | √ | √ | √ |
| | APX | √ | √ | √ | √ |
| | OMEL | √ | √ | √ | √ |

The clearing and settlement of off-exchange contracts is currently not supported by any electronic OTC market. Power computer exchanges, by definition, support the entire transaction chain, i.e., they offer clearing and settlement services not only to exchange but also to OTC transactions. In summary, the automation in existing electronic OTC markets is limited. Only the first two transaction phases are well-supported. The electronic support for the negotiation phase in electronic OTC markets is rudimentary.

# 7 A Concept for an Electronic Electricity Trading System

Our concept aims to combine market microstructure theory and auction theory with electronic markets since the automation of price discovery mechanisms has been discussed in the context of financial markets [21, p. 139] as well as electronic commerce [13, p. 468].

The implementation of an automated dynamic pricing depends on the degree of contract standardization. Highly standardized contracts (e. g. certain electricity forward contracts) with fixed contract terms leave only price and quantity to be negotiated. Price discovery mechanisms for highly standardized contracts are well-known in form of auction mechanisms [22]. The automation of auctions has been shown in computerized stock exchanges, e. g., the system XETRA (eXchange Electronic TRAding) and retail auctions, e. g., ebay.com. Auction mechanisms have also been applied to electricity trading [23].

Semi-standardized contracts differ from standardized products in only a single contract term, e. g. delivery period. A standardized peak product typically covers a constant load of 1 MW from 8am to 8pm while a semi-standardized peak may cover 7am to 9pm. Individualized contracts differ from standardized contracts in two or more contract terms. In fact, individualized contracts may contain arbitrary agreements over an arbitrary number of contract terms. An automated price discovery for non-standardized contracts must therefore enable negotiations over an arbitrary number of contract terms and, hence, renders auction mechanisms which depend on "a well-defined object or contract" [24] inappropriate. Therefore, alternative price discovery mechanisms need to be implemented to electronically support the negotiation phase with non-standardized contracts. Price discovery mechanisms known to work with non-standardized contracts are bulletin board systems, sometimes called "hit and take" markets, where market participants "hit" an offered contract to conclude a deal without re-negotiation of any contract term [18, p. 29]. If a market participant wants to re-negotiate, e. g., on the price, a "hit and chat" market allows market participants to hit a specific offer and re-negotiate contract terms through a chat system, possibly supported by a guided user interface.

Further automation can be achieved by automated negotiations "when the negotiating function is performed by (networked) computers", i. e., "a process in which two intelligent software agents negotiate a solution electronically [...]" [25, p. 263]. Automated negotiations using software agents have been discussed in literature [26] and applied to electricity trading [27]. Besides the actual price dis-

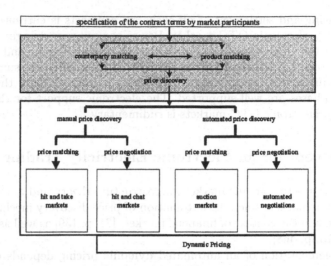

**Fig. 2.** Market Models in ELTRAS

covery mechanisms, the market organization, legal framework, information technology and custom and usances, among others, influence the market efficiency and price quality [28]. A particular combination of (market micro-) structural features (e. g. market transparency: closed or open orderbook; trading frequency: periodically or continuously; price discovery: auction or market maker market) of a specific market constitutes a "market model". A term which originally refered to the market structures, i. e., the rules and regulations, of stock exchanges [29]. Market participants make different demands on market models in different trading situations, i. e., market models must comply with the heterogeneity of market participant's transaction desires. Static market models enjoin a set of concrete structural features and, therefore, meet only predetermined transaction desires. As an extension, dynamic market models enable market participants to choose (from a range of) structural features for each transaction (e. g. bilaterally negotiate an tailor-made contract and use an auction for a highly standardized contract) [30].

Our concept for an EETS, called ELTRAS (Electricity Trading System), approaches standardized as well as non-standardized contracts, i. e., we investigate bulletin board systems, then expand our focus on auction mechanisms (see also [23]) and finally, we will transfer insights from our agent-based bond trading system, AMTRAS (Agent-Mediated Trading System) [16] to ELTRAS (see Fig. 2). Before the latter, we will empirically analyze the market demand for automated negotiations using software agents in the context of electricity trading. ELTRAS aims to verify our working hypothesis that insights into the market structure and trading processes of financial markets can be transferred to electricity markets. Our main focus is on designing dynamic market models and extending them to allow an automation of the negotiation phase in electricity trading.

# 8 Synopsis and Future Research

In this paper, we argue that OTC trading in the German wholesale electricity market lacks electronic support for the most important transaction phase within the trading process, the negotiation phase. While electricity trading in Germany is dominated by OTC transactions, the full potential for an automated off-exchange trading process is not being exhausted. Concerning the German wholesale electricity market, a lack of electronic trading systems as the vital component of electronic markets has been unfolded, both in exchange and off-exchange markets. A concept for an Electronic Electricity Trading Systems was introduced which is based upon our vision of an automated dynamic pricing. Future research will be concerned with the implementation of price discovery mechanisms reflecting the commodity's peculiarities and the market participant's requirements for an Electronic Electricity Trading System. We consider the evaluation of our design by Internet experiments as the final destination in our endeavor.

# References

[1] Meller, E.: Chancen und Risiken der Liberalisierung im Strommarkt. Brennstoff Kraft Wärme 7/8 (1998)
[2] Schmidtchen, D., Bier, C.: Liberalisierte Strommärkte. Mohr Siebeck, Tübingen (1997)
[3] Pfaffenberger, W., Münch, D., Salge, K.: Liberalisierung des Strommarktes in Deutschland. In et. al., H., ed.: Liberalisierung des Energiemarktes. Volume 8 of Schriften des Forschungszentrums Jülich, Reihe Energietechnik / Energy Technology., Jülich, Forschungszentrums Jülich, Zentralbibliothek (1999) 113–147
[4] Bundesministerium für Wirtschaft und Technologie: Energie Daten 1999. On-line at http://www.bmwi.de, Bonn (1999)
[5] Finsterbusch, S.: Die Liberalisierung des Strommarktes nimmt Gestalt an. Frankfurter Allgemeine Zeitung (1999)
[6] Preußer, P.: Stromverkauf an Großkunden. In Weizäcker, C., ed.: Energiehandel und Energiemärkte. Volume 30 of Tagungsberichte des Energiewirtschaftlichen Instituts., München, Energiewirtschaftliches Instituts an der Universität Köln, Oldenbourg (1998) 219–241
[7] Drasdo, P., Drillisch, J., Hensing, I., Kreuzberg, P., Nolden, A., Perner, J., Riechmann, C., Schulz, W., Schuppe, T., Starrmann, F., eds.: Konzentration und Wettbewerb in der deutschen Energiewirtschaft. Volume 52 of Schriften des Energiewirtschaftlichen Instituts an der Universität Köln. Oldenbourg, München et. al. (1998)
[8] Gomber, P., Budimir, M., Kosciankowski, K., Urtheil, R.: Elektronisierung des außerbörslichen Rentenhandels auf Basis von Softwareagenten. In Weinhardt, C., Meyer zu Selhausen, H., Morlock, M., eds.: Informationssysteme in der Finanzwirtschaft. Springer, Heidelberg (1998) 253–267
[9] Frost, J.C.: The Software Acquisition Process. Power Marketers Online Magazine (1999) On-line at http://www.powermarketers.com.
[10] Schmid, B., Lindemann, M.A.: Elements of a Reference Model for Electronic Markets. In Sprague, E., ed.: Proceedings of the 31st Haiwaii International Conference on Systems Sciences (HICSS'98). Number 4 (1998) 193–201

[11] Picot, A., Bortenlänger, C., Röhrl, H.: The Automation of Capital Markets. Journal of Computer-Mediated Commerce 1 (1995) On-line at http://www.ascusc.org/jcmc/vol1/issue3/picot.html.

[12] Schmid, B.: Elektronische Märkte - Merkmale, Organisation und Potentiale. In Hermanns, A., Sauter, M., eds.: Managementhandbuch Electronic Commerce: Grundlagen, Strategien, Praxisbeispiele. Vahlen, München (1999)

[13] Schmid, B.: Elektronische Märkte. Wirtschaftsinformatik 35 (1993) 465–480

[14] Gerke, W.: Computerbörse für den Finanzplatz Deutschland. Die Betriebswirtschaft 53 (1993) 725–748

[15] Picot, A., Bortenlänger, C., Röhrl, H.: Börsen im Wandel. Fritz Knapp, Frankfurt am Main (1996)

[16] Weinhardt, C., Gomber, P.: Agent-Mediated Off-Exchange Trading. In Sprague, E., ed.: Proceedings of the 32nd Hawaii International Conference on Systems Sciences (HICSS'99). Number 5 (1999)

[17] Domowitz, I.: Automating the Price Discovery Process: Some International Comparisons and Regulatory Implications. Journal of Financial Services Research (1992) 305–326

[18] Schenk, N.: Informationstechnologie und Börsensysteme. Gabler, Wiesbaden (1997)

[19] Gomber, P.: Elektronische Handelssysteme. Physica, Heidelberg (2000)

[20] Securities and Exchange Commission: Regulation of Exchanges and Alternative Trading Systems, Final Rule, Release No. 34-40760 (1999)

[21] Gerke, W., Rapp, H.W.: Strukturveränderungen im internationalen Börsenwesen. Die Betriebswirtschaft 54 (1994) 5–23

[22] McAfee, R.P., McMillan, J.: Auctions and Bidding. Journal of Economic Literature 25 (1987) 699–738

[23] Zimmerman, R., Thomas, R.J., Gan, D., Murillo-Sachnez, C.: A web-based platform for experimental investigation of electric power auctions. Decision Support Systems 24 (1999) 193–205

[24] Branco, F.: The design of multidimensional auctions. RAND Journal of Economics 28 (1997) 63–81

[25] Beam, C., Segev, A.: Automated negotiations: a survey of the state of the art. Wirtschaftsinformatik 39 (1997) 263–268

[26] Sandholm, T.: Automated Negotiation. Communications of the ACM 42 (1999) 85–85

[27] Maifeld, T., Sheblé, G.B.: Computer Simulation of an Electric Marketplace Using Artificial Adaptive Agents. In: Proceedings of the 1995 Midwest Electro-Technology Conference. Number 4 (1995) 68–71

[28] O'Hara, M.: Market Microstructure Theory. Blackwell Publisher, Cambridge, Mass. (1997)

[29] Braue, C., Hille, L.: XETRA - Elektronisches Handelssystem am Finanplatz Deutschland. Die Bank (1997) 140–145

[30] Budimir, M., Gomber, P.: Dynamische Marktmodelle im elektronischen Wertpapierhandel. Wirtschaftsinformatik 41 (1999) 218–225

# On the Competition between ECNs, Stock Markets and Market Makers *

Eric Benhamou[1] and Thomas Serval[2]

[1] Financial Markets Group, London School of Economics,
Houghton Street,London WC2A 2AE, UK
e.ben-hamou@lse.ac.uk
[2] Ecole Normale Superieure and GREMAQ, Université Toulouse I
Manufacture des Tabacs - Bâtiment F - 21 Allé de Brienne
31000 Toulouse Cedex- France
serval@clipper.ens.fr

**Abstract.** Favored by the Security Exchange Commission, Electronics Communication Networks (ECNs) have grown as alternative trading systems that enable to bypass the markets makers on the stock markets and allow investors to directly compensate and execute their orders with more discretion and at a lower cost.

In this paper we underline the fragile character of the current ECNs and question their competitive advantages through empirical evidences. We find a rationale for market makers and ECNs' excessive spreads and overreactions. The use of network theory highlights notions of critical mass, open interface and alliances. Moreover, since competition between market makers and ECNs is based on volume, the emergence of ECNs has been mainly possible because of the growth of the American stock market. Furthermore, strategies of new ECNs are built on anticipated future growth. Should the market shrink, ECNs would rapidly be forced to merge and most of them would disappear.

## 1 Introduction

An ECN is a communication network designed to match orders. Instead of having a supply side that provides Bid and Ask prices, the matching system consists in a book where limited buy and sell price orders are displayed. When the latter match, a deal is made and reported to the quoting system. Consequently, ECNs compete with stock exchanges by providing an alternative trading structure and to market makers by offering lower transaction costs.

Though considered by stock exchange authorities as broker dealers, they have acquired a special statute from the Security Exchange Commission (SEC) since 1997. Consequently, the SEC's regulatory change as well as technology, have

---

* We would like to thank Grigorios Mamalis for careful reading, Robert Dornau for interesting comments. All our errors are indeed ours.
A longer electronic version of this article is available at
http://cep.lse.ac.uk/fmg/people/ben-hamou/publication.html

revolutionized interactions between market makers, brokers, dealers, and stock exchanges, leading to more complex settings with multiple players and divergent interests.

The current paper examines the exact nature of the competition between ECNs, market makers, brokers, dealers and stock exchanges using a network economics framework. We will focus on the nine ECNs that have been officially registered by the SEC and NASD in order to look at the competition inside Nasdaq. However many results can be transposed to the case of other Alternative Trading Systems like the Arizona Stock Exchange.

The remainder of this paper is organized as follows. In section 2, we examine key features of current ECNs. In section 3, we give insights on the composition of future marketplaces. Last section concludes giving possible extensions to our paper.

## 2 The ECNs from financial information networks to electronic stock markets

As its name explicitly shows, an Electronic Communication Network is not an electronic stock market. This has sometimes led to confusion especially in the Press. ECNs were sometimes called e-bourses or e-markets. One should, however, not mix the two terms. The fact is that there is still a difference between ECN and electronic stock markets.

It is obvious that both are supported by a set of terminals linked by a specific protocol and a communication network. Both enable to trade stocks. However looking further, an electronic stock market gives a price for each product traded and guarantees execution and delivery of the trades. This is not the case of an ECN. Basically an ECN gathers orders from its members and matches them when possible, it also posts its own quote on Nasdaq. It doesn't have a direct impact on the real price discovery process but it may have some influence on the prices through the quote display. An ECN replicates the prices given by the stock markets. It does not guarantee delivery and execution. If by any chance, an ECN turns out (or wants) to offer such services, the ECN can not any more be defined as an ECN. It becomes a real electronic market and has therefore to apply for a status change.

### 2.1 The connectivity of the financial networks

When dealing with networks, the issue of critical mass is of fundamental importance. A financial network like any other network needs to reach a critical mass in order to experience positive externalities network effects as Economides and Himmelberg mentioned [10]. Using current network theory classification, we can characterize financial networks as two way networks i.e. where messages can be conveyed in the two directions and therefore each user can send and receive information. When plugging in a new user to a two-way network, of size $n$, the number of potential goods (or connections) increases by $2n$. The new user can join the existing $n$ members and the old $n$ members can join him. A network externality appears when being linked to the network is more profitable than being outside the network. The standard example is the public phone network, who can afford in those days not having a phone line ? In network theory, the word connectivity describes the number of potential terminals linked together on the network. Increasing therefore the number of users for an ECN is vital since it intensifies the connectivity of the networks.

**The importance of the installed basis** Building a new network is expensive and generates a lot of fixed costs. If the cost function of the firm that builds the network is highly non convex (with high fixed cost), the optimal size of the network would be theoritically infinite and lead to a natural monopoly. However technology can lower the fixed costs and allow an oligopolistic market structure to emerge.

This is precisely, the situation we are experiencing nowadays on Nasdaq where several ECNs are competing for order flow.

In network economics, history matters. To be the first on the market requires obtaining a significant installed basis. This situation is self reinforced with network effects, even if the technology used is not of the state of the art. This is examplified by the current market share of Instinet. In the competition between ECN, the installed basis is a key factor to differentiate the networks and their ability to reach quickly a critical mass. Network economics is often seen as a winner-take-all economy.

**Interconnection between networks** Another way of dealing with critical mass and competition is to establish alliances to benefit from network interconnections. From a theoretical point of view, we can consider that the move of the big Wall Street firms towards the ECNs is a way to interconnect their network with the ECN. Vertically integrated firms are formally equivalent to a one way network. For example, Datek owns Island and provides the ECN with order flow. This can be characterized as a vertical alliance.

But there is also horizontal alliances through interconnection between ECNs network. In order to avoid a lack of liquidity, if a match cannot be found internally, the Archipelago technology can sweep to other ECNs and market makers in order to find the best possible match. This horizontal interconnection does not relies on an official agreement between the firm but on the open interface provided by Nasdaq communications tools.

## 2.2 Anonymity and transaction costs

Anonymity and transaction costs are two main issues for customers.

**The interest of being anonymous on a market and the trade-off with liquidity** Important investors fear sometimes that the market get aware of their position on a given stock. It is difficult for a trader to indicate an interest in buying or selling a large block of stock without causing the price of that stock to move ahead of his/her order - a phenomenon known as "market impact." This is especially true if the order is from a large institutional investor.

Market analysts have estimated that the cost of market impact associated with buying and selling significant blocks of stock - as institutional investors do every days - can be more or less ten times the transaction fees.

The number of intermediaries in the regular way of making order makes it difficult to stay anonymous. On the contrary, anonymity is guaranteed on a fully electronic matching service like the ECNs. However this anonymity has a price if the ECN cannot provide enough liquidity.

The difference in the spreads is mostly due to the lack of liquidity of the smaller ECNs. This trade-off between anonymity and liquidity reinforces the stronger players such as Instinet. In order to survive, the smaller players have allowed their system to search the best prices on all networks. However this won't provide them, on the long run, a sustainable model of growth because they will be charged for the deals made on others systems that theirs. If there is a dominant player on the market, he can successfully foreclose the market to the others by charging a high rate for the use of its matching system.

**Key feature of the ECN : the matching service** Buy and sell orders which are represented in Nasdaq through ECN quotes are either public orders forwarded to the ECN by subscribing broker/dealers, or orders from institutions subscribing to an ECN. The best ECN buy and sell orders, or "top of book," will frequently drive the inside market, meaning they represent the best bid and ask prices for a security. In order to provide more informative data, the SEC has recently ordered the ECNs to provide their three best prices and not only their best one.

**The price of immediacy on real time market** One of the services provided by the market makers is immediacy. Since they guarantee in their quote a buy and a sell price, everyone can act immediately. But not all traders need a real time deal. Sometimes it can be cheaper to use an ECN, if the cost of transaction is lower.

Economides and Schwartz [9] have summarized a survey from the traderforum of the Institutional Investor in 1994. They found that the majority of traders are willing to trade patiently if this reduces execution costs. Many traders indicate that they frequently delay trades to obtain better prices. Most respondents indicate that they are typically given more than a day to implement a large order, that they typically break up more than 20% of their large orders for execution over time, and that they regularly take more than a day for a large order that has been broken into lots to be executed completely.

## 2.3 The race towards Liquidity

Liquidity is alleged to give competitive advantage for market efficiency purpose. It has been argued after the article of Glosten that, Electronic market should provide better edge for liquidity efficiency purposes. As Glosten [11] pointed out, an electronic open limit order book is more efficient in providing significant trading volume. Using a theoretical model of an idealized electronic open limit order book, Glosten found that an open limit order book mimics competition among anonymous exchanges.

Consequently, there is no incentive to set up a competing anonymous dealer market. On the other hand, any other anonymous exchange will invite "third market" competition. The conclusion that electronic open limit order book should turn out to be superior in providing liquidity should be tempered by the very specific hypotheses used in the model.

**Liquidity as a network externality** Liquidity is the measure of the time needed to sell or buy a certain stock. The natural provider of liquidity is the number of people on the market Economides [7] and [8], defines the liquidity as a composite good generated by the adjunction of a buy order and a sell order. The liquidity is the main network externality that appears on a financial network.

**Compensation or transmission of orders** One of the key issues of the electronic network is to determine who is able to compensate the orders and who has just to route the orders. Being the counterpart or compensating orders is the only difference between a regular stock exchange and a financial information network. The market makers are defined as making the market for some stocks. Hence, they must hold an inventory of this stock and part of their fees are linked to the inventory charges. Thus, the move from broker dealer to exchange appears to be a natural evolution of the ECNs. Being a regular exchange will allow them to avoid the inventory fees from the market makers.

**Future mergers** Apart from Instinet who has already reached a significant market share, all the other ECNs are fighting for liquidity. And because they are for-profit companies, there is a tendency for them to merge to reach a critical mass.

These moves will be soon to come especially for the ECNs who have a very small market share but a brand new technology. Most of the new ECNs can be seen as technological start ups as indicated by their current size and creation date

## 3  The future of the marketplace

In 1999, the OptiMark Trading System will be integrated as a facility of Nasdaq Stock Market trading network. With OptiMark, investors can indicate their interest in trading across a range of price and size parameters based on their trading strategies. With the frequency of two minutes, the OptiMark system will match large orders anonymously. Nasdaq is then moving toward becoming a big ECN. If this change of nature of Nasdaq happen rapidly, the very existence of the ECN will be threatened. Actually, the part of the ECNs in all trades is about 30 percent that gives a big advantage to the regular Nasdaq trades as far as liquidity is concerned.

## 3.1 The diffusion of technology

Paradoxically, Nasdaq which trades most of the IT stocks of the market is far from being computerized. The artificial introduction of the ECNs has made the market makers evolve to more digitalized tools of communication. As pointed out in figure 1, technology is to be introduced everywhere, from the communication networks to the matching algorithms. Ten years ago, most of the trades were negociated through the public telephone networks, now they are more or less done through computers. However, if the email-like system (SelectNet) is used to broadcast orders through the market makers or to send direct agency order, these orders are not matched automatically. This matching service remains the key feature of the ECN, until the introduction of Optimark on Nasdaq.

**Partially compatible networks** The first ECNs have been designed as proprietary systems, i.e., systems were software and hardware belong to the operator. The new competitors, because they had to reach a critical mass, have chosen an open interface by providing only additional privately owned softwares. However the need for liquidity gives a strong incentive to firms to set up compatible networks.

The strategic question of the compatibility between networks have been addressed by Katz [16].

They show that if the costs of achieving compatibility are lower for all firms than the subsequent increase in profits, then the industry move towards compatibility is socially optimal. However, it may be true that the (fixed) cost of achieving compatibility is larger than the increase in profits for some firms, while these costs are lower than the increase in total surplus from compatibility. Then profit-maximizing firms will not achieve industry-wide compatibility while this regime is socially optimal. Further, if a change leads to less than industry-wide compatibility, the private incentives to standardize may be excessive or inadequate. Similarly, the incentive of a firm to produce a one-way adapter, that allows it to achieve compatibility without affecting the compatibility of other firms, may be deficient or excessive because the firm ignores the change it triggers on other firms' profits and on consumer surplus.

These results, show us that in the network economy, the question will not be who owns what, but who sets up the standards. Standard setting will be the new monopoly and will provide the true rent for the economics sector. Right now technologies are competing among the ECNs but because of the network effect, the winner of this war can expect substantial benefit from the electronic exchange.

**The effects of the Internet** The Internet has often been described as the source of the changes on the financial networks. As it has been previously underlined, market forces and regulatory incentives have played a central role in the phenomenon.

Nevertheless, we can see three major implications of the Internet in the evolution of marketplace : The Internet as an investment tool : The financial news freely provided through the Internet have a direct effect on quotes. Since the origin of the information on small chat rooms or web sites are difficult to monitor, the risk of false information or insider trading is a great concern for regulators (see SEC regulations on exchange).

The Internet as a support for on-line brokers : Thanks to the Internet, new intermediaries known as on line brokers have emerged (E-trade, Datek), others have experienced a significant growth (Charles Schwab). Actually, the Internet is a powerful tool that can aggregate demand for stocks and then reach an important volume with a huge number of small accounts. These new brokers have already a fully integrated electronic interface and find it more convenient to route their orders through electronics alter ego like the ECNs. These can explain the investment of E-trade in Archipelago. Moreover new brokers could have some incentives to bypass the existing exchanges and to join the new exchanges.

The Internet as a means of communication : The newer ECNs miss the critical mass. In order to have a sustainable business model, they need to grow fast at a low cost, using the Internet as a means of communication significantly reduces the fixed cost of developing an alternative network. They only develop a secured user interface while all the data transit through the Internet. It allows them to concentrate on the competition on quality of services and gives them a great potential connectivity.

We must also underline that the influence of the Internet on the financial market is part of a broader phenomenon where all intermediaries that were designed to make a price are changed into electronic smart agents. This trend is very strong especially in the Business to Business relationships.

Paradoxically, the exchanges have been among of the first in the world to introduce computers and networks but they have assigned them the function of communicating and not negociating. With the emergence of the Internet, the electronization comes back from the business world to the exchanges with the goal of achieving market efficiency through electronic matching services.

**New competitors : the existing information networks** As it has been pointed out before, the connectivity and the liquidity are key features of the ECNs. Thus, the new competitors can be the institutions who own their own proprietary financial information networks such as big banks or broker dealers who can be interested in vertical integration. The providers of liquidity such as important Internet brokers can also take part in the game. They have already done it by taking staking in various ECNs. But they can move a step further by opening their own networks to their clients becoming, de facto, powerful players on the ECN market. They can also buy one of the ECN to merge their network with technology of the ECN.

Another competitor is Nasdaq itself which can become fully computerized. The introduction of Optimark systems as an open interface provides all Nasdaq participants with a anonymous electronic matching service. The choice of an open interface, that is to say that doesn't exclude any users of Nasdaq terminals (to be compared with the limited and selected clients of the ECNs), will make the system a real threat for the survival of the ECNs inside Nasdaq.

## 3.2   Convergence and globalization of financial networks

**Competition between networks in the US may lead to worldwide leaders** By allowing several private systems to compete each other, the regulator favors the emergence of strong and efficient electronic marketplaces. This can be considered as a threat for other foreign markets with strong institutional connections between exchange and government. Once a critical mass is reached in any parts of the world, the electronic exchange can be a very aggressive competitor on all other markets because the marginal cost of adding a new terminal is close to zero whereas the benefit of being linked to the network is positive.

Due to the numerous network effects and unregulated market will lead to a monopolistic structure of the trading networks. Nevertheless, the optimal choice does not coincide with the strategic choices as Katz and Shapiro [16] have proved it.

**Trade-off between fair prices and high fixed costs : a regulatory problem to come** If we assume that the economics of the electronic for-profit exchange leads to a monopoly, it is not sure that this structure would be socially optimal

Actually, there is a trade-off between lowering transaction costs by sharing infrastructure and avoiding the monopoly prices. These problems have already been addressed in the literature on natural monopoly. We can expect a need for a stronger regulation on the infrastructure, that is to say the norms and protocols that will have to be used on the networks. Should the electronic exchanges spread worldwide, national regulators legitimacy would then be questioned.

**The signs of the convergence** With the emergence of electronic market places all around the world, the fundamental differences between the market tends to disappear. Because of the ECNs, Nasdaq is becoming more order-driven and consequently closer to the NYSE. The evolution of exchange towards continuous market has been undertaken under the ECNs pressure. In a near future, the biggest stock markets in the world will be open 24 hours a day. The fact that orders are now routed through homogeneous systems, irrespective of the time, the distance, or the regulatory environment, could be seen as the premises for a global electronic market. However, the need for immediacy is not crucial for most of the orders. Since liquidity varies with time, people will also trade-off between immediacy and liquidity. For instance, if the market for a Microsoft stock is not very liquid on Saturday night, a trader may prefer to delay this order to have a better execution price rather than interfere with the current quote.

We have previously shown that the difference between existing exchange, ECNs and financial information networks mainly relies on the ability for the former to guarantee the delivery of stocks. It is very likely that once the ECNs will have enough volume, they will be able to guarantee the stock delivery and then bypass the whole exchange. They will compete like any exchange in the world in stocks listing and they will have a significant technological advantage because of the natural selection process, they are experiencing now.

## 4 Conclusion

In this article, we have seen that the competition between ECNs, stock markets, market makers is intensive and complex. This environment is fast moving, volatile and at the same time it is the interest zone of many actors.

Built as a communication network between market makers, to trade OTC stocks, Nasdaq was the designated place for electronic matching services to emerge. Paradoxically, the computerization of Nasdaq was designed to achieve better communication between market makers but not to match orders. And, indeed, the emergence of ECNs has not resulted from the market structure but from regulatory changes.

Due to the strong network effects that characterize any communication network, all competitors are fighting for liquidity, so as to reach a critical mass. ECNs promote their low transaction costs and the anonymity of their trading process. However, empirical research tends to prove that ECNs'spreads are wider than market makers' ones because of the lack of liquidity. From the client point of view, the trade-off tends to be between anonymity and liquidity.

The current "informational" revolution has also played a great role in market nature changes. By lowering communication costs, the Internet has allowed new ECNs, based on open interface, to enter the market. As demand agregator, the Internet has also favored the growth and development of on-line brokers, who would rather face electronic counterparts to process their order homogeneously. Finally, the continuous growth of stock markets has permitted higher volume to be shared with the new entrants. Should the market collapse now, all ECNs under the critical liquidity market size would disappear. Looking at figures, this would include most of them. Apart from Instinet, ECNs can be seen as technological start-ups similar to the numerous smart ones found in other industries. They actually compete for market share and technology. As a result, the winner of this competition is going to be a serious competitor for all institutional stock markets.

# References

1. Biais, B.T. Foucault, F. Salanie " Floors, dealer market and limit order markets", Journal of Financial Markets, No. 1. (1998), pp. 253-284.
2. Barclay, M. J., Christie W.G., Harris J. H. , Kandel E, Schultz P. "The Effects of Market Reform on the Trading Costs and Depths on Nasdaq Stocks", Journal of Finance. Vol LIV, No 1 (February 1999) pp 1-35.
3. Christie, W. G . and P.H. Schultz, "Why do Nasdaq market makers avoid odd eighth Quotes?" Journal of Finance (December 1994), 1813-1840.
4. Chung, K.H.;Van Ness, B.F.;Van Ness, R.A. "Limit Orders And The Bid-ask Spread - A Paired Comparison Of Execution Costs On Nasdaq And The Nyse" Journal of Financial Economics 53 (1999), pp 255-287.
5. Demsetz, Harold, "Limit orders and the alleged Nasdaq collusion", Journal of Financial Economics 45 (1997), pp 91-96
6. Dutta, Prajit, and Ananth Madhavan, "Competition and collusion in dealer markets", Journal of Finance 52 (1997), pp 245-276
7. Economides, N., Liquidity and Markets, in: The New Palgrave Dictionary of Finance (1992)
8. Economides, N., Network Economics with Application to Finance, Financial Markets, Institutions. (1993)
9. Economides, N. and R.A. Schwartz, Equity Trading Practices and Market Structure: Assessing Asset Managers? Demand for Immediacy, Financial Markets, Institutions (1995).
10. Economides, Nicholas and Charles Himmelberg, (1995), "Critical Mass and Network Size with Application to the US Fax Market," Discussion Paper no.EC-95-11, Stern School of Business, N.Y.U.
11. Glosten Lawrence R. "Is the Electronic Open Limit Order Book Inevitable?" Journal of Finance, Vol. 49, No. 4. (Sep., 1994), pp. 1127-1161.
12. Godek, P.E. "Why Nasdaq market makers avoid odd-eighth quotes", Journal of Financial Economics, 41 (1996), pp. 465-474.
13. Grossman, Sanford J. , "The Informational Role of Upstairs and Downstairs Trading", Journal of Business, Vol. 65, No. 4. (Oct., 1992), pp. 509-528.
14. Hendershott Terrence and Haim Mendelson "Crossing Networks and Dealer Markets: Competition and Performance" forthcoming in the Journal of Finance (1999)
15. Huang, R.D.;Stoll, H.R. ."Dealer Versus Auction Markets: A Paired Comparison Of Execution Costs On Nasdaq And The Nyse" Journal of Financial Economics (1996) 41, pp 313-357
16. Katz, Michael and Carl Shapiro, (1985), "Network Externalities, Competition and Compatibility," American Economic Review, vol. 75 (3), pp. 424-440.
17. Klock Mark and D. Timothy McCormick. "The Impact of market maker Competition on Nasdaq Spreads", NASD Working Paper 98-01, August 1998
18. LaPlante, M.;Muscarella, C.J. "Do Institutions Receive Comparable Execution In The Nyse And Nasdaq Markets? A Transaction Study Of Block Trades" Journal of Financial Economics 45 (1997) pp 97-134.
19. Reilly, Frank K. , William C. Slaughter, "The Effect of Dual Markets on Common Stock Market Making", Journal of Financial and Quantitative Analysis, Vol. 8, No. 2. (Mar., 1973), pp. 167-182.
20. Securities and Exchange Commission, Regulation of Exchanges and Alternative Trading Systems. December 8, 1998. Effective Date: April 21, 1999

# Internet Advertising: Market Structure and New Pricing Methods

Andrea Mangàni

Department of Economics – University of Siena
Piazza S.Francesco 7 53100 Siena (0039 050 43270)
mangania@unisi.it

**Abstract.** In this paper the Internet advertising market is analyzed. Data and estimates confirm that the Web represents a real threat to television and newspapers. Therefore, the main characteristics of the advertising market are described in order to point out the differences between Internet and traditional mass media. In particular, pricing methods appear to be the most peculiar innovation carried out by on-line advertisers. It is shown how these new business models may substantially change the quantity of advertising which maximizes web publishers' profits.

## 1 Introduction

The Internet is the fastest growing medium and it has great potential as an advertising medium. The use of the World Wide Web will improve dramatically in the coming years, gradually making the Web a mainstream medium. Advertisers are showing great interest in this new medium, because of the large and growing number of users spending time on it: with Internet, it is possible to differentiate the advertisement to meet users' requirements, and online advertising is becoming part of many companies marketing strategy.

In the early days of advertising on the Internet, the only vehicle for delivering advertising messages was a banner. Now the range of advertising formats has expanded greatly: this expansion is due to increase of the number and type of advertisers, greater bandwidth, sophistication of the Internet audience, and the creative strength of digital technology.

Publisher Web sites that function as ad-supported media vehicles, just as with advertising in the print and broadcast media, must serve the dual demands of two groups: Web consumers and Web advertisers. Therefore the role of the publisher's site includes enabling and encouraging the consumer to interact with advertising appearing with content at its site. Yet, the World Wide Web is intrinsically different from the mass media traditionally used as advertising channels. An understanding of the differences is essential to explaining market structures and new business models.

The Internet combines the ability of the mass media to create a message reaching a wider audience with the feedback and interaction possibilities deriving from providing individualized information: traditional advertising is consumed passively, whereas on the Internet users have to actively select an advertisement. In addition, the

Internet offers unlimited low cost space compared to the limited capacity and high costs found in traditional media.

In the next section we introduce the main concepts concerning Internet advertising, while in the third section we show the extent of the emerging Internet advertising industry. In the section four, with the background of main theoretical contributes on media advertising markets, we discuss the choice of the optimal quantity of advertising by the web publishers, given some advertising formats and under different assumptions with respect to pricing methods. We show that the equilibrium outcomes may be different from those obtained in the case of traditional mass media. Some concluding remarks are provided in the last section.

## 2 What Is Internet Advertising?

Firstly, let's try to capture what we mean by Internet advertising. Sometimes the whole process of producing and maintaining a corporate Web site is called "Internet advertising". Nevertheless, there is a clear distinction to be made between maintaining a Web site, as part of a firm's marketing communications strategy, and maintaining a Web site in order to sell advertising space on the site and generate revenues.

Using a narrow definition, Internet advertising means the Web banner, i.e. when a World Wide Web site owner offers to display an advertisement on its Web pages, by placing the advertisement in a box somewhere on the page. With a broad definition, we take into account all sort of methods of product, brand and corporate promotion, including the Web banner, buttons, links, and other devices used on Web pages, site-sponsorship deals, cross-media promotion involving branding of the Web site as part of the package, e-mail distribution lists and many others. In what follows, we are mainly interested in analyzing the former definition of Internet advertising, and theoretical considerations will be based on it.

Web advertising has two components - passive and active. These passive and active components are differentiated by the amount of control exercised by the consumer over their exposure. Consumers are automatically exposed to passive ads when they visit a publisher's Web site. Passive ads act as a gateway to active ads, since they provide the links that the consumer clicks to view the active ads.

The most famous advertising format is the banner, a small rectangular ad placed within another content-filled page. *Banners* can be static or animated and interactive. The newest banners allow users to interact with ads without leaving the current web site. Advertisers are devoting increasing amounts of resources to creating ads that will attract attention, especially as click-through rates for traditional banner ads decline. Recent estimates show that click-through rates have fallen below 1% from 3% several years ago. The decline in click-throughs has been attributed to several factors, including consumer advertising overload, a wear-out of the novelty effect, and more directed search on the Internet by consumers.

*Interstitials* are animated ads that appear suddenly in full screen without any user action to activate them. They are short messages which may interrupt the user's current task, or more often, fill time between scheduled events. With *sponsorships*, advertisers offer content that is somehow related to their products or services and valued by the target audience. Sponsorships are expected to grow in both volume and share of spending because of their potential for relatively unobtrusive and continuing contact with the consumer. Banners, interstitials and sponsorships account for most of what is included in estimates of Internet advertising currently available.

Other formats are the *directories*, listing sites such as "Yahoo!" where users search for specific categories of products or services, *enhanced links*, which may be purchased (enhancement stands for moving the listing to the top of the screen, enlarging it, or highlighting it with different labels, fonts, or colors), *electronic mail*, which may be *direct* e-mail and *sponsored* e-mail. Direct e-mail is usually sent to consumers who have requested product-related news, while sponsored e-mail is sent to consumers who are subscribers to a specific content-focused electronic publication.

A number of other advertising formats are usually excluded from estimates of Internet advertising, perhaps because they are not priced in the same standard unit. *Affiliate programs* utilize performance-based compensation for advertising. For example, any Web site can become an Amazon "affiliate" and establish a link to Amazon books on its site. *Barter* or *link exchange programs* imply the trading of links between Internet sites without any exchange of money. Bartering and trade are estimated to account for approximately 5% of current advertising placement.

## 3 The Extent of the Market

U.S. online advertising revenues reached $1.709 billion in the fourth quarter of 1999 [4]. Fourth quarter 1999 revenues grew 161% over the same period in 1998, and $497 million (40%) over the third quarter of 1999. Advertising revenues for 1999 have now hit $4.553 billion, more than doubling (141%) the revenues of 1998 (see also figures 2-4).

Web advertising revenues are doubling each quarter and are predicted to reach $5 billion by 2000. This demonstrates the strength of the medium as it attracts increasingly larger portions of advertiser budgets. However, on line advertising revenues represent only a fraction, even if increasing, of advertising revenues across all media.

The 10 leading online publishers accounted for 75 percent of total 1999 second quarter revenues, the same as 1999 first quarter, and up from 67 percent reported for the second quarter of 1998. The 25 and 50 leading publishers accounted for 86 percent and 90 percent of 1999 second quarter revenues respectively.

Internet advertising continues with a mix of formats being used by advertisers. Banner advertisements are reported as the main type of advertising in the fourth quarter of 1999, accounting for 53%. Sponsorships account for 25%, interstitials for 4%, and email for 3%, with all others at 15%.

When looking at pricing models, hybrid pricing (combination of impression-based pricing combined with performance-based compensation) accounted for 52% of 1999 fourth quarter revenues, with CPMs or impression-based dealing at 40% and performance-based accounting for 8% of revenues.

An effect of the rapid expansion of supply, Internet advertising prices have declined over time. The decline of Internet cost for impression has been attributed to the increasing oversupply of advertising space in the market. Actually, the number of Internet sites accepting advertising has dramatically increased, as many publishers have learned that this kind of revenue is critical for their long-term survival, in a market where subscriptions are difficult to generate. It has been estimated that approximately 10% of Internet sites are trying to sell advertising space[1].

The products which lead online spending during the fourth quarter of 1999 were: consumer-related (31%), computing (16%), financial services (17%), new media (12%) and business services (7%). The greatest share of revenue transactions (94%) are cash-based with barter/trade and packaged deals accounting for 5% and 1% of total revenues respectively [4].

In the first three quarters of 1998, almost 50% of Internet advertising was placed by sellers of computer-related products and services. Nonetheless, over time there has been a significant broadening of the advertising base on the Internet. Table 1 compares the percentages of expenditures in different media accounted for by the major categories of Internet advertisers.

Several features of these service categories bear noting. The Internet functions as both a communication and distribution channel for many services. Besides, the advertised services are characterized by both search and experience attributes. The Internet is appropriate to deliver information required to assess search attributes, and through bulletin boards and newsgroups, it permits the exchange of consumption experiences. For example, automobiles, which is the dominant product category, consist of both search and experience attributes.

The major categories of Internet advertising seem to most closely be similar to those of newspapers – a medium in which a substantial quantities of information can be delivered. As may be seen from Table 1, the leading advertisers in newspapers in 1998 were financial services, computers and software, automobiles and travel. Aside from automobiles, the leading advertisers on network TV in 1998 tended to be non-durable experience goods: toiletries, medicine, and food. As expected, experience goods tend to be more intensively advertised than search goods. Accordingly, as the number of people spending time on the Internet increases, we expect to see a greater proportion of advertising for experience goods and services, particularly high-cost items involving great amounts of pre-purchase information search. It may also be that search goods and non-durable experience good will rely more heavily on Internet formats such as directory listings, sponsorships, and Web sites, in order to achieve the different goals of their Internet marketing campaigns.

## 4 The Optimal Choice of Advertising Quantity

### 4.1 Advertising and Broadcasting: Theoretical Literature

Media industries are unusual because they operate in what is called a dual product market: media firms "offer" their products to the viewers, listeners, and readers, and they sell access to audiences to advertisers, who try to use the proper media in order to attract the greatest number of final customers. In particular, advertisers attempt to select those media and vehicles whose characteristics are most compatible with the advertised brand in reaching its target audience and conveying the intended message.

---

[1] The apparent infinite supply of Internet advertising space contrasts drastically with the short-term inelasticity of supply in the television market; even newspapers face short-run constraints on ad space.

Advertising support changes the nature of the final product being sold and hence the nature of final demand. In the case of radio and television broadcasting, the final product of advertising supported broadcasters is access to audience which is sold to advertisers. Programming is an intermediate input supplied to consumers in order to generate an audience for the advertising. Performance in each market affects performance in the other: the demand for the product sold depends on the willingness of advertisers to pay for exposures to this audience, which in turn depends on the effectiveness of the advertising.

In the last 50 years theorists have developed several hypotheses on the relationships between market structure, product diversity and audience size in mass media markets. Theoretical models suggest that those links are especially important in advertising-financed broadcast programming such as radio and television.

The majority of theoretical work is mainly concerned with the diversity of programming. In particular, a lot of attention has been devoted to analyze how an increase of the number of the firms in the market affects the diversity of programming. In spite of the heterogeneity of these contributes, the analytical results can now help to explain many characteristics of broadcasting markets[2].

From the point of view of a welfare analysis, the choice between pay television and advertising supported television is a choice between second best outcomes. In fact, under any system the marginal cost of supplying the program to an additional viewer is almost zero. With advertising support, the per program charge per viewer is zero, and pricing is efficient. However, the program is not broadcast unless revenues cover the cost of producing it, a cost that is independent of the number of viewers. Under pay television, there will be an efficiency loss because of pricing above marginal cost (price higher than zero). Therefore the trade-off is between the failure of advertising supported television to reflect the intensities of preference on the one hand, and inefficient pricing on the other. In general, a mixed revenue support from both advertising and subscription would be optimal, because it might provide a good compromise between the lower price allowed by advertising support and the mechanism for conveying the preferences allowed by subscription payments.

On the other hand, little has been said about how the oligopolistic interaction between media affects the equilibrium in the advertising market. Masson et al. [7] utilize the classic Bertrand and Cournot models in order to describe competition between television channels for the sale of advertising time. Their analysis shows that, under certain conditions, the quantity of advertising produced and sold in equilibrium may be lower under duopoly than in monopoly, which is not what one should expect in "normal" markets. As a consequence, increased competition may lead to a higher price of advertising with the duopoly than with the monopoly.

In Kehoe [6] the choice variables of a broadcaster are the quantity of advertising, the price of the advertising, and the amount of investments in "talent". Talent is a variable which includes all that may increase the size of audience: good disc jockeys, journalists, etc. The author examines only the case of a monopolistic firm, but the model represents an improvement over the previous literature on media markets, since in former works the cost of broadcasting was assumed equal to zero.

---

[2] See, for example, [1], [8], [11], [12].

Finally, Hackner, Nyberg [3] analyze media markets by means of a Bertrand duopoly differentiated model. Their analysis is concerned with a framework where the media product is a private good. The results show that there exist symmetric and asymmetric equilibria, where the latter can be interpreted as natural monopolies. The tendency towards natural monopolies is weaker the more differentiated the products are and the higher the quality of the product. As television and radio broadcasting are concerned, if advertising externalities are negative, only symmetric equilibria are feasible, while with positive externalities the public good property strengthens the tendency towards natural monopoly. However, there are some questionable assumptions in this model, such as positive advertising externalities.

## 4.2 Theoretical Literature on Internet Advertising

There is few theoretical literature on Internet advertising. The greatest part of it belongs to marketing studies and is concerned with marketing applications of advertising models. With respect to this approach, [5] provide a very comprehensive survey of all reasons to advertise on the Web. They also discuss some myths and popular wisdom concerning Internet advertising which sometimes affect marketing studies of the new medium.

In a paper by Silk et al. [9] it is explored the substitutability between Internet advertising and other media advertising. Their work suggests how different Internet advertising formats compare with respect to the factors hypothesized to influence intermedia choices. The comparisons serve to emphasize that the Internet is an adaptive, hybrid advertising medium. The evidence reported shows that alternative formats available on the Internet offer advertisers a great range of options with respect to audience addressability, audience control, and contractual flexibility. This kind of adaptability suggests that the Internet may be employed as a substitute or complement for virtually any of the conventional media, for both national and local advertisers.

Chatterjee et al. [2], propose a model for predicting advertising click response at an advertiser-supported Web site using "clickstream" data gathered at the individual level. Empirical analysis of clickstream data collected over a seven month period at an ad-supported site was used to study the effect of other advertising stimuli encountered by the consumer during navigation and heterogeneity in within-visit and across-visit click behavior at the Web site. The results suggest that increasing the number of same passive ad insertions will lead to negative returns initially and level off at higher level of exposures. The negative impact will increase with increase in frequency of visits to the site. The publisher can accommodate many different advertisers at the site, without adverse effects as long as a single passive ad is placed on a page.

## 4.3 Advertising Supported Media: CPM Pricing Methods

Here we want to discuss the optimal choice of advertising quantity by broadcasters (television and radio), extending the discussion to the case of Internet site publishers. In particular, we want to analyze the different outcomes resulting from different pricing methods: the CPM (cost for exposure) method and the "cost per action" (clicks) method. Naturally, in television, radio and Internet, the total audience response function would be dependent upon various parameters, not only advertising. Formally we have

$$q_{Ni} = q_{Ni} \ (PC_i, \ FC, \ q_{Ai}, \ q_{Aj}) \tag{1}$$

where $q_{Ni}$ is the number of viewers (listeners, visitors) of program (web site) $i$, $PC_i$ is the production cost of program (web pages) $i$, $FC$ are the fixed costs of broadcasting (connecting the site to the web), $q_{Ai}$ and $q_{Aj}$ are the quantities of advertising broadcast (shown) by $i$, with $j \neq i$.

Within the framework of a partial model, the audience response function may be set up as a function of just the advertising quantity chosen by the single firm: $q_{Ni} = q_{Ni}$ $(q_{Ai})$. It seems reasonable to assume that members of the audience feel that the smaller the number of advertising messages, the better for them. Then we have $\partial q_{Ni} / \partial q_{Ai} < 0$.

In a market in which the only private source of revenue for broadcasting is the sale of advertising, because of the public goods characteristic of broadcasting service, the choice variable of the broadcaster is then the quantity of advertising or, better, the time dedicated to advertising during the day programming or within the web pages. The problem of $i$ is then Max $\pi_i = p_{Ai} \ q_{Ai}$, w.r.t. $q_{Ai}$, where $p_{Ai}$ is the price paid by the advertisers to firm $i$ for a minute (or a banner) with advertising. The advertising price can be expressed as $p_{Ai} = p_{Ai} \ (CPM, \ q_{Ni})$, where CPM is the cost for impression and $q_{Ni}$ is the number of viewers, listeners, readers or visitors in the case of Internet.

We are assuming that the price of advertising is a function of the size of audience: the greater the size of audience, the higher the price paid by advertisers, e.g. $\partial p_{Ai} / \partial q_{Ni} > 0$. This is a considerable simplification, since audience characteristics, such as age, sex, and wealth also matter to advertisers.[3]

Also, in a competitive market the CPM (cost for impression) will be constant. So we can write $p_{Ai}(q_{Ni}) = kq_{Ni}$, with $k > 0$. The value of $k \equiv CPM$ is obviously determined by demand and supply. Given that the advertisers market is not competitive but oligopolistic, one may say that the strategies of firms will affect $k$. Anyway, in the short run, and with respect to price choice, $k$ is given, and the single firm can not affect it too much. This characteristic seems to be confirmed by some empirical observations.

Given this general framework we have that Max $p_{Ai} \ q_{Ai}$ = Max $q_{Ni} \ q_{Ai}$, i.e., the profit maximizing quantity of advertising is the quantity which maximizes the number of impressions (the product between the audience and advertising time). We can see these relationships in figure 1, where we assume that $q_{Ni}(q_{Ai}) = a - bq_{Ai}$, with $a, \ b > 0$. The profit maximizing quantity of advertising is where the marginal revenue curve is zero.

We suppose that the firm faces zero production costs. Actually, there are no costs for "producing" advertising time. The costs relate to the production of television

---

[3] Advertisers will want their messages to be delivered to the audiences most likely be interested in purchasing their product or services. Advertising agencies accordingly attempt to find programs or stations attracting the best target audience, defined by demographic, income and ethnic mix. In addition, various methods of price discrimination between advertisers are the norm in these markets, whereas we assume a uniform price if the size of audience is the same for different stations. We need the simplification in the text in order to concentrate on the advertising market.

programs, radio programs or Internet pages, in which advertising space is then going to be sold. In addition, these are often fixed costs, with variable costs close to zero. In other words, we are not considering investments in quality or variety[4]. With linear specifications of the audience response function, the maximization problem leads to $q^*_{Ai} = a/2b$, $q^*_{Ni} = a/2$ and $p^*_{Ai} = ka/2$.

### 4.4 Advertising Supported Media: New Pricing Methods

Driven by advertisers' desires for greater accountability, the pricing of Internet advertising appears to be evolving in ways that depart from existing print and broadcast models. Some years ago, Procter and Gamble created a stir by insisting that Internet vehicles be paid for "click-throughs" rather than for exposures. After the immediate uproar, this practice has become more common and has generated even more precise measures of response: "price per action" relates charges to specific consumer actions such as subscribing to an e-mail list or downloading software to qualify for compensation; "cost-per-lead", is a popular pricing option for higher-priced services such as insurance and financial services ([10], [14]).

The implicit assumption that more passive impressions is better may not hold true in generating advertiser-desired outcomes in the Web medium. Aggregate counts of clickthroughs or click rates (i.e., the ratio of passive ad clicks to passive ad impressions) are actually preferable, since they measure actual exposure to passive ads and a commitment by the consumer to view the active advertising content[5].

If we consider a method of payment of advertising space based on click-through rates, we have that the expression above becomes $p_{Ai} = p_{Ai} (q_{Ni}, q_{Ai}) = h\alpha\, q_{Ni}\, q_{Ai}$, where $h$ is the "cost of a click", that we continue to assume constant given the competitive advertising market, and $\alpha$ is the share of people visiting the site presumably seeing the banner (i.e. the number of impressions) who click on the banner. The number of clicks depends on the number of impressions, and we assume a linear relationship between these two variables, with $h>0$ and $0 < \alpha < 1$. The maximization problem for the single firm becomes Max $\pi_i = h\alpha\, q^2_{Ai} (a - bq_{Ai})$. The problem leads to $q^*_{Ai} = 2a/3b$. Therefore, in the case of linear audience response functions, we have that

$$q^*_{A(click)} > q^*_{A(impression)} \cdot \tag{2}$$

---

[4] The assumption of zero production costs seems to be appropriate when we analyze the performance in the advertising market, but is also a common assumption of program choice analyses. In reality, in the latter case the people who select programs for stations and networks also make decisions that affect the costs of the program they air. One would expect that viewers will find programs with large budgets more appealing than programs with small budgets, because program producers will spend money deriving from advertising on things that viewers like. Spending more to get more popular performers, better program writers and directors will generally result in a more popular program.

[5] Widespread adoption by the Internet of these pricing methods portends the use of the Internet not as a general awareness-building medium, but as a means to influence behavior directly, much like direct marketing and quite different from television. These trends further suggest that, not only will Internet advertising be a threat to mass media advertising because of its higher audience targeting capability, but that it will also spur efforts to improve advertising measurement methods by traditional media in order to remain competitive.

This could be the reason why Web publishers refuse to adopt a method of payment of advertising space based on click through rates: as the advertising quantity increases, the number of visitors will decrease. But it should be noted that it is not clear if publishers' profits are higher with a pricing method based on the number of exposure. It clearly depends on the form of the "visiting response function".

## 5 Conclusions

The Internet has great potential as an advertising medium. The use of the World Wide Web will improve dramatically in the coming years, and advertisers are showing great interest in this new medium: online advertising is becoming part of many companies marketing strategy. As a marketing medium, the Internet presents many advantages over traditional media. With the Internet capability to target customers, advertising it's more efficient; with its flexibility in interacting with customers, the web combines many functions of marketing in an organizationally superior process.

The range of advertising formats has expanded greatly. Also, Internet is creating new pricing methods for advertising space, and this seems to be the most innovative and peculiar characteristic of the advertising market: pricing methods are evolving in ways that depart from existing print and broadcast models.

In section 4, by means of an example, we have shown how different pricing methods affect equilibrium outcomes in the advertising market. Obviously the analysis has to be extended to consider the interaction between different firms in an more realistic environment. The results depend on the characteristic of the audience response function, particularly on the relationship between the number of visits at the Web site and the quantity of advertising utilized by Web publishers. Therefore empirical investigations are needed in order to achieve a realistic and more precise framework in which it is possible to develop new theories for the new medium.

## References

1. Beebe, J.H.: Institutional Structure and Program Choices in Television Markets. Quarterly Journal of Economics, 91, (1977) 15-37.
2. Chatterjee, P., Hoffman, D.L., Novak, T.P.: Modeling the Clickstream: Implications for Web-Based Advertising Efforts. Rutgers University, Department of Marketing, May (1998).
3. Hackner, J., Nyberg, S.: Price Competition, Advertising and Media Market Concentration. Paper presented at the 25th Annual Conference of E.A.R.I.E., Copenaghen, (1998).
4. Internet Advertising Bureau: Internet Advertising Revenue Report; 1999 Fourth Quarter Results. Pricewaterhouse Coopers, New Media Group (2000).
5. Kalakota, A., Whinston, R.: The Economics of Electronic Commerce. Addison Wesley Longman Inc. (1999).
6. Kehoe, M.R.: The Choice of Format and Advertising Time in Radio Broadcasting. PhD. dissertation, University of Virginia (1996).

7. Masson, R. T., Mudambi, R., Reynolds, R.J.: Oligopoly in Advertiser-Supported Media. Quarterly Review of Economics and Business, 30 (2), (1990) 3-16.
8. Owen, B.M., Wildman, S.S.: Program Competition, Diversity, and Multichannel Bundling in the New Video Industry. In: Regulation, Economics, and Technology, Noam Eli-M. ed., Columbia University Press, New York, (1985) 244-273.
9. Silk, A.J., Klein, L.R., Berndt, E.R.: Restructuring in the U.S. Advertising Media Industry. Paper presented at the Second Berlin Internet Conference, Berlin (Germany) (1999).
10. Snyder, B.: Pay-Per-Lead Makes Inroads as Online Ad Pricing Method. Advertising Age, 69, March (1998).
11. Spence, M., Owen, B. M.: Television Programming, Monopolistic Competition, and Welfare. Quarterly Journal of Economics, 51, (1977), 103-125.
12. Steiner, P.: Program Patterns and Preferences, and the Workability of Competition in Radio Broadcasting. Quarterly Journal of Economics, 66, (1952) 194-223.
13. Stewart, D.W., Furse, D.H.: Effective Television Advertising. Lexington, MA: Lexington Books (1986).
14. Wool, A.: Pricing Web Site Advertising. Advertising Media Internet Center, April (1996).

**Fig. 1**

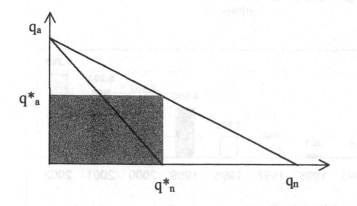

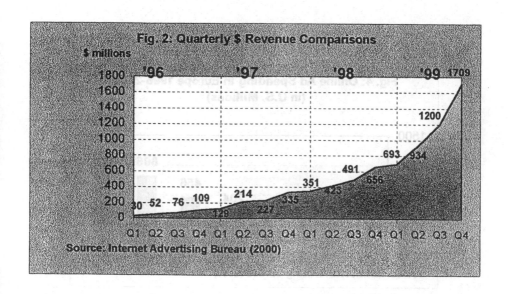

Fig. 2: Quarterly $ Revenue Comparisons

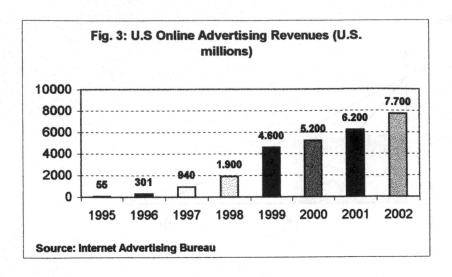

Fig. 3: U.S Online Advertising Revenues (U.S. millions)

Source: Internet Advertising Bureau

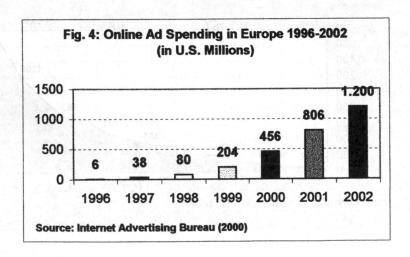

Fig. 4: Online Ad Spending in Europe 1996-2002 (in U.S. Millions)

Source: Internet Advertising Bureau (2000)

### Table 1: U.S. Expenditures for Advertising on the Internet and Selected Media (first 3 quarters 1998)

| Category | Internet | National Adv. in Major Media | Network TV | National Newspapers | Consumer Magazines |
|---|---|---|---|---|---|
| Automotive | 4.5% | 18.2% | 15.7% | 9.9% | 14.1% |
| Retail | 2.7% | 14.6% | 6.4% | 2.8% | 3.2% |
| Entertainment | 5.0% | 5.1% | 5.2% | 3.3% | 3.8% |
| Financial Services | 8.8% | 4.5% | 3.8% | 24.4% | 3.8% |
| Airlines & Cruises | 2.8% | 3.8% | 1.0% | 8.7% | 4.3% |
| Tlc | 2.7% | 3.5% | 3.4% | 3.7% | 1.3% |
| Computers & Software | 47.3% | 2.8% | 2.3% | 14.3% | 7.8% |
| Direct Response | 7.0% | 2.6% | 0.2% | 3.9% | 8.6% |
| Insurance & Real Estate | 1.2% | 2.4% | 1.4% | 4.5% | 1.5% |
| Games, Toys, Hobbies | 0.8% | 1.2% | 1.7% | 0.1% | 0.5% |
| Government & Organizations | 1.1% | 1.0% | 0.7% | 1.5% | 0.6% |
| Cumulative Percentage of Total Expenditures Represented by these categories | 83.9% | 59.7% | 41.8% | 77.1% | 49.55 |
| Total $ Expenditures (Millions) | $200 | $73,214 | $15,225 | $1,650 | $12,701 |

Sources: Intermedia Advertising Solutions, Internet Advertising Bureau, Advertising Age.

# Dynamic-Agents, Workflow and XML for E-Commerce Automation

Qiming Chen, Umesh Dayal, Meichun Hsu, Martin Griss

HP Labs, Hewlett-Packard, 1501 Page Mill Road, MS 1U4, Palo Alto, CA 94303, USA
{qchen,dayal,mhsu,griss}@hpl.hp.com

**Abstract.** Agent technologies are now being considered for automating tasks in e-commerce applications. However, conventional software agents with pre-defined functions, but without the ability to modify behavior dynamically, may be too limited for mediating E-Commerce applications properly, since they cannot switch roles or adjust their behavior to participate in dynamically formed partnerships. We have developed a Java-based dynamic agent infrastructure for E-Commerce automation, which supports dynamic behavior modification of agents, a significant difference from other agent platforms. Supported by dynamic agents, mechanisms have been developed for plugging in workflow and multi-agent cooperation, and for dynamic service provisioning, allowing services to be constructed on the fly. We treat an agent as a Web object with an associated URL, which makes it possible to monitor and interact with the agent remotely via any Web browser. XML is chosen as our agent communication message format. Dynamic agents can carry, switch and exchange domain-specific XML interpreters. In this way, the cooperation of dynamic agents supports plug-and-play commerce, mediating businesses that are built on one another's services. A prototype has been developed at HP Labs.

## 1 Introduction

This work focuses on providing a multi-agent cooperation infrastructure to support E-Commerce automation. Before discussing our solutions, we first present a typical E-Commerce scenario and the requirements for E-Commerce automation.

E-Commerce applications operate in a *dynamic and distributed environment*. An E-Commerce scenario typically involves the following activities: identifying re-quirements, brokering products, brokering vendors, negotiating deals, and making purchase and payment transactions. Today, these activities are initiated and executed primarily by humans. In the future, with the increasing automation of e-commerce, we see them being conducted by software agents (Figure 1).

Software agents are personalized, continuously running and semi-autonomous computational entities. They can be used to *mediate* users and servers to automate a number of the most time-consuming tasks in E-Commerce [7,8]. Agents can also be used for *business intelligence*, such as discovering patterns (e.g. shopping behavior patterns or service providing patterns) and reacting to pattern changes. Moreover, agents can selectively preserve data and themselves become *dynamic information sources.*

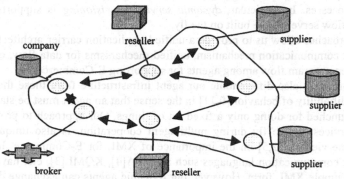

**Figure 1:** E-Commerce automation through multi-agent cooperation

E-Commerce is also a *dynamic plug and play environment.* Business processes and agent cooperation are embedded in each other. Services need to be created dynamically on demand. Business partnerships (e.g. between suppliers, resellers, brokers, and customers) need to be created dynamically and maintained only for the required duration such as a single transaction. Agents need to flexibly switch roles and adjust their capabilities to participate in such dynamic business partnerships. Furthermore, agents may cooperate in different application domains. The dynamic nature of E-Commerce also requires multi-agent cooperation to be based on *dynamic ontology.*

At HP Labs, we have developed a Java based *dynamic agent* infrastructure for E-Commerce that supports *dynamic behavior modification* of agents, a significant difference from other agent platforms [1]. A dynamic agent does not have a fixed set of predefined functions, but instead, it *carries application-specific actions,* which can be loaded and modified on the fly. This allows a dynamic agent to adjust its capabilities and play different roles to accommodate changes in the environment and requirements. Through messaging, dynamic agents can expose their knowledge, abilities and intentions, present requests and exchange objects. They can move to the appropriate location for high-bandwidth conversation. They can also manage their own resources across actions. Such an infrastructure supports dynamic service construction, modification and movement, and allows a dynamic agent to participate in multiple applications and dynamically formed partnerships. With these features, dynamic agents fit well into the dynamic E-Commerce environment.

Dynamic agents are designed as Web objects. Each agent contains or connects to a Web server, and has a dedicated Web page, accessed via a URL, on which is posted information about the agent's state and the tasks it is carrying.

Dynamic agents communicate using XML[5], and can *dynamically load and exchange different ontologies and XML interpreters* for tasks in different domains.

Finally, we introduce mechanisms for *modeling and enacting agent cooperation* as *workflow processes,* and *plugging in cooperating agents to execute tasks* of workflow processes. In particular, *dynamic service provisioning* is supported, allowing workflow servers to be built on the fly.

These approaches allow us to provide a unified application carrier architecture, a unified agent communication mechanism, unified mechanisms for data flow, control flow, and even program flow among agents for supporting E-Commerce.

These approaches also differentiate our agent infrastructure from those that lack dynamic modifiability of behavior [9,11] in the sense that an agent must be statically coded and launched for doing only a fixed set of things. Our approach to providing workflow services on the fly during multi-agent cooperation, is also unique. We share the same view as [2,5] on the importance of XML for E-Commerce. In fact, several agent communication languages such as FIPA[4], KQML[3], etc, have been converted to simple XML form. However, our dynamic agents can exchange domain specific ontology, and even XML interpreters, so as to participate in multiple applications, to switch domains, and to form dynamic partnerships.

The rest of this paper is organized as follows. Section 2 outlines the dynamic agent infrastructure. Section 3 shows how to build agents as Web objects. Section 4 describes the use of XML messaging with dynamic ontology to support multi-agent cooperation. Section 5 illustrates how to plug workflow processes into multi-agent cooperation, and vice versa. Finally in section 6, some concluding remarks are given.

## 2 Dynamic Agents

To realize E-Commerce automation, agents need to have dynamic behavior while maintaining their identity and consistent communication channels, as well as r e-taining data, knowledge and other system resources to be used across applications.

It is neither sufficient for an agent to be equipped with a fixed set of application-specific functions, nor practical for the above capabilities to be developed from scratch for each agent. This has motivated us to develop a *dynamic-agent* infrastructure [1]. The infrastructure is Java-coded, platform-neutral, light-weight, and extensible. Its unique feature is the support of *dynamic behavior modification* of agents; and this capability differentiates it from other agent platforms and cli-ent/server-based infrastructures.

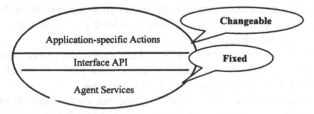

**Figure 2:** Dynamic Agent as Program Carrier

A dynamic-agent has a *fixed part* and a *changeable part* (Figure 2). As its fixed part, a dynamic-agent is provided with light-weight, built-in management facilities for distributed communication, object storage and resource management. A dynamic agent is capable of carrying data, knowledg, and *programs* as objects, and executing the programs. The data and programs carried by a dynamic agent form its change able part. All newly created agents are the same; their application-specific behaviors are gained and modified by dynamically loading Java classes representing data, knowledge, and application programs. Thus dynamic agents are general-purpose *carriers* of programs, rather than individual, application-specific programs.

The architecture of a dynamic agent is described in more detail below.

*Built-in facilities.* Each dynamic agent is provided with several light-weight built-in facilities for managing messaging, data and program object storage, action activation, GUI, etc. A carried application, when started, is offered a reference to the underlying built-in management facilities, and can use this reference to access the APIs of the facilities.

A *message-handler* is used to handle message queues, for sending, receiving and interpreting inter-agent messages. The interaction styles include one-way, request/reply, and publish/subscribe (selective broadcast). Message forwarding is also supported. An *action-handler* is used to instantiate and execute application programs (Java classes). One dynamic agent can carry multiple action programs. An *open-server-handler* is used to provide a variety of continuous services, which can be started and stopped flexibly at dynamic agent run-time. A *resource-handler* is used to maintain an object-store for the dynamic agent; it contains application-specific data, Java classes, and instances, including language interpreters, addresses and any-objects (namely, instances of any class).

Applications executed within a dynamic agent use these built-in dynamic agent management facilities to access and update application-specific data in the object-store, and to perform inter-agent communication through messaging.

**Dynamic Behavior.** Enabled by corresponding messages, a dynamic agent can load and store programs as Java classes or object instances, and can instantiate and execute the carried programs. Within these programs, built-in functions can be invoked to access the dynamic agent's resources, activate and communicate with other actions run on the same dynamic agent, as well as communicate with other dynamic agents or even stand-alone programs.

**Mobility.** Two levels of mobility are supported. A dynamic agent may be moved to or cloned at a remote site. Programs carried by one dynamic agent may be sent to another, to be run at the receiving site.

**Coordination.** Every dynamic-agent is uniquely identified by its symbolic name. Similar to FIPA [4], a coordinator agent is used to provide a naming service, mapping the name of each agent to its current socket address. The coordinator itself is a dynamic agent, with the added distinction that it maintains the agent name registry and, optionally, resource lists. When a dynamic agent, say $A$, is created, it will first attempt to register its symbolic name and address with the coordinator by sending a message to the coordinator. Thereafter, $A$ can communicate with other dynamic agents by name. When $A$ sends a message to another dynamic agent whose address is unknown to $A$, it consults the coordinator to obtain the address. If $A$ is instructed to load a program but the address is not given, it consults the coordinator or the request sender to obtain the address. Each dynamic agent also keeps an address-book, recording the addresses of those dynamic agents that have become known to it, and are known to be alive.

In a multi-agent system, besides a naming service, other types of coordination may be required, and these are provided either by the coordinator or by other designated dynamic agents that provide brokering services for resources, requests and events.

Dynamic agents form a dynamic distributed computing environment for E-Commerce. In the following sections we shall show how to take advantage of the dynamic agent infrastructure for E-Commerce automation.

## 3 Agents as Web Objects

The reach of the World Wide Web (WWW) has extended out from all varieties of computing platforms into the domain of small appliances. Web-enabled appliances can be monitored or interacted with remotely. We see this trend moving from hardware boxes to software modules. A dynamic agent with an embedded web server can deliver a web page to a browser on a remote computer, and this page can be used to interact with the agent and to monitor or manage the agent remotely. The advantage of doing so goes far beyond providing a more flexible GUI.

The main difference between treating agents as Web objects and as other Java objects is that each agent has a Web page, which is accessed via a URL. This Web page contains information about the agent itself and about the task it is doing. With this mechanism we can build a virtual market where clients and servers are all connected to the Web, have Web-facing representations, and are able to offer and participate in services on the Web.

As a Web object, an agent connected to the Internet is accessible via HTTP or XML. This typically requires that the agent embeds, or accesses, a web server. An agent is provided with at least one web page (HTML or XML page) that provides an interface for it to be accessed via any browser. The agent "publishes" on that page, a set of control, maintenance and application operations that can be accessed or invoked via Web browsers.

For example, an agent carrying seller functionality has a web page that shows what it sold, for which price, to whom, and when. The control operations can be represented on the Web page. An authorized person can adjust the price range via the Web page.

As with the agents' names, the URLs of dynamic agents are maintained by the coordinator as a kind of resource in case the agents move, but the coordinator's URL (host + port) is left stable.

An operation request issued from a Web browser to a dynamic agent looks the same as a traditional form request. For example, operation requests may be sent over HTTP using the GET or POST method. In the case of a POST request, the operation name and argument data will be sent in the body of the request. In a standard Web request, the arguments in the URL (including the operation name and return value) will be URL-encoded, which is a simple text encoding scheme. More complex encoding schemes can be used to support integration with non-Web based systems or for the passing of private information types. Note that inter-agent communication using messages does not require the involvement of a Web server. Interaction with an agent via a Web browser can easily interface to agent communication messaging facilities. For example, such a facility may be configured as a programmatic gateway supported on a Web server, which is easy to do by specifying the corresponding MIME table.

## 4 Multi-agent Cooperation with XML Messaging

Autonomous agents cooperate by sending messages and using concepts from a domain ontology. A standard message format with meaningful structure and semantics, and a mechanism for agents to exchange ontologies and message interpreters, are key issues. The message format should be accepted not only by the agent research community, but should be an industry standard that is likely to be adopted by information providers.

### 4.1 Document-driven Agent Cooperation

The extensive markup language, XML, is fast becoming the standard for data interchange on the Web. We chose XML, therefore, as the primary message format for dynamic agent communication.

In fact, an XML document is an *information container* for reusable and customizable components, which can be used by any receiving agent. This is the foundation for document-driven agent cooperation. By making the Web accessible to agents with XML, the need for custom interfaces for each consumer and supplier will be eliminated. Agents may use an XML format to explain their BDI, defining new performatives in terms of existing, mutually understood ones. Based on the commonly agreed tags, agents may use different style DTDs to fit the taste of the business units they mediate. Further, a dynamic agent can carry an XML front-end to a database for data exchange, where both queries and answers are XML encoded.

The power of XML, the role of XML in E-Commerce, and even the use of XML for agent communication, have been recognized. Although XML is well structured for encoding semantically meaningful information, it must be based on the ontology. As ontology varies from domain to domain, and may even be dynamic for dynamically formed domains. A significant issue is how to exchange the semantics of domain models, and how to interpret messages differently in different problem domains.

Generally speaking, a domain ontology provides a set of concepts, or meta-data, that can be queried, advertised and used to control the behavior of cooperating agents. These concepts can be marked using XML tags, and then a set of commonly agreed tags, underlie message interpretation. The structures and the semantics of the documents used in a particular problem domain are represented by the corresponding DTDs and interpreters.

We use different languages, all in XML format, for different problem domains, such as product ordering, market analysis, etc. Accordingly, we use an individual interpreter for each language. Dynamic agents can exchange the DTDs together with documents, and exchange the corresponding interpreters as programming objects, in order to understand each other.

## 4.2 DTD based Program Generation

Since information sources are evolving, it is unlikely that we can use fixed programs for information accessing and processing. Our solution is to let a dynamic agent carry program tools that generate XML oriented data access and processing programs based on DTDs. A DTD (like a schema) provides a grammar that tells which data structures can occur, and in what sequence. Such schematic information is used to automatically generate programs for basic data access and processing, i.e. creating classes that recognize and process different data elements according to the specification of those elements. For example, from an XML document including tag UNIT_PRICE, it is easy to generate a Java method "getUnitPrice", provided that the meanings of tags are understood, and an XML parser is appended to the JDK classpath. The XML parser we use is the one developed by Sun Microsystems that supports SAX (Simple API for XML) and conforms to W3C DOM (Document Object Model [2]).

The advantage of automatic program generation from DTDs, is allowing tasks to be created on the fly, in order to handle the possible change of document structures. Thus for example, when a vendor publishes a new DTD for its product data sheet, based on that DTD, an agent can generate the appropriate programs for handling the corresponding XML documents. Agents use different programs to handle data provided by different vendors.

## 4.3 Ontology Model Switching

Different application domains have different ontology models, with different agent communication languages and language interpreters, although they are in XML format. In a particular application domain, agents communicate using domain sp e-cific XML language constructs and interpreters.

In our implementation, a dynamic agent can participate in multiple applications. It communicates with other agents for the business of one domain, say $D_a$, using $D_a$'s language and language interpreter; for the business of another domain, say $D_b$, using $D_b$'s language and language interpreter. A dynamic agent can carry multiple inte r-preters. It switches application domains and ontologies by switching the DTD's and interpreters it uses.

We load an interpreter, say, *xml_shopping*, to an agent by sending it a message:

```
<MESSAGE type="LOAD" from="A" to="B" interpreter="xml.default">
  <CONTENT> <LOAD_INTERPRETER
      class="da.XMLshoppingInterpreter" url="file:host.hp.com/Dmclasses">
      xml_shopping
  </LOAD_INTERPRETER> </CONTENT>
</MESSAGE>
```

Supporting the switching of problem domains and handling dynamic ontology, are the key mechanisms we use to approach the dynamic requirements of E-Commerce.

## 5  Multi-agent Cooperation with Plug-in Workflow Support

Workflow systems provide flow control for business process automation. Business processes often involve multilevel collaborative and transactional tasks. Each task represents a logical piece of work that contributes to a process. A task at leaf-level is performed by a *role*. A role is filled at run-time with a user or a program. Business processes may be considered as a kind of multi-agent cooperation [6], in the sense that a software agent can be used to fill a role for performing a task in a workflow, and workflow can be used to orchestrate or control the interactions between agents. However, many related activities in E-Commerce automation do not form synchronized, traditional workflow, but require more dynamic agent cooperation. In order to combine the strength of workflow and agent cooperation for supporting E-Commerce, it is necessary to understand their relationship and differences.

First, workflow supports task integration with pre-defined flow control. In contrast, agent cooperation is more dynamic, flexible, and decentralized. Focusing on a general goal, the task performed by agents may be dynamically selected, depending on the run-time situation such as the results of previous tasks. For example, choosing a purchase task depends on the results of negotiation with multiple seller agents, and the negotiation itself is a cooperative, asynchronous multi-agent process.

Next, the role of a software agent played in E-Commerce automation should be closer to that played by a human user (rather than a program) in the workflow co ntext. In conventional workflow, a program task has a designated execution life span, it exists only during the execution time, and cannot receive messages before and after that task. On the contrary, a human user has memory and knowledge, and can work across multiple tasks and multiple business processes, even simultaneously. These properties are required for cooperative software agents. As a simple example, a buyer agent may simultaneously participate in several business partnerships with different vendors and brokers.

Our conclusion is that agent cooperation and workflow cannot replace each other, but may plug into each other.

**Plugging Multi-agent Cooperation into a Workflow.** By this we mean that a particular part of the workflow process, such as a single task, may be accomplished by multiple agents working cooperatively. As an example, a purchase task may include bargain search and negotiation involving multiple agents. Such activities are handled by autonomous agents rather than under centralized workflow control. As another example, task reallocation among self-interested agents aimed at balancing work-load, is also not centrally controlled. These tasks are performed through multi-agent cooperation.

Our dynamic agent infrastructure is suitable for plugging agent cooperation into workflow. This is because a dynamic agent is not simply a task, but a *carrier* of tasks that represents steps of a business process. Compared with a normal task, a dynamic agent is a continuous running object with persistent communication channel and knowledge across tasks and processes. In these aspects a dynamic agent can behave more similar to a human user than to a normal program task. This allows, for example, an auction agent to use the above capabilities to combine requests from multiple buyers, and to make intelligent decisions by cooperating with other agents. From the workflow point of view, "selling items by auction" may be considered a single task, but it actually involves multi-agent cooperation.

**Plugging in Workflow to Multi-agent Cooperation.** Multi-agent cooperation is more general than workflow. However, in some cases there exists a need for workflow support, in order to synchronize agent cooperation[6]. Particularly, the transactional workflow features such as ACID and failure recovery, may be required.

**Dynamic Workflow Service Provisioning.** The most promising feature of plugging workflow in agent cooperation is not launching a process to be executed by a *stand-by* workflow server, but establishing workflow services on the fly.

In statically structured distributed systems, service is provided by stationary servers. The introduction of dynamic agents can liberate service provisioning from such a static configuration. Given the underlying support for communication, program-flow, action-initiation, and persistent object storage, dynamic agents can be used as the "nuts and bolts" to integrate system components on the fly, and thus to provide services dynamically. Consider the following scenario. Some agents watch inventory and sales trends. Other agents watch supply chain changes. When an agent, say $A$, that correlates information from multiple sources, discovers an inventory shortage, it configures a purchase process, *order_proc* to order new products. This job includes two general steps: $A$ first downloads and sets-up a workflow engine on the fly, and then sends it *order_proc* for execution. This process involves multiple tasks on remote sites, performed by agents as well as human users. After the process is completed, the dynamic workflow servers may be shut down, or even removed from the carrying dynamic agents.

# 6 Conclusions

E-Commerce is a dynamic, distributed, and a plug and play environment for which we expect software agent-based technologies to become increasingly important. However, agents with static capability are not really suitable for the highly dynamic E-Commerce applications.

In this paper we presented our solutions for E-Commerce automation using a dynamic agent infrastructure. Dynamic agents are carriers of application programs, they can be loaded with new functions, change behavior dynamically, and exchange program objects. As a result, dynamic agents can switch roles, participate in multiple problem solving domains, and form dynamic partnerships. With these features, we have developed mechanisms for plugging workflow and multi-agent cooperation into each other. In particular, we support dynamic workflow service provisioning, allowing workflow servers to be built on the fly. XML is chosen as our agent communication message format. Since different problem domains have different underlying ontology, we allow agents to communicate with domain specific languages (all in XML format) and act using corresponding interpreters.

A very practical and significant development is to build our dynamic agents as Web objects, which allows them to be monitored, accessed and controlled remotely in a unified way. This mechanism represents two steps towards the virtual marketplace, mediating physical resources with agents, and mediating agents via the Web.

# References

1. Q. Chen, P. Chundi, Umesh Dayal, M. Hsu, "Dynamic Agents", International Journal on Cooperative Information Systems, 1999, USA.
2. Document Object Model, http://www.w3.org/DOM/
3. T. Finin, R. Fritzson, D. McKay, R. McEntire, "KQML as an Agent-Communication Language", Proc. CIKM'94, 1994.
4. Foundation for Intelligent Physical Agents(FIPA)- FIPA97 Agent Specification, http://www.fipa.org/
5. R. J. Glushko, J. M. Tenenbaum and B. Meltzer, "An XML Framework for Agent-based E-Commerce", CACM 42(8), March, 1999.
6. M. Griss, G. Bolcer, L. Osterweil, Q. Chen, R. Kessler "Agents and Workflow -- An Intimate Connection, or Just Friends?", Panel, TOOLS99 USA, Aug 1999.
7. P. Maes, R. H. Guttman and A. G. Moukas, "Agents that Buy and Sell", CACM 42(8), March, 1999.
8. A.G. Moukas, R. H. Guttman and P. Maes, "Agent Mediated Electronic Commerce: An MIT Media Laboratory Perspective", Proc. of Int. Conf. on Electronic Commerce, 1998.
9. Odyssy, "Agent Technology: Odyssey", General Magic, http://www.genmagic.com, 1997.
10. B.Perry, M. Talor, A. Unruh, "Information Aggregation and Agent Interaction Patterns in InfoSleuth", Proc. of CoopIS99, UK, 1999.
11. Voyager, "Voyager Core Package Technical Overview", Object Space, http://www.objectspace.com/voyager/technical_white_papers.html, 1997.

# Towards a Foundation for XML Document Databases

Chutiporn Anutariya[1], Vilas Wuwongse[1],
Ekawit Nantajeewarawat[2], and Kiyoshi Akama[3]

[1] Computer Science & Information Management Program,
Asian Institute of Technology, Pathumtani 12120, Thailand
{ca, vw}@cs.ait.ac.th
[2] Information Technology Program, Sirindhorn International Institute of Technology,
Thammasat University, Pathumtani 12120, Thailand
ekawit@siit.tu.ac.th
[3] Center for Information and Multimedia Studies, Hokkaido Unversity,
Sapporo 060, Japan
akama@cims.hokudai.ac.jp

**Abstract.** This paper develops a theoretical framework for modeling and managing XML documents by employment of *Declarative Description (DD)* theory. In the framework, the definition of an *XML element* is formally extended by incorporation of variables in order to represent inherent implicit information and enhance its expressive power. An XML document - a set of XML elements - is simply modeled as an *XML declarative description* which consists of *object descriptions*, representing XML elements in the document, and *relationship descriptions*, specifying relationships among the elements as well as integrity constraints. DTDs and complex queries can also be expressed and evaluated.

## 1 Introduction

Modeling and managing XML [8] data have several challenges. An obvious difficulty is that XML is considered as a variation of *semistructured data* - data that may be varied, irregular and unrestricted to any particular schema. An XML document must only be *well-formed* but need not conform to a particular *Document Type Definition (DTD)*. Mapping of semistructured data into well-defined and highly-structured schemas, such as those in the relational and object-oriented models, often requires a lot of efforts and frequent schema modifications. This difficulty has obstructed the use of relational and object-oriented approaches to XML data modeling. Therefore, development of an appropriate and efficient data model for XML documents has become an active research area. Major current models are based on *directed edge-labeled graphs* [7,9,10,13,16], *hedge automaton theory* [14,15] and *functional programming* [12].

A *declarative description data model* for XML documents is developed by employment of *Declarative Description (DD)* theory [1–3], which has been developed with generality and applicability to data structures of a wide variety of domains, each characterized by a mathematical structure, called a *specialization system*. An appropriate *specialization system for XML elements* is formulated and a framework for their representation, computation and reasoning is constructed. XML elements defined in this paper can represent both explicit and implicit information through the employment of variables. Conventional XML elements are directly represented in the proposed model as ground (variable-free) XML elements, with no translation needed. An *XML declarative description* (*XML-DD*) comprises a set of *XML elements*, called *object descriptions* (*ODs*), and a (possibly empty) set of their relationships, called *relationship descriptions* (*RDs*). The meaning of such an XML-DD will not only yield all the explicit information, represented in terms of ODs, but will also include all the implicit information derivable by application of the RDs to the set of ODs, whence complex queries about both kind of information can be formulated and executed [6].

RDs not only represent relationships among XML elements, but can also be used to define *integrity constraints* that are important in a document, such as data integrity, *path and type constraints* [10]. Moreover, in order to restrict XML elements to only those that satisfy a given DTD, a simple and effective mechanism is to directly map the DTD into a corresponding set of RDs for checking the validity of an element with respect to the DTD [5].

Sect. 2 reviews major approaches to modeling semistructured/SGML/XML documents, Sect. 3 develops a declarative description data model for XML documents, Sect. 4 presents approaches to modeling XML documents and their DTDs, Sect. 5 outlines how to formulate and evaluate queries, and Sect. 6 draws conclusions and presents future research directions.

# 2 Review of Data Models for Semistructured/SGML/XML Documents

Three important approaches to modeling semistructured/SGML data before 1995, i.e., *traditional information retrieval, relational model* and *object-oriented approaches*, have been reviewed in [19]. This section reviews the more recent ones which are based on graphs, hedge automaton theory and functional programming.

In *graph-based models*, an XML document is mapped into a directed, edge-labeled graph [7, 9, 10, 13, 16] consisting of nodes and directed edges, which, respectively, represent XML elements in the document and relationships among the elements, e.g., element-subelement and referential relationships. Although a graph-based model provides an effective and straightforward way to handle XML documents, it exhibits a difficulty in restricting a document to a given DTD. The proposal [7], for instance, only provides a way to query XML documents but does not facilitate a means of representing the structure imposed by a DTD. A substantial extension to the model is required to overcome this difficulty. For example, by application of *first-order logic theory*, the proposal [10] has incorporated the ability to express *path and type constraints* for specification of the document structure; the integration of these *two different formalisms* also results in an ability to reason about path constraints.

Employing *hedge automaton* theory [14] (aka. *tree automaton* and *forest automaton* theory), developed by using the basic ideas of *string automaton* theory, the proposals [15] have constructed an approach to formalizing XML documents and their DTDs. A *hedge* is a sequence of trees or, in XML terminology, a sequence of XML elements. An XML document is represented by a hedge and a set of documents conforming to a DTD by a *regular hedge language* (*RHL*), which can be described by a *regular hedge expression* (*RHE*) or a *regular hedge grammar* (*RHG*). By means of a *hedge automaton*, one can validate whether a document conforms to a given RHG (representing some particular DTD) or not.

A *functional programming approach* to modeling XML documents and formalizing operations upon them has been developed in the proposal [12] by introduction of the notion of *node* as its underlying data structure. An algebra for XML queries, expressed in terms of *list comprehensions* in the functional programming paradigm, has also been constructed. Using list comprehensions, various kinds of query operations, such as navigation, grouping and joins, can be expressed. However, this approach has considerable limitations as it does not possess an ability to model a DTD, whence a mechanism for verifying whether a document conforms to a given DTD or not is not readily devised.

## 3 Declarative Description Data Model for XML Documents

*XML declarative description* (*XML-DD*) theory, which has been developed by employment of *Declarative Description* (*DD*) theory [1–3] and serves as a data model for XML documents [4], is summarized.

In XML-DD theory, the definition of an XML element is formally extended by incorporation of variables in order to represent inherent implicit information and enhance its expressive power. Such extended XML elements, referred to as *XML expressions*, have similar form as XML elements except that they can carry variables. The XML expressions without variable will be precisely called *ground XML expressions* or XML elements, while those with variables *non-ground XML expressions*.

There are several kinds of variables useful for the expression of implicit information contained in XML expressions: *name-variables* (*N*-variables), *string-variables* (*S*-variables), *attribute-value-pair-variables* (*P*-variables), *expression-variables* (*E*-variables) and *intermediate-expression-variables* (*I*-variables). Every variable is preceded by '$' together with a character specifying its type, i.e., '$N', '$S', '$P', '$E' or '$I '.

Intuitively, an *N*-variable will be instantiated to an element type or an attribute name, an *S*-variable to a string, a *P*-variable to a sequence of attribute-value pairs, an *E*-variable to a sequence of XML expressions and an *I*-variable to a part of an XML expression. Such variable instantiations are defined by means of *basic specializations*, each of which is a pair of the form (*var*, *val*), where *var* is the variable to be specialized and *val* a value or tuple of values describing the resulting structure. There are four types of basic specializations:

  i) rename variables,
 ii) expand *P*- or *E*-variables into sequences of variables of their respective types,
iii) remove *P*-, *E*- or *I*-variables, and
 iv) instantiate variables to some values corresponding to the variables' types.

Let $\mathcal{A}_X$ denote the set of all XML expressions, $\mathcal{G}_X$ the subset of $\mathcal{A}_X$ comprising all ground XML expressions in $\mathcal{A}_X$, $\mathcal{C}_X$ the set of basic specializations and $\nu_X : \mathcal{C}_X \to partial\_map(\mathcal{A}_X)$ the mapping from $\mathcal{C}_X$ to the set of all partial mappings on $\mathcal{A}_X$ which determines for each $c$ in $\mathcal{C}_X$ the change of elements in $\mathcal{A}_X$ caused by $c$. Let $\Delta_X = \langle \mathcal{A}_X, \mathcal{G}_X, \mathcal{C}_X, \nu_X \rangle$ be a *specialization generation system*, which will be used to define a *specialization system* characterizing the data structure of XML expressions and sets of XML expressions.

Let $V$ be a set of *set variables*, $\mathcal{A} = \mathcal{A}_X \cup 2^{(\mathcal{A}_X \cup V)}$, $\mathcal{G} = \mathcal{G}_X \cup 2^{\mathcal{G}_X}$, $\mathcal{C} = \mathcal{C}_X \cup (V \times 2^{(\mathcal{A}_X \cup V)})$, and $\nu : \mathcal{C} \to partial\_map(\mathcal{A})$ the mapping which determines for each basic specialization $c$ in $\mathcal{C}$ the change of elements in $\mathcal{A}$ caused by $c$.

In the sequel, let $\Gamma = \langle \mathcal{A}, \mathcal{G}, \mathcal{S}, \mu \rangle$ be a *specialization system for XML expressions with flat sets*, where $\mathcal{S} = \mathcal{C}^*$ and $\mu : \mathcal{S} \to partial\_map(\mathcal{A})$ such that

$$\mu(\lambda)(a) = a, \text{ where } \lambda \text{ denotes the null sequence and } a \in \mathcal{A},$$
$$\mu(c.s)(a) = \mu(s)(\nu(c)(a)), \text{ where } c \in \mathcal{C}, s \in \mathcal{S} \text{ and } a \in \mathcal{A}.$$

Elements of $\mathcal{S}$ are called *specializations*. Note that when $\mu$ is clear in the context, for $\theta \in \mathcal{S}$, $\mu(\theta)(a)$ will be written simply as $a\theta$.

The definition of *XML declarative description* together with its related concepts can be given in terms of $\Gamma = \langle \mathcal{A}, \mathcal{G}, \mathcal{S}, \mu \rangle$. An XML declarative description (simply referred to as an *XML-DD*) on $\Gamma$ is a set of *descriptions*, each having the form

$$H \leftarrow B_1, B_2, ..., B_n. \tag{1}$$

where $n \geq 0$, $H$ is an XML expression in $\mathcal{A}_X$ and $B_i$ an XML expression in $\mathcal{A}_X$, a *constraint* or a *set-of reference* on $\Gamma$. Such a description, if $n = 0$, is called an *object description* or an *OD*, and, if $n > 0$, a *relationship description* or an *RD*.

A *constraint* on $\Gamma$ is a formula $q(a_1, \ldots, a_n)$, where $q$ is a constraint predicate and $a_i$ an element in $\mathcal{A}$. Given a ground constraint $q(g_1, \ldots, g_n), g_i \in \mathcal{G}$, its truth and falsity is assumed to be predetermined.

A *set-of reference* on $\Gamma$ is a triple $r = \langle S, f_{x,a}, P \rangle$ of a set $S \in 2^{(\mathcal{A}_X \cup V)}$, a set-of function $f_{x,a}$, and an XML declarative description $P$, which will be called the *referred description* of $r$. Given $x, a \in \mathcal{A}_X$, a set-of function $f_{x,a}$ can be defined as follows: For each $X \in 2^{\mathcal{G}_X}$,

$$f_{x,a}(X) = \{x\theta \in \mathcal{G}_X | a\theta \in X, \theta \in \mathcal{C}_X^*\}. \tag{2}$$

In other words, for each $X \in 2^{\mathcal{G}_X}$, $x\theta \in f_{x,a}(X)$ iff there exists $\theta \in \mathcal{C}_X^*$ such that $a\theta$ and $x\theta$ are ground XML expressions in $X$ and $\mathcal{G}_X$, respectively. Intuitively, $a$ and $x$ are used, respectively, to define the condition for the construction of a set and to determine the elements comprising that set, i.e., $x\theta \in f_{x,a}(X)$ iff

```
<!ELEMENT Person      (Name, BirthYear, Parent?)>
<!ATTLIST Person      ssn ID #REQUIRED
                      gender (Male | Female) #REQUIRED>
<!ELEMENT Name        (#PCDATA)>
<!ELEMENT BirthYear   (#PCDATA)>
<!ELEMENT Parent      EMPTY>
<!ATTLIST Parent      father IDREF #IMPLIED
                      mother IDREF #IMPLIED>
```

**Fig. 1.** An XML DTD example

$a\theta \in X$. The objects $a$ and $x$ will be referred to as *filter* and *constructor* objects, respectively.

Given a specialization $\theta \in \mathcal{S}$, application of $\theta$ to a constraint $q(a_1, \ldots, a_n)$ yields the constraint $q(a_1\theta, \ldots, a_n\theta)$, to a reference $\langle S, f_{x,a}, P \rangle$ the reference $\langle S, f_{x,a}, P \rangle\theta = \langle S\theta, f_{x,a}, P \rangle$ and to a description $(H \leftarrow B_1, B_2, \ldots, B_n)$ the description $(H\theta \leftarrow B_1\theta, B_2\theta, \ldots, B_n\theta)$. The head of a description $D$ will be denoted by $head(D)$ and the set of all objects (XML expressions), constraints and references in the body of $D$ by $object(D)$, $con(D)$ and $ref(D)$, respectively. Let $body(D) = object(D) \cup con(D) \cup ref(D)$.

Given an XML-DD $P$, its meaning, $\mathcal{M}(P)$ is the set of all the ground XML expressions that can be derived from the descriptions in $P$. Intuitively, given a description $D = (H \leftarrow B_1, B_2, \ldots, B_n)$ in $P$, for every $\theta \in \mathcal{S}$ that makes $B_1\theta, B_2\theta, \ldots, B_n\theta$ true with respect to the meaning of $P$, the expression $H\theta$ will be derived and included in the meaning of $P$.

# 4 Modeling XML Documents and DTDs

## 4.1 XML Document Modeling

A conventional XML element is represented directly as a ground XML expression in $\mathcal{G}_X$. A class of XML elements sharing certain similar components and structures can also be represented as an XML expression with variables. These variables are used to represent unknown or similar components (which could be tag names, attribute-value pairs, subexpressions or nesting structures) shared by the elements in the class.

A collection of XML documents can be modeled by an XML-DD consisting of *ODs* and *RDs*. The meaning of such an XML-DD yields all the directly represented XML elements in the document collection, i.e., those expressed by ODs, together with all the derived ones, which may be restricted by constraints.

*Example 1.* Let $P$ be an XML-DD which represents an XML document encoding demographic data and conforming to the DTD given in Fig. 1. Assume that such a document contains three **Person** elements and $P$ comprises the following seven descriptions, denoted by $D_1 - D_7$:

$D_1$:
```
<Person ssn="99999" gender="Male">
        <Name>John Smith</Name>
        <BirthYear>1975</BirthYear>
        <Parent mother="55555"/>
</Person>.              ←
```

$D_2$:
```
<Person ssn="55555" gender="Female">
        <Name>Mary Smith</Name>
        <BirthYear>1950</BirthYear>
        <Parent father="11111"/>
</Person>.              ←
```

$D_3$:
```
<Person ssn="11111" gender="Male">
        <Name>Tom Black</Name>
        <BirthYear>1920</BirthYear>
</Person>.              ←
```

$D_4$:
```
<Ancestor ancestor=$S:Father descendent=$S:Person/>
    ←   <Person ssn=$S:Person $P:PersonAttr>
            $E:Subexpression
            <Parent father=$S:Father $P:ParentAttr/>
        </Person>.
```

$D_5$:
```
<Ancestor ancestor=$S:Mother descendent=$S:Person/>
    ←   <Person ssn=$S:Person $P:PersonAttr>
            $E:Subexpression
            <Parent mother=$S:Mother $P:ParentAttr/>
        </Person>.
```

$D_6$:
```
<Ancestor ancestor=$S:Father descendent=$S:Desc/>
    ←   <Ancestor ancestor=$S:Anc descendent=$S:Desc/>,
        <Person ssn=$S:Ancestor $P:PersonAttr>
            $E:Subexpression
            <Parent father=$S:Father $P:ParentAttr/>
        </Person>.
```

$D_7$:
```
<Ancestor ancestor=$S:Mother descendent=$S:Desc/>
    ←   <Ancestor ancestor=$S:Anc descendent=$S:Desc/>,
        <Person ssn=$S:Anc $P:PersonAttr>
            $E:Subexpression
            <Parent mother=$S:Mother $P:ParentAttr/>
        </Person>.
```

Descriptions $D_1 - D_3$ represent **Person** elements in the document; Descriptions $D_4 - D_7$ derive ancestor relationships among the individuals in the collection. Descriptions $D_4$ and $D_5$ specify that both **father** and **mother** of an individual are ancestors of such individual. Descriptions $D_6$ and $D_7$ recursively specify that the **father** and the **mother** of an individual's ancestor are also the individual's ancestors. This ancestor relationship represents an example of complex, recursive relationships which can be simply expressed in the proposed approach.       □

## 4.2 XML DTD Modeling

An XML DTD is represented, in the proposed approach, as an XML DD comprising a set of RDs [5]. Such RDs, referred to as *DTD-RDs*, are obtained directly from translating each of the element type and attribute-list declarations contained in the DTD into a corresponding set of DTD-RDs and then combining these sets together.

The head expression of such a DTD-RD only imposes the general structure of its corresponding element type and merely specifies the valid pattern of the associated attribute list. Restrictions on the element's content model, e.g., descriptions of valid sequences of child elements, and on its associated attribute list, e.g., attribute type and default value constraints, are defined by appropriate specifications of constraints and XML expressions in the DTD-RD's body. An XML expression contained in a DTD-RD's body will be further restricted by the DTD-RDs the head of which can be matched with that XML expression.

An XML element is valid with respect to a given DTD, if such element can successfully match the head of some DTD-RD translated from the DTD and all the restrictions specified in the body of such a DTD-RD are satisfied.

*Example 2.* This example demonstrates a translation of the DTD given in Fig. 1, which will be referred to as myDTD, into a corresponding set of DTD-RDs:

```
V1:    <myDTD_Person>
            <Person ssn=$S:SSN gender=$S:Gender>
                <Name>$S:Name</Name>
                <BirthYear>$S:BirthYear</BirthYear>
                $E:Parent
            </Person>
       </myDTD_Person>
                ←    <myDTD_Parent>
                         $E:Parent
                     </myDTD_Parent>,
                     IsMemberOf(<Value>$S:Gender</Value>,
                         {<Value>"Male"</Value>,
                          <Value>"Female"</Value>}).
V2:    <myDTD_Parent>
            <Parent father=$S:FatherSSN $P:MotherAttr/>
       </myDTD_Parent>
                ←    <myDTD_Parent>
                         <Parent $P:MotherAttr/>
                     </myDTD_Parent>,
V3:    <myDTD_Parent>
            <Parent mother=$S:MotherSSN/>
       </myDTD_Parent>        ←    .
V4:    <myDTD_Parent>
            <Parent/>
       </myDTD_Parent>        ←    .
```

$V_5$:    `<myDTD_Parent>`
          `</myDTD_Parent>`          ←

Description $V_1$ imposes restrictions on the **Person** element. The head expression of $V_1$ specifies that every conforming **Person** element must contain **ssn** and **gender** attributes as well as **Name** and **BirthYear** elements as its first and second subelements, respectively. The only restriction on **Name** and **BirthYear** elements stating that their contents must be textual data is simply represented by the $S$-variables **\$S:Name** and **\$S:BirthYear**, respectively, and is defined within the restrictions on the **Person** element, i.e., within the head of $V_1$. The $E$-variable **\$E:Parent** is defined such that, following the **Name** and **BirthYear** subelements, a **Person** element can optionally contain a **Parent** element. The **myDTD_Parent** element contained in the body of $V_1$ specifies that such **Parent** subelement will be further restricted by the descriptions the heads of which are **myDTD_Parent** expressions, i.e., descriptions $V_2 - V_5$.

The constraint **IsMemberOf** enforces that the value of the **gender** attribute, represented by **\$S:Gender**, must be either **"Male"** or **"Female"**.

Moreover, it should be noted that since validation of *uniqueness* and *referential integrity constraints* defined by means of attributes of types ID and IDREF/IDREFS, respectively, requires additional concepts of *id* and *idref/idrefs references* [5] which are beyond the scope of this paper, this example omits validation of such constraints.

Descriptions $V_2 - V_5$ can be interpreted in a similar way as description $V_1$.  □

## 5   Query Processing

As details of the query formulation and evaluation based on the proposed data model are available in [6], this section merely sketches the basic ideas.

A query is formalized as an XML DD, comprising one or more RDs, called *query RDs*. Each query RD is written as a description $D$, where $head(D)$ describes the structure of the resulting XML elements, $object(D)$ represents some particular XML documents or XML elements to be selected, $con(D)$ describes selection criteria and $ref(D)$ constructs sets or groups of related XML elements to be used for computing summary information. This syntax intuitively separates a query into three parts: a *pattern*, a *filter* and a *constructor*, where the pattern is described by $object(D)$, the filter by $con(D)$ and $ref(D)$, and the constructor by $head(D)$. The five basic query operations [11, 17, 18]: *extraction, selection, combination, transformation* and *aggregation*, can be formulated [6].

Given an XML-DD $P$ specifying a collection of XML documents together with their relationships, a query represented by an XML-DD $Q$ is evaluated by transforming the XML-DD $(P \cup Q)$ successively until it becomes the XML-DD $(P \cup Q')$, where $Q'$ consists of only *ground object descriptions*. In order to guarantee that the answers to a given query are always preserved, only *semantics-preserving transformations* or *equivalent transformations* [1–3] will be applied in every transformation step. The equivalent transformation is a new computational model which is considered to be more efficient than the inference in the logic paradigm and the function evaluation in the functional programming paradigm. The *unfolding transformation*, a widely used program transformation in the conventional logic and functional programming, is a kind of equivalent transformation.

*Example 3.* Referring to XML-DD $P$ of Example 1, a query which lists the names of all the John Smith's ancestors can be formulated as:

```
D:    <JohnAncestor>$S:Name<JohnAncestor/>
        ←    <Person ssn=$S:JohnSSN $P:JohnAttr>
                <Name>John Smith</Name>
                $E:JohnSubExp
             </Person>,
             <Ancestor ancestor=$S:Anc descendent=$S:JohnSSN/>,
             <Person ssn=$S:Anc $P:AncAttr>
                <Name>$S:Name</Name>
                $E:AncestorSubExp
             </Person>.
```

By means of unfolding transformation, XML-DD $(P \cup \{D\})$ can be successively transformed into XML-DD $(P \cup \{D', D''\})$, where

```
D':   <JohnAncestor>Mary Smith<JohnAncestor/>    ←    .
D'':  <JohnAncestor>Tom Black<JohnAncestor/>     ←    .
```

Since $\mathcal{M}(P \cup \{D\}) = \mathcal{M}(P \cup \{D', D''\})$ and the heads of $D'$ and $D''$ are the only **JohnAncestor** elements in $\mathcal{M}(P \cup \{D', D''\})$, such elements are the only answers to the query. □

## 6   Conclusions

This paper has proposed and developed an expressive, declarative framework which can succinctly and uniformly model XML elements/documents, integrity constraints, element relationships, DTDs as well as formulate queries. By integrating the framework with an appropriate computational model, e.g., the Equivalent Transformation (ET), one will be able to efficiently manipulate and transform XML documents, evaluate queries, and validate XML data against some particular DTDs. The framework, therefore, provides a foundation for representation and computation of as well as reasoning with XML data.

A Web-based XML processor which can help demonstrate and evaluate the effectiveness of the proposed framework has been implemented using *ETC* - a compiler for programming in ET paradigm. The system has been tested against a small XML database and preliminary good performance is obtained; and a more thorough evaluation with a large collection of XML documents is underway. Other interesting future plans include development of indexing and query optimization techniques for XML document databases.

**Acknowledgement**  This work was supported in part by Thailand Research Fund.

# References

1. Akama, K.: Declarative Semantics of Logic Programs on Parameterized Representation Systems. Advances in Software Science and Technology, Vol. 5. (1993) 45–63
2. Akama, K.: Declarative Description with References and Equivalent Transformation of Negative References. Tech. Report, Information Engineering, Hokkaido University, Japan (1998)
3. Akama, K., Shimitsu, T., Miyamoto, E.: Solving Problems by Equivalent Transformation of Declarative Programs. Journal of the Japanese Society of Artificial Intelligence, Vol. 13 No.6 (1998) 944–952 (in Japanese)
4. Anutariya, C., Wuwongse, V., Nantajeewarawat, E., Akama, K.: A Foundation for XML Document Databases: Data Model. Tech. Report, Computer Science and Information Management, Asian Institute of Technology, Thailand (1999)
5. Anutariya, C., Wuwongse, V., Nantajeewarawat, E., Akama, K.: A Foundation for XML Document Databases: DTD Modeling. Techn. Report, Computer Science and Information Management, Asian Institute of Technology, Thailand (1999)
6. Anutariya, C., Wuwongse, V., Nantajeewarawat, E., Akama, K.: A Foundation for XML Document Databases: Query Processing. Tech. Report, Computer Science and Information Management, Asian Institute of Technology, Thailand (1999)
7. Beech, D., Malhotra, A., Rys, M.: A Formal Data Model and Algebra for XML. W3C XML Query Working Group Note (1999)
8. Bray, T., Paoli, J., Sperberg-McQueen, C.M.: Extensible Markup Language (XML) 1.0. W3C Recommendation. (1998)
9. Buneman, P., Deutsch, A., Tan, W.C.: A Deterministic Model for Semi-Structured Data. Workshop on Query Processing for Semistructured Data and Non-Standard Data Formats (1998)
10. Buneman, P., Fan, W., Weinstein, S.: Interaction between Path and Type Constraints. Proc. ACM Symposium on Principles of Database Systems (1999)
11. Fankhauser, P., Marchiori, M., Robie, J.: XML Query Requirements, January 2000. W3C Working Draft, (2000)
12. Fernández, M., Siméon, J., Suciu, D., Wadler, P.: A Data Model and Algebra for XML Query. Draft Manuscript (1999)
13. Goldman, R., McHugh, J., Widom, J.: From Semistructured Data to XML: Migrating the Lore Data Model and Query Language. Proc. 2nd Int. Workshop on the Web and Databases (WebDB'99), Pennsylvania (1999)
14. Murata, M.: Hedge Automata: A Formal Model for XML Schemata. Technical Report, Fuji Xerox Information Systems (1999)
15. Murata, M.: Transformation of Documents and Schemas by Patterns and Contextual Conditions. Principles of Document Processing '96. Lecture Notes in Computer Science, Vol. 1293 (1997)
16. McHugh, J., Abiteboul, S., Goldman, R., Quass, D., Widom, J.: Lore: A Database Management System for Semistructured Data. SIGMOD Record, Vol. 26, No. 3 (1997) 54–66
17. Quass, D.: Ten Features Necessary for an XML Query Langauge. Proc. Query Languages Workshop (QL'98), Boston, MA, (1998)
18. Robie, J., Lapp, J., Schach, D.: XML Query Language (XQL). Proc. Query Languages Workshop (QL'98), Boston, MA, (1998)
19. Sacks-Davis, R., Arnold-Moore, T., Zobel, J.: Database Systems for Structured Documents. IEICE Transactions on Information and System, Vol. E78-D, No. 11 (1995) 1335–1341

# An XML/XSL-based Software Architecture for Application Service Providers (ASPs)

Oliver Günther*[†] and Olivier Ricou*

* Pôle Universitaire Léonard de Vinci
92916 Paris La Défense, France
{Oliver.Gunther, Olivier.Ricou}@devinci.fr

† Humboldt-Universität zu Berlin
Spandauer Str. 1, 10178 Berlin, Germany

**Abstract.** Application Service Providers (ASPs) are changing the way software is being used and distributed. Using ASP technology, users do not have to own software anymore, nor do they have to install it on their local computing environment to use it. Instead, the software is installed by the ASP on some remote server that also performs the necessary data management. Customers use the software via the Internet and pay a usage fee, where applicable. Our longer-term vision is an open ASP marketplace where anybody can offer their software modules with little technical and administrational overhead. This paper presents an XML/XSL-based approach to support this paradigm. In order to make software available for ASP-style execution, providers only need to write a simple XML wrapper that states the location and the input/output specifications of the module. We also propose a new XSL command to control software execution and we discuss its possible integration into the current XSL standard.

## 1 Introduction

Up to now, most of the information published on the World Wide Web is presented in the form of static pages. However, dynamic documents that involve the execution of programs are quickly becoming more popular. Typical technologies used in this context include the Common Gateway Interface (CGI) for server-based execution, and Java applets for client-based execution. For more complex applications, the use of an object request broker architecture, such as CORBA, may be advantageous.

Server-based approaches have recently become very popular under the label *Application Service Provider (ASP)*. Using ASP technology, users do not have to own their software anymore, nor do they have to install it on their local computing environment in order to use it. Instead, the software is installed by the ASP on some remote server that also manages the required data management. Users ("consumers") use the software (the "service") via the Internet and pay for each individual usage ("software leasing"). Typical services amenable to the ASP paradigm include linear optimization programs, enterprise resource planning (ERP) systems, visualization tools, or statistical software packages.

Let us consider a simple example. John, a Ph.D. student, has developed a complex mathematical method for the analysis and forecasting of stock quotes. First experiments yield encouraging results. John may decide to make his method publicly available, i.e. to become a computational service provider. He may use an ASP to register his method; as a result it is immediately visible to a large group of potential customers and it will be indexed by a variety of search engines. On the other hand, there is Susan who is always interested in new techniques to optimize her private portfolio strategy. Browsing or searching the web (e.g. by using a mainstream search engine), Susan one day comes across a link to the ASP, in particular its large selection of financial analysis and forecasting services including John's method. With a few operations, Susan can test this method on some of her own portfolio data. Because Susan uses a standard format to manage her portfolio (e.g. Excel or Yahoo Finance), required data conversions are performed automatically by the system. The portfolio data is sent to John's computer and fed into the method. After the computation has finished, the results are sent back to Susan, who then pays the applicable fee for using this service.

The ASP paradigm offers some major advantages for both service consumers and service providers. *Consumers* do not need to provide a local computing infrastructure to run the software in question. Moreover, they avoid the burden that is usually associated with installing and maintaining somebody else's software. Costs are variable, i.e., they correspond to the frequency and intensity of utilization. *Providers* maintain more control over who uses their software and which version and service level users request. They extend their potential market to customers who do not have the financial or technical means to install the software locally. And finally, they can cut distribution costs by reducing their sales force and hotline personnel.

Regardless which technology is used, however, there still exist considerable limitations concerning the creation and use of dynamic documents and services. Both CGI and Java are difficult to handle for a non-expert user, and services based on this techniques are relatively difficult to implement. Java applets are slow, and the technology does not extend to software written in languages other than Java. Both CGI and Java applets usually handle their data input using HTML forms, which restricts the volume and complexity of input data. The flexible combination and reconfiguration of multiple program modules in order to implement more complex functionalities is rarely possible, unless one integrates the modules in an object request broker (ORB) architecture. The implementation and use of an ORB architecture, however, is anything but trivial. Major investments in hardware, software and human expertise are necessary to implement an infrastructure such as CORBA and to integrate new software modules into such an infrastructure.

In order to have a truly open electronic market for computational services, posting and using services has to be much easier than it is with the techniques described above. In fact, it should be no more difficult than posting or reading a web page, and no major skills in web programming should be required. Market entry could thus be easy for anybody who has some interesting software to offer. Our longer-term vision is an open ASP marketplace where anybody can offer their software modules with little technical and administrational overhead.

In this paper, we present some XML- and XSL-based techniques to facilitate the registration of new services on such an open marketplace. After a short overview of XML, Section 2 describes our proposed architecture. We show how providers can declare a new application service, how consumers can then execute this service and how it can be chained to other services. Section 3 compares our method to other XML-based approaches to ASP, including XML-RPC, a variation of the classical Remote Procedure Call (RPC) protocol, and MMM, a middleware for method management. Section 4 is devoted to possible extensions of our architecture.

## 2 An XML/XSL-based Architecture for Open ASP Marketplaces

### 2.1 Overview

The main *active* feature of classic HTML concerns the possibility to link one document to another one, based on browsers' ability to interpret an HREF tag. When SUN Microsystems proposed Java, the key idea was to allow the execution of programs on the client's computer and to display the result inside the output of an HTML page. This was made possible by a new tag called APPLET. Considering ASP as a new class of web services in this tradition, we propose to add a new type of tag, which controls the execution of remote software. Given recent developments, it makes more sense to explore such an extension in the context of XML rather than HTML.

The eXtensible Markup Language (XML) is a subset of SGML, the Standard Generalized Markup Language, defined by the W3C[1]. It uses markup tags like HTML, while strictly separating content from presentation. The XML file represents the content and an XSL [8] file describes how to display this content. The

---

[1] World Wide Web Consortium, http://www.w3c.org/

combination of these two files produces a document in whatever format (HTML, TEX, Java, ...) has been specified in the presentation file.

For example, let us consider a company that has chosen XML to represent its product list. With two different XSL files, the company can then use this XML-based list to produce a postscript-based printed catalog and an HTML-based web presentation. This shows one of the key features of XML: to associate any content with any kind of presentation format, depending on the particular requirements of the application.

However, the use of XML/XSL is not restricted to the representation and presentation of data sets. Services (also called "methods") can also be described using this framework. If one chooses XML/XSL for this purpose, one may as well control the execution of services with these tools. To this end, service providers will be expected to write XML-based descriptions of their offerings, and consumers will have to describe their input data sets in the same manner.

Figure 1 shows a possible XML/XSL-based interaction between providers and consumers. Here the provider (dark shading) makes a service available by writing an XML Document Type Description (DTD). Consumers (light shading) write XML files to control the execution. They may also rewrite an XSL file if they want to display the result differently.

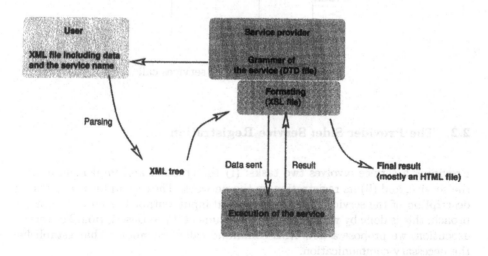

**Fig. 1.** XML/XSL-based architecture for an open ASP marketplace

Consumers can also call more than one service at once. These services may be sequential or nested. In the latter case, calls are processed one by one, starting with the innermost call. The result is sent to the XSL module after the last call. Figure 2 gives an overview.

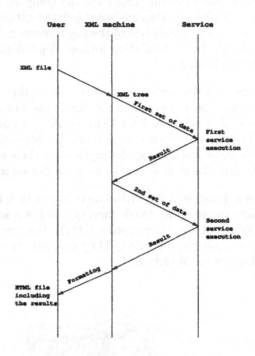

**Fig. 2.** Time scheme of services call

## 2.2   The Provider Side: Service Registration

Providing a service involves two tasks: (i) the creation and implementation of the service, and (ii) its registration on the network. The second task requires the description of the service's functionality and input/output behavior. In our approach, this is done by writing an XML Document Type Description. For service execution, we propose a new XSL command called connect [2] that establishes the necessary communication.

For example, let us consider a simple service that doubles a given input value. Writing a program to perform this service is a trivial task:

---

[2] This command is now included in the Lotus XSL Processor of IBM, cf http://www.alphaworks.ibm.com/. We aim to include it in the browser Mozilla, cf http://www.mozilla.org/

```
#include<iostream.h>

int main()
{
    double x;

    cin >> x;
    cout << 2*x;
    return 0;
}
```

**Fig. 3.** The times2 program written in C++

Then a computer has to be assigned to run this service. On a UNIX server, for example, this could be done by an entry in the /etc/inetd.conf file. In this case, any data sent to the port 1618 of this computer will be returned doubled through the same port.

```
1618  stream  tcp  nowait  nobody  /home/ricou/XML/prog/times2
```

**Fig. 4.** The line in the /etc/inetd.conf file under UNIX to support the times2 service.

Then one has to provide an XML description of the service's input/output behavior. This can be done by the following DTD:

```
<?xml encoding="UTF-8"?>

<!ELEMENT times2 (#PCDATA)>
<!ATTLIST times2 address #CDATA "test.devinci.fr">
<!ATTLIST times2 port #CDATA "1618">
```

**Fig. 5.** The DTD file of the times2 service

Hence, to use the `times2` service, the client should write in his XML file
`<times2>234</times2>` or
`<times2 address="mine.devinci.fr" port="2345">234</times2>`. In the first
case, the client does not give an address and therefore uses the default computer,
`test.devinci.fr`, to perform the service. The second case shows how to choose
a different server.

Input formats can be more complex. Here is the DTD of the `mean` service,
which computes the mean value of $n$ values:

```
<!ELEMENT mean (n, val)>
<!ATTLIST mean address CDATA "127.0.0.1">
<!ATTLIST mean port CDATA "1619">
```

**Fig. 6.** The DTD file of the `mean` service

Note that customers have to encapsulate the number of values within the tag
`n` and the values themselves within the tag `val` (cf. Fig. 8).

The last step is to explain to the translator how to manage the XML file of
the client, i.e., what to do with the data and how to display the result. This is
done in the corresponding XSL file:

```
<xsl:template match="times2">
  <P><xsl:apply-templates/> times 2 = <STRONG>
  <xsl:connect address="{@address}" port="{@port}"><xsl:apply-templates/>
  </xsl:connect>
  </STRONG></P>
</xsl:template>

<xsl:template match="mean">
  <P>The mean value of <xsl:value-of select="val"/> is <STRONG>
  <xsl:connect address="{@address}" port="{@port}">
      <xsl:value-of select="n"/> <xsl:value-of select="val"/>
  </xsl:connect>
  </STONG></P>
</xsl:template>
```

**Fig. 7.** The XSL file for the services `times2` and `mean`

This file explains how to transform and display any XML data using the times2 and mean XML command it introduces. To do so, it uses the usual XSL commands [7] plus the xsl:connect command we added to the XSL processor. For times2, for example, it states to write to the output file:

- "<P>" for paragraph in HTML
- the data between the times2 tags, which is the meaning of XSL command <xsl:apply-templates/>,
- " times 2 <STRONG>", hence the result will be in bold,
- the result of the connect call to the times2 service as we will explain more precisely later,
- "</STRONG></P>" to close the bold region and the paragraph.

## 2.3 The Consumer Side: Service Execution

In order to execute the service, consumers have to write an XML file with the input data, following the data protocol that is given in the provider's DTD. Then the XML file is translated. Figures 8 and 9 demonstrate this technique on the example services times2 and mean.

```
<?xml version="1.0" ?>
<!DOCTYPE cours SYSTEM "math.dtd">
<doc>
   <times2 address="127.0.0.1">2.2</times2>
   and
   <mean><n>5</n><val>3 6 12.4 6 -9</val></mean>
</doc>
```

**Fig. 8.** An XML file corresponding to the specifications in the DTD

2.2 times 2 = **4.4**

and

The mean value of 3 6 12.4 6 -9 is **3.68**

**Fig. 9.** The resulting HTML document, as it is presented in a web browser

## 2.4 Service Chaining

Calling services becomes more interesting if it is possible to chain services (similar to the UNIX pipe command), i.e., to plug the output of one service as input into another service. Or even better, one should have a language to store service outputs in variables and to use them later as inputs to other services. This language could itself be a service.

Let us consider an example based on the mathematical script language Matlab. To obtain a visualization of the pollution over Paris one hour from now, one would have to :

1. contact the Paris weather service to obtain the wind over Paris between now and one hour from now;
2. get of a mesh over Paris;
3. contact the Paris pollution center;
4. solve the Navier-Stokes equations on these data to get an approximation of the pollution in one hour;
5. draw this pollution.

To perform this task, one thus has to call on a variety of information providers. The three first calls are to *data providers*, the next two calls are to *application service providers*. Note that the fourth call involves a highly complex matrix calculation (Navier-Stokes), which is likely to be assigned to a more specialized *computational service provider*, who has dedicated hardware and software available for this purpose.

This could be written as follows

```
<Matlab>W0=</meteo where="Paris" what="wind" when=0 type_data="Matlab">;
W1=</meteo where="Paris" what="wind" when=1 type_data="Matlab">;
Mesh=</meteo where="Paris" what="mesh" type_data="Matlab">;
Pol=<Paris-Pollution when=0 type_data="Matlab">Mesh</Paris-Pollution>;
Sol=<NSsolver type_equation="transport" typedata="Matlab">
    <mesh>Mesh</mesh>
    <time><begin>0</begin> <end>1</end> <dt>0.02</dt></time>
    <velocity data="linear"> <init>W0</init> <end>W1</end> </velocity>
    <unknown> <init>Pol</init> </unknown>
    </boundary_condition type="Neumann">
    </NSsolver>;
contour(Mesh(1,:),Mesh(:,2),Sol)
</Matlab>
```

**Fig. 10.** How a pollution forecast could be make

The following example shows how calls to different services can be nested. It also shows how our modified XML parser can be called from a web server via a

343

form. The services provided in this example are identical to the ones introduced above, except that their result is not embedded in a text output anymore but just piped into the next service in line. In addition, we employ Scilab [1] as a service. Scilab is an open mathematical software similar to Matlab, which has been made available by INRIA, the French National Research Institute of Control and Computer Science.

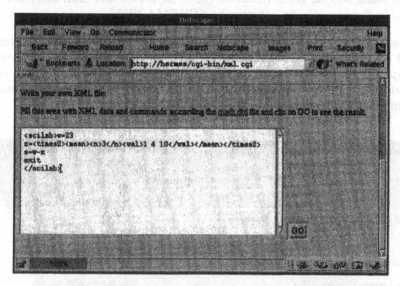

**Fig. 11.** HTML form to write XML files

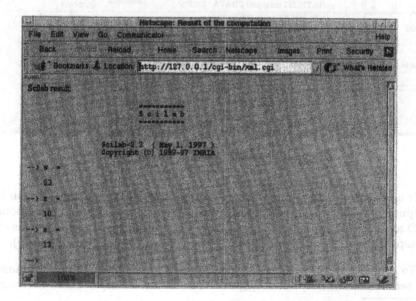

**Fig. 12.** Result of the call to Scilab via the form of Fig. 11

## 2.5   A Service Engine Registry

As XML will become popular, the most common services and presentation files will be integrated in the browser, just like new HTML extensions quickly migrate into new browser versions. Other services will have to be referenced and indexed in the same way as XML resources (such as DTDs and XSL files) are made available, for example, by category by SCHEMA.NET[3].

Such tools have to provide a human readable interface, a web server, but could also offer computer-to-computer communication like a DNS system. An example of web server indexing services is illustrated in Figure 13. Any service provider can add the description files of a new service, or modify or erase an existing description of one of his own services.

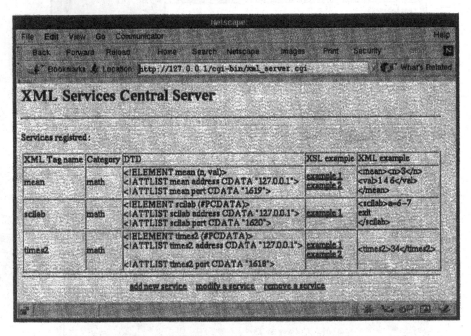

**Fig. 13.** An XML services engine registry

If users wish to execute an XML command that is not available on their local computer, the computer-to-computer interface will request the corresponding DTD and XSL files from the associated XML service engine registry. This could be implemented in a similar manner as the Domain Name System (DNS).

To avoid duplicate XML name commands, we could add package names in the headers of the XML files. Figure 14 shows an example where information

---

[3] http://www.schema.net/

about the `matrixSquare` service will be searched first in the A.M.S. XML Service Engine Registry, then in IBM's registry.

```
<servicePackage name="IBM">
  <servicePackage name="AMS">
...
    <matrixSquare><line>2</line><column>2<column>
    <val>1 2 3 4</val></matrixSquare>
...
  </servicePackage>
</servicePackage>
```

**Fig. 14.** Directing the search among service engine registries

## 3 Related work

Several recent research projects have focused on simple and interactive interfaces to register services in distributed computing environments. *CorbaWeb* [6], for example, proposes a script language called CorbaScript to write CGI scripts which can call CORBA objects. This facilitates considerably access to CORBA objects for non-expert users. Nevertheless, some programming (in particular, for writing the CorbaWeb scripts) is still required. To reduce this burden, one could imagine a library of CorbaWeb pages to use different CORBA services to simplify their use. The interface for service users ("consumers") could then be based on forms, which makes the chaining of services (like, for example, `specialFFT(superSolver(A,b))`) much more difficult.

This chaining possibility is a strength of our own service infrastructure, which is called *MMM (Middleware for Method Management)* [3, 5]. MMM supports service providers by giving them an interface that is based on generic technology (web browser, XML) and that is relatively easy to use. Simple services can be registered within minutes by filling out a simple form, thus generating an XML record that describes the service in question (cf. Fig. 15). More complex services may require additional metadata in order for potential users to find, evaluate, and run the service. Consumers are supported by a variety of other tools. On the one hand, MMM offers a specialized search engine that supports users in finding the right method for a given problem. On the other hand, applying a method to a given data set typically takes no more than a few mouseclicks. Essentially, it only takes entering the input data (directly or via an URL) and specifying the mode of payment (typically credit card or some micropayment system).

```
<OBJECT><MSO><ID>ADJPH</ID>
<GENERAL>
<AUTHOR><PERSON> ... </PERSON></AUTHOR>
...
</GENERAL>
<ACCESS location="extern" decompression="none" tarfile="">
http://www.aos.princeton.edu/WWWPUBLIC/tapio/arfit/adjph.m</ACCESS>
<SIGNATURE>
<CALL>adjph(x)</CALL>
<INPUT>
  <PARAMETER> <ID>x</ID><DESCRIPTION>complex matrix</DESCRIPTION></PARAMETER>
...
</INPUT>
<OUTPUT>  ... </OUTPUT>
</SIGNATURE>
<ENVIRONMENT> <ENGINE><MATLAB></MATLAB></ENGINE> </ENVIRONMENT>
<CONTENT>
<TYPE><MSO_TYPE> <SCRIPT format="ascii" language="matlab"></SCRIPT> </TYPE></MSO_TYPE>
<DESCRIPTION>
<URL>http://www.aos.princeton.edu/WWWPUBLIC/tapio/arfit/</URL>
%       ox=ADJPH(x) produces a complex matrix ox ...
</DESCRIPTION>
<KEYWORDS> <KEYWORD>autoregressive model</KEYWORD> .. </KEYWORDS>
<ABSTRACT>
<URL>http://www.aos.princeton.edu/WWWPUBLIC/tapio/papers/arfit.html</URL>
<URL>http://www.aos.princeton.edu/WWWPUBLIC/tapio/papers/arfit_alg.html</URL>
</ABSTRACT>
</CONTENT></MSO></OBJECT>
```

**Fig. 15.** XML record describing a Matlab program for time series analysis (some parts intentionally left out)

Another project, *Zope* [2], resembles CorbaWeb. It is a web server with a new language that includes calls to functions, computations, and other data manipulations to produce HTML pages. Is has the possibility to include packages like "COM External Method" to bind COM servers to the Zope server as Zope's methods. The new version also understands XML and includes XML-RPC which we will discuss in more detail later on.

All these approaches require some reconfigurations at the central server site where the ASP market is located. Some techniques use forms to send input data to the central server, which forwards them to the application server where the requested service is implemented. In the case of MMM, the MMM central server stores the necessary routing information (cf. Fig. 15), hence there is no need to know their address.

On the other hand, the approach proposed in this paper aims at bypassing the central server site when it comes to method execution. This resembles well-known middleware architectures, such as ORB, RMI and RPC. These approaches are more rigid in some respects: input and output values are checked for consistency and there is exception possibility. However, it requires serious programming skills to employ them, which is not consistent with the needs and requirements of our target audience.

The last approach we present is the one that is closest to our own. The *XML Remote Process Control (XML-RPC)* [4] is a simple method to call remote services using XML tags. To use it, one has to send the input data to some server that understands XML-RPC. At this point, one needs to use an ad hoc client program for this purpose, but, in the near future, browsers should understand XML-RPC input directly. There are a variety of different implementations of XML-RPC, including a package for the Zope server. Here is an example of the XML-RPC syntax to call the service provided on betty.userland.com that gives the name corresponding to the number of a state:

```
OST /RPC2 HTTP/1.0
User-Agent: Frontier/5.1.2 (WinNT)
Host: betty.userland.com
Content-Type: text/xml
Content-length: 181

<?xml version="1.0"?>
<methodCall>
   <methodName>examples.getStateName</methodName>
   <params>
      <param>
         <value><i4>41</i4></value>
      </param>
   </params>
</methodCall>
```

**Fig. 16.** Call to a service implemented in XML-RPC

The XML-RPC syntax is strict, easy to understand, and identical for all the services. At the same time, it is comparatively heavy and it is difficult to chain services. Just for comparison, consider the call to a similar service with our approach, given that betty is not the usual computer for this service:

```
<getStateName address="betty.userland.com">41</getStateName>
```

**Fig. 17.** Comparable call in our approach

# 4 Conclusions and Future Work

This article proposes a simple method to provide and use services over the Internet through a web browser. It represents one step towards a web environment where the registration of services is as easy as the writing of HTML pages is today. Several more features are needed to make our approach easier to use and to make it more attractive for commercial use.

The first such feature would be to reference all services in the same way web crawlers and engines index HTML pages. Hence users know which services are available and can use them without having to download the XSL file of the service. The XML Services Engine Registry presented above is a first step into this direction but more work is required.

The second feature to add is security. Users may want to protect their data and therefore our method should give them this possibility. In our approach, two aspects of security need to be addressed: 1. the protection of the data during transportation on the net; 2. the hiding of the client data from the service provider.

The first problem can be solved using available cryptography techniques. An easy way to do so is to use slogin of SSH instead of telnet in our connect command. It is also possible to use SSL or any other cryptographical method but it should stay simple to use for the provider. The second problem is more difficult to solve. Hiding client data from the service provider means that the service has to work with encrypted data. The result of this computation then has to be transformed into the "real" result by the consumer. This problem is not within the scope of this paper; see [5] for a more detailed discussion.

The third class of features to consider concerns server and user authentification, consistency problems with input and output data, locking problems if the server does not answer, and exceptions the application service may send. Since all these problems are already addressed with common remote process control like ORB and RMI for example, our method should use them instead of calling directly the application server via a simple socket.

# References

1. J.P. Chancelier, F. Delebecque, C. Gomez, Ma. Goursat, R. Nikoukhah, and S. Steer. Scilab home page. http://www-rocq.inria.fr/scilab/.
2. Digital Creations. Zope home page. http://www.zope.org/, 1999.
3. Oliver Günther, Rudolf Müller, Peter Schmidt, Hemant Bhargava, and Ramayya Krishnan. Mmm: A www-based method management system for using software modules remotely. *IEEE Internet Computing*, 1(3), 1997.
4. UserLand Software Inc. Xml-rpc home page. http://www.xmlrpc.com/, 1999.
5. Arno Jacobsen, Oliver Günther, and Gerrit Riessen. Component leasing on the world wide web. *Netnomics*, 2000.
6. P. Merle, C. Gransart, and J.M. Geib. Corbaweb. http://corbaweb.lifl.fr/.
7. W3C. Xsl draft. http://www.w3.org/TR/WD-xsl/, 1999.
8. W3C. Xsl home page. http://www.w3.org/Style/XSL/, 1999.

# A Search Engine for Indian Languages

Ashwani Mujoo, Manoj Kumar Malviya, Rajat Moona, TV Prabhakar

(mujoo, manojkm, moona, tvp)@cse.iitk.ac.in
Department of Computer Science and Engineering,
Indian Institute of Technology, Kanpur, India

**Abstract.** There is a great need for a search engine for web documents written in languages other than English. In this paper, we describe the design issues of a Search Engine for Indian Languages. We also describe the implementation of two Search Engines for Indian Languages, one for documents in ISCII and the other for documents in Unicode. The software allows full-text indexing and searching of a database of documents written in any Brahmi-based Indian Language. The Search engine gathers the HTML documents from the web, indexes and compresses the documents and then searches for the given keywords. The main features of the search engines are phonetic tolerance, morphological analysis, compression and indexing, leading and trailing substring matches for keywords, search through compressed documents. The implementation includes a search server architecture, which can be accessed from a WYSIWYG front end, which is a Java swing applet. Performance results show that the search engine achieves a compression of almost 80 percent and has an appreciable precision and recall.

## 1 Introduction

The Internet in India is growing by more than 300% a year, and poses some unique problems not found elsewhere. There are 15 officially recognized languages and various sites with localized content in multiple languages are coming up rapidly. Though there are search engines that search documents in different languages of the world, none of them are enabled to search documents written in Indian Languages. Another problem is that many Indian Language documents take the route of using the FONT FACE tag in HTML along with a glyph set for Indian Languages. This is sufficient for displaying documents but is a major obstacle for searching. Encoding schemes like ISCII and Unicode not only facilitate display but also give a handle on indexing and searching.

In this paper we describe the implementation of two Search Engines that can search documents written in Devanagari (Deavanagari is a script used by several Indian languages like Hindi, Marathi, Sanskrit etc.). First we describe the Search Engine for documents in ISCII encoding where we handle the major linguistic issues and then for Unicode documents where we take care of the compression of the web documents.

## 2 Design Issues

Language specific features can be expected to have a significant influence on the architecture of an Internet search engine. We identify some of the issues that need to be considered when building an Indian language search engine.

- **Different Forms of the Words**: Almost in every language grammatical markers (like *s*, *es*, *ing* etc in English and  Ä, ´ÉÉ ÉÉ, ^ÉÉÄ in Hindi) are used with a word stem (or root word) and new words are made. These new words called morphological variants of the stem, present the same concept but differ in tense, plurality etc. An example, ÉC EÄÒ, ÉC EÒÉÅ are morphological variant of the root word ÉC EÒÉ. It is possible that a document contains a root word, say ÉC EÒÉ and the user gives a morphological variant of the root word, say ÉC EÄÒ for searching. The search engine should be able to handle such conditions and should give matches for all the morphological variants of the word.

- **Phonetic Tolerance**: Indian languages alphabet contains many characters ( Ä, Æ , ØX ), which sound similar, i.e. they are phonetically equivalent. These characters are often used interchangeably. For example, ZÉÆB É, ZÉHB É, ZÉXB É, ZÉÄB É are phonetically equivalent words. Users may use any phonetically equivalent word of a keyword for searching. So the search engine should be able to support some form of phonetic tolerance. If the user gives the word ZÉÆB É for searching, the search engine should be able to get matches for all its phoneme equivalent words ZÉHB É, ZÉXB É, ZÉÄB É

- **Font Independence**: Due to lack of standardization, Indian language documents on the Web are being written in different fonts. Each web author uses her own font encoding in the HTML documents using the FONT FACE tag. There is no universally accepted font or display encoding. A user can see the Hindi content only when he has the same fonts as were used by the web page author. So the character sequence in a web page is a function of the fonts used for viewing the web page. To search a word in such documents is not possible, since the font encoding is not a standard.

- **Language Independence**: Since there are a number of spoken and written languages in world, a user may want a search engine with no language barriers. A truly internationalized search engine will be able to search for different sites having content in any language of the world.

- **Indian Language Front End**: Since the content that is being searched and gathered by the search engine is in an Indian Language, it is expected that the user would like to give the query in an Indian Language. So the front end of the search engine should be able to support typing keywords in an Indian script.

# 3 Design and Implementation of Search Engine for ISCII documents

The Indian Script Code for information Interchange, ISCII, specific a 7-bit code table, which can be used in 7 or 8-bit ISO compatible environment [4]. The ISCII code table is a super-set of all the characters required in the ten Brahmi-based Indian scripts. It allows English and Indian script alphabets to be used simultaneously. ISCII retains the ASCII character set in the lower half and provides the Indian script character set in the upper 96 characters in the 8-bit code. Our search engine is primarily designed to index and search Indian language documents that have ISCII character encoding. It can also index and search English documents simultaneously. Its design is language independent. Only one module is language specific and that is the morphological analyzer. We used a morphological analyzer of Hindi language in this implementation. The morphological analyzer of any other Indian language can easily replace this Hindi morphological analyzer. With this replacement our search engine can work for any other Indian language.

At the top level our search engine can be divided into three parts - gatherer, indexer and search processor. We now discuss each part in detail.

## 3.1 Gatherer

Gatherer works as a regular web user, sends HTTP requests to the remote server for collecting the documents. It starts its journey of the web from a set of specified URLs. The search engine maintainer chooses these URLs manually. It follows all hyper links that it comes across, visits those links and fetches the corresponding web pages. The pages fetched should have been written in an Indian language. The web pages should be in ISCII encoding which can be viewed with an ISCII plugin in the browser.

## 3.2 Indexer

Everything the gatherer finds goes into the indexer. The indexer of our search engine works in two phases. The first phase runs with the gatherer. It takes documents from the gatherer, parses those documents and collects information about each word of the document. Root word generation and stop word removal are also performed in the first phase. Information collected in the first phase is stored locally for use by the second phase. The first phase creates two files - a list of all words and a database of URLs. The main task of the second phase of the indexer is to build the indexing structure.

### 3.2.1 Document Parsing and Weight calculation
Document parsing involves the separation of text from the HTML tags. The parser also separates Hindi text from English. Words occur with different HTML tags in the HTML documents. We are assuming that the words coming in headings, title and keyword tag represents the

subject of the document. So the words occurring with these tags are assigned a higher weighting factor. After determining the weighting factor the next task is to determine the language of the word. In this process, program checks the parameters of the <FONT FACE> tag. If a <FONT FACE> tag surrounds word with font name as some Hindi font, then it means the word belongs to Hindi language otherwise some other language. If the word belongs to Hindi, it is converted into ISCII encoding.

Now the weight of the word is calculated using the following formulae:

```
weight = (1000 - location) * weighting_factor

location = offset  * 1000 / content_length and
```

*weighting_factor* is the weight of the tag in which the word is coming. *content_length* is the size of the document and *offset* is the offset of the word in the document.

The sum of the weights of each occurrence of the word gives the weight of the word in the particular document; weight, document id, and word frequency are the fields of the data record, which have to be stored in database with the word as indexing key. This word is passed to the morphological analyzer for further processing

**3.2.2 Morphological Analyzer** The primary task of morphological analyzer is to return the root word of a given input word [6]. This is necessary to search the different forms of a word. For example, if the word  ÉC    EÄÒ appears in the document then its root word  ÉC    EÒÉ and the original word ÉC    EÄÒ will be stored in the database. Now, if the user gives the word ÉC    EÒÉÅ for searching, search is performed for the root word of the search word as well ( ÉC    EÒ), giving a match.

After generating the root word from the given input word, the stop word list is checked to filter. If any of the words exist in the stop word list, both these words (root word and original word) are not included in the database.

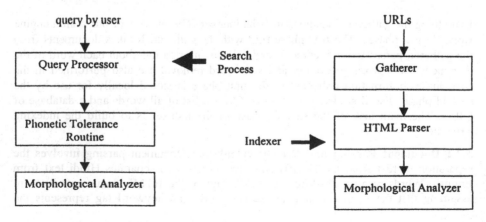

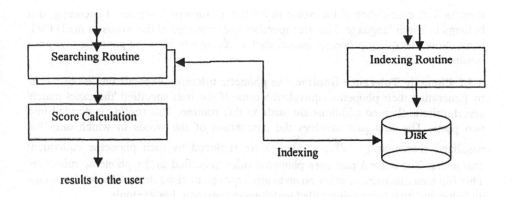

**Fig. 1.** Design of the Search Engine

**3.2.3 Indexing Data Structure.** The second phase of the indexer creates a URL database and word database from the intermediate files that were created in the first phase. This word database is accessed via an index of the keywords. The index file is organized as a variant of basic tries referred as compressed tries.

A *basic trie* is an m-ary tree (m is a size of alphabet set) in which the root node points to another node for each of the possible alphabets a word may have. Each of these nodes likewise contains a pointer to a node for each possible second alphabet and so on. The basic trie is space inefficient; therefore we used a compressed version called a *Compressed Trie*. Details of this data structure can be found in [5]

**3.3 Search Processor**

The Search processor is the actual search engine of the search system. We implemented it as a CGI program, which can be invoked by an HTML form. It will accept both GET and POST methods of passing data to the CGI program. An HTML form is the primary interface for the search processor. When the form is submitted, the search program will take values from the form and perform the actual search in the indexing structure. The HTML form contains an input text field where the user will enter the search words. This form has other options for controlling the search criteria and for formatting the results. The search process is divided into the following four modules, which execute in the given sequence.

**3.3.1 Query processor** The search processor gets a list of words from the HTML form that invoked it. The query processor takes this list and if the searching program was invoked with the Boolean expression parsing enabled, it does syntax check in that list. If there are syntax errors, it displays the syntax error. If the Boolean parser was not enabled, the list of words is converted into a Boolean expression by putting either ANDs or Ors between the words. This depends on the search type specified by the user. In both cases, each of the words in the list is converted into ISCII encoding, if it belongs to Hindi language. The user specifies the language of the words in the HTML form. Now, the query processor passes each of these words to the phonetic tolerance routine.

**3.3.2 Phonetic Tolerance Routine** The phonetic tolerance expands the list of words by generating their phoneme equivalent words. If the user specified 'the exact match' search criteria then no additions are made to this routine. This routine is divided into two parts. The first part involves the generation of the words in which only the nasalized characters ( Æ, Ä, ) are replaced by their phoneme equivalent characters. The second part uses phoneme rules specified in the phoneme rules file. This file contains pairs of other phonetically equivalent characters of Indian Language alphabet and an integer value called matching percentage. For example

$$[GA] \Rightarrow [GA][NUKTA] \Rightarrow 70$$

indicates that if MÉ occurs in a word then generate a new word in which MÉ will be replaced with MÉ. And if this new word is later found in the index, its final weight will be 70% of the weight value stored in the data record. This file can be changed according to the requirements of various Indian Languages.

**3.3.3 Morphological Analyzer.** The words generated in the last step are passed to the morphological analyzer for generation of the root words. Since among all the phoneme equivalent words only one word is grammatically valid, the root word will be returned only for that valid word. The Morphological analyzer ignores other words. Here a grammatically valid word means a word that is present in the dictionary e.g. !ÆEÒÉÅ !ÄEÒÉÄ !XEÒÉÄ are phonetically equivalent words but only !ÆEÒÉÄ is grammatically valid. So Morphological analyzer recognizes only this word and returns root word !ÆEÒ for it.

**3.3.4 Stop Word Removal** Before searching the words in the indexing structure, it would be better if we remove all the stop words from the list. This improves the searching time, as non-relevant words are not searched.

**3.3.5 Searching the Database** Searching the database involves searching the compressed trie. The algorithm is described in [5].

**3.3.6 Results, Ranking and Display.** Before ranking the results are combined according to the Boolean expression of the query. The rank of the match is determined by the weight of the word that caused the match. The document is which the keyword has a higher weight is given a higher rank. A word's weight is determined by the importance of the word and by the phoneme rules. For example, words in the title of a document have a much higher weight than words at the bottom of the documents. Finally when the document ranks have been determined, the resulting matches are displayed in the order of ranks

### 3.4 Performance

This software has been tested on a database of 780 Hindi documents spanning 14 MB of disk space. We found that the index size is 11.3% of the total document size.

**3.4.1 Recall and Precision of Search Engine** In order to measure the recall and precision of our search engine, following tests were conducted.

We indexed 34 Hindi documents out of which 21 documents were relevant to a keyword !ÉÄJÉÅ and 11 documents were relevant to a query SÉÉÄNÙ SÉÉÄNÙXÉÒ. When the keyword !ÉÄJÉÅ is given for searching, our search engine retrieved 18 documents of which 17 documents were relevant to that keyword i.e. 80% recall and 94% precision. Our search engine retrieved 9 documents for the query SÉÉÄNÙ SÉÉÄNÙXÉÒ out of which 8 documents were relevant to this query i.e. 72% recall and 80% precision.

In the second test total indexed documents were 100 out of which 21 documents were relevant to the keyword !ÉÄJÉÅ and 13 documents were relevant to the query SÉÉÄNÙ SÉÉÄNÙXÉÒ. Search engine retrieved 22 documents for the keyword !ÉÄJÉÅ out of which 17 documents were relevant. This gave 80% recall and 77% precision. For the query SÉÉÄNÙ SÉÉÄNÙXÉÒ our search engine retrieved 19 document out of which 11 documents are relevant i.e. 80% recall and 57% precision

## 4 Design and Implementation of Search Engine for Unicode documents with Compression

Unicode is the universal character-encoding standard used for the representation of text for computer processing [7]. The Unicode standard provides the capacity to encode all of the characters used for the written languages of the world. UTF-8 [3] encodes Unicode characters as a varying number of octets, where the number of octets and the value of each, depend on the integer value assigned to the character in Unicode Standard. The UTF-8 encoding allows Unicode to be used in a convenient and backward compatible way in environments that, like Unix, were designed entirely around ASCII.

The basic idea behind the design is to use the commonality between dictionary coding and the inverted indexing to unite compression and text retrieval into a common framework. A technique similar to Huffman coding at word level has been used. The result is a search engine that is efficient in terms of storage requirement and has the capability of searching directly through compressed text. In the design of the Search Engine it is assumed that the gathering process has already been done and the web pages, which are written in UTF-8 encoding for Unicode, are stored in some location on the local disk. But since UTF-8 encoding takes one to three bytes for each character, depending upon the character repertoire, we need to compress the gathered data with no loss of information and still be able to search the web pages without actually decompressing it.

There are two passes over the database. The first pass deals with the creation of word lists from the data set and to organize it suitably for the second pass. The second pass deals with the compression and indexing where each word is converted into dictionary id. The key words are searched in the index created and the search report is given out by decompressing the compressed database at any particular context. Decompression is feasible and is scaleable since the user doesn't want all the relevant pages to be seen at the same time.

## 4.1 Unicode Compression

In UTF-8 encoding a Devanagari character takes as many as three bytes. It is possible to reduce this to one byte by Unicode compression [2]. This scheme divides the Unicode code space into a set of windows. Byte values are interpreted relative to the position of the window currently in force. Each window size is equal to 128. For all the windows, which will be in use, tag bytes are assigned. Tag byte 0x01 for the Basic Latin window (0x0020 -- 0x007F and CR, LF, TAB), tag byte 0x02 for the Devanagari window (0x0900 – 0x097F) and tag 0x03 for the Private User Area (0xE900 -- 0xE97F).

Initially a window in the Basic Latin Range is defined. Each character in the Unicode string is then checked to see in which window does that fit. If that window is currently in use, no tag bytes are inserted. Otherwise the tag byte for that window is inserted. Then the Unicode character is represented as a byte in range of 0x80 and 0xFF as shown below:

```
Compressed byte = (Unicode Character Value) -
(Conversion factor)
```

Where the Conversion factor for various windows used are 0x0000, 0x0880, 0xE880 for Basic Latin, Devanagari, Private User Area respectively. This approximates the storage requirements to the storage size of traditional character sets like ISCII.

## 4.2 Indexing, Compression and Search

A shrink and search (SASE) [1] framework has been used for implementing the indexing combined with compression. This technique uses the same dictionary for both indexing and compression. The granularity of compression is a word, which gives lesser compression ratios than methods like Lempel-Ziv but integrates pattern matching (searching) with compression. For a detailed description of this method see [1], [8].

### 4.3 Search Client

The Search Client is the actual CGI program that is invoked from the web server. It receives the encoded keyword from the front end, which is decoded into the UTF-8 encoded word. The encoded keyword is actually a string of numbers. Breaking the encoded keyword in four number strings and five number strings and changing them to Unicode values forms a Unicode string out of it. This UTF-8 encoded word is then passed onto the phonetic tolerance routine for further processing.

### 4.4 Front End and Display Rendition

The Front end is a Java Swing applet, the interface of which includes the text field for entering the keyword and other components for setting of the options as described earlier in the Search Server. In the text field the keyword is entered in Devanagari script, which is stored as a font encoded string. This string is converted into a Unicode string by mapping from font to Unicode. There is a submit button that sends the keyword and the options to the web server as a URL encoded string. But since only ASCII values can only be passed in the URL, the Unicode values need to be encoded as the string of numbers (Unicode values) and passed on to the web server as encoded keywords. The results displayed on the Client's browser are UTF-8 encoded, as are the documents that have been searched and can be seen only if the browser has support for Unicode. The browser settings for viewing the results include the character set encoding to be set to Unicode (UTF-8) and the font settings to be Unicode font.

### 4.5 Performance

The software has been tested on a large text database of 4820 Hindi HTML web pages, which include the whole Gita Super Site and the *Corpora*, the content for educational use from the Ministry of Information Technology, Govt. of India, with a total data size of 80 MB. The documents are in UTF-8 encoding for Unicode. On removing the tags from the html pages, we get a size of 46 mb for the actual documents. The search results don't contain the tags that are present in the original web pages, so we don't consider the tags in finding the compression and index sizes. The total unique number of words turns out to be 1,72,342.

**4.5.1 Compression Performance.** Compression Ratio is defined as:

```
Compression Ratio = 1 - (Compressed File Size /
Original File Size)
```

The compressed format of the files was found out to be 8.2MB when Unicode compression for storing the dictionaries was used giving us a compression ratio of 82%, and 10.1MB when Unicode compression was not used, which gives a compression ratio of 77.8%. This means an extra 5% compression is achieved because of Unicode Compression. The inverted index size was found out to be 9.8 MB, which is 21% of the original document size.

## 5 Further Work

Search engines in Indian languages demand interesting features like phonetic tolerance, morphological analysis, font independence, flexible user-interfaces, powerful compression schemes etc. In this paper we presented two experimental search engines addressing some of these needs. They can be extended in several dimensions like:
- A front end that allows data entry in any Indian language script
- Synonym searches
- More robust indexing and compression techniques for larger scale-up
- Advanced indexing techniques
- Incremental indexing

This would form a basis for a universal search engine that can index and search across all languages in the world.

## References

1. S.Varadrajan and T.Chieuh, SASE: Implementation of a Compressed Text Search Engine, Proceedings of the USENIX symposium on Internet Technologies and Systems, 1997.
2. M Wolf, K Whistler, C Wicksteed: Unicode Technical Report #6, A Standard Compression Scheme for Unicode, http://www.unicode.org.
3. RFC Archive, UTF-8, A transformation format of ISO 10646, Network Working Group, SunSite, Denmark.
4. Indian Script Code for Information Interchange – ISCII standard. Bureau of Indian Standards, New Delhi, December 1992.
5. Puneet Chopra: An Efficient Concurrency Control Model for Compressed Tries, Department of Computer Science and Engineering, Indian Institute of Technology, Delhi.
6. Dr. Vineet Chaitanya and Dr. Rajeev Sangal: Morphological Analyser for Anusarka, Indian Languages Translation Project, IIT Kanpur Center for National Language Processing, University of Hyderabad, Hyderabad.
7. Unicode Home page http://www.unicode.org
8. Mujoo, A.: A Search Engine for Devanagari in Unicode with Compression, M.Tech. Thesis, IIT Kanpur, March 2000

# Metadata Based Web Mining
# for Topic-Specific Information Gathering

Jeonghee Yi[1], Neel Sundaresan[2,3], and Anita Huang[2]

[1] Computer Science, University of California, Los Angeles
405 Hilgard Av. LA, CA 90095, USA
jeonghee@cs.ucla.edu
[2] IBM Almaden Research Center
650 Harry Rd. San Jose, CA 95120, USA
nsundare@yahoo.com, anhuang@almaden.ibm.com
[3] Current Affiliation: NehaNet Corp., San Jose, CA 95131, USA

**Abstract.** As the World-Wide-Web grows at an exponential rate, we are faced with the issue of rating pages in terms of quality and trust. In this siutation, with significant linkage among web pages, what other pages say about a web page can be as important as and more objective than what the page says about itself. The cumulative knowledge of such recommendations (or lack of them) can help a system to decide whether to pursue a page or not. This metadata information can also be used by a web robot program, for example, to derive summary information about web documents written in a foreign language. In this paper, we describe how we exploit this type of metadata to drive a web information gathering system, which forms the backend of a topic-specific search engine. The system uses metadata from hyperlinks to guide itself to crawl the web staying focused on a target topic. The crawler follows links that point to information related to the topic and avoids following links to irrelevant pages. Moreover, the system uses the metadata to improve its definition of the target topic through association mining. Ultimately, the guided crawling system builds a rich repository of metadata information, which is used to serve the search engine.

## 1 Introduction

The size of the World Wide Web has reached over 800 million pages and is growing at an exponential rate [13]. As the number and complexity of pages grow, it becomes increasingly expensive and complex to rate these pages based upon their content. An alternative approach is to rate the relevance or quality of each page based upon what other pages that point to the page say about it. This approach can be compared to a recommendation-based market system, where buyers do transactions with sellers based on recommendations from other buyers. In general, it is a system of learning from other people's experience.

Typical web crawlers crawl the web seamlessly paying little attention to the quality of search information. These crawlers have the goal of getting to as many

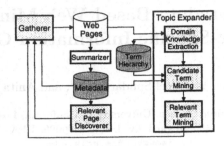

**Fig. 1.** System Architecture. The *gatherer* visits web pages and the *summarizer* produces metadata on the hyperlinks and the content of the pages. The *topic expander* discovers new topics relevant to the topic. The *relevant page discoverer* determines relevant pages to the topic based on the metadata.

pages as possible, regardless of topic. Topic-directed crawlers have a different objective. They aim to get to as many *relevant* pages as fast as possible without deviating to pages unrelated to their topic of interest.

In our work on topic-specific crawling, we start with the HITS (Hypertext Induced Topic Search) premise and enhance it using descriptive information found around hyperlinks. HITS is a pioneering work in classifying web pages based on the link structure of hypertext documents [10]. HITS identifies strongly connected components in this structure to find good *authority* and *hub* pages. Introduced by HITS, good hub pages *point to* good authority pages, and good authority pages are *pointed to by* good hub pages. In our work, we enhance HITS by assigning weights to the edges of the link topology. The weights are based on the occurrences of certain topic words in the metadata. We also use the metadata to expand the definition of our target topic through association mining.

The experiments we discuss in this paper were conducted using the Grand Central Station (GCS) web gathering system [7]. Figure 1 shows the GCS system. The system includes i) a *gatherer* that crawls the web, ii) a *summarizer* that produces metadata for the crawled pages, iii) a *topic expander* that discovers relevant topics, and iv) a *relevant page discoverer* that selects and prioritizes the URLs to crawl. The metadata for a web page describes what other pages say about it and what it says about the pages that it points to.

The rest of the paper is organized as follows. Section 2 introduces metadata in Web pages. Section 3 discusses how topic specific gathering can be enhanced with hyperlink metadata. Section 4 analyzes related work. Section 5 discusses conclusions and future work.

## 2  Metadata in Web Documents

*Hyperlink metadata*, or simply *metadata*, is the information that a web page provides (through its hyperlinks) about the documents that it refers to. Like the citations of a research paper, which provide summaries or evaluations of the

| Metadata Type | Hyperlinks | Pages |
|---|---|---|
| ALT Tag | 1,890 (0.9%) | 281 (1.5%) |
| Anchor Text | 147,745 (72%) | 14320 (76%) |
| HREF Tag | 176,412 (85%) | 16313 (87%) |
| NAME Tag | 5,487 (27%) | 779 (4.1 %) |
| ONMOUSEOVER Tag | 9,383 (4.5 %) | 1523 (8.1%) |
| Surrounding Text | 49,138 (24%) | 8424 (45%) |
| Title | 885 (0.4%) | 249 (1.3 %) |

**Table 1.** This table lists various attributes associated with a hyperlink. The numbers in the column "Hyperlinks" gives the number (and the percentage) of hyperlinks that are referenced with a particular metadata type. The column "Pages" gives the number of pages that contain at least one particular metadata type.

papers that they reference, the hyperlinks in a web page provide information, in their associated text and attribute values, about the web pages that they point to. In this paper, we focus on analyzing and using the metadata found around the hyperlinks of HTML documents to drive our information gathering system.

## 2.1 HTML Metadata

In HTML documents we find five types of hyperlinks: anchor tags (A), image tags (IMG), map tags (MAP), area tags (AREA), and frame tags (FRAME, IFRAME). Each of the tags have attributes associated with them. For example, the anchor, area, and map tags each have a set of main attributes, which include name, title, alt, on-mouse-over, and href. These attributes provide metadata information about the page that the hyperlink points to. This metadata is also found in the text surrounding and contained inside the hyperlink tags. We begin our experiments by identifying the attributes and text that are most appropriate for use as hyperlink metadata for our system.

## 2.2 Metadata Extraction

In order to extract metadata from hyperlinks in an HTML document, we first convert the HTML documents to well-formed XML documents using an HTML-to-XML filter. The filter performs extensive error recovery in the case of poorly formed HTML documents. Once we have a well-formed XML document, we look for the hyperlink elements (A for anchor tags, IMG for image tags, and so on) and extract their attribute values. For surrounding text, we extract the XML nodes of type PCDATA that are the left and right siblings of the tags. For the text contained inside the tags (e.g., anchor text), we extract the PCDATA nodes that are children of the tags.

To identify the most appropriate hyperlink metadata, we studied the metadata extracted from a sample set of 20,000 HTML pages. In these pages, over

206,000 hyperlink references were found. These hyperlinks pointed to pages both within and outside of the sample set. Table 1 lists characteristics of several types of hyperlink metadata. It can be seen that, second to href, anchor text is the most common metadata type. In addition to frequency of occurence, we measured the quality of a metadata type by the number of relevant topic terms discovered by its use during mining. We also measured the absolute and relative reliabilities of metadata types by comparing what the metadata says about the referenced page and what the page really contains (taking into account outdated or expired references). From our experiments we found that anchor text, href, and surrounding text, in that order, provide the best metadata. The results reported in this paper were based on anchor text, which occurs most frequently and is most reliable. Alternative schemes (such as choosing weighted averages of different metadata type occurrences) may also be applied.

# 3 Topic-Directed Information Gathering using Metadata

This section discusses the use and effectiveness of hyperlink metadata in two information gathering applications: topic-directed crawling and topic expansion. It begins with a brief description of the metadata database.

## 3.1 The Metadata Database

As a crawler visits a page it extracts all the links (with their metadata) in the page and adds them to a URL database. A summarizer produces Resource Description Framework (RDF) [12] metadata for the page, which includes what the page says about other pages and what other pages say about it. With its XML serialization syntax, RDF can be incorporated into query systems that understand XML structures. For each URL, the crawler stores the URL text, crawl history, and other information to be used for future visits of a URL in the database. It also keeps an additional table of link metadata information, as (URL, parent-URL, metadata) triples, which is used to rank the URLs based on their relevance to the target topic.

## 3.2 Topic-Directed Crawling

The goal of topic-specific information gatherers is to stay focused on pages that pertain to the target topic. We have developed various algorithms for guiding topic-specific gatherers on the basis of hyperlink metadata. In this paper, we outline the algorithms and summarize their performance on crawling relevant pages. More in-depth discussions of the algorithms, relevance metrics, and results from the crawling experiments may be found in [17–19].

*1) Simple Heuristics (SH)*
SH gives the highest crawl priority to those URLs that contain a predetermined set of relevant topic terms in their href metadata (i.e., the URL itself). Using SH, the crawler visits higher priority URLs first and ultimately crawls all the URLs descended from the seed set.

## 2) Relevance Weighting (RW)

RW selects and prioritizes URLs to crawl based on the relevance of all of the hyperlink metadata associated with the URL. Unlike SH, RW selects a page to crawl only if its metadata surpasses a relevance threshold for the topic. The RW relevance score for a page $w$, $\Theta_{RW}(w)$, is computed as follows:

$$\Theta_{RW}(w) = \begin{cases} max(\Theta(t)_{t \in M(w)}) & \text{if } max(\Theta(t)_{t \in M(w)}) \geq c \\ 0 & \text{otherwise} \end{cases}$$

where $\Theta(t)$ denotes the relevance of a term $t$ to the target topic (discussed in detail in [19, 18]). $M(w)$ is the hyperlink metadata of the in-link of $w$, and $c$ is a user defined threshold for relevance.

## 3) Relevance Weighting with Boosting (RWB)

To avoid stagnation and get out of local clusters, *RWB* modifies RW by deliberately increasing the relevance score of some pages that fail to meet the relevance threshold. First, for pages selected by random boosting, it recalculates relevance scores based on entire page content (rather than just the in-link metadata). In addition, it boosts the scores of randomly selected pages that do not qualify even after this recalculation. The RWB relevance score for a page $w$, $\Theta_{RWB}(W)$, is computed as follows:

$$\Theta_{RWB}(w) = \begin{cases} \Theta_{RW}(W) & \text{if } max(\text{if } \Theta_{RW}(W) > c \text{ or } R_1 < b \\ max(\Theta(t)_{r \in w}) & \text{if } R_1 \geq b \text{ and } max(\Theta(t)_{t \in w}) \geq c \\ R_2 & \text{if } R_1 \geq b \text{ and } max(\Theta(t)_{t \in w}) < c \end{cases}$$

where $R_1$ and $R_2$ are random variables with uniform distribution, and $b$ is a user-defined boosting factor.

## 4) HITS with RW (HITS-RW)

*HITS-RW* enhances the HITS algorithm by adding weights based on hyperlink metadata to the uniform link topology used by HITS. By itself, HITS is known to drift from the target topic [2] because the algorithm uses uniform link weights for all web pages. By constrast, HITS-RW computes the *authority* scores of pages using link weights based on the relevance scores of the incoming links. With HITS-RW, an incoming link contributes more to a web page's authority score than do other links, if it has a higher relevance score.

## Experiments

Figure 2 shows the effectiveness of the various crawling techniques—SH, HITS RW, RWB, and HITS-RW—measured by the total number of relevant pages identified by each technique as the crawl progresses. RW gathers the highest quality web pages by avoiding unpromising hyperlinks. 92% of the web pages collected by RW were related to the target topic. In other words, decisions based on anchor-text metadata were accurate 92% of the time. This result was achieved without page lookups (i.e., downloading the pages). The algorithm, however,

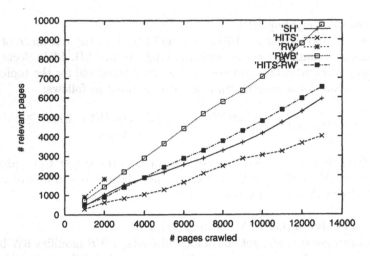

**Fig. 2.** Quality of Crawling. The graph shows the total number of relevant pages discovered by each algorithm as the crawl progresses. RW achieves the highest accuracy, with 92% of pages crawled relevant to the topic, but suffers from stagnation. RWB achieves the next best accuracy (75%) and avoids stagnation. Using relevance edge weighting, HITS-RW (50%) improves the performance HITS (31%) by a notable margin.

causes the crawler to run out of pages to crawl quickly, after about 3K pages. The reason is that, being too selective, RW over-prunes potential URLs to crawl.

Overall, RWB performs the best. While the noise introduced by RWB's boosting reduces crawl accuracy, it allows the crawler to discover new clusters and thereby increases the scope of relevant resources. Moreover, even with the noise, compared to SH and HITS, RWB does not extensively chase irrelevant links. As evidenced by the graph, RWB surpasses HITS-RW, SH, and HITS by wide margins. HITS, by itself, performs the worst, fully neglecting page relevance.

These results confirm that topic-specific crawlers should take into account page relevance to focus the crawl. Moreover, they support the use of hyperlink metadata as an inexpensive and effective approach for determining page relevance in this context.

### 3.3 Topic Expansion

The notion of a *topic* in a topic-specific search engine is not clearly defined in many cases. For instance, should all HTML pages be in an XML-specific search engine because HTML may be considered an instance of XML? Obviously not. We would, however, like to include other non-proliferating instances of XML and information about these instances in the search engine. Hence, our information gathering system should discover new topics related to the target topic as it crawls the web. In this section we present the utility of hyperlink metadata on the learning of relevant topics using association mining[1]. Association mining involves identifying relevant topic terms based upon the co-occurrences of topic terms with terms that are known to be relevant to the target topic. For instance, if XSL has a high frequency of co-occurence with XML in metadata, XSL will be identified as a term relevant to XML.

## Topic Expansion by Association Mining

To discover terms, called *candidate topics* (ct), that have a high probability of being relevant to the target topic, we look for terms that frequently co-occur in hyperlink metadata with the known terms of the target topic. To do so, we apply association mining techniques to the metadata. The mining algorithm identifies candidate topics by finding strong association between the target topic and the terms appearing in the metadata. Significant association rules are those that have confidence and support values higher than selected threshold values. The use of metatdata for topic expansion has several advantages over the use of the entire text of web pages. First, association mining that uses the entire page content increases computational complexity but does not guarantee improved accuracy. In fact, the use of the entire text degrades accuracy in many cases due to the *curse-of-dimensionality* problem [8]. Second, association mining that uses metadata requires a significantly smaller number of web pages to be downloaded. The reason is that it does not require the lookup of all linked pages (of which a significant number are irrelevant).

We formulate association mining on link metadata within the following framework:

1. Each web page is considered to be a market-basket (or transaction).
2. Each topic, included in the metadata of hyperlinks, is considered to be a transaction item.
3. Given that $r$ is a significant association rule, a candidate topic term is a term that appears in the antecedent of the rule $r$.

Detailed descriptions of the mining algorithms may be found in [18, 19].

## Filtering to Verify the Relevance of Candidate Topics

Strong association of terms does not always guarantee the relevance of terms. To compensate, we developed and used various filtering techniques to identify and extract *relevant topics* from the set of ct. A detailed discussion of these filtering techniques may be found in [19, 18]. In this paper, we present a brief overview of two filtering techniques and their accuracy in order to discuss the overall quality of relevant-term learning.

### 1) Filtering by Term Hierarchy (Specialization Filter)

The specialization filter utilizes a term hierarchy, similar to [15], to determine topic relevance. It concludes that a candidate topic term, $t_1$, is relevant to the target topic term, $\tau$, if any of the following conditions holds:
- $t_1$ is $\tau$,
- $t_1$ is a specialization of another topic $t_2$, and $t_2$ is relevant to $\tau$,
- $t_1$ is specialization of $t_2$, and $t_2$ is a generalization of $\tau$ in the topic domain.

| | $1^{st}$ Iteration | $2^{nd}$ | $3^{rd}$ | $4^{th}$ |
|---|---|---|---|---|
| 1. # of Pages | 2 K | 5 K | 10 K | 17 K |
| 2. Candidate Topics | 130 | 110 | 79 | 67 |
| 3. Actual Relevant Topics | 29 (24%) | 37 (34%) | 41 (52%) | 54 (81%) |
| 4. Relevant Topics by Filtering | 24 (83%) | 34 (92%) | 37 (90%) | 49 (91%) |

**Table 2.** Number of Candidate Topics Discovered by Association Mining and Filtering: The number of candidate terms are 130 after the $1^{st}$ iteration, and 110, 79, and 67 in the subsequent iterations [item 2]. Out of the candidate terms, 29, 37, 41, and 54 terms are indeed relevant [item 3]. The ratio of relevant terms out of candidate terms has improved from 24% after the $1^{st}$ iteration to 81% after $4^{th}$ iteration [item 3]. By filtering, consistently, over 90% of relevant terms are extracted, except the first iteration [item 4].

## 2)Filtering by Sampling (Sampling Filter)

In topic-specific crawling, the gathered web pages, $P$, are biased towards $\tau$. The sampling filter exploits this bias to determine whether each $ct$ is indeed relevant. To test each $ct$, a sample set $S$ is gathered for $ct$ rather than for $\tau$. The sampling filter measures the difference between the data distributions of $P$ and $S$.

A new topic $ct$ is not relevant to $\tau$, if

$$r = \frac{p_S(\tau \mid ct)}{p_P(\tau \mid ct)} < c \tag{1}$$

where $c$ is the user-defined threshold. $p_P(\tau|ct)$ and $p_S(\tau|ct)$ measure the proportions of web pages with term $ct$ that also contain the topic term $\tau$ in the sample sets $P$ and $S$, respectively. The more dependent (thus relevant) the terms $ct$ and $t$ are, the more $p_P(\tau|ct)$ and $p_S(\tau|ct)$ will be similar. For example the probability that one would find the topic term XML in web pages about XML is higher than the probability of finding it in web pages about Picasso.

## Experiments

The experiments were conducted on a set of over 17,000 web pages. The topic expansion experiments started with an initial set of 2K pages with more pages added as crawling proceeded through subsequent iterations.

The mining experiment is summarized in Table 2. Association mining on metadata discovered 130 $ct$ in the $1^{st}$ iteration, followed by 110, 79, and 67 in subsequent iterations (item 2). By manual inspection, we found 29, 37, 41, and 54 terms of $ct$ to be indeed relevant to $\tau$ (item 3). As shown, the rate of discovering relevant topic terms was accelerated as the mining iterations continued. Initially, only 24% of candidate terms were relevant. After 4 iterations, 81% of candidate terms were topic related (item 3). This level of accuracy is impressive. Even the initial accuracy of 24% in the first iteration is impressive in comparison to text mining of the entire text. In our experiments of association mining on the entire text, less than 2% of relevant topics were discovered from the top 200 most significant association rules due to excessive noise in the HTML text.

The filters extracted 83%, 92%, 90%, and 91% of relevant topics from the set of candidate terms in the $1^{st} \sim 4^{th}$ iteration (item 4). Some of the XML-related concepts we learned in the process included BSML, XQL, XMTP, XHL, XDK, XAF, WIDL, VML, SPDL, SDQL, SAX, which are XML vocabularies or names for XML processing software technologies.

These experiments imply that association mining on the basis of hyperlink metadata is very effective. Combined with filtering, 90% of relevant topic term discovery was achieved without human involvement.

## 4 Related Work

HITS[10] introduces a novel mechanism to rate web documents by identifying good authority pages based on link connectivity. Subsequent work on classification [3], focused crawling (FC) [4], and identifying micro-web communities [11] are based on HITS. We enhance HITS using metadata around hyperlinks. To direct the crawl, we classify pages based on this metadata, in constrast to FC, which relies on the entire text. Different from our system, FC visits all pages pointed to by each relevant page regardless of the relevance of the pointed to pages [9]. Our experiments show that using metadata rather than the entire text saves significant time and effort by not looking at unpromising pages.

In [6], the authors describe a system where important pages are first visited based on both content and link similarity measures. They keep two different queues to give higher priority to the pages with the topic word. However, they do not learn new topics, and their similarity decision is based on the entire text.

Cora [14] defines domain-specific search engine for computer science papers. It uses machine learning techniques to improve the crawls. Chen *et. al.* [5] also refine the techniques of utilizing metadata for information retrieval. ParaSite[16] exploits link information (not just hyperlinks) to build applications like finding individuals homepages, or expired or moved pages.

## 5 Conclusion

In this paper we described our work on using metadata to build a topic-directed search engine for XML based concepts. We use metadata to direct our crawler to a particular topic of interest and to improve the topic definition by extending it with relevant topic terms.

The use of hyperlink metadata in our crawling strategies resulted in a significant improvement in the proportion of relevant pages that were gathered—with RW and RWB gathering 92% and 75% relevant web pages, respectively. While RW suffered from stagnation, RWB did not. Moreover, the use of metadata for relevant term mining resulted in the successful discovery of over 50 relevant topic terms from about 17K web pages. It thereby significantly extended the topic definition for further gathering and, combined with filtering, suffered from almost no *curse-of-dimensionality* problem.

# References

1. Agrawal, R., Srikant, R.: Fast Algorithms for Mining Association Rules. The $20^{th}$ VLDB Conference. Santiago, Chile, (1994)
2. K. Bharat, M. Henzinger: Improved Algorithms for Topic Distillation in Hyperlinked Environments. Proc. of $21^{st}$ Int. ACM SIGIR Conference. Melbourne, Australia, (1998)
3. Chakrabarti, S., Dom, B., Raghavan, P., Rajagopalan, S., Gibson, D., Kleinberg, J.: Automatic Resource Compilation by Analyzing Hyperlink Structure and Associated Text.
4. Chakrabarti, S., van den Berg, M., Dom, B.: Focused Crawling: A New Approach to Topic-Specific Web Resource Discovery. The $8^{th}$ Int. World Wide Web Conference. Toronto, Canada, (1999)
5. Chen, H., Chung, Y.M., Ramsey, M. and Yang, C.C.: A Smart Itsy Bitsy Spider for the Web. Journal of American Society of Information Science. **49(7)** (1998) 604–618
6. Cho, J., Garcia-Molina, H., Page, L.: Efficient Crawling through URL Ordering. The $7^{th}$ Int. World Wide Web Conference. Brisbane, Australia, (1998)
7. Matthias Eichstaedt, Daniel Ford, Reiner Kraft, Qi Lu, Wayne Niblack, Neel Sundaresan: Grand Central Station. IBM Research Report. IBM Almaden Research Center, (1998)
8. R. Feldman, H. Hirsh: Mining Associations in Text in the Presence of Background Knowledge. The $2^{nd}$ Int. Conference on Knowledge Discovery and Data Mining. Portland, Oregon. (1996) 343–346
9. B, Huberman, P. Pirolli, J. Pitkow, R.Lukose: Strong Regularities in World Wide Web Surfing. Science. **280** (1998) 95–97
10. J. Kleinberg: Authoritative Sources in a Hyperlinked Environment. Proc. of $9^{th}$ ACM-SIAM Symposium on Discrete Algorithms. (1997)
11. Kumar, R., Raghavan, P., Rajagopalan, S., Tomkins, A.: Trawling the Web for Emerging Cyber-Communities. The $8^{th}$ Int. World Wide Web Conference. Toronto, Canada, (1999)
12. Lassila, O., Swick, R.R.: Resource Description Framework (RDF) Model, Syntax, Recommendation. W3C, (1999), "http://www.w3.org/TR/REC-rdf-syntax/"
13. Lawrence, S., Giles, L.: Accessibility and Distribution of Information on the Web. Nature. **400**, (1999) 107–109
14. McCallum, A., Nigam, K., Rennie, J., Seymore, K.: Building Domain-Specific Search Engines with Machine Learning Techniques. AAAI Spring Symposium. (1999)
15. Miller, G.: Nouns in WordNet : A Lexical Inheritance System. International Journal of Lexicography. **2(4)** (1990) 245–264
16. E. Spertus: ParaSite: Mining Structure Information on the Web. The $6^{th}$ Int. World Wide Web Conference. Santa Clara, CA, (1997)
17. Sundaresan, N., Yi, J., Huang, A.: Using metadata to enhance a web information gathering system. The $3^{rd}$ ACM SIGMOD Workshop on the Web and Databases. Dallas, TX, (2000) 11–16
18. Yi, J., Sundaresan, N., Huang, A.: Automated Construction of Topic-specific Web Search Engines with Data Mining Techniques. IBM Research Report. IBM Almaden Research Center. (2000)
19. Yi, J., Sundaresan N.: Metadata Based Web Mining for Relevance. International database Engineering and Applications Symposium, *forthcoming*. Yokohama, Japan, (2000)

# Advanced Studies on Link Proposals and Knowledge Retrieval of Hypertexts with CBR

Ernst-Georg Haffner[1], Andreas Heuer[1], Uwe Roth[1],
Thomas Engel[1], Christoph Meinel[1]

[1] Institute of Telematics, Bahnhofsstr. 30-32
D-54292 Trier, Germany
{Haffner,Heuer,Roth,Engel,Meinel}@ti.fhg.de

**Abstract.** In this paper, several problems in associating hyperlinks to text and the diverse possibilities to overcome these problems are discussed. At the current stage, an important aspect is knowledge retrieval of hypertexts. Our advanced studies on hyperlink management focus mainly on a concept similar to Case-Based Reasoning (CBR) systems as a possibility for the automatic generation of links for hypertexts in addition to traditional textual based methods. A detailed discussion of the basic ideas of CBR and an evaluation of its usefulness follows. Finally, methods to evaluate the quality of the proposals are described.

## 1 Introduction

The need for high quality hypertexts is increasing as a result of the growing of the World Wide Web (WWW). One of the most difficult tasks when writing hypertexts is the finding of appropriate links. Modern web authoring systems should not only provide possibilities to check link consistencies and help to manage any changes that might occur, but should also propose links in order to improve the usefulness of the documents, which are, in most cases, HTML-files.

It is very difficult to generate hyperlinks based on text semantics without making use of some human interaction. Authoring tools integrate documents of a web site and add structural links which are used to navigate through the various pages of a web site. Often, these web tools provide means for storing files in special folders (departments) according to their content [1].

The reason for these difficulties is the knowledge retrieval of the hypertexts to be able to make meaningful link suggestions. Automatic link proposals possess several advantages. Suggestions can be made very fast and with a minimum of user interaction.

Several possibilities to derive link proposals on a textual base are known, but all of them have their weaknesses, especially concerning the usefulness of the derived link suggestions [2], [3]. To improve the accuracy of the proposals, some approaches apply semantic analyses but all of these systems require user feedback of a high quality because it is the job of the web author to create the appropriate semantic model for the pages [4].

In this paper, we focus on a technique derived from *Case-Based Reasoning (CBR)* [5] as a possibility to provide high quality link proposals. The knowledge retrieval used is also based on CBR. Even though our main focus deals with the textual analysis of documents, the same ideas can also be applied to semantic-based approaches.

In a first step, we will discuss the most important areas of current hyperlink research. Next, a short summary of the main ideas of CBR systems and their principles will follow. After this, we will give a detailed description of the methods for retrieving knowledge from hypertexts in order to propose links of high quality. Ideas dealing with the evaluation of these results are mentioned next. Finally, we will present a conclusion and give a short outlook on future work.

## 2  Progress made in Hyperlink Retrieval

It is very important yet difficult to provide hyperlinks in a (HTML-) document. Hyperlinks dramatically improve content quality by presenting related work, contradictory positions, further information or simply by the continuation of the next page or by giving similar navigational information [6]. The question of how a web author can easily find such information remains, though.

Research on the area of hyperlinks has been carried out since the introduction of the World Wide Web service to the Internet. Kaindl et. al. present a compact history of the progress made so far [7].

Link retrieval research aims at generating hyperlinks if not completely automatically, at least with as little user interaction as possible. Very serious problems arise, though, when trying to retrieve hyperlinks of texts on a statistical base without any semantic knowledge. The results are of low quality [8]. Allan classified link types into three major groups: *manual, automatic* and *pattern-matching* [9]. The idea is to retrieve at least the easy-to-find links of the two latter groups and leave most of the former one to the user. This consideration is very useful even though it contains a disadvantage: the classification only works "a posteriori".

In this paper, we will describe methods to retrieve some of the "manual" links with CBR techniques and focus on the mechanisms to retrieve the corresponding knowledge from the hypertexts. Good examples for classical solutions without using CBR can be found in [10] or [11].

The dilemma of hyperlink retrieval is that a fully automated generation of links on a statistical base [12] leads to relatively bad results in terms of precision and recall, while semantic approaches with very good results require a high degree of user interaction [13]. If hyperlink retrieval is to be used as a tool for supporting web authors in easily adding up links, it would not be appropriate to require the time consuming formulation of a complete model of the semantic dependencies of a text.

Web authors and users (readers) of hypertexts can also be supported without a generation of links. Zellweger et. al. introduce the concept of *fluid links* as a convenient way to deal with temporarily visible information [14].

The technique based on CBR presented in this paper can easily be adapted as part of a web authoring system like *DAPHNE* [1]. It is also appropriate to extend hyperlink management systems such as *Microcosm* [15] with CBR-methods. Another possibility would be the use of CBR in combination with *Distributed Link Services* (DLS) presented by Carr et. al. in [16].

## 3 Foundations of Case-Based Reasoning Systems

Research in the area of Case-Based Reasoning begun in the early years of the last decade [17]. CBR-systems are well known means of representing knowledge in form of *cases*. Each case can be regarded as a *problem* together with its *solution*. A problem consists of its *description* in form of attributes and one or more *solutions* which refer to it. A typical environment of CBR is the area of diagnostics. Here, the attributes are the *symptoms* and the solution is the *diagnosis* [18].

In general, CBR-systems store their cases in a knowledge database called *case-base*. To solve a new problem, CBR-systems try to find the most similar cases in the case-base. Next, the solutions of these results are transferred to the new problem or are simply regarded as solutions of it. Remarkable efforts have been made to find out how to store only really usable cases (to avoid storage overflow) and how to learn to adapt the rules to compare cases for calculating their similarities [19].

CBR work can be divided into two different phases. The first process, the *learning phase*, builds up the case-base with reasonable cases, e.g. problems together with their solutions. The quality of the resulting case-base is better particularly after the learning phase if the according cases cover the scope of the problem.

The second process, the *classifying phase*, compares a new problem with the existing problems of the cases in the case-base. The solution of the most similar case found is a good proposition for a solution of the new problem. In practice, both phases are combined. The learning of new cases (new "knowledge") will continue as long as the (real) solutions of formerly posed problems are being recognized.

A main idea of this paper is to model hyperlink generation problems as a case-base and to use the experiences of CBR-systems to retrieve high quality links as proposals for the web author. The written texts of the web authors are regarded as the "problems" and the hyperlinks within are considered to be the "solutions". A complete hypertext can be viewed as a *case*. The advantages of CBR-systems to generate hyperlinks are:

- CBR research proves serviceable for extended use (several years) and for use in many areas
- It requires no special user interaction

- The learning process takes place implicitly (i.e. while the user accepts or rejects a link proposal)
- Core functions of CBR are fast and easy to implement
- CBR-systems "learn" to adapt personalized link favorites
- Due to the case model all kinds of (typed) links can be found - not only those that point to documents on the local web side
- The link proposal system can be applied to existent web sites by filling the case-base with hypertexts
- CBR can be used in conjunction with other methods (e.g. the concept model of [4])
- It is not restricted to language characteristics as described in [7][1]
- Link proposals of CBR do not determine non-ambiguous sources of the hyperlinks so that the same keyword can (implicitly) generate more than one link for the hypertext[2]

On the other hand, there are also some disadvantages of CBR-systems:

- The proposed links do not belong to a small fragment of text but to the whole page so that special link positions must be adapted manually
- CBR generates (many!) link proposals ordered by the probability of their usefulness. Therefore, the classical measurements of recall and precision cannot simply be applied
- The quality of the proposals depends on the structure of the case-base. If it is empty, the system cannot make any proposals. If it overflows, some cases will be "forgotten"

The use of CBR systems can be applied to hyperlink management systems in a straightforward manner. In order to verify the quality of the CBR-system, we scan web pages and take their links as solutions of the problem described by the (raw) text. Before learning those cases we try to classify them first. In the next step, the links proposed by the classifying module are being compared to the really existent hyperlinks of the HTML-pages. Finally, the complete page (text attributes together with the actual hyperlinks) is learnt as a new case for the case-base.

It is clear that at the beginning of such a process the resulting proposals – if any – are not too useful. The quality of the proposals will only improve while increasing the knowledge base and filling it with reasonable cases.

In the area of diagnostics, there are two unusual adaptations of CBR. The first difference arises from a special treatment of hypertexts: a hyperlink that points to the HTML-file forming a case should be added to the number of links (solutions) of the case-base as well, even though there is no single document which contains this hyperlink already. To a certain extent, this means that the problem itself is a part of the solution – of no relevance for the original case but very important for future classification steps of other texts. The other and even more essential difference to classical

---

[1] Even though we only tested the system for English and German pages
[2] The exact final location of the hyperlink can be replaced by the user

CBR-systems consists in the storage of the cases themselves. We calculate the most probable link proposals *implicitly* by considering the weights of the according symptoms to the regarded links. Usually, CBR-systems are looking for the most similar cases in the case-base *explicitly* and then transfer the results found to an existing problem.

# 4 Knowledge Retrieval of Hypertexts

A very crucial question in the context of CBR-systems is the transformation of the problem into certain properties that represent it. Therefore, it is necessary to retrieve the relevant information of the according hypertexts. In this section, we present a technique for knowledge retrieval that is based on statistical and syntactical considerations. Usually, a problem is modeled as an n-vector $P$ where n is the number of attributes used to describe the problem. Every element of $P$ must be normalized into the interval $[0..1]$. The solutions of a case are also represented that way. Here, we speak of an m-vector $S$, which is mostly a binary vector with elements set to 1 if and only if solution i solves the Problem $P$, and 0 otherwise. The variable m is the number of all solutions available from the according case-base. Obviously, a problem $P$ can have up to m solutions. In the presented concept, the solutions are hyperlinks within the (problem-) files. To specify the attributes of hypertexts we chose the following settings (if available):

- Every important (weighted) *keyword* of the document is regarded as an attribute
- Every *author* of the document forms an attribute
- The creation date and expiration date of a document are subsumed to one attribute *"validation"*
- The publishing state[3] and the version are combined to form the attribute *"availability"*
- The department information is one attribute *"structure"*, but we make the restriction that each document must not belong to more than one department

Thus, we made a statistical approach to apply CBR-ideas. Semantic methods could have been modeled at this point too. An evaluation of our settings will be given in section "5 Evaluation of the CBR-Approach".

## 4.1 Keyword Extraction

A very difficult problem is the extraction of keywords from a document on the basis of statistical distribution [20]. We decided to carry out a full text analysis with a special treatment of HTML-tags. All words beside HTML tags, comments and the stop-

---

[3] Allowed states are for instance: *generation in progress, reviewed, exported to the Internet, published ...*

words (e.g. a multilingual list from CD-ISIS [21]) were treated as potential keywords[4]. Beside the classical stopwords we regard in the context of hyperlink management also terms as "homepage" and the company's name as unusable for classification of whole web pages by keywords. A "word" in this context is a sequence of letters without special characters (e.g. hyphens). The following table 1 shows the - arbitrary chosen - weights we attached to every word in a text depending on its relative position between tags. These settings reflect that keywords in titles or headlines are more important than those in the body. In the next version of our CBR-approach, the weights of the keywords should also be part of the learning process.

| Position within tag | Weight |
|---|---|
| <TITLE> | 50 |
| <META> (description) | 10 |
| <H1> | 5 |
| <H2> | 4 |
| <H3> | 3 |
| <H4> | 2 |
| <BODY> | 1 |
| <A HREF> | 0 |

Table 1: Distribution of keyword weights

The number of occurrences of a word in a document multiplied with the settings of table 1 results in an absolute weight. Words within the anchor-tag for hyperlink references (HREF) are unconsidered because their information results already in a concrete link.

Only the words that exceed a minimum threshold (depending upon the document length) are treated as keyword attributes. In addition - if there are too many keywords - only the ones with the highest weights are selected[5]. At the end all weights are proportionally transformed into the interval [0..1]. Thus, all weights are divided by the maximum value among them.

Some essential points of the keyword extraction are:

- Keyword extraction does not consider ambiguities in the meaning of the words that are spelled the same
- Abridgments and acronyms can be defined in the text itself and will thus be treated like stopwords
- Even if two texts only have few keywords in common, they can share their solutions in CBR-systems
- The use of full form lexicons for treating different kinds of word-flexion [22] should be applied in the future

---

[4] We made our studies for English and German documents. For the latter, we have an additional restriction: only words with beginning capitalized letter (beside the first word of a sentence) are regarded as potential keywords. In German nouns always start with a capitalized letter.

[5] The number of keywords varied between five and hundred.

## 4.2  Author Information

If the author of an HTML document is known, this information will form an additional attribute for the according CBR-case. If there is more than one author, the system is able to take care of the varying relevance of the different authors (e.g. the first author is weighted by 1, the second by 1/2, the third by 1/3 and so on; or all authors are weighted by 1 in case of alphabetically sorted authors).

## 4.3  Document Validation

The idea to consider the "age" of a HTML-file as an attribute to form a CBR-case arises from the perception that the relevance of the content depends on its creation and expiration time. This is also true for the links contained in these documents. To get a linear value between 0.0 and 1.0 for the validation of a file we calculate the "distance in time" between now and the lifetime of the document. There are three possibilities as described in figure 1:

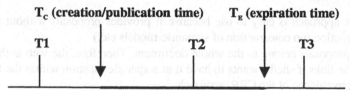

Figure 1: Timeline to calculate validation

If the creation or publication time of a document $D$ is in the past and the expiration time is in the future (T2 = "now"), the "validation" value v of $D$ will result in:

$$v = 1.0 \quad (1)$$

If the publication time of $D$ is in the future, e.g. $D$ is not yet visible in the Internet/Intranet (T1 = "now") the validation v is calculated as:

$$v = \frac{T_E - T1}{T_C - T1} \quad (2)$$

If the document is already obsolete the validation attribute of the corresponding documents will obtain the following value (T3 = "now"):

$$v = \frac{T3 - T_C}{T3 - T_E} \quad (3)$$

## 4.4  Departmental Information

If possible, additional information of the document structure is also used as an attribute for CBR. Here, the idea is that those documents that are positioned "deeper" in the (tree) structure of a web-site obtain a lower value as those on the top level. The usability of links with regard to structure depends on how general the contents of the concerned web pages are. It is more probable that links on the top level are not as specific as those in other positions, even though this is not always true. Very often, files all over the web-site refer to the root of the tree (the "home" link).

# 5 Evaluation of the CBR-Approach

The presented link proposal method implemented as a pure Java application should be a module of a complete hyperlink management system or a standalone program. Even though it is not meant to be used "a posteriori" on finished hypertexts, we think that the comparison of the system proposals with the real links inside existing documents is an appropriate possibility to measure the performance of the system. Therefore, we chose several existing web pages, extracted the links within, classified the texts without considering the link information, and compared, finally, both results. The model we presented is not easy to classify with regard to the terms *precision, recall, thoroughness* and *ease of use* [4].

- The CBR approach is easy to use because it provides proposals without any prior user interaction (no construction of semantic models etc.)
- All link proposals belong to the whole document. Therefore, the web author has to replace the links if she/he wants to have it at a specific location within the text. This is an inconvenience of the CBR-approach
- CBR can only be as accurate as the according cases in the case-base. It can never propose a link which has not already been learnt
- The system makes many proposals, ordered by the probability of their usefulness. An evaluation in terms of recall and precision this is rather problematic

Therefore, we introduced new terms on base of the probabilities of the link proposals. On the one side, the *"Quantified Cumulating Recall (QCR)"* describes the sum of all probabilities in the set of proposed links that were really found in the hypertext divided by the number of those links. If applied on every link in the hypertext, the QCR becomes an increasing curve. On the other side, the *"Quantified Cumulating Precision (QCP)"* describes the share of hits among those proposals (the "good" links of [4]). The gradient of both curves signals the quality of the proposals. The best curve would be the diagonal.

As a practical evaluation example, we show below the link proposal results for the first ninety pages[6] of the *Association for Computing Machinery (ACM)* (www.acm.org), the *World Wide Web consortium (W3C)* (www.w3.org) and the *Institute of Telematics (TI-FHG)* (www.ti.fhg.de)[7] (figures 2 and 3).

---

[6] ... with a depth first search tree scan beginning with the document root. No other than HTML-files were considered. For external web scans only the keyword attributes were available.

[7] We did not begin with the document root here, but with the "no frames" root page.

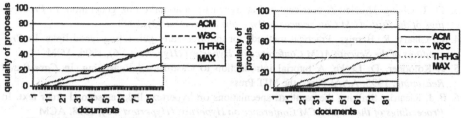

Figure 2: Quantified Cumulating Recall    Figure 3: Quantified Cumulating Precision

The QCP of the TI-FHG proposals was higher because we could use here the complete set of attribute values (keywords, author information, validation etc.). The overall recall and precision results are rather good, but a lot of effort has still to be done in order to become perfect.

## 6 Conclusion and Outlook

We presented a method similar to Case-Based Reasoning to propose links in the context of hyperlink management systems. After a general introduction of CBR-systems we focused on a special model for hyperlink suggestions with some differences to classical approaches. Especially, we decreased the importance of the cases themselves and operated with implicit similarities instead of explicitly looking for the best matching element in the case-base. The difficult task of retrieving knowledge from a hypertext was split into several parts. The most important attributes are the weighted keywords.

In order to adequately measure the quality of the system proposals we refined the terms of recall and precision. In the evaluation part, we presented some promising results of "a posteriori" classifications of web pages.

Even though the proposal mechanism works rather well, several improvements are possible. Our future work aims at increasing the efficiency of the learning algorithm and the finding of the best parameter values. The method must be extended by considering not only proposal acceptance but also the rejection of hyperlink suggestions to improve precision.

## References

1. A. Heuer, Z. Zhang, T. Engel and C. Meinel. DAPHNE - Distributed Authoring and Publishing in a Hypertext and Networked Environment. In *Proceedings of the International Conference IuK99 - Dynamic Documents*, 1999. Jena
2. M. Bernstein. An apprentice that discovers hypertext links. In *Proceedings of the First European Conference on Hypertext (ECHT-90)*, 1990

3. D. T. Chang. HieNet: A user-centered approach for automatic link generation. In *Proceedings of the Fifth ACM Conference on Hypertext (Hypertext '93)*, 1993

4. C. Cleary, R. Bareiss. Practical methods for automatically generating typed links. In *Proceedings of the Seventh ACM Conference on Hypertext (Hypertext '96)*, 1996. ACM

5. J. Kolodner, D. Leake. A tutorial introduction to Case-Based Reasoning. In *Case-Based Reasoning*, 1995. AAAI Press, the MIT Press

6. F. J. Ricardo. Stalking the paratext: speculations on hypertext links as second order text. In *Proceedings of the Ninth ACM Conference on Hypertext (Hypertext '98)*, 1998. ACM

7. H. Kaindl, S. Kramer. Semiautomatic generation of glossary links: A Practical Solution. In *Proceedings of the Tenth ACM Conference on Hypertext (Hypertext '99)*, 1999. ACM

8. R. J. Glushko. Design issues for multi-document hypertexts. In *Proceedings of the Second ACM Conference on Hypertext (Hypertext '89)*, 1989. ACM

9. J. Allan. Automatic hypertext link typing. In *Proceedings of the Seventh ACM Conference on Hypertext (Hypertext '96)*, 1996. ACM

10. C. Marshall, F. Shipman. Searching for the missing link: discovering implicit structure in spatial hypertext. In *Proceedings of the Fifth ACM Conference on Hypertext (Hypertext '93)*, 1993. ACM

11. M. H. Andersen, J. Nielsen, H. Rasmussen. A similarity-based hypertext browser for reading the UNIX network news. *Hypermedia,* 1(3), 1989

12. J. Gordesch, A. Zapf. Computer-aided foramtion of concepts. In *Quantitative text analysis, (Quantitative linguistics, Vol. 52)*, 1993. WVT Trier

13. C. Petrou, D. Martakos, S. Hadjiefthymiades. Adding semantics to hypermedia towards link's enhancement and dynamic linking. In *Hypertext - Information Retrieval - Multimedia '97 (HIM 1997)*, 1997. Universitaetsverlag Konstanz

14. P. Zellweger, B.-W. Chang, J. Mackinlay. Fluid links for informed and incremental link transitions. In *Proceedings of the Ninth ACM Conference on Hypertext (Hypertext '98)*, 1998. ACM

15. W. Hall, H. Davis, G. Hutchings. *Rethinking Hypermedia: The Microcoms Approach*. Kluwer Academic Publishers, 1996

16. L. A. Carr, W. Hall, S. Hitchcock. Link services or link agents? In *Proceedings of the Ninth ACM Conference on Hypertext (Hypertext '98)*, 1998. ACM

17. D. W. Aha. Case-Based Learning algorithms. In *Proceedings of the DARPA Workshop on Case Based Reasoning*, 1991. Morgan Kaufmann

18. K.-D. Althoff, S. Wess. Case-Based Reasoning and Expert System Development. In *Contemporary Knowledge Engineering and Cognition (Schmalhofer, Strube, Wetter)*, 1992. Springer

19. D. Joh. CBR in a changing environment. In *Case-Based Reasoning Research and Development (LNAI 1266)*, 1997. Springer

20. R. J. Chitashvili, R. H. Baayen. Word frequency distributions of texts and corpora as large number of rare event distributions. In *Quantitative text analysis, (Quantitative linguistics, Vol. 52)*, 1993. WVT Trier

21. CD/ISIS Wageningen Agricultural University Library
ttp://www.bib.wau.nl/isis/docum.html (multilin.) 1999

22. R. Sproat. *Morphology and Computation*. The MIT Press, 1992

# Virtual Tendering and Bidding in the Construction Sector

Simon Kerridge[1], Christos Halaris[2], Gregory Mentzas[2], and Susan Kerridge[1]

Project Manager, Centre for Electronic Commerce, University of Sunderland, Informatics Building-201, St. Peter's Campus, St. Peter's Way, Sunderland, SR6 0DD, United Kingdom.
{simon.kerridge, susan.kerridge}@sunderland.ac.uk
Senior researcher, Department of Electrical and Computer Engineering, National Technical University of Athens, 9, Iroon Politexniou Str., 15780 Zografou, Greece
chala@cc.ece.tnua.gr, gmentzas@softlab.ntua.gr

**Abstract.** The tendering/bidding process is vital for companies in the construction sector. This sector includes a number of actors performing at each stage of the process three different roles (client, info provider, provider). Based on e-commerce technologies numerous systems have been developed, aiming at the electronic support of this process. A short review of those systems indicates that they mainly focus on providing information about tenders. However, they don't cover much of the bidding process, where the formation of a virtual consortium is often required and the preparation of the final bidding document requires bids from subcontractors and suppliers. SupplyPoint is an innovative European-wide research and development effort partly funded by the European Commission under the ESPRIT Programme. The SupplyPoint system will support the whole tendering and bidding process, electronically providing - in addition to what existing systems provide - services for forming virtual consortia that bid for construction projects.

## 1 Introduction

The rapid evolution of e-commerce in the past few years has introduced new ways for organizations to perform tendering processes and participate in biddings. The term tendering is used to describe all the actions performed by the awarding authority to produce, publish and manage tendering documents, while bidding incorporates the effort of interested organisations to win contracts by responding to tenders. In this context, the value adding functionalities related to e-commerce technologies include for example electronic publication of tenders, electronic search of tenders as well for partners and suppliers, electronic submission of biddings, electronic notification of award and so on.

Those abilities are especially important for industries, where business is performed on a project-by-project basis and in many cases by consortia formed especially for the project. This is the case of the construction sector, where timely opportunity identification and adequate consortium formation are the key factors for winning a contract. As a result the main actors of the sector, i.e. tendering authorities, construction companies, suppliers of materials, and manufacturers can gain substantial benefits, by using these new electronic mechanisms.

## 1.1 Aims of the paper

- To analyse the opportunities (and risks) of electronic commerce for electronic tendering and bidding in the construction sector, by examining the chain of business processes and reviewing the pros and cons of existing systems;
- To present SupplyPoint, an innovative European-wide research and development effort (SUPPLYPOINT: *Electronic Procurement using Virtual Supply Chains* is partly funded by the European Commission under the ESPRIT Programme - project EP-27007 - see [1]). The SupplyPoint system (which is currently under the final stage of development and testing) will support the whole bidding process electronically providing - in addition to what existing systems provide - services for forming virtual consortia that bid for construction projects.

## 1.2 Structure of the paper

The next of the six sections presents the value chain actors and processes in the construction sector and reviews the pros and cons of existing tendering/bidding systems. Section three presents the rooms concept used. The fourth section covers the main functionalities and the technical architecture of the SupplyPoint system, while the fifth section presents the way the SupplyPoint system facilitates the formation of virtual consortia [VCs] with the use of alternative business scenarios. Finally some concluding remarks and outlines for further research directions are given.

## 2. Managing Virtually the Tendering/Bidding Process in the Construction Sector

The tendering/bidding process in the construction sector is characterised by the involvement of a large number of actors and requires a substantial investment of time and effort often with a limited success ratio. The set of actors involved includes the contracting authority, architectural and engineering firms, general contractors, specialised contractors, suppliers, manufacturers etc.

Those actors perform different roles during the tendering/bidding procedure. Based on the nature of the activities three roles have been identified:

- Client,
- Info Broker and
- Provider.

As shown in figure 1 the main subject of the Client role is the successful completion of the tendering/bidding procedure. The Client prepares tender documents, evaluates bids and assigns the contract to the winner of the tender. This role is performed by the contracting authority but also by any other actor who wishes to purchase services or products for the implementation of their work within a project. An example would be a general contractor searching for suppliers or subcontractors.

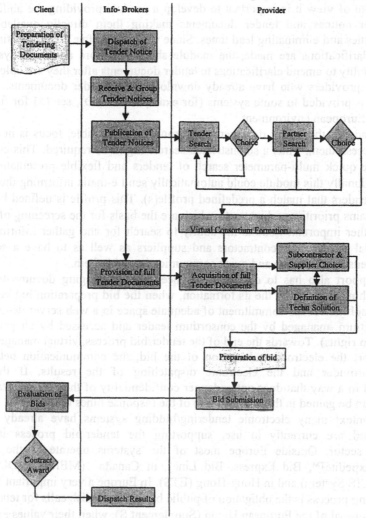

**Fig. 1.** Breakdown of tendering/bidding process by roles.

The role of Info Broker is to collect, organise, amalgamate and dispatch information about tenders in progress, potential partners, contract awarded and so on. As will as the above mentioned typical Info Brokers, this role is also performed by the contracting authority and occasionally by any of the actors when for example passing information to partners or subcontractors.

A typical provider could be a general contractor, who after searching for tenders and choosing one to bid, forms with others a Virtual Consortium (VC – see [6]). The VC then prepares and submits a bid to the client. However, this is also the case when specialised contractors, suppliers or manufacturers send their bids to a general contractor that is preparing a bid for a tender.

Managing virtually the tender/bidding process consists of supporting electronically the execution, partially or in total, of the activities executed by the above roles. From the client point of view it is important to develop a module providing the ability to upload tender notices and tender documents making them directly available to interested parties and eliminating lead times. Since very often after the publication of the tender, clarifications are made, the module should in more advanced systems provide the ability to amend clarifications to tender documents after they are uploaded and to notify providers who have already downloaded the tender documents. This functionality is provided in some systems (for example ELPRO), see [5] for further details of the European environment.

Having made all the tender documents electronically accessible, focus is now on the way to access them. Thus a sophisticated search engine is required. This engine should enable quick multi-parameter search of tenders and flexible presentation of results. Additionally this module could automatically send e-mails informing the user of any new tenders that match a predefined profile(s). This profile is defined by the user and contains priorities and interests, which are the basis for the screening of new tenders. Another important issue is the ability to search for and gather information about potential partners, subcontractors and suppliers as well as to have a secure environment ensuring on-time and quick communication with them.

Virtual support also has to deal with the need for exchanging documents and messages within the VC after the its formation, when the bid preparation bid begins. An effective solution is the commitment of adequate space in a web server dedicated to the consortium, managed by the consortium leader and accessed by all partners (depending on rights). Towards the end of the tender/bid process, virtual management should support the electronic submission of the bid, the communication between client and provider and the electronic dispatching of the results. If this is accomplished in a way that does not endanger confidentiality of the bids, substantial advantages can be gained in the minimisation of the response times to tenders.

In this context many electronic tendering/bidding systems have already been developed and are currently in use, supporting the tender/bid process in the construction sector. Outside Europe most of the systems operate in the USA (Trns•port Expedite™, Bid Express, Bid Line), in Canada (MERX, BIDDs) in Australia (DCIS System) and in Hong-Hong (ETS). In Europe a very important factor in the tendering process is the obligation of public bodies to publish calls for tender in the Official Journal of the European Union (Supplement S), when their values exceed the established thresholds. Thresholds vary, depending on the subject of the tender (e.g. services, procurement, works). In the case of public works the threshold is set at 5.000.000 Euro. In other words Europe has developed a database of medium and high value tenders fed daily by member states. This has resulted in the development of two categories of systems supporting the tendering/bidding process in the construction sector; pan European systems based on TED (Tenders Electronic Daily, the electronic version of Supplement S) and national systems fed by tenders published by national and local authorities.

Functionalities provided by these systems vary from system to system and include:
- electronic search of ongoing or assigned tenders,
- tender documents download,
- search for partners in the systems database

- e-mail exchange between primes, subcontractors and suppliers,
- automatic search of new tenders based on defined user profile and user notification
- electronic creation and submission of bids

Most of the non-European systems are initiated by and focus on the support of tendering authorities, whereas systems in Europe aim more often to support companies, including the construction sector. The main scope of most existing systems is to support the search for tenders and the acquisition of tender documents. Few of them provide also the ability to search for potential partners through a database containing companies validated by the authority, or members of local official construction companies records.

Some systems offer also ability to submit electronic documents after appropriate registration. With the exception of systems operated by tendering authorities, where services are provided for free, the most common pricing policy is to provide free tender search and requiring subscription to the service before providing access to the full service package. However, many of the systems covering the national level in European countries require subscription before proving any service.

Closing this section, it is important to note that none of the systems reviewed provide a solid collaboration platform that can support - in a virtual manner - the formation of a consortium. Another area that these systems lack is the integration and automation of the whole tendering/bidding process. Such integration could be obtained by incorporating technologies like workflow management systems; see for example [3], [4], [7] & [9].


# 3 Rooms

The concept of "Rooms" (e.g. BSCW, see e.g. [2]) has been developed and this provides the users with a readily comprehensible metaphor for their "location" within the SupplyPoint system. A Room is a place in the system, where information (documents) and users that have access to those documents are stored. Rooms can contain rooms and documents in a hierarchical manner analogous to most computer directory tree structures. Similarly each room has rights for visibility and access. Again, documents have rights for view, edit and delete. A top level Room is automatically created when an organisation is registered to SupplyPoint. This is the "Home Room" of the organisation. Users can create (and subsequently edit and delete) new Rooms and store information (e.g. contracts and potential partners) concerning the formation of Virtual Consortia. They can also add edit, view and remove both documents and user access from the Rooms. The GUI representing the notion of rooms is currently implemented as a tree structure in much the same way as for example windows explorer (see Figure 3 in section 4).

Each entity (a subscribing organisation or a virtual consortium) in the system owns a top level home room, which by default contains two sub rooms: "Bookmarked Organisations" and "Bookmarked Contracts". These Rooms help to organise information that concerns contracts and organisations and will be used for the formation of a Virtual Consortium.

## 4. SupplyPoint Architecture

Figure 2 shows the main components of the SupplyPoint (SPP) architecture. The system consists of two main parts, the SPPClient and the SPPServer. It also allows for integration with external systems (ELPRO is shown as an example).

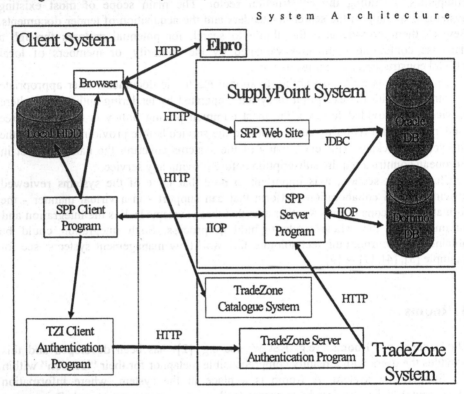

**Fig. 2.** SPP Architecture

It should be noted that the Common Object Request Broker Architecture (CORBA) is used to provide a communications protocol. The SPPClient establishes a connection with the SPPServer via IIOP. The Lotus Notes Domino Server is used to provide the basic workflow components and infrastructure. The visual element is mirrored in the client using a Java GUI thus providing a high degree of integration.

### 4.1 SPPClient

The SPPClient delivers services to the users of the SupplyPoint system. It provides a Graphical User Interface developed in Java 1.2 that allows the user to access the required functionality from almost any workstation. Within the SPPClient the user is able to communicate with other SupplyPoint system users via a communication/E-mail system developed (or rather integrated) for that purpose. The Rooms concept (see Section 3 above) provides the users with a readily comprehensible metaphor for

385

their "location" within the SupplyPoint system. Both documents and users are associated with Rooms. The GUI representing the notion of rooms is a tree view similar to windows explorer as shown in Figure 3 below.

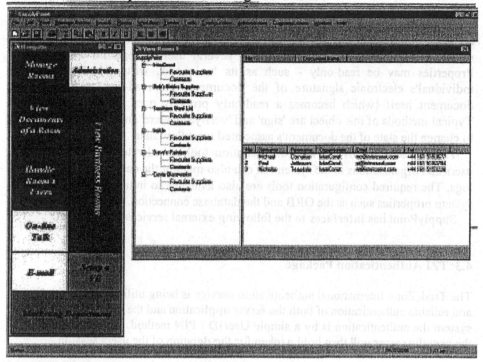

**Fig. 3.** The SPP Client Graphical User Interface

Using the SPPClient the user is able to handle documents belonging to those rooms depending on the permissions that have been set for the specific documents / rooms. A number of external facilities are also access via the SPPClient including: an Electronic catalogue that enables the users to purchase through the world wide web and an electronic procurement system that enables users to look for available contracts on the web and prepare tenders.

The SPPClient is installed on the user's machine but it invokes methods, through IIOP, that are implemented on the SPPServer. This thin client approach has been followed in the SupplyPoint system thus offering a minimal footprint for the client program and reducing the computing requirement on the SMEs computer system.

## 4.2 SPPServer

The server provides all the functionality for querying, inserting and updating the database for permissions, documents, user details, etc. The SPPServer connects to the Oracle database via a Thin JDBC driver in order to be able to query the database. Requests from the SPPClient are received via the IIOP and the SPPServer executes a specific method related to the request and queries the database via the JDBC driver.

As indicated, the connection between the SPPServer and the SPPClient is via IIOP for CORBA objects, however in order to provide support for workflow and authentication, an XML (see for example [3] & [9]) wrapping technique for documents is used. XML is used as a transport mechanism since it can carry any (Base64 encoded) document within it and also any associate document management or state information. The wrapper may be considered as a persistent object serialisation and, when de-serialised, has several useful properties and methods. Properties may be read-only - such as its 'unique-id', write-only - such as an individual's electronic signature of the document, and read-write - such as the document itself (which becomes a read-only property once it has been signed). Typical methods of this object are 'sign' and 'verifySignature' and others may be used to change the state of the document's associated workflow state.

The SPPServer provides an Administration tool in order to be able set-up new users and organisations in the system. It can also monitor the database and the system logs. The required configuration tools are also available to initialise the SupplyPoint system properties such as the ORB and the database connection.

SupplyPoint has **interfaces** to the following external services and systems:

## 4.3 TZI Authentication Package

The TradeZone International authentication service is being utilised to provide secure and reliable authentication of both the server application and the user. In the prototype system the authentication is by a simple UserID / PIN method. Having authenticated the user the server will then hold a token for the duration of the users session.

## 4.4 TZI Payment Package

Within the SupplyPoint project the TradeZone payment service is being developed as a means of on-line payment for registration fees. It is envisaged that as a stand alone plug-in service this can be utilised for other payment requirements at a future date.

## 4.5 ELPRO Public Procurement System

Under EU Legislation, public bodies are obliged to invite tenders from across Europe for [Works] contracts over 5.000.000 Euro, and give notice of this in the Official Journal of the EU (sometimes referred to as the OJ). Tenders are also currently announced electronically via TED (Tenders Electronic Daily) – see [5] for further details. The ELPRO system provides support to the entire procurement cycle for both procurers and suppliers, starting with the announcement of intention to invite tenders through to the award of the contract. There is an interface to the ELPRO system.

# 5 Formation of Virtual Consortia (VCs) Using SupplyPoint

The formation of virtual consortia within the SupplyPoint system involves the direct interaction and collaboration between potential partners, who enter into discussions, through the system, to form a collaboration to deal with a specific tender/project. The concepts behind this process are described in [6].

An organization can identify potential partners using various searches or through suppliers/partners already known to them (bookmarked). Discussions with these potential partners can be carried out and agreements made to form a virtual consortium by creating a shared work area containing various collaboration sections.

Within this on-line business area, or virtual company building, the partners are given access to discussion rooms, data storage rooms and workflow procedures to facilitate in the collaborative processes to prepare and submit a bid for tender.

In creating the virtual consortium (and virtual company building), information needs to be supplied including; the VC name, a list of partners, access rights (for partners and individuals from the partners), a management structure and of course a "contract" of interest to the VC (i.e. that it intends to tender for).

From this a virtual company building containing a room of partner details and a contract room for the contract of interest to the VC is formed.

Once formed, anything that a single company can do within the SupplyPoint system can be done by the VC. However, internal workflow will be required to ensure that all the relevant parties have agreed on a particular action. For example, the partners must electronically agree any tender documents before they can be submitted as a bid. To prepare a bid a workflow procedure is used allowing all partners to contribute and agree to the bid before it is sent to the awarding body. This workflow procedure includes:

- From within the contract room a workflow procedure can be initiated
- A tender bid document is created and circulated to all partners in turn
- Tender details are entered into the document by each partner
- After each partner has contributed the final document is prepared for submission
- Each partner must access the final document and approve or modify it
- If a document is modified the approver list is reset and all partners must re-approve
- A manager must ensure that a document if fully approved before submission
  These processes are supported by the workflow facilities of SupplyPoint.

# 6. Conclusions and further research

Tendering and bidding in the construction sector is a very important process involving a large number of actors in three different roles. In order to support the process taking advantage of e-commerce technologies numerous systems have been developed. The majority of those systems support search for tenders and the acquisition of tender documents and few of them provide additional services such as search for potential partners, electronic submission and so on. However, existing systems do not provide a solid collaboration platform that can support the formation of a virtual consortium.

That was the opportunity for the development of SupplyPoint, a new system aiming to support the whole bidding process.

The SupplyPoint system is available for validation and verification from June 2000 and a critical mass of users has been identified in France and the UK. The project will end in late 2000, when the system will be available for commercial purposes.

Currently SupplyPoint provides access to above the line procurement, however there are many opportunities for contracts below this figure of 5.000.000 Euro (Construction Works). There are a number of regional and sector specific systems that provide this type of information - interfaces to these sources would be extremely beneficial, as would the ability to be able to place sub-contracts onto them.

Further work will be required on many issues, including for example the close integration with new and existing 3$^{rd}$ party services, in order to provide a seamless environment for the SupplyPoint user.

The virtual rooms concept is being utilised in the education arena to form a virtual campus with students and tutors being able to upload notes, tutorials etc online.

Although this paper does not address the legal implications of virtual company formation the SupplyPoint consortium have done extensive research into the subject. The final report will be publicly available shortly.

# References

1. Kerridge, S. Slade, A., Kerridge S.R. & Ginty K., (1998) SUPPLYPOINT: Electronic Procurement using Virtual Supply Chains - an overview, International Journal of Electronic Markets, University of St. Gallen, Switzerland, Vol 8, No3 1998, p28-31
2. Klöckner, K.: (1999) Cooperative Activities and Distributed Communication - E-Commerce, Global Learning and CSCW. In: Hofer, S.; Beneder, M. (ed.): Proceedings of the IDIMT '99, 7th Interdisciplinary Information Management Talks, Sept. 2-3, Zadov. Linz, Österreich: Universitätsverlag Rudolf Trauner, 1999, S. 115-126.
3. Laplante, M.F. (1997) 'Accelerating Electronic Commerce: Making EDI accessible with XML', Document Software Strategies Analysis, Vol2, No 29, August 1997.
4. Mentzas, G.N. and Halaris, C. (1999) Workflow on the Web: Integrating E-Commerce and Business Process Management, *International Journal of E-Business Strategy Management*, November/December 1999, Vol. 1, No. 2, pp. 147-157.
5. Slade, A. (1998) Electronic Procurement in Europe. Chapter in Doing Business Electronically, pp121-137, Springer Verlag. ISBN 3 540 76159 4
6. Tsakopoulos, S. Bokma, A. and Kerridge, S.R. (1999) SUPPLYPOINT: Towards a Framework for Virtual Enterprises in Contracting, Business and Work in the Information Society: New Technologies and Applications, J.-Y. Roger et al (Eds.). pp223-229. IOS Press. ISBN 90 5199 491 5
7. Van Dyke Panurak H. (1997) Technologies For Virtual Enterprises, Industrial Technological Institute, Ann Arbor, MI, 1997
8. Weijgers, E and Kerridge S., XML A successor to EDI? A case study in the health care sector. International Journal of E-Business Strategy Management, Vol 1, August 1999.
9. Workflow Management Coalition (1998) Workflow and Internet: Catalysts for Radical Change, White Paper, June 1998.

# Using Genetic Algorithms to Enable Automated Auctions

E. Wolff, M.T. Tu, and W. Lamersdorf *

Distributed Systems Group, Computer Science Department
University of Hamburg, Germany
Vogt–Kölln–Str. 30, 22527 Hamburg, Germany
[3wolff,tu,lamersd]@informatik.uni-hamburg.de

**Abstract.** In this paper, an approach to implement automated auctions as a negotiation mechanism for Business-to-Business electronic commerce applications is presented. It is based on Genetic Algorithms (GAs) that evolve FSMs (Finite State Machines). Each of these FSMs represents an auction strategy that competes on the market and is modified over time according to the outcome of this competition by using GA principles.
The paper gives an overview of auctions, especially in the Business-to-Business domain, and other work related to this paper. Then, the application of Genetic Algorithms to automate auctions is presented and relevant details on the prototype implementation are given. In addition, some key results obtained from experiments using this implementation are discussed.

**Keywords:** auctions, genetic algorithms, negotiation strategies, E-Commerce.

## 1 Introduction

Internet auctions are becoming more and more popular as they offer a means of doing business that has the potential to replace fixed price mechanisms of conventional commerce by those that are truly based on the *dynamic* demand for the respective goods. Presently, auction sites on the Internet mostly focus on the needs of *end-consumers*, i.e. they can be classified as a part of the Consumer-to-Consumer or Business-to-Consumer commerce. However, providers are emerging that offer auction mechanisms for the Business-to-Business domain which certainly has an enormous economic potential. With respect to this domain, possibilities of automating auctions would be of great benefit, e.g. for enterprises that belong to or depend on the supplying industry and therefore need to negotiate on many items to get best prices.

This paper presents an approach to automated auctions in the Business-to-Business domain using Genetic Algorithms. Genetic algorithms (GAs) are a

* This work is supported, in part, by grant no. La1061/1-2 from the German Research Council (Deutsche Forschungsgemeinschaft, DFG)

kind of optimization technique based on evolution principles. Due to their main feature of *self-adaptation*, negotiation strategies that are based on GAs seem to fit very well to dynamic markets in general. In [TWL00], we presented an approach to use this technique in bilateral negotiations. In this work, GAs are applied to auctions as an example of multilateral negotiations. So this work can be seen as a first step to prove the applicability of GAs to the very diverse domains in the field of E-Commerce.

The remainder of the paper is organized as follows: Section 2 gives an overview of auctions with emphasis on computer-aided or automated auctions. Then, the essentials of Genetic Algorithms, especially those based on FSMs, and how they can be applied to auctions are described in Section 3. The next section 4 gives details on the implementation of the prototype system and reports some of the results achieved from experiments done with this system. The last section 5 gives a summary and an outlook on possible future work.

## 2  Auctions

Generally speaking, auctions are a form of multilateral negotiations on one issue (price). Kumar and Feldman [KF98] present a classification of auctions by three key attributes:

**Interaction format** *Open cry auctions* are similar to auctions that take place in a public meeting. Every participant learns about every bid from the other participants and must response to a bid in a few seconds time. For internet auctions, this would mean that every participant must be online at the same time. This is almost impossible especially if the participants live in different time zones. Another problem is that this kind of auction needs a reliable distribution of the offers with low latency. Given the often unreliable and high latency connections in the Internet, it is very hard to guarantee these properties.

In a single-round *sealed bid* auction, all offers are collected until a certain deadline and afterwards evaluated. In multiple-round sealed bid auctions, there is a deadline for each round of bids and then either the auction is closed or a new round of bids is started. This kind of auctions appears to be much better suited for Internet applications because it is inherently asynchronous and thus, not all participants need to be online at the same time and offers do not need to be broadcasted with a low latency.

**Control of bids and offers** Either the auctioneer can announce a bid and see if one of the participants is willing to pay it or he can ask the participants to submit their bids. If the auctioneer announces the bids, he can either start with a very high bid and lower it or he can start with a low bid and raise it until only one participant is left in the auction.

**Setting the trade price** After the bidding phase, the bidder with the highest bids gets the auctioned item. But the price he has to pay needs not necessarily be the same as his bid. If there are multiple auctions with identical items, all winners could be allowed to pay the price of the lowest winning bid. Another alternative is to let them pay the highest non-winning bid (Vickrey auction).

Apart from these key attributes, there are many other specific characteristics of auctions such as how much information about the other offers is disclosed to each participant. The end of the auction is another example of such a characteristic: It can be closed after a certain number of rounds or at a specific point of time. Another possibility is to end the auction when the frequency of new bids decreases below a certain threshold.

For the auction system presented here, a multiple-round sealed bid auction was chosen. The auctioneer announces a minimum bid and can lower the bid if no participant is willing to pay this minimum bid. Each subsequent bid must be higher then the previous bid. The final bid is also the price the participant has to pay for the item. During the bidding process, each participant is only given the information whether his bid is currently the highest bid. The bids of the other participants are not disclosed to him. The end of the auction is reached after a certain number of auction rounds.

As mentioned above auctions are multilateral negotiations. The main motivation for implementing such an auction system is to try GAs on the rather complex field of multilateral negotiations as compared to the work already done by us in the field of bilateral negotiations [TWL00]. So this is the first step to tackle the area of multilateral negotiations using GAs.

Another reason is the rise of Business-to-Business auctions where an enterprise and its potential suppliers form a marketplace to negotiate about the price of items. In this kind of auctions, a lot of identical items are traded between two or more parties. Conducting an auction for each of these items seems impractical due to the high costs for such auctions with human participants unless there is a convenient way for the automation of these auctions. To accomplish this, there needs to be a large group of agents that take part in the auctions on behalf of the original parties. Each of these agents should then buy or sell one of the items in an auction. Note that such a technique does not depend on the fact that the price is found using an auction but could be applied to every kind of mechanism to determine a price.

## 3 Using FSM-based Genetic Algorithms for Auctions

To optimize groups of items, *Genetic Algorithms* (GAs) can be used. GAs are inspired by the evolution taking place in nature. This process is based on very simple principles: selection together with reproduction, crossover and mutation. Selection means that only the fittest individuals survive. Reproduction is the ability to breed new individuals and mutations are deviations during this reproduction process. Crossover is the ability to take two individuals (parents) to breed one new individual that shares some attributes with each parent.

In GAs, these basic principles of evolution are used to create objects that are optimized for a certain function. To carry out this process, a set of objects (the *population*) is evaluated at discrete points in time (between the *generations*). Each individual has a certain probability to be taken into the next generation. This probability depends on its quality (*fitness*) measured in terms of the property that should be optimized. The individual can be propagated into the next generation either unchanged (reproduction), mutated or as resulted from a crossover with another individual. The evolutionary approach can be used for the optimization of numerical problems (*Genetic Algorithms*) as well as for the automatic generation of programs (*Genetic Programming*) [BNKF98]. A benefit of these techniques is that they can be used for tasks that require the capability to adapt to a changing environment, i.e. to optimize individuals even if the criteria for the optimization change over time as in changing market places.

For auction scenarios as those described above, the optimization of a population of agents by means of Genetic Programming (GP) appears to be a good approach. An important decision in applying Genetic Programming is determining the data-structure that is used to represent the programs such as the auction strategies in this example. For the system described in this paper, Finite State Machines (FSMs) are used because they are a simple, yet enough powerful model in comparison to other approaches of applying GAs to the E-Commerce field. For example, in [Oli96] simple linear structures are used.

Usually, FSMs just accept regular sets. But in order to be applied to auctions, they must also generate some output (bids) as response to some input (state of the auction). This can be achieved by using FSMs with output such as Mealy automata [HU79]. An example of a strategy modeled as a FSM can be seen in Figure 1. After bidding the initial offer (not shown in the figure), the FSM is in the initial state (the black circle in the middle). In case the initial offer is successful — i.e. it is the highest offer in the first round — the FSM is given an input of 1 and thus continues to the right state and outputs 100 as the increase of the offer, i.e. it will increase the offer by 100 in the next round. If the initial offer was not successful, the FSM is given an input of 0 and continues to the left state, this time increasing the offer by 200. The left and right states are almost identical, the only difference is that a successful bid in the left state result in a raise of 150 while in the right state, this results in a raise of only 50. So the strategy presented here depends very much on the outcome of the initial offer: If it was successful, the FSM continues in the right state and raises the offer by relative small amounts compared to the case where the initial offer was not successful. This represents a strategy where the participant believes that in case the first offer was successful, it is likely that afterwards only relative small increases are needed to stay successful.

Note that the strategy presented here can also be given a semantics that suites the role of an auctioneer: The initial offer can be interpreted as a minimum bid and the outputs of the FSMs as amounts by which the minimum bid is decreased. So if an auctioneer follows the strategy presented in Figure 1, he will lower the minimum bid by 200 if no participant was willing to pay the initial minimum bid. In case the initial offer was successful, the minimum bid will be decreased by 100 but this will not influence the outcome of the auction as there are already participants that agreed to pay the initial minimum bid. This shows that in the system implemented, the strategies for both auctioneers and bidders are really identical; they only have different semantics depending on the role of the participant.

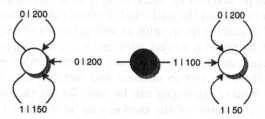

**Fig. 1.** A strategy for auctions as an FSM.

Besides the semantics of the FSMs, there must also be a definition of the genetic operators for crossover and mutation. Mutation on FSMs is implemented in this system by changing the states and edges. So for example, the input symbol of an edge can be modified or a state can be connected to different edges. For crossover, the sets of states of two FSMs are taken and each is divided into two subsets. Then the subsets are interchanged and edges are created as a connection between the subsets.

To calculate the fitness of a specific FSM, auctions are simulated. During each generation, every FSM takes part in at least one auction and according to the outcome of these auctions, it is assigned a fitness that determines whether it will be in the next generation or not. For the participants of the auction, each successful auction is rewarded with a fitness value of $\frac{2000}{p}$ where $p$ is the price that the participant payed in the auction[1]. If the participant did not succeed in the auction, it is assigned a fitness value of 0 for that action. As mentioned above, FSMs can also be used to implement the strategy of auctioneers. In this case, the fitness is calculated as $\frac{p}{2000}$ because it is better for an auctioneer to achieve a higher price.

To simulate a multifaceted market, there are also *fixed strategies*. For auctions, these strategies can only choose when to increase the bid by which amount. Most often, the maximum bid the participant is willing to pay is fixed by means such as the value the participant assigned to the item. Thus, the decision how high the maximum bid can be should not be made by the strategy but rather by some external source such as the participant himself. In the MarketMaker system [MIT], a way to generate strategies for auctions is proposed: The user of the system can decide what the graph between the initial and the maximum bid should look like. For instance, one can choose to use an exponential function.

---

[1] The constant 2000 is chosen because the bids in the experiments done are in the order of 2000 and this fitness value will be in the order of 1.

That would mean that at the beginning of the auction, the bid is increased at lower rates than at the end of the auction. This represents a strategy where the participant wants to be cautious at the start of the auction but is willing to risk more at the end. An alternative would be to raise the bid linearly.

For the system presented here, fixed strategies with a linear increase of the bid are used. The parameters for these strategies are the amount by which the bid is raised each round and the initial bid. Both of these values are taken from a normal distribution and the mean value as well as the standard deviation of these values can be set to model a market with certain price ranges. The percentage of agents with fixed strategies to take part in each auction can be set and so a complete market with a certain demand and certain prices can be simulated. Again, the same kind of strategies can be used for auctioneers, so apart from the demand, also the supply of the market can be simulated using these fixed strategies.

## 4 Implementation and Results

To implement the concepts presented in the last section, an object-oriented approach was chosen and the Java programming language was used. In this section, the prototype auction system based on GAs will be presented. Then, some experiments done using this prototype system and their results will be described.

The prototype auction system consists of a part that is responsible for auctions in general. Within this part, it is defined how the auction should be carried out and the functionality to implement bidders and auctioneers with fixed strategies is implemented. However, the implementation of the auction itself makes no assumptions about the bidders and auctioneers and thus, FSMs can easily take part in these auctions. Every time an auction takes place, not only the bidders are assigned a fitness but also the auctioneer. Both the auctioneers and the bidders can be FSMs that are optimized by a Genetic Algorithm. Most of the functionality for general negotiations and GAs was provided by a framework for the implementation of Genetic Algorithms that was built at the University of Hamburg to study GAs in the context of negotiations and auctions (see [TWL00] for more details on the framework). After this system was implemented, a number of experiments, also called *scenarios*, were performed and results were measured. These scenarios share the parameters shown in Table 1.

Each scenario was run with values for the mutation and crossover probability in the range from 0 to 0.5 in steps of 0.05. In the 20th generation, the prices for the bidder with strategies optimized by a GA and for the bidders with fixed strategies was measured. In addition, the ratio between auctions where a fixed strategy succeeded and auctions where a strategy optimized by a GA succeeded was measured. The same was done for the strategies of the auctioneers. For the auctioneers, the chosen parameters for both the fixed and the genetically optimized strategies can be found in Table 3 while the parameters for the bidders can be found in Table 2.

| parameter | value |
|---|---|
| size of population | 20 |
| generations | 20 |
| iterations (for mean values) | 100 |
| auctions per generation | 4 |
| rounds per auction | 5 |

**Table 1.** Common parameters for all scenarios.

| | genetically optimized strategies | fixed strategies |
|---|---|---|
| participant per auction | 2 | 50 %=2 |
| initial offer | 0-2000 | $N(900, 100)$ |
| increase per round | 0-120 | $N(100, 10)$ |
| | FSM have $\leq$ 10 states initially. | linear increase |

**Table 2.** Parameters for the bidders. $N(x, y)$ denotes a normal distribution with mean value $x$ and standard deviation $y$.

The first relevant result achieved is that with respect to the auctioneer, both fixed strategies and strategies optimized by a genetic algorithm perform equally well in all scenarios. This is not surprising since auction is a market type where bidders determine the price by outbidding each other. What the auctioneer does during the auction can not influence this.

For the bidders, first a scenario was implemented where in each auction, there were two strategies that were optimized by a Genetic Algorithm. This resulted in a competition in which these strategies tried to outbid each other. The reason for this is that the strategy that succeeds in an auction is assigned a fitness > 0 while the strategy that does not succeed is assigned a fitness of 0. So an evolution takes places where the strategies with lower maximum bids are slowly extinguished because of their lower fitness values. At the same time, the genetically optimized strategies succeed in virtually every auction. So there is a close connection between the maximum offers and the rate of success in the auction: If the maximum bid is very high, one can succeed in almost all auctions. This translates to a high market share in the market of the auctioned items.

| | genetically optimized strategies | fixed strategies |
|---|---|---|
| initial minimum offer | 0-2000 | $N(900, 100)$ |
| decrease per round | 0-100 | $N(100, 10)$ |
| | FSM have $\leq$ 10 states initially. | linear decrease |

**Table 3.** Parameters for the auctioneers.

So for the next scenario, only one strategy that is optimized by a Genetic Algorithm is allowed in each auction. In that case, the market share of the strategies optimized by a genetic drops to about 80 %-90 % and the prices paid by them also drop, but they are still higher than the prices for fixed strategies. Again, this is not surprising because higher maximum bids lead to higher market shares as stated above.

The real problem of these scenarios is that the implemented system has not taken into account the actual goal or the value function of the person or company that wants to use the strategies. Two simple goals can be considered: purchase as many items as possible for a certain total price *or* purchase a certain number of items for a price as low as possible. A certain number of purchased items translates to a certain number of purchased items. For example, if the market share is 40 % and there are 1000 auctions, then 400 items are bought. Once the market share and the price can be controlled, more complex value functions representing a relationship between price and market share can be specified by the user. Therefore, in the next scenario, the strategies were assigned a fitness > 0 only if they bought the item for a price *below* a certain threshold, and in fact then, the strategies are really optimized by the Genetic Algorithm to fulfill this requirement because the evolution leads to a population of strategies with a mean price well below this threshold. To control the *market share*, a scenario was implemented in which the strategies were assigned a fitness of 0 if they purchased more items than specified by the user. This led to a population that did not exceed the specified market share. However, at the same time, the fixed strategies achieved a higher market share with lower bids. So even though the goal was reached by the population, they performed worse than the fixed strategies. At least, it was shown that GAs can fulfill the goals of a user.

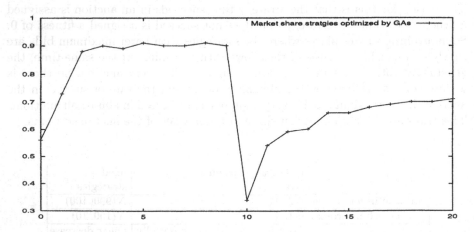

**Fig. 2.** Market share for the strategies optimized by Genetic Algorithms in each generation.

Another important point to take into account is the question how fast the population can adapt to changes in the market. To answer this question, the values for the fixed strategies were changed in the 10th generation: Instead of an initial offer of 900, the fixed strategies now make an initial offer of 1500. This means they are willing to pay 600 more for the items and thus a change in the marketplace is simulated. Also the number of auctions per generation was lowered to two. The changes for the market shares and the prices are given in Figures 2 and 3. From the first generation, it takes 3 generations (6 auctions) until the market share reaches a value that stays constant until generation 10. At that point, the market share drops because of the price increase. This time, it takes 4 generations (8 auctions) until a stable value is reached again. This gives some hints on how long the results of the strategy population stay sub-optimal if a change occurs in the market. However, it is important to note that in real markets, the changes are usually not as dramatic as the changes presented here. So in a slowly changing environment, the Genetic Algorithms could perform even better than the values presented here suggest.

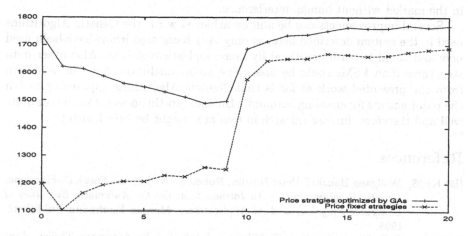

**Fig. 3.** Prices for the fixed strategies and the strategies optimized by a Genetic Algorithm in each generation.

# 5 Summary and Outlook

In this paper, a method to make a population of agents learn strategies for multilateral negotiations (i.e. auctions) in Business-to-Business E-Commerce based on Genetic Algorithms (GAs) has been presented. To model the strategies, Finite State Machines (FSMs) are used as the basic data structure processed by the GAs.

To explore the applicability of GAs as a negotiation mechanism, especially as strategies for auctions, a corresponding prototype auction system was built and several experimental scenarios were implemented. The first scenarios lacked the possibility for the user of the strategies to specify his preferences. It was realized that the most important values for the auctions are the maximum price one is willing to pay and themarket share he wants to reach. In the scenarios implemented later, the user could specify the market share he wants to achieve. This is closely related to the number of items the user wants to purchase. The other possibility is to specify the maximum price the user is willing to pay for the items. In both cases, the strategies behaved as specified by the user. However, at least in a few cases, fixed strategies are still more successful, i.e. reach a higher market share while paying lower prices. Other experiments showed that the population is able to adapt quite quick to changes in the market.

These results show that Genetic Algorithms might provide good strategies for automated negotiations — which can be performed by mobile agents for example (see [TGML98]) — in E-Commerce systems in cases where larger quantities of items are traded in regular time intervals. Auctions are only one way of implementing such systems; other mechanisms to agree on a price could also be tackled by this technique. The main benefit is the automatic adaption to changes in the market without human interference.

Several improvements can be still be achieved w.r.t. the Genetic Algorithms used in the system described here, as only very basic algorithms have been used now and could be easily replaced by more sophisticated GAs. Also other data structures than FSMs could be used. The main conclusion that can be drawn from the presented work so far is that Genetic Algorithms apparently match the requirements for enabling automatic Business-to-Business E-Commerce quite well and therefore, further research in this area might be very fruitful.

# References

[BNKF98] Wolfgang Banzhaf, Peter Nordin, Robert E. Keller, and Frank D. Francone. *Genetic Programming — An Introduction: On the Automatic Evolution of Computer Programs and its Applications*. Morgan Kaufmann Publishers, 1998.

[HU79] J. E. Hopcroft and J. D. Ullman. *Intrduction to Automata Theory, Languages and Computation*. Addison-Wesley, 1979.

[KF98] Manoj Kumar and Stuart I. Feldman. Business negotiations on the internet. Technical report, IBM T.J. Watson Research Center, 1998.

[MIT] MIT Media Lab. Marketmaker. http://maker.media.mit.edu/.

[Oli96] J. R. Oliver. *On Artificial Agents for Negotiation in Electronic Commerce*. PhD thesis, The Wharton School, University of Pennsylvania, 1996.

[TGML98] M.T. Tu, F. Griffel, M. Merz, and W. Lamersdorf. A Plug-In Architecture Providing Dynamic Negotiation Capabilities for Mobile Agents. In K. Rothermel and F. Hohl, editors, *Proc. 2. Intl. Workshop on Mobile Agents, MA'98, Stuttgart*, Lecture Notes in Computer Science. Springer-Verlag, 1998.

[TWL00] M.T. Tu, E. Wolff, and W. Lamersdorf. Genetic Algorithms for Automated Negotiations: A FSM-based Application Approach. In *Proceedings of the 11th International Conference on Database and Expert Systems Applications (DEXA 2000) — e-Negotiations Workshop*, 2000.

# Keeping a Very Large Website Up-to-Date: Some Feasibility Results

HAIFENG LIU   WEE-KEONG NG   EE-PENG LIM

Centre for Advanced Information Systems, School of Computer Engineering
Nanyang Technological University, Singapore 639798, SINGAPORE
awkng@ntu.edu.sg

**Abstract.** As websites grow large and become more sophisticated, organizations use structured database systems as a source of base data for information on the website. Thus, it has become critical to keep a very large website up-to-date in response to the frequent changes in base data. This gives rise to an important issue: Can a website be timely refreshed by executing a set of queries against the base data? In this paper, we investigate the feasibility of scheduling a set of queries to refresh a very large website. Based on two types (*tight* and *loose*) of feasibility requirements, we present feasibility results when the base data change with uniform, regular and random periods. We found that tight feasibility depends on the interval length between two consecutively raised cell refresh requests while it is NP-Hard to determine loose feasibility when the base data have regular or random update periods. For the case when the base data have the uniform update periods, loose feasibility of a set of refresh queries depends on the sum of execution times of the refresh queries.

## 1 Introduction

The popularity of WWW has made it a prime vehicle for disseminating information. More and more corporations and individuals advertise themselves through websites in recent years. Compared to static and dynamic Web pages which are dynamically created by a CGI script at run-time, we focus on *semi-dynamic* Web pages whose contents are extracted from source databases and the contents change in response to updates to the source databases. An example of such a page (Figure 1) can be found at http://www.fish.com.sg where a list of stock information is refreshed frequently with respect to updates to base data. A crucial problem arises when base data change frequently and there is a need to keep a large set of semi-dynamic pages up-to-date in response to source changes since no one is interested in stale data on the Web; an investor may suffer great losses relying on obsolete stock price on the Web.

To perform update on a website that hosts semi-dynamic Web pages, fresh data are "pulled" to the website by executing queries against the source database since the freshness cannot be guaranteed by "pushing" base data from the source databases to the websites. To differentiate between the contents derived from base data and the *trivial* contents of a Web page, we refer to that portion of

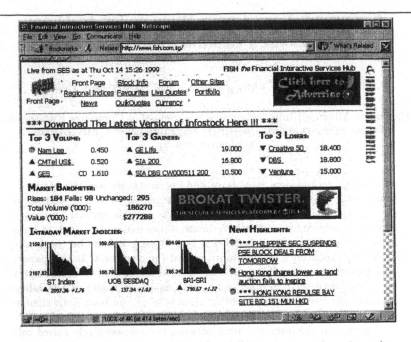

**Fig. 1.** A semi-dynamic Web page whose content comes from base data

a page derived from base data a *Web cell*. Each cell has an associated *refresh query*. The task of refreshing a website is to schedule refresh queries to refresh the Web cells in the website. In our approach, we collect and materialize all cells of a website into a logical *cellbase*. A cellbase functions like a cache and provides fresh data whenever the Web pages must be re-generated.

Generally, a cell is *timely refreshed* once if a single execution of the corresponding refresh query can be started after an update to the base data and completed before the next update to the base data. The aim of website refresh is to timely refresh all the cells in a cellbase constantly. However, this is not easily achievable due to the *update pattern* of base data and the constraint of resources. We approach this problem by considering the case when each base table in the source databases is updated with finite frequency.

According to the "timeliness" or response speed to the update on base data, it is possible to classify cell freshness into two levels: *tight freshness* and *loose freshness*. A cell is *tight fresh* if the corresponding refresh query can be executed instantaneously whenever an update event occurred on the base data, (assuming that the query execution time is far less than the update interval of the base data) . Otherwise, the cell is *loose fresh* if the execution of the refresh query starts with some delay after an update event occurred on the base data but is nevertheless completed before the next source update. For the set of cells in a cellbase, we refer to the corresponding set of refresh queries as the *candidate query set* of the cellbase. If all cells in the cellbase can be kept tight fresh by scheduling the

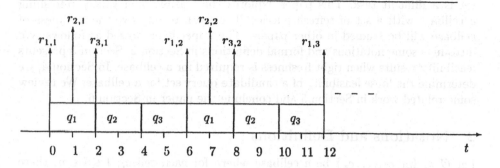

**Fig. 2.** A tight infeasible but loose feasible candidate query set.

queries in the candidate query set, we say that the candidate query set is *tight feasible*. Likewise, if the cells can be kept loose fresh, the candidate query set is *loose feasible*. Note that a tight feasible candidate query set is also loose feasible, but the converse is not true.

For each cell in the cellbase, whenever a relevant update event occurred on the base data, a cell *refresh request* is raised. When tight freshness is required, the refresh request is *timely satisfied* if the corresponding refresh query executes instantaneously; otherwise, the request is *missed*. When loose freshness is required, the request is missed when the execution of the refresh query cannot be started after the request has been raised and completed before the next request is raised. Thus, no refresh requests would be missed for a (tight/loose) feasible candidate query set. Note that since a cell may be derived from multiple base tables that are updated with different periods, the constant interval between the raised refresh requests for the cell, called the *refresh period* of the cell, is restricted to the minimal update period among all base tables. The base table having the minimal update period is called the *feature table* of the cell. Now let us use a simple example to illustrate the tight and loose feasibility of a candidate query set as follows:

*Example 1.* Let $C = \{c_1, c_2, c_3\}$ be a cellbase, where each cell has the same refresh period 6 time units and the first update events on their feature tables occurred at time instants 0, 1, 2 respectively. Queries in its candidate query set $Q(C) = \{q_1, q_2, q_3\}$ take the same 2 time units to execute. As shown in Figure 2, $Q(C)$ is tight infeasible since $q_2$ cannot be executed instantaneously when the first refresh request of $c_2$, denoted as $r_{2,1}$, is raised at time 1. However, $Q(C)$ is loose feasible because for each refresh request of $c_1$, $c_2$ and $c_3$, the execution of the corresponding refresh query can be successfully completed before the next refresh request of the cell is raised. ∎

The example above is simple enough for us to directly tell the feasibility of the refresh query set. However, when we have a large cellbase and cells have different refresh patterns, to determine the feasibility of the corresponding refresh query set is a difficult task. This paper explores the feasibility of timely refreshing a cellbase with a set of refresh queries. The work to improve the freshness of cellbase will be studied in other papers. The paper is organized as follows: We introduce some notations and formal definitions in Section 2. Section 3 presents feasibility results when tight freshness is required for a cellbase. In Section 4, we determine the loose feasibility of a candidate query set for a cellbase. We review some related work in Section 5 and conclude the paper in Section 6.

## 2 Notations and Definitions

Let $C = \{c_1, c_2, \ldots, c_n\}$ be a cellbase where for each cell $c_i$, $1 \leqslant i \leqslant n$, there exists a refresh query $q_i$ that takes $E_{q_i}$ time units to execute to yield $c_i$. Let $\Phi(q_i)$ denote the result set of query $q_i$. Then, $\Phi(q_i) = \{c_i\}$, $1 \leqslant i \leqslant n$, and we refer to $Q(C) = \{q_1, q_2, \ldots, q_n\}$ as the candidate query set of $C$.

**Definition 1 Update Pattern of Feature Table.** Let $b_i$ be the feature table of cell $c_i$. If $b_i$ is updated at a constant period $U_i$, the duration of each update is assumed to be the same and the first update completes at time $t_{i,1}$, then we know the time instants when the subsequent updates complete $t_{i,j} = t_{i,1} + U_i(j - 1)$ ($t_{i,j}$ is the completion time of the $j$th update). Therefore, the tuple $\langle U_i, t_{i,1} \rangle$ is the set of all time instants when the updates on $b_i$ finish and we denote the tuple as the update pattern of $b_i$. ∎

A *refresh request* for a cell is raised whenever its feature table has finished one update. We denote $r_{i,j}$ as the $j$th refresh request for cell $c_i$ raised at time $t_{i,j}$ when $b_i$'s $j$th update finishes.

**Definition 2 Refresh Pattern.** The update pattern $\langle U_i, t_{i,1} \rangle$ of the feature table of cell $c_i$ is the refresh pattern of $c_i$.

**Definition 3 Refresh Pattern Set.** Let the collection of refresh patterns of all cells in cellbase $C$ be represented as $R(C) = \{r_i | r_i = \langle U_i, t_{i,1} \rangle, 1 \leqslant i \leqslant n\}$. Then $R(C)$ is the refresh pattern set for $C$. ∎

The task is to determine the feasibility of $Q(C)$ for a cellbase $C$ with refresh pattern set $R(C)$. Throughout this paper, we assume the following:

1. At any time instant, only one query is executed.
2. The execution of a query cannot be interrupted before it finishes (non-preemptive).
3. The processor minimizes execution waiting time by scheduling outstanding queries for executions as quickly as possible.
4. The execution time of any one query is much less than the update period of any one base table.
5. We assume a logical discrete time unit (clock ticks) where refresh requests are raised and query executions begin and terminate at clock ticks; parameters are expressed as multiples of a clock tick.
6. The first refresh request of a cell is raised at or after time 0 and before its refresh interval elapses, i.e., for any cell $c_i$, $0 \leqslant t_{i,1} \leqslant U_i$.

# 3 Feasibility Results for Tight Freshness Required

In this section, we determine the tight feasibility of $Q(C)$ depending upon different types of refresh pattern set $R(C)$ which is determined by the update pattern of feature tables. Currently, we consider the following cases of refresh periods of cells in the cellbase:

1. All feature tables are updated the same period. Thus, all cells have the same refresh period.
2. Let $U_{min}$ be the minimum among the update periods of all feature tables. Then the update period of other feature tables is a multiple of $U_{min}$; i.e., the refresh period of a cell is a multiple of $U_{min}$.
3. All feature tables are randomly updated with arbitrary periods. Thus, all cells have random refresh periods.

Another factor which plays an important role for feasibility determination is the time instants when the first updates of feature tables complete, i.e., the time instants when the first refresh requests of cells are raised. These requests may be asynchronously raised while satisfying $t_{1,1} \leqslant t_{i,1} < t_{1,1} + U_i$ for any request $r_{i,1}$ from cell $c_i$ where $U_i$ is the refresh period of $c_i$ and $t_{1,1}$ (usually it is set to 0) is the starting time of refresh work (i.e., $c_1$ is the first among all cells who raises the refresh request).

We present the feasibility results for three sub-cases of refresh periods below. Note that due to the space limitation, we omit all proofs of results.

## 3.1 Uniform Cell Refresh Periods

We begin with the simplest case where all $n$ cells in the cellbase $C$ have the same refresh period $\mu$. Thus, the refresh pattern set $R(C) = \{\langle \mu, t_{1,1} \rangle, \langle \mu, t_{2,1} \rangle, \ldots, \langle \mu, t_{n,1} \rangle\}$ where we assume that $t_{i,1} \leqslant t_{j,1}$ for all $i < j$. The feasibility of $Q(C) = \{q_1, q_2, \ldots, q_n\}$, where the execution time for $q_i$, $1 \leqslant i \leqslant n$, is known as $E_{q_i}$ and $E_{q_i} \ll \mu$, depends on the length of time interval between two adjacent starting requests in $R(C)$. We formulate this dependency as a necessary and sufficient condition for feasibility of $Q(C)$ in the following theorem:

**Theorem 4.** *For cellbase $C$ with refresh pattern set $R(C) = \{\langle \mu, t_{1,1} \rangle, \langle \mu, t_{2,1} \rangle, \ldots, \langle \mu, t_{n,1} \rangle\}$, its candidate query set $Q(C) = \{q_1, q_2, \ldots, q_n\}$ is tight feasible $\iff t_{i,1} + E_{q_i} \leqslant t_{j,1}$ for all $i < j$ and $t_{n,1} + E_{q_n} \leqslant t_{1,2}$.* ∎

Clearly, in Example 1, $Q(C)$ is infeasible because $t_{1,1} + E_{q_1} > t_{2,1}$.

## 3.2 Regular Cell Refresh Periods

In reality, it is impractical to require all cells in cellbase to have the same refresh period. So, we relax the restriction such that $U_i = k_i U_{min}$ for all $1 \leqslant i \leqslant n$, where $k_i \in \mathbb{Z}^+$ and $U_{min}$ is the shortest refresh period among all cells in $C$. For

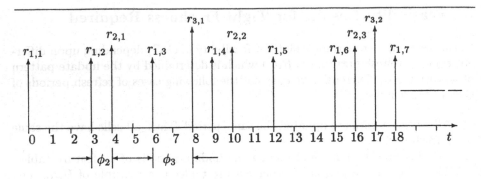

**Fig. 3.** Sequence of refresh requests in Example 2.

convenience, we assume that $c_1$ is the cell which has the shortest refresh period among all cells and the starting time of 0 is used when the first refresh request $r_{1,1}$ of $c_1$ is raised, i.e., $U_{min} = U_1$ and $t_{1,1} = 0$. Then, for all $1 \leqslant i \leqslant n$,

$$t_{1,i} = (i-1)U_1 \tag{1}$$

Next, we introduce the concept of *request phase* of cells to describe the time instants of the first refresh requests of other cells except $c_1$:

**Definition 5 Request Phase.** For all $i \neq 1$, if $t_{1,s_i} < t_{i,1} < t_{1,s_i+1}$, then we define $\phi_i = t_{i,1} - t_{1,s_i}$ as the request phase of $c_i$. ∎

Thus, we have

$$t_{i,1} = t_{1,s_i} + \phi_i \tag{2}$$

. Together with the restriction $t_{i,1} < t_{1,1} + U_i$ and $t_{1,1} = 0$, we have $t_{1,s_i} < U_i$ which leads to

$$s_i < k_i + 1 \tag{3}$$

We illustrate the concept of request phase with the following example.

*Example 2. Given a cellbase $C = \{c_1, c_2, c_3\}$ with refresh pattern set $R(C) = \{\langle 3, 0 \rangle, \langle 6, 4 \rangle, \langle 9, 8 \rangle\}$, the sequence of refresh requests raised is shown in Figure 3. We observe that $t_{2,1} = t_{1,2}+1$, $t_{2,2} = t_{1,4}+1$, ... and $t_{3,1} = t_{1,3}+2$, $t_{3,2} = t_{1,6}+2$, .... Therefore, $\phi_2 = 1$ and $\phi_3 = 2$.* ∎

A candidate query set is tight feasible if the time difference $t_{j,y} - t_{i,x} = \phi_j - \phi_i$ ($t_{j,y} > t_{i,x}$) between any two adjacent requests $r_{i,x}$ and $r_{j,y}$ during $[t_{1,i}+E_{q_1}, t_{1,i}+U_1]$ is greater than $E_{q_i}$, i.e., the request phase difference between $c_i$ and $c_j$ is larger than $E_{q_i}$. Otherwise, there is insufficient time to execute the query $q_i$ to satisfy $r_{i,x}$ and a conflict results if $q_j$ is started to satisfy $r_{j,y}$ at $t_{j,y}$. With these results, we now study the conditions that determine the feasibility of $Q(C)$ when cellbase $C$ has regular cell refresh periods in the following theorem:

**Theorem 6.** *For cellbase* $C = \{c_1, c_2, \ldots, c_n\}$ *with refresh pattern set* $R(C) = \{\langle U_1, t_{1,1}\rangle, \langle U_2, t_{2,1}\rangle, \ldots, \langle U_n, t_{n,1}\rangle\}$ *where* $t_{1,1} = 0$ *and* $U_i = k_i U_1$ $(1 \leqslant i \leqslant n,$ $k_i \in \mathbb{Z}^+)$, *its candidate query set* $Q(C) = \{q_1, q_2, \ldots, q_n\}$ *is tight feasible* $\Longleftrightarrow$

1. *for all* $i \neq 1$, $\phi_i \geqslant E_{q_1}$ *and* $\phi_i + E_{q_i} \leqslant U_1$;
2. *for all* $i \neq j \neq 1$, $t_{i,1} = t_{1,s_i} + \phi_i$, $t_{j,1} = t_{1,s_j} + \phi_j$, *if*
   (a) $s_i = s_j$ *or*
   (b) $s_i \neq s_j$ *and* $\gcd(k_i, k_j) = 1$ *or*
   (c) $s_i \neq s_j$, $g = \gcd(k_i, k_j) \neq 1$ *and* $(s_i - s_j) \bmod g = 0$,
   *then* $\phi_i \neq \phi_j$ *and* $\phi_j - \phi_i \geqslant E_{q_i}$ *if* $\phi_j > \phi_i$; *Otherwise*, $s_i \neq s_j$, $g = \gcd(k_i, k_j) \neq 1$ *and* $(s_i - s_j) \bmod g \neq 0$. $\blacksquare$

In Example 2, because $\gcd(k_2, k_3) = 1$, $\phi_2 = 1$ and $\phi_3 = 2$, according to the above theorem, if $E_{q_2} > (\phi_3 - \phi_2) = 1$, $Q(C)$ would be tight infeasible. Only when $E_{q_2} = 1$ can $Q(C)$ be tight feasible.

## 3.3 Random Cell Refresh Periods

Now we come to the most complicate case where the cells in a cellbase have random refresh periods. However, there is a basic relationship between refresh periods of any two cells: they are either relatively prime or not. Based on this observation and results derived in previous cases, we may still determine the tight feasibility of a candidate query set for the cellbase with random cell refresh periods.

**Lemma 7.** *Given two cells* $c_i$ *and* $c_j$ *with respective refresh pattern* $\langle U_i, t_{i,1}\rangle$ *and* $\langle U_j, t_{j,1}\rangle$, *where* $t_{j,1} > t_{i,1}$, *if* $U_i$ *and* $U_j$ *are relatively prime, then there exist two refresh requests respectively from* $c_i$ *and* $c_j$ *which meet together at the same time.*

For tight feasibility determination, if two refresh requests are raised at the same time, then the candidate query set would not have a feasible schedule because it is impossible to execute two queries at the same time to instantaneously satisfy the requests. Therefore, from the above lemma, if there are any two cells in the cellbase whose refresh periods are relatively prime, then the corresponding candidate query set is tight infeasible. We have the following theorem:

**Theorem 8.** *Given a cellbase* $C = \{c_1, c_2, \ldots, c_n\}$ *with refresh pattern set* $R(C) = \{\langle U_1, t_{1,1}\rangle, \langle U_2, t_{2,1}\rangle, \ldots, \langle U_n, t_{n,1}\rangle\}$ *and candidate query set* $Q(C) = \{q_1, q_2, \ldots, q_n\}$, *if* $Q(C)$ *is tight feasible, then all* $U_i$*s have the common divisor, i.e.,* $U_i = k_i U$, $1 \leqslant i \leqslant n$, $k_i$ *is an integer and* $U$ *is a constant integer.* $\blacksquare$

This theorem is straightforward proved from Lemma 7.

Therefore, after excluding the infeasible cases led by relatively prime cell refresh periods, the case is similar to that in Section 3.2; hence, we shall not rewrite the same result here.

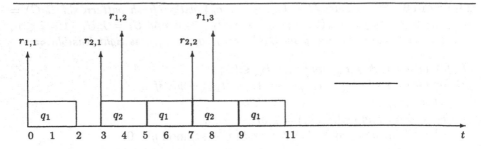

Fig. 4. $Q(C)$ in Example 3 is loose feasible.

# 4 Feasibility Results for Loose Freshness Required

In Section 3, all results are based on the requirement that a cellbase should be kept tight fresh, now we relax the restriction in this section and allow a refresh query to be executed with some delay provided that its execution can be completed before the next update on base data finishes. Thus, cells in the cellbase are kept loose fresh. In this case, multiple refresh requests from different cells may be *pending* (having been raised but not satisfied yet) at the same time instant. Some previous tight infeasible candidate query sets may become loose feasible. We use an example below to illustrate this situation.

*Example 3. Given a set of cells $C = \{c_1, c_2\}$ with refresh pattern set $R(C) = \{\langle 4,, 0\rangle, \langle 4, 3\rangle\}$ and candidate query set $Q(C) = \{q_1, q_2\}$ where $E_{q_1} = E_{q_2} = 2$, $Q(C)$ is tight infeasible according to Theorem 4. However, it is loose feasible (see Figure 4) and all refresh requests can be timely satisfied without any missed requests.* ∎

In rest of the section, we determine the loose feasibility of candidate query set according to three sub-cases of the refresh periods of the corresponding cells: cells with uniform refresh periods, cells with regular refresh periods and cells with random refresh periods.

## 4.1 Uniform Cell Refresh Periods

We start from the simplest case where all cells in cellbase have the same refresh period $\mu$. We determine the loose feasibility of the candidate query set with the following theorem:

**Theorem 9.** *For cellbase $C$ with refresh pattern set $R(C) = \{\langle \mu, t_{1,1}\rangle, \langle \mu, t_{2,1}\rangle, \ldots, \langle \mu, t_{n,1}\rangle\}$, where $t_{1,1} = 0$ and $t_{i,1} < \mu$, its candidate query set $Q(C) = \{q_1, q_2, \ldots, q_n\}$ is loose feasible $\Leftrightarrow \sum_{i=1}^{n} E_{q_i} \leqslant \mu$ where $E_{q_i}$ is the execution time of query $q_i$.* ∎

That is, the feasibility of the query set depends on the sum of query execution times. Example 1 shows such a feasible candidate query set.

## 4.2 Regular and Random Cell Refresh Periods

Now we relax the refresh periods of cells in cellbase $C$ to the regular and random cases as we did in Section 3.2 and 3.3. However, unlike the case when tight freshness is required, it is not a simple task to determine the feasibility of scheduling refresh queries in $Q(C)$ when loose freshness is required. It has been shown in [6] that determining the feasibility of a period task set with arbitrary task releasing times and arbitrary task periods is a NP-Hard problem. We extend the result here.

**Theorem 10.** *Given a cell set $C$ with request pattern set $R(C) = \{\langle U_1, t_{1,1}\rangle,$ $\langle U_2, t_{2,1}\rangle, \ldots, \langle U_n, t_{n,1}\rangle\}$, where $U_i = k_i U_1$ ($k_i \in Z^+$) or randomly generated and $t_{i,1} < U_i$ for all $1 \leqslant i \leqslant n$, to determine the feasibility of $Q(C)$ is NP-Hard in the strong sense.* ∎

## 5 Related Work

Since refreshing cell is performed with a strict timing constraint such that the execution of refresh query must be completed within the interval between two consecutive changes of base data, we may view the refreshing cell as a typical *recurring task* [8] in a *real-time system* that makes repeated requests for processor time. A real-time system is one in which the correctness of the system depends not only on the logical results, but also on the time at which the results are produced [11]. An important goal in real-time scheduling theory is to determine the *feasibility* of the given system that is composed of a set of recurring tasks. Some published feasibility results concerning *preemptive* and *non-preemptive* scheduling over a single processor are collected in [7]. A non-preemptive scheduling policy does not interrupt the execution of any task whereas a preemptive scheduling policy does.

Recurring task systems may be *periodic* or *sporadic*. Because the base data is updated periodically, we are dealing with the case of a periodic task system [1, 4] where each task makes a request for processor time at regular periodic intervals. For non-preemptive scheduling, which is our case, work has been done with *inserted idle time* allowed or not. Without inserted idle time, when a task has been released, it cannot wait before being scheduled if the processor is not busy. As shown in [6], when inserted idle times are not used, feasibility of a periodic task system for all start times can be determined in pseudo-polynomial times. They have also shown that determining feasibility for given start times is NP-Hard in the strong sense. When inserted idle times are allowed, the problem of determining feasibility of a periodic task system for all start times and to find out whether there exist start times for which a given periodic task system is feasible, are both NP-Hard in the strong sense [8].

In our work, we schedule the refresh queries with non-preemptive policy and do not allow inserted idle time. The big difference between our work and previous work is that we distinguish the tight feasibility and the loose feasibility which is concerned by all previous work. Also we derive results for specific (uniform or regular periods) task systems with given task start times. More related work on real-time scheduling can be found in [2, 3, 5, 9, 10].

## 6  Conclusions

To refresh semi-dynamic Web pages whose contents are derived from a source database is a important issue due to the arbitrary update patterns of base data and a large number of refresh queries scheduled on a single processor. In this paper, we view a website as a set of Web cells, each of which is derived by executing a refresh query against the source database. Then, assuming all base tables are periodically updated, we study the feasibility to successfully schedule a set of refresh queries to timely refresh a set of cells. In our future work, we will focus on dealing with the infeasible case such that the maximum freshness of a set of cells can be achieved.

## References

1. C. L. LIU, J. LAYLAND. Scheduling algorithms for multiprogramming in a hard-real-time environment. *Journal of the Association for Computing Machinery*, 20:46–61, 1973.
2. I. BATE, A. BURNS. Schedulability analysis of fixed priority real-time systems with offsets. In *Proceedings of 9th EuroMicro Workshop On Real-Time Systems*, pages 11–13, June 1997.
3. J. LEHOCZKY, L. SHA, J. STRONIDER. Enhanced aperiodic responsiveness in hard real-time environments. In *Proceedings of the Real-Time Systems Symposium*.
4. J. LEUNG, M. MERRILL. A note on preemptive scheduling of periodic, real-time tasks. *Information Processing Letters*, 11:115–118, 1980.
5. J. R. HARITSA, M. LIVNY, M. J. CAREY. Earliest deadline scheduling for real-time database systems. In *Proceedings of Real-Time Systems Symposium*, December 1991.
6. K. JEFFAY, D. STANAT, C. MARTEL. On non-preemptive scheduling of periodic and sporadic tasks. In *Proceedings of the 12th IEEE Real-Time Systems Symposium*, pages 129–139, 1991.
7. LAURENT GEORGE, NICOLAS RIVIERRE, MARCO SPURI. Preemptive and non-preemptive real-time uniprocessor scheduling. Technical Report RR-2966, Inria, Institut National de Recherche en Informatique et en Automatique.
8. R. HOWELL, K. VENKATRAO. On non-preemptive scheduling of recurring tasks using inserted idle times. *Information and Computation*, 117:50–62, 1995.
9. K. RAMAMRITHAM. Allocation and scheduling of precedence-related periodic tasks. *IEEE Transactions on Parallel and Distributed Systems*, 6(4):412–420, April 1995.
10. S. BARUAH, R. HOWELL, L. ROSIER. Algorithms and complexity concerning the preemptive scheduling of periodic, real-time tasks on one processor. *Real-Time Systems*, 2:301–324, 1990.
11. J. A. STANKOVIC. Strategic directions in real-time and embedded systems. *ACM Computing Surveys*, 28(4), December 1996.

# LRU-Based Algorithms
# for Web Cache Replacement

A. I. Vakali

Department of Informatics
Aristotle University of Thessaloniki, Greece
*E-mail: avakali@csd.auth.gr*

**Abstract.** Caching has been introduced and applied in prototype and commercial Web-based information systems in order to reduce the overall bandwidth and increase system's fault tolerance. This paper presents a track of Web cache replacement algorithms based on the Least Recently Used (LRU) idea. We propose an extension to the conventional LRU algorithm by considering the number of references to Web objects as a critical parameter for the cache content replacement. The proposed algorithms are validated and experimented under Web cache traces provided by a major *Squid* proxy cache server installation environment. Cache and bytes hit rates are reported showing that the proposed cache replacement algorithms improve cache content.

*Key-Words :* Web-based information systems, Web caching and proxies, Cache replacement algorithms, Cache consistency.

## 1 Introduction

The continuously rapid growth and worldwide expansion of the Internet has introduced new issues such as World-Wide Web (WWW) traffic, bandwidth insufficiency and distributed objects exchange. Web caching has presented an effective solution, since it provides mechanisms to faster web access, to improved load balancing and to reduced server load. Cache efficiency depends on its content update frequency as well as on the algorithmic approach used to retain the cache content reliable and consistent. Several approaches have been suggested for more effective cache management and the problem of maintaining an updated cache has gained a lot of attention recently, due to the fact that many web caches often fail to maintain a consistent cache. Several techniques and frameworks have been proposed towards a more reliable and consistent cache infrastructure [5, 7]. In [2] the importance of various workload characteristics for the Web proxy caches replacement is analyzed and trace-driven simulation is used to evaluate the replacement effectiveness. The performance and the homogeneity of Web caching is studied in [1] where a new generalized LRU is presented as an extension to the typical SLRU algorithm. Hit ratios and robustness of the proposed replacement algorithm is compared with other Web replacement policies using both event and trace-driven simulations.

Performance improvements due to Web caching have been investigated in order to estimate the value and importance of Web caching. Research efforts have focused in maintaining Web objects coherency by proposing effective cache replacement policies. A number of Web replacement policies are discussed in [3], and compared on the basis of trace-driven simulations. A web-based evolutionary model has been presented in [12] where cache content is updated by evolving over a number of successive cache objects populations and it is shown by trace-driven simulation that cache content is improved. A Genetic algorithm model is presented in [13] for Web objects replication and caching. Cache replacement is performed by the evolution of Web objects cache population accompanied by replication policies employed to the most recently accessed objects.

This paper presents a new approach to Web Cache replacement by proposing a set of algorithms for cache replacement. The proposed set of algorithms is based on the popular *Least Recently Used* (*LRU*) algorithm which replaces from the Web cache the objects that have not been requested for the longest time. Thus LRU uses only the time of the last request to a Web object and this time is the critical factor for an objects purge from the Web cache. Here, we introduce a variation of LRU which considers a "history" of Web objects requests. A similar approach was presented in [10] for the page replacement process in database disk buffering. The main idea is to keep a record for a number of past references to Web objects, i.e. a history of the times of the last $h$ requests is evaluated for each cached Web object. This approach defines a whole set of cache replacement algorithms called History LRU (notation *HLRU(h)*). A number of HLRU algorithms is experimeneted under Squid proxy cache traces and cache log files.

The remainder of the paper is organized as follows. The next section introduces and formulates the cache replacement problem. Section 3 presents the typical LRU and the proposed HLRU algorithms whereas Web proxies ans their performance issues are presented in Section 4. Section 5 discusses implementation and validation details and results from trace driven experimentation are presented. Section 6 points some conclusions and discusses potential future work.

## 2 The Cache Replacement Problem

Web proxies define a limited cache area, for storage of a number of Web objects. Once the cache area is almost filled there has to be a decision to replace some of the cached objects with newer ones. Therefore, a cached Web object "freshness" has to be determined by specific rules and in Web caching terminology an object is considered *stale* when the original server must be contacted to validate the existence of the cache copy. Object's staleness results from the cache server's lack of awareness about the original object's changes. Each proxy cache server must be reinforced with specific staleness confrontation. The most important parameters corresponding to attributes of each cached object are summarized in Table 1.

| parameter | description |
|-----------|-------------|
| $s_i$ | server on which object resides. |
| $b_i$ | object's size, in KBytes. |
| $t_i$ | time the object was logged. |
| $c_i$ | time the object was cached. |
| $l_i$ | time of object's last modification. |
| $f_i$ | number of accesses since last time object $i$ was accessed. |
| $key_i$ | objects original copy identification (e.g. its URL address). |

**Table 1.** The most useful attributes of each cached object $i$.

**Definition 1** : The cached object's *staleness ratio* is defined by,

$$StalRatio_i = \frac{c_i - l_i}{now - c_i}$$

where the numerator corresponds to the time interval between the time of object being cached and the time of the object's last modification and the denominator is the cache "age" of the object i.e. it determines the time that the object has remained in cache. It is always true that $StalRatio_i \geq 0$ since $c_i - l_i \geq 0$ and $now - c_i > 0$ (*now* is the current time). The lower the value of $StalRatio_i$ the more stale the object $i$ is, since that indicates that it has remained in cache for longer period.

**Definition 2** : The cached object's *dynamic frequency* is defined by

$$DynFreq_i = \frac{1}{f_i}$$

since $f_i$ is the metric for estimating an object's access frequency (Table 1). It is true that the higher the values of $DynFreq_i$, the most recently was accessed.

**Definition 3** : The cached object's *retrieval rate* is defined by

$$RetRate_i = \frac{lat_s}{band_s}$$

where $lat_s$ is the latency to open a connection to the server $s$ and $band_s$ is the bandwidth of the connection to server $s$. $RetRate_i$ represents the cost involved when retrieving an object from its original storage server.

**Definition 4** : The cached object's *action function* is defined by

$$act_i = \begin{cases} 0 \text{ if object } i \text{ will be purged from cache} \\ 1 \text{ otherwise} \end{cases}$$

**Problem Statement** : If $N$ is the number of objects in cache and $C$ is the total capacity of the cache area, then the cache replacement problem is to :

$$\text{MAXIMIZE} \quad \sum_{i=1}^{N} act_i \times StalRatio_i \times \frac{DynFreq_i}{RetRate_i}$$

$$\text{subject to} \quad \sum_{i=1}^{N} act_i \times b_i \leq C$$

where the fraction $\frac{DynFreq_i}{RetRate_i}$ is used as a weight factor associated with each cached object, since it relates the objects access frequency with its retrieval rate.

## 3  LRU and HLRU Cache Replacement

LRU cache replacement is based on the Temporal Locality Rule which states that "The Web objects which were not referenced in the recent past, are not expected to be referenced again in the near future". LRU is widely used in database and Web-based applications. For example, in Squid, the LRU is used along with certain parameters such as a *low watermark* and a *high watermark* to control the usage of the cache. Once the cache disk usage is closer to the low watermark (usually considered to be 90%) fewer cached Web objects are purged from cache, whereas when disk usage is closer to the high watermark (usually considered to be 95%) the cache replacement is more severe i.e. more cached Web objects are purged from cache. There are several factors as of which objects should be purged from cache.

**Definition 5 [ LRU Threshold ]** : A value identified as *threshold* is needed for estimating the expected time needed to fill or completely replace the cache content. This threshold is dynamically evaluated based on current cache size and on the low and high watermarks. When current cache size is closer to low watermark the threshold gets a higher value, otherwise when current cache size is closer to high watermark the threshold value is smaller.

One of the disadvantages of the LRU is that it only considers the time of the last reference and it has no indication of the number of references for a certain Web object. Here we introduce a scheme to support a "history" of the number of references to a specific Web object.

```
for (i=left boundary; i<=right boundary; i++)
{     if (hashTable[i]. OldtimeOfAccess = = 0)
      {     ++counterOfObjectswithOneAccess;
            if (counterOfObjectswithOneAccess > 1)
                  break;
      }
}
if (there is >1  object with only 1 access)
      for (i=left boundary; i<=right boundary; i++)
            if (the object i had more than one accesses)
                  age[i] = CurrentTime – hashTable[i]. OldtimeOfAccess;
            else
                  age[i] = CurrentTime – hashTable[i]. NewtimeOfAccess;
else
      for (i=left boundary; i<=right boundary; i++)
            if (the object i had more than one accesses)
                  age[i] = CurrentTime – hashTable[i]. OldtimeOfAccess;
            else
                  hashTable[i].empty = true;

qsort(hashTable);

for (i=left boundary; i<=right boundary; i++)
{     if (not an emergency purge)
      {     if (position is full)
                  if (the age of object i > LRU threshold)
                  {
                        object is purged;
                        time the object stayed in cache =
                              CurrentTime - hashTable.timeOfFirstAccess;
                        current cache swap - = object's size;
                  }
      }
      else   // the case of an emergency purge
      {     if ( i <= left boundary of the bucket + 8 )
                  if ( position i is not empty )
                  {
                        purge the object;
                        time the object stayed in cache =
                        CurrentTime – hashTable.timeOfFirstAccess;
                        current cache swap - = object's size;
                  }
      }
}
```

**Fig. 1.** The History LRU cache replacement algorithm.

**Definition 6 [ History Function ] :** Suppose that $r_1, r_2, \ldots, r_n$ are the requests for cached Web objects at the times $t_1, t_2, \ldots, t_n$, respectively. A history function is defined as follows :

$$hist(x, h) = \begin{cases} t_i \text{ if there are exactly } h-1 \text{ references} \\ \quad \text{between times } t_i \text{ and } t_n \\ 0 \text{ otherwise} \end{cases}$$

The above function $hist(x, h)$ defines the time of the past $h$-th reference to a specific cached object $x$.

Therefore, the proposed HLRU algorithm will replace the cached objects with the maximum $hist$ value. In case there are many cached objects with $hist = 0$, the typical LRU is considered to decide on which object will be purged from cache. The same idea of the threshold value (to decide when the cache replacement will occur) still holds. In Table 2 the main structure of the cache hash

| LRU | HLRU |
|---|---|
| struct *HashTable* | struct *HashTable* |
| {   long *LRU_age* | {   int *OldTimeOfAccess* |
|     long *positionInFile* |     long *positionInFile* |
|     boolean *empty* |     boolean *empty* |
|     long *timeOfFirstAccess* |     long *timeOfFirstAccess* |
| }   *hashTable*[50000] | }   *hashTable*[50000] |

**Table 2.** The main LRU and HLRU data structure

table is presented. For LRU each cached object is assigned an *LRU_age* to indicate the time since its last reference. Variable *positionInFile* declares the position the specific object has in the file, whereas the boolean type variable *empty* indicate whether the specific cache location is empty or not. Finally, variable *timeOfFirstAccess* is used for the time the specific object was cached. The HLRU data structure is quite similar, there are two different times kept for each cached object. *OldTimeOfAccess* is the time the cached object was first referenced whereas *NewTimeOfAccess* is the time of the last reference to the cached object. Similarly, Figure 1 presents the implemented HLRU algorithm in a pseudocode format, for the case of two ($h = 2$) past references. Under HLRU a linked list has been used for each cached object in order to keep track of the times of past references.

## 4   Web Proxies - Performance Issues

The performance metrics used in the presented approach focus on the cached objects cache-hit ratio and byte-hit ratio :

- **Cache hit ratio :** represents the percentage of all requests being serviced by a cache copy of the requested object, instead of contacting the original object's server.
- **Byte hit ratio :** represents the percentage of all data transferred from cache, i.e. corresponds to ratio of the size of objects retrieved from the cache server. Byte hit ratio provides an indication of the network bandwidth.

The above metrics are considered to be the most typical ones in order to capture and analyze the cache replacement policies (e.g. [3, 1, 2]).

Furthermore, the performance of the proposed cache replacement algorithms is studied by estimating the strength of the cache content. This strength is evaluated by the consideration of the cached objects retrieval rates as well as their frequency of access and their "freshness". In order to evaluate the HLU algorithms we have devised a function in order to have a performance metric for assessing the utilization and strength of the cache content. The following formula $F(x)$ considers the main web cache factors as identified in the Cache replacement problem statement in Secion 2. Here, we consider a cache content $x$ of $N$ individual cached objects :

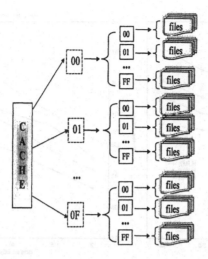

**Fig. 2.** Structure of the Squid proxy cache area.

$$F(x) = \sum_{i=1}^{N} act_i \times StalRatio_i \times \frac{DynFreq_i}{RetRate_i} \qquad (1)$$

The above function has been introduced in the present research effort in order to consider the effect of staleness, access frequency and retrieval cost in the overall cache replacement process.

## 5 Experimentation - Results

Aristotle University has installed Squid proxy cache for main and sibling caches and supports a Squid mirror site. The present paper uses traced information provided by this cache installation for experimentation. A simulation model was developed and tested by Squid cache traces and their corresponding log files. Traces refer to the period from May to August 1999, regarding a total of almost 70,000,000 requests, of more that 900 GB content. A compact log was created for the support of an effective caching simulator, due to extremely large access logs created by the proxy. The reduced simulation log was constructed by the original Squid log fields needed for the overall simulation runs.

A track of the proposed HLRU algorithms has been tested. More specifically the notations $HLRU(2)$, $HLRU(4)$ and $HLRU(6)$ refer to the HLRU implementations for 2, 4 and 6 past histories respectively. Furthermore, the typical LRU cache replacement policy applied in most proxies (e.g. Squid), has been simulated in order to serve as a basis for comparisons and discussion.

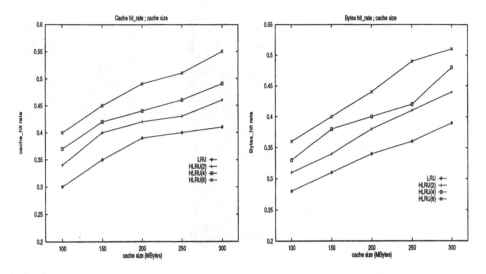

**Fig. 3.** Cache and Bytes hit; cache size

The performance metrics used in this simulation model focus on the cached objects cache-hit ratio, byte-hit ratio and the strenth function $F(x)$ (equation 1) normalized to the interval [0,1]. Figure 3 depicts the cache hit and the bytes hit ratio for all four algorithms with respect to cache size. More specifically, the left part of Figure 3 presents the cache hit ratio for a cache size of $100, 150, \cdots, 300$ MBytes. The cache hit under $HLRU(6)$ policy outperforms the corresponding metric of all other policies whereas all $HLRU$ algorithms have better cache hits than the corresponding typical LRU approach. This was expected due to the ability of the $HLRU$ approach to keep track of a history of past references. It should be noted that the cache hit ratios seem to get to a peak and remain closer to this peak value as the cache size increases. This is explained due to the fact that the larger the cache size, the less replacement actions need to be taken since there is more space to store the cached objects and the cache server can "afford" to accommodate them there with less replacement actions. Figure 3 (right part) depicts the byte hit ratio for the four different cache replacement policies with respect to the cache size. The byte hit ratios follow a similar skew as the corresponding cache hit ratios, but they never get in as hit high values as cache hit ratios. a smoother curve as the cache size increases. Again $HLRU(6)$ algorithm is the best of all and as the byte hit rates decrease as the number of past references (history set) decreases.

Figure 4 depicts the cache hit and the bytes hit ratio for all four algorithms with respect to the number of requests. More specifically, the left part of Figure 4 presents the cache hit ratio for a cache of $50, 150, \cdots, 250$ thousands of requests. Again, the cache hit under $HLRU(6)$ policy outperforms the corresponding metric of all other policies whereas all $HLRU$ algorithms have better cache hits than the corresponding typical LRU approach. It is important to note

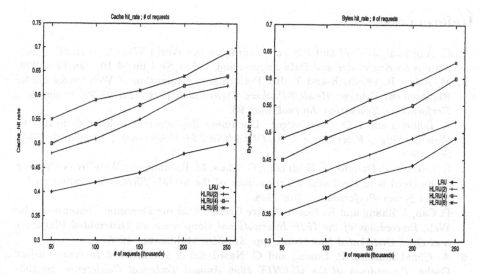

**Fig. 4.** Cache and Bytes hit; # of requests

that all approaches show better results as the number of requests increases and
the cache hit rates do get to considerable hit rates of almost 70%.

## 6  Conclusions - Future Work

This paper has presented a study of applying a history based approach to the
Web-based proxy cache replacement process. A history of past references is associated to each cached object and a track of algorithms has been implemented
based on a number of past histories. Trace-driven simulation was used in order
to evaluate the performance of the proposed cache replacement techniques and
the simulation model was based on the Squid proxy cache server. The experimentation indicated that all of the proposed HLRU approaches outperform the
conventional Least-Recently-Used (LRU) policy adopted by most currently available proxies. Results have shown that the HLRU approach significantly improves
cache hit and byte hit ratios.

Further research should extend current experimentation and the present
scheme in order to integrate most popular cache replacement algorithms. More
specifically, different schemes such as SLRU, MFU, RR algorithms could be introduced in the proposed cache replacement in order to study their impact and
effectiveness on the Web cache content replacement.

## Acknowledgments

The author thanks Panayotis Junakis (System administrator) and Savvas Anas-
tasiades (technical staff) of the Network Operation Center at the Aristotle University, for providing access to the Squid cache traces and trace log files.

# References

1. C. Aggarwal, J. Wolf and P.S.Yu: Caching on the World Wide Web,*IEEE Transactions on Knowledge and Data Engineering*, Vol.11,No.1,pp.94-107,Jan-Feb 1999.
2. M. Arlitt, R. Friedrich and T. Jin: Performance Evaluation of Web Proxy Cache Replacement Policies, *Hewlett-Packard Technical Report HPL 98-97, to appear : Performance Evaluation Journal*, May 98.
3. A. Belloum and L.O. Hertzberger : Document Replacement Policies dedicated to Web Caching , *Proceedings ISIC/CIRA/ISAS'98 Conference* , Maryland, USA, Sep. 1998.
4. R. Caceres, F. Douglis, A. Feldmann, C. Glass, M. Rabinovich : Web Proxy Caching : The Devil is in the Details, *Proceedings of the SIGMETRICS Workshop on Internet Server Performance*, Jun 1998.
5. P. Cao, J. Zhang and K. Beach: Active Cache : Caching Dynamic Contents on the Web, *Proceedings of the IFIP International Conference on Distributed Platforms and Open Distributed Processing* , pp. 373-388, Middleware 1998.
6. A. Chankhunthod, P. Danzig and C. Neerdaels: A Hierarchical Internet Object Cache, *Proceedings of the USENIX 1996 Annual Technical Conference*, pp.153-163,San Diego,California,Jan 1996.
7. S. Michel, K. Nguyen, A. Rosenstein and L. Zhang: Adaptive Web Caching : Towards a New Global Caching Architecture, *Proceedings of the 3rd International WWW Caching Workshop*, Manchester, England, Jun 1998.
8. A Distributed Testbed for National Information Provisioning, http://ircache.nlanr.net/, 1998.
9. M. Nottingham: Web Caching Documentation, http://mnot.cbd.net.au/cache_docs/, Nov 1998.
10. E. J. O'Neil, P. E. O'Neil, and G. Weikum : The LRU-K Page Replacement Algorithm For Database Disk Buffering, *Proceedings of the ACM SIGMOD Conference*, pp.297-306, Washington DC, USA, 1993.
11. Squid: Squid Internet Object Cache, mirror site, Aristotle UNiversity, *http://www.auth.gr/Squid/*, 1999.
12. A. Vakali: A Web-based evolutionary model for Internet Data Caching, *Proceedings of the 2nd International Workshop on Network-Based Information Systems, NBIS'99*,IEEE Computer Society Press, Florence,Italy, Aug 1999.
13. A. Vakali: A Genetic Algorithm scheme for Web Replication and Caching, *Proceedings of the 3rd IMACS/IEEE International Conference on Circuits, Systems, Communications and Computers, CSCC'99*, World Scientific and Engineering Society Press, Athens, Greece, Jul. 1999.

# A Step towards a Suite of E-commerce Benchmarks

Dawn Jutla[1], Peter Bodorik[2], and Yie Wang[2],

[1]Faculty of Commerce, Saint Mary's University
dawn.jutla@stmarys.ca
[2]Faculty of Computer Science, Daltech, Dalhousie University
{bodorik, ywang}@cs.dal.ca

**Abstract.** A benchmark is used to measure and compare the performance of like systems. It is also used to estimate the scalability of a system in terms of the number of users and/or transactions that a system can support and system response times under different loads and hardware/software deployment platforms. Because of the multidimensional aspects of e-commerce and the various emerging and distinct e-commerce business models, one single benchmark is not suitable for the purposes of examining scalability and determining throughput and response time of e-commerce applications. This paper advocates development of suites of benchmarks based on distinguished business models that represent existing and emerging e-commerce applications in terms of their distinct features. In particular, the paper develops a benchmark for one such business model, a model that is based on a cybermediary or electronic broker, e-broker. Two implementations of the benchmark specification are described: one based on Microsoft's COM technology while the other one is based on CORBA technology. Sample benchmark results are presented and discussed. The paper also proposes a framework for development of a suite of e-commerce benchmarks.

## 1 Introduction

Benchmarking is important as it is used to measure and compare the performance of like systems under controlled conditions. Equally importantly, it is also used to determine the characteristic performance of a system under various scenarios. Typical use of a benchmark is in determining the scalability of a system in terms of the number of users and/or transactions that a system can support and system response times under different loads and hardware/software deployment platforms.

Benchmarks for individual components are currently available. Webperf is a benchmark for web servers [1]. It calculates throughput in HTTP operations per second and client response times per HTTP operation. WebSTONE [2] measures the performance of an HTTP server, which facilitates the evaluation of different implementations of HTTP specification. The Wisconsin Benchmark [3] systematically measures and compares the performance of relational database systems with database machines. Benchmark Factory [4] provides prepackaged scalable benchmarking and load-testing tools.

The Transaction Processing Performance Council (TPC) defines a suite of benchmarks, including TPC-C, TPC-H, TPC-R, and TPC-W [5]. Earlier benchmarks, TPC-A and TPC-B are outdated. The TPC-C benchmark models a typical business OLTP environment, the TPC-H (Ad-hoc, decision support) benchmark represents decision support environments, while the TPC-R (Business Reporting, Decision Support) benchmark represents decision support environments where users run a standard set of queries against a database system. The TPC-W is a transactional web benchmark. It emulates business activities of a web server while accessing DBs and external servers.

E-commerce exhibits multidimensional aspects and operates in various environments and, consequently, different e-commerce business models have been developed. The models exhibit distinctive characteristics in terms of the user-server interaction, the number of DBs accessed, transactions' characteristics, and the business rules employed. One single benchmark is thus unsuitable for the purposes of examining scalability and determining throughput and response time of diverse e-commerce applications. As a consequence of this, we argue that one benchmark, such as TPC-W, is not sufficient for e-commerce, but rather a suite of benchmarks is required. We propose that a framework for a suite of benchmarks be developed based on e-commerce business models.

Three distinct classes of e-commerce business models were described in [6]: e-broker, manufacturer and auction models. Each model represents a category of existing e-commerce applications. Michael Rappa [7] provides a taxonomy of nine forms for business models for the web. We advocate development of a suite of benchmarks based on distinguished business models that represent existing and emerging e-commerce applications in terms of their distinct features. To start learning about development of benchmarks for business models, we created and used the benchmark for a business model that we were familiar with, the cybermediary or electronic broker model, or e-broker model for short. The objective was to learn about the process in order to develop an appropriate framework for development of a suite of benchmarks. Two implementations of the benchmark specification are described: one based on Microsoft's COM technology while the other one is based on CORBA technology. Sample benchmark results are also presented and discussed in order to demonstrate the usefulness of the benchmark when examining the effect of distinct technologies on performance and also when examining the scalability of the application.

The paper is organized as follows. Section 2 very briefly describes the e-broker business model and the proposed benchmark. Section 3 briefly outlines the two implementations while Section 4 presents and compares the benchmarking results. Section 5 proposes an e-commerce benchmark framework for development of a suite of benchmarks based on business models. The final section provides a summary and concluding remarks.

## 2 WebEC Benchmark for the E-broker Model

The intermediary (e-broker) business model includes querying multiple online supplier databases, requesting services from third party businesses and responding to the consumer. In addition to the online consultation of the suppliers' databases, credit verification at a third party financial-service company (e.g. bank) is required. For further details on the e-broker business model, see [6].

The e-broker model benchmark is targeted to the small-to-medium enterprises (SMEs). Business transaction definitions (browse, user registration, buy, shopping cart and order status), except for the buy transaction, are generic to any e-commerce site that serves as an e-broker. The benchmark design includes page navigation, a set of internal and external relations/tables, and transactions. They are discussed here only briefly – for further details interested readers should consult [8].

The set of web pages that users navigate through includes: Welcome Page, Category Page, Products by Category Page, Product Page, Shopping Cart Contents Page, User Registration Page, Credit Card Info Page, Order Status Page, Order Confirmed and Thank-you Page. With the exception of the pages for user registration and credit card information, pages have search and browsing to other pages and from pages transactions are invoked.

DBs accessed by the e-broker are either local or remote. The local database consists of twelve individual tables. The e-broker accesses remote DB of a finance company and tables of remote DBs of four suppliers. The partner suppliers hold trusted relationship with the e-broker.

The benchmark specifies a web e-commerce transaction processing (OLTP) workload. Some transactions are simple in that they result in a simple request-reply interaction between the customer/browser and the web-server. Some transactions cause access to a single either local or remote DB. Examples are Stock Level Update and Order Status transactions. The complex nested Buy transaction is a heavyweight read-write transaction that triggers several sub-transactions, namely the registration transaction, the credit verification check, the online supplier contact, the internal delivery, the customer history update, and the order confirmation. Paying by credit card is chosen as the payment method and the Secure Socket Layer (SSL) is used as the security protocol.

When a transaction accesses a remote DB, it is a distributed transaction spanning different remote resource managers, e.g., remote database management systems (DBMSs) residing on the partner suppliers. In case of the distributed Buy transaction that spans a number of DBs, 2-Phase Commit protocol is used. (The 2-Phase Commit is assumed as the organizations operate as trusted partners.)

# 3 WebEC Benchmark DCOM and CORBA Implementations

This section briefly describes two implementations of the benchmark, one using Microsoft's COM/DCOM technology while the other one using Iona's CORBA technology. Both implementations use the same Java transaction generator and are based on the standard three-tier client/server model, as described in [9], containing the data services, business services, and user services tiers. The transaction generator and the two implementations are described in this section. For further details on the COM and CORBA implementations see [10] and [8], respectively.

The transaction generator is written in Java to manage the running of the WebEC benchmark. The generator decides navigation of pages and which transactions are to be executed. The transactions are generated based on the percentages of a mix of transactions that is specified in the input workload. A deck card algorithm is used to generate the appropriate number of transactions of each type. One or more cards in a deck are associated with each transaction type. The required mix is achieved by selecting each new transaction uniformly at random from a deck whose content guarantees the required transaction mix. Pages are navigated through the browser while the generator waits a "key time" period to simulate user input and waits a "think time" period to simulate the user's examination of the page and decision making on the next action (navigation, input, or transaction).

Next described is an example implementation of the WebEC benchmark using Microsoft's Component Object Model (COM) / Microsoft Transaction Server 2.0 (MTS) / Internet Information Server 4.0 (IIS) / ActiveX Server Page 2.0 (ASP) platform (see Figure 3.1). The client accesses the Web server through the Internet. The client application is implemented using Active Server Page technology that adopts server-side scripting to dynamically create HTML responses. The clients' application is written using the ASP script language. IIS serves as the web server that accepts ASP requests from the ASP page sent from the client's browser.

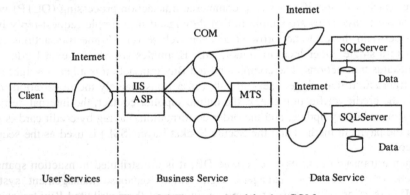

**Figure 3.1** Three-tier Model using COM

The business service subsystem consists of Microsoft Internet Information Server (IIS), Active Server Page (ASP) engine, Component Object Model (COM) elements, and Microsoft Transaction Server (MTS). Although only two DBs are shown in the figure, they represent more then two. Along with the IIS and ASP servers that reside on the middle tier, we include the Microsoft Transaction Server (MTS) as transactional middleware. MTS groups and manages the COM objects that consist of the business logic components that interact with various transactional systems, such as remote SQL Server or Oracle databases. Interaction with the DBs is using ActiveX Data Objects (ADOs) through Open Database Connectivity (ODBC). MTS is tightly integrated with IIS and the ASP engine.

Next described is an example implementation of the WebEC benchmark using Iona's CORBA technology. The client is a Java applet downloaded by a Web browser. The middleware is the OrbixOTS server and business components. These business components are shopping cart component, customer registration component, buy component, order status component, category browsing component, product by category browsing component, product browsing component, and stock level component. All business components are implemented as C++ classes. The third tier consists of RDBMSs.

Figure 3.2 illustrates the typical workflow of the WebEC benchmark. It demonstrates how the Web-based client interacts with its server.

1. The client makes the initial requested for a page.
2. Web browser receives and downloads an HTML page that includes references to embedded Java applets.
3. Web browser requests the Java applet from the HTTP server.
4. The HTTP server retrieves the applet and downloads it to the browser in the form of bytecodes. Web browser loads applet into memory.
5. Applet invokes CORBA server objects. The Java applet includes the IDL-generated client stub classes, which let it invoke objects on the ORB server.
6. Server objects access the database according to the defined business logic.
7. Server objects return the results back to the Web client, and the results are displayed on the client's browser.

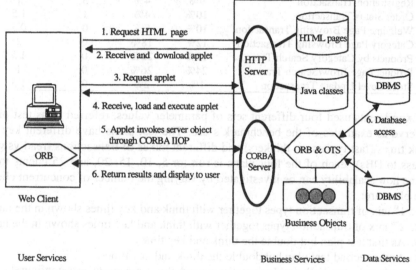

**Figure 3.2** The Workflow of WebEC Benchmark for CORBA Implementation

# 4 Experiments

The purpose of the experiments is to examine the usefulness of the benchmark when considering deployment technology of an e-commerce application and when examining the issue of scalability. It should be noted that the experiments were performed in a university lab setting with low-end equipment.

The performance metrics, response time and transaction throughput are measured while varying the "think time", the "key time", the transaction mix, and the number of clients. The percentages of transaction types are illustrated in Table 4.1. The first mix of transactions supports a ratio of 32% order-related transactions (Shopping Cart, Buy, User Registration and Stock Update) and 68% browse-type transactions (Welcome Page, Category Page, Products by Category, Product Page, Search and Order Status). The second transaction mix represents 22% order related and 78% browse type transactions. The $1^{st}$ mix has almost twice the number of buy transaction than the $2^{nd}$ one (11% vs. 6%). Transaction types are selected at random while maintaining the required percentage-mix for each transaction type over the measurement interval. The table also illustrates the think and keys times used in experiments.

**Table 4.1** Percentages of Mixed Transactions

| Business Transaction Types and Key and Think Times | $1^{st}$ Mix | $2^{nd}$ Mix | Key Time(sec) | Think Time(sec) |
|---|---|---|---|---|
| Shopping Cart Transaction | 11% | 10% | 0 | 1.5 |
| Buy Transaction | 11% | 6% | 1 | 2 |
| Registration Transaction | 9% | 4% | 3 | 1 |
| Order Status Transaction | 10% | 4% | 1 | 1.5 |
| Welcome Page Browsing Transaction | 10% | 8% | 0 | 0.5 |
| Category Page Browsing Transaction | 12% | 18% | 0 | 2 |
| Products by Category Search Trans. | 12% | 22% | 0 | 1.5 |
| Product Page Brow/Search Trans. | 24% | 26% | 0 | 1 |
| Stock Level Update Transaction | 1% | 2% | 0 | 1.5 |

Experiments used four different sets of parameter values, referred to as test plans, to serve as examples of the benchmark's use. The test plans have different key and think times (fast typists vs. thinkers) and different mixes of transactions (read vs write access to DBs). Each of the four plans is run for 5, 10, 15, 20, and 25 clients to examine how scalability can be investigated by varying the number of concurrent clients. The plans are:

1. $1^{st}$ mix of transaction types together with think and key times shown in the table.
2. $2^{nd}$ mix of transaction types together with think and key times shown in the table.
3. As first test plan but double the think and key times.
4. As the second test plan but double the think and key times.

Experiments for both implementations used the same hardware configuration of low-end platforms consisting of three 133 MHz Intel PCs with 32 MB RAM, and one 233 MHz Intel PC with 128 MB EDO SIMMS and EIDE hard disks. One of the 133 MHz PCs was running both the web server and also the local DB server. Configuring both web and DB server on one platform is not recommended in general (reasons why we did this will become apparent later). The other PCs were running the bank's and the suppliers' DB servers. The network configuration was identical in both cases. The difference between the two implementations was the middle-tier layer. One implementation was based on COM/DCOM with the components implemented using Visual Basic, while the other one was based on CORBA with the business logic implemented using C++ classes. [10] and [8] present detailed specification for the hardware and software platforms.

Figures 4.1 and 4.2 show the respective throughput and response time for the COM and CORBA implementations. In both cases the first four bars are for the COM cases while the last four bars for the CORBA ones.

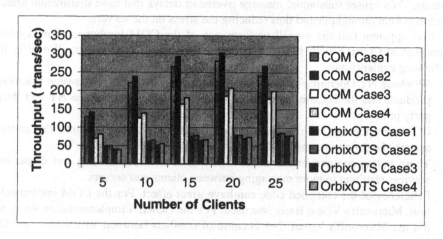

**Figure 4.1** Throughput for COM and CORBA Implementations

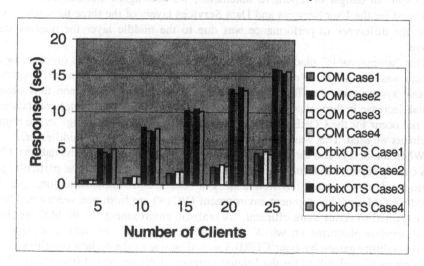

**Figure 4.2** Response Times for COM and CORBA Implementations

For COM implementation, the throughput is almost twice as high in test plans 1 and 2 as opposed to 3 and 4 that are for "slower" users. The distinction between case 1 and 2 (and between 3 and 4) is that the former is more write oriented, containing more of the buy transactions that stress the system and lead to lower throughput. Also, note that the throughput appears to peak for 20 users and additional users actually cause decline in throughput! The reason is the "strange arrangement" of housing both the web and DB server on one system.

For CORBA, the throughput rises almost in a linear fashion. The distinction between the slow and fast users is not as pronounced as for the COM implementation. The response time increases in what appears to be linear fashion with the number of clients. OTS causes substantial message overhead delays that have detrimental affects on the system throughput and thus reducing the stress on the servers.

It is apparent that the overall performance of the COM implementation is better than that of CORBA both in terms of throughput and response time. We offer the following explanations:

- Windows NT Operating system was used. Clearly, interactions between Microsoft products and the NT are far more efficient than those between the NT and third-party products.
- COM components are dlls, which means that they are linked into the address spaces of existing processes while CORBA components are not.
- There is less communication under COM. CORBA uses naming and dispensing services resulting in more messaging between clients and servers.
- Efficiency of the compiled code can have great effect. For the COM implementation, Microsoft's Visual Basic was used. For the CORBA implementation we could not use Mircosoft's Visual C++ because of conflicts between Visual C++ and Orbix.

In spite of danger of repetitive statements, we note again that the same software was used for the User Services and Data Services layers of the three-tier architecture. Thus the difference in performance was due to the middle layer for reasons stated above.

Our "unreasonable" placement of both web and local DB servers on one low-end system was intentional. We expected to observe saturation of CPU and disk resources on that system with a sufficient increase in the number of clients and thus observe actual decrease in throughput. This indeed occurred for the COM implementation. It did not occur for the CORBA implementation at least not for the range in the number of clients we used. This was due to high messaging overhead in the middle tier.

When the delays and throughput are compared for the two implementations, COM was clearly superior in terms of efficiencies. This was expected for the particular platforms and development environment. For the COM implementation, the OS, COM/DCOM, and development environment (VC++) are from one vendor and hence are expected to result more efficient. A realistic environment for WebEC would include various platforms on which clients and servers run. In such a scenario, the interoperability gained by using CORBA would be one of the highest priorities.

In terms of scalability, for the limited number of clients tested (maximum of 25), the CORBA implementation did not appear hit bottleneck when scaling up to 25 clients. For the COM implementation, the throughput clearly peaks at 20 clients.

Obviously, we do not claim that the quantitative results are representative in terms of the magnitude of numbers - the experiments were performed in a university lab setting with low-end equipment. The experiments, however, clearly demonstrate the usefulness of benchmarking on the two fronts examined in detail here: choice of technology and scalability.

# 5 Application Framework for E-commerce Suite of Benchmarks

The WebEC benchmark differs from the TPC-W benchmark in the composition of DBs, transactions, and load generated on the system. Yet, it is also similar to TPC-W, in general, in terms of the type of DBs, transactions and user behavior. Without a supporting argument we claim that both benchmarks, WebEC presented here and the TPC-W benchmark, are instances of the e-broker model. Thus, if an application framework can be developed for benchmarks based on the e-broker model, then both WebEC and TPC-W could be generated "easily" using the framework. (An application framework is generic software targeted for a particular application domain. It provides interfaces and structures in such a way that it can be (easily) customized into a complete application.) Based on the implementation experiences, we propose that a framework for benchmarks based on the e-broker model be developed. Furthermore, the framework must provide for customization of the following components:

- *Internal and external DBs*: Definition of DBs housed internally by the organization and also externally (DBs of trusted or un-trusted partners).
- *External services*: External services need to be used, for instance for credit checks and payments.
- *User related*: How information is presented to users (e.g., composition of pages) and user-behavior need to be emulated as they impact the system performance.
- *Load generation* (internal and external): Load can be generated internally, for instance for the purposes of report generation and data mining, or externally, as a result of user requests or execution of agents. Generation of transaction mixes is needed.
- *Transactions representing business logic*: User requests result in invocation of transactions that can range in complexity from very simple to very complex.
- *System structure*: The framework's generic software must be able to generate a system structure that captures the major system implementation decisions dealing with the implementation technologies.

The objective of the framework is not only the generation of the benchmark load but also generation of a software system that closely represents the final e-commerce application. We are currently developing an application framework that satisfies such requirements.

# 6 Summary and Conclusions

This paper described WebEC, a benchmark for the e-broker business model of e-commerce. The benchmark's transactions, databases, navigational layout, security, and mix of transactions were presented. Implementations using Microsoft's COM/DCOM technology and also CORBA technology were also described. The two implementations of the WebEC comprise first steps towards a framework for development of a suite of benchmarks for e-commerce. The suite should be viewed as an initial tool towards selecting appropriate technology and platforms and examining potential performance and scalability of chosen solutions.

An e-commerce platform can be assembled from various combinations of web servers, transaction servers, commerce servers, web browsers, security protocols, database connectivity solutions, and operating and DBMS systems. E-commerce benchmarks are of value to IT professionals and managers in the decision making process for final IT investment. The benchmarks aid IT managers in determining the number of users that a system can support, system response times under various loads, and estimations of scalability.

# References

1. Webperf, http://playground.sun.com/pub/prasadw/webperf, (1997)
2. Trent, G. and Sake, M., "WebSTONE: The First Generation in HTTP Server Benchmarking," White paper, MTS Silicon Graphics, (1995)
3. Wisconsin Benchmark, http://benchmarkresources.com/ handbook/4-1.html
4. Benchmark Factory, http://www.benchmarkfactory.com (1997)
5. Transacion Processing Council, http://www.tpc.org.
6. D. Jutla, P. Bodorik, C. Hajnal, C. Davis, Making Business Sense of Electronic Commerce, IEEE Computer, March 1999, pp. 65-76.
7. M. Rappa, *Business Models on the Web*, in http://ecommerce.nscu.edu/business_models.html.
8. Cao Lihong., "CORBA Implementation Of the WebEC", Masters of Computer Science, Faculty of Computer Science, Dalhousie University, Halifax, Nova Scotia, Canada, 1999.
9. R. Jennings, *Database Workshop – Microsoft Transaction Server 2.0*, SAMS Publishing, Indianapolis, Indiana (1997)
10. Wang Y., "WebEC: An Electronic Commerce Benchmark", Masters thesis, Faculty of Computer Science, Daltech, Dalhousie University, Halifax, Nova Scotia, Canada, December 1998.

# A Business Model for Charging and Accounting of Internet Services

Helmut Kneer[1], Urs Zurfluh[1], Gabriel Dermler[2], Burkhard Stiller[3]

[1]Institut für Informatik IFI, University of Zürich, Switzerland, {kneer, uzurfluh}@ifi.unizh.ch
[2]IBM Research Laboratory, Zürich, Switzerland, dermler@zurich.ibm.com
[3]Computer Engineering and Networks Laboratory TIK,
Swiss Federal Institute of Technology, ETH Zürich, Switzerland, stiller@tik.ee.ethz.ch

**Abstract.** The fast growing development of electronic commerce within the past few years and the increasing number of multimedia applications for the Internet contribute to traffic congestion and bottlenecks on the Internet. Since bandwidth is and will remain a scarce network resource in the future, the demand for charging and accounting mechanisms for the Internet arose.

Besides from the implementation of charging and accounting mechanisms for Internet services, it is essential to define a business model for electronic business applications. This paper introduces a business model that defines and characterizes the business entities and describes their roles and functions within an e-commerce scenario. Based on these definitions, a technology model applies the different Internet technologies available today.

## 1 Introduction

Within the field of electronic commerce a variety of services and products is offered and purchased by means of an underlying network infrastructure that connects customer and merchant. Since the Internet was introduced in 1969 by a military project of the American Defense Department (ARPANET), it was developed to span most parts of the world today. Hence, the Internet as a global network infrastructure is ideal to do business electronically.

The critical point with Electronic Business is the delivery and the performance across the Internet since too much traffic traverses through the backbones of the ISPs' networks. Packet-switched Internet applications are very susceptible to congestion since their quality strongly depends on network parameters such as data throughput, bandwidth, and latency. Unfortunately, packet forwarding in today's Internet only works on a best-effort base which results in a poor quality for multiplexed audio or video streams, especially in times when the network is congested.

One solution to overcome this problem is to classify Internet traffic and charge the customers according to the transport service the ISPs provide. Usage-based pricing schemes consider charges for the actual amount of consumed network resources [17]. Charging and accounting of Internet services effects the Internet traffic in such a way that the classified traffic of the different applications is treated fairly according to their service level and price [19]. This means that the ISPs have to establish a basis for a multi-service-level Internet in which different service levels are offered and the desired Quality-of-Service (QoS) can be guaranteed. This would help (1) the ISPs to cover their operating costs by collecting usage fees from their customers and (2) the customers to receive the desired QoS that they chose and paid for. IP telephony, as an example for such a multi-level Internet application, was investigated in [20].

Apart from the implementation and realization of charging and accounting mechanisms, there has to be a business model that defines processes and phases from the initiation of the electronic business to the final payment for a product or service. Three levels of abstraction are proposed within this paper that are essential for charging and accounting of Internet services, (1) the business level, (2) the contract level, and (3) the network level. The business model describes on the business level what parties there are, what roles and functions they have, and what business relationships are essential for performing electronic business. Contracts and agreements are necessary between the parties to stipulate the business conditions and to declare the service performance. On the contract level, the parties are considered liable entities that are responsible for the delivery of the service according to the defined service conditions. Network components and architectures are explored on the network level forming the underlying network infrastructure and implementing designed business processes of the business model that were contractually defined on the contract level.

It is the cooperation of the many entities, the widespread business environment, and the competition among the parties that make the whole business model a challenge for charging and accounting on the Internet. There are trusted and un-trusted relationships among the business entities and some parties do not even know each other, e.g., the end-customer does not know all of the intermediate ISPs that are engaged in establishing the network connection to the ESP. There are security risks and threats for all involved parties, which are analyzed and identified in order to develop a security architecture [12] based on the business model [10] and the trust model [23]. The security architecture introduces a concept for secure business transactions based on five security-relevant aspects.

This paper is organized as follows. Starting on the business level, the business model is described in Section 2 for the e-commerce scenario between an end-customer, an ESP, and intermediate ISPs. Section 3 illustrates on the network level technical possibilities and characteristics of the Internet protocol architecture, which is important for the actual implementation of charging and accounting mechanisms. Section 4 introduces on the contract level the usage of Service Level Agreements (SLA) as a mechanism to ensure QoS based end-to-end communication, before a summary of results will conclude the paper in Section 5.

## 2 Business Model

A business model includes the course of business events and reflects the processes within an economic system. The economic system introduced in this paper consists of a simple business relationship between a customer and a merchant doing business over the Internet. In terms of electronic business systems, the merchant can be modelled by an Electronic Commerce Service Provider (ESP), and the customer by an end-customer, which simply means that this is an end point of a communication connection (cf. Figure 1).

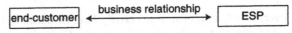

**Figure 1:** E-commerce business relationship.

The ESP offers products, contents, and services online via the World Wide Web (WWW) and represents the merchant or the seller of a good. Products offered by the ESP include physical goods that could also be purchased in stores, *e.g.*, books, cars, CDs, etc. Contents offered by the ESP comprise digital information as non-tangible goods in form of bits and bytes. Content includes for example the digital content of an online book or the digital version of a CD that can be downloaded onto the end-customer's local disk. Furthermore, there is a broad spectrum of multimedia contents and services (*e.g.*, audio-on-demand or video-on-demand) offered by the ESP online to the customers across the Internet. A CD online shop could offer the service to pre-listen to a CD before the customer decides to make the purchase. Another form of electronic commerce service offered by the ESP is the possibility for the end-customer to make data backups onto the ESP's storage medium.

The offers of the ESP can be retrieved by end-customers from all over the world using a web browser. Thus, the end-customer represents the buyer of a good. The end-customer may be a private individual or a commercial customer such as an enterprise or a university.

The basic idea of an economic system between an end-customer and an ESP is well understood and theoretically feasible. Problems arise with the introduction of performance and QoS for the delivery of Internet services. Internet Service Providers (ISP) provide the physical infrastructure for the Internet but also the technical network equipment like routers, switches, and network management software and form the basic foundation of all electronic commerce activities. ISPs provide the transport of data packets over the Internet between end-customer and ESP. However, traffic congestion and unreliable connections on the best effort Internet describe a problem for transmitting data, especially if high bandwidth and reliable throughput is required (*e.g.*, multimedia applications). ISPs could overcome this problem by charging the end-customers according to the transport service they request.

The focus of this paper is on the business model for realizing the business relationship between the ESP and the end-customer using ISPs for charging and accounting of transport services. Therefore, an e-commerce scenario was developed with an end-customer and an ESP on both ends, and several intermediate ISPs. Figure 2 shows the business relationships between all the involved parties of such a scenario. There might also be a payment provider involved in this scenario that is responsible for the financial clearing between the parties. The payment provider can be represented by a bank, a credit institution, or a Trusted Third Party (TTP).

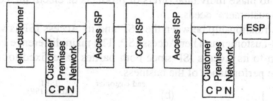

**Figure 2**: Relationships between involved parties of an e-commerce scenario.

The ISPs are divided into Access ISPs and Core ISPs according to their scope of duties. Access ISPs support Local Access Networks and provide Internet connections to the end-customer, be it directly or through a Customer Premises Network (CPN). Core ISPs increase the reach of Access ISPs to a global extent and form the backbone of the Internet. They perform the data transport service interconnecting Access ISPs. There may be more than one core ISP involved in a communication connection between end-customer and ESP, depending on the connectivity of ISPs and their local distances. In case there is only one ISP involved between end-customer and ESP, it acts as both Access ISP and Core ISP providing the data transport service. Thus, Access ISPs and Core ISPs may be physically similar.

It is possible that end-customers are affiliated to a Customer Premises Network (CPN), *e.g.*, a LAN of an enterprise or a university. A CPN represents a group of users in terms of a common policy and conceals the individual end-customer from the Access ISP. A CPN may offer additional private applications or extra conditions for data transport services to its end-customers. An end-customer can be connected either to a CPN or directly to the Access ISP, if the end-customer is a residential user. There may be multiple end-customers involved in one communication connection in case of a conference system.

## 2.1 Phases of the Business Model

In order to realize such an e-commerce scenario, as described in Figure 2, the involved parties need to cooperate and interact with each other. General rules and business conditions have to be set up between the end-customer, the ESP, and the involved ISPs. The business processes within the business model can be described by four coherent phases, an initial contracting phase, a reservation phase, a service phase, and a final clearing phase. Figure 3 (a) shows graphically the coherence of the different phases that are described in the following.

**Contracting Phase.** The contracting phase is the initial phase for the business entities before any products or contents are purchased or any services are performed. The different cooperating parties need to get to know each other, establish or maintain business connections to their partners, and arrange business conditions and contractual agreements for later businesses and services. Four different kinds of business relationships are investigated within this paper that need to be set up before any electronic business can be done, assuming that there is no CPN involved and the end-customer is a residential user connected directly to her Access ISP. There are relationships between (1) end-customer and ESP, (2) end-customer and Access ISP, (3) Access ISP and Core ISP, and (4) Access ISP and ESP (as can be seen in Figure 2).

The relationship between the end-customer and ESP does not require contracts or agreements. The end-customer simply logs in at the ESP's homepage to buy products or contents or to order a service. The log in process could be performed anonymously where the end-customer does not reveal any personal information about her identity. If the ESP offers the service to register its frequent customers, the end-customer can sign up declaring personal business related data. The ESP might have user profiles of its customers to keep track of their records in order to make individual offers of products or electronic commerce services tailored to the end-customers' needs.

The business relationship between the ESP and its Access ISP is very similar to the one between the end-customer and her Access ISP. The main difference is the fact that the ESP is always known to its Access ISP since both parties have fixed locations and anonymity would hinder the performance of the business.

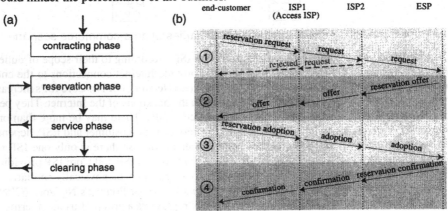

**Figure 3**: (a) Sequence of coherent phases of the business model.
(b) Reservation messages exchanged between the different parties.

The relationship between the end-customer and the Access ISP is established as soon as data needs to be transferred between the ESP and the end-customer. It is a special relationship since the Access ISP works as a broker or general contractor that offers the end-customer access to the Internet and represents a contact point for any data transport service to a sending or receiving ESP. Skeleton agreements are set up between the end-customer and the Access ISP that stipulate future business conditions and legal aspects. Within the contracting phase, the Access ISP creates user accounts for the end-customer which contain among others charging and billing information, monthly spending limits, or special types of reservations (*e.g.*, fixed weekly reservations of a data transport service). If the end-customer wants to remain anonymous and unknown to the Access ISP, the contracting phase may be skipped.

The relationship between Access ISP and Core ISP, or two general ISPs respectively, is formed by negotiations on traffic contracts and SLAs that regulate on the contract level the amount of incoming and outgoing traffic through the network of an ISP. The ISPs strive for maintaining a dense network infrastructure for their customers in order to deliver a data transport service with a guaranteed QoS. SLAs between the ISPs are made statically before any data transport service is performed but they can be changed and adjusted dynamically during operation if the network situation changes throughout the service delivery or the end-customer wants to change service parameters. Service Level Agreements for QoS-based communication is discussed in detail in Section 4 on the contract level.

**Reservation Phase.** The end-customer has decided to buy a content or service with the ESP and thus needs an Internet connection to exchange data with the ESP. Within the reservation phase, the end-customer reserves network resources with her Access ISP since it represents the starting point for subsequent network transport.

In a first sub-phase, the login phase, the end-customer chooses her Access ISP and requests a data transport service to the ESP. In a second sub-phase, the specific information phase, the Access ISP could provide its end-customer some interesting information about the short-term market situation, network traffic, or price comparisons with other ISPs. This information could vary for different registered or anonymous end-customers. Auctions could be used to find the best/cheapest/shortest connection between the end-customer and the ESP on a market where bandwidth and network resources are offered and sold [17]. The Access ISP, as a broker or a general contractor for the end-customer, is responsible for the execution and maintenance of the delivered service. Traffic contracts and SLAs were set up in the contracting phase already to organize traffic flows through the networks of the ISPs.

The actual reservation of a data transport service or a simple price query takes place within the negotiation phase, as a third sub-phase of the reservation phase. The reservation of network resources for single flows on the Internet is performed in four steps according to the RSVP protocol [25], [7].

In the first step, the end-customer sends out a signal to her Access ISP to indicate a reservation request (cf. Figure 3 (b)). This request contains information about the kind of reservation (*e.g.*, application, point of time, and duration), a scheme for charge sharing (end-customer pays only, ESP pays only, both pay), and parameters defining the QoS for the application. These parameters could include among others the bandwidth indicating the performance (bit/s), the transfer quality (max. fault-probability, encryption), routing parameters, or the maximum delay time. The flow specification, or flowspec, of RSVP contains the service requirements for the application and characteristics of the traffic stream or flow [3], [21], [14]. The request is sent across other (Core/Access) ISPs (in case there are other ISPs) to the ESP, which replies with a reservation offer, if it accepts the end-customer's request. If one ISP or the ESP does not agree upon the request, it may reject the request and send the denial back to the end-customer (dotted line in Figure 3 (b)). In this case, the negotiation starts anew.

In the second step of the negotiation process, the ESP replies to the reservation request with a reservation offer informing the end-customer on acceptance or denial of the reservation request. The reservation offer is sent the same way back to the end-customer, where different ISPs reserve the requested resources for that particular flow or they add pricing information in case it was only a price request [20]. If one party does not accept the reservation offer, the end-customer must re-send the reservation request with different parameters.

The third and fourth step of the negotiation phase (reservation adoption and confirmation) are optional and can be used to add sender or receiver provided electronic payments if, for example, reservation fees are required or payments have to be made in advance [7]. This four-step negotiation phase has to be run through for every newly requested service or if the end-customer wants to extend the currently performed service.

**Service Phase.** After the data transport service has been reserved within the previous reservation phase, the actual service can be performed within the service phase. The data transport service is delivered by the Access ISPs and eventually several intermediate Core ISPs according to the previously defined QoS parameters.

Of particular importance for ISPs and the payment of the service is the question, whether the end-customer is a known business partner, and thus can be trusted, or whether she decided earlier in the contracting phase to remain anonymous. In case the end-customer has registered with her Access ISP earlier in the contracting phase, charging, billing, and eventually payment for the service is done in the subsequent clearing phase (by post-paid payments).

If the end-customer is an anonymous business partner, she has to pay before the service is performed due to a lack of trust and security. Pre-paid payments could be made (1) from pre-paid accounts, (2) online with debit, credit, or some pre-paid money card, or (3) by some sort of electronic money that could eventually be included in the reservation adoption message (for end-customer payments) or the reservation confirmation message (for ESP payments). Depending on the charge sharing scheme, both end-customer and ESP pay their share for the service. If ISPs do not get money from the end-customer/ESP beforehand, they can immediately release the allocated resources for the reserved service. After the delivery of the service, the end-customer can go back to the reservation phase and request a new service or try to extend the currently performed service with similar QoS parameters.

**Clearing Phase.** The clearing phase contains the charging, billing, and the payment for the delivered data transport service. If the end-customer decided to remain anonymous, payments were made already within the service phase and thus the clearing phase can be skipped. Charging and billing includes the process of transforming the collected accounting records for the end-customer into monetary units and summarizing them on a bill [7]. The bill contains the used network resources and the delivered services within a certain period of time (e.g., one month) and the corresponding pecuniary value.

Different billing and payment schemes are possible and discussed in [9]. The best possibility is to perform billing and payment through the Access ISP who collects single bills from ISPs to combine them to one bill and redistributes the payment back to corresponding ISPs. Another possibility is that every involved ISP sends a separate bill to the end-customer and receives the payment for the service. There might even be a payment provider involved in the whole clearing process as a Trusted Third Party (TTP) assuming control over billing and payment. Payments can be made with debit or credit card, or simply by a transfer of funds.

The clearing phase is terminated when every ISP received its money. The end-customer can go back to the reservation phase and start reserving a new service again. An optional sub-phase for customer support could be appended which gives the ISP(s) the chance to receive feedback from the end-customer (*e.g.*, via questionnaire) regarding the performance of the service or special customer-related problems and suggestions (*e.g.*, special services for frequent customers).

435

## 2.2 Billing of the Content

Although this paper is focusing on charging and accounting mechanisms for transport services on the Internet, it is important to consider charges for the content combined with the transport. This subsection gives a quick description of relevant factors that decide, whether it is favorable to charge content together with the transport service or not. Figure 4 (a) shows the primary influencing factors, namely the relative value of content (defined as the value of content divided by the cost of transportation) and the required end-customer anonymity. Not the amount of bytes settle the value of the content, but the market price.

For low values of content it is more efficient to charge and bill the content together with the transport service either on one bill or through a pre-paid calling card. A separate bill for the content will be provided for registered end-customers, if the relative value of content is higher than the middle threshold (approximately around 10). If the end-customer likes to be anonymous and the relative value of content is between the low and the high threshold (approximately between 5 and 50), pre-paid money cards can be used to pay for the content. Extremely valuable content (above the high threshold) requires pre-paid accounts on the ESP's side with secret access codes. Both middle and high values of content should only be charged when the transfer was successful, e.g., a big data file was received correctly.

Figure 4 (b) shows secondary influencing factors deciding, whether to bill separately for the content or together with the transport service. There is the number of logically independent content blocks per time and the value of content per time. Logically independent blocks of content are discrete and contain direct useful information. A feed of financial information (e.g., stock rates) consists of many independent data packets which are billed continuously. A backup file or a high resolution image file can be seen as one big block of content. If only one intermediate packet gets lost, the transmission failed and no billing should be performed.

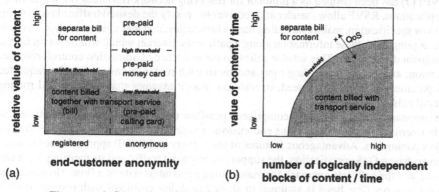

(a) end-customer anonymity

(b) number of logically independent blocks of content / time

**Figure 4**: Influencing factors for a separate billing of the content.

Transmission of a high number of logically independent blocks of content with a low value of content (lower right corner of Figure 4 (b)) is billed together with the transport service, if the QoS for the transport service is below a certain threshold. If the QoS for the transport service increases (QoS threshold moves to upper left in Figure 4 (b)), the relative value of content decreases and billing of the content is performed with the transport service.

## 3 Internet Protocol Architectures

Providing charging and accounting services on the Internet requires a number of technical prerequisites. As of recently, the Internet has performed on a non-commercial basis and charging services have not been necessary or foreseen. However, with the commercialization of the Internet as a networking infrastructure and the Internet services offered, this point of view changes. In particular, once an end-customer has to choose from, say, two different service classes, a best-effort one and another one delivering some sort of bandwidth guarantees, a purely technical solution of providing these classes is not sufficient anymore. The reason is hidden in the greedy nature of almost every, certainly the majority of end-customers – they will choose the service class with the best QoS. Of course, if this is the case, the service class with less QoS will become obsolete, since it is not used. In turn, users encounter similar problems within the better class of service due to its heavily congested usage. This situation will remain unchanged as long as no financial incentives on choosing a service class, which is perfectly suited for the end-customer's needs, are provided by the Internet.

Today's Internet does not offer any service differentiation mechanisms, since the best-effort type of service still dominates. In addition, the basic protocol is defined by the Internet Protocol (IP) [16], which is currently used in its version 4 and does not provide any service class differentiation features besides the Type-of-Service (TOS) field. Nevertheless, this field is only optionally used within IPv4 on a broad scale. Some future enhancements, or better changes, to determine IPv6 is being prepared by the IETF [5], including a flow label field [15] and an extended TOS field. However, today two distinct Internet protocol architectures are used as approaches towards a service discriminated Internet.

### 3.1 Integrated Services Internet (IntServ)

IntServ defines a networking framework, which supports unidirectional end-to-end flows [4]. These flows may request a certain QoS and may use a Controlled Load Service [24] or a Guaranteed Service [18]. However, every flow needs to establish a context between the sender, the receiver, and intermediate nodes. Therefore, the Resource ReSerVation Protocol (RSVP) [3] has been defined as a protocol for reserving network resources for single flows of applications. RSVP allows sender and receiver to specify the desired traffic class in terms of a flow specification, mainly including bandwidth, delay, and loss characteristics. Furthermore, it propagates these information along a path in the Internet which will be set up for the subsequent data packets. This scheme relies on the existence of admission control, resource allocation, and packet forwarding mechanisms in each router to ensure that the requested QoS parameters can be guaranteed. In addition, RSVP assumes that a QoS-based routing protocol exists.

In summary, the IntServ model comprises a per-flow reservation of network resources for single Internet applications from one end-customer to another with a certain pre-defined set of QoS parameters. Advantageous features of the IntServ and RSVP approach encompass a receiver-driven QoS specification, the support of multicast traffic and its merging for reservations, and the soft state approach for maintaining the context data of a flow. However, the support on a per flow-basis is assumed to show scalability problems with respect to large number of flows and states to be kept in large backbone routers. The per-flow granularity imposes overhead which may not be necessary for a certain number of situations. Service classes in IntServ distinguish between best-effort and guaranteed services. The application of the business model as described in Section 2 has been performed for guaranteed services, which require a resource reservation based on RSVP.

### 3.2 Differentiated Services Internet (DiffServ)

Due to these assumed scalability and overhead problems in case of many single flows, a different framework was developed recently. Instead of treating a single flow as the entity of interest, the Differentiated Services Internet (DiffServ) handles Internet traffic based on the notion of aggregated flows and fixed numbers of service levels in terms of service profiles [2]. This approach minimizes the state to be kept in routers. In addition, this is supported by a domain-concept, where a group of routers implements a similar number of service levels and the appropriate set of policies. This DiffServ domain is defined by a fixed boundary, consisting of ingress and egress routers. However, traffic traversing such a DiffServ domain is required to be marked. This marking happens on a per IP packet-basis at the ingress routers and utilizes the DiffServ (DS) field in an IP packet [13]. This DS field replaces the TOS field from the IPv4 protocol and allows the definition of per-hop behaviors (PHB), which in turn determines the service level such a packet will be treated by. Once the DS Code Point as part of the DS field has been set, the packet "tunnels" through the DiffServ domain being treated equally in every interior router. Similarly as within IntServ, an aggregated DiffServ flow of flows is considered to be unidirectional.

Since single end-to-end flows are bundled to aggregated flows with a similar behavior within a DiffServ domain, the DiffServ approach requires less overhead. However, the need to mark IP packets at the DiffServ borders remains. In addition, a longer termed service contract may be required between different DiffServ domains, since a certain service level may be required. This type of flow aggregation in conjunction with service guarantees require some sort of admission control, since an over-utilization may lead to service degradations. Regularly, so-called Service Level Agreements (SLA) are set-up between interconnecting ISPs in order to maintain the desired service level for the aggregated flows. An initial SLA needs to be set up between interconnected ISPs before any service is performed. SLAs can also be adjusted dynamically. Basic details on SLAs are provided in Section 4.

### 3.3 Comparison and IntServ over DiffServ

As presented above, IntServ as well as DiffServ show a number of advantages and drawbacks. Based on six classification criteria, Table 1 depicts the main differences for IntServ, DiffServ, and best-effort traffic types in the Internet.

**Table 1** Comparison of IntServ and DiffServ

|                    | Best-effort    | IntServ                    | DiffServ                        |
|--------------------|----------------|----------------------------|---------------------------------|
| QoS Guarantees     | no             | per data stream            | aggregated                      |
| Configuration      | none           | per session (dynamic)      | long-term (static)              |
| Zone               | entire network | end-to-end                 | domain-oriented                 |
| State Information   | none           | per data stream (in router) | (none, in BB, in edge router)   |
| Protocols          | none           | signalling (RSVP)          | bit field (DS Byte)             |
| Status             | operational    | matured                    | worked on                       |

The integration and combination of IntServ and DiffServ advantages is possible. Local Area Networks (LAN) tend to show an overprovisioning of bandwidth, which does not require a sophisticated resource management and signalling, if a certain topology and traffic considerations are taken into account. The Access Network, however, utilizes RSVP to signal flow requirements from senders to the Core Network. Edge routers perform a mapping of these requirements onto particular flow aggregation types available in the DiffServ core and represented by a dedicated SLA. Since core routers purely perform traffic forwarding based on PHBs, they are able to cope with many aggregated flows. Only edge routers need to keep the state of flows from their local domain.

# 4  Service Level Agreements for QoS-based Communication

Inter-provider agreements are employed between ISPs to capture the terms of service for exchanged traffic. As in a commercial environment, an offered service is an item which may be sold or purchased. An inter-provider agreement represents a contract-like relationship indicating the characteristics of the covered service and implied financial settlements.

Traditionally, within the Internet, ISPs engage in interconnection agreements in order to assure each other pervasive Internet connectivity. Such agreements allow engaging ISPs to exchange traffic at an interconnection point, either with or without financial settlements [1]. Traditionally, these agreements do not consider QoS related issues.

More recently, Service Level Agreements (SLAs) are used as a means to establish a provider/customer type of relationship between two providers. While the exact content of an SLA often depends on the specific business and technology context, the core of an SLA always includes a description of the traffic covered by the SLA and the service level which is to be applied. SLAs provide the contractual envelope for QoS based assurances.

## 4.1  DiffServ SLAs

The mentioned IntServ approach of the IETF does not refer to business related entities. In contrast, the DiffServ approach is based on the notion of network domains which can be operated by different ISPs. In a pure DiffServ world, both access and core domains would use DiffServ technology to transfer data within their domains as well as between domains. In order to indicate service commitments between domains, Service Level Agreements (SLAs) are employed.

DiffServ SLAs are defined on the contract level, abstracting from the type of underlying physical network connectivity, which is assumed to be given per se. Due to the ability of DiffServ to classify traffic, SLAs can be defined for various aggregations of flows, for instance based on the source or destination IP addresses. According to the envisaged support of DiffServ for multiple service classes, an SLA also specifies a selected service class. Thus, a DiffServ SLA includes:

- a description of the aggregated flow to which the SLA is applicable,
- the corresponding throughput, and
- the corresponding service class (*e.g.*, assured/premium service, determining QoS, delay or loss characteristics).

In principle, DiffServ SLAs can be defined at any granularity level, including the level of application flows. As DiffServ pursues the goal of high scalability, only a limited set of SLAs is likely to exist between any two domains, such that explicit support of individual flows through DiffServ SLAs will likely be an exception.

## 4.2  Commercial SLAs

SLAs have emerged in the commercial domain as a result of increasing customer demand to reliably understand what kind of service they actually can expect from an Internet Service Provider. Such SLAs are typically tied to the provision of a network service on a long-term basis. Service provision includes both the installation of physical equipment (*e.g.*, routers, access lines) as well as the provision of a data transport service (*e.g.*, based on IP protocols).

In order to capture QoS aspects, SLAs include similar parameters as considered in the DiffServ case. As an example, the SLA employed by UUNET [22] foresees the following:

- the throughput offered to customers (*e.g.*, T1),
- round-trip latency across the provider's network,
- the availability of the service,

- outage notification duration,
- duration between order and installation, and
- reimbursement procedure in case of non-compliance.

Both mentioned SLA approaches tend to serve the same purpose: establish *longer-term service* relationships between adjacent ISPs and provide assurances for *traffic aggregates* exchanged between them. These approaches avoid the overhead implied by a high number of concurrent SLAs and frequent changes in the terms of agreements.

### 4.3   Flow-based SLAs

In principle, the SLAs above may be applied at the service interface between Access ISPs and their end-customers. However, given that in the access domains per-flow handling of traffic is a viable option, a different approach is feasible which offers superior flexibility in applying charging schemes to QoS based traffic.

First, it is likely that QoS support within the Internet will, for a long time, not be pervasive. Whenever a QoS based flow is requested, the availability of such support has to be established depending on the source and destination end-points as well as the sequence of ISPs involved. Providing SLAs dynamically on a per-flow basis allows to take such dependencies into consideration and automatically adapt to increasing Internet support for QoS.

Second, considering QoS automatically implies a strong differentiation among Internet services. QoS can be provided at multiple levels (e.g. to support various audio qualities). In consequence, there is a need for differential, QoS dependent pricing in order to prevent users from making use of the best QoS level only. Similarly, applying differential pricing is required in order to reflect the communication path (i.e. ISPs) traversed including the source and destination locations. Both aspects lead to service prices which can be established only if the characteristics of a requested flow are known, i.e. on a per-flow basis.

Third, there is an ongoing discussion about pricing schemes that should be applied to Internet traffic. Dynamic pricing of offered services based on a current level of network usage was shown to improve the service characteristics a network can provide, for instance reduce congestion and smooth traffic [8], respectively. Assuming such an approach, both the implied QoS level and the provided price are to be established dynamically for each new flow.

Providing flow-based SLAs captures all the mentioned issues. Such SLAs are in strong contrast to the ones considered in the previous section. They directly concern application level flows and not aggregations of traffic. Furthermore, they are likely to be set up for the required duration of communication only.

Flow based SLAs are in line with the service model proposed by IntServ, as far as the end-customer's point of view is concerned. We find a significant difference in the motivation stated above. The motivation of considering single flows by IntServ is that customers want to have selectable QoS on a per-flow basis. In contrast, the arguments mentioned above are driven by economic considerations: ISPs want to provide incentives for end-customers to make use of more or less resources in the network and, in case of dynamic pricing, ISPs want to consider the availability of free resources when setting prices. These aspects are best considered in the context of individual demand units, i.e. flows.

## 5   Summary and Conclusions

Within this paper, a business model was introduced illustrating independent and coherent phases necessary for charging and accounting of Internet services. The business model was developed for an e-commerce scenario with an end-customer, an ESP, and several ISPs. Each of the players has a well-defined and integrated role within the scenario. Different levels of abstraction are necessary to implement the business model for charging and accounting of Internet services. On the top most level, the business level, there is the business model with interacting players doing business with each other. On a second level, the contract level, Service Level Agreements (SLA) are essential in order to provide reliable and accountable QoS-based end-to-end communication. The base of the entire business model is a technology model for the network infrastructure (covering IntServ and DiffServ models) carrying data across the Internet according to the contractual agreements of the contract level. The fact that multiple dynamic ISPs with heterogeneous resources are assembled for the delivery of a guaranteed service justifies the business model with its underlying network model for the communication infrastructure.

One of the key conclusions of this paper is the special role of the Access ISP within the entire business model. The fact that only the Access ISP is visible to the end-customer makes electronic business (1) easier and more trustworthy for the end-customer, since the Access ISP is a well-known point of reference, and (2) easier for the ISPs to charge and account the end-customer for the use of the transport service. If the end-customer decides to be anonymous to the Access ISP, she is invisible to the Access ISP and, thus, has to make payments in advance. The business model included two kinds of payments that have a big influence on the phases of the business model: (1) account-based post-paid payments or (2) immediate pre-paid payments. Depending on whether the end-customer wants to remain anonymous to the Access ISP or not, payments have to be made in advance or the end-customer will receive a bill with a list of the cost for the used services. Consequently, the payment scheme has an important influence on the business model.

Open issues in this area of work are the full end-to-end provisioning of services trespassing multiple core ISPs, which need to offer guaranteed services. These tasks will be an integral part of future investigations of Service Level Agreements and their definitions in a commercial and highly dynamic environment. Particularly, the different views of integrating the advantages of IntServ and DiffServ need to be studied with respect to signalling protocols and their efficient usage for e-commerce scenarios.

**Acknowledgements.** This work has been performed in the framework of the project Charging and Accounting Technology for the Internet – CATI (CAPIV 5003-054559/1 and MEDeB 5003-054560/1) which has been funded by the Swiss National Science Foundation, SNF, Berne, Switzerland. The authors like to acknowledge many discussions with project colleagues.

## References

[1]     J. P. Bailey: *The Economics of Internet Interconnection Agreements*, Internet Economics, MIT Press, Cambridge, 1997.

[2]     S. Blake, D. Black, M. Carlson, E. Davies, Z. Wang, W. Weiss: *An Architecture for Differentiated Services;* IETF, Request for Comments RFC 2475, December 1998.

[3]     R. Braden, S. Berson, S. Herzog, S. Jamin: *Resource ReSerVation Protocol (RSVP) – Version 1 Functional Specification;* IETF, Request for Comments RFC 2205, September 1997.

[4]     R. Braden, D. Clark, S. Shenker: *Integrated Services in the Internet Architecture: An Overview;* IETF, Request for Comments RFC 1633, June 1994.

[5]     S. Deering, R. Hinden: *Internet Protocol, Version 6 (IPv6) – Specification;* IETF, Request for Comments RFC 2460, December 1998

[6]     G. Dermler, G. Fankhauser, B. Stiller, T. Braun, M. Günter, H. Kneer: *Integration of Charging and Accounting into Internet Models and VPN;* Public CATI Deliverable CATI-IBM-DN-P-004-1.5, June 30, 1999.

[7] G. Fankhauser, B. Stiller, C. Vögtli, B. Plattner: *Reservation-based Charging in an Integrated Services Network;* 4th INFORMS Telecommunications Conference, Bocca Raton, Florida, U.S.A., March 1998, Session MC-2.

[8] A. Gupta, D. Stahl, A. Whinston. *The economics of network management,* Communications of the ACM, Vol. 42, No. 9, 1999.

[9] U. Kaiser: *Sicherheits- und Kostenaspekte in elektronischen Zahlungssystemen für RSVP;* Institut für Technische Informatik und Kommunikationsnetze, TIK, ETH Zürich, Student's Thesis, August 1998.

[10] H. Kneer, U. Zurfluh, C. Matt: *Business Model (RSVP);* Public CATI Deliverable CATI-UZH-DN-P-001-2.0, March 12, 1999.

[11] H. Kneer, U. Zurfluh, C. Matt: *Business Roles and Relationships;* Public CATI Deliverable CATI-UZH-DN-P-003-2.0, June 30, 1999.

[12] H. Kneer, U. Zurfluh, C. Matt: *Security Architecture;* Public CATI Deliverable CATI-UZH-DN-P-002-3.0, June 30, 1999.

[13] K. Nichols, S. Blake, F. Baker, D. Black: *Definition of the Differentiated Services Field (DS Field) in the IPv4 and IPv6 Headers;* IETF, Request for Comments RFC 2474, December 1998

[14] C. Partridge: *A Proposed Flow Specification;* BBN, Request for Comments RFC 1363.

[15] C. Partridge: *Using the Flow Label Field in IPv6;* IETF, Request for Comments RFC 1809, June 1995.

[16] J. Postel (Edt.): *Internet Protocol;* IETF, Request for Comments RFC 791, September 1981.

[17] P. Reichl, S. Leinen, B. Stiller: *A Practical Review of Pricing and Cost Recovery for Internet Services;* 2nd Berlin Internet Economics Workshop (IEW'99), Berlin, Germany, May 28–29, 1999. Session "Survey I".

[18] S. Shenker, C. Partridge, R. Guerin: *Specification of Guaranteed Quality of Service;* IETF, Request for Comments RFC 2212, September 1997.

[19] B. Stiller, T. Braun, M. Günter, B. Plattner: *The CATI Project – Charging and Accounting Technology for the Internet;* Springer Verlag, Berlin, Germany, Lecture Notes in Computer Science, Vol. 1629, 5th European Conference on Multimedia Applications, Services, and Techniques (ECMAST'99), Madrid, Spain, May 26–28, 1999, pp 281–296.

[20] B. Stiller, G. Fankhauser, G. Joller, P. Reichl, N. Weiler: *Open Charging and QoS Interfaces for IP Telephony;* The Internet Summit (INET'99), San Jose, California, U.S.A., June 22–25, 1999, Track 4 "Technology", Session "IP Audio".

[21] C. Topolcic: *Experimental Internet Stream Protocol, Version 2 (ST-II);* CIP Working Group, Request for Comments RFC 1190.

[22] *UUNET Service Level Agreements;* available at URL: www.uunet.com/customer/sla

[23] N. Weiler, G, Joller, B. Stiller, G. Fankhauser: *Trust Model;* Public CATI Deliverable CATI-TIK-DN-P-010-2.0, May 28, 1999.

[24] J. Wroclawski: *Specification of the Controlled-Load Network Element Service;* IETF, Request for Comments RFC 2211, September 1997.

[25] L. Zhang, S. Deering, D. Estrin, S. Shenker, D. Zappala, *RSVP: A New Resource Reservation Protocol,* IEEE Networks Magazine, Vol. 31, No. 9, pp 8-18, September 1993.t

# Facilitating Business-to-Business Electronic Commerce for Small and Medium-Sized Enterprises

Christoph Quix and Mareike Schoop

Informatik V (Information Systems), RWTH Aachen, 52056 Aachen, Germany
{quix,schoop}@informatik.rwth-aachen.de

**Abstract.** One way to facilitate effective business-to-business electronic commerce (EC) for small and medium-sized enterprises (SMEs) is to provide a brokering service that is tailored to the needs of SMEs. While many of the larger companies use EDI for their electronic business exchanges, SMEs have to be more flexible and demand a less rigid system. In this paper we will present an architecture of a modular broker system that supports the whole EC process. Such a broker system thus requires facilities for mediating the exchange of information. The mediating role is fulfilled by a repository that manages the data of the modules. The repository also provides access to heterogeneous information coming from external sources using sophisticated metadata management. Furthermore, the repository allows to monitor the contents of the external sources and provides notification services to the users of the broker system.

## 1 Introduction

One of the advantages of business-to-business electronic commerce (BtB EC) is the electronic integration of negotiation and ordering processes with the rest of the business process. The integration can help to reduce costs and will probably speed up the buying or selling process. However, such an integration has yet only taken place in large enterprises, e.g. in the automobile industry. A large enterprise can set a requirement for its smaller suppliers to install a certain software for electronic data interchange (EDI), thereby forcing them to adhere to a certain standard. The (implicit) threat is that the smaller companies will not be considered as future business partners if they do not use the standard.

A small or medium-sized enterprise (SME) usually conducts business with various companies, on the one hand as a buyer, on the other hand as a seller. For example, in the building and construction industry wholesalers buy from producers and act as sellers for contractors. It would be very difficult to keep track of all the business exchanges if communication were to take place directly. On the other hand, EDI systems do not offer an appropriate solution either for two reasons. Firstly, EDI systems are only semi-standards as there exist many variations for different industrial sectors. Secondly, these systems are very rigid and do not allow for individuality and flexibility. Both reasons can be considered as serious obstacles for effective BtB EC for SMEs.

Thus, it will be argued in this paper that more flexible and open solutions are required for facilitating BtB EC in SMEs. In [11], a framework for business-to-business EC for SMEs is presented. The key element of this framework is a broker system which acts as a mediator between two business partners.

In the present paper an architecture for a business data repository that forms the memory of such a broker system will be presented. The business data repository will offer a uniform access point to existing data sources and storage facilities for the different modules. Moreover, ownership of data and access rights for different user groups will be managed. Finally, notification services will be offered to keep the users of the broker system informed about products and companies.

In the next section the framework of the EC broker system will be described in detail and some requirements for the business data repository will be outlined. We will discuss the architecture of the repository in section 3 before exemplifying our approach in section 4. Finally, concluding remarks will be given in section 5.

## 2 Business-to-Business Electronic Commerce for SMEs

In this section, the context of the present work will be established. In section 2.1 we will summarise the situation of BtB EC as it is today. Based on the problems described, we will then present a new approach to effective BtB EC for SMEs (section 2.2). The core of the present work is a broker system that fulfils a mediating role. Its modular architecture will be discussed in section 2.3. As will become obvious, the broker system requires facilities for mediating the exchange of information between the different modules. A metadata repository is proposed for that purpose. Concrete requirements concerning its functionality will be presented in section 2.4.

### 2.1 Current State

There is a large number of EC approaches both in the academic and the industrial realm. However, most approaches concentrate on the later stages of an EC process. For example, standards for ordering and payment are developed [9] but there is hardly any support of the early phases of an EC process. For example questions such as "Which company can supply this product?", "What is the current situation on the market for my product?", "How can I find new respectable business partners?" are often answered only partly or indeed not at all.

EDI systems have been in use for a considerable time, especially for larger companies in certain sectors such as the automobile industry. For SMEs, there are a number of problems related to EDI systems [9]: (i) They are relatively expensive to develop and operate which is a problem for SMEs. (ii) EDI systems have a limited accessibility in that they do not allow transaction between buyers and sellers in an easy way. EDIFACT is a semi-standard which is so complex that there are usually different sub-standards for different domains. Therefore, one-to-one solutions are often in place. (iii) EDI systems are rigid and do not allow for intuitive interactions or flexible exchanges whereas a key characteristic of SMEs is their flexibility. (iv) EDI systems are partial solutions, i.e. they only automate one part of the EC process. Consequently, we argue that a new approach to BtB EC for SMEs is required which is based on solid database technology and on empirical data showing SMEs' concrete demands regarding BtB EC. EDI can be part of such approach (as indeed it will be in our approach) but it must not be used on its own.

### 2.2 A new Approach

Our vision of an effective support of business-to-business EC processes takes the problems described in the previous section into account and seeks to overcome them. Based on an analysis of existing business processes, we argue that for SMEs a mediator for information exchange is not only helpful but indeed vital for effective BtB EC. SMEs have many business associates and it would be very difficult to keep track of all business exchanges if there was only direct communication. The core of the approach presented in this paper is a broker system which is tailored to the needs of SMEs. The broker mediates the exchanges of business partners. Its architecture will be introduced in the next section.

## 2.3 Architecture of the Broker System

The broker system consists of four modules, i.e. search, negotiation, fulfilment, and data management (see figure 1). Firstly, business partners need to have intelligent search facilities including keyword and semantic search [10]. Buyers can thereby find suppliers of certain products easily and quickly; sellers can look for possible buyers efficiently and can be found easily by prospective clients. The search engine provides a number of companies satisfying the search conditions.

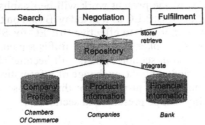

**Fig. 1.** Architecture of the broker system

Then the phase of contract negotiation starts. We envisage negotiation support by providing structured Email messages based on speech act terms [12, 13] and EDIFACT which provides a run-time specification of SMEs' interactions [17]. A company will start parallel negotiation with some of the companies they found in the search phase, i.e. parallel message threads will be created. During the parallel negotiation, one company will be selected as the business partner for the particular EC process.

After an agreement has been reached, the fulfilment phase starts. A contract is drawn up and commits the parties to certain actions.

As can easily be imagined, a large amount of data is created and amended and needs to be maintained during the EC process. To manage the data efficiently, we propose a metadata repository which acts as the memory of the broker system. Just as the broker system mediates the communication between the companies, the metadata repository mediates between the different broker modules that the business partners use during their exchanges.

The second role of the repository is to provide access to heterogeneous information coming from external sources. For example, chambers of commerce can provide extensive information about companies in certain regions; companies offer detailed characteristics of products; banks might offer financial information. Such external information is useful for an intelligent search module. For example, a company might want to look for suppliers from Greater Manchester with a reliable credit history selling bubble-jet printers in the price range of 200-230 Euro. The integration of such heterogeneous data sources will be discussed in section 3.

## 2.4 Requirements for a Metadata Repository

Based on our vision of an effective BtB EC process for SMEs, the following requirements have been drawn up in discussion with user groups. The repository should

**facilitate information exchange across modules;** The results from the search process are the basis for negotiations with certain companies, thus information must be passed on, for example, from the search module to the negotiation module.
**provide extensible data structures;** It is possible that further requirements will be uttered by user groups which must then be embedded in the existing data structures.

**make flexible workflows possible;** The workflow of "search-negotiate-fulfil" is not the only possible order of events. For example, if a company is regarded as an established business contact, negotiation might start without any search.

**enable traceability of negotiation and fulfilment phases;** To show the history behind an agreement, it is vital that the different steps of negotiation and fulfilment are stored and are accessible for the business partners. This facility can serve as a memory aid and as a medium of communication between employees of the same company; it can help to evaluate different business strategies etc.

**monitor the fulfilment;** Once an agreement has been reached, a contract will be drawn up with clear responsibilities for all parties involved. A monitoring facility could help to anticipate conflicts and be used, for example, to issue certain predefined messages automatically as reminders, penalities etc.

**integrate external data sources;** Data coming from external sources is helpful for effective EC processes and should, therefore, be used in a repository.

**manage access rights and data ownership;** External information providers might not want to provide accessibility to their data to everybody. Rather, they want to grant access only to their business partners. Furthermore, the owners of external information want to retain the control over their data, e.g. update or remove data.

## 3 Architecture of the Repository System

In the previous section, we have discussed the framework and the requirements for a business data repository. We will now explain what functionalities the repository has to provide to fulfil the requirements.

One of the core functionalities of the repository is to provide information to the search, negotiation and fulfilment modules. The repository must, therefore, offer flexible data structures which are able to store the data provided by the modules and external data sources. This function is realised by an extensible object oriented data model and a hierarchy of views which allows the base data to evolve independently of the applications. The view mechanism is also used to map the data structures of the repository to the client data structures and to provide notification services for client applications. These issues will be addressed in sections 3.1 and 3.2.

Another requirement is the integration of external data sources into the repository. Our approach to this problem is based on the idea of federated database systems. A federation of databases is a combination of locally administered databases to a distributed system that allows application programs to access the data without having to resolve the semantic and structural heterogeneity of the local databases [14]. Instead, a virtually integrated database is constructed by recombining the local databases into a central database schema (also called global schema). Structural and semantic conflicts are resolved by appropriate definitions in the global schema. In section 3.3, we will show how this idea is technically implemented in our framework. Section 3.4 will then address the problem of syntactic and semantic integration.

The repository is implemented with the ConceptBase system [6] which is a knowledge-based repository that is mainly used for metadata management. The client-server architecture allows clients to access the repository via the Internet. The repository can notify clients on certain events that have occured.

### 3.1 Business Data Structures

The repository should manage all data relevant for BtB EC between SMEs. We have identified the following data items that have to be managed by the repository: (i) *company and product profiles* as they are used by the search engine to find business partners,

(ii) *search results* are stored to be used during the negotiation phase or for later similar searches, (iii) *negotiation details and contracts* are stored to resolve later legal conflicts and to trace a negotiation process, and (iv) *user profiles* which store information about users, such as access rights, personal search results, ongoing negotiations etc.

All member companies of the EC broker system have to provide a company profile to become a member of the system. Additional company profiles can be provided by organisations such as the chambers of commerce. If a company has been registered, it may provide information about its products to the system. Two key problems of company and product profiles are that they are heterogeneous and that international standards are not available or rarely supported.

Our approach to this problem is to map the profiles to standards as far as possible. For example, the European Business Register [3] is an international organisation that tries to build up a register of companies in many European countries. The register includes information about contact address, registration authority, company type and description, and financial data. Such information is offered by the chambers of commerce in Germany (e.g., see Internet Business Network of IHK Aachen [5]). In section 4 we will show how the information from IHK Aachen can be mapped into the EBR.

For product profiles, some industry-specific organisations offer product ontologies that can be used to classify products into a hierarchy of concepts. For example, the Dutch organisation HCP-EDIBouw [4] has developed an ontology for the building and construction industry in the Netherlands. One goal is to facilitate the EC between producers, wholesalers, building companies, and architects. Therefore, HCP-EDIBouw's product ontology is divided into several perspectives as the different user groups use different terminologies.

Although all this data is extracted from different sources, it must be integrated into a coherent data model, e.g. product profiles are linked to the company profiles of their producers. Figure 2 gives an overview of the data model of the business data repository[1].

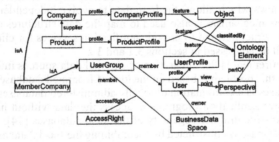

**Fig. 2.** Data model of the business data repository [8]

Figure 2 describes the relationship between companies, products and their profiles. Companies and products may have several profiles for different user groups. The structure of the profiles is not further defined, they may have several *features*. The semantics of these features is defined by linking the relationship to the corresponding element in the ontology.

Furthermore, figure 2 describes how we manage the "dynamic" information in the repository, i.e., search results and details about negotiations and contracts. For each business transaction and each user involved in this transaction, we construct a *business*

---

[1] ConceptBase has an object-oriented data model: types are represented as classes; relationships between classes are attributes of the classes; data are object instances of these classes.

*data space* (BDS) [8]. A BDS will contain all data that is the result of a transaction. The owner of the BDS can allow other users to access her or his BDS. Furthermore, the owner can update and remove data in the BDS. Thus, the BDS fulfils the requirement for managing access rights and retaining data ownership.

## 3.2 Support for Client Applications

The repository supports client applications in several ways. Firstly, the repository allows to define views on top of the base data defined in section 3.1. The views allow the client application to extract that part of the repository which is of interest to the application. Furthermore, the structure of the view is independent of the base data. Thus, it can be defined in a way that is best-suited for the client application.

Secondly, the output format of the repository for a certain view can be defined by the administrator of the repository. By doing so, the application does not have to know about the internals of the repository system and the repository can easily be integrated into existing environments. The result of a view can be transformed into any ASCII string, e.g., XML document, HTML page, or an EDI message.

Finally, the repository is able to maintain and update the views for the client applications if necessary. The repository uses a view maintenance algorithm [15] to compute the changes for the view whenever an update to the base data has occurred and then notifies the client applications about these changes [16]. This mechanism can be used to keep the user informed about the information (s)he has requested [1]. For example, the user might want to get notified if a company publishes a new product, or if the price of a product goes below a certain limit.

## 3.3 Integration of External Information Sources

We propose a federated architecture for the integration of external information sources in the repository. In such an architecture, the repository plays the role of an information trader: all requests by the client applications are sent to the repository. The repository then looks up the metadata of external sources and sends the query to the appropriate source. The result is received by the repository and then sent back to the client application in the desired format.

The advantage of a federated architecture is that local databases can remain unchanged while allowing application programs to operate on a central virtual database providing the data of all participating databases. Such an architecture is especially useful for a loosely-coupled system we envision for the EC broker system. The data sources are not controlled by the administrator of the EC broker system, and access to these sources might be limited. Within our architecture, it will be possible to materialise a snapshot of a data source in the repository (e.g., if access to the sources is very inefficient, or if the sources are rarely updated), or to keep the integration *virtual*, i.e., there is no materialisation and every query to the data is delegated to the source.

It has been argued that federated databases are a technologically attractive solution to the problem of distributed databases [14]. However, practice has shown some disadvantages and risks when they are applied in a too comprehensive way. Structural and semantic conflicts are often underestimated. Especially semantic conflicts may arise if the local databases are maintained for diverging goals (e.g. the semantics of concepts like 'order' or 'product' might differ in different departments or companies). Therefore, it is necessary to analyse the business processes that operate on the local databases. The problem of structural and semantic integration is also addressed in data warehousing [7]. Structural conflicts are solved by special data cleaning programs. Semantic conflicts require a careful analysis of the data sources and their semantics. The result of such an analysis is a conceptual model of the information which is available in the enterprise and the data sources [2].

Our technical solution to the problem is as follows. The repository stores the metadata about the location of the source data, how it can be accessed, and its schema. To be able to access the heterogeneous databases, these systems must either offer a standard interface to their data (e.g., JDBC, XML) or a *wrapper* has to be implemented that provides access to the source data.

In our 'trader architecture', ConceptBase provides added value for the client applications without preventing them to access the business information sources directly. To access external information sources such as relational database systems or XML documents, ConceptBase uses the JEBserver (Java External Binding).

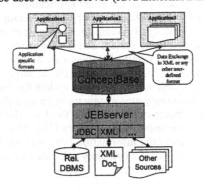

**Fig. 3.** Federated architecture of the repository system

The JEBserver has an architecture that is similar to a driver manager in an ODBC/ JDBC architecture. The core of the JEBserver manages the connection with the ConceptBase server and translates the data from the sources into the format required by ConceptBase. For each type of source, a specific *driver* (or *wrapper*) is necessary. The drivers are implemented as Java classes and they have to support an interface that is defined by the JEBserver. This interface is similar (and yet much simpler) to the driver interface in JDBC.

To know how and when external information sources need to be accessed, ConceptBase manages some metadata about the sources such as the relations stored in the sources and the access method. The integration process is incremental, i.e., not all sources have to be integrated at one step and additional sources may be added later.

### 3.4 Syntactic and Semantic Integration

*Syntactic* integration is the part of the integration process which resolves the syntactic heterogeneity of the data source, i.e., different names for data types and attributes, different metrics for values, etc. *Semantic* integration deals with the heterogeneity of conceptual models, e.g., even if two data types from different sources have the same name, they can represent different "real-world" objects.

In our approach, the integration is done by building a *global schema* for the data available in the sources. This global schema is a *view* that is constructed from the base data that is imported from the sources (see figure 4). The base data, as it is stored in the repository, does not necessarily have the same schemata as in the sources.

Syntactic conflicts in the different sources are resolved in the repository by defining views on top of the base data, i.e., unifying different syntactic representations of

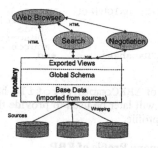

**Fig. 4.** Hierarchy of schemata and views for syntactic and semantic integration

data types. These views form the global schema of the repository. On top of the global schema, further views are used to extract a part of the repository which is useful for a client application. This means that a client application does not need to know the whole global schema of the repository, it just needs to know the part of the global schema (or the view on the global schema) which is relevant for the application.

The problem of semantic integration can be solved by creating a conceptual representation of the global schema and the sources, following the approach we have developed in the ESPRIT project DWQ (Foundations of Data Warehouse Quality) [7]. In DWQ, an enterprise-wide conceptual schema (called Conceptual Data Warehouse Model) is constructed. The conceptual models of the sources are then expressed in terms of the conceptual enterprise model. A semantically rich language is used to express relationships between the entities of the different models.

## 4   Example: Integration of Company Profiles

### 4.1   Data Structures

We will show a straightforward integration of the company profiles of IHK Aachen [5]. The company profiles of IHK Aachen are stored in a relational database. We do not explain here the internal format of the database but focus instead on the views which are exported by the database. The database exports two views: one view contains the company profiles, and the second view contains the descriptions of activity codes (based on the NACE code, an international standard for the classification of companies).

The contents of both views will be loaded into the business data repository. Therefore, it is necessary to specify in ConceptBase how the data sources can be accessed. This is done by defining an instance of `ExternalDataSource`. This instance describes how the data can be accessed by defining a Java class which implements a wrapper for JDBC data sources. Furthermore, it is specified where the database server is running by defining a URL.

```
IHKDatabase in ExternalDataSource with
url exturl :
   "JEB-JDBC:twzl.jdbc....:jdbc:z1MySQL://host:1234/mysql"
driver
  extdriver : "i5.cb.jdbc.JEBJdbcDriver"
end
```

If this data has been entered into ConceptBase, the metadata of the data source, i.e., table definitions, are loaded automatically. For company profiles and the NACE Code, the following classes will be created in ConceptBase.

```
IHKCompanyProfile in ExternalObject      NACECode in ExternalObject
  with field                               with field
    Name : String;                           Code : String;
    Street : String; [...]                   Description : String;
    Branch : String                          source extSource : IHKDatabase
  source extSource : IHKDatabase           end
end
```

The attribute `Branch` of `IHKCompanyProfile` has a foreign key relation to the table `NACECode`. This will later be used to provide the description of the branch together with the company profile.

### 4.2 Mapping to the Company Profile of EBR

Most of the fields in the database of IHK Aachen can be mapped directly to the corresponding fields of the EBR's company profile. This mapping is established using a view on the company profile data of the IHK database.

```
View EBR_CompanyProfileOnIHK isA IHKCompanyProfile with
  computed attribute
    Name : String;          Type : String;
    Country : String;       ActCode : String;
    RegDate : String;       ActDescription : String
  constraint c:$(this Name ~Name) and (~Country == "Germany") and
    (exists y/Int (this Year y) and (~RegDate in IntToStr[y/int]))
    and (this LegalForm ~Type) and (this Branch ~ActCode)
    and (exists n/NACECode (n Code ~ActCode)
    and (n Description ~ActDescription)) $
end
```

In ConceptBase, a view can be seen as a derived class. In this example, the instances of this class are inherited from the class `IHKCompanyProfile`. It is also possible to inherit the attributes from this class, but as the attributes for a company profile in EBR are slightly different to the ones in the IHK database, we have to "compute" them. The computation is done in the constraint of the view. In this constraint, the attributes of the view can be used as variables, their names are prefixed with ~. For example, the statement (`this LegalForm ~Type`) assigns the attribute value of the attribute `LegalForm` of the superclass to the attribute `Type` of the view. ConceptBase also supports functions like `IntToStr` for data type conversions. In addition, users can specify their own functions for more complex computations. The view mechanism can also be used to map the repository data to client data structures, e.g. corresponding to a DTD of an XML document.

## 5 Conclusion

In this paper we have argued that one way to facilitate effective business-to-business electronic commerce for small and medium-sized enterprises is to provide a brokering service that is tailored to the needs of SMEs. While many of the larger companies use EDIFACT for their electronic business exchanges, SMEs have to be more flexible and demand less rigid systems that match their business situations and support the whole EC process, i.e. providing intelligent search mechanisms for locating new business partners, supporting electronic negotiation via structured message exchanges, and coordinating the fulfilment of the contract.

Our approach is based on a semantically rich business data repository. The repository manages the data of the modules by using an extensible object-oriented data model. Thus, the repository serves as a technical mediator between the modules of the EC broker system. It can be helpful for SMEs engaging in BtB EC to be able to access data from other sources such as product catalogues and company profiles. Therefore, the repository must integrate heterogeneous data from external sources and store the data in a coherent data model whilst retaining the data ownership.

Future work will concentrate on the refinement of data structures for company and product profiles to handle multilinguality and more complex ontologies. The concept of business data spaces will be enhanced to improve the management of access rights and data ownership. Furthermore, we will refine the data structures for tool integration with the negotiation process and the fulfilment phase. These data structures will be used to trace and monitor a business transaction. We will continue to work in close cooperation with several SMEs to provide effective support of BtB EC tailored to the real needs of SMEs.

**Acknowledgements** The research is supported by the European ESPRIT Project "MEMO: Mediating and Monitoring Electronic Commerce", No. 26895. We would like to thank our project partners for the useful discussions.

# References

1. S. Abiteboul, B. Amann, S. Cluet, A. Eyal, L. Mignet, T. Milo. Active Views for Electronic Commerce. $25^{th}$ Conf. Very Large Data Bases (VLDB'99), Edingburgh, pp. 138–149, 1999.
2. D. Calvanese, G. De Giacomo, M. Lenzerini, D. Nardi, R. Rosati. Source Integration in Data Warehousing. Proc. $9^{th}$ Int. Workshop on Database and Expert Systems Applications (DEXA'98), pp. 192–197, 1998.
3. European Business Register. http://www.ebr.org.
4. HCP-Edibouw. Branchemodel Elektronische Communicatie. HCP-EDIBOUW, Driebergen, Netherlands, November 1998.
5. IHK Aachen: Internet-Business-Network. http://www.aachen.ihk.de/.
6. M. Jarke, R. Gallersdörfer, M. Jeusfeld, M. Staudt, S. Eherer. ConceptBase – a deductive object base for meta data management. Journal of Intelligent Information Systems, 4(2), pp. 167–192, 1995.
7. M. Jarke, M. Lenzerini, Y. Vassiliou, P. Vassiliadis. Fundamentals of Data Warehouses. Springer-Verlag, 1999.
8. M.A. Jeusfeld. Business Data Structures for Business-to-Business Electronic Commerce. Technical Report, Infolab, Tilburg University, 2000 (forthcoming).
9. R. Kalakota, A.B. Whinston. Readings in Electronic Commerce. Addison-Wesley, 1997.
10. C.J. Leune, M.P. Papazoglou. Classification Mechanisms and semantic searches for trading-information. Deliverable 1.1, MEMO project, available at http://www.abnamro.com/memo/
11. M.P. Papazoglou, M.A. Jeusfeld, H. Weigand, M. Jarke. Distributed, interoperable workflow support for Electronic Commerce. In Proc. GI/IFIP Conf. Trends in Electronic Commerce (TREC'98), Hamburg, Germany, June 3-5, 1998.
12. M. Schoop, D.G. Wastell. A Language-Action Approach to Cooperative Documentation Systems. $6^{th}$ Eur. Conf. Information Systems (ECIS'98), Aix-en-Provence, pp. 984–987, 1998.
13. J.R. Searle. Speech Acts – An Essay in the Philosophy of Language. Cambridge University Press, 1969.
14. A.P. Sheth, J.A. Larson. Federated Database Systems for Managing Distributed, Heterogeneous, and Autonomous Databases. ACM Computing Surveys, 22(3), pp. 183–236, 1990.
15. M. Staudt, M. Jarke. Incremental Maintenance of Externally Materialized Views. Proc. $22^{nd}$ Intl. Conf. on Very Large Data Bases (VLDB'96), Bombay, India, pp. 75–86, 1996.
16. M. Staudt, C. Quix, M.A. Jeusfeld. View Maintenance and Change Notification for Application Program Views. ACM Symposium on Applied Computing, Atlanta, Georgia, USA, 1998.
17. H. Weigand. Formal Models of Negotiation. Proc. Workshop on Formal Models of Electronic Commerce (FMEC), Erasmus University Rotterdam, June 1999.

# Next Generation Business-to-Business E-Commerce

M. O'Connell, P. Nixon

Computer Science Department, University of Dublin, Trinity College, Dublin 2, Ireland.
{Marcus.OConnell, Paddy.Nixon}@cs.tcd.ie

**Abstract.** Most discussion on the current hot topic of e-commerce focuses either on the relationship between the customer and the supplier or on the security of these interactions. This paper presents business-to-business e-commerce as collaborations between parties, in the form of virtual enterprises. The paper presents a review of business-to-business technology issues.

## 1 Introduction

Modern business practices are undergoing a dramatic shift. Business imperatives such as accelerating product cycles and improved product targeting imply that both fundamental (long-term) and market-driven (short-term) collaborations are critical to a business' continued competitiveness. Moreover, downsizing and narrow niche markets suggest that collaboration has great potential for reducing costs and fostering interoperability of products and services within the global marketplace.

Although the Internet, and e-commerce in particular, promise to enhance the way we do business their most significant contribution to date has been in the one-to-one direct selling domain. However, e-commerce is much more than just direct sales. It is about harnessing technology to support every aspect of business. An area of particular interest is how supply chains, or business-to-business relationships, can be improved through the use of the Internet. Particularly, Internet technology promises to make the process of building such supply chains faster, more open and more profitable. A number of problems manifest themselves immediately when considering how to implement such supply chains over the Internet to realise these promises. The location of potential collaboration partners is complicated, as is the logistics of agreeing a suitable collaborative contract. Once formed, large project consortia, and those with highly dynamic populations, are notoriously hard to administer and control. Finally there are important legal and commercial issues in the accessibility of information between partners, both during the project and (equally importantly) when it has been formally completed

The rest of this paper is organised as follows. Section 2 provides a concise definition and an overview of business-to-business e-commerce realised as virtual enterprises(VE). Section 3 outlines some of the characteristics of a typical VE, section 4 discusses two VE life-cycle models. Section 5 discusses the issues and problems of VEbusiness processes. Section 6 discusses some work related to virtual enterprises.

## 2 Virtual Enterprise Overview

Ouzounis et al [9] define a virtual enterprise to be a set of legally independent performers of varying types who voluntarily co-operate to seize a market opportunity. They are represented by at least one partner to the external world and they agree to produce a common output, e.g. a product or service, based on a common understanding of their business rules and business processes. To achieve this, they should share their resources, core competencies, skills and know how in order to become quicker, flexible and more global.

According to Fischer [3], the term virtual enterprise is generally attributed to Mowshowitz [7,8], who established a parallel between it and the term virtual memory as it is used in information technology. It derives from the early days of computing when the term described a way of making a computer act as if it had more storage capacity that it really possessed. The term virtual was used for the first time to describe a business organisation by Jan Hopland of Digital Equipment Corp. (DEC) some ten years ago, where he was responsible for plotting strategy for DEC's information technology business. Hopland, who is often credited with coining the phrase virtual enterprise, had been inspired to use the adjective 'virtual' by the world of information technology. His use of the term virtual corporation describes an enterprise that could marshal more resources to bear on any given situation than are currently available by collaboration, not growth or expansion.

Virtuality is achieved through co-operation of independent enterprises, which together realise the complete field of goods and services. Each enterprise realises in this connection only one special part of the value chain. However, this is no regular co-operation. Partners in a virtual corporation bring in their critical, core competencies. Thus, a virtual organisation is ideally a combination of best-of-class (complementary) core competencies. This co-operation - bringing together suppliers, producers and developers with their customers - renders the virtual organisation practically merged with the environment. This removes all kinds of boundaries between the organisation and the environment and thus leads to its overall unbounded character.

## 3 Virtual Enterprise Characteristics

For an organisation to be referred to as virtual, it needs to base its co-operation or rather sheer existence on the use and application of information technology (IT). Hence, the use of IT is a constitutive feature of the virtual organisation. This allows it to be differentiated from other types of networked organisations - The virtual organisation is a network organisation but, in addition to implementing various forms of co-operation, it makes a heavy and critical use of information technology. Hence, IT emerges as the primary integrator of the virtual corporation. Information technology transcending organisational boundaries spans companies together into an agile and re-configurable network of high efficiency and adaptability. Only recent developments in network computing and the Internet have made a truly global and efficient virtual organisation a viable idea.

The two main reasons for organising activities in the form of a virtual enterprise may be described as:

- an increasing need for flexibility, in addition to which the necessary core competencies can only be obtained on collaborating with external partners
- the need for efficiency by sharing resources with other partners

Virtual enterprises can be catagorised into two separate types, stable or dynamic. In a stable virtual enterprise, collaboration has a more stable character. Usually, there is one organisation that is the core partner and that lays down the rules for collaboration. Dynamic virtual enterprises on the other hand, embark on a common action the moment the customer approaches them with an order or a problem. Here, temporary collaboration relations are involved with shared leadership.

The virtual corporation is not just a collection of partners, but a collaborative structure, and this amplifies its apparent lack of boundedness. This is because co-operation ties the collaborators together to such an extent that they are practically merged into one, though re-configurable, structure. Since each constituent realises only a special fraction of the value chain, on their own, constitutive parts are nothing. The whole situation is further amplified by the fact that virtual partners share their resources, infrastructure, personnel, research, information and knowledge.

Virtual organisations have two key structural characteristics: interdependence between the constituent operations, and distribution of responsibility between constituent operations. They are globally distributed, and exploit information and communication technologies to support their operation. Information systems allow virtual organisations to monitor feedback and refine their configurations, allowing them to constantly evolve [1].

Appel [1], states that there are five key types of virtual organisation:

1. alliances of organisations
2. alliances of individuals
3. established decentralised companies
4. central companies seeking to adapt
5. single organisations

Virtual organisations have at least one of the following four characteristics: geographic separation, functional specialisation with separate reporting hierarchies, transitory membership driven by evolving needs over time, and separation of production across different time dimensions [1].

The virtual organisation does not need to be any more temporary than other conventional organisations. It appears that what makes virtual organisations dissimilar from "regular" companies is not that they are temporary, but what rather counts is their strong re-configurability, continuous reconstruction and design aspect, as well as element substitutability. A virtual organisation can mutate so much that it is beyond recognition, but it is still a virtual corporation, albeit completely transformed. Thus virtual corporations have continuence and longevity beyond a single project and this is what differentiates them, among other things, from project organisations. At the same time, virtual organisations have a different life cycle from conventional companies. The virtual organisation actively pursues opportunities and undertakes new projects. In the course of those activities, it often modifies its partners, co-operative arrangements and the available resources. This process seems endless rather than a one-off occasion like in the case of a project-driven setup.

However, it must be noted that virtual organisation literature leaves the impression that they are only business, profit-driven types of organisation. This impression is further amplified by the use of the words, corporation or enterprise, and not organisation. While it is probably true that the bulk of writing about the virtual organisation is devoted to money-making virtual ventures, virtual organisations operate with a great deal of success also in not-for-profit areas. The Open University in the UK is an example of this, which is for its students, only a conceptual space, not a physical one.

Research suggests [10] that virtual organisations need to be tackled from four key aspects: connectivity, purpose, technology and boundary.

**Connectivity** - the creation of unity or linkage through structural change, breaking of constraints or overcoming of previously existing barriers. Many virtual organisations break distance barriers. Another barrier to be broken is legal separation, i.e. separate legal entities operating as if they were a single legal unit (the virtual corporation). Another form of connectivity is the creation of unity between different parties with significantly different goals, e.g. two or more 'players' in a competitive situation who decide to set aside their win/lose conflict in order to fend off another party. Connectivity needs to be examined both in terms of selectivity (how important the connectivity is for success) and in terms of difficulty (how difficult it is to achieve). Selectivity will foster a virtual organisation; difficulty will hinder it.

**Purpose** - the objective that provides the incentive for creating the new organisation and which servers as the cohesive force to hold the virtual organisation components at least temporarily together. Purpose addresses the issue of value of the virtual organisation. It answers the question of what benefits are to be derived from the virtual organisation arrangement. Purpose is the basic drive for virtual organisation creation. The stronger the purpose (higher value) and the more selective the arrangement (only the virtual organisation form will achieve it), the more stable the virtual arrangement will be.

**Technology** - the enabling factor that allows the breakthrough and makes the virtual form possible.

**Boundary** - the separation of those who are part of the virtual organisation and those who are not, in the absence of any clearly visible physical border lines. It defines who can share its activities and who receives benefits. As traditional physical boundaries become meaningless for virtual organisations, new and less physical, yet similarly effective, boundaries have to be created to separate those who are part of the virtual organisation from those who are not. Only in this way can it be ensured that outsiders cannot tamper with the organisation or derive benefits from it that they are not entitled to. With the advancement of computer and telecommunication technologies, boundaries of virtual organisations have become stronger and, at the same time, less visible. The invisibility of a virtual organisation would be one of the important indicators to measure the virtuality of the organisation. The more invisible the boundary is, the more virtual the organisation will be. Less visible boundaries may result in more inviting business posture for organisations.

Taken together, the four key characteristics give guidance for the assessment of virtual organisation stability and for the design of new virtual organisations.

A key question is when should companies organise for innovation by using virtual approaches, and when should they rely on internal organisation? The approach depends on the innovation in question. Some innovations are autonomous - that is, they can be pursued independently from other innovations. In contrast, some innovations are fundamentally systemic - that is, their benefits can be realised only in conjunction with related, complementary innovations. The distinction between autonomous and systemic innovation is fundamental to the choice of organisational design. When innovation is autonomous, the decentralised virtual organisation can manage the development and commercialisation tasks quite well. When innovation is systemic, members of the virtual organisation are dependent on the other members, over whom they have no control.

The virtual companies that have demonstrated staying power are all at the centre of a network that they use to leverage their own capabilities. Few virtual companies that have survived and prospered have outsourced everything. Rather, the virtuous virtuals have carefully nurtured and guarded the internal capabilities that provide the essential underpinnings of competitive advantage. And they invest considerable resources to maintain and extend their core competencies internally. The very reliance of virtual companies on partners, suppliers, and other outside companies exposes them to strategic hazards.

Many companies with superior capabilities have prospered as the dominant player in a network. Companies that are much larger that their suppliers, can compel those suppliers to make radical changes to their business practices. In a more egalitarian network, suppliers can demand a large share of the economic benefit of innovations, using what economists call hold-up strategies. Strong players are rarely vulnerable to such tactics and are thus in a better position to drive and co-ordinate systemic innovation. The most successful virtual companies sit at the centre of networks that are far from egalitarian.

The leader of a virtual enterprise is an individual, or a small group, with a will to accomplish something. Consciously or intuitively, the leader creates a strategic map showing how a new business arrangement will be put together in a virtual organisation. The leader also has a conception of the core competence of his own unit. This competence is later supplemented by the contributions of the partners and partner enterprises co-operating in the arrangement. The leader's unit is called the leader enterprise. One or more partners or partner enterprises are added, which are managed and held together by the leader enterprise [6].

The virtual organisation is held together primarily by cohesive forces other than those used for conventional companies, such as capital, laws and contracts, customs, and tradition. Trust is probably the most important ingredient in the "organisational glue" that keeps the virtual organisation from coming apart. Synergies constitute an important class of cohesive forces. Synergies may relate to the customer base, market communication, the delivery system, the production system, purchasing, or input goods. Another major category of cohesive forces is in information technology. IT can make co-ordination possible over an area that otherwise would be too large from an economic or practical standpoint.

## 4 Virtual Enterprise Life-Cycle

This section provides an overview of two life-cycle models for virtual enterprises. The life-cycle model is key to determining the services that are required to allow collaboration between parties in a virtual enterprise. There are technology challenges at each stage of the life-cycle and also in the transitions between the stages.

Van Wijk et al [11] propose a virtual enterprise life cycle model consisting of seven stages, as follows:

1) Modification of strategy: As a result of several trends and developments or as a continuing process, a company may decide to think about repositioning its strategy. This strategy may consist of many different topics, like the position of the company versus its competitors, its own human resources, product development, ICT support of the organisation in the market. Depending on the situation of the company, the focus will be on one or more of these topics.

2) Co-operation strategy: By a number of causes, for example forced by increased competition, a focus on core competition or the willingness to expand on new markets, the repositioning of the strategy may result in a stronger focus on co-operation.

3) Weigh co-operation alternatives: Several forms of co-operation are possible, all different in flexibility, stability and juridical aspects. There is a range of co-operation forms to meet with the specific demands and strategy of an organisation, from discrete transactions to acquisition. One of them is the virtual organisation.

4) Selection of partners: Once a company has decided to focus on co-operation in a virtual organisation form, one has to select partners, or make sure to be selected by other companies.

5) Design and integration: The virtual organisation, consisting of the selected partners, must integrate to a certain extent to be able to work together effectively towards the goals. Choices in the design of the virtual enterprise have to be made.

6) Management: During the functioning of the virtual enterprise, whether it is a virtual enterprise with or without a core partner, the tuning and co-operation between the partners has to be co-ordinated in a certain way.

7) Dissolution and evaluation: When the goals are reached, the virtual enterprise can be dissolved and evaluated. The partners can evaluate themselves as partners in the virtual enterprise and adjust the impression that they have of the network partners.

Ouzounis et al [9] present an alternative life-cycle model, consisting of just three phases:

**Built In Phase:** During which members of the virtual enterprise are establishing, integrating and configuring the linkage between them. This phase includes:
- Initial negotiations between organisations to agree on a specific set of business processes, as well as on a set of business process interfaces provided by one member to another under certain terms and conditions involving security, control and management, reliability and fault tolerance.
- Specification, and creation of electronic contracts that specify all the available services and conditions of service provision process between members
- Modification of access rights to allow restricted and secure access to services and business processes based on the electronic contracts developed.
- Configuration and customisation of access control, authentication and authorisation systems for the secure provisioning of business processes, and services to the virtual enterprise members according to electronic contracts.
- Business processes re-engineering of current business processes so as to be adopted to the new business model. Business process re-engineering is achieved by re-using and extending business components. In that way, business processes can span different business domains. This phase includes modelling, simulation, and performance evaluation.
- Testing and performance analysis of the new developed processes to remove bottlenecks and de-efficiencies

**Execute/Manage Phase:** During which the provided services can be accessed and invoked in a secure and modest way. This phase includes the:
- Invocation of business processes transparently by each member of the virtual enterprise according to the contracts established in the first phase.
- Management and control of invoked business processes during real time operation so as to increase reliability and fault tolerance and identify bottlenecks.

- Business event management and performance evaluation of business processes.
- The possible change/alteration of internal implementations of business processes and services without changing the provided interfaces so as interoperability can be preserved
- The insurance that the provided business process semantics remains constant throughout the whole virtual enterprise life-cycle

**Terminate Phase:** During which the virtual enterprise members may alter the access rights, interfaces and implementations of the provided services and business processes.

# 5 Supply Chain Management

Supply chain management is the operations system of the virtual corporation. It is concerned with the management and control of the flow of materials and information across separate entities forming the supply chain. Supply chain management is the integration of business processes from end users through original suppliers that provides products, services and information that add value for customers. The supply chain is a network of organisations that are involved, through upstream and downstream linkages, in the different processes and activities that produce value in the form of products and services in the hand of the ultimate consumer. To implement supply chain management, some level of co-ordination across organisational boundaries is needed. This includes integration of processes and functions within organisations and across the supply chain.

A virtual web is an open-ended collection of pre-qualified partners that agree to form a pool of potential members of virtual corporations. An effective web must have a way of identifying the evolving core competencies of its members as well as of its changing membership. The way a web identifies and qualifies opportunities for a virtual corporation instance is critical to its success. Webs may use central or distributed marketing capabilities, but when a market opportunity is identified, the mechanism for choosing partners must be clearly established. Regardless of the amount of structure used in creating a web, the key goal is to permit a virtual corporation to be formed very quickly.

The main emphasis of a virtual corporation is to produce a competitive output as fast as possible. Therefore it is essential that the logistics management systems of the partnering companies are compatible. This includes, in particular, the linkage of computer systems such as order entry, capacity resource planning, master production planning, material resource planning, inventory and distribution resource planning systems. This information sharing is important for reliable deliveries for just-in-time manufacturing within the supply chain. Semich states that information sharing replaces inventory in the virtual corporation. Joint planning reduces the risk of waste and facilitates the synchronised production.

The virtual web is a vehicle to facilitate and accelerate the formation of virtual corporations. One key issue of the virtual web is the design of the supply chain. It is essential for the success of a virtual corporation that the leader (or broker) has chosen the right combination of companies with complementary core competencies, sufficient capacity and compatible business processes to create a competitive supply chain. It is necessary that a virtual web has a broker who identifies market opportunities, administrates core competencies of member companies and designs the supply chain. Furthermore, the virtual corporation needs a leader, whether it is a leading company or the broker itself, to manage the integrated planning, scheduling, administration and controlling of the supply chain.

# 6 Virtual Enterprise Business Processes

A business process is a set of one or more linked procedures that collectively realise a business objective or policy goal, normally within the context of an organisational structure.

In a virtual enterprise, the co-operating units mainly contribute their core competencies. The independent units contribute partial business processes which are combined together to form the global business process describing the virtual enterprise. Because in a virtual enterprise individual enterprises fulfil only parts of the value chain to produce the product, the main problem in assembling a virtual enterprise is the mapping of the partial processes to the individual enterprises. It can be divided into two phases: In the first phase, a suitable business process partitioning is worked out. In the second phase, the process chain of the virtual enterprise is assembled and instantiated.

The problem in the first phase is at what positions of the value chain is such a partitioning sensible. A solution to this problem, proposed by Fischer et al. is facilitated by a uniform description formalism for partial processes.

In the second phase, the partners for the virtual enterprise are selected. It can be divided into four sub-phases:

- Identification of potential partners
- Generation of alternative mappings from partners to partial processes
- Evaluation of the strategic interest and risk, respectively
- Finalisation of partners and mapping to partial processes

Ouzounis et al. [9] present an interoperable distributed business domain architecture than enables the integration, automation and management of business processes located in different business domain boundaries. This architecture provides a platform on which applications, business processes, and service components can be integrated and managed. It is composed of the following layers:

- Secure interoperable infrastructure: provides the environment for accessing services, invoke them, make transactions, perform business critical tasks across the net in an interoperable, modular, and extensible way.
- Enterprise wide infrastructure: Provides the interoperable environment and framework required in supporting business processes and business objects. It provides the interfaces and protocols for the application components to collaborate and the support mechanism for plug and play application component integration.
- Common business objects: Provide the basic common operations that can be used by specialised business processes and needs. These objects can support different administrative domains and business departments, like sales, production, electronic commerce, financial.
- Electronic commerce business processes: Support and provide primary electronic commerce business processes such as ordering, contracting, payment, negotiation, order tracking, between the different parties.
- Electronic commerce applications and VE support environment: These are front-end enterprise-wide applications that provide the ability to various parties to co-operate and effectively perform business electronically within a secure service provisioning and management framework.
- Service provisioning and management framework: Provides the appropriate services for secure access to services, dynamic service execution and service management, accounting, trouble ticketing, performance control and configuration.

Ouzounis et al. also propose a set of virtual enterprise enabling services which support the integration, sharing and management of business processes in virtual enterprises. The functional behaviour and the services that they provide are:

- Access control: Ensures the authorised access to services. It is a general purpose authentication and authorisation mechanism to increase security levels during service invocation and event notifications.
- VE contract manager: Manages all VE member contracts. A VE member contract specifies all the agreed services that this member will provide to other members.
- Business process directory: Maintains information about existing business processes registered in this business domain.
- Business process broker/trader: Manages all the service invocation requests issued by other business domains.
- Event manager: Manages all the incoming events and notifies business processes that register for them. Also manages registration and de-registration of specific events. The event manager works locally in a single business domain, and serves event management operations related only to this domain.
- Business processes: Are the basic functional components that provide specialised business logic functions. Every business component provides a well defined interface which is stored in the business process manager.

# 7 Related Work

This section provides an overview to some areas that are related to virtual enterprises.

## 7.1 The Industrial Virtual Enterprise

An industrial virtual enterprise is a temporary consortium of independent member companies coming together to quickly exploit fast-changing world-wide product manufacturing opportunities [5]. Industrial virtual enterprises assemble themselves based on cost-effectiveness and product uniqueness without regard for organisation sizes, geographic locations, computing environments, technologies deployed, or process implemented. The National Industrial Information Infrastructure Protocols (NIIIP) Consortium, formed in 1994, is a team of organisations co-operating with the U.S. government to develop open industry software protocols allowing manufacturers and their suppliers to interoperate as if they were part of the same enterprise, even though many of their interactions are unscheduled and occur between both sophisticated and relatively unsophisticated users with a range of computer systems, operating environments, and business processes.

NIIIP will allow systems from various manufacturers to be linked, so several companies and their suppliers can work as a single, integrated virtual enterprise to address a business opportunity. Much of the NIIIP work involves consolidating and "harmonising" numerous existing protocols. The protocols are being designed to give the systems used by and industrial virtual enterprise the following characteristics:

- Non-interference: The new protocols should not preclude running existing applications with current data
- Availability: Each member of an industrial virtual enterprise should be able to share product data with the other members.
- Open access: The equipment and applications members bring to a virtual enterprise can vary widely. The entry cost should be small, but more sophisticated members should be able to gain the advantage of working with larger machines and applications.
- Load balancing: An industrial virtual enterprise data server would be overwhelmed if asked to run a large number of challenging applications for a large number of clients.
- Controlled publication: Each member must be able to control the parts of its product database that are added to the industrial virtual enterprise product database
- Seamless integration: The boundaries between data contributed by the various members should be seamless for applications processing it.
- No replication: The members should not be required to place copies of their data in servers they do not control.

## 7.2. Modelling a Virtual Enterprise

A key area in virtual enterprises is the need to understand and support the structured, competitive or even adversarial interactions that are characteristic to commerce, trade and inter-organisational interaction - interactions that are governed by well-formed rules of engagement and enforcement [12].

Wood and Milosevic [12] believe that some advanced object-based concepts can be added to traditional object modelling methodologies to assist in the rigorous specification and construction of virtual enterprises. These concepts can be used to describe the dynamic and normative aspects of virtual enterprises.

Object modelling is primarily concerned with the information and computational aspects of a system. Is it possible to describe a virtual enterprise in terms of classes of objects and interactions between objects, but this is not intuitive, and furthermore, does not capture some of the significant aspects of virtual enterprises. These include - the specification of the policies that govern the behaviour of enterprise objects, the goal seeking behaviour that enterprise objects display, the notion of trust that is often implicit between enterprise objects, and the reality that a virtual enterprise can be considered to exist if it is only partially instantiated at a given point in time.

Role is a modelling concept that describes behaviours. As a modelling concept, it is removed from the computational definition of objects that will implement these behaviours. It is sufficiently general to specify the behaviour of entities, which can be with IT system components or people.

Wood and Milosevic propose the RM-ODP Enterprise Viewpoint [13] as presenting a basic framework for expressing many of these concepts. The enterprise viewpoint specification focuses on the purpose, scope and policies for that system. The enterprise language introduces concepts and terminology necessary to represent both the functional and non-functional behaviour expected of an ODP system by other entities within the enterprise. Community is a key enterprise concept, which is defined as a configuration of objects formed to meet an objective. The objective is the purpose of the configuration, expressed as a contract that specifies how the objective can be met. A contract specifies an agreement governing part of the collective behaviour of a set of objects. A contract specifies obligations, permissions and prohibitions for the objects involved. A contract specification may also include the specification of different roles engaged in the contract, the interfaces associated with the roles, quality of service attributes, indications of periods of validity and behaviour that invalidates the contract.

## 7.3 Intelligent Agents and the Virtual Enterprise

Agents are autonomous or semi-autonomous hardware or software systems that perform tasks in complex, dynamically changing environments [3]. Autonomy means the ability to make decisions based on an internal representation of the world, without being controlled by a central instance. Agents communicate with their environment and effect changes in their environment by performing actions. A multiagent system (MAS) consists of a group of agents that can take specific roles within the organisational structure. The step from isolated single-agent scenarios to open multi-agent systems offers the new quality of emergent behaviour: the group of agents is more than the sum of the capabilities of its members. In order to cope with basic tasks, agents need basic capabilities such as reactivity, deliberation, efficiency, the ability to interact with other agents, and adaptability.

Fischer et al. [3] describe intelligent agent support in setting up a virtual enterprise. The assembly of a virtual enterprise is carried out in two phases. The first phase consists of the definition of the product and the partial processes, while in the second phase, partners are selected and mapped to partial processes. The formation of a virtual enterprise may be considered as a multi-agent decision process. The solution to which is carried out in four steps:

1. Goal specification: description of the global process to be delivered by the virtual enterprise. Intelligent agents can assist a human product manager in the design of the goal specification.
2. Decomposition: mapping of the goal specification into partial processes.
3. Allocation: selection of potential partners and mapping of partners to the partial processes identified in the decomposition step. This involves three subsequent activities:
   - Selection of potential partners
   - Distribution of the partial processes to potential partners
   - Selection of partners to perform the individual processes

Syntheses: definition of the global processes by the composition of the partial processes instantiated in the allocation step. A major practical problem in this context is that the partial processes to be connected may run in different geographical and organisational environments at different enterprises within the virtual enterprise. Thus, connecting two partial processes $P_i$ and $Q_j$ performed by enterprises i and j, respectively to a global process $\Pi = f(P_i, Q_j)$ in general cannot be obtained by simple composition of the form $\Pi = Q_j \quad P_i$. Rather, it is a complex business process re-engineering task, as both processes need to be modified to fit together smoothly.

# 8 Discussion

In this paper we have reviewed how a virtual enterprise, which may be defined as an association constructed from both administratively and geographically distributed business units or organisations, may be considered to be the essence of a business-to-business relationship. A virtual enterprise may be considered to be either stable or dynamic, depending on its lifespan and collaborative structure. When examining virtual enterprises, four key aspects must be considered, namely: connectivity, purpose, technology, and boundary. It is these four characteristics taken together provide a guide as to the stability and the life-cycle of the virtual organisation. These fundamental characteristics of the virtual enterprise show how they mirror business-to-business e-commerce as it exists today. However, from another perspective, virtual enterprises can be seen as fundamentally different from existing business-to-business e-commerce systems, as it revolves around collaboration between parties rather than just transaction-based interaction. The parties in a virtual enterprise interact in a closely coupled, but well-defined, way. It is this close coupling and collaboration which will provide new business opportunities and ways of operating on the Internet to businesses.

However it raises some deeper questions about trust management and contract obligation. Now that companies can *collaborate* on the Internet how can we ensure they are who they say they are? How can we force them to meet their obligations through contracting? How do we audit the overall process and how do we manage the ownership of product data and data after the lifetime of the collaboration. A hint to the answer for the more tangible problems lies in the encapsulation of services provided by participants in the virtual enterprise as a software interface that can be (although not easily) rigorously specified and verified and hence can be expressed as a machine readable and auditable contract. The intangibles, such as building trust relationships, are harder to fathom and will probably be solved by brokers who vouch for the track record of a company.

# References

1. Wolfgang Appel. Towards the theory of Virtual Organisations: A description of their formation and figure. virtual-organization.net Newsletter Vol. 2, No. 2.
2. William H. Davidow, Michael S. Malone. The Virtual Corporation. HarperBusiness. 1992.
3. Fischer K, Muller JP, Heimig I, Scheer A-W. Intelligent Agents in Virtual Enterprises. Proceedings of the First International Conference on the Practical Application of Intelligent Agents and Multi-Agent Technology. Practical Applications Company. 1996.
4. Charles Handy. Trust and the Virtual Organization. Harvard Business Review. May/June 1995.
5. Martin Hardwick, Richard Bolton. The Industrial Virtual Enterprise. Communications of the ACM, Vol. 40, No. 9. September 1997.
6. Bo Hedberg, Goran Dahlgren, Jorgen Hansson, Nils-Goran Olve. Virtual Organizations and Beyond. John Wiley & Sons. 1997.
7. Abbe Mowshowitz. Virtual Organization: A Vision of Management in the Information Age. The Information Society, Vol. 10, No. 4. 1994.
8. Abbe Mowshowitz, guest editor. Virtual Organization. Communications of the ACM, Vol. 40, No. 9. September 1997.
9. Vaggelis Ouzounis, Volker Tschammer. Integration of Electronic Commerce Business Processes in Virtual Enterprises. European Multimedia, Microprocessor Systems and Electronic Commerce, EMMSEC'98. September 1998.
10. Y.P. Shao, S.Y. Liao, H.O. Wang. A Model of Virtual Organizations. Journal of Information Science, Vol. 24, No. 5. 1998.
11. ir Jacoliene van Wijk, drs Daisy Geuerts, ing Rene Bultje. 7 steps to virtuality: understanding the Virtual Organisation processes before designing ICT-support. 'Objects, Components and the Virtual Enterprise', OOPSLA'98. 1998.

12. Andrew Wood, Zoran Milosevic. Describing Virtual Enterprises: the Object of Roles and the Role of Objects. 'Objects, Components and the Virtual Enterprise', OOPSLA'98. 1998.
13. ISO/IEC JTC1/SC33/WG7, "Information Technology – Open Distributed Processing – Reference Model – Enterprise Viewpoint". ISO ISO/IEC 15414 | ITU-T Recommendation X.9ff, January 20 1998.

# Security Issues in Mobile eCommerce

Do Van Thanh

Product Line Mobile e-commerce, Ericsson Norway,
P.B. 34, N-1375 Billingstad, Norway
van.thanh.do@eto.ericsson.se

**Abstract.** With Mobile e-commerce the mobile user can buy and pay for things, pay his bill or make a bet via his mobile phone when on the move, anywhere and at any time. Mobile e-commerce will bring convenience and contribute to improve life quality of the users. However, in order to be su c-cessful, security measures must be strong enough to protect the user from ill e-gal abuses and to get confidence from him. Unfortunately, current security measures for mobile phones are not yet sufficient. This paper describes the R&D activities in mobile e-commerce at Ericsson, which aim at making m o-bile e-commerce applications secure and enabling a full-scale development and deployment of them. The paper starts with a definition of mobile e-commerce. Next are a summary of the Wireless Application Protocol (WAP) and its achievements. The problems related to security in mobile e-commerce are then described. Thereafter, the solution to the problems is presented. The paper concludes with a look on the future and discussions on what can be done.

## 1 Introduction

The convergence of mobile communications network and Internet has paved the way for a range of brand-new applications called wireless Internet applications. Which one of them will be the killer application is still unclear. However, there is one type of wireless Internet applications that are getting more and more popular and may even surpass their counterpart in the fixed Internet. They are called mobile electronic commerce applications. They enable the user to buy small things such as soft drinks, cinema tickets, train tickets, etc. or to pay his bills via mobile devices, i.e. mobile phones, PDAs (Personal Data Assistant), palmtops, etc. In a time when people are much on the move and focus is on life quality improvement, mobile e-commerce applications will bring both convenience and save a lot of time for the mobile user. However, in order to be successful, security measures must be strong enough to pr o-tect the user from illegal abuses and to get confidence from him. Unfortunately, current security measures for mobile phones are not sufficient. This paper describes the R&D activities in mobile e-commerce at Ericsson, which aim at making mobile e-commerce applications secure and enabling a full-scale development and deplo y-ment of them. The paper starts with a presentation of mobile e-commerce. Next are a summary of the Wireless Application Protocol (WAP) and its achievements. The problems related to security in mobile e-commerce are then described. Thereafter, the solutions to the problems are presented. The paper concludes with a look on the future and discussions on what can be done.

## 2 What is mobile e-commerce?

Mobile e-commerce is e-commerce brought to mobile users via mobile devices such as palmtops, PDAs or most dominantly mobile phones. With an ever-increasing number of devices in the market, mobile phones will undoubtedly play a crucial role in promoting mobile e-commerce. Mobile e-commerce allows users to conduct e-commerce on their mobile devices: obtain marketing and sales information, receive ordering information, make a purchase decision, pay for it, obtain the service or product and finally, receive customer support required.

Mobile e-commerce is more than a mobile and wireless extension of the Web-based e-commerce. It is an entirely new sales and promotion channel, and is the enabler for a whole range of new services such as buy a Coke, pay for parking, buy train ticket, etc. via mobile phone. Most importantly it is tailored to the users in many aspects. It follows the user and is available anytime and anywhere. Although mobility is a valuable characteristic to the user in general, it is especially precious for e-commerce because it enables a key factor, which is missing in other e-commerce forms, namely the ability to adapt to the user, his humor and his demands. In fact, the essence of commerce is to be able to satisfy the demands of the users. It is i m-portant not only to be able to offer whatever the user wants but also whenever he wants. Mobile e-commerce can also be customised such it fits the preferences of the user in combination with time and location.

Another important aspect of mobile e-commerce is the ability to mix electronic media with other media such as newspaper, TV, radio, natural communication in any of the commerce phases i.e. presentation, selection, ordering, payment, delivery and customer care. For example, the mobile user can browse on his mobile phone and obtain the location of the closest shop. He goes there and buys a Coke. In this case, the presentation and selection are done electronically via the mobile phone while the rest is done in a traditional way via natural communication. In another situation, the user buys groceries and pays via his mobile phone. The presentation, selection, ordering, delivery and customer care phases are carried out in traditional way and only the payment phase is done electronically.

## 3 Mobile e-commerce and WAP

The Wireless Application Protocol (WAP) promoted by the Wap forum enables the access to the Internet for mobile devices. Taken into account the limited bandwidth of the wireless link, the limitation of mobile devices concerning processing, storage, battery life, size and weight, WAP is optimised for the wireless environment. The architecture of WAP is shown in Figure 1.

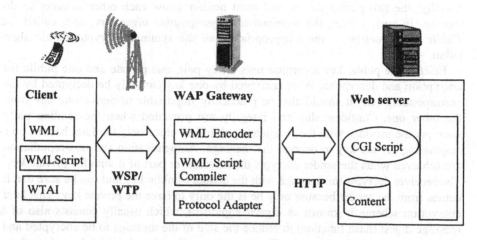

**Figure 1** The WAP architecture

Of course, WAP will contribute to the success of mobile e-commerce but it is worth noting that mobile e-commerce exists also without WAP. For example, the first m o-bile e-commerce application in Norway, "The cinema ticket" that was jointly deve l-oped by Ericsson and Telenor Mobile is not based on WAP. It is based on SIM appl i-cation toolkit where the commerce application is implemented on the SIM (Su b-scriber Identity Module) of the mobile phone. In the future, mobile e-commerce can be extended further through the adoption of newer technology such as Bluetooth, which allows local communications between devices without the need of an on-line connection with the network.

# 4 Security requirements in e-commerce

In e-commerce where the consumer and the merchant communicate indirectly via software entities and the Internet, trust must be somehow established between the two parties. In order to achieve trust the following security functions must be pe r-formed:

- **Authentication:** Each party needs to be able to authenticate its counterpart, i.e. to make sure that the counterpart is the one he claimed to be.
- **Integrity:** Each party needs to make sure that the received messages are not a l-tered or fabricated by other than their counterpart.
- **Confidentiality:** Each party wants to keep the content of their communication secret.
- **Message authentication:** Each party wants to make sure that the received me s-sages do really come from his counterpart.

- **Non-repudiation:** Each party wants to prevent that the counterpart later on denies the agreements that he has approved earlier.

Usually, the two parties do not and must neither know each other in order to do trading. In such a case, the *asymmetric cryptographic algorithm*, also called the *Public key algorithm* is more appropriate than the symmetric cryptographic algorithm.

Briefly, the public key algorithm uses a key pair, one private and one public for encryption and decryption. What encrypted by one key can only be decrypted by the corresponding one. It should also be practically impossible to derive one key from the other one. Confidentiality and integrity are prevailed when the sending party encrypts the message with the recipient's public key since only the later has the corresponding private key to decrypt the message. Authentication and non-repudiation are achieved when the sender encrypts the message or part of it with his private key. The receiver decrypts the message with the sender's public key and can be sure that it comes from the sender because only he is the only to have the private key. This later encryption scheme is known as *digital signature*, which usually consists also of a message digest (hash function) to reduce the size of the message to be encrypted and to optimize the signing process. There are currently several public key algorithms such as RSA [1], Elliptic curves.

The issue now is to be certain who owns what key pair. A certificate issued by a trusted authority also called *Certificate Authority* (CA) attests that a public key belongs to an entity or individual with a certain name and attributes. Both certificates and keys need to be managed, i.e. generated, revoked, updated, recovered, etc. and a *Public Key Infrastructure* (PKI) is necessary for that.

# 5 Commerce for the mobile user

## 5.1 Ideal mobile e-commerce system

At first glance, mobile e-commerce may appear to be identical to "fixed" e-commerce extended with mobile wireless access and the solutions used in Web commerce, e.g. Web shopping, Web banking can be applied directly to mobile e-commerce. However, mobile e-commerce differs to "fixed" e-commerce in the following respects:

**Instantaneous delivery:** The mobile user is of course interested in having service like web shopping where the delivery of non-electronic goods is carried out later. But, in addition he may want to have the goods delivered to him immediately or in a short delay. For example, after paying for a Coke via his mobile phone he expects the can to run out from the Coke automate. When paying for a cinema ticket he expects to be able to collect the ticket within the same day. It is therefore necessary to have user authentication and also receipt delivery.

**Micro payment:** For mobile users it is also to be able to buy small things and to pay small amount of money. The fees for such payments must be small compared to the payments.

**Mobile context:** The mobile user in many situations must be able to operate the services with only one hand. The user may be in environments that are distracting, e.g. crowded, noisy and interactions with the e-commerce services must both simple and small in numbers. The payment scheme of Web shopping described earlier where the user has to enter his personal data and his credit card number is hence not appropriate for the mobile user. A user-friendly payment scheme is required.

An ideal mobile e-commerce as shown in Figure 2 should support the following features:
-   user authentication
-   merchant authentication
-   secure channel i.e., encrypted channel
-   user friendly payment scheme supporting micro payment
-   receipt delivery
-   simple user interface

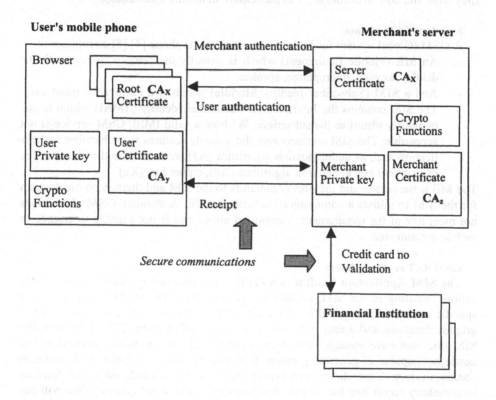

**Figure 2** An ideal mobile e-commerce system

## 5.2 Limitations of the mobile phones

An ideal e-commerce system puts severe requirements that are difficult to be met by the mobile phone itself as follows:
- It must also be equipped with a browser that has interface to the cryptographic functions.
- It must be capable of digitally signing a message using the user private key in order to participate to the user authentication. For that, it must have public key cryptographic functions such as RSA. It must have a tamper-proof storage for storing the user's private key. It must also have enough storage for the user's certificate.
- It must be capable of authenticating the merchant. For that, it needs to have enough storage for root certificates. It must have public key cryptographic fun c-tions.
- It must also have symmetric cryptographic functions for the establishment of the secure channel between the mobile phone and the merchant' server.

Let us consider successively different type of mobile phones and see what capabilities they have and how to enable them to participate in mobile e-commerce.

### Standard GSM phones

A GSM (Global System for Mobile communication) phone [4] [5] co mprises of:
- An **ME** (Mobile Equipment) which is actually the "empty" phone with the display, keypad, microphone, speaker.
- And a **SIM** (Subscriber Identity Module) which is a removable smart card. The SIM contains the International Subscriber Identity ( **IMSI**) which unam-biguously identifies the subscriber. Without a valid IMSI, GSM service is not accessible. The SIM contains also the security features for subscriber authe n-tication such as authentication algorithm (A3), subscriber authentication key (Ki), cipher key generation algorithm (A8), cipher key (Kc)

The ME is the master and initiates commands to the SIM and there is no mechanism for the SIM to initiate a communication with the ME. A standard GSM phone does not meet nay of the requirements mentioned above and is not capable to engage in mobile e-commerce.

### GSM SAT enabled phones

The **SIM Application Toolkit (SAT)** provides mechanisms, which allows appl i-cations, existing in the SIM, to interact and operate with any ME supporting the specific mechanisms required by the application. A browser, the public key crypt o-graphic functions and a user private key can be installed in the SIM. However, the SIM does not have enough storage capacity for all the certificates needed and is hence not capable of generating complete digital signature. In addition, in order to communicate with merchant's web server, the SAT phone needs assistance from an intermediary server that has similar functionality as the WAP gateway. We will not consider pure SAT phones since more powerful WAP phones have emerged.

**WAP phones**

The WAP phone is a mobile phone that has a WML browser and a WAP protocol stack on the ME. It is hence capable of communicating with any Web servers via the WAP gateway. The connection with the WAP gateway can be based on different bearers such as GSM circuit-switched connection, GPRS, SMS, USSD, etc.

The first version of WAP phones, called WAP 1.1 phones do not have public key cryptographic functions for digital signature. However, a combined WAP-SAT phones will both have a WML browser in the ME and public key functionality in the SIM. The only problem is the lack of the interface between the browser and the cryptographic functions on the SIM. The browser is hence not able to invoke the cryptographic functions necessary for user authentication.

In the WAP 1.2 phone, there will be a Wireless Identity Module (WIM), which incorporates both the SIM and also local memory in the ME. Public key cryptographic functions and also the user private key can both be stored in the WIM. There will also be implemented an interface, which allows the browser to communicate with the cryptographic functions. WAP 1.2 phones will be capable of generating digital signature according to the PKCS#1 standard [6], but they will not able to generate an electronic signature according to the PKCS#7 that are required in the validation process of the signature. It is possible to say that even WAP phones are not capable to participate in mobile e-commerce by themselves but they need assistance from the system.

## 5.3 The Mobil ePay

To allow mobile phones to perform digital signature, we introduce a proxy server, called **Mobile ePay**. The Mobile ePay is responsible to perform on behalf of the mobile phones the tasks that the latter are not capable such as:
- Storing the user's certificates
- Generating electronic signature, e.g. PKCS#7 message format from digital signature, e.g. PKCS#1 format, generated by mobile phones.
- Validating of the merchant's servers

In addition to the security functions the Mobile ePay has also payment functions such as:
- Prepaid account supporting micro payment
- Interfacing with the systems of the financial institutions

To illustrate the role of the Mobile ePay in our payment system two operations namely user authentication for WAP 1.1 phones and payment from WAP 1.1 phones are described.

**User authentication**

The user authentication as depicted in Figure 3 comprises of the following steps:
1. The user visits a merchant site.
2. The merchant server sends the content to the mobile phone via the WAP gateway.

3. The user wants to authenticate himself toward the merchant. The authentic a-tion request is sent to the WAP gateway, which sends to the Mobile ePay. The M o-bile ePay sends it to the merchant server.

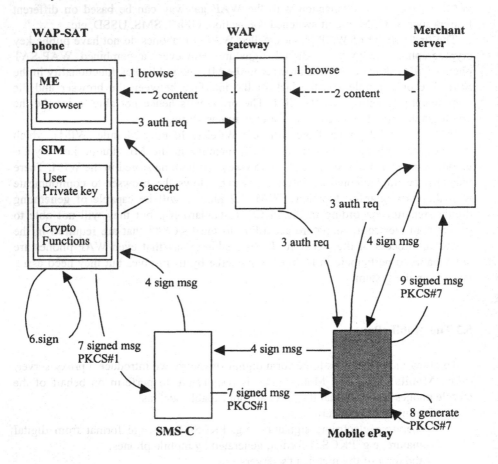

**Figure 3** Mobile ePay role in user authentication

4. The merchant server generates an authentication message, e.g. a random nu m-ber and sends it to the Mobile ePay, which sends to the SMS-C (Short Message Center). The SMC-C delivers it to the SIM on the mobile phone.

5. The SIM asks for permission to sign.

6. If the user accepts the SIM performs the signing, i.e. generating a digital si g-nature in PKCI#1 format.

7. The SIM sends it back to the SMS-C, which sends it to the Mobile ePay.

8. The Mobile ePay generates an electronic signature in PKCS#7 format by using the received digital signature in PKCS#1 format.

9. The Mobile ePay sends the complete electronic signature to the merchant server.

## Payment from WAP 1.1 phones

1. The user visits a merchant site.
2. The merchant server sends the content to the mobile phone via the WAP gat e-way.

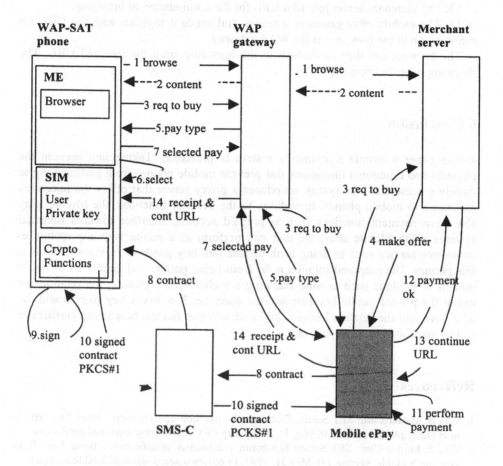

**Figure 4** Payment from WAP 1.1 phones

3. The user wants to buy. The request is sent to the WAP gateway, which forwards it to the Mobile ePay. The Mobile ePay delivers it to the merchant server.
4. The merchant server sends an offer to the Mobile ePay.
5. The Mobile ePay sends a request for payment type to the browser via the WAP gateway
6. The user selects the payment type, e.g. prepaid account, credit cards, etc. and
7. The payment type is sent to the Mobile ePay via the WAP gateway.
8. The Mobile ePay sends the contract to the SIM via the SMS-C.
9. After asking for confirmation from the user, the SIM performs the signing
10. The SIM sends the digital signature back to the Mobile ePay via the SMS-C.

11. The Mobile ePay executes the necessary transactions according to the payment type. This may include transactions towards financial institutions in case of payment by credit card.

12. The Mobile ePay sends a confirmation to the merchant server.

13. The merchant server returns a URL for the continuation of browsing.

14. The mobile ePay generates a receipt and sends it together with the URL for continuation to the browser via the WAP gateway.

The browser can then continue with the browsing from the received URL. The shopping is hence completed.


# 6 Conclusion

In this paper a mobile e-commerce system is presented. Taking into account the physical and functional limitations that prevent mobile phones from participating to mobile e-commerce, the system introduces a proxy server that offers the necessary assistance to mobile phones. In addition to the security functions, the Mobile ePay also have payment functions such as prepaid account, interface towards financial systems. With Mobile ePay, the user can perform in a secure way any mobile e-commerce service such as doing bank transaction, buy goods or services, from m o- bile phones. The proposed solution is far from being perfect and quite a lot of issues remain to be done such as time stamping for electronic signature, the relation b e- tween the private public key pair and the user, i.e. how many key pair should the user have and the relation between key pair and certificates, how many certificates can be associated to a key pair, etc.


# References

1. Visa & Master Card: SET Secure Electronic Transaction Specification - Book One: Bus i-ness Description, version 1.0, May 31, 1997, http://www.setco.org/download.html/#spec
2. Visa & Master Card: SET Secure Electronic Transaction Specification - Book Two: Pr o-grammer's Guide, version 1.0, May 31, 1997, http://www.setco.org/download.html/#spec
3. Visa & Master Card: SET Secure Electronic Transaction Specification - Book Three: Fo r-mal Protocol Definition, version 1.0, May 31, 1997, http://www.setco.org/download.html/#spec
4. ETSI: GSM 02.17 V8.0.0 Digital cellular telecommunications system (Phase 2+); Su b-scriber Identity Modules (SIM); Functional characteristic
5. ETSI: GSM 11.14 Digital cellular telecommunications system (Phase 2+); Specification of the SIM Application Toolkit for the Subscriber Identity Module - Mobile Equipment (SIM - ME) Interface
6. RSA Laboratories. PKCS #1: RSA Encryption Sta ndard. Version 1.5, Nov 1993
7. RSA Laboratories. PKCS #7: Cryptographic Message Syntax Standard. Version 1.5, Nov 1993

# Mobile Electronic Commerce: Emerging Issues

Aphrodite Tsalgatidou[1] and Jari Veijalainen[2]

University of Jyväskylä,
Department of Computer Science and Information Systems/
Information Technology Research Institute,
P.O.Box 35, FIN-40351 JYVÄSKYLÄ, FINLAND
{afrodite,veijalai}@jyu.fi

**Abstract.** There are many definitions for Mobile Electronic Commerce (M-Commerce). We define M-Commerce as any type of transaction of an economic value having at least at one end a mobile terminal and thus using the mobile telecommunications network. The Wireless Application Protocol (WAP) plays an important role in m-commerce by optimizing Internet standards for the constraints of the wireless environment and thus bridging the gap between Internet and mobile world. Mobile Network Operators can play a major role in m-commerce by being strategically positioned between customers and content/service providers. In this paper we investigate the roles the operator can play in m-commerce and discuss respective problems and emerging issues.

## 1 Introduction

Internet has made available a wide range of applications and services over the World Wide Web at a low cost. Millions of users enjoy the benefits accrued by Internet, by using their desktop computers or portables. At the same time, the number of users of mobile terminals (phones, PDAs[3], and communicators[4]) is continuously increasing. The miniature size of mobile terminals and the fact that they can easily fit in a pocket and carried everywhere makes them an ideal channel for offering personalized and localized services to the continuously increasing number of mobile users. We define Mobile electronic commerce (M-Commerce) as any type of transaction of an economic value having at least at one end a mobile terminal and thus using the mobile telecommunications network. This means, that E-Commerce transactions performed by a mobile customer via a fixed terminal (e.g. from a hotel room) or via a portable computer that is connected to the Internet via a modem and wired network are not

---

[1] The research was supported by the Finnish National Technology Agency under contract 750/401/99. Aphrodite Tsalgatidou is on leave of absence from Department of Informatics of the University of Athens, Greece.

[2] The research was supported by the Finnish National Technology Agency under contract 330/401/99.

[3] PDA=Personal Digital Assistant, like the Palm products by 3Com, or the PDAs by Psion etc.

[4] Examples include the Nokia Communicator 9000 and 9110 products.

included in our definition of M-Commerce. The same applies for personal SMS communication sent by one person to another.

M-Commerce creates new business opportunities for players in the field, like content and service providers and especially for Mobile Network Operators who can play a more active role in a m-commerce transaction and become more profitable and competitive. This paper investigates the role of the mobile network operator in m-commerce in a number of scenarios, discusses respective billing scenarios and identifies open issues and problems in the current billing process. The rest of the paper is organised as follows. Section 2 briefly describes the Wireless Application Protocol (WAP) [6] which plays an important role in m-commerce. Section 3 describes the participating entities and roles in the m-commerce value chain. Since the role of the Mobile Network Operator is very important in this value chain, this is separately discussed in section 4 that examines a number of roles that a Mobile Network Operator can play in m-commerce. Associated billing issues are discussed in section 5 that is followed by a discussion on the open issues in section 6. Finally section 7 concludes the paper.

## 2 The Wireless Application Protocol (WAP)

The Wireless Application Protocol (WAP) is the de-facto standard for the presentation and delivery of wireless information and telephony services on mobile terminals. WAP was developed by the WAP Forum, an industry association founded by Nokia, Ericsson, Motorola and Unwired Planet in June 1997 with the goal to open Internet for wireless mobile access by creating a 2G+[5] network technology. Today, WAP Forum comprises over 200 members from all segments of the wireless industry value chain, including Hewlett Packard, Microsoft, IBM, etc. aiming to ensure product interoperability and growth of wireless market.

Internet standards such as HTML, HTTP, TLS and TCP are inefficient over mobile networks as they require large amounts of mainly text-based data to be sent. Standard HTML content cannot be effectively displayed on the small-sized screens of pocket-sized mobile terminals and pagers. WAP optimizes these standards for the unique constraints of the wireless environment, i.e. low bandwidth, high latency and not stable connection. The WAP Specifications define a lightweight protocol to minimize bandwidth requirements and to guarantee that a variety of wireless networks can run WAP applications. The lightweight protocol stack is designed to minimize the required bandwidth and maximize the number of wireless network types that can deliver WAP content. Multiple networks can be targeted, these include GSM 900, 1800, 1900 MHz, DECT, TDMA, PCS, FLEX and CDMA. All network technologies and bearers will also be supported, including SMS, USSD, CSD, CPDP and GPRS.

The interface between the operator's network and the Internet is realized by the WAP gateway which includes HTML to WML filters, the HTTPS interface to an online Web Server as well as interface to the WAP handset via the PSTN and GSM networks over circuit switched data. Requests from the mobile device are sent as a

---

[5] 2G+ is an acronym for amended second generation (2G) networks, like WAP.

URL through the operator's network to the WAP gateway. Responses are sent from the web server to the WAP Gateway in HTML which are then translated in WML and sent to the mobile terminals over WST/WST. The role of the WAP gateway can be clearly seen in Figure 1.

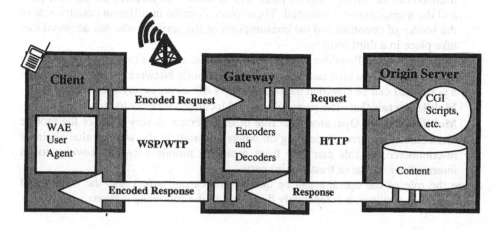

**Figure 1.** The role of WAP Gateway in M-Commerce

In this way WAP establishes the mobile terminal as the trusted, personalised delivery channel for many kinds of services like financial services, travel services, information services, news alerts, retailing services, entertainment services and so on. The penetration of the market by WAP is slowly but steadily increasing the possibilities and creates challenges and competition among network operators and service providers in providing a constant stream of new services.

# 3 Participating entities in M-Commerce Value Chain

The participating entities in an e-commerce transaction depend on the underlying business model. For example, in Internet e-commerce, if the business model is an e-shop, e.g. amazon.com, the customer interacts directly with the merchant or service provider, while in other business models, the intermediaries/brokers or portals, play an active role in the value chain. There might be also other entities that support a specific function in the value chain, such as electronic payment, logistics or distribution, e.g. FedEx [2] or UPS [5]. It is common for a business to use third parties for specific parts of the value chain (e.g. e-payment), as in this way they can modernize their operation and offer advanced services to their customers a low cost.

Since we consider mobile terminals as an access technology to Internet, the structures at the Internet side remain the same and the main entities in M-Commerce are similar with the entities participating in an Internet Commerce transaction. The main addition in the participating entities is the Mobile Network Operator. Furthermore, due to the peculiarities of the mobile e-commerce as regards the customer's needs and the way of accessing the services, a couple of more entities appear in the value chain and additional roles are assigned. Thus, the main entities in the m-commerce value chain are the following:

- **Customer** who is mainly mobile. The place s/he is when the transaction is initiated can be different from a place s/he is when s/he receives the service, pays and the transaction is committed. These places can be in different countries or in the border of countries and the consumption of the services s/he has acquired can take place in a third country.
- **Content/Service Provider** who provides specific contents to a customer through a WAP Gateway which can be hosted at the Mobile Network Operator or though a portal that can be hosted at the operator's WAP server or anywhere else.
- **Mobile Portals** that offer personalized and localized services to customers.
- **Mobile Network Operator:** The role of the operator is very vital for the mobile electronic commerce. Depending on where it stands in the whole value chain of m-commerce, its role can vary from a simple mobile network provider to an intermediary, portal or trusted third party.

Since the role of the operator can be quite complex and affect also the billing and payment of m-services, it is separately discussed in the following sections.

## 4  The Role of the Mobile Network Operator in M-Commerce

M-Commerce brings challenging opportunities for the Mobile Network Operator, the role of which can vary from very simple and passive to very active and dynamic by being strategically positioned between customers and content/service providers and offer portal or trusted third party services.

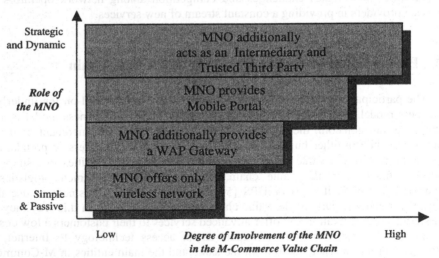

**Figure 2.** The Mobile Network Operator (MNO) in the M-Commerce Value chain

Figure 2 depicts the various roles of the MNO in relation with the degree of its involvement in the m-commerce value chain and the degree of the importance of its role. It seems that the simplest and most passive role that the Mobile Network Operator (MNO) can play is to just provide the mobile network infrastructure and let the customer communicate and negotiate directly with the various content/service providers or other portals (scenario 1). Profits of the MNO come from the offered wireless connection. In addition to this, the operator can have three escalating roles:

- host a WAP gateway for enabling the exchange of information between a customer holding a WAP terminal and an Internet merchant who doesn't provide WAP compliant contents (scenario 2)
- Act as a portal offering advertising services and providing search facilities while enabling connection with the content/service provider (scenario 3)
- Act as an intermediary and trusted third party (scenario 4)

The last two scenarios are very interesting and they are analysed in the following.

## 4.1 The Mobile Network Operator offers Portal Services

Instead of simply facilitating transactions between customers and content providers, the operator can have an escalated role by providing portal services. In other words, the operator can act as a portal, facilitating customers to locate appropriate service providers and at the same time enabling content providers to reach customers via the operator's portal. Mobile portals differ from Internet portals, as the needs of mobile customers and the characteristics of a mobile terminal differ from those of a customer sitting in front of his/her desktop or portable computer. A mobile portal (m-portal) is characterized by a greater degree of personalization and localization. Localization means that a mobile portal should supply information relevant to the current location of the user. Information requirements may include for example, restaurant bookings, hotel reservations, nearest petrol station, yellow pages, movie listings and so on. Personalization applies to any kind of information provided by m-portals including location-specific information. User's profile, past behavior, situation and location should be taken into account for the provision of such personalized and localized services. Yourwap.com [7] is a representative example of a mobile portal.

Mobile network operators have a number of advantages over other portal players as they have an existing customer relationship and personal data and they can identify the location of the subscriber. Usual Internet portals are neither able to incorporate location-specific information nor do they have the data and knowledge of each customer that the mobile operator has. In many instances, the 'traditional' portal player knows only an email address that can also be virtual without any information about customer's identity. Moreover, the traditional portal doesn't usually have a billing relationship with the customer (with the exception of portals like Compuserve who are also Internet Service Providers). Therefore, it is very natural for a mobile network operator to offer mobile portal services to its customers and additionally offer services similar to the ones offered by Internet portals, for example search services, lists of content and service providers with provided services, products and prices, respective comparisons, etc. In other words, the operator can be the front end for a number of suppliers. The customer in this way can choose the supplier with the best offer from Quality of Service (QoS) and financial point of view.

The operator can make profit by making special agreements with content/service providers. Direct contact of the customer with a provider, after the first contact through the portal, can be allowed or not depending on the operator's policy.

## 4.2 Operator acts as an Intermediary/Trusted-Third-Party (TTP)

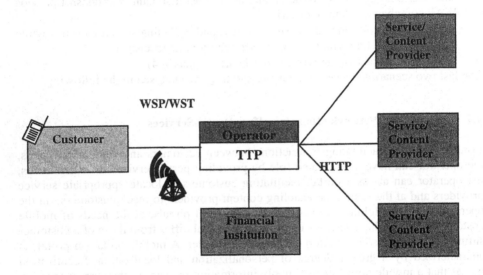

**Figure 3.** The role of Telecom Operator has escalated to Intermediary and Trusted Third Party (TTP)

In this case the role of the operator has been escalated into a more dynamic one in the m-commerce market and provides whatever a portal provides and in addition:

- *Provides bundle services*, i.e. provides offers with a combination of various purchases from different suppliers with discounts. So, for example, if customer wants to buy product A from supplier X, s/he may find an offer by the Telecom Operator about two products A and B from different supplier at a lower price.
- *Acts as a front- end to the bank*, i.e. the customer pays to the operator who, in this case, is also responsible for payment refund to the customer if the latter is not satisfied with the products.
- *Acts as Trusted Third Party* in cases the customer wants to buy a number of goods from various suppliers that must interoperate. Fulfillment is a critical part of an e-commerce transaction and essential for building trust relationships with customers. If the product arrives in bad condition or too late or doesn't arrive at all the customer has to be protected and the liability issues must be very clear. For example, say that a customer wants to buy a digital camera and a computer from two different suppliers and that the customer requires these two products

interoperate in order to easily download images from the camera to the computer. The operator can guarantee properties such as money atomicity and product atomicity[6], i.e. the operator guarantees that the customer pays only if both products are delivered in good condition and are interoperable. This alleviates the customer from negotiating with different suppliers and from trying to find liabilities in case that something goes wrong. The operator is responsible in this case for the whole billing process, thus the customer pays just the operator who is then responsible for distributing the money to the IPR[7] owners and to the content providers. Depending on the underlying agreement, some IPR owners may get paid by the content providers rather than the operators.

The role that the operator eventually plays is dependent on what is allowed by the relevant legislation. For example, current legislation in Finland doesn't allow Telecom Operators to charge for contents/services exceeding a certain amount of money (60mk). This means, that the operator may need to found subsidiary companies in order to act as TTP and/or acquire licenses for a bank.

In addition to this role, the Mobile Network Operator can act as Internet Service Provider. It is clear that the operator can play such a role not only in M-Commerce but also in Internet Commerce.

## 5 Billing

Billing of mobile services is a complicated issue. Whom the customer is going to pay? When? How? How much? For what? How money is going to be distributed among the operator, service provider, IPR owners, tax administration authority etc.? Here we examine some of these issues:

- **What the customer pays for?**
  The customer pays for the mobile connection service and the acquired contents/services/goods received:

  1. Billing for the mobile connection service
     The customer pays the operator for the connection and/or the transactions or sessions s/he has performed while connected. This billing can be:
     - *connection time based:* this can be very expensive for the customer, as in order to get what s/he needs s/he may have to be connected for a long time to the network.
     - *transaction based:* customer pays according to the number of transactions[8] s/he has performed.

---

[6] Money atomicity, product atomicity and other transactional requirements are extensively discussed in [3,4].

[7] IPR = Intellectual Property Rights

[8] In WAP and more specifically in the Wireless Transaction Protocol (WTP), a transaction is a unit of interaction between an Initiator and a Responder. A transaction begins with an invoke message generated by the Initiator. The Responder becomes involved with a transaction by receiving the invoke message. In WTP several transaction classes have been defined. The

- *session based:* customer pays for a whole session[9], irrespectively of the number of transactions performed
- *a combination of the above:* customer pays a basic rate for the connection and for the transactions or sessions s/he has initiated.

2.  Billing for the acquired contents/provided service
    In addition to the billing for the mobile service, the customer has to pay for the acquired contents/goods/services. Contents are either provided for free or a certain fee is charged per acquired content. Services and tangible goods are always charged. The question that arises here is whom the customer pays for this. This is discussed next.

– **To whom the customer pays?**

The customer normally pays:

- The operator for the mobile connection service and
- The service/content provider for the acquired contents/service/goods

Depending on the business model supported by the operator, the customer either pays the operator for both connection service and the acquired contents/goods or s/he pays the operator just for the wireless connection and the service provider for the rest. In the Durlacher's report [1] it is estimated that in future advertising, sponsoring and subscription models will also be realised.

– **How the money is distributed?**

Another important issue in the billing and payment process is the distribution of money. We assume that the money acquired for a m-commerce transaction has to be distributed among the mobile operator, the content/service provider and IPR owners and discuss two different billing scenarios. We note that we do not tackle issues associated with tax. These are not simple especially when the participants of m-mobile transactions (i.e. customer, content provider, operator, IPR owners, etc.) are in different countries. Some of the taxation issues are defined by European Union's legislation, while others depend on national legislation.

- *$1^{st}$ Billing Scenario:*

The customer pays directly the operator for the connection time used and for the content/service acquired. The operator then distributes the money to the content provider who subsequently is responsible for giving the corresponding amount to the IPR owners. The operator can also make profit by holding some percentage of the money per committed transaction and send the rest to the content provider or get a monthly fee from the content provider depending on the number of committed transactions.

- *$2^{nd}$ Billing Scenario:*

The customer pays directly to the operator only for the connection time and then pays directly the content provider for the acquired contents/service. In this case, the

---

invoke message identifies the type of transaction requested which defines the action required to complete the transaction.

[9] In WAP and more precisely in the Wireless Session Protocol (WSP), a session is a long-lived communication context established between two programs for the purpose of transactions and typed data transfer.

service/content provider is again responsible for paying the appropriate fees to IPR owners.

## 6 Discussion

The role that the operator can play depends a lot from the current legislation. For example, in Finland, operators can not charge services more than 60FIM. The rationale for this is that since the customer pays the operator monthly or bi-monthly, the operator would play the role of a credit bank. This means that the operators need to found new companies to play more dynamic roles, like Trusted Third Parties and gain more profit, as we have also mentioned before.

Most portals run by the mobile network operators, like Sonera and Radiolinja (Finland), Telia (Sweden), Telenor Mobil (Norway), Orange and Vodafone (UK), have limited the access to their own subscribers. It is expected that sooner or later they will open their portals to customers of other networks too. This is very important, otherwise m-commerce becomes problematic from many points of view. If for example Sonera's and Radiolinja's portals can only be accessed by their customers, what is going to happen with 'roaming' customers, i.e. customers coming to Finland from Greece with Greek mobiles. Will they be able to access any Finnish portal? If not, the location-based services are of no use for 'roaming' customers. Further problems that have to be resolved are related with the billing of 'roaming' customers. Will they pay their 'home' operator for services received in another country?

Other issues have to do with the pricing of services which should be known to the customer before acquiring any content or service, in order to avoid unpleasant surprises. Also, should the customer pay for the connection if s/he didn't receive any contents? At the moment this is the case, and operators have the first complains by customers who have been charged for the connection while trying to acquire a service without any success.

What about the language? For example, at the moment, Sonera's portal is only in Finnish. This means that Sonera's WAP solution is useless for non Finnish speaking people.

Furthermore, some operators do not allow their customers to directly contact any other portals or content providers. All communication goes through the operator's portal. This restricts the customer's options.

These are some of the issues which are open at the moment and require further investigation and cooperation between Telecom Operators.

## 7 Conclusion

The potentials of m-commerce are enormous. Mobile terminals seem to be the ideal channel for offering personalized and location-based services as well as for one-to-one marketing. Other very popular applications are mobile advertising, mobile financial services (stock exchange, bank payments, insurance services), mobile entertainment, emails based on SMS and alert services to mention a few.

Regarding the m-terminals, PDAs and smart phones including a WAP microbrowser for wireless Internet access are becoming very popular. We will soon have a wide range of mobile terminals from simple voice terminals to multi-purpose terminals incorporating MP-3 player or video player that can handle in parallel voice, data and video services, depending on customer demand.

The mobile network operators have a competitive advantage in the m-commerce market due to the fact that they possess information about customers, they have an established billing relationship with them and they can easily locate the subscriber's geographical location. Thus, location-based services such as advertising, shopping, reservations and information provisioning can be easily offered. Also, they can be strategically positioned between content/service providers and subscribers and have an upgraded role in the m-commerce value chain by acting as mobile portals or information brokerage. They can also play the role of Internet service provider and even acquire a bank or a banking license and play the role of a Trusted Third Party. It is very likely that operators will keep only mobile voice services and found subsidiary companies for the mobile portal services in order to comply with existing legislation and also because of the different business models required for serving respective demands. In this paper we investigated some of the roles that that the mobile network operator can play and discussed associated issues. A more extensive discussion on the associated business, legal and technical issues as well as on transactional aspects may be found in [4].

At the moment there is still a small number of applications and content available, the WAP phones are not widely available and the call set-up time is too long. But, there is a lot of work going on by many industries, network operators and software providers and, it is estimated that, at the beginning of 2002, as GPRS[10] start to become more widespread, m-commerce will start to take off on a larger scale [1]. However, in order for m-commerce to flourish, related business and legal issues should also be resolved.

# References

1. Durlacher Research Ltd.: Mobile Commerce Report, Feb. 2000. www.durlacher.com
2. FedEx, http://www.fedex.com
3. Schuldt, H., Popovici, A., Schek, H.-J. (1999). Execution Guarantees in Electronic Commerce Payments. *Proceedings of TDD '99*, Dagstuhl, Sept., 27, 1999.
4. Tsalgatidou, A., Veijalainen, J.: Requirements Analysis for Billing Transactions in M-Commerce. Internal Report, University of Jyväskylä, (2000).
5. UPS http://www.ups.com
6. Wireless Application Protocol (WAP). http://www.wapforum.org
7. Your Wap. www.yourwap.com

---

[10] GPRS (General packet Radio Service) is a packet switch wireless protocol the main advantage of which is that it provides a "always on" connection between the mobile terminal and the network and thus enables instant IP connectivity.

# Author Index

488

# Lecture Notes in Computer Science

For information about Vols. 1–1825
please contact your bookseller or Springer-Verlag

Vol. 1865: K.R. Apt, A.C. Kakas, E. Monfroy, F. Rossi (Eds.), New Trends Constraints. Proceedings, 1999. X, 339 pages. 2000. (Subseries LNAI).

Vol. 1866: J. Cussens, A. Frisch (Eds.), Inductive Logic Programming. Proceedings, 2000. X, 265 pages. 2000. (Subseries LNAI).

Vol. 1867: B. Ganter, G.W. Mineau (Eds.), Conceptual Structures: Logical, Linguistic, and Computational Issues. Proceedings, 2000. XI, 569 pages. 2000. (Subseries LNAI).

Vol. 1868: P. Koopman, C. Clack (Eds.), Implementation of Functional Languages. Proceedings, 1999. IX, 199 pages. 2000.

Vol. 1869: M. Aagaard, J. Harrison (Eds.), Theorem Proving in Higher Order Logics. Proceedings, 2000. IX, 535 pages. 2000.

Vol. 1872: J. van Leeuwen, O. Watanabe, M. Hagiya, P.D. Mosses, T. Ito (Eds.), Theoretical Computer Science. Proceedings, 2000. XV, 630 pages. 2000.

Vol. 1873: M. Ibrahim, J. Küng, N. Revell (Eds.), Database and Expert Systems Applications. Proceedings, 2000. XIX, 1005 pages. 2000.

Vol. 1874: Y. Kambayashi, M. Mohania, A M. Tjoa (Eds.), Data Warehousing and Knowledge Discovery. Proceedings, 2000. XII, 438 pages. 2000.

Vol. 1875: K. Bauknecht, S.K. Madria, G. Pernul (Eds.), Electronic Commerce and Web Technologies. Proceedings, 2000. XII, 488 pages. 2000.

Vol. 1876: F. J. Ferri, J.M. Iñesta, A. Amin, P. Pudil (Eds.), Advances in Pattern Recognition. Proceedings, 2000. XVIII, 901 pages. 2000.

Vol. 1877: C. Palamidessi (Ed.), CONCUR 2000 – Concurrency Theory. Proceedings, 2000. XI, 612 pages. 2000.

Vol. 1878: J.P. Bowen, S. Dunne, A. Galloway, S. King (Eds.), ZB 2000: Formal Specification and Development in Z and B. Proceedings, 2000. XIV, 511 pages. 2000.

Vol. 1879: M. Paterson (Ed.), Algorithms – ESA 2000. Proceedings, 2000. IX, 450 pages. 2000.

Vol. 1880: M. Bellare (Ed.), Advances in Cryptology – CRYPTO 2000. Proceedings, 2000. XI, 545 pages. 2000.

Vol. 1881: C. Zhang, V.-W. Soo (Eds.), Design and Applications of Intelligent Agents. Proceedings, 2000. X, 183 pages. 2000. (Subseries LNAI).

Vol. 1882: D. Kotz, F. Mattern (Eds.), Agent Systems, Mobile Agents, and Applications. Proceedings, 2000. XII, 275 pages. 2000.

Vol. 1883: B. Triggs, A. Zisserman, R. Szeliski (Eds.), Vision Algorithms: Theory and Practice. Proceedings, 1999. X, 383 pages. 2000.

Vol. 1884: J. Štuller, J. Pokorný, B. Thalheim, Y. Masunaga (Eds.), Current Issues in Databases and Information Systems. Proceedings, 2000. XIII, 396 pages. 2000.

Vol. 1885: K. Havelund, J. Penix, W. Visser (Eds.), SPIN Model Checking and Software Verification. Proceedings, 2000. X, 343 pages. 2000.

Vol. 1886: R. Mizoguchi, J. Slaney /Eds.), PRICAI 2000: Topics in Artificial Intelligence. Proceedings, 2000. XX, 835 pages. 2000. (Subseries LNAI).

Vol. 1888: G. Sommer, Y.Y. Zeevi (Eds.), Algebraic Frames for the Perception-Action Cycle. Proceedings, 2000. X, 349 pages. 2000.

Vol. 1889: M. Anderson, P. Cheng, V. Haarslev (Eds.), Theory and Application of Diagrams. Proceedings, 2000. XII, 504 pages. 2000. (Subseries LNAI).

Vol. 1890: C Linnhoff-Popien, H.-G. Hegering (Eds.), Trends in Distributed Systems: Towards a Universal Service Market. Proceedings, 2000. XI, 341 pages. 2000.

Vol. 1891: A.L. Oliveira (Ed.), Grammatical Inference: Algorithms and Applications. Proceedings, 2000. VIII, 313 pages. 2000. (Subseries LNAI).

Vol. 1892: P. Brusilovsky, O. Stock, C. Strapparava (Eds.), Adaptive Hypermedia and Adaptive Web-Based Systems. Proceedings, 2000. XIII, 422 pages. 2000.

Vol. 1893: M. Nielsen, B. Rovan (Eds.), Mathematical Foundations of Computer Science 2000. Proceedings, 2000. XIII, 710 pages. 2000.

Vol. 1895: F. Cuppens, Y. Deswarte, D. Gollmann, M. Waidner (Eds.), Computer Security – ESORICS 2000. Proceedings, 2000. X, 325 pages. 2000.

Vol. 1896: R. W. Hartenstein, H. Grünbacher (Eds.), Field-Programmable Logic and Applications. Proceedings, 2000. XVII, 856 pages. 2000.

Vol. 1897: J. Gutknecht, W. Weck (Eds.), Modular Programming Languages. Proceedings, 2000. XII, 299 pages. 2000.

Vol. 1898: E. Blanzieri, L. Portinale (Eds.), Advances in Case-Based Reasoning. Proceedings, 2000. XII, 530 pages. 2000. (Subseries LNAI).

Vol. 1899: H.-H. Nagel, F.J. Perales López (Eds.), Articulated Motion and Deformable Objects. Proceedings, 2000. X, 183 pages. 2000.

Vol. 1900: A. Bode, T. Ludwig, W. Karl, R. Wismüller (Eds.), Euro-Par 2000 Parallel Processing. Proceedings, 2000. XXXV, 1368 pages. 2000.

Vol. 1901: O. Etzion, P. Scheuermann (Eds.), Cooperative Information Systems. Proceedings, 2000. XI, 336 pages. 2000.

Vol. 1902: P. Sojka, I. Kopeček, K. Pala (Eds.), Text, Speech and Dialogue. Proceedings, 2000. XIII, 463 pages. 2000. (Subseries LNAI).

Vol. 1906: A. Porto, G.-C. Roman (Eds.), Coordination Languages and Models. Proceedings, 2000. IX, 353 pages. 2000.

Vol. 1912: Y. Gurevich, P.W. Kutter, M. Odersky, L. Thiele (Eds.), Abstract State Machines. Proceedings, 2000. X, 381 pages. 2000.

Vol. 1913: K. Jansen, S. Khuller (Eds.), Approximation Algorithms for Combinatorial Optimization. Proceedings, 2000. IX, 275 pages. 2000.

Vol. 1923: J. Borbinha, T. Baker (Eds.), Research and Advanced Technology for Digital Libraries. Proceedings, 2000. XVII, 513 pages. 2000.

Vol. 1924: W. Taha (Ed.), Semantics, Applications, and Implementation of Program Generation. Proceedings, 2000. VIII, 231 pages. 2000.

Vol. 1926: M. Joseph (Ed.), Formal Techniques in Real-Time and Fault-Tolerant Systems. Proceedings, 2000. X, 305 pages. 2000.